Jimmy Carter,
the Politics of Family,
and the Rise of the
Religious Right

SINCE**1970**
Histories of Contemporary America

J. BROOKS FLIPPEN

Jimmy Carter, the Politics of Family, and the Rise of the Religious Right

The University of Georgia Press
Athens and London

© 2011 by the University of Georgia Press

Athens, Georgia 30602

www.ugapress.org

Set in Minion by Graphic Composition, Inc.

Printed digitally in the United States of America

Library of Congress Cataloging-in-Publication Data

Flippen, J. Brooks, 1959–

    Jimmy Carter, the politics of family, and the rise of the religious right / J. Brooks Flippen.

        p. cm. — (Since 1970 : histories of contemporary America)

    Includes bibliographical references and index.

    ISBN-13: 978-0-8203-3769-2 (hardcover : alk. paper)

    ISBN-10: 0-8203-3769-2 (hardcover : alk. paper)

    ISBN-13: 978-0-8203-3770-8 (pbk. : alk. paper)

    ISBN-10: 0-8203-3770-6 (pbk. : alk. paper)

    1. Carter, Jimmy, 1924– —Political and social views.

2. Carter, Jimmy, 1924– —Religion.

3. United States—Politics and government—1977–1981.

4. Families—Political aspects—United States—History—20th century.

5. Religious right—United States—History—20th century.

6. Christian conservatism—United States—History—20th century

7. Christianity and politics—United States—History—20th century.

8. United States—Social conditions—1960–1980. I. Title.

    E873.2.F57 2011

    973.926092—dc22   2010032599

British Library Cataloging-in-Publication Data available

For my parents, Jim and Nancy Flippen

Contents

Acknowledgments

THE AMERICAN NOVELIST SHERWOOD ANDERSON once remarked, "The whole glory of writing lies in the fact that it forces us out of ourselves and into the lives of others." In my case, at least, the truth of this sentiment is probably more than Anderson intended. While over the last several years my writing has brought me into the lives of Jimmy Carter and the prominent figures of his day, my research has forced me—perhaps more directly—into the lives of librarians, archivists, researchers, and editors without whom all of my efforts would have been in vain. At Southeastern Oklahoma State University, Ken Chinn, my department chair, has supported me in more ways than I can count. From the start Ken has encouraged my work and helped arrange my schedule for the time it required. At the Henry G. Bennett Memorial Library, librarian Dennis Miles assisted in my research and, just as important, was always a friendly face when I needed one. Archivist Albert Nason at the Jimmy Carter Library patiently answered my e-mails and always led me to just the right file, the right record, or whatever. This book would not have been possible without archivists such as Bert and his dedicated colleagues. Independent Atlanta researcher Lynne Watson-Powers also aided in locating key sources. I want to thank all those who agreed to oral histories and quietly endured my endless questions. I also thank the photographic staff at the National Archives, Liberty University, and the Christian Broadcasting Network. The editors at the University of Georgia Press, including Nancy Grayson, Beth Snead, and Jon Davies, did a fantastic job in the production of this book. Together with John McLeod in the marketing department, they demonstrated why so many writers regard the University of Georgia Press as among the best academic publishers in the nation. In the end, I want to thank those whose lives were most affected by my work: my wife, Celeste, and my daughters, Maya and Emily. Their patience and love while I toiled away always reminded me that family is, indeed, the most important thing in life.

Jimmy Carter,
the Politics of Family,
and the Rise of the
Religious Right

Washington for Jesus

THE CROWDS BEGAN TO ASSEMBLE early, some arriving on busses, a line of which remained parked on the streets nearby. Others took the Metro, Washington's new subway system, chartered during the morning rush hour for the occasion. Despite the gray and chilly weather, the thousands arriving remained enthusiastic, congregating on the Mall, where a large stage constructed in red, white, and blue dominated the rally. Posters and signs declared, "America, You Need Jesus!" and "The Bible—It's True." Swarms of people strolled or held hands and prayed or sang, their arms waving to the sky in celebration. By evening, twelve hours after it had begun, the rally closed, estimates of participation varying but all acknowledging that hundreds of thousands of people from across the nation had attended. Whether the police estimate of two hundred thousand or the organizer's claim of half a million, the crowd surpassed the throngs who had turned out recently to welcome the new pope, John Paul II. The rally was, some suggested, one of the largest ever on the Mall, the most impressive since Martin Luther King Jr.'s famous March on Washington a decade and a half before. As one observer put it, the rally was "the largest single assemblage of Christians in American history." It was a "Christian Woodstock."[1]

The Washington for Jesus rally on April 29, 1980, certainly met the expectations of its organizers. The idea for the rally had begun more than two years before with Pastor John Gimenez, a Harlem-born Puerto Rican who had overcome drug addiction and a criminal conviction to lead Rock Church, an independent charismatic congregation in Virginia Beach, Virginia. America had lost its way, Gimenez asserted, and needed to return to its theological moorings, to accept Jesus and repent before it was too late. America's sins were manifold—homosexuality, abortion, feminism, and what some termed "secular humanism." A repugnant cultural liberalism in all of its manifestations had for almost two decades rapidly consumed the traditions that had made America special in God's eyes. Indeed, the very core of America—the nuclear family—was in danger. Gimenez said that he had received a "vision" from God calling him to stage a rally in the shadow of the Capitol, a rally that would "dramatize to the nation and the world that the church of Jesus Christ means business." In Gimenez's vision, conservative Christians clearly played the role of the biblical David. "Even as David aimed at Goliath's head and slew him, so we have to go to the capitol—the head of government—where unrighteousness is being legislated," he insisted. Despite all their historic differences, conservative Christians "share a common concern that the United States has gone off course spiritually and is consequently facing a serious crisis." A "common ground" existed where all concerned could "stand together and seek God in humility and repentance."[2]

Gimenez shared his vision with Pat Robertson, who as a fellow charismatic also believed in the inner workings of the Holy Spirit, in, for example, faith healings and the speaking of tongues. Robertson was a fifty-year-old neighbor, a friend, and as Gimenez undoubtedly knew, a man who enjoyed a larger platform as founder of the Christian Broadcasting Network and host of the popular television ministry *The 700 Club*. The Yale-educated son of a senator, Robertson thought Gimenez's idea brilliant but had loftier aspirations. To attract noncharismatics, Robertson asked one of his former film producers, John Gilmore of Virginia Beach, to approach his acquaintance Bill Bright, the fifty-nine-year-old founder of Campus Crusade for Christ, the well-known evangelical youth ministry on college campuses across the nation. No charismatic, Bright had been quietly planning a similar rally in conjunction with his ongoing Here's Life campaign but quickly agreed to scrap his plans in lieu of a coordinated, larger effort. Most important, Bright had connections in virtually all Christian denominations, and with some luck the rally might even attract Catholics as well as Protestants. It might cross all racial and socioeconomic divides. The ambitious trio formed a nonprofit organization, One Nation Under God, to coordinate fund-raising and planning, with Gimenez the chair of its national steering committee. The rally would be, Robertson told all who would listen, a "once-in-a-lifetime celebration of holy communion in a worship service at the foot of the Washington Monument."[3]

One Nation Under God established a toll-free telephone line and opened

380 offices around the country; it then raised over half a million dollars in contributions. Almost every congressional district had an office, which ensured wide grassroots participation. Ministers received fliers, while congregations learned of the planning process through sermons. "Your help is needed now," read a flier distributed to pastors. "Exhort each congregation, each audience, each group you address to become involved."[4] Despite theological disputes and a history of frequent antagonism, Christians across the denominational spectrum rushed to join. A number of conservative Baptists, Methodists, Presbyterians, Lutherans, and members of independent "Bible churches," among others, planned to attend. Christians both within and outside the Pentecostal tradition agreed to put aside their differences to unite against what they believed to be a common enemy. Fundamentalists, those who insisted upon a literal interpretation of scripture, planned to attend in force even as their less restrictive evangelical cousins made arrangements as well. Catholics proved more reticent, their conflict with many in the Protestant fundamentalist community especially bitter. In the end the United States Catholic Conference did not endorse the rally but acknowledged the participation of a number of priests, a position that, perhaps, implied its approval.[5]

The list of the rally's supporters grew into a virtual Who's Who of American evangelicalism. Dr. Ben Armstrong, executive director of the National Religious Broadcasters, brought extensive connections in both the theological and political realms. Notable participants included D. James Kennedy of Coral Ridge Presbyterian Church in Fort Lauderdale, Florida; Charles Stanley of First Baptist Church in Atlanta, Georgia; and Adrian Rogers of Bellevue Baptist Church in Memphis, Tennessee, the newly elected president of the Southern Baptist Convention. Rex Humbard, whose launching of the massive Cathedral of Tomorrow in Cuyahoga Falls, Ohio, foreshadowed the rise of the "megachurch" so common in later years, planned to attend, as did Robert Schuller of Crystal Cathedral in Garden Grove, California, an enormously popular televangelist known to mix patriotism into his sermons. James Robison, a Dallas Baptist broadcaster and one of the most respected evangelists in Texas, agreed to participate, although he still planned to convene a large gathering of conservative Christians in Dallas in August. Jim Bakker, the smooth host of PTL, the Praise the Lord network, which had grown to over 170 stations, sought a leadership position, as did Demos Shakarian, head of the popular Full Gospel Businessmen's Fellowship. Internal strife, every minister agreed, should not divert the faithful from their common problem. All promised to use their mailing lists, program audiences, or personal contacts to further recruitment. With its diversity as its strength, the group together hoped to save the American family.

Unity, however, was not easy. Despite the worrisome societal trends of the previous decade, many evangelicals still hesitated to enter the political realm, a sentiment born of their history. The Baptist faith, for example, had long stressed the principle of the separation of church and state. During the denomination's formative era many early Baptists were poor frontiersmen who feared the hegemony of rich, eastern Anglicans in the Colonial assemblies. Two centuries later, when fundamentalists had taken the lead in combating the teaching of evolution in public schools, the famous Scopes Trial discredited them in the eyes of many Americans. Their political activism had cast them as uneducated, unsophisticated hillbillies. More significantly, perhaps, many evangelicals still believed that attempting to influence worldly affairs diverted attention from their primary mission of converting, and thus saving, individual souls. The prominent evangelist Jerry Falwell, minister of Thomas Road Baptist Church in Lynchburg, Virginia, had explained this view as late as 1965 in a sermon dubbed "Ministers and Marchers." Men of God should preach "the pure saving gospel of Jesus Christ" and avoid politics, Falwell remarked. "Preachers are not called to be politicians but to be soul winners."[6]

To overcome such resistance, One Nation Under God remained persistent and focused. Ultimately, only two notable evangelists did not plan to attend the Washington for Jesus rally. The famed preacher Billy Graham, known to work with every president since Harry Truman, endorsed the idea but declined to participate personally. The sixty-one-year-old dean of evangelists had never shared any fundamentalist hesitancy to embrace politics but had always tried to avoid legislative specifics or the partisanship politics engendered. Graham cited scheduling difficulties with a crusade he planned in Indianapolis, although any new evangelism with political overtones undoubtedly would have given him pause. Graham, after all, was still reeling from his close association with President Richard Nixon, disgraced in the infamous Watergate scandal six years before.[7]

Jerry Falwell, now forty-seven and ambitious as ever, also declined to attend. In one sense, at least, Falwell's absence appeared odder than Graham's. In an amazing theological reversal Falwell had renounced his "Ministers and Marchers" sermon and endorsed political activism. Attributing his shift to the spread of secularism and cultural liberalism in the 1960s,

Falwell now intended to launch "a holy war for the survival of the family."[8] Falwell knew the rally's participants personally and had even recruited several of them to his newly formed religious and political lobby, the Moral Majority. Kennedy and Stanley, for example, had agreed to serve on the Moral Majority's first board of directors. Like Gimenez and Robertson, Falwell also now acknowledged the advantages of reaching across denominational lines. Just weeks before, he had met with Catholic cardinal John O'Connor, and the two had agreed that homosexuality and abortion were sins to battle. Nevertheless, Falwell still harbored reservations about Washington for Jesus. Even as Robertson pressed for his involvement, Falwell replied that he feared the rally would fizzle, discrediting its architects. In fact, Falwell had other reasons, which he confessed in later years. "The rally appeared too heavily charismatic," he admitted, referring to the flamboyance of many charismatic pastors. "I was afraid of a loose cannon in an uncontrolled environment saying something that would hurt us." It was, in short, an admittance that, even as Washington for Jesus loomed, he still had problems overcoming the historic animosities that had divided the Christian community. After the rally concluded, however, he never experienced any reluctance again. Falwell had, it appeared, learned his lesson.[9]

Robertson selected April 29 as the date of the rally because of its historic political significance. On that day in 1607 the first settlers of the Jamestown colony landed and erected a cross on the new shore. Two hundred and fifty-six years later, in 1863, President Abraham Lincoln proclaimed the date the National Day of Humiliation, Fasting, and Prayer. America, the date seemed to suggest, was a Christian nation from the start. Politicians, of course, were one of the rally's intended targets. Washington for Jesus had strong political overtones from the outset, although One Nation Under God continued to portray the rally as nonpartisan. "We are coming to support no candidate for public office," Robertson told the media, "but to repent our sins as a nation."[10] Left unstated was that the rally's backers also coordinated with Intercessors for Congress, a group that planned to recruit "1,000 believers in each congressional district." On the day of the Washington for Jesus rally, Intercessors planned to flood the offices of each congressman with "prayer partners."[11] One Nation Under God issued a four-page statement of its objectives titled "Christian Declaration." The statement declared that "[Americans] have turned from God" and then listed the "slaughter of unborn children" and the prevalence of "adultery, rape and homosexuality" as evidence. It openly endorsed the Family Protection Act, a broad bill that not only supported "traditional families . . . and the role of women as traditionally understood" but also prohibited funds for any agency or function that might advance abortion, homosexuality, or feminism. In sum, the document outlined positions on a host of economic, diplomatic, and social issues, many politically controversial, morally ambiguous, and not normally considered the direct purview of religion. The declaration stated, for example, that the government "has become bloated at the expense of the citizens" and stifled freedom and initiative. "Our government has aided our enemies and destroyed our friends." Leaders had forgotten that they were "first servants of God, then servants of the people." Even when addressing issues long of concern to conservative Christians (for example, humanism in education), the document appeared to take a tone intended to provoke. Satanism and other sins, it explained, "are taught [in schools] at public expense."[12]

Such sentiments worried the Reverend Robert Maddox; in fact, he had warned his superiors about them for months. A Southern Baptist minister, Maddox had agreed less than a year before the rally to serve as a liaison to the religious community for the administration of Democratic president Jimmy Carter. Working out of the Old Executive Office Building adjacent to the White House and under the jurisdiction of the Office of Public Liaison, Maddox learned quickly the difficulty of his new job. Most of Carter's staff, Maddox recalled, "didn't understand what deep trouble he was in with these [religious-oriented] issues." The staff tended to discount the "number and intensity" of religious conservatives and their anger. Those who recognized the growing hostility tended to dismiss its political significance.[13]

The staff's complacency was, perhaps, understandable. Carter remained one of the most famous evangelicals in the world, a man whose faith defined not only his person but also his policies. After losing his bid to become Georgia's governor in 1966, a depressed Carter had famously become "born again." Already an ardent Southern Baptist, he had rededicated his life to Christ.[14] When the *Washington Post* reported on this conversion experience ten years later during his presidential campaign, an explosion of national coverage resulted. Carter later estimated that by May 1976 over one hundred articles had explored his religion.[15] As most evangelicals cheered the publicity Carter garnered for their faith, reporters now spoke of the "religious issue." According to *Newsweek* magazine, 1976 was "The Year of the Evangelical."[16]

Not surprisingly, therefore, much of the same constituency that supported the Washington for Jesus movement in 1980 had supported the refreshing candidacy of Jimmy Carter four years before. With the stain of Watergate still fresh, the born-again Southern Baptist who promised never to lie appeared to the faithful to be just what the doctor ordered. When Carter spoke of his born-again faith, Falwell remembered, it was "a flash card to Christians and gave comfort to many." While he personally still harbored reservations, "two-thirds of our people supported Carter."[17] Late in the 1976 campaign Robertson invited Carter to appear on his *700 Club* broadcast. In the interview Carter turned the conversation to the state of the American family. "One of the reasons that we have begun to rely much more heavily on the government to provide our needs is because of the destruction of relationships within the family or within the church," Carter stated. The government could not legislate morality, but the president "needs to set an example, not only himself, but members of his family." Robertson then asked Carter if he would appoint people of "godly counsel." Appointees, Carter replied, should have as an "important prerequisite" a "commitment to the principles expressed to us by God." Robertson responded with a simple "amen."[18]

It seemed a natural alliance. Robertson, who still considered himself a Democrat like his powerful father, asked Carter to do a promotion for a coming television revival and applauded when Carter promised to convene a White House conference on the American family if he were elected. While Robertson claimed a dozen years later that he had voted for the incumbent Republican, Gerald Ford, in the election, he also admitted, "I thought it would be wonderful to have a man who was a born-again Christian as president." He acknowledged that he voted for Carter in the primary and, reminiscent of his rhetoric at the Washington for Jesus rally four years later, proclaimed after the election that Carter offered "an unprecedented opportunity for America to fulfill the dream of the early settlers who came right here to Virginia in 1607, that this land would be used to glorify God." In fact, at one point Robertson even boasted that he had done everything short of violating Federal Communications Commission (FCC) regulations to ensure Carter's victory.[19] Whatever his later comments, Robertson was hardly alone among evangelicals in supporting Carter. In a keystone address to the Southern Baptist Convention, pastor Bailey Smith stated directly that the United States needed "a born-again" in the White House.[20] *Christianity Today*, whose readers included a wide array of theological conservatives, stopped short of endorsing Carter but noted the importance both of his faith and of a "religious qualification in the electoral process that is too dear to yield." If nothing else, when the 1976 election closed, its results suggested that Carter's religion had indeed played a critical role. Carter had expanded the Democrats' evangelical vote by approximately 50 percent, undoubtedly significant in a close election won by a slim margin of 1.7 million votes.[21]

Now, four years later and with the Washington for Jesus rally rapidly approaching, Maddox knew that the past was not necessarily prelude. The fact that most members of One Nation Under God had voted for Carter before meant nothing now that he was running for a second term. The brief tenure of the Carter administration, Maddox insisted, had somehow witnessed a profound change in the attitude of many conservative Christians. Nevertheless, oddly to Maddox, the White House staff still appeared oblivious to or at least unconcerned about this change. In the words of Carter friend Bert Lance, who briefly headed the Office of Management and Budget, many advisors still assumed that "the religious community belonged to Carter."[22] This belief had to change, Maddox insisted. It was still not too late.

The situation, Maddox told all who would listen, demanded an embrace or at least an acknowledgment of the Washington for Jesus rally. Residual goodwill remained. One Nation Under God still, officially at least, proclaimed itself politically impartial. If the administration moved quickly, there was reason for hope. The White House had received a number of requests from Robertson and Bakker to interview Carter, Maddox reported. It was wise to accept. "Millions in the conservative/evangelical community still want to vote for the President but need assurances that he is indeed a devoted Christian who relies heavily on the leadership of the Lord as he makes his difficult decisions," Maddox lobbied White House press secretary Jody Powell.[23] Powell's assistant, Ray Jenkins, agreed that the interview might not be a bad idea. It would be best to conduct it before the annual meeting of the National Religious Broadcasters, which would show excerpts on closed-circuit television. The potential audience might be in "excess of 100 million," and *ABC News* might use some of the interview as well, even allowing beforehand for a White House veto of the portions selected. "I recommend these undertakings," Jenkins agreed.[24]

Receiving no response and sensing both an urgency to act and the hesitancy of his superiors, Maddox broadened his ideas and recommendations in a much longer memo to Powell a week later. The memo's title made Maddox's concern obvious: "The Religious Aspects of the Campaign." Maddox began by noting that "conservative groups will vote in greater blocks than ever before," with the television preachers helping millions to decide their vote. "Many of these conservatives will vote for the President only if they are convinced that his stands on certain key issues are compatible with theirs." Carter's born-again faith had raised their expectations four years before, but this now made him "vulnerable to charges of inconsistency if he does not lift up selected issues." Maddox noted that Carter's positions on issues such as abortion and prayer in schools were difficult for many evangelicals to grasp. Carter still needed to explain that his stance on public policy did not mean that he personally favored abortion or that he thought children should not pray. If Carter would address these complex issues in more detail, "conservatives would at least have the advantage of understanding his true positions." Maddox now also recommended that Carter, besides granting the television interviews that Maddox had previously recommended, directly address the annual meeting of the National Religious Broadcasters scheduled to be held in the nearby Capital Hilton. Carter should invite leading evangelical ministers to personal meetings, Maddox wrote, adding that many had already met with the Republicans. Perhaps most important, Maddox reiterated, "a huge 'Washington for Jesus' rally is being organized for the Smithsonian Mall." Many conservative groups planned to participate, and "hundreds of buses will bring the people to the city." Hotels were already booked for the weekend. "The President, as President, will be invited to speak, the only political leader invited." He should quickly accept, Maddox argued.[25]

In fact, organizers had already reached out to Maddox. Robertson did not attend the meeting, but Gimenez and Shakarian joined Robertson's friend Ted Panteleo and noted developer and Christian activist Paul Toberty in pressing for Carter's participation. One Nation Under God genuinely intended the rally to bridge all divides, the delegation insisted, political as well as religious. Carter was the president; he would receive a warm welcome. The group impressed Maddox, who recalled them as "four of the finest gentlemen I've ever met." Gimenez invited Maddox to attend his church several weeks later, and Maddox readily accepted. Once in Virginia Beach, Maddox attended a dinner of the rally's organizers but found many of the charismatics annoyed with Carter. "I didn't even taste my food," Maddox later wrote, "so intense was the interrogation." After the dinner, however, at a church service and formal planning session for the rally, Maddox found a different reception. The service, for one, was "delightful." Maddox agreed to preach, and he was well received by the audience. The organizers explained that they invited Carter to speak as a president, not as a candidate. Republican challenger Ronald Reagan would receive no invitation. "I was moved by their dream and excited about the spiritual—and I must say, political—potential for the rally," Maddox admitted.[26]

Much to Maddox's dismay, the White House declined. Carter never attended the Washington for Jesus rally, nor did he ever publicly acknowledge it. He never embarked on a full-fledged campaign to win back religious conservatives, despite another, more detailed Maddox plea four months after the rally. As the rally approached, the administration did agree to invite a dozen religious conservatives to a breakfast meeting at the White House, but the meeting did not go well. Robertson declined to attend, but One Nation Under God members Kennedy, Bakker, Shakarian, and Humbard agreed to come. The meeting accomplished little, however, and the only result was a public dispute between the White House and Falwell over comments Carter had allegedly made about homosexuals. Similarly, Carter agreed to address the annual meeting of the National Religious Broadcasters several weeks before the rally, but that too appeared fruitless. Afterward, in the months that followed Washington for Jesus, Maddox often received explicit instructions when conservative pastors pressed for a meeting with Carter: "If they call again, the answer is no!"[27] Maddox did what he could to close the rift, attending a smaller Jesus '80 rally at Anaheim Stadium in California. He knew, however, that he was fighting an uphill battle, his superiors apparently lost without a political roadmap. On the one hand, Maddox bemoaned, the rally had emboldened conservatives to promote their "morality by decree," their "virtue with a vengeance." On the other hand, Carter's staff still did not understand "how born again translates." They still did not understand the situation.[28] Sadly, for Maddox, the political die appeared to have been cast.

Rally festivities began the night before the anointed day. Thousands of young participants attended a "youth rally" held in Robert F. Kennedy Memorial Stadium just east of the Capitol, the home of the Washington Redskins National Football League club. There they heard prayers and entertainment from singer Pat Boone, former Mr. Universe Bob Birdsong, and professional soccer player Kyle Rote Jr., among others. For the older participants, the midtown headquarters of the Daughters of the American Revolution hosted a prayer vigil and gathering. A number of the almost sixty speakers the next day avoided controversy, obviously worried about overt partisanship. In the words of one participant, the rally was "similar to a 'repentance' rally analogous to those of Old Testament days." Speakers read scripture and pleaded for redemption. "The Washington for Jesus rally was not a condemnation of non-Christian people, but a spiritual renewal for those that attended."[29]

While some spoke of the forgiveness of sin and God's love and hope for America, specific complaints about federal policy on abortion, homosexuality, sex education, and the prohibition of prayer in schools resonated with the crowd, drawing large applause. The American family was in grave danger, all agreed. Gimenez spoke of the need to "reverse the trend of the nation away from God." He noted that when critics complained about evangelicals' positions on public policy, the faithful should take no heed: "We are standing on biblical truth."[30] A degree of urgency, of crisis, underlay many speeches, the speakers pronouncing that problems were too pressing to be ignored any longer. "America has one last chance," bellowed Bakker to cheers from the crowd.[31] Added Robertson, "There is one ruler over the affairs of man, God Almighty. Every leader in this city holds his tenure only so long as God wills it." The nation was angry, Robertson continued, and the time was ripe for action. "We have enough votes to run this country. And when people say, 'We've had enough,' we are going to take over."[32] It was James Robison, however, who threw the crowd the reddest meat: "I am sick and tired of hearing about all the radicals and the liberals and the leftists and the Communists coming out of the closet. It's time for God's people to come out of the closets, out of the churches, and change America." With gay rights protesters within shouting distance, Robison's inflammatory statement resonated with his audience, which roared its approval.[33] In the end, one participant summed up the sentiments of the zealous multitude: "You feel [excitement] all around you, people raising their hands to God and praying for Him to spare the country, and singing the old, soul-stirring hymns, not through a little speaker in a TV set, but from all around you."[34] It was, he hoped, the dawn of a new day.

The crowd's preference for Republicans was hard to deny. For one, if the government was legislating unrighteousness, to paraphrase Gimenez, and the Democrats held all branches of government, then it stood to reason that the Democrats were unrighteous. Even when sticking directly to scripture, most speakers avoided the sins of war, poverty, and racial bigotry, undoubtedly aware of their Democratic associations. While not invited to speak, a number of notable Republicans welcomed the crowd, including Utah senator Orrin Hatch and New York congressman Jack Kemp.[35] The National Gay Task Force, a group of gay and lesbian activists predictably hounding One Nation Under God, documented that not only had many Intercessors lobbied for specific bills, as they had promised not to do, but their efforts had focused overwhelmingly on Republicans.[36] Moreover, one did not have to look far to note that many pundits and advocates not directly involved in the rally but publicly supportive of it had long Republican associations. Phyllis Schlafly, the fifty-six-year-old antifeminist crusader and onetime Republican candidate for the Senate, then embroiled in a fight against ratification of the equal rights amendment, spoke strongly in favor of Washington for Jesus. Former beauty queen Anita Bryant, who had increasingly embraced Republicans in her well-publicized struggle against homosexuality, lent her support as well. "I am not just concerned about one issue," she stated. The nation's drift away from God had to stop. "All of these issues are just symptoms of the moral decadence of America."[37]

Not only were Republican associations obvious, but the rally promised that they would grow stronger in the future. It was, after all, no coincidence that a presidential election loomed just under seven months away. Bumper stickers supporting the likely Republican presidential candidate, former California governor Ronald Reagan, were omnipresent at the rally. Reagan had worked to cultivate many of the rally's organizers and planned to attend Robison's Dallas event in August. As many participants learned from the campaign fliers Reagan volunteers handed out during the Washington for Jesus rally, the Republican candidate clearly had potential.[38] Nevada senator Paul Laxalt, Reagan's campaign committee chairman, directed his volunteers to focus on the evangelical vote at the rally but, aware of the many obstacles, tried not to rely too heavily on a theological appeal. "I hope that they can turn out the votes, but I don't know," he explained a week before the rally. "It's never been tried before." David Keene, who at the time of Washington for Jesus still directed the campaign of Reagan's chief Republican challenger, George Bush, was even more dubious: "I expect there's a potential source of some vote power there, but I don't know if it's ever been demonstrated." Theological conservatives had yet to prove that they could overcome their many differences or the historical disdain many still held toward politics. On the other hand, Keene acknowledged, the new issues of homosexuality, abortion, and feminism—"what they now are calling traditional moral values"—might reshuffle the political deck.[39] Only the future would tell.

Before the National Park Service employees had even begun to clean up the Mall after the Washington for Jesus rally, debate over its impact had begun. In the end, Washington for Jesus was nothing but a futile exercise in self-righteousness, critics concluded, nothing that had any long-term consequences. Robertson had promised that the rally would raise so much money that proceeds would go to a Cambodian refugee fund, but it appeared that the charity had received little money. In fact, the skeptics claimed, the rally had not even covered its own expenses.[40] The rally, they laughed, had not received a great deal of media coverage. Indeed, after front-page coverage the day following the rally, the event seemed to fade rather quickly from public consciousness, the political spin notwithstanding. The resignation of Cyrus Vance as secretary of state and his replacement with Maine senator Edmund Muskie undoubtedly diverted coverage, but the lingering Iranian hostage crisis (Americans had already suffered five months of bondage at their embassy in Teheran) continued to dominate the news cycle. This was all predictable sour grapes, organizers countered; the rally was a seminal event. Engaging in a little hyperbole, Bright confidently declared the rally "the most important day in the nation's history apart from its founding." Robertson had the same sentiments, although he was more measured in his comments. "I believe this is an historic moment for our nation," he exclaimed.[41] For his part, Robison simply observed the obvious. Washington for Jesus was "one of the first times that mainline denominations joined hands with Charismatics and Pentecostals and said 'Let's stand up together.'" The future, he promised, would see continued coordination.[42]

Certainly, for both the ambitious ministers and the equally ambitious Republicans who wooed them, Washington for Jesus demonstrated the wisdom of their new alliance. Whatever the media coverage, they had clearly touched a nerve among many Americans. "God isn't a right-winger or a left-winger," Robertson still exclaimed on occasion, even as he enjoyed the fact that for the first time people approached him advocating that he run for the Republican presidential nomination.[43] Every religious television network had carried the rally, reaching into thousands of homes across the land. The rally's participants left Washington enthused and, obviously, focused on the upcoming election. The press and much of the public may not have recognized the symbolism or significance of the Washington for Jesus rally, but in retrospect it proved that the strengthening alliance of conservative Christians and the Republican Party was here to stay. With critics' cries of a "right-wing agenda" still ringing in the air, *Christianity Today*, at least, was inspired by the rally to write of the "New Political Right," the new "Religious Right."[44]

The Washington for Jesus rally in 1980 hardly created the modern Religious Right, but its story—the motivations and actions of its key players, the manner in which events unfolded—tells a lot about the social and political movement that has so defined American conservatism for the past generation. It illustrates both the complex nature of the movement and the forces that drove its growth. Supreme Court Justice Potter Stewart famously remarked in a 1964 case concerning pornography, "I will know it when I see it." The same, one might suggest today, is true for the Religious Right. Like obscenity, the Religious Right is controversial, and defining it is no easy task, the definition inevitably reflecting as much about the assumptions of the person describing it as the movement's actual characteristics. Nevertheless, like obscenity in a court of law, a definition is necessary if one is to discuss the movement's origins and history.

Critics, such as those opposed to the rally, have described the Religious Right as a "motley group of ultra-conservative, self-defined 'Christian fundamentalists' who decided that the United States was losing its heritage." They have "roared into the political arena to make what they see as the law of God the law of the land." They were "born-again fascists," the "new subversives." Not only is this characterization unduly harsh, it makes a mistake common to less biased reviewers. It limits the Religious Right to fundamentalists, a term somewhat promiscuous. The journalist Elizabeth Drew, for example, described the Religious Right as a "new form of an old element in American political life . . . the fundamentalist religious movement." It was, in the words of another, a "fundamentalist phenomenon" that sought to weaken church-state barriers.[45]

To many members of the Religious Right, on the other hand, the movement was broader than Christianity, encompassing America's "Judeo-Christian" heritage and dedicated to traditional values. Supporters often preferred descriptors such as "profamily," some even objecting to the term "Right" as too connected to the Republican Party. To them the movement was broad and nonpartisan, just as the organizers of Washington for Jesus claimed. Ralph Reed, a leader of one of the most prominent Religious Right organizations of recent years, the Christian Coalition, characterized the movement in such sweeping terms that it almost lost any meaning. The Religious Right, Reed insisted, "encompasses much of what was good about

America for most of the history of the republic and adds to this some more recent gains."[46]

Its advocates and critics aside, the movement's theological foundations are clearly complex. The movement has elements of Catholicism and Mormonism and even a smattering of Orthodox Judaism, but its membership, in the words of author Matthew Moen, hails primarily "from the conservative wing of Protestantism." This "phalanx of the pure in heart," scholars Samuel Hill and Dennis Owen concur, finds its roots in the "evangelical and fundamentalists families of Protestantism."[47] The movement draws most heavily from the evangelical community, once again a rather nebulous description. In its broadest sense evangelicalism simply implies the authority of scripture and a belief in salvation by grace through faith. As an expression of the Reformation, it has existed since the sixteenth century. In the more accepted modern sense and in its application to American history, it connotes a faith internalized by a conversion experience and externalized in moral and spiritual discipline, including mission work. In general, one accepts an individual commitment to Christ during a "born-again" conversion experience, although some have noted that not all evangelicals self-identify as "born again." Fundamentalists, while hardly the movement's only engine, are indeed a major component. Overlapping with evangelicals, their insistence that scripture is inerrant is, to some, "orthodoxy gone cultic," their revivalist traditions reactionary and militantly antimodernist.[48] The Religious Right contains a number of members from the Pentecostal and charismatic communities as well as denominations such as the Church of Christ and the American Lutheran Church. Conservatives within the "mainline" Protestant faiths, such as Presbyterianism and Methodism, have contributed, while the Religious Right continues to draw heavily from the Southern Baptist Convention and the growing number of independent Bible churches. The Washington for Jesus rally was only a case in point.

None of this is to imply, however, that every member of these religious constituencies is a member of the Religious Right. To some extent opinions vary within all faiths; all religions risk fracturing. Fundamentalists, one writer explains as an example, "may be apocalyptic or nonapocalyptic, political or apolitical." Some abhor politics, while others enmesh themselves in it. Of the latter, some share an historic allegiance to the Democratic Party, while others embrace the Grand Old Party.[49] Moreover, the issue of race remains. Many African Americans have not joined the movement, just as they were largely absent from the rally. While undoubtedly many share a conservative Christianity, if not a political activism, with their colleagues in the Religious Right, their political identity remains forged in the civil rights struggles and the Democratic allegiances those struggles encouraged. One could suggest that while the Religious Right extends across all geographical boundaries, it maintains its strength in the rural and suburban communities of the South, the so-called Bible Belt. In the words of one observer, "In large part, [members of the Religious Right] are new arrivals to the rapidly expanding cities and growing suburbs of the New South, many having moved from smaller towns and rural areas to take advantage of the educational and employment opportunities of the late postwar period." In the words of another, they are members of the "first modernized generation," traditional people struggling to maintain rural religious values in an increasingly urban and secular society.[50] While in general the Religious Right rejects the liberal theology that grew during the era of the Vietnam War and civil rights, perhaps most famously represented by the theologian Reinhold Niebuhr, its theological foundations are clearly diverse, the movement built more on a house of shifting sand than rock.[51]

Reactive to society's dynamism, its fragile unity dependent upon events of the day, the Religious Right is as much a loose political coalition as a cohesive religious reformation. As one observer put it, "It is a delicate exercise . . . to attempt in any way to describe the 'Religious Right' except by the positions on issues they have taken and the groups with whom they have chosen to associate themselves." In the words of another, "The identity of the Religious Right is determined by the specific 'for or against' campaigns it wages."[52] Throughout American history the sentiments that drive the Religious Right have manifested themselves in reform movements as diverse as Prohibition and anti-Communism. Not surprisingly, therefore, political scientists, historians, sociologists, and theologians have produced a great volume of literature on the Religious Right, with its present incarnation a continuing interest to scholars.[53]

The modern Religious Right certainly inherited its predecessors' concerns for education, even if its struggle against modernity appears broader than simply combating evolution, pornography, or alcoholism. It continues to merge faith with triumphant nationalism, a potent combination since the days of evangelist Billy James Hargis and his Christian Anti-Communist Crusade in the 1950s. To fail America, one of the Lord's special creations, is to blaspheme God. Communism, the Religious Right continues to assume, threatens Christianity. Not only did Karl Marx proclaim religion the opiate of the masses, but Communism promises a "heaven on earth," a perfect society founded on communal, not individual, rights. In obvious contrast, Christianity denies perfectibility in the absence of God and stresses individual worth.[54] Just as during the 1950s, the modern Religious Right stresses a strong military if not a diminution of the United Nations, sometimes feared as the beginning of a one-world government. Some believe on eschatological grounds that America must stand firmly behind Israel. In their view the Middle East will prove the focal point for Armageddon, the final battle between the forces of good and evil and the signal for the Second Coming of Christ. It is essential, therefore, that the United States stand with Israel, God's people, for salvation. Israel, Falwell concluded, was a "shining testimony to the faithfulness of God."[55] Moreover, the Religious Right continues to stress laissez-faire capitalism as, in the words of historian John Kater, "inherent in American identity, and therefore a part of the divine greatness of the country and its culture." While Pat Robertson noted that the Bible admonished the faithful to stay out of debt, Jerry Falwell argued that the book of Proverbs endorses the free enterprise system. "Ownership of property is Biblical," Falwell claimed. "Competition in business is Biblical. Ambitious and successful business management is clearly outlined as part of God's plan for His people."[56]

Some evangelists and scholars have cast the modern Religious Right as a reaction to specific acts of government. In this vein the Supreme Court's 1962 ruling in *Engel v. Vitale*, which declared that a New York statute allowing voluntary recitations of nondenominational school prayers was a violation of the "establishment" clause of the First Amendment, frequently emerges as a seminal event. Others give more weight to an Internal Revenue Service ruling in 1970 that revoked the tax-exempt status of racially discriminatory private schools, a ruling enforced seven years later.[57] According to Falwell, the IRS "made us realize that we had to fight for our lives." It was "dynamite" to Robert Billings, founder of Christian School Action, and to Robert Grant it was a direct cause of his organization, Christian Voice.[58] Debates over textbook selection or school curriculum, most notably the 1974 battle over sex education in the Kanawha County, West Virginia, school district, also play a prominent role.[59] Obviously, almost all scholars note the influence of the rebellious 1960s and the equally tumultuous 1970s. In the words of author Robert Zwier, the era offered any number of "specific triggers," from the general, such as the youth counterculture and the withering of sexual inhibitions, to the specific, such as the famous 1973 ruling in *Roe v. Wade* that declared the option of a first-trimester abortion a constitutional right and the simultaneous battle over ratification of the equal rights amendment.[60]

Scholars have not forgotten the presidency of Jimmy Carter. According to Zwier, Carter was a "facilitator" for the rise of the Religious Right: "His campaign for national office in 1976 first demonstrated the possibility of mobilizing evangelicals." Carter initially energized conservative Christians, drawing many of the reluctant back into the political sphere. His actions as president, however, disillusioned them, turning their new political ardor to the Republicans. "If Carter's political ascendancy represents one of the most dramatic stories in the history of American politics, the rapid turning against Carter by many of the same evangelicals who had supported him in 1976 is one of the most striking paradoxes of American politics," Randall Balmer writes. The Carter candidacy, Clyde Wilcox concurs, had important consequences for the future of the Christian Right. "The mobilization of previously apolitical evangelical voters by the campaign demonstrated to secular political elites the existence of a new potential voting bloc," Wilcox concludes. "Leaders of the secular New Right immediately began to devise strategies to further mobilize these evangelicals and woo them to Republican activism." In the end, author Moen adds, Carter "was of great symbolic importance to the fundamentalist community." Facing an "aura of high expectations," his presidency "proved to be a major disappointment."[61]

Despite the importance that almost all serious students of the Religious Right ascribe to Carter, his record on the issues critical to the movement and, in general, his larger influence on the movement's infancy remain only partially explored. Rice University's William Martin offers the most detailed explanation of Carter's role, devoting portions of two chapters to Carter in his broad survey of the movement's long history. Martin gives particular emphasis to the conference on the American family that Carter promised during the 1976 campaign and that took place, with much dissension, in a series of regional conferences four years later.[62] While these conferences were indeed critical, the issue of family—and the politics that surrounded it—was much broader, involving secular humanism in education, homosexuality, abortion, and feminism, among others—in short, the very issues that animated the Washington for Jesus rally. Taken individually, not one of these issues caused the Religious Right. Not one explains its birth. Balmer, for example, is correct when he states that any claim that abortion was the movement's main emphasis "collapses beneath historical scrutiny." Ed Dobson, an assistant to Falwell at the time, was accurate when he remarked, "I sat in the smoke-filled back room of the Moral Majority, and I frankly do not remember abortion being mentioned as a reason why we ought to do something." At the time of Carter's election in 1976, abortion still constituted a relatively new issue that had not yet fully resonated with members of the Religious Right. While a few evangelical voices, including the journal *Christianity Today*, mildly protested *Roe v. Wade* in 1973, most evangelicals remained silent, with many Southern Baptists maintaining that the decision was an appropriate articulation of the separation of church and state. "Religious liberty, human equality and justice are advanced by the Supreme Court decision," the Baptist press reported at the time.[63] Taken collectively, however, all of these issues had, by the end of the Carter years, begun to define the threat to the family that drove Dobson's and Falwell's followers. Together they laid the foundations for theological—and ultimately political—unity out of denominational diversity. Separately, not one of these issues caused the modern Religious Right, but without them as a whole, without the issues of gender and sexuality, without the politics of the family that exploded during the Carter era, the movement would not have flourished as it did. "Over the course of the post–World War II period, the 'family' has been assuming an ever more central role within evangelical belief systems," sociologist Duane Murray Oldfield notes. "The importance evangelicals attached to the family can scarcely be exaggerated," added religious historian David Watt. It had come to replace expectations of the Second Coming as a source of hope in a hopeless world.[64]

Carter contributed mightily to the dawn of partisan family politics. His contribution was made up of more than just his conferences on the family, and it speaks to the diversity of the American religious experience. In one sense Carter could not have avoided these issues. Carter may have unwittingly precipitated the debate by calling the conferences that Martin so ably describes, but he could not have avoided, say, the ratification struggle over the equal rights amendment or the controversial political rise of gay activist Harvey Milk. Whoever occupied the Oval Office, Illinois congressman Henry Hyde was going to propose contentious legislation prohibiting federal funds for abortion, an amendment that ultimately took his name. Local communities were going to debate divisive ordinances on gay rights regardless of whether Carter was president. The Internal Revenue Service had already threatened to remove schools' tax-exempt status. The issue already simmered. Nevertheless, to Carter these issues spoke to morality, and as such, he reacted to them according to his own faith. This alone assured that Carter magnified the politics of family and infuriated the Religious Right.

Carter, domestic advisor Stuart Eizenstat explained, "wanted to be a different type of President." He found political considerations distasteful. He saw himself "above that [political] system."[65] Another White House staffer recalled a meeting with Carter: "The President went around the room asking each staff member what they thought he should do. When he got to me, I started by saying, 'Mr. President, I think that politically . . .' I got about that far and he shut me up." Academics have agreed. In the words of the University of Virginia's Charles O. Jones, Carter "interpreted his representational role as that of trustee—an official entrusted to represent the public or national interest, downplaying short-term [political] considerations."[66] This was especially true for matters related to religion. Robert Maddox concluded that Carter "was loath to talk about a religious strategy," his experience with the Washington for Jesus rally illustrative of his position. "In fact, only rarely did we persuade President Carter to make any direct political overture to the religious community, so sensitive was he to the cherished Baptist tradition of separation of church and state."[67] Maddox understood that most members of the Religious Right held different theological interpretations of "family issues" and what it meant to be a born-again evangelical. He understood that Carter's faith lay in a different strain of evangelicalism, a fact perhaps lost in all the coverage his religion had received during the 1976 campaign. "To many folks in the conservative religious community, 'born-again' connoted a set of social beliefs," Maddox concluded, beliefs that did not necessarily characterize Carter. These beliefs were "anti-abortion, anti-homosexual, anti-ERA, anti-SALT, pro–military build-up, and anti–Tri-Lateral Commission."[68]

It is fair to say that Carter and the Religious Right fell on opposite sides of what some authors have delineated as two broad camps within American evangelicalism. One side reads the Bible literally, distrusts intellectualism, and fears modernity. The other, more open to change and political interaction, encourages critical reasoning and cherishes mystery and beauty as attributes of the holy. While the first group believes that Satan is a real creature and that eternal life is an actual heaven reserved for defenders of the one true faith, the second assumes that Satan is a metaphor for the potential for evil and that heaven is simply an indefinable unity with God.[69] These groups constitute two "American Christianities," author Garry Wills concludes, one of the "heart" and the other of the "head." These "two polls of American religion . . . have tugged against each other" since the nation's founding.[70] They are not necessarily mutually exclusive, however. Sharing a number of attributes, they have always interacted and occasionally overlapped, their alignment dynamic depending upon the events of the day. However they shuffle denominations, however similar or disparate they appear at any given moment, they remain distinct strands within the American evangelical experience.

"While Carter was an evangelical, believing it his responsibility to spread the word of God," Carter biographer Peter G. Bourne writes, "he was not a fundamentalist."[71] When it came to the vortex of religion and politics, Carter accepted Niebuhr. Niebuhr's writings, one Carter acquaintance surmised, were Carter's "political Bible."[72] If Carter accepted social activism in his interpretation of scripture, he did not think that it was the role of government to define and regulate matters of individual morality, such as abortion and homosexuality. Carter was "willing to struggle with the ambiguities that exist between private views and public policy," Maddox concluded. Because of this he "ran afoul of many sincere people who could not or would not operate in the middle ground."[73]

None of this made for a coherent political strategy. In the 1976 election Carter may have won many conservative Christians who did not fully understand his religious views and thought him one of their own, but he had also raised the expectations of social liberals, the same feminists, abortion rights supporters, and homosexual activists, among others, who now prepared to battle the emerging Religious Right. On the "family issues" critical to both sides, Carter eschewed politics, relied on his own moral compass, and steered a middle route. Compromising on what both sides viewed as issues of morality was not high on either side's agenda, however, and thus Carter floundered and pleased neither. As a number of scholars have noted, Carter was unable to hold together his Democratic coalition, which began to fracture by 1980.[74] Washington for Jesus and all that it entailed was only part of a larger problem Carter faced. In the words of advisor Eizenstat, "Constituent members refused to recognize economic realities, continued to make maximum demands on the administration and therefore governance became very difficult for a Democratic President at a time of high inflation and inadequate resources." With a decline in party identification and the growth of divisive issues, Carter had constantly to "assemble interest group support ad hoc." In retrospect, "we had the worst of all possible worlds because of the avaricious quality of many of the interest groups." Many "were never satisfied because we did not give them everything."[75]

Carter had unintentionally magnified the issues that drove the Religious Right. During the Carter years issues such as abortion and homosexuality, still relatively new on the national stage, became more partisan, advocacy or opposition more associated with specific parties.[76] Just as he had reacted to the Washington for Jesus rally, Carter never fully embraced one side or the other, ultimately suffering the wrath of both. To make matters worse, issues that had animated earlier manifestations of the Religious Right, for example, issues surrounding government bureaucracy, taxation, regulation, and national power, issues not directly related to the family, continued to resonate. Here too Carter angered conservative Christians, ultimately contributing to the rise of the Religious Right. "Carter's religious faith," political scientist Gary M. Fink wrote, "helped to meld a conservative mentality and a liberal social outlook into a practical political philosophy."[77] Practicality born of Carter's brand of faith, however, was sure to anger many conservative Christians. Events on the international stage proved only the most obvious example. "The Christian thing," Eizenstat reflected, "had some real impact on his sense of unwillingness to use force," and it underlay Carter's emphasis on human rights. Carter was no pacifist, but his foreign policy "was incorrectly interpreted by people as a sign of weakness." In Maddox's view, the Religious Right pressed for a "macho image" for America. With a different theological perspective, however, Carter sought a different image.[78]

It is no coincidence that the Carter years witnessed the formation of the most prominent Religious Right organizations. Prior to the Carter administration, activist evangelicals were, in the words of one author, "politically unsophisticated." Many shared a revulsion at the cultural tumult of the day, but "their activism remained disorganized and diffuse."[79] Recognizing both the breadth of this discontent and its potential political power if properly harnessed, a group of professional conservative strategists, dissatisfied with the moderation and complacency of the Republican Party, began to play off Carter. They sought to lure the discontented religious conservatives to the Grand Old Party, invigorating both conservatism and the nation simultaneously. This group of Republican masterminds included Howard Phillips, who launched the Conservative Caucus; Paul Weyrich, the driving force behind the Committee for the Survival of a Free Congress; and Richard

Viguerie, a leader in political direct mailing with a reported database of 20–30 million names. Collectively, the group approached school activist Billings and the Christian Freedom Foundation's Ed McAteer with their plan for a new Republican majority. Out of this union grew organizations such as the Religious Roundtable, Christian Voice, and Falwell's celebrated Moral Majority, among others.[80] By the end of the Carter era, author Steve Bruce notes, "Viguerie, Weyrich, and Phillips had created a mass of organizations so interlocked that any diagram . . . looks like an octopus shaking hands with itself."[81] To one Republican activist, Viguerie's database was the critical factor, essentially making him "the Godfather of the New Right."[82] Whoever deserved the most credit, author Michael Lienesch concludes, these powerful strategists at least initially "set much of the agenda for their politically less sophisticated recruits."[83]

If the Religious Right was a top-down movement, Carter had set the stage for its movers and shakers. He had proved the perfect foil. By the end of the Carter era, no doubt existed that Washington's political world had shifted, the Washington for Jesus rally only one of many indicators. Carter returned to Georgia, continuing to live his life according to the dictates of his own religious conscience. Meanwhile, Robertson, Falwell, and the others associated with the Washington for Jesus rally joined with their new Republican mentors for what they hoped would prove a successful crusade to save the American family, to save America before it was too late. The modern Religious Right had arrived. Indeed, the Carter administration had baptized it.

CHAPTER ONE

The Times They Are a-Changin'

JAMES EARL CARTER JR.'S LOVE of family was no charade, and his frequent professions of faith were no political ploy. Faith and family formed the foundation of Carter's life, the key to his character, and the explanation for many of his actions. From his birth in 1924 in the small southern town of Plains, Georgia, Carter inherited the Bible Belt morality of his devout parents. His mother, Lillian, abandoned her Methodist upbringing for the Southern Baptist faith of her strict husband, Earl, who taught the young Carter in the Sunday school his parents required him to attend. Earl and Lillian established a nurturing environment for Carter and his siblings, Gloria, Ruth, and Billy. The structure suited Jimmy. "We felt close to nature, close to members of our family, and close to God," Carter recalled in a campaign biography. Later, in a campaign interview, he elaborated. "You know I had stability there," he explained. "When things started going wrong in my life, my mother and father were there, and my community was there—which never did change; never has changed yet—but there was something there around which I built my life. In the modern-day world, you don't have that."[1]

Throughout his life Carter recalled his youth fondly. In an exit interview as he left the Oval Office in 1981, his nostalgia was obvious. Plains, Carter recalled, "had a very developed sense of family." The community noticed the arrival of a new family. "The first question anybody asked was, 'Are they Methodist or Baptist?' and then the next question was, 'Who's going to go and see them?'"[2] Carter's wife, Rosalynn, three years younger and also born in Plains, agreed. The family was critical, and life in the small town "centered around church activities and school activities."[3]

When Carter, a good student, left for the United States Naval Academy, he did not leave his faith and family behind. While a young midshipman at Annapolis, Carter taught a Sunday school class for children from the academy community. Upon graduation and stationed aboard a nuclear submarine, Carter continued his classes, this time with his congregation sitting on folding bunks between torpedoes. If his commitment was not already obvious, Carter married his hometown sweetheart and, upon the untimely death of his father from cancer in 1953, gave up a promising naval career to return to Plains and manage the family's peanut farm. His father's death had reminded him of the importance of community—a sense of place, a sense of roots, and the faith that tied it all together and gave it all meaning.[4]

Carter had not given up his ambition, however, and he set his sights on politics. Becoming active in the local Democratic Party, he won a seat in the state legislature and in 1966 launched a campaign for the governorship. His subsequent defeat hit him hard but set the stage for perhaps the most celebrated born-again conversion experience in modern American history. The term was familiar to evangelicals, who traced it back to the Gospel of John. In the third chapter of this Gospel Jesus tells a follower that he must be "born again" to see the Kingdom of Heaven. Although to many evangelicals this meant official baptism with water, most recognized the term as a profound spiritual experience during which one accepted Christ as one's individual savior. Depressed by his loss and walking with his sister Ruth Stapleton, who had become the first in her family to be born again and now counted herself as an ardent missionary, Carter asked how she appeared so happy and peaceful. The two discussed her faith, which included an unordained ministry that advocated "inner healing." Combining psychology and spiritualism with her strong Baptist faith, Ruth sought out society's pariahs and offered to restore them by "healing the wounds of the inner child" and returning to the worst moments of their life while "taking Jesus with [them]." Impressed, Carter explained that he wanted the same tranquility. Ruth asked Carter if he would give up everything for Christ, and Carter, crying, according to his sister, replied that he would. She then asked if he would give up politics, and after a long period of thought, Carter replied that, honestly, he would not.[5]

Carter's born-again experience was, without a doubt, genuine, but, as his discussion with Ruth indicated, he did not see politics and religion as mutually exclusive. Two years later, returning from one of his many religious retreats with his friend Hoyt Robinson, a former Plains resident, Carter explained his perceptions of the two. Religion should inform politics, Carter explained, but he had to guard against the reverse. Government should reflect strong religious morals; its goal, to paraphrase Reinhold Niebuhr, was to "establish justice in a sinful world." Drawing from the lessons of his parents, the separation of church and state inherent in the Baptist tradition, and theologians such as Paul Tillich, Søren Kierkegaard, Dietrich Bonhoeffer, and Karl Barth, Carter melded a rather activist existentialism in his Christian faith. He had met people from all religions at Annapolis and understood not only that good people could disagree but also that civil society required tolerance. He would evangelize, therefore, serve as an example, but avoid mandates. Carter spoke fondly and frequently of Niebuhr's "Christian Realism," a belief that sin prohibits the fulfillment of a moral ideal—pure love—in history. Humanity had to come to terms with the relativeness of human moral endeavors, with the paradoxical and contradictory nature of human existence. In practical terms this meant that humans had to be realists, always attentive to all the forces at play and always working to elicit the greatest possible justice from any given situation. Demanding perfection was impractical.[6] Advisor Stuart Eizenstat recalled that once when a supporter gave Carter a biography of Niebuhr, Carter immediately underlined the key quotes. "He knew Niebuhr," an amazed Eizenstat chuckled.[7] One of Carter's speech writers, Patrick Anderson, recalled how Carter had revised an early draft of an address, removing sections that sounded too political and adding lines that stressed the importance of "translating Christian love into justice." Anderson remarked that the change was "wonderful." Carter replied, "It ought to be. It's Niebuhr."[8]

In the years that followed his famous conversion experience, Carter never shied away from his faith or acknowledging how it guided his policies. In the words of author Erwin Hargrove, "It is plausible that between 1966 and 1970 Carter attained a certain serenity . . . by deepening his religious faith to cope with the crisis of middle life." He planned still to pursue his ambition but now was willing to accept failure "so long as he was secure in the belief that he had done his best and acted according to his principles."[9] When Carter challenged Governor Carl Sanders in 1970, the campaign turned ugly when the incumbent accused the challenger of dirty, immoral politics. Frustrated, Carter instinctively turned to his religion for a defense. "I'm a Christian, I love God," Carter remarked, denying the specifics of the charges. After his victory Carter's speeches frequently referenced his faith. In a 1972 speech before Atlanta Youth for Christ, for example, he noted the need for "a Christian approach to people." Two years later, in a speech in Macon, Georgia, he concluded that a man needs only "two loves in his heart: one is a love for God; the other is a love for the person who happens to be in front of [him]." In Orlando only a week after this address, he spoke of the need for a "completely childlike commitment to Christ." Still later, in 1974, he told the Christian Business Men's Committee of Detroit, "I am a businessman and a Christian; I am a father and a Christian; I am a Governor and a Christian." To the Southern Baptist Convention he spoke of the need to "continually strive for perfection as commanded by God." Christians should do so, however, cognizant that they will never fully achieve it and thus should guard against pride. "The best evangelism can come only when we have a personal relationship with Christ which deserves to be imitated." By the end of his term as governor, Carter, it appeared, had emerged as one of the most outspoken evangelicals in state politics.[10]

Accepting the imperfectability of human beings in a sinful world, Carter saw his mission to serve as an example for others. This meant, of course, that while he recognized that he might not attain all he sought politically, it was important for him to demonstrate pure motives. He could not be just another politician operating out of electoral self-interest. His actions had to be worthy of emulation. As Carter launched his political career, his longtime friend Charles Kirbo was blunt about Carter's intentions and the limitations they might pose for his career. "He's not a politician," Kirbo remarked before adding somewhat prophetically that if Carter were ever elected to the highest office in the land, "he may be a one-term president." Driven by his strong faith, Carter was going to do what he thought was right, whether his actions were politically popular or not.[11]

Across the denominational spectrum, Governor Carter appeared to be a champion of Christian values. At closer inspection, however, the complex nature of Carter's Christianity was evident as well, if occasionally hidden in his rhetoric or overlooked by many of his constituents. One of Carter's first acts as governor was to end the religious services that had been held every morning in the statehouse since the days of Governor Lester Maddox a decade before. He moved on to oppose state "blue laws" outlawing the sale of liquor on Sundays. Early in his term he supported family-planning programs that included abortion, and he authored the foreword to a book, *Women in Need*, that favored abortion rights. Moreover, he encouraged the plaintiffs in the case of *Doe v. Bolton*, filed against the state of Georgia to overturn its rigid abortion restrictions. The case joined with the famous *Roe v. Wade* and eventually became part of the basis for the landmark Supreme Court decision that defined abortion rights.[12] Perhaps most egregious to many in the South, he supported the integration of the Baptist Church. Segregation was "in contravention of biblical teachings," he argued unsuccessfully.[13] At the time Carter admitted, "We thought seriously about leaving the church and finally decided that we wouldn't." Because a number of young people had voiced their support, however, Carter hoped that ultimately he would be able to convince the others of the need for reform. One should always employ reason, the governor responded to a reporter who asked him if he believed everything in the Bible was literally true. "I don't think the earth was created in seven days as we know it now and I reserve the right to make my own interpretation." The Bible was an important tool for Carter in the search for the truth, but clearly he was uncomfortable with unquestioning faith.[14]

Rosalynn, Carter recalled, was always "an equal partner with me." When he worked as a peanut farmer "she not only answered the phone but she kept the books, she sent out bills, she helped me make decisions about the kinds of credit to extend and where we should get loans and identify customers." In short, "she kept up with the status of our business." Later, as Carter entered politics, Rosalynn was "obviously a key person and helped plan strategy, helped me evolve campaign platform planks, and helped me how best to approach the news media." Rosalynn and Carter had four children, Jack, Chip, Jeff, and Amy, and both of them cherished their family life, the most important aspect of their lives, as they regularly noted. Rosalynn, however, was clearly no shrinking violet; her interest, if not her influence, was as broad as her husband's.[15]

Carter had many critics, but by the mid-1970s he had established himself as a formidable politician, his disdain for the inevitable nature of elected representatives aside. He was known for his honesty and his strong Christian ideals, and he was perceived as a man who understood the importance of family. He had an acceptable record as governor and an obviously large and loving brood, Amy still a cute preteen living at home. He was not known nationally, but it was enough for Carter and his allies to begin to entertain the thought of higher office. It was a long shot, but Carter already had his eyes set on the White House.

"The times they are a-changin'," sang Bob Dylan as Carter launched his political career. The cold war raged, and nuclear Armageddon, it appeared, remained a real possibility. It had only been a decade since Wisconsin senator Joseph McCarthy's infamous anti-Communist witch hunts had exposed the underbelly of cold war politics, and while the frenzy of paranoia had ebbed, fear remained. "McCarthyism made the anti-Communist message that many fundamentalist preachers had espoused for decades suddenly popular, and it made the formation of political organizations profitable," noted Clyde Wilcox, speaking of the Religious Right of the 1950s.[16] Now, a decade later, not only did Communism still pose an obvious threat to faith and family, but America appeared to be eroding from within, perhaps the gravest threat to both. Born of postwar affluence and the maturing baby boom generation, a new emphasis on individual rights grew throughout the 1960s. This system of rights underscored not only the black struggle for an end to Jim Crow, perhaps evidenced in Carter's actions as governor, but a new counterculture. Young Americans grew more receptive to open lifestyles centered on self-gratification along with experimentation in morals, manners, and dress.

The era's emphasis on rights produced the "sexual revolution," a welcomed development for many American women who saw it as another step on their long journey to equality. While Carter was still a young politician, a Connecticut housewife named Betty Friedan authored the seminal best seller *The Feminine Mystique*.[17] In doing so she gave voice to the disillusionment of many women barred from equality in the realm of politics and business. Launching the National Organization for Women (NOW), Friedan protested the societal double standard and began to demand reform. NOW emphasized the right to equal pay and employment but also, more controversially, the right to reproductive self-determination, including legal abortions. Moreover, as historian Daniel Bell has noted, feminism was an ideology. It "raised questions of the definition of roles, status, and occupations by gender, and the problem, particularly in the character of the family, of the historically subordinate role of women."[18] The sexual divisions of labor within the family constituted "one of the oldest features of social structure," and, thus, feminism struck at the heart of the traditional family.

Feminism and its attendant reforms constituted a powerful challenge to the status quo. Paralleling the "Second Reconstruction," the burgeoning movement for African American civil rights, feminism diversified as it gained momentum. As terms such as "sexism" and "male chauvinism" became part of the popular vernacular, protests included such direct actions as sit-ins at all-male clubs, the symbolic crowning of a sheep as Ms. America, and the donning of rabbit costumes to protest *Playboy* magazine.[19] While some women lobbied quietly and patiently for equal pay, equal job opportunities, and flexibility for working mothers, others became more radical. Demanding immediate and more revolutionary action, they burned their bras, shaved their heads, and talked of overturning the patriarchal structure of society.[20] In 1970, for example, Kate Millet published *Sexual Politics*. In a male-dominated society, she wrote, the family was the principal unit for brainwashing, inculcating in young girls a sense of inferiority. New relationship patterns had to be formed. For the outspoken feminist Germaine Greer, the family was "the prison of domesticity," the "patriarchy's chief institution."[21]

These claims could be offensive, especially to stay-at-home mothers who bristled at charges of being "just a housewife." Recognizing the potential for alienation, for appearing a foe of the family, Friedan increasingly spoke of "women's rights" and not "feminism," which she had come to see as a term unfortunately tinged with radicalism. Indeed, as radical groups such as the Red Stockings mocked traditional families and even implied that all heterosexual sex was a form of rape, Friedan tried to defend housewives. "All women's work is work," she declared. It wasn't always an easy case to make. In writing that housewives, if paid, would have only the salary of "common bus drivers," a Friedan ally unintentionally insulted nonprofessional workers.[22]

Given the spectrum of views, women's advocates never walked in lockstep with ideological or political unity. Nevertheless, by the early 1970s there was enough consensus and popular support to make the long-desired equal rights amendment (ERA) a reality. Despite its differences, the movement slowly rallied around issues not only of economic equality but also of reproductive freedom.[23] To many in the women's movement, the ERA represented the Holy Grail, the cornerstone of their agenda. First proposed in 1923 by advocates such as Alice Paul, the amendment had languished in Congress for almost half a century, buried in the House Judiciary Committee.[24] Between 1940 and 1970 it emerged from Senate committees ten times. Twice, in 1950 and 1953, the full Senate passed it, but with a rider added by Arizona senator Carl Hayden. The Hayden rider declared directly that the ERA "would not be construed to impair any rights, benefits, or exemptions now or hereafter conferred by law upon the female sex," wording ultimately designed to defeat the amendment's purpose.[25]

With the burgeoning women's movement giving renewed momentum to the amendment, however, the eighty-two-year-old Paul began coordinating with NOW in 1967. The press began to highlight the effort when various civil rights groups began to announce their support. Finally, in the summer of 1970 Michigan congressman Gerald Ford helped the House Judiciary Committee report out the bill for the first time. Debate soon centered on the addition of the so-called Wiggins amendment. Similar to the earlier Hayden rider, the new wording declared that the ERA would "not impair the validity of any law" that "promotes the health and safety of the people." Obviously open-ended, it too could easily emasculate the ERA's intent. After a bitter battle in the House and Senate, Congress defeated all riders and amendments and in 1972 passed the ERA as its supporters cheered.[26] The final version was relatively simple: equality of rights under the law shall not be denied or abridged by the United States or by any state on account of sex. The law was clear, perhaps, but, as its advocates well knew, it was still controversial. As a proposed amendment to the Constitution, it needed thirty-eight states to ratify it by March 1979. At first, all indications were positive for ratification. By 1973 thirty states had approved the measure.[27] For the remainder, however, the battle promised to be fierce.

With its long history, abortion promised no less a struggle. Before 1821 American courts followed English common-law tradition, which did not condemn abortion before "quickening," the point at about sixteen to eighteen weeks when the mother could begin to feel the fetus move. After the British Parliament passed a statute restricting abortion in 1803, a few state legislatures followed, beginning with Connecticut and New York in the 1820s. These early laws, however, were concerned more with the elimination of incompetent practitioners than with the principle of abortion itself. By the 1840s this began to change as advancing science questioned the old assumptions of quickening. A growing antiabortion movement, led by physicians, resulted in broader and more restrictive statutes in many states. By the Civil War twenty-three states had laws banning all abortions, and by 1880 abortion had become illegal virtually across the country. Practitioners faced punishment but, in many states, so did the women who sought the abortions. In general, these bans remained in place until the 1960s.[28]

Beginning in the 1950s, a new movement to weaken the antiabortion statutes began among physicians who had dealt with the tragic results of botched illegal and unprofessional abortions. The doctors argued that the existing restrictions kept them from deciding what was in their patients' best medical interests. Along with environmentalists who noted the threat of overpopulation, the new feminists protested that American laws were more restrictive than in many Catholic countries. They argued that medical science had made abortion a safe and simple procedure if conducted early enough. The argument fit in well with the growing emphasis on individual rights, and by the time Carter was elected governor of Georgia, polls indicated that a strong majority of people favored abortion when the mother's health and life were threatened.[29]

Litigation naturally followed, NOW and other feminist groups viewing the courts as a promising avenue in which to address inequities in the law as well as a way to garner publicity to help guide public opinion. The 1965 case *Griswald v. Connecticut* suggested that a majority of the Supreme Court shared feminists' broad, legal-realist view of the Constitution. Although rarely enforced, laws against the use of contraceptives were still in place and supported by many conservative denominations. The *Griswald* decision declared that these laws were unconstitutional in part because of a "right to privacy" inherent in the Fifth and Fourteenth Amendments and, in general, the "constitutional scheme under which we live." Individual rights came not only from specific guarantees but also from the Constitution's guiding principle of liberty from government intrusion into the family.[30]

By 1970 state courts faced a flood of abortion litigation, and the Supreme Court had a number of writs for certiorari. It was apparent that the Court could no longer simply ignore the issue. The case that began in 1971, *Roe v. Wade*, was a class-action suit that represented the interests of many women. The Court, rearguing the case the following year and finally deciding in 1973, accepted Justice Harry Blackmun's division of pregnancies into three trimesters. During the first trimester women's rights prevailed, and the states could not outlaw abortion. During the second trimester the states could regulate but not prohibit abortions. During the third trimester the states could rule that the fetus's interests predominated over the woman's desire to terminate her pregnancy. This delicate balancing of interests pleased few, most notably many Catholics who believed that the fetus in all stages of development was a human being. In this view abortion was not only a grave threat to the family but constituted murder. Many legal scholars, strict constructionists of the Constitution, suggested that the Court had overstepped its boundaries; by twisting the Constitution beyond recognition, the judiciary had supplanted the legislature.[31]

The movement for individual rights did not stop with the issues of feminism and abortion. It also emboldened homosexuals, perhaps the most obvious challenge to the gender-specific world of the traditional nuclear family. Present in virtually all societies throughout history, homosexuality had held different meanings over the centuries. Some non-Western cultures, such as Japanese warriors in early modern times, Chinese men and women during the Yuan and Ming dynasties, and several Native American tribes in the pre-Colonial era, had recognized and institutionalized same-sex unions.[32] Although there was some limited recognition of homosexual rights in ancient Greece and Rome and to a lesser extent even in medieval Europe, homosexuals had faced persecution throughout most of Western history.[33] The Catholic Church institutionalized prohibitions against homosexuality, and the Reformation faiths did little to alter the orthodoxy.

According to social historian Michael Bronski, "homosexuality struck at the heart of Western cultures in societies." Because it posited a sexuality justified by pleasure, it stood "in stark and frightening contrast to the entrenched belief that reproduction alone legitimized sexual activity," a belief "enshrined in religious and civil law and the foundation for society's limiting gender roles," in short, the foundation for the family.[34] This was a difficult bar to overcome. Most gays, either internalizing society's prohibitions or simply remaining clandestine about their sexual orientation, did not challenge the emerging consensus. The Scientific Humanitarian Committee in Germany became the first organization to fight publicly for gay rights in 1897, and the Society for Human Rights followed in the United States in 1924. Just over two decades later, researcher Alfred Kinsey suggested that homosexuals comprised up to 4 percent of the population.[35] None of this, however, altered public perceptions. Hitler's Third Reich brutally included homosexuals in the Holocaust, and the Society for Human Rights quickly folded, the wife of one of its members reporting the group to Chicago police. The New York Supreme Court upheld regulations against gays and lesbians congregating in bars, while the State Liquor Authority threatened to withdraw the license of anyone who served gay patrons, both actions quelling what little gay subculture had grown in Greenwich Village during the 1920s. The Motion Picture Production Code officially banned all homosexual references and depictions from Hollywood films. After World War II McCarthy equated homosexuality with Communism and the cold war's McCarran Act prohibited the immigration not only of Communists but also of "sexual deviates," a term the Supreme Court later confirmed applied to homosexuals.[36] For his part, Kinsey faced criticism both inside and outside the academy. When a group of men in 1952 formed the Mattachine Society, a new gay rights group, its leader, Dale Jennings, faced prosecution for indecent behavior.[37] While gay activists argued fervently that homosexual unions constituted a family that was as real as any heterosexual family, much of the public seemed to disagree. Any gay rights movement appeared destined to failure, gays and lesbians effectively driven underground.

Society, however, was on the verge of the shifting cultural tides of the 1960s. Jennings decided to fight the indecency charges facing him, ultimately getting them dropped when the jury was unable to reach a verdict. The Mattachines also won in the Supreme Court the right to publish their newsletter, *One Magazine: The Homosexual Viewpoint*, which the postmaster general had banned as obscene. Joining in their fight was the Daughters of Bilitis (DOB), a lesbian group formed in San Francisco in 1955. The DOB's newsletter, the *Ladder*, soon reached thousands, and both groups formed chapters across the nation.[38] The American Psychiatric Association removed homosexuality from its list of mental disorders, and in 1961 Illinois became the first state to decriminalize homosexual acts between consenting adults. A number of states began to repeal their laws against sodomy, including Connecticut (1971), Colorado (1972), Oregon (1972), Delaware (1973), Hawaii (1973), North Dakota (1973), and Ohio (1974). While a sodomy law remained on the books in Massachusetts, the state's supreme court ruled in 1974 that the law's prohibition of "unnatural and lascivious acts" did not apply to private, consensual adult behavior. By the time Carter mobilized for a presidential campaign, six additional states (New Hampshire, New Mexico, California, Maine, Washington, and West Virginia) had repealed sodomy laws, which meant that effectively homosexual activity had been decriminalized for approximately one-third of the American population. In 1973 a class-action lawsuit raised the possibility of reform in federal civil service policy, and in the next several years openly gay candidates began to win local elections, most notably in Michigan and Massachusetts. Minnesota state senator Allan Spear declared his homosexuality publicly—now known as "coming out"—while in office, but his declaration did not prevent his reelection.[39]

Protests for homosexual rights began slowly. In 1965 a handful of gay men picketed the White House. Although their vigil paled in comparison to the thousands marching against the Vietnam War, many observers considered it the first public gay political protest in American history. As the decade neared its end, the Gay Activist Alliance (GAA) debated the next step in civil disobedience, an alliance with the larger youth rebellion if not the radicalism of such organizations as the Black Panthers.[40] It was, however, the Stonewall Riot in June 1969 that first introduced homosexuality as an issue at the forefront of political debate. "Stonewall became ground zero for an explosion of gay activities," reflected National Public Radio.[41] Police routinely raided gay bars in New York City, and the raid at the Stonewall Inn in Greenwich Village began just as many others. The police entered the grimy and dimly lit bar, a regular for so-called drag queens, and after asking the customers for identification, began to force them outside and into squad cars. As a crowd began to form and jeer, the officers became rougher, which in turn enraged the onlookers. Bottles, trash, and even a burning garbage can replaced the insults thrown at the police. The officers retreated into the bar and called for the riot squad. For the next three days the police kept the street open, but during the nights clashes continued. The confrontation became front-page news nationally, quickly becoming a symbol of persecution for the gay community. The Gay Liberation Front (GLF), representing a more radical element than the GAA, used the riot to garner support. By the end of 1970 the GLF claimed nineteen "cells," a word with an intended political tinge. Its newspaper, *Come Out!* demanded further action. The *Advocate*, a less angry but more influential gay newspaper founded in 1967, began to extend its circulation beyond just New York City. Obviously, the issue was not about to fade. Just like their ideological cousins, the larger feminist movement, homosexual activists ensured that the struggle for the American family was only in its infancy.[42]

The times may have been changing, as Dylan sang, but the rights revolution of the 1960s had already proved an unmitigated disaster, according to its conservative critics. The impact of feminism and its attendant reforms on the American family was, they claimed, already obvious. By the time Carter prepared for national office, a number of pundits, sociologists, and politicians had begun to tie increasing rates of juvenile delinquency, school dropout, drug use, divorce, teenage pregnancy, and crime to the decline of the traditional nuclear family. Such complaints were nothing new, as historian James Gilbert notes, going back to the "latch-key" children and rebellious youth of the 1950s.[43] After the tumultuous 1960s, however, the problem appeared worse, and the criticism had grown. While Daniel Patrick Moynihan's seminal 1965 report, *The Negro Family: The Case for National Action*, noted the destruction of the two-parent family as the primary challenge for the African American community, the following years indicated that the problem was not limited to just one race or segment of society; it was more universal and growing fast.[44] A Cornell University study in 1975, for example, noted that student test scores had plummeted over the previous two decades, while teenage suicides had almost tripled. This, together with similar figures on crime, paralleled an increase in the divorce rate and the prevalence of single-parent homes. Such homes, usually a single mother, tended to earn on average less than $4,000 per year. The resulting poverty was devastating. In the words of the report's author, Urie Bronfenbrenner, children growing up in such single-parent homes were at "especially high risk—physically, emotionally, and socially."[45]

The new cultural liberalism had to stop, critics complained. "Militant homosexuals exploit disillusionment with marriage," responded one psychiatrist, obviously disagreeing with his colleagues that homosexuality was not a mental disorder. "Homosexuality is a sign of the family's failure to be what the society needs it to be: a force for stability, the locus of affection, and the place where children must learn love, trust and belief." The tolerance and laissez-faire attitude that homosexuality encouraged destroyed the social fabric. Abortion, others added, spoke to an individualism that undermined marriage. It deemphasized the importance of family and children.[46] The most important factor, some argued, was rampant feminism, whose narcissistic individualism mocked the traditional role of housewife. Perry Shoemaker, father of four and the president of the Lackawanna and Central Railroad Company of New Jersey, undoubtedly spoke for many when he reminisced that a stay-at-home mother used to be "busy but happy in enjoying her family's development." The women's rights movement, however, had encouraged despondency and "distorted our values." Without discipline, permissiveness ruled the day. Feminist individualism had even distorted many traditional faiths. "The church is not without blame," Shoemaker concluded, "and must now reassert and restore the dignity of the family as a basic institution."[47]

In fact, feminism, abortion, and homosexuality had begun to tear at the fabric of many faiths. Their rather rapid evolution as theological and political controversies left many religions divided, tentative in their official reactions. Some saw the work of Satan. "Feminists desire to eliminate God-given differences that exist between the sexes, that is why they are pro-homosexual and lesbian," one minister claimed.[48] In several states congregations opposed to the ERA lobbied against ratification by distributing jars of homemade jelly with gift tags that read "Preserve the family unit." In other congregations the faithful organized in support, claiming that the amendment strengthened families. Opponents exclaimed that differences between the genders made some options of equality out of the question, such as women in combat roles. "Man has the physical strength," concluded one critic. "God decreed that. I didn't. You didn't. And God decreed that women would have the children." The ERA, they feared, would augment the troublesome societal changes that had been taking place, undermining the traditional "masculine" and "feminine" roles that had served as a foundation for the family, the key to a stable society throughout the ages. In the narrowest sense the amendment might force building owners to provide unisex bathrooms, while in the broader sense it might erode a man's responsibility to support his wife and children. This was nonsense, supporters countered, for a proper reading of the New Testament, if not the Old, encouraged equality, love, and acceptance.[49]

While some feared that the ERA would endanger "protective" legislation (various laws that tended to favor women, such as child custody), much resistance to the amendment was religious. One study in Texas found that over 98 percent of women opposed to the ERA attended a church regularly, with over two-thirds belonging to a fundamentalist denomination. This led the authors to conclude that "fundamentalist religion is a principal source of political attitudes of the anti-ERA women."[50] In addition, a strong overlap existed in opposition to the ERA and abortion.[51] Opposition was strongest in southern and rural areas but extended far beyond southern fundamentalists. The Church of Jesus Christ of Latter-day Saints—the Mormons—strongly opposed the ERA, while the Roman Catholic Church hardly endorsed it. Conservative wings in such denominations as the Lutheran Church and Orthodox Judaism also opposed ratification. Many individual Catholics may have supported ratification, but most service organizations with the church, such as the Knights of Columbus, vehemently opposed it. At the same time, however, polls indicated that not only did a majority of members of the Unitarian Universalist Church, the United Church of Christ, and the Jewish faith support ratification, but a sizeable percentage of the "mainline" Protestant faiths did as well.[52]

The most ardent theological conservatives insisted that the Bible prescribed a specific role for women, that of homemakers and helpmates. They claimed that women had the weaker will but were the principal vessels of virtue in society, important but in need of protection. Men were to lead, women to submit. Those who adhered to this more literal interpretation cited Genesis, noting that God created a man first and that a woman was the first to fall to Satan's temptations. They noted that Jesus took only men as his twelve disciples. Most notably, they cited the apostle Paul's letter to the Ephesians. "Wives, submit yourselves unto your husbands, as unto the Lord," the verse read. "For the husband is the head of the wife, even as Christ is head of the church."[53] The Reverend John Percley of the Baptist Bible College of Springfield, Missouri, declared such scripture immutable. God made men and women "with a difference," he preached. "We don't represent a religious group, but we are the Christian people."[54]

God was clear about abortion and homosexuality as well, Percley and his theological allies agreed. The Fifth Commandment and biblical passages such as Luke 1:40–44 and Psalm 139:13, 16 spoke clearly about life in the womb. They made clear that abortion was immoral and against God's will. At the same time the conservatives noted that Christianity was not the only religion that denigrated homosexuality as a sin. The Bible, they explained, was explicit at three points: the story of the destruction of the city of Sodom, the priestly codes of Leviticus, and the letters of Paul.[55] The apostle Paul mentioned homosexuality in the same vein as murder or other serious crimes (1 Timothy 1:8–11). Scripture identified sodomy as a sin on fifteen occasions, including "abomination" (Leviticus 18:22), "lusts" (Romans 1:24), "wicked" (Genesis 13:13), "vile affections" and "against nature" (Romans 1:26), "unseemly" (Romans 1:27), "strange flesh" (Jude 1:6–7), and "reprobate mind" (Romans 1:28). In one instance the Bible labeled homosexual prostitutes "dogs" (Deuteronomy 23:18), while in another it told homosexuals that they would not "inherit the kingdom of God" (1 Corinthians 6:10).[56]

All of this was a misrepresentation of scripture, theological liberals replied, embracing the equality and freedoms of the era as a reflection of the tolerance and love inherent in the Christian message. For one, they countered, Jesus never preached about abortion, nor did the Bible ever explicitly mention it. In regard to the verses cited against homosexuality, one had to take their condemnations in context. Often, they insisted, the verses cited were ambiguous, especially given differences in translation. Christians, for example, had interpreted the verses from 1 Corinthians eight different ways over the centuries, including several that did not involve homosexuality. Moreover, none of the verses cited referred to homosexuality as it is known today. The verses assumed that the people engaging in same-sex acts were heterosexuals acting in a way contrary to their nature. The Gospel writers associated homosexuality with the idolatrous religious worship of their pagan neighbors and could not fathom healthy, normal, God-centered, same-sex relationships. At the same time, many Jews equated homosexual practices with temple prostitution. In any event, the Bible's condemnations of homosexuality were part of a long list of Old Testament laws routinely ignored today. These antiquated laws included, for example, prohibitions on the consumption of shellfish and on the planting of two types of crops in the same field. As Methodist writer Bruce Hilton explained it, "Taking the priestly codes literally in the twentieth century raises some real problems."[57] Finally, the liberals responded, Jesus never mentioned homosexuality as a sin. When he condemned human behavior, he did so against the hardness of heart of religious insiders. Judgment, these liberals insisted, should be left to God. In the broadest sense, a loving, merciful, and magnanimous God may even have intended gay people as his special instruments in reaching out to the outcasts of society.[58]

In 1972 the General Conference of the United Methodist Church declared homosexuality "incompatible with Christian teaching," a direct response to the arguments of several gay rights Methodist ministers. The declaration hardly settled the matter. Several years later *Christianity Today* declared, "Methodists Grope for a Common Center." Gay rights supporters within the church, the article noted, complained bitterly that the leadership had reaffirmed its opposition to homosexuality even as it claimed to celebrate its differences. The church was "united in its diversity," some argued, only partly sarcastic. "Rumble of Realignment in U.S. Presbyterianism" read another headline, describing a push by some Presbyterian leaders to promote the ordination of women, a proposal that rankled conservatives and threatened a "major realignment" of the denomination. "We would rather not go," explained one church member about leaving the denomination, "but we have lost the battle from within."[59] As for homosexuality, the Presbyterian Church refused to recognize a newly formed gay caucus. Proponents of the caucus noted that the church's constitution recognized unofficial groups if they were "organized for . . . the instruction of religion and the development of Christian nurture." Any gay caucus, the Reverend Arthur McKay declared, did not qualify, since "the scriptures as understood in our tradition do not condone their sexual orientation and lifestyle."[60] To challenge such views, a group of ministers in 1965 drew from a number of Protestant denominations to form the Council on Religion and the Homosexual (CRH). Although police disrupted some of its initial meetings, the CRH represented a shot across the theological bow of conservatives. Three years later the Reverend Troy Perry founded the Metropolitan Community Church in Los

Angeles, often considered the first fully gay church in America. Within a few years the church had branches across the country.[61]

Known for its all-male priesthood and its dedication to pastoral celibacy, if not its centuries-old liturgy, the Catholic Church appeared in one sense a model of stability. In another respect, however, its divisions ran even deeper. Some reformers pressed for the right of priests to marry, while others argued for the ordination of females. Radicals even questioned the infallibility of the pope. In regard to homosexuality, the Vatican issued a six-thousand-word declaration in the mid-1970s that reasserted the church's traditional condemnation of homosexuality but illustrated that it too recognized the difficulty of the matter. The declaration drew a distinction between homosexuals "whose tendency comes from a false education, from a lack of normal development, from habit, from bad example or other similar causes" and those "who are definitely such because of some kind of innate instinct or pathological constitution judged to be incurable." Of the latter, priests should be "understanding and maintain hope." In essence, therefore, the Catholic Church recognized that not all gays and lesbians were personally responsible for their orientation but also that homosexuality was, for whatever reason, inherently sinful.[62] This was not enough for Dignity, a group of approximately five thousand Catholics who advocated open acceptance of homosexuality. Founded in Boston in 1968, Dignity called the Vatican statement a "narrow understanding of human sexuality." The Reverend John McNeill, a Jesuit theologian and Dignity leader, claimed that the Catholic Church should have a "broader" interpretation of scripture. God's destruction of Sodom, McNeill argued, was not because of homosexuality but rather inhospitality. The essence of the scriptures was "unselfish love."[63]

To make matters worse, media reports described a hierarchy in disarray over abortion, with many American leaders opposing the church's official stance rejecting the procedure. "Intra-church disputes over sexuality," the New York Times reported, "have played a crucial role in [the church's] slump." The Catholic hierarchy had not to this point made a large issue of abortion, the matter still relatively new. There were indications, however, that the Vatican might change course and plan a more public offensive, just what many America Catholics feared. According to commentator William Shannon, the bishops risked harming "the spirit of mutual charity and tolerance that should prevail in political discourse" if they tried to enforce a more rigid doctrine.[64]

Many denominations such as the Episcopalians attempted to remain relatively quiet on all such controversial matters, perhaps recognizing their divisive nature and hoping to avoid the public spats growing in other faiths. The ordination of women in the Episcopal Church passed without a great degree of controversy several years after the Carter era, and it was not until the late 1990s that a schism developed over the ordination of a gay priest. For his part, the famous evangelist Billy Graham hardly condoned issues such as abortion and homosexuality, but, perhaps trying to maintain his broad, interdenominational, nonpartisan appeal, he did not stress them as central tenets.[65]

The different paths followed between Graham's own denomination, the Southern Baptists, and the National Council of Churches were particularly noteworthy. The former, the largest Protestant denomination in America, with 12.7 million members, had a long tradition of individual autonomy and did not adopt a strong resolution stressing homosexuality as a sin or urging societal restrictions until after the Carter presidency. In 1971 and 1974 the Southern Baptists debated abortion and in each instance defeated a statement of condemnation. They reaffirmed their principle of freedom of conscience and thus once again approved of the separation of church and state. At the same time, however, it was obvious that conservative forces, accepting a more literal interpretation of the Bible and more ardently opposed to the rights revolution, were gaining in strength. As early as 1963 the Southern Baptist Convention weakened its anticreedal sentiment by revising its official "Statement of Faith and Message." Meeting in Norfolk, Virginia, more than a decade later, just as Carter campaigned for the White House, the convention first acknowledged homosexuality as "contrary to biblical truth" and prohibited the ordination or hiring of overt homosexuals. Delegates defeated a statement that urged "compassion for all persons whatever their lifestyle," but even this did not placate conservatives who sought a harsh condemnation.[66] Several years later the convention passed overwhelmingly a resolution to "preserve the doctrinal integrity of the seminaries and other institutions," demanding that all faculty "believe in the divine inspiration of the whole Bible, the infallibility of the original manuscripts and that the Bible is truth without error." Liberals countered that the resolution would have little clout, noting that many of the most outspoken faculty had tenure. Nevertheless, the conservative evolution of the denomination was obvious.[67]

The opposite, however, was the case with the National Council of Churches (NCC), a loose organization representing approximately thirty Protestant denominations. As Carter began his campaign for the White House, the governing board of the NCC called for "full civil rights" for homosexuals. While this resolution still prohibited gays and lesbians from the clergy, opponents complained bitterly that the board, growing more liberal by the day, had surrendered the omnipresent truth to the politically expedient. In another move liberal theologians in the NCC recommended "nonsexist" language in new editions of the Bible, appointing a committee to "update this version of Scripture." The committee quickly adopted the reforms, explaining, "It is possible to minimize the use of He for God and accept a distinct theological style where one refrains from pronouns." Replacing "God the Father" with "God the Creator" did not sit well with conservatives. "I am not willing to cut myself off from the Judeo-Christian tradition," complained one critic, clearly on the losing end. Driving reform in the NCC were denominations such as the United Church of Christ, which had long championed gender equality and had already ordained a gay minister, the Reverend William Johnson.[68]

If more liberal elements appeared to have the upper hand theologically within the NCC, the organization acknowledged the task it faced. In 1976 the NCC published a new edition of its *Yearbook of American and Canadian Churches*, an annual compilation of statistics and theological data. Citing polls by the Gallup Organization, the Roper Public Opinion Research Center, and the National Opinion Research Center, the anthology documented that "Americans are more likely to change their membership in a church denomination for theological reasons now than they were in the past." The beneficiaries of this trend were the evangelical and "very conservative churches." The Southern Baptists had gained over 113,000 new members as it had begun drifting to the theological right, while the other eight largest church bodies—the "mainstream" strongly represented in the NCC—had all lost membership.[69]

Nowhere was this as evident as in the case of Richard Neuhaus. On January 26, 1975, Neuhaus led eighteen prominent clergymen representing nine major Christian denominations in issuing the "Hartford Manifesto." A Lutheran priest well known for his activism on behalf of civil rights and against the Vietnam War, Neuhaus had never been a conservative leader. Nevertheless, when the clergymen's three-day gathering concluded at Con-

necticut's Hartford Seminary, their manifesto bemoaned a retreat from religious orthodoxy and called for a more pious awareness of the Almighty.
The group did not reject social activism but rather a growing spiritual relativism among many Americans. Too many people, Neuhaus complained,
believe that "modern thought is superior to all past forms of understanding
reality." They mistakenly equated all religions and assumed that "being true
to one's self is the whole meaning of salvation." America needed to return to
the word of God, return to the scriptures. Americans should get involved,
but they could not marry the spirit of the times with God's truth; the latter
was immutable and omniscient, impervious to society's dynamism.[70]

Neuhaus had no grand political scheme, and he shared little in common
with many of the theological conservatives similarly upset by the cultural
drift of the nation. He had abhorred the extremes of the Religious Right
of the 1950s and did not envision himself a vanguard of political rebirth.
Nevertheless, his own personal evolution spoke volumes about the direction of many American Christians. Arrested at the 1968 Democratic Convention, Neuhaus had a long record of political activism that suggested an
embrace of the liberalism of the period. He had supported liberals such as
Robert Kennedy and had even run for office as a Democrat. Now, however,
he spoke out against the NCC and lobbied against abortion rights. Nothing in the "Hartford Manifesto" was overtly partisan or even political, but,
given his background if nothing else, the manifesto obviously had implications for both domestic and foreign policy. It seemed to foretell that the disputes over family policy, over issues such as education, feminism, abortion,
and homosexuality, among others, would only grow in importance, that the
past was only prelude. It seemed to suggest that Neuhaus and his colleagues
sought a man of faith to help right the ship of state.[71]

In theological terms, if not in the larger culture, the immediate postwar era
of the 1950s had appeared relatively placid, the Religious Right of the day
notwithstanding. Two decades later, with Carter's national ambitions now
as obvious as his Christian faith, nothing, religious or otherwise, seemed
calm. If religious discourse appeared increasingly stringent, lacking the
"spirit of mutual charity and tolerance" that William Shannon thought vital,
it was not alone. America was angry. Gas prices soared, the "energy crisis"
obviously more than the relatively brief 1973 Arab oil embargo that had followed the Yom Kippur War of the same year. Clearly, Americans were not
the only ones wrestling with religious schisms. Economists now spoke of

"stagflation," a brutal combination of high unemployment and high inflation that challenged the post–World War II affluence that Americans had
come to take for granted. The television carried pictures of American dip-
lomats and military frantically fleeing from their embassy in Saigon as the
North Vietnamese troops advanced to celebrate their long-sought victory,
the Vietnam War now a memory but also a national humiliation. A president who had won office due in part to his defense of law and order now
sat sick and disgraced in California, the first president in American history
to resign, his lies documented for all to see. With a country that appeared
frayed at the edges, the threat to the family was not the only problem America faced. For many Americans, however, it was the basis for all the others.
Without a strong and stable family life, without morals and universal truths
able to withstand the passage of time and the many crises the nation faced,
all was lost.

Everything the government did, conservatives complained, seemed to
backfire. At first, government involvement was relatively benign. In May
1948 over 125 national organizations sponsored the National Conference
on Family Life. Although it was not officially an administration operation,
President Truman wrote a letter commending the conference and held a
White House reception for participants.[72] By the 1960s, however, it was a
different story. In the decade's first year the Food and Drug Administration approved the birth control pill, an impetus for the sexual revolution.
Lyndon Johnson may have intended his Great Society to help American
families, conservatives continued, but reforms such as Medicaid, food
stamps, and even revisions of the tax code encouraged, not discouraged, the
prevalence of single-parent homes. These reforms encouraged dependency
on the government. Worse still, federal funds for family planning and the
spread of sex education into high school hygiene and health classes encouraged promiscuity.

The latter was particularly galling to conservatives, for it represented an
obvious federal intrusion into a matter best left to religion and the family, in
fact *their* religion and *their* family. Together with the *Engel v. Vitale* decision
against school prayer, the addition of sex education to the public schools
led to a proliferation of private Christian schools. By the time Carter began
his campaign for the presidency, the number of members in the California
Association of Christian Schools, for example, had jumped almost fivefold
from a decade earlier, to a total of more than 350 academies. Several magazines ran headlines proclaiming a "Boom in Protestant Schools." In general,

the media reported, a growing number of conservative Christians had begun to believe that the government was intent on undermining parental control and on indoctrinating a secular agenda that ran counter to their own morals. For this reason, the IRS's decision to revoke the tax-exempt status of racially discriminatory private schools was, in effect, pouring gas on a fire. The fact that the IRS did not immediately begin enforcement—inaction that, according to one scholar, was "difficult to explain"—muted somewhat the initial protest but seemed nevertheless to confirm for conservatives their worst assumptions. Also suggesting the worst was a similar IRS decision, a ruling to revoke the tax-exempt status of the Christian college Bob Jones University, which had denied blacks admission until 1971 and still prohibited interracial dating. As the university sued, conservatives assumed that enforcement at the secondary level was imminent.[73]

Issues surrounding school curriculum have always been, in the words of political scientist Fred Inglis, "both the text and context in which production and values intersect." They were always the "twist point of imagination and power." Even as late as the mid-1970s some members of the American Legion still pressed for schools to teach "one hundred percent Americanism," an obviously vague concept popular in the 1950s that assumed traditional values. The introduction of sex education spoke more directly to traditional values and brought out conservative groups such as the John Birch Society and religious organizations such as the Christian Crusade. It all encouraged new levels of emotion.[74]

California's Family Life and Sex Education Program was a case in point. The program sought to help form "a family with strong bonds of affection, loyalty and cooperation." When conservative parents learned in 1968, however, that the four-and-a-half-week program taught that ambiguous sexual feelings were common and that homosexuality was natural, a well-publicized protest followed. "There were more homosexuals made in that sex-education classroom than would ever have been here today if they hadn't told them, 'it's just an alternative lifestyle,'" testified one critic. "Well, they tried it and they didn't knock it, and a lot of them became homosexuals as a direct result of being taught that in the classroom. That's a fact."[75] The battle waged for months, the program's critics even screening the movie *Pavlov's Children*. The film depicted Communists in government-run sex education classes using Pavlovian conditioning techniques to tear their youthful charges from their families and thus open them to totalitarianism. This was to the program's creators simply the rants of "Bible-thumping right-wing kooks and nuts," but it proved effective. California dramatically reduced the program and deleted its controversial segments.[76]

More famous was the Kanawha County school case in 1974. The introduction of sex education into the West Virginia school district annoyed conservative parents. One of the parents, Alice Moore, won a seat on the school board after describing sex education as an outside attempt to bring "a humanistic, atheistic attack on God" into the classroom. Moreover, the broader school emphasis on the racial, cultural, and philosophical diversity of American society was "anti-Christian, anti-American, anti-authority, depressing and negative."[77] Undoubtedly, there were a number of factors that contributed to the Kanawha controversy, including the recent consolidation of rural schools and the urban-rural tensions it created. In any event, what began as a small protest by a determined band of parents grew into a huge public spectacle involving school boycotts and even violence. Moore and her allies largely prevailed in the end, ensuring that the entire episode emerged as a cause célèbre for conservative religious groups. She defended herself by decrying the media's preoccupation with the struggle as a fight between the rich urbanites and the poor, ignorant coal miners. She denounced not only the televised coverage of the protest but the programming of American media in general. Television had helped make the sick and perverse acceptable, she claimed, and thus her fight was not only local but one that good citizens should wage across the land.[78]

Perhaps inspired by Moore, conservatives began to organize. The American Library Association documented a dramatic increase in textbook controversies in the years that followed. Polls began to show that the number of citizens who trusted public education had begun to dip. Politicians such as Reagan reacted by becoming more vocal in defending private schools from government oversight. The question of requiring state certification of private school teachers was particularly troublesome for many activists, and several states began to press for removing or weakening the requirements. A year after the Kanawha episode, Arizona congressman John Conlan introduced a bill that would have eliminated federal support for all courses that taught secular humanism, legislation obviously unenforceable and doomed to failure but a proposal that received a great deal of publicity.[79] Perhaps in response to this momentum, the National Education Association (NEA) began its own lobbying campaign in defense of universal compulsory education. Public education was not atheistic but "nontheistic," the group claimed, as the founding fathers intended. The social and religious conservatives were not defending their faith as much as attacking science and secularism. "We are fighting like hell to save our public schools," noted one NEA spokesperson.[80]

Outside the issues of school curriculum, conservative Christians attacked federal support for child-care centers as another factor in the demise of the American family. In 1971 Congress passed legislation subsidizing day care for families earning between $3,900 and $7,000 annually. This infuriated Connaught "Connie" Marshner, a member of the conservative Young Americans for Freedom and a recent graduate of the University of South Carolina. Marshner sent out fliers from a group she called the Emergency Committee for Children. Although initially Marshner was the only member of the group, her fliers had the intended effect. She began corresponding with other conservative mothers and soon published the *Family Protection Report*. The report monitored feminists and what Marshner saw as their effort to involve government in family life. Using her new connections, she organized a letter-writing campaign to the White House to lobby against the child-care centers. As a direct result of her efforts, President Nixon vetoed the measure.[81]

The issue would not die, however, and was ready to explode again by the time Carter ran for the White House. Marshner, her opponents claimed, did not grasp modern reality. There were single-parent homes, poor homes, and others that desperately needed child-care assistance to survive. Moreover, child care was no longer just for the working poor.[82] Feminism had launched more women into the workforce, and not simply because of economic necessity. The nation needed high-quality and comprehensive care where, in the words of one advocate, "mothers could drop off a child early in the morning and be sure that he or she would receive a hot breakfast, schooling, lunch, a rest period, medical attention if needed, and supervised play until the end of the day." It was an admirable "community style of child-rearing" that had proved quite successful in Israel and Western Europe.[83]

"Faced with these realities," Indiana senator Birch Bayh concluded, "we must persist in our goal of quality child care services for all children." Government involvement did not hurt families but would actually "cement family relationships." It would decrease the societal trends that all agreed were alarming. Taking another approach, writer Russell Baker argued that the antiabortion movement itself hurt families: "Success for the right-to-life movement would mean more unwanted children." In this sense, the right-to-life movement's own argument supported federally funded child care. Agreeing with such a philosophy, a number of independent groups, such as the Foundation for Child Development, raised private capital for child-care centers. In the fall of 1973 Minnesota senator Walter Mondale, who had sponsored the measure Nixon vetoed, chaired hearings of the Subcommittee on Children and Youth. The hearings, entitled "America's Families: Trends and Pressures," led to no legislation, but, two years later, Mondale once again chaired hearings, this time promising to revive bills for comprehensive child care in the near future.[84]

Almost every day seemed to bring more reasons for conservative Christians to complain. For one, many school districts had begun to offer classes in comparative religions, a particularly sore subject. They now taught the Bible as literature, presenting it along with the scriptures of other faiths such as the Koran. "Religion was out," the *New York Times* reported, but "religions were in." This belittled the truth, many evangelicals complained, by equating all religions when salvation required devotion to the one real faith. Moreover, in early 1975 a California appellate court ruled that closing state offices early on Good Friday was unconstitutional given that the offices remained open on dates sacred to other religions. This was an affront to tradition, a chorus of critics complained.[85] Later that year, in another egregious example for conservative evangelicals, the American Civil Liberties Union protested a decision of the Jackson, Mississippi, city council to appropriate $1,000 for a visit of the famed evangelist Billy Graham. While Graham heard of the ACLU suit and worked to defuse tensions, many in the community remained flabbergasted. What better way to spend public money than assist an exemplar of Christ's love? How could the ACLU possibly object? As the Jackson debate faded, reports surfaced that the Central Intelligence Agency (CIA) had been using clergymen as its agents, a situation that many feared would undermine evangelism. In response, George Bush, head of the CIA, announced that the agency would no longer employ missionaries. The protests faded, but for many the problem that it represented did not. Indeed, government at all levels seemed so out of hand that any unsupported rumor appeared ominous. As the end of 1975 approached, thousands of letters poured into the FCC protesting plans to ban religious programming. There was no such plan, however, the rumor having grown from an unsuccessful 1974 petition by two broadcasting consultants to freeze new broadcasting licenses. For months the FCC had denied the allegation, but as the year came to a close it still received almost five thousand letters daily. "This is the greatest number we've ever received on any single issue," remarked an exasperated Wallace Johnson, the chief of the FCC's Broadcast Bureau.[86]

At all levels and in all respects government seemed to many on the theological Right to be impotent, incompetent, or worse, corrupt. Society seemed to celebrate the hedonism of the "Me Decade," which, by its very definition, appeared a challenge to the Golden Rule. Nixon, it appeared, was not the only leader willing to bend rules. Joining him in Watergate infamy was his vice president, Spiro Agnew, who had earlier resigned over allegations of tax evasion. Far from challenging the selfish and indulgent cultural consensus, the two former government leaders seemed to exemplify it. Nixon's successor as president, Gerald Ford, at least appeared an honest man, but he was inept at moving the country in the right direction. His slogan WIN, an acronym for "Whip Inflation Now," appeared a lame excuse for a real policy solution to the continuing economic crisis. In foreign policy even Cambodia appeared to mock America, seizing the merchant marine vessel *Mayaguez*. Ford launched a military rescue mission that saved the thirty-nine crewmen but cost the lives of forty-one servicemen. For every step forward, it appeared to many conservative Christians, America took two steps backward. Like many of its leaders, the once great nation needed to be reborn.

The troublesome social and political milieu of the mid-1970s certainly was an impetus for conservative Christians to unite politically. As the election year 1976 dawned, with so many new issues simmering, with disgust at government never far below the surface, and with the fate of the American family seemingly threatened, one columnist adroitly observed, "While large numbers of theological conservatives object to the idea of the church becoming involved in politics, a nucleus of evangelical leaders have begun taking steps that could foreshadow a larger role for their constituents."[87] This nucleus, undoubtedly aware of the Religious Right of previous decades, could draw more recent inspiration from the accomplishments of their liberal brethren. The National Black Evangelical Association had been active in the struggle for civil rights, joining liberal clergy from across the spectrum. On Thanksgiving Day in 1973 the Evangelicals for Social Action had formed in Chicago, an effort to continue what amounted to a modern version of the Social Gospel. Perhaps taking their cue from such activism, conservative evangelical leaders from around the globe met the following year in Lausanne, Switzerland, near the epicenter of the ministry of Francis Schaeffer. An eccentric with long hair, a goatee, and knickers, Schaeffer was an author and lecturer who appeared to echo the same sentiments that the theologian Neuhaus had voiced in the "Hartford Manifesto," only with a more obvious and specific political tinge. Christians who accommodated modernity, Schaeffer and his colleagues warned, were "in danger of having the ground cut from under them." Without firm theological foundations, they would certainly be lost.[88] The Gospels acknowledged a political dimension, Schaeffer continued, and politics was indeed an appropriate venue for solutions to society's ills. As if to prove this point, Schaeffer joined in 1975 with fellow theologian Harold O. J. Brown and pediatrician C. Everett Koop to form the Christian Action Council, which promised to lobby Congress for limits to abortion. While many conservative evangelicals had not yet stressed abortion as a central issue, the Christian Action Council represented one of the first Protestant-based organizations committed to the fight against it.[89]

The ever-present threat that the IRS might suddenly enforce its 1970 ruling against segregated private schools was, of course, a major impetus for conservative clergy to unite politically. They viewed their schools as an extension of their ministries. There was no division. If the government could interfere with their educational component, it could regulate their religion. Individual clergy in a number of denominations had been active in, for example, the efforts of Alice Moore in Kanawha County and those of Connie Marshner against federal child care, but the threat of IRS action appeared more directly ominous and thus a greater force for unity. Robert Billings, president of Hyles-Anderson College, an independent, fundamentalist Baptist college in Crown Point, Indiana, published *A Guide to the Christian School* and attracted ministers across the denominational spectrum. After a failed congressional run, he formed Christian School Action, later renamed the National Christian Action Coalition, and actively began recruiting ministers for his cause. A close friend of his, Ed McAteer, a former salesman with Colgate Palmolive, became national field director of the Christian Freedom Foundation (CFF) in 1974 and immediately began applying his sales experience with pastors. Originally founded during the 1950s, CFF benefited tremendously from McAteer's efforts. Traveling from one congregation to another, McAteer developed an impressive list of concerned conservative clergy willing to wage a cultural war to save the country.[90]

Bill Bright's Campus Crusade for Christ (CCC) remained an obvious venue for conservative pastoral coordination. Founded in Los Angeles in 1951 by the then thirty-year-old Bright, CCC by the mid-1970s had chapters across the nation and in virtually every state. Speaking more pointedly than ever before about a nation gone astray, running from God, Bright was one of the most ardent and early critics of abortion, condemning it almost immediately following *Roe v. Wade*, unlike many of his evangelical colleagues. In the words of biographer Michael Richardson, Bright quickly "included an indictment of abortion as sin in almost every public remark."[91] His sermons also increasingly spoke ill of homosexuality and feminism, not to mention Hollywood, which he thought contributed to both. CCC's membership exploded as the organization launched a number of new initiatives, including the Here's Life campaign to help churches expand discipleship training, in essence to create a "Christian Peace Corps" of new lay ministers. Thousands of people attended CCC's evangelical gatherings, including 1972's Explo '72 in Dallas and Explo '74 in South Korea. Bright continued to insist that he and his organization were nonpartisan, and indeed, Bright did not officially endorse any presidential candidate. Moreover, he knew Jimmy Carter. In Atlanta Carter had helped launch a CCC "prayer chain" with a reception at the governor's mansion. Rosalynn had participated more directly, speaking favorably of Bright to the media. Nevertheless, even as some conservative pundits complained that Bright was not partisan enough, his son Zac worked for the Republican National Committee. His wife, Vonette, battled the American Civil Liberties Union in her efforts to promote public prayer. In late 1975 Bright founded the Christian Embassy in Washington as an outreach to elected officials. After purchasing a regal building worthy of the term "embassy," Bright's staff lobbied congressmen, held prayer breakfasts, and engaged in frequent Bible study sessions as a way to counsel legislators. He acknowledged the goal of electing "Godly" Christians to public office, an effort that brought him into direct contact with other political-oriented evangelicals, many with more partisan agendas.[92]

Facilitating unity was, of course, technology. In 1975, according to Pulitzer Prize–winning journalist Charles E. Shepard, "religious services broadcast from local churches still dominated religious programming in America."[93] Satellite technology and networking that included hundreds of affiliates promised to revolutionize the ministries, however, expanding the influence of the industry leaders. Several ministers were already out in front, anticipating the seismic shift in broadcasting and best prepared to spread their message. Pat Robertson, most notably, had founded the Christian Broadcasting Network (CBN) after purchasing a small UHF station in Portsmouth, Virginia, in 1960. Within only a few years he had mastered the art of telethons, at first asking several hundred listeners to pledge ten dollars per month in order for the station to meet its seven-thousand-dollar budget. Robertson referred to these original contributors as his 700 Club. By the mid-1970s CBN's future appeared bright. Robertson distributed tapes of his programs to an extensive list of affiliates and, hardly surprising given his blue-blood pedigree, harbored grander ambitions for the future.[94] As part of his operations, Robertson hired Jim and Tammy Bakker to lead CBN's children's programming. The Bakkers proved an immediate hit and soon launched their own rival broadcast, Praise the Lord, or more commonly, PTL. Seeking a truly national audience, Bakker recognized that CBN had the advantage in larger markets and thus began focusing on the mid- and smaller-sized cities, sending videotapes to PTL's own affiliates.[95]

Joining Robertson and Bakker among the pantheon of evangelical broadcast stars were, among others, Rex Humbard, Oral Roberts, Jerry Falwell, Charles Stanley, and James Robison. Humbard and Roberts arguably represented the "old school," having begun televising their ministries in 1953 and 1955, respectively. Humbard's broadcasts extended almost fifty years, and by the mid-1970s he was near his peak of popularity, leasing several hundred television stations. Roberts's broadcasts likewise reached thousands, allowing him to raise enough money to establish Oral Roberts University in Tulsa, Oklahoma, in 1963.[96] If Humbard and Roberts appeared near their professional zenith, Falwell, like Robertson and Bakker, had loftier ambitions. A graduate of Missouri's Bible Baptist College, Falwell returned to his Lynchburg, Virginia, home in 1956 and rented an old Coca-Cola bottling plant on Thomas Road in which to begin his church, whose membership grew rapidly. Located in one of the older, middle-class sections of Lynchburg, the church was a large octagonal brick building fronting the street with a supermarket-sized parking lot around it, hardly impressive from the outside. If the facilities were not the attraction, the energetic and magnetic Falwell was. With his flock growing, Falwell quickly began a radio and television ministry whose growth matched that of his church. His *Old Time Gospel Hour* aired weekly and by the mid-1970s was one of the largest syndicated television ministries in the country.[97] Charles Stanley was a newer arrival to the world of broadcast evangelicalism, having launched his program, *The Chapel Hour*, only in 1972, a year after becoming senior pastor at the large First Baptist Church in north Atlanta. Robertson recognized

Stanley's popularity and acquired the show for his CBN. Joining Stanley as a new face was the youngest broadcaster, James Robison. Just over thirty years old by the mid-1970s, the Texas evangelist had established the popular television ministry *Life Today* in 1971. With his audience rapidly growing, Robison, like the others, now enjoyed considerable influence.

The largest audience, of course, remained Billy Graham's. Known more for his famous connections and impressive crusades than his command of budding technology, Graham remained the most potent force for conservative Christian unity. Graham had been a young radio preacher in 1945 when a group of ministers from around the country formed Youth for Christ International (YFC) and selected him as its first official field representative. This position had won Graham an audience with Truman in 1950, famously ending with Graham kneeling to pray on the White House lawn. The event, dutifully broadcast by the press corps, constituted a breach of protocol, angering Truman. In the years since then, Graham had actively cultivated a relationship with each successive president, clearly enjoying the platform it offered him.[98] By the mid-1970s his name recognition and popularity dwarfed those of his telegenic competition, and he openly courted Christians far from his own traditions. "There's not much difference between me and Catholics theologically," Graham declared, overlooking the historic animosity that had existed for centuries. Both groups shared a "hunger for simple faith." Those in the Pentecostal traditions, meanwhile, were equal brothers: "God had used the charismatic movement to arouse dead Christians in many parts of the world." *Christianity Today*, which Graham helped launch, reflected its founders' sentiments, always espousing a conservative Christianity but never endorsing one brand or ritual over another. In short, Graham's interdenominational reach was as obvious as the political influence it carried.[99]

Little doubt existed about Graham's politics, although he strove to cultivate friendships on both sides of the aisle and always avoided the extremes. Like Bright, he never endorsed candidates and always insisted that he and his ministry were nonpartisan. By the mid-1970s he already knew Carter both as a committed Christian and as a possible presidential contender. Carter had served as chairman of a "film crusade" that Graham's ministry had held in Americus, Georgia, years before, and, Graham remembered, Carter had given "the invitation every night for people to come and receive Christ." Carter, while governor of Georgia, had invited the famed preacher on numerous occasions to lead prayer breakfasts at the state capitol and, most notably, had served as chairman of his 1973 Atlanta crusade.[100] Nevertheless, Graham's background still spoke strongly to Carter's political opposition. YFC was famously nationalistic and anti-Communist, with its membership overlapping with the more zealous and Republican-leaning organizations of the day, most notably, evangelist Billy James Hargis's Christian Anti-Communist Crusade. Graham criticized Truman's Korean policies and became an obviously close confidant of his successor, Republican Dwight Eisenhower. He occasionally made, author William Martin adds, "Republican flavored comments."[101] Graham refused to participate in the civil rights struggles of his fellow member of the clergy, Martin Luther King Jr., and during his ill-fated friendship with Richard Nixon uttered anti-Semitic remarks in private.[102]

After the social upheavals of the 1960s, Graham shared many of the concerns of conservative Christians that the United States had lost its way from God. In 1975 he even had good words for Communist sexual mores. "In terms of sexual morality, the Communists are teaching us some lessons wherever they take over," he stated. "They close down brothels, eliminate prostitution, and eliminate pornography." Although he attempted to avoid overtly fanning the political flames that had begun to spring up around issues such as homosexuality, abortion, and feminism, he spoke that same year in glowing terms of the "new evangelism," which was hardly so reticent.[103]

Of all the well-known preachers, Graham had spoken out most often and directly in regard to politics and was clearly in the best position to forge a new political force. He was, however, not about to lead any overt partisan movement. His actions and words might, in varying degrees and at different times, give any such movement credence, but he was no political revolutionary. Likewise, Humbard and Roberts had avoided any similar partisan alliance during their long careers, if not from any fundamentalist hesitancy to delve into the political world, then out of a pragmatism that recognized the potential negative impact on church membership and fundraising. Like Graham, both sought to cast the widest possible net. Clearly, their theology spoke more strongly to a potential Religious Right than did their direct political rhetoric.

Robertson and Falwell had never particularly focused on politics, although for both men the libertine 1960s and its rights revolution pressed for a change in course. They shared the fundamentalist tradition of abstaining from the political world, but each recognized a growing threat to the

American family that begged for intervention. Robertson had never made any "Ministers and Marchers" sermon denouncing political involvement, as had Falwell, and given his prominent father's background, politics was not exactly a stretch. Nevertheless, by the mid-1970s Robertson remained for the most part only titillated by politics, not ensconced in it. His most important goal remained building his ministry, that is, saving souls and raising money. In 1975 Robertson said that as he considered purchasing five acres for a new CBN headquarters, he heard the "unmistakable" word of God while attending a charismatic conference in California. God, Robertson stated, told him to purchase a 142-acre tract of land in Virginia Beach, Virginia, to "build a headquarters and school for My glory." Robertson consummated the purchase on December 31, 1975, and after that the enormous task of establishing a university from scratch consumed the majority of Robertson's time.[104]

Falwell, having officially retracted his "Ministers and Marchers" sermon, was more ready to brandish a political sword, but in most respects he was less prepared to do so. Falwell later wrote that legalized abortion was a major factor in his reversal. Praising the antiabortion street protesters, he wrote, "For the first time in my life I felt God leading me to join them."[105] In reality, Falwell had made few comments on abortion by the mid-1970s. The broader issue of family, by contrast, had already become a central tenet of his critique. "It is my conviction that the family is God's basic unit in society," Falwell told his congregation. "No wonder then . . . we are in a holy war for the survival of the family." Without strong families, the United States could not survive: "The people who are leading the anti-family efforts in America today are failures." The feminists and homosexuals "are trying to bring everybody else into their position of misery and failure."[106] In his book *Listen America!* Falwell was clear about what constituted the family: "The family is the God-ordained institution of the marriage of one man and one woman together for a lifetime with their biological or adopted children." Along with the church and government, it was one of "only three institutions God ordained in the Bible." Scripture "declares that God has called the father to be the spiritual leader in his family." Unfortunately, this "fundamental building block" was facing a "vicious assault." The family, Falwell insisted, had to be protected. No wonder, then, that by the mid-1970s he was preparing for political battle.[107]

By the time he shifted to public advocacy, Falwell's ministry had come far since its founding almost two decades before. Nevertheless, moving into the public realm carried real risks. For one, the ministry was not yet self-supporting, given the high costs of its rapid expansion. A bond program offered hope for stability but was poorly run. After an investigation, the Securities and Exchange Commission found numerous mistakes and irregularities and filed suit against the ministry in 1973. In the end the court appointed an oversight committee, and the ministry suffered numerous reductions in personnel and expenses. "We grew too quickly," Falwell later reflected. Until the ministry was able to purchase new high-speed duplication technology, Falwell's programs suffered significant delays from filming to airing. At that point, despite its outward signs of success, Falwell still employed only three professional production personnel and had to rely on untrained volunteers for much of the work.[108] Not only did Thomas Road Baptist Church face significant debt, but Liberty Baptist College, the new school launched by Falwell, had to hold classes in a nearby middle school scheduled for demolition. While the college, still in its infancy, its future uncertain, desperately needed student housing and a higher-quality faculty, Falwell still quietly had hopes for purchasing land on, as he named it, "Liberty Mountain." The purchase and construction would cost millions, however, and thus Falwell, like Robertson, had a great deal on his plate.[109]

Lost among the baying broadcasters was an individual with perhaps the greatest academic background for a battle in the politics of the family, the child psychologist James Dobson. The son of an evangelist with the Church of the Nazarene, Dobson earned a master's degree in education and a doctorate in child development. While a professor at the University of Southern California School of Medicine, Dobson wrote several popular best sellers that appealed to conservative Christians threatened by the changing society. His first book, *Dare to Discipline*, set the tone for his career in espousing a combination of biblical principles, developmental psychology, and a nostalgia for the 1950s. Other books included *What Wives Wish Their Husbands Knew About Women*, which exhibited an obvious disdain for modern feminism.[110] Ignoring the well-documented negative aspects of the 1950s, Dobson portrayed the decade as an era of contented domestic bliss. The traditional nuclear family was the nation's bedrock, and the country flourished as a direct result. The 1960s, however, brought a cultural revolution that undermined the family and posed a grave risk to children. This threat included, in Dobson's words, "the secularization of society, value-neutral schools, homosexual activism, easy-divorce laws, pornography, crime, and violence on television and in the movies, 'safe-sex' ideology, socialistic and humanistic colleges and universities, governmental bureaucracies with destructive purposes, oppressive tax laws, radical feminism, abortion on demand, the drug culture, and overworked and exhausted parents." The threat was expansive enough that everyone could find at least one point of agreement. Employing a folksy persona that personified the very decade he embellished, Dobson sprinkled his message with anecdotes and in general appeared a wise figure worthy of admiration. While his books sold well, Dobson left no doubt that feminists and homosexuals were the most egregious offenders. They were, in short, "influential people who hate families." Against such satanic evil "we must defend the family from the assault of hell." By the mid-1970s Dobson remained in academia, largely known only among his professional colleagues and conservative family activists. The latter, however, represented fertile ground, as Dobson recognized. Resigning his professorship, Dobson, like Carter at the same time, sought greener fields in which to expand his influence.[111]

For Paul Weyrich and his colleagues, it all represented fertile ground—the groundswell of revulsion to feminism and cultural liberalism, the problems of government and the disdain they generated, and the phalanx of conservative Christian ministers now anxious, if not ready or prepared, to change the course of the country. If anyone sought for conservative Christians to unite politically, it was Paul Weyrich. Raised in Wisconsin by an immigrant Catholic father and a mother from an evangelical Protestant family, Weyrich learned early from family conversations that religion and politics intertwined. A lifelong Republican, Weyrich recognized that if his party could get working- and middle-class Catholics and Protestant evangelicals together, the coalition could dominate. The Republican Party appeared to Weyrich weak-kneed in response to Democratic dominance. It needed new issues, a new audience, and a new focus, in short, a new, fresh wave of true conservatism. Nixon had laid the foundation with his famous "Southern Strategy," a campaign to win traditionally Democratic southern whites, but now the party should follow up, if not on the racial issues that underlay Nixon's strategy, then certainly on the social issues that overlapped the same demographic. The "Rockefeller Republicans," the moderates such as Ford, did not represent the direction the party should take. Combining true fiscal and regulatory restraint and a resurgence of military power with the social issues that animated the likes of Robertson, Falwell, and Dobson promised a bright future for the Grand Old Party. Never one to let an opportunity pass, Weyrich received generous support from Colorado brewer

Joseph Coors and established in 1973 a conservative policy organization—a think tank known as the Heritage Foundation—to provide intellectual heft to his revolution. As the Heritage Foundation gained momentum, Weyrich added a political action committee (PAC), the Committee for the Survival of a Free Congress, the following year. Weyrich's close friend Howard Phillips, a former Nixon administration official, often discussed over casual lunches with Weyrich their plan for a new Republican majority. Following in Weyrich's footsteps, Phillips led his own PAC, the Conservative Caucus, to press their joint cause.[112]

Ironically, given the pair's distaste for government, Democratic-sponsored legislation assisted their efforts. A 1974 post-Watergate law regulated campaign contributions and contributed to the importance of PACs. The new law limited individual contributions to $1,000 per election, with an overall annual individual ceiling of $25,000. A PAC, however, could contribute up to $5,000 per election with no overall limit. First to recognize the potential of the legislation, conservatives were quick to take advantage. Joining the Committee for the Survival of a Free Congress and the Conservative Caucus were the Conservative Political Action Committee, founded by operative Terry Dolan, and the Christian Voice Moral Government Fund. Moreover, the law created a system of public financing of presidential elections, the money going only to those candidates who succeeded in raising small amounts of money across several states. This put a premium on direct mailings and played into the hands of established fund-raisers such as Richard Viguerie.[113] Viguerie, who shared Weyrich's and Phillips's vision, had been active in conservative politics since working for the organization Young Americans for Freedom and the 1964 presidential campaign of arch-conservative Arizona senator Barry Goldwater. As much a visionary with technology as Robertson, Viguerie recognized the potential of databases and computers to political organizing. For years he had tried to access Graham's extensive mailing lists, but each time the evangelist had rebuffed him, recognizing that it would cast him as the partisan he sought to avoid being. Nevertheless, Viguerie persisted in trying to lure disgruntled, if often still reluctant, conservative pastors to his fold.[114]

An acquaintance of all three ambitious Republican operatives helped. Congressman Conlan, who had introduced the anti–secular humanist legislation in the wake of the Kanawha County debate, was as much a devout evangelical as an ardent Republican. As such, he had been a key supporter of the Christian Freedom Foundation and the Christian Embassy, a legislator frequently willing to give the speeches that both organizations requested. He had become a friend of both McAteer and Bright and through them developed a relationship with a large number of conservative pastors. The Heritage Foundation, meanwhile, had inserted itself into the Kanawha County debate as well, which had offered an entrée for Weyrich and, through him, Phillips to Billings and his Christian school cohorts. Impressed by Weyrich, Billings invited him to deliver a political pitch in Washington to a number of conservative ministers. The group was hesitant until the wily Weyrich collected money from them to conduct a survey of their congregations. The pastors knew that their flocks feared government control of their schools, but now the results of the survey proved that their followers were ready for the broader battle, the very alliance that promised to change everything. By the mid-1970s the seeds were in the ground. Weyrich, Phillips, and Viguerie had close connections with Bright, Billings, and McAteer and an array of evangelical leaders. From these seeds would grow new acquaintances with the emerging broadcast stars who were itching for a political fight.[115]

As the United States entered its bicentennial year, the country just did not seem its old self. Gone was the self-confident swagger, the moral certitude, that spoke to its "exceptionalism," as Alexis de Tocqueville had written a century and a half before. Racked by inflation, embarrassed by scandal and defeat, the United States appeared to be a country on the wane. To recover, many conservative Christians assumed, it needed both the new and the old. The United States needed new leaders with moral clarity and the old values and traditions that had served the nation so well in the past. It needed to reject the changing times that suddenly appeared to be such a threat to the very foundation of society, the traditional nuclear family. Few at the time spoke of any modern Religious Right. Any political unity for conservative Christians still appeared elusive, theological or denominational differences far from overcome. Nevertheless, concerns about society's ills crossed traditional divides once thought impenetrable, suggesting new alliances equally unimaginable. Taken together, they held the potential to reshuffle the nation's political deck.

CHAPTER TWO

The Year of the Evangelical

IF JIMMY CARTER HOPED TO PROVE himself a different sort of president, a man above narrow electoral self-interest, he first had to win the Oval Office. His 1976 campaign staff, which included experienced political advisors and fellow Georgians Hamilton Jordan and Jody Powell, had no naïveté about what this involved. They well knew that while their candidate disdained politics for politics' sake, no one aspiring to the highest office in the land could simply ignore the political landscape. Successful campaigns required a certain level of dodging, weaving, and spinning of issues to make their man as attractive as possible. They required a certain vagueness when controversy dictated. As any challenger knew, specifics invited criticism, and Carter, like those before him, was not above couching matters in the most advantageous way. He would never lie, never contradict his religious beliefs, but his campaign was not about to forget the political context. For the voter, speechwriter Patrick Anderson recalled, Carter cast himself as a "southerner, Baptist, peanut farmer, naval officer, nuclear physicist, friend of Bob Dylan and fan of Dylan Thomas." In short, he was Everyman, perfectly cast for the cynical post-Watergate, post-Vietnam world.[1] Everyone saw something to like, which was certainly no coincidence. Carter, biographer Betty Glad noted, was adept at making "abstract statements of principles to which few could object." He exhibited considerable "skills in escaping controversy," so much so that polls indicated that Carter more than his opponents represented "traditional American values."[2] Carter's "usual strategy," historian Kenneth Morris added, "was to make a general statement of principle and then qualify it with contradictory specifics."[3] He would stress one aspect of a controversial issue to one target audience and take a completely different tack with another group.

This strategy suited the emerging "family issues" well. For one, Carter's own beliefs helped. He did, for example, genuinely believe that abortion and homosexuality were sinful, and thus when he stressed this sentiment to conservative audiences, he was telling the truth. When he emphasized to conservative Christians that he was a born-again evangelical, he was nothing but honest. At the same time, however, he was not lying when he spoke positively before more liberal crowds about abortion or homosexual rights. He was sincere when he stressed before feminists or civil rights advocates the importance of the separation of church and state. This too was a central tenet of his faith. He honestly did not believe it was his role to mandate personal morality. Carter was not lying in either instance, nor did he ever contradict his religious beliefs. He was, as Jordan and Powell encouraged him to do, simply practicing smart politics. Carter did not relish the fact that presidential campaigns often resembled as much Sun Tzu's ancient assumptions on the art of war as Niebuhr's musings on Christian ethics, but he recognized that it would all come to naught if he were not successful. To do great good, he first had to win. Moreover, the family issues were as relatively new in the political arena as they were in the theological arena. Not as prominent as they would become in later years, they were not as partisan. Simply put, little partisan machinery yet existed to mandate political purity or magnify debate. While his opponents complained that Carter was having it both ways, his statements always had supporters on the opposite side of the aisle. It was easier to be vague when all sides were just beginning to flush out their political positions.

By the time Carter announced his candidacy, the foundation for a partisan divide certainly existed. A growing number of feminists favored the Democrats if for no other reason than because Lyndon Johnson's War on Poverty had included birth control and other family-planning services under Medicaid. The Democratic Party appeared in many respects more sympathetic to the changing social mores, and many Democrats had been in the forefront of the battle to ratify the ERA and defend abortion and homosexual rights. Indiana Democratic senator Birch Bayh, for example, had been a key supporter of the ERA, and every Democratic member of the Senate Judiciary Committee had spoken out in favor of ratification. Leading the popular opposition, meanwhile, was Republican Phyllis Schlafly. Schlafly had twice run for an Illinois House seat and had also campaigned for the presidency of the National Federation of Republican Women. Armed with a law degree and a sharp intellect, she attacked the evils of feminism in her books *The Power of Positive Women* and, later, *The Power of the Christian Woman*. She also had a monthly newsletter, the *Phyllis Schlafly Report*. Schlafly, whose writings included praise for a hero of modern conservatism, Barry Goldwater, actively sought to encourage Republican alliances. Her organization, the Eagle Forum, coordinated with the Republican Party, and her campaign to defeat the ERA, called Stop-ERA and run from her home in Alton, Illinois, included a network of Republican committees. According to Schlafly, liberals degraded the homemaker and the "pleasure in being female." There was oppression of women "only in their [the liberals'] distorted minds."[4] Indeed, when the final Senate vote on the ERA arrived in 1972, six of the eight senators voting against passage were Republicans. While the numbers perhaps indicated that Schlafly had her work cut out for her, it also indicated that she had a partisan base from which to build.[5]

In the five years of its existence, the National Abortion Rights Action League (NARAL) had pressed access to abortion as a fundamental "right." In doing so it had tied abortion to the civil rights movement of the 1960s, obviously associated with the Democratic Party since the presidency of John Kennedy. Indeed, scholars had tied race and class to abortion. Studies indicated that black and poor women had significantly higher rates of abortion than national levels. By the early 1970s hostility toward such women had replaced the idealized liberalism of the Great Society. Many Americans no longer pitied these women as unfortunate victims in need of assistance but rather as "welfare queens," lazy, drug-addicted ghetto matriarchs scamming the system and robbing the taxpayers. Indeed, Nixon had recognized as much in his famous "Southern Strategy."[6]

Nixon had come to the conclusion that he could not pry away women's rights voters from the Democratic Party and had accepted the advice of advisor Patrick Buchanan that public opposition to abortion was wise politically. "Women's libbers will moan and groan," Buchanan wrote, "but this group we never had, and never will have." More importantly, Buchanan argued, criticizing abortion "will engage us on the moral side of an issue" and thus offset the effects of the Watergate scandal. In the end, therefore, Nixon reversed a regulation making abortions easily available in military hospitals and proclaimed unequivocally that the "unborn have rights also."[7] He became more vocal in criticizing broad constructionists on the Supreme Court, the very judicial philosophy that had produced *Roe v. Wade*. With the impact of Roosevelt- and Johnson-era appointments now painfully obvious to conservatives, Nixon, perhaps foretelling George W. Bush's criticism of "activist judges," began campaigning for a conservative judiciary and thus against the intellectual justification upon which legal abortion rested.[8]

Leading the effort to pass a constitutional amendment to ban abortion were two Republicans, senators Jesse Helms of North Carolina and James Buckley of New York. The former's resolution provided that "every human being shall be deemed, from the moment of fertilization, to be a person and entitled to the right to life." The latter's resolution declared that "all human beings, including their unborn offspring at every state of their biological development irrespective of age, health, function or condition of dependency," possessed a right to life. Of the more than fifty proposals to amend the Constitution to prohibit abortion, the overwhelming majority came from Republicans. In reaction, the American Civil Liberties Union, long a bane to the GOP and an ally to the Democrats, moved to embrace abortion rights. In 1968 its leadership publicly called for the repeal of restrictive state antiabortion laws and, six years later, created the Reproductive Freedom Project.[9]

Leading the fight for a federal homosexual civil rights bill was a Democratic New York congresswoman, Bella Abzug. During the 1972 election Democrats had gay delegates at their convention, and many Democrats favored repealing state sodomy laws. Joining Schlafly as an opponent of gay rights was the Republican Ronald Reagan, undoubtedly associating the gay rights movement with the cultural liberalism he abhorred. This sentiment was hardly unsupported in the Republican Party, which resisted Abzug's bill and did not recognize gay delegates at its convention.

Despite all these indications of partisanship, however, it is a gross oversimplification to suggest that in 1976 the family issues were completely partisan. In fact, they strongly divided both parties just as they divided so many denominations. The roots for partisanship were present, but the issues were simply too new. In one sense, despite growing concern, other momentous events of the day still largely overshadowed them. The Vietnam War and the Watergate scandal frequently kept abortion and homosexuality off the front page. As if to prove this point, the announcement of the *Roe v. Wade* decision did not lead the news the day of the Court's decision. Lyndon Johnson's death on that same day dominated coverage. In another sense, however, the family issues had already galvanized extremists on both sides. To try to win publicity and converts, battling activists showed little restraint in appealing to emotions. Critics of abortion, for example, displayed horrific pictures of fetuses aborted during the third trimester. Not to be outdone, their opponents waved bloody coat hangers as a symbol of the dangers of continued abortion restrictions. The emotional nature of the debates made politicians wary. The majority still believed that victory demanded winning the moderate middle, mandating compromise. The high emotions, however, did not readily lend themselves to accommodation. Many politicians assumed that if they took a side, they risked inflaming a vocal opposition. The debates had only recently sprouted; polls were conflicting; the best tactic was to avoid the matter as much as possible.[10]

Democrats, of course, had particular reasons for caution when it came to stressing abortion rights. Urban Catholics remained one of their key constituencies, and yet, just as many had earlier feared it would, the Catholic Church issued its first strong antiabortion declaration as the 1976 campaign commenced. The National Conference of Catholic Bishops overwhelmingly adopted the eight-page "Pastoral Plan for Pro-Life Activities." The bishops called for "all Catholic-sponsored or identifiable Catholic national, regional, diocesan and parochial organizations and agencies" to support "a comprehensive pro-life legislative agenda," including a constitutional amendment prohibiting abortion.[11] In a similar vein, polls indicated that African Americans, another key Democratic constituency, also opposed abortion at rates higher than the general public. Explanations for this varied, some claiming that abortion was genocide for the race and ensured minority status, while others pointed to higher levels of doctrinal orthodoxy in black religion. Regardless, many Democrats recognized that too vocal a support for abortion rights risked alienating key constituencies.[12]

Although there were few polls at the time accurately measuring views on abortion by state, scholars recently have employed data from a National Center for Health Statistics computer simulation model. From 1968 to 1972 opposition to abortion was strongest in the South, states that traditionally voted Democratic. In the states of the old Confederacy almost two-thirds of the public opposed abortion. While in most states this opposition decreased slightly over the four-year span, in six of the southern states it slightly increased. Democratic politicians' raw data may not have been as accurate as this computer model, but they undoubtedly knew the direction of the political winds.[13]

Women's rights advocates had tried to write an abortion rights plank into the 1972 Democratic Party platform but had failed. Antiabortion forces remained too strong within the party. Early in the election that year Democratic presidential candidate George McGovern had clearly struggled with the issue. When women's organizations pressed him, he reluctantly acknowledged his support for abortion rights but refused to see them as constitutionally protected. "In my judgement abortion is a private matter which should be decided by a pregnant woman and her doctor," McGovern stated at the time. "I do believe, however, that abortion is a matter to be left to the states." A few months later, pressed by abortion opponents, he denied that he favored eliminating all abortion restrictions. "That is a lie and my critics know it is a lie. I have never advocated federal action to repeal those laws, and if I were elected President, I would take no such action."[14] One could understand McGovern's predicament; postelection polls indicated that Democratic voters were evenly split on abortion: 37 percent favored outlawing the practice, while 41 percent thought the decision best left to the woman.[15]

While the majority of the Democratic leadership in 1976 favored abortion rights, a number of Democrats in the House of Representatives led the opposition, most notably New York congressman James Delaney. Delaney, working with Maryland Republican Robert Bauman, insisted that any prohibition against abortion not include exceptions, even when the pregnancy threatened the life of the mother. Less stringent but no less committed Democrats included Edward Boland and Joseph Moakley of Massachusetts, both obviously reacting to their strong Catholic constituencies. Joining them were Clement Zablocki of Wisconsin, Romano Mazzoli of Kentucky, James Oberstar of Minnesota, and Fernand St. Germain of Pennsylvania. In the Senate Democrats James Eastland of Mississippi, Edward Zorinsky of Nebraska, and William Proxmire of Wisconsin led the fight against abortion rights. One of the most consistent critics of abortion was Thomas Eagleton of Missouri, McGovern's own running mate for much of the 1972 campaign.[16] In short, abortion divided the Democratic legislators as much as the party's rank and file.

Not all Republicans resisted abortion rights. The issue divided the GOP no less than the Democrats. While Helms and Buckley pressed for a constitutional amendment banning abortion, their party colleagues on Bayh's Subcommittee of the Senate Judiciary Committee helped the chairman defeat the proposals. Many Republicans worried that conflicts might arise between the rights of the woman and the rights of the fetus. They also feared that the proposed amendments required a significant shift in constitutional philosophy. If one accepted the premise that the Constitution guaranteed a right to life and not simply "equal protection," Democrats might argue that the Constitution guaranteed government support for life from conception to the grave. It might, therefore, be the justification for a Republican nightmare, the ultimate welfare state.[17]

If the abortion issue in 1976 were not completely partisan, neither was the issue of homosexual rights. Several years earlier the Democratic administrations of John Kennedy and Lyndon Johnson had led a Democratic congressional majority in defeating a more open gay immigration policy, and many in the homosexual movement still complained about the Warren Court's failure to move more forcibly to protect gay rights. While the Democrats allowed gay delegates at their 1972 convention, they did so under pressure and then restricted the number to only five. When one of the five, longtime activist Jim Foster, made a passionate plea for the inclusion of gay rights into the party platform, the leadership scheduled his speech for after midnight. The platform committee defeated all gay proposals. While Abzug introduced her civil rights bill, a number of prominent Democrats argued against it and assisted in its demise.[18] Key Democratic constituencies, including leading black civil rights leaders, resisted the gay movement or, at best, remained lukewarm in their support. Even the National Organization for Women, which declared in the early 1970s lesbian rights a priority, had earlier been reticent. Betty Friedan had once labeled the gay rights movement "diversionary" and even accused it of being encouraged by the CIA to disrupt the women's movement.[19]

At the same time, many Republicans joined Democrats in supporting the repeal of sodomy laws. In fact, it had been the Nixon-appointed National Commission on Reform of Federal Criminal Law that had first recommended repeal. When litigation over civil service restrictions began, many Republicans lobbied for reform, if only to minimize the uncomfortable debate.[20] Reagan undoubtedly spoke for the majority of Republicans when he denounced gay rights, but many other leaders in the GOP remained open to reform. In the House congressmen Paul "Pete" McCloskey of California, Joel Pritchard of Washington, and James Jeffords of Vermont supported gay rights legislation. In the Senate John Tower of Texas and Edward Brooke of Massachusetts, among others, spoke openly of their support. At the state level Republican support was greater. Governors Otis Bowen of Indiana, Robert Ray of Iowa, and Daniel Evans of Washington all took a lead in the fight to repeal sodomy laws. In Alaska governor Jay Hammond pressed his state's Equal Employment Opportunities Commission to investigate anti-gay discrimination, while in Hawaii Republican legislators took the lead in supporting homosexual rights legislation. In Oregon, Maryland, and even Kansas, known for its social conservatism, Republican state legislators split almost evenly on gay rights. Homosexuality was not completely partisan because for many Republicans it was not the business of government, no matter how repugnant the activity. In the words of California Republican state senator Howard Way, "Government has no business sticking its nose into what goes on in private between consenting adults."[21]

There was support for, as well as opposition against, the ERA in both political parties. After Congress passed the amendment, both the Democratic and Republican parties officially endorsed ratification. In the Senate key support came from Democrat Bayh and Republicans William Broomfield and Marlow Cook. South Carolina senator Strom Thurmond, then still a Democrat, joined Republican Gerald Ford, soon to become the House minority leader, in supporting the ERA. Senator Bob Dole, serving as chair of the Republican National Committee in 1972, noted that his party "has championed women's rights for nearly one hundred years." At the same time Nixon added, "I have not altered my belief that equal rights for women warrant a constitutional guarantee." On this issue, at least, many of his most fierce Democratic critics agreed. In Alabama former governor and presidential candidate George Wallace supported ratification, as did the Southern Christian Leadership Conference and the American Civil Liberties Union. First Ladies Lady Bird Johnson and Betty Ford, influential women in their respective parties, both endorsed the measure.[22]

The same was true when it came to the opposition. In the Senate leading critics were North Carolina Democrat Sam Ervin, who coordinated resistance, and fellow Democrat James Eastland from Mississippi. Among many others, however, their allies included the outspoken Republicans Helms and Goldwater. The archconservative John Birch Society opposed passage, as did, until 1973 at least, the AFL-CIO, the powerful labor lobby that had strongly supported Democrats since the days of Franklin Roosevelt. Carl Hayden, who had earlier proposed a rider to weaken the amendment, was a Democrat, as was Edith Green from Oregon, one of the few women in Congress and, before her conversion later, noted for her resistance.[23]

If convoluted, the political scenario appeared dynamic, with the potential for significant impact on party politics. In one respect, at least, the Democratic Party appeared particularly divided. While its leadership used the leverage it enjoyed as the majority to usher the ERA through Congress, the ratification process suggested something else. Among many of the states that had already rejected ratification, Democrats controlled the legislatures. The Democrats still dominated the South, after all, where opposition to the amendment was the most fierce. In the words of political scientist Janet K. Boles, "Even though each party was in control of comparable numbers of adopting legislatures, a disproportionate number of the laggards were in the Democratic South."[24]

Neither party opposed the concept of women's rights, of course, the question of the ERA aside. When the United Nations designated 1977 as International Women's Year, Gerald Ford, by then president, led both Republicans and Democrats in creating a commission to plan for a conference. When preparations took longer than expected, Bella Abzug successfully sponsored bipartisan legislation extending the commission through March 1978 and providing $5 million to hold a series of state planning conferences and the official national conference. The president was to appoint commission members and report to Congress on the conference's final recommendations, a plan that members of both parties supported. As the 1976 election approached, organizers tentatively planned the conference for Houston in November of the following year.[25]

In the end, perhaps the most obvious indicators of a lack of true partisanship on the issues of abortion, homosexuality, and the ERA were the groups advocating one side or the other. Most directed their lobbying at both parties. While Schlafly's Eagle Forum clearly focused on Republicans, ERAmerica, an organization formed to coordinate ratification efforts, had two female cochairs, one a Republican and the other a Democrat. While Abzug had helped form the National Women's Political Caucus, the new NWPC deliberately recruited bipartisan membership.[26] The National Gay Task Force (NGTF), formed in August 1973 to lobby lawmakers at all levels for gay rights, advised its members to focus on Republicans in the lower houses of state government and to press particularly hard on those in urban districts, in large part because of their narrower constituencies.[27] The National Right to Life Committee, one of the largest antiabortion groups and only three years old in 1976, still believed its key goal was to identify allies and opponents, to force incumbent politicians of both parties to make unequivocal statements that could guide further actions. The Watergate scandal had led to a wave of new Democratic legislators in the 1974 congressional elections, many with no records or making ambiguous comments. Alienating potential allies with precipitous and presumptuous criticisms was unwise. In a similar vein, one of the oldest antiabortion political groups, New York's

Right to Life Party, founded three years before the National Right to Life Committee, clearly drew its membership from both sides of the aisle.[28] On all the issues surrounding the family, the controversial waters were simply too murky. Advocates on both sides sought to cast the broadest net, few dismissing one party or the other in their efforts to shift the debates to their advantage.

Carter was one of the first Democrats to declare his candidacy, with his sights set on the first primary in Iowa in January 1976. He faced stiff competition for the Democratic nomination, including Indiana senator Birch Bayh, Arizona congressman Morris Udall, Kennedy relative and former Peace Corps leader Sargent Shriver, Alabama governor George Wallace, Oklahoma senator Fred Harris, Minnesota senator Eugene McCarthy, and Texas senator Lloyd Bentson, all of whom, like Carter, announced their candidacies early. Carter sought to position himself as the Washington outsider, challenging the status quo much as he had done in his successful run for governor. For liberals, he hoped to cast himself as a moderate southern alternative to Wallace, known for his segregationist past, and for southerners and conservatives, as an honest government reformer. By the time of the first primary in Iowa, Carter had spent almost a year campaigning in the state. His victory, in turn, set in motion a strong showing in Oklahoma and a victory in New Hampshire. By this point, in February 1976, Washington senator Henry "Scoop" Jackson had entered the race and quickly claimed a victory in Massachusetts, which halted Carter's apparent momentum. By mid-March Carter had won Florida but lost Mississippi, and his campaign was low on cash. In short, the nomination still appeared wide open.[29]

In these early primaries the first to wade into the issue of families was the long-shot candidate Shriver, who proposed a revision of the tax code. As the Democratic vice presidential candidate four years before, Shriver well knew that the plight of American families played prominently in the media and obviously hoped to get out front on the issue. Shriver proposed to extend the child-care tax deduction to those who cared for their own children. Noting that the deduction applied only when both parents worked outside the home and the children were in daycare, Shriver asked why the rules "penalized those who try to keep parenting within the family." Similarly, Shriver proposed that stay-at-home mothers receive credits toward later Social Security benefits. At the very least, government and private industry should experiment with part-time jobs and flexible working hours, thereby allowing working parents greater leeway in coping with their family responsibilities.[30]

Championing the family was, perhaps, as obvious as touting one's patriotism or at least professing a love for apple pie and baseball. As all the leading Democrats paid rhetorical homage to the family, Carter exhibited a degree of exigency that his competition lacked. One of his first campaign speeches, historian Perry Deane Young noted, "was a speech on the family that Jerry Falwell could have written." In this speech Carter described the "breakdown of the family" as an "urgent priority for the next administration."[31] Nevertheless, throughout the early primaries Carter ensured that his remarks avoided the specifics that Shriver offered. "We are going to reverse the trend that we've experienced in the past that has destroyed the American family," Carter stated in one speech. "I pledge to you that every statement I make, every decision I make, will give our families a decent chance to be strong again." Offering no specifics but frequently citing the importance of his own family, Carter exhibited sentiments with which few could find fault, and the crowds invariably cheered. It little mattered what different perceptions of "family" members of the audience might hold.[32]

Helping Carter was the fact that all major Democratic candidates supported ratification of the ERA, allowing Carter to voice his support without engendering much controversy. Asked early in the primary season about his position, Carter grinned and replied, "I can answer that in three words. I'm for it."[33] Here, at least, Carter could be clear and unequivocal. Moreover, the issue of homosexuality remained surprisingly quiet, at least in regard to him. Throughout the early primaries Carter made passing comments that he disapproved of all discrimination, adding sexual orientation quickly in passing, a public position that risked a political backlash. The issue had never come up in his gubernatorial campaign, however, and both the multitude of Democratic contenders and the obvious economic travails diminished the matter in the new year. Properly presented and with any luck, Carter hoped, the issue might prove a net positive. He might win the gay vote without incurring the wrath of its political opponents. If anyone appeared to suffer from the issue, it was Jackson. Gay activists had begun to appear at Jackson's rallies, heckling the candidate, who was known for his opposition to Abzug's civil rights bill. When protesters interrupted one of his speeches on unemployment in New York, Jackson, obviously fatigued, became combative. "Go on and have your own rally," he snapped. "Our people want hard work. We don't want gay work. We don't want gay jobs.

You have your gay jobs. You just do your own thing and stay away." Perhaps recognizing that his comments unnecessarily inflamed emotions, Jackson tried to back away. "All people are entitled to human dignity," he added, "all entitled to jobs."[34] The damage was done, however, which Carter undoubtedly recognized.

Abortion, however, was not so easy for Carter. Just as voters in Iowa came to the polls, over 65,000 people rallied in Washington to protest legalized abortion. Several days before the primary Carter told a reporter for a Catholic publication that he personally opposed abortion but also the proposed antiabortion amendment to the Constitution. When the reporter pressed him, Carter added that he might support some sort of "national statute" but included no details. Carter's Democratic rivals, all opposed to the antiabortion amendment, immediately pounced, suggesting that Carter was intentionally vague in order to attract the antiabortion vote without alienating abortion rights supporters.[35] Columnists Rowland Evans and Robert Novak added to the debate by writing that after Carter had stated his opposition to the antiabortion amendment in an Iowa speech, he had quietly—"even more softly than usual"—told a woman in the audience that "under certain circumstances I would" support such an amendment. To diffuse the growing controversy, Carter tried to blame the media. "The confusion in Iowa," he suggested, "did not originate because of any change of position on my own." Ultimately, however, Carter had, in a broader sense, helped define himself for the coming general campaign. In the words of comedian Pat Paulson, officials had wanted to put Carter on Mount Rushmore, "but they didn't have room for two faces."[36]

Bayh continued to press the charge that Carter was holding out "false hopes" to the antiabortion forces; he was trying to be all things to all people or waffling to avoid the matter entirely. Since he had been instrumental in the Senate in killing the antiabortion amendment the previous year, Bayh had faced protesters at every turn. They yelled "murderer" at him to drown out his speeches and, wearing surgical gowns stained with imitation blood, played taps for the children aborted. Bayh knew more than most that the issue was difficult to finesse, and he was not about to let Carter off lightly.[37] When Shriver began picking up on this theme, reporters began pressing the matter. Already on the defensive, Carter was clearly agitated but kept calm. "When [Carter] was asked at least the 500th time about his position on abortion," one report noted, "he stared blankly and it was apparent he resented hearing the question again." Regaining his composure, however,

Carter finally responded, "Well, okay, if you want to go through that again, I will."[38] Despite the criticism, Carter was not alone in trying to manipulate the issue. Fellow candidates Humphrey, McCarthy, and Udall all searched for an acceptable middle ground. The positions of all three mirrored Carter's, although McCarthy clearly resented the questions as much as Carter, complaining that they were irrelevant because there was little any president could do. Only long-shot candidate Wallace, who had initially supported *Roe v. Wade*, adopted a position firmly in favor of an antiabortion constitutional amendment.[39]

On the Republican side, abortion appeared to play a larger role as well, perhaps magnified by incumbent Gerald Ford's apparent vulnerability. Weakened by his pardon of Nixon and a lingering inflationary economy, Ford faced a stiff challenge from Reagan. Finally forced to take a position, Ford claimed that he opposed the *Roe v. Wade* decision and was against abortion on demand. However, in a clear move to the center, he added that exceptions to a ban were necessary in cases of rape or when the mother's life was in danger. When it came to a matter of a constitutional amendment, he did not favor a ban but rather an amendment to return the question to the states. Despite his obvious efforts, his stance pleased few people. The Catholic Church complained from the political right, while women's groups did the same from the left. Complicating matters for Ford was First Lady Betty Ford, an outspoken supporter of abortion rights. Given the nature of the debate, reporters sought out the views of all of the candidates' wives. Each woman, except Jackson's wife, dutifully—and quietly—supported her husband's position. Betty Ford, however, remained as adamant as she was vocal, which soon earned her a regular following of protesters. "Abort Betty," read one sign. "Betty Ford favors the killing of unborn children," read another just above a small white baby's coffin.[40]

In many respects, Reagan was the exception among the leading presidential contenders. Rather than seeking a middle ground or simply attempting to avoid the issue like many of the others, he positioned himself as the champion of the prolife voter. Only when the mother's life was in grave danger would he even consider the possibility of abortion. While his rhetoric was unequivocal in support of a constitutional amendment to ban all abortions, he still had his own problems. In 1967, his first year as governor of California, he had signed legislation that allowed abortions when either a mental or physical threat existed and when the pregnancy was the result of a rape or incest. Antiabortion activists complained that the vague and broad wording of the bill, particularly the mental health provisions, opened the door to abortion on demand. Now backtracking, Reagan apologized and termed his signature on the bill a "mistake." He had not fully understood the bill's implications and the manner in which activists might subvert its intent. "If I had it all to do over again, I would have more restrictions than I agreed to," Reagan said to reporters. "I placed too much faith in those who were entrusted with insuring that the patient met the terms of the bill."[41]

The 1976 election season had only just begun, but pundits already claimed that abortion was an issue that could determine the election's outcome. It appeared, the *New York Times* editorialized, "to be playing the role that gun control, race, and the war in Vietnam did in the sixties." Perhaps sensing that the high emotions evoked might help sell copy, the media fanned the flames. Complaining about the efforts of politicians on both sides to equivocate, one critic remarked, "Do we want a President who will talk out of three sides of his mouth?"[42] To take advantage of the publicity and thereby promote her prolife cause, New York housewife Ellen McCormick decided to run what amounted to a single-issue campaign and entered the Democratic primaries in New Hampshire and Massachusetts. Denying that her Catholic faith influenced her, McCormick explained that a slide show she had seen on abortion framed the debate for her. "I couldn't believe what was happening and that some people called it a fetus," she remembered. "I was convinced it was a human life being taken. It was a baby, and it was a terrible thing to do."[43] Working with her group, the Pro-Life Action Committee, McCormick soon announced that she sought federal campaign funds. The new Federal Election Campaign Act of 1974 promised matching funds to any candidate able to raise at least $5,000 in contributions of $250 or less in each of twenty states. After McCormick claimed she qualified, the NARAL filed a complaint with the Federal Election Commission (FEC). The money she raised was for her committee, the NARAL argued, not specifically her campaign. The FEC disagreed, however, and the NARAL announced that it would challenge her in court. Although she performed poorly in the two primaries, she had the publicity she sought and vowed to continue the struggle in other states. Abortion as a campaign issue, it appeared, might remain significant news through the November general election.[44]

Balancing competing interests was not going to be easy for any candidate. As if to pour gas on the embers of the cultural war, the atheist Madalyn Murray O'Hair successfully fought a number of school districts who claimed that Bible readings were constitutional because no government had composed them and because they were more ethical than religious. This was hogwash to O'Hair, whose resistance was colorful and garnered significant publicity just as the primary season opened. The Bible, O'Hair stated, was "nauseating, historically inaccurate, and replete with the ravings of madmen." God was "sadistic and brutal."[45] At the same time, the Heritage Society published a well-publicized study, *Secular Humanism and the Schools: The Issue Whose Time Has Come.* Secular humanism, the conservative think tank wrote, undermined families: "The humanist philosophy of moral relativism and situational ethics teaches that moral and social beliefs and behavior are not necessarily based upon Judeo-Christian principles being taught by most families at home, but should be fashioned instead to the wishes and convenience of the majority or society as a whole." Conflicting values threatened "the family adjustment of the student."[46] Also in the midst of the primary season evangelist Francis Schaeffer published a new book titled *How Should We Then Live?* and also produced a film series that took his message to broader audiences. If families did not educate their children in the traditions of Western civilization and the Christianity it fostered, Schaeffer argued, the humanist conception of culture would ultimately destroy society.[47] For her part, Phyllis Schlafly increased her lobbying as the "voice of the home-loving, family-oriented American woman."[48] Together with Adm. Chester Ward, she published an election-year critique titled *Ambush at Vladivostok* and endorsed early in the primaries the candidacy of Ronald Reagan. Ford, she insisted, was not conservative enough.[49]

The early primaries signaled a starting gun for Weyrich, Phillips, and the other Republican partisans seeking a new coalition with conservative Christians. Just after the Iowa primary, the National Association of Evangelicals (NAE) met at the Shoreham Americana Hotel in Washington, D.C. According to one report, "The program featured an unprecedented mix of politicians and preachers." Actively working the crowd was Arizona congressman James Conlan, who trolled the convention for converts. "There are some fifteen million unregistered voters who are evangelical and could turn the tide of this nation," he argued. Others, however, had reservations. Senator Mark Hatfield, an evangelical and a Republican as well, warned against too close an alliance of theology and government. The NAE should avoid a "Christian political platform," he pleaded. "Which of you would like to decide which of us has the Christian position on a given issue?" Perhaps Conlan assumed that he did, but perhaps the board of the National

Council of Churches assumed otherwise. It was a tricky situation, Hatfield understood.[50]

With the nomination races still wide open, it was at this point, in mid-March, that Carter's religion exploded into the national spotlight. Carter had of course spoken of his religion before, for example, mentioning in Iowa that God was first in his life, his family and friends second, and his own interests third, but his statement had received little attention. Similarly, his campaign biography, *Why Not the Best?* had painted an almost idyllic portrait of his family and noted the importance of his faith. It too, however, had received little attention.[51] Then, on March 12, eleven days before the North Carolina primary, Ruth Carter gave an interview to the *Washington Post* outlining Carter's born-again experience. The newspaper dispatched the reporter Jules Witcover to North Carolina to investigate. Carter confirmed the story with Witcover, whose subsequent reporting magnified it.[52] No presidential candidate had spoken so ardently of his faith since John Kennedy deflected criticism of his Catholicism sixteen years before, and no one had ever professed to have been "born again." The national media now had a unique angle on a leading presidential contender. Unlike many evangelists, the national media were hardly familiar with the term, which, if anything, conjured up for them images of fundamentalist ignorance and the infamous Scopes evolution trial of the 1920s. An explosion of national coverage resulted, Carter later acknowledging that all the attention surprised him.[53] Columnist James Reston claimed that interest in Carter's faith came from three sources: "from skeptics who cannot quite believe a Presidential candidate can be a true believer; from religious fanatics who don't think a man should be a Presidential candidate unless he is a true believer; and from reporters who are honestly curious about the effect of a candidate's religion on his politics." All three ensured great stories. Accordingly, reporters now spoke of the "religious issue."[54]

In many respects, Carter could not avoid the topic. When Carter appeared on public television soon after he raised the issue of his religion, interviewer Bill Moyers began with a fairly innocuous question: "What drives you?" When Carter quite naturally included his faith as one of his motivations, Moyers followed with a question unprecedented for a presidential candidate. "How do you know God's will?" asked Moyers, seemingly ignoring that Carter had never implied that he did. What followed was a lengthy discussion of theology and philosophy, including intimate disclosures previously considered beyond legitimate political inquiry.[55] Other reporters pressed Carter in a more superficial way. How would Jewish voters react? Given the historic tension between Catholics and Southern Baptists, could he expect to win the Catholic vote? Would the fact that he was a Southern Baptist hurt him with northern voters?[56]

Now, at almost every stop, Carter faced questions about his faith. The day following the initial report, for example, Carter attended a fund-raiser in Winston-Salem, North Carolina. He told the story of his born-again experience with Ruth but conveniently left out the part about refusing to give up politics. The next day, in Wake Forest, it was obvious that Carter was becoming worried that the magnitude of the coverage might cast him as a zealot. He acknowledged that he was a Christian but this time did not go into specifics. He did, however, assure reporters that he was no eccentric. After a victory in the North Carolina primary, it was on to Wisconsin and more questions. "The most important thing in my life is Jesus Christ," Carter told a crowd in Kenosha, quickly adding that he was a staunch believer in the separation of church and state. In any event, he followed, no one should vote for him simply because he was a Christian.[57]

Initially, the effect of all the coverage was debatable. Carter won Wisconsin but lost New York, in the latter performing poorly among Jewish and Catholic voters and suggesting, perhaps, that Carter still needed to refine his new message. After these contests and a victory in Illinois, however, it was on to the southern states, which had larger evangelical and conservative Christian constituencies. Here the coverage was largely positive, throngs of reporters gathering at Carter's Plains church and interviewing its parishioners. Each, invariably, spoke well of the candidate. Tourists even stopped by to view the spectacle. Carter, meanwhile, told *NBC News* that he had never prayed for a political victory but only asked God to help him do what was right.[58]

As the campaigns entered the South, pundits and columnists noted that appealing to evangelical voters was wise. "Every indication is that evangelicalism is skyrocketing," wrote Gerald Strober, author of a book on the rising tide of political evangelism. Speculating on Carter's chances, religion scholar Martin Marty of the University of Chicago agreed. By stressing his southern religious roots, Carter had the potential to win a "huge constituency."[59] Carter already had advantages other candidates lacked. For one, he went by the name Jimmy, not James. "Evangelicals are intimate to the point of folksiness," concluded the *New York Times*. Ruth, Carter's sister, agreed:

"What I like about [evangelicalism] is all the hugging." Carter's informality implied the intimacy evangelicals cherished while reminding them of their hero, Billy Graham. In time, the name James Carter would become as unthinkable as William Graham.[60] In addition, help came from an unlikely source—Charles Colson. As one of Nixon's most trusted political advisors, Colson had been intricately involved in the Watergate crimes. Now out of prison, he had been born again, devoted to evangelicalism. In the middle of the primary season he published his memoir, *Born Again*, which quickly became a best seller, not only helping him reclaim his good name but also helping to popularize the term.[61] While renouncing his earlier career and stressing personal salvation, he still did not deny the importance of the political process. He certainly did not agree with Carter's policy positions, but by stressing the need for his fellow born-again Christians to become active and to value the faith of the candidates, he helped, perhaps unintentionally, drive them into the Carter camp. They were born again; Carter was born again. It was, quite literally, an easy leap of faith.[62]

Carter certainly had his critics, some of whom claimed that his public spirituality was contrived. The Episcopal priest and social critic Malcolm Boyd noted that Carter appeared to "surround himself with the accouterments of Christianity." A crucifix was always nearby during interviews, or a priest or preacher was always nearby in photographs.[63] Carter hardly contrived his faith, but he did craft the way he presented it. Speaking in Indiana, for example, Carter defended the separation of church and state even as he touted "men of faith" as necessary for the nation's recovery from Watergate. "I'm not a preacher," he reminded the audience, suggesting that no one had a monopoly on God. At the same time, undoubtedly implying his own candidacy, he added, "God has work for each one of us as individuals and wants us to demonstrate as best we can the life of Christ."[64] He insisted that members of the press who wanted to interview him first had to read *Why Not the Best?* which highlighted his faith. "When talking about his Christianity," biographer Glad wrote, "Carter used language that would ring bells of recognition in diverse religious groups."[65] At times, his language hinted at a literal interpretation of the Bible. At others, however, he quoted Niebuhr, Kierkegaard, and Barth, which implied a more nuanced stance. At times, he implied his faith without bringing it up directly. Speaking of his boyhood, for example, he explained that he was raised in an environment that "resembled farm life of fully 2,000 years ago."[66]

Carter's use of his faith and its apparent success in the South annoyed his opponents, their hope for the nomination diminishing rapidly. One Carter supporter, for example, contrasted his candidate's faith with Udall's Mormonism, even though Udall had left the church years before and the church had undergone numerous reforms. Speaking to a black audience, the supporter remarked, "I'm asking you to make a choice between one man from Georgia who fights to let you in his church, and a man from Arizona who won't even let you in the back door." When Udall demanded an apology, Carter refused until Udall "apologized for all the misleading statements [Udall] has made against me." For his part, Jackson tried to fan the flames of doubt. "When people go around telling how religious they are, I generally get suspicious."[67]

As the summer approached and along with it the conventions, Carter continued to raise his religious beliefs but remained aware of the delicate balance he had to achieve. At a national gathering of the Disciples of Christ at Purdue University, Carter gave a speech that sounded more evangelical than political. "The biggest blessing we have is our belief in Christ," Carter told the crowd. Carter's aides, meanwhile, had clearly learned the jargon to win the evangelical vote. Carter was "witnessing his faith in Christ," explained one aide to a church member.[68] While such religious rhetoric helped portray Carter as the "different" candidate he sought to be, the campaign knew that it also carried the risk of alienating Catholics, many already concerned over his position on abortion. To mitigate this, Carter promised to find "ways to provide aid to parents whose children attend non-segregated private schools, so that those children can benefit fully from federal education programs."[69] He also began to provide more specifics in his defense of the American family, another concern that both Protestant evangelicals and Catholics shared. Not only did he begin to speak more frequently on the importance of family, he tied it into the need for reforms in welfare, public housing, and tax regulation, suggesting many of the ideas Shriver had earlier proposed if in somewhat less detail. Aware that his religious rhetoric might also alienate Jewish voters, Carter now regularly included Russian Jews in his litany of human rights abuses, an obvious appeal to the American Jewish vote but a tack that risked angering the Soviets.[70] It was, indeed, a delicate balancing act.

Victories in many of the southern primaries still did not assure Carter of the nomination. Although Hubert Humphrey, former vice president under Lyndon Johnson and the first choice of many in the party, announced that he would not join the campaign, two new candidates threw their hats into the ring: Idaho senator Frank Church and California governor Edmund "Jerry" Brown Jr. After narrowly escaping defeat in Michigan in late May, Carter lost Oregon and Idaho to Church and Nevada to Brown. Carter subsequently lost California, but with other victories his delegate count was almost insurmountable, and by late June, as the convention approached, all of his opponents had conceded. In the end, the religious issue undoubtedly played a role in Carter's nomination. Observed columnist James Reston, it was not just southern voters "impressed by [Carter's] religious faith." Deftly balancing his "ethical and political philosophies," he stood an excellent chance in the general election to "gain more support by his faith than he will lose."[71]

At the very least, Carter's rhetoric won the support of Richard Neuhaus, who not only promised to vote for the former governor of Georgia but also organized on his behalf. "Carter is an embarrassment to the press because he prays for his campaign in public," Neuhaus explained. "I'm supporting him because it's important to our national health that we rediscover American character." The civil rights and antiwar movements of the previous decades had advanced God's agenda, but the rest of the decade had devolved to debauchery. Problems such as abortion and homosexuality undermined the family: "These are historic times when evil is so clearly defined that all Christians are called to witness." It was time to address the "excesses and mistakes of the [cultural revolution]."[72] Neuhaus was hardly alone. The Gallup Organization conducted a poll at the time of the conventions and reported that 94 percent of those polled believed in God, and "nearly all people" belonged to a church or faith. In reporting on the poll, the *New York Times* referenced Carter, a sign of just how prominent the coverage of his faith had become. "Most of this [religious] activity has been in the evangelical style shared by Jimmy Carter, the Democratic Presidential nominee," the paper reported before going on to describe Carter's beliefs. Another poll several weeks later indicated that Carter was the overwhelming choice of those who described themselves as born again and that this segment of the electorate was greatest in Carter's native region, the South.[73]

Carter had clearly touched a nerve among evangelicals. Before the conventions, *Christianity Today* editorialized in referencing Carter's chances: "The question is whether in a political sense . . . a candidate who promises to be honest can survive." The journal did not endorse Carter but appeared to set the stage for his candidacy. "There is a growing resentment among Southern Baptists over the way Carter is being treated by some of the secular media," the journal concluded.[74] Although granting no formal endorsement, the journal was not above defending Carter in both its news and its editorial pages. When *Time* magazine reported Carter's born-again conversion, noting that he would not give up politics, *Christianity Today* complained that the story lacked context. Carter's remarks reflected his religious integrity: "Carter went beyond just this negative answer," and readers "should carefully scrutinize campaign verbiage."[75]

One Southern Baptist, at least, had his doubts. Jerry Falwell thought Carter a "good moral man" and welcomed the candidate's religious rhetoric and his emphasis on the family. Nevertheless, Falwell remembered, "I felt nervous about him throughout much of the campaign, fearing that he represented moderates in the Southern Baptist Convention, which I had come to oppose theologically."[76] Falwell knew, however, that most of his congregation did not share his reservations and warmly embraced Carter. For the moment, at least, he would grant Carter the benefit of the doubt and recognize his positive potential. If nothing else, Falwell recognized that Carter's rhetoric aided his own agenda. Carter's success garnered publicity for his larger cause and aided in fund-raising. After seeing a musical titled *I Love America*, Falwell decided to stage musical rallies around the country, the nation's bicentennial providing a way to tie nationalism with traditional morality. Falwell selected seventy students from his college and purchased busses to carry them. Behind the busses came tractor trailers carrying stage equipment and costumes. The evangelist himself flew to each city, meeting with pastors and political leaders and urging them to "take a stand against the forces of evil at work in their towns and around the country."[77] In all, Falwell's I Love America rallies visited 141 cities, including 44 of the state capitals. Falwell invited legislators from both political parties but always found Carter popular. "There probably wasn't a single rally [where] we criticized Carter," Falwell recalled.[78]

James Dobson undoubtedly understood Falwell's position. As Carter began to stress the importance of family, Dobson founded a small nonprofit, Focus on Family. The organization was housed in a rented office with a part-time secretary, but it found a receptive audience. As ambitious as Falwell, Dobson began planning for a thirty-minute radio broadcast. He offered to write a book and donate proceeds to anyone who would advance him the $35,000 needed to purchase airtime for the first year. The result was the best seller *The Strong-Willed Child*, which sold over a million copies, and a broadcast that grew tremendously from forty-three stations once a week.[79]

In a similar vein, Pat Robertson found his audience growing, Carter helping to lay the foundation for his religious empire. Robertson admitted to
"giving some quiet help behind the scenes in the Democratic primary that
may have been responsible for [Carter] winning Pennsylvania for him." For
his part, Bill Bright endorsed the book *In the Spirit of 76*, published by the
conservative Third Century Publishers. The book contained an article by
Conlan that spoke of a plan to elect "real Christians" into power as Republicans. When the more liberal magazine *Sojourners* blasted Bright as a result,
Bright was livid. He had not read the article or known of the book's slant,
he insisted. Carter was a fine Christian man worthy of respect, and both his
candidacy and his rhetoric had done much to advance the cause of Christ.
The period of Carter's candidacy "marked a high point in [Bright's] personal walk of faith." If nothing else, most evangelists recognized, Carter was
helping to break down the traditional hesitancy of many religious Americans to join the political fray. He was helping to highlight the problems facing the nation's families and the importance of religion in their solutions.
His candidacy was a welcomed development.[80]

Watching with growing concern, of course, were the feminists and supporters of abortion and homosexual rights. The more Carter spoke of his strong
evangelical faith, the more conservative pastors characterized him in positive terms, the more complex Carter's delicate balancing act became. Carter
still hoped to win the vote of these more liberal activists, but the appearance
of too close an alliance with conservative evangelicals threatened the fragile
and unlikely coalition he hoped to achieve. For every overture he made to
one side, he had to mitigate it to the other. With the conventions and the
general campaign looming, the task was challenging, to say the least.

Only weeks before the conventions, thousands of gay rights advocates
in New York City marched from Greenwich Village to Central Park, a fifty-
two-block, one-hour walk that took them past the Stonewall Inn. The chanting crowd carried placards and banners, and the media took notice. Indeed,
magazines such as *Time* and *Newsweek* had begun to run more favorable
stories on homosexual issues. "The love that dare not speak its name,"
quipped one writer, "now can't seem to keep its mouth shut."[81] The marchers
complained to the media that neither the Democratic nor the Republican
candidates had sufficiently raised the issue. According to organizer Robert
Halstead, who suggested that almost eight hundred thousand homosexuals

lived in New York City alone, civil rights for gays and lesbians "should be a rallying point for equal rights for all."[82] As if to complicate Carter's task, the Supreme Court ruled 6–3 that states may prosecute and imprison people for committing homosexual acts even when both parties were consenting adults and the acts were in private. The Court acted without hearing oral arguments and without issuing an opinion, suggesting that even it was uncomfortable with the matter. Rather, it simply confirmed a lower court's 2–1 ruling. Only weeks later, however, the Civil Service Commission (CSC) announced that government offices could not discriminate in the hiring of homosexuals, an obvious attempt to circumvent the ongoing civil service litigation. The policy applied to all federal workers except for those in sensitive posts, where, the CSC maintained, the possibility of blackmail existed.[83] These conflicting events each had its critics. A spokesman for the NGTF called the Supreme Court's ruling "shocking" and "insensitive" while correctly noting that it stood counter to the recent trend in judicial decisions.[84] The NGTF inundated the Civil Service Commission with what it called a "coordinated campaign."[85] Abzug, its champion in Congress, increased her pressure for candidates to endorse her bill to protect the civil rights of gays and lesbians, and the National Women's Political Caucus added its support. "Any issue pertaining to the right of women to control their own bodies, including sexual preference, is a women's issue," it declared.[86] In noting that the CSC's policy seemed to condone homosexuality, opponents of gay rights once again sought to characterize the decision as a direct assault on the traditional family. "It is no accident that increasing acceptance of homosexuality parallels increasing attacks on the family," wrote one pundit, thereby increasing the trend of lumping gay rights with feminism and abortion rights.[87]

Undoubtedly hoping that his public professions of faith offered a degree of cushion against criticism, Carter moved to placate the homosexual community. In a Los Angeles appearance that Ed Edelson, Carter's California coordinator, arranged, Carter faced a direct question from the gay minister Troy Perry. Would Carter ban discrimination against homosexuals in four areas: the military, housing, immigration, and civilian contracts that required security clearance? The candidate's answer surprised Perry, who well knew of Carter's overtures to conservative Christians. "I only have a problem with one of those," Carter replied, "and that's only in the area of having security clearances where the person's not out and open." Perry had his candidate, and he let his followers know, asking for a photograph with Carter at the end of the evening. Carter did not appear with Perry in the picture, but Rosalynn did.[88]

The fact that Carter's wife appeared but the candidate himself did not was telling. Trying to win both sides, Carter portrayed gay rights as a matter of public discrimination to liberal audiences and as a matter of negative private morality to conservatives. His campaign wrote the NGTF that Carter would sign Abzug's bill if it reached his desk but that Carter "was not comfortable with homosexuality for personal reasons." Left unstated was the question if Carter would actively lobby for the bill while president.[89] Even while he publicly acknowledged homosexuality as a sin, he invited one of the gay community's staunchest supporters, Margaret "Midge" Costanza, to join his campaign. The liberal vice mayor of Rochester, New York, and onetime congressional candidate appeared an odd supporter of the moralist Carter, but Carter's surprising remarks to activists such as Perry were difficult for Costanza to ignore. The reality was that despite Carter's efforts to appeal to some of the gay community's opponents, he had spoken out more forcibly than any other candidate against discrimination. He had, for example, written to a local gay group in Philadelphia. "I oppose all forms of discrimination on the basis of sexual orientation," the letter had stated. "As president, I can assure you that all policies of the federal government would reflect this commitment."[90]

With the Democratic National Convention approaching and his campaign thriving, Carter began to face more scrutiny. Tom Snyder of NBC's *The Tomorrow Show* pressed Carter about his promise not to discriminate while insisting that homosexuals not hold positions in national security. As Carter replied that such persons might be subject to blackmail, Snyder insisted that certain heterosexual relationships—an adulterous relationship, for example—might also be of concern. "That's true," Carter answered, "but the blackmail attempt might be much more successful in the case of homosexual acts." Sensing, perhaps, that Snyder's questioning cast doubt on his careful balancing act, Carter sought to move the discussion onto another matter. "Look," he snapped, "I think my position is fairly advanced on the subject."[91]

By the time of the convention, his nomination assured, Carter had no intention of letting controversial issues such as homosexual rights disrupt the party. When the platform committee met at the Democratic National Convention, Carter's gay supporters pressed for a platform plank endorsing homosexual rights. The campaign, however, actively resisted it. To many homosexual activists this came as a shock, given Carter's earlier comments, and Jean O'Leary, an NGTF leader, drove overnight to protest directly to Midge Costanza and the platform committee. Costanza listened, promised that the committee would at least take a vote and not simply ignore the matter, and finally complained to one of Carter's top political advisors, Stuart Eizenstat. "Midge, let's do what we have to for the gay rights movement but let's do it after we get to the White House," Eizenstat replied. "For God's sake, don't let us carry this albatross going into the [general] campaign. We have to win this election."[92]

The convention, held in New York's Madison Square Garden, proceeded smoothly, to Carter's relief, and did not adopt a platform endorsing gay and lesbian rights. Constanza got her vote, but it failed 52–27. The platform remained conspicuously quiet on the issue, and while the delegates accepted a gay caucus, they ignored it in official schedules and programs. The convention appeared to reflect Carter's finessing of the issue. Inside, aware of Carter's position, the NGTF "opted for a moderate position," in the words of the *Advocate*. It circulated a petition signed by over six hundred delegates that endorsed homosexual rights but did not publicly complain that only four of those delegates were openly homosexual. More important, it resisted the urge to criticize Carter. In the words of one delegate, the gay community should "get with a winner and work to improve the winner rather than be doctrinally pure and work with a loser." According to the *Advocate*, "Did [the gay lobbying] accomplish anything? That's a good question."[93]

Outside, in a series of protests around the city, a group calling itself the New York State Coalition of Gay Organizations was not so restrained but, thankfully for most Democrats, received almost no publicity. The protests angered Carter's staff. In an unguarded moment one Carter aide expressed his frustration: "Most of the radical gay political people are not clever enough to recognize the difference between an enemy and a friend. Yes, they have been fucked over by a number of politicians. But Jimmy has spoken on the gay issue. What more do they want?"[94]

The aide might have said the same thing about many of the feminists. Carter remained clear in his support of the ERA, and the platform committee at the Democratic convention ensured a similar stance by the national party. Carter created the 51.3% Committee, named for the percentage of females in the overall population and appointed to give women's rights advocates a voice in the campaign. Just as the Democrats began their convention, the

Supreme Court ruled 6–3 that states could not require women to get their husband's permission before getting an abortion and 5–4 that states could not issue "blanket" restrictions requiring all single women under the age of eighteen to get parental approval. The decisions were "monumental" to Ilse Darling, executive director of the newly formed Religious Coalition for Abortion Rights, and "negative and defensive" to Cardinal Terence Cooke, Catholic archbishop of New York. Some antiabortion groups even began to call rather ominously for a "congressional investigation of the Supreme Court." When the Democrats adopted a plank that opposed a constitutional ban on abortion, Ellen McCormick led a rally in Central Park of over ten thousand protesters. Her delegates attacked Carter personally, claiming that "Carter backs baby murder."[95]

In spite of this, many feminists remained leery of Carter's evangelical rhetoric. Adding to their suspicion was the fact that when legislators began to consider restricting federal funds for abortion, Carter avoided the matter and did not join the opposition. He remained uncomfortably vague. Moreover, many feminists complained that a deeply embedded southern attitude that questioned the position of women in authority still pervaded the campaign. Several competent women staffers, including Barbara Blum and Connie Plunkett, found themselves excluded from key campaign strategy sessions, while the venerable White House correspondent Helen Thomas complained that campaign staff regularly dismissed her. Recalling the campaign years later, another female reporter stated, "The Carter campaign was where I learned what male chauvinism was all about." Much of the discontent centered on Hamilton Jordan. After a female volunteer leaked a story on the prevailing internal attitude toward women in the campaign to the *Wall Street Journal*, Jordan called a meeting with staffers, beginning it with a derogatory statement about the role of women. Plunkett protested, and an argument ensued. To the surprise of the women, the meeting was simply to find the leaker, not to address the content of the leak.[96]

Before the convention, the women's caucus demanded that in four years, at the 1980 convention, a gender quota should divide the delegates exactly even, 50 percent for each sex. Aware that this would face certain opposition from the more conservative elements in his party and receive a lot of unwanted publicity, Carter met privately with Jane Patterson and Abzug, the former the primary architect of the 50–50 proposal and the latter in the middle of a campaign for the Senate after resigning her congressional seat. He privately promised both to appoint a large number of women to high positions in his new administration and to lobby personally for equality at the 1980 convention. This compromise eventually produced a heated, hour-long debate among the women's caucus before the majority voted to accept. Carter, it appeared, was proving successful at cultivating one constituency without embittering another.[97] At the convention Carter's strong rhetoric in support of women was hard to ignore, and many leaders of the women's movement spoke out ardently in support of his candidacy. Outwardly, at least, there was a show of unity even if many women still quietly harbored concerns over misogyny and abortion.

Perhaps aiding Carter was the media attention given to the Republicans, who, surprisingly, given the political demographics, appeared in many respects more divided than the Democrats. Phyllis Schlafly's efforts had begun to pay dividends, and before the Republican convention in Kansas City, her allies worked to repeal the party's endorsement of the ERA and to win an endorsement of a constitutional ban on abortion. At the same time, the *New York Times* reported, "Republican feminists are prepared for a fight." It all promised to become a public brawl. Schlafly testified before the platform committee that because the Democrats had embraced abortion, homosexuality, and the ERA, "religious and family-oriented Americans" would gladly support the planks she advocated. In regard to the ERA, a subcommittee recommended that the party take no stance, ending over thirty years of official endorsement.[98] Prominent delegate Patricia Goldman, who had been active in the NWPC, fought back, complaining that women's rights advocates were only "occasionally seen and hardly ever heard." While such sentiments were undoubtedly hyperbole born of frustration, they were difficult to ignore. In the end, the platform committee voted "in an emotional battle" 51–47 to continue the party's endorsement.[99] Schlafly thought that the vote was unfair but that it was "bad politics" to complain. If Reagan won the nomination, Schlafly assumed, he would take up the fight, and the platform would be meaningless.[100] In regard to abortion, however, Schlafly and her allies had more success pressing for a plank that supported a constitutional ban. Debate lasted until 2:00 a.m., when the feminists finally surrendered, muttering to the press that continued fighting "was just not worth it."[101]

"Next to the fight between President Ford and Ronald Reagan, the women's fight has been the best and most skillfully waged political contest on view here," the *New York Times* reported from the convention. "Normally proper GOP women" were now quite angry.[102] The struggle could get personal, and it all made for good press. According to one Republican feminist, Schlafly in no way represented American housewives. "I know perfectly well that Phyllis Schlafly has domestic help to scrub her own kitchen floors," delegate Betsy Griffith declared. "I scrub my own floors and some day we can compare dishpan hands." Privately, Griffith and her allies acknowledged that Schlafly's strength was impressive and that they had decided to wear dresses and high heels for the convention. Pantsuits would appear too masculine. For their part, Schlafly's supporters taunted ERA advocates. "Do you hate men?" asked one. "Hardly" came the reply. "I'm pregnant."[103]

Ford had hoped to avoid such a public division and, just before the convention, worked to shore up his support among women voters. Perhaps anticipating the frustration of Goldman, Griffith, and others, he ordered a review of all federal laws to identify and eliminate those that had unwisely or unjustifiably discriminated on the basis of sex. Reiterating his support for the ERA, he declared, "Injustice cannot wait upon politics." Likewise, First Lady Betty Ford rejected direct criticism from Schlafly. "I'm going to stick to my guns and will continue to do what I can [in lobbying for the ERA]," she confidently declared. Even as she spoke, however, thirty-five members of Schlafly's organization picketed outside with signs reading "Happiness Is Stopping ERA."[104] The Fords undoubtedly felt the need to reiterate their support of women's rights because Schlafly had proven quite adept at tying both traditional conservative distaste for government and concern for the American family with the fight against the ERA, often with sensational headlines. In one instance, for example, she claimed that ERA advocates wanted to "turn over the care of children to the government." Her "new evidence" was an Ohio panel's recommendation for federally funded universal child care. Even as Schlafly spoke, Ford publicly celebrated the anniversary of the birth of Susan B. Anthony. It appeared a direct counter.[105]

By appearing to direct her fire primarily at Ford, not Carter, and by publicizing the divisions within the GOP, Schlafly arguably assisted Carter in his efforts to avoid controversy. As Carter stressed his born-again religious beliefs in an appeal to the conservative religious vote, Schlafly's efforts seemed to point out that Ford was no friend to the same constituency. Carter was able to garner even the most radical feminist voters while holding on to his party's traditional southern base. In any event, while hardly intending to aid Carter, Schlafly's efforts had clearly paid off in regard to the ERA. As the election approached, news reports implied that the ratification process had ground to a halt. "Equal Rights Amendment Slipping," read one headline. "Approval on Rights Bid Held Dim," read another. A national labor strike called by NOW to protest the resistance to ERA ratification fizzled. In reporting on the failure of women to join what was referred to as the "Alice Doesn't" strike, from the 1974 film *Alice Doesn't Live Here Anymore*, the *New York Times* commented dryly, "Alice Did."[106]

In the end, the nominations of Jimmy Carter and Gerald Ford to square off in the fall's general election campaign were, of course, due to a multitude of factors, much more than simply religion or family issues. Liberals failed to coalesce around a Democratic alternative, while Carter proved adept at both raising money and winning influential backers. Carter emerged as the "outsider" candidate when the nation appeared disgusted with "insiders." In this, Carter's use of religion and his ability to finesse controversial issues undoubtedly played a role. For many, however, it was simply the assumption that Carter stood the best chance of defeating Ford. This was, for most Democratic primary voters, the bottom line. Ford hardly enjoyed the advantage of appearing something new, but he did have the awesome power of incumbency and all that it entailed. Populists such as Schlafly sought to steer the party away from what she termed its "eastern establishment," but the majority of primary voters did not yet share her more ardent conservatism.[107]

In his first major speech after the convention, Carter traveled to an outdoor rally in Manchester, New Hampshire, to stress once again his plans to save the American family. Aides insisted that such a large rally was inappropriate for an issue as serious and complex as family policy, but Carter overruled them. "The American family is in trouble," Carter declared to the crowd, and it was "clear that the national government should have a pro-family policy." Noting the importance of reform in welfare, child care, and the tax code, Carter invoked the Bible to large applause. "Honor your father and mother," he stated. To advance the cause of the family further, Carter announced that he had asked Joseph Califano Jr., an attorney and former aide to Lyndon Johnson, to serve as a "special advisor on how Federal programs can aid and support the American family." The press praised the speech, leading speechwriter Patrick Anderson to remark to Carter, "The family material went over really well." Many conservatives, of course, thought otherwise. Carter's speech had lofty rhetoric, they responded, but as long as he embraced feminism, homosexuality, and abortion, he would never really be a champion of the family.[108]

In the wake of the convention the abortion issue flared once again. A number of Catholics complained that the Carter campaign had not invited Cardinal Terence Cooke or Archbishop Joseph Bernardin because of their views on abortion. It was tradition, they insisted, that the bishop of the diocese in the convention city give an invocation. Moreover, they claimed, aide Stuart Eizenstat had even remarked that the Catholic hierarchy "was out of it."[109] In short, it was clear that Carter once again had to recalculate his delicate political balancing act. Accordingly, on August 31 Carter accepted the advice of running mate Walter Mondale that a meeting with six Catholic bishops at Washington's Mayflower Hotel might calm the waters. Carter began the meeting by reiterating that he was personally against abortion. While he did not support a constitutional amendment outlawing it, he did disavow the Democratic Party's own stance on the issue. He would not oppose people who tried to enact an antiabortion amendment. Under no circumstances, he insisted, should the government do anything to encourage abortion. Carter clearly hoped that this would pacify his listeners, but Bernardin did not take the bait. When Carter attempted to steer the conversation toward other issues on which the candidate and the church agreed, Bernardin stated that until they had resolved the abortion matter, there was no point in discussing anything else. The conversation then grew a bit strained, with Carter defending himself by claiming that he really could not comment on any constitutional amendment without reading its specific wording. Afterward, while Carter claimed that the meeting was successful, Bernardin told reporters that he was "disappointed" in what Carter had to say. "Personal opposition is not enough," Bernardin declared before the cameras.[110] In the end, the entire episode simply added to the sense that Carter was trying to appease both sides. A Carter aide lamented, "In a sense, Jimmy's not much different in the way he runs now than when he was running for state legislator. He still places heavy emphasis on pleasing the people who are in the room with him at that moment."[111] At the very least, historian Garland Haas concluded, "the religious issue created a number of awkward moments for Carter." For one, it made him sound awfully defensive in declaring it a "mistake to see the issue as myself against the Catholic Church."[112]

Catholicism and abortion proved a continuing problem for Carter's campaign. The following month, in September, the campaign scheduled Carter to speak at Our Lady of Pompeii Roman Catholic Church in Philadelphia. Just before the event, however, its sponsor, the Coalition of Organizations for Action (COA), announced that the Philadelphia archdiocese would not let the meeting take place without the abortion issue in the forefront. Since the group wanted to hear Carter speak on matters pertaining to urban decay, the COA arranged for a nearby Lutheran church to host the meeting. While the campaign diffused a more embarrassing situation, the change in venue still contributed to a sense that the Catholic Church held Carter in low esteem. His relationship, the *New York Times* concluded, "had sunk to a new low point." With reporters pressing him, Carter aide Jody Powell replied, "We think the real problem with the abortion issue is not the issue of abortion itself, but on how Jimmy handles it. We know that this fuzziness thing is hurting him and we don't want to be fuzzy on the issues."[113]

Complicating matters was the issue of federal funding for abortions. New York Republican representative Angelo Roncallo had first attached an antiabortion rider to an appropriations bill two years before without much success. In the wake of the political conventions, however, Illinois Republican representative Henry Hyde thought the time advantageous to press the matter again as part of the annual Department of Labor–Health, Education, and Welfare (HEW) appropriations. Medicaid, the joint federal-state program funding medical services for the poor, paid for over a quarter-million abortions per year at the cost of approximately $50 million. The Hyde Amendment, abortion rights supporters insisted, would, therefore, have severe ramifications in both health and fiscal terms. It enforced one religious view over another; it violated equal protection by singling abortion out from other, still-funded medical procedures; and it rendered abortion rights meaningless for women too poor to pay for the procedure. To supporters of abortion rights, it was simply a matter of fairness.[114]

In a sense, at least, Hyde was correct. With critical funding for two departments at stake, pressure was enormous to pass the bill. Debate centered on what, if any, exemptions might exist, for example, cases of medical necessity or cases of rape or incest. As the summer progressed the House passed the amendment, but the Senate balked, the appropriations bill ending in a conference committee. After the conference could not agree, the matter returned to the respective chambers. The House proceeded to pass the amendment with broader support, and in the end, the Senate finally agreed with one exemption—instances where carrying the fetus to term threatened the life of the mother. Led by Abzug and Texas attorney Sarah Weddington, the latter having played a key role in the *Roe v. Wade* decision three years before, abortion rights advocates sought an injunction in federal court. With the elections only weeks away, the federal court in Washington agreed. The issue of federal funding would, apparently, have to wait for a new Congress—and a new president.[115]

Reporters naturally pressed Carter for his position on the debate. Undoubtedly hoping that his decision would please conservative Catholics, their feathers already ruffled, Carter announced that he supported Hyde's amendment. He reminded Catholics that he personally opposed abortion and did not agree with the Democratic Party's platform. The campaign also dispatched vice presidential nominee Mondale to the University of Notre Dame. Informing the audience that he had come to the Senate the same year as Robert Kennedy, Mondale reminded them that in 1960 many voters had worried that John Kennedy's Catholicism was "a different religion than most of the citizens." It was not an issue for Kennedy, and, he implied, the same was true for Carter's evangelicalism. Mondale worked to be cordial with his hosts, referring to the university's president, the Reverend Theodore Hesburgh, as "Father Ted." The crowd responded warmly. Mondale avoided controversy and deliberately focused on those issues on which the Catholic clergy and the campaign agreed. Carter might profess his evangelical faith, the unstated message was obvious, but he shared the same concerns as the majority of Catholics.[116]

Helping Carter overcome the controversy was the simple fact that the two candidates' official positions on abortion were remarkably similar. If Carter annoyed conservative Catholics, Ford did as well. Ford claimed that he was personally against abortion on demand but favored abortion in limited cases such as the Hyde Amendment allowed. With the amendment bogged down in the courts, Ford requested his Domestic Council to study ways to keep federal spending on abortion "to the minimum required by law." He claimed that he supported the Republican Party platform even as some interpreted its abortion plank to endorse a total ban, something Ford claimed that he did not support. Attempting to take advantage of the controversy, a tack that Carter warned would backfire, Ford requested a meeting with the same bishops Carter had met.[117] This time Bernardin declared himself "not totally satisfied" with the meeting. Facing criticism from both sides, as did the Carter campaign, Ford had to disavow a television commercial that displayed a skull and crossbones to lambaste abortion rights. "Some of the pro-life groups used very bad judgement," declared vice presidential candidate Bob Dole, perhaps annoying many conservatives. As he crisscrossed the nation, Ford, like Carter, had to guard against protesters from both sides of the great abortion divide. The protesters were, according to the media, angry and well organized, requiring the Secret Service to "form a protective ring" around the respective candidates.[118]

Carter's efforts to mitigate conservative criticism on abortion meant, of course, that he angered social liberals. The delicate balancing act continued. The newly formed Religious Coalition for Abortion Rights, composed of both Jewish and Protestant liberals, expressed "dismay" over Carter's apparent refusal to fight a total constitutional ban and his recent overtures to the Catholic clergy. "We are asking him to hear the voice of the religious community which supports the 1973 Supreme Court decision on abortion," said Rabbi Richard Sternberger.[119] As if in response, Carter spoke out more forcibly in favor of women's rights. If elected, he stated, he would "tear down the walls that have kept women out of the decision-making process." He declared that he favored affirmative action on behalf of women and criticized Ford for opposing federal funding of child-care centers and for tepid enforcement of Title IX, the equal access statute of the 1972 Educational Opportunity Act.[120] When the National Women's Agenda Conference, held just outside Washington, invited him to speak, his language appeared designed to win the hearts of even the most radical elements of the women's movement. Women, he declared, should be "tough" and "militant" in their fight for equal rights.[121] Before conservative audiences such stringent comments vanished. There was no "disharmony among us," he described the women's movement from one pulpit. "We all share a constant love for Thee."[122]

Carter also moved to shore up his support in the homosexual community, rattled no less than the feminists. He appointed the NGTF's Jean O'Leary to his 51.3% Committee. "It marks," a press release noted, "the first time that a known gay person has been appointed to an important national advisory committee."[123] A group known as Gays for Carter formed, with Troy Perry and O'Leary actively involved. The two kept in close contact with Midge Costanza, who remained the gay community's central liaison. A central task was to reassure wary homosexuals, which Carter encouraged. "I happen to be a Baptist," Carter reminded them, "and one of the central tenets of the Baptist Church is the separation of Church and State."[124] The election only months away, the Carter campaign purchased advertisements in several gay publications. "[Carter] has deep religious beliefs," the ads read, "but doesn't believe in legislating morals."[125] Carter's twenty-six-year-old son, Chip, participated in a benefit tricycle race sponsored by the Mint Tavern, a prominent San Francisco gay bar.[126] Supporters of gay rights suggested that the campaign "get Mondale more involved with gay issues." This would help solidify the gay vote while not directly implicating Carter.[127]

Watching it all was Billy Graham, a man with his own balancing act. On the one hand, Graham, still reeling from his association with Nixon, knew that he had to appear nonpartisan. He did not want to get burned again. On the other hand, he enjoyed his reputation as the nation's evangelical leader and the entrée it offered him to the powerful elite. He did not want to lose his status. In one sense, Carter genuinely appeared a different sort of politician, a man whose faith was as real as Graham's own. Carter indeed appeared to offer the chance for a new national awakening. In another sense, however, Carter's vague and sometimes contradictory statements and his confusing positions on issues such as abortion and homosexuality were worrisome. Graham needed Carter, but Carter needed Graham as well. An endorsement from the famed preacher would help mute continuing reservations among conservative Christians as Carter's campaign courted the supporters of abortion and gay rights. With both Graham and Carter balancing their own interests, the result was an odd flirtation between the two. At times during the campaign they seemed allied, at others conflicted. In the end, the relationship between the two served both men well. Graham remained in the national eye, and his reputation, in the aggregate, served Carter well.

As the general campaign got under way, Graham's comments were ambiguous. He promised to stay "totally out of any partisan politics" but allowed that "people are going to demand moral integrity and some spiritual strength in public leaders in a way they have not done before."[128] He planned to "stay a million miles away from politics this year" but, in what some took as a jab at Carter, added that attempts to organize an evangelical partisan voting bloc "would be very detrimental to America and the church," something he would "fight." When Bill Bright asked that he serve as chairman of the Christian Embassy, a staging ground for evangelizing legislators, Graham refused.[129] On the other hand, he appeared proud that forty million evangelicals "would be enough to turn a presidential election," something he was "sure Mr. Carter has not been unaware of."[130] With Carter stressing his faith, Graham concluded, "It is refreshing to have candidates come along and talk about their devotion to God, especially if they back it up with their lives." Leaving for a crusade in San Diego in late summer, Graham went further. "We need to know what political leaders believe religiously, morally, and sociologically." While in San Diego, Carter telephoned Graham to wish him good luck with his crusade. Graham was obviously pleased, telling a reporter from Atlanta, "Well, you might be interested to know that I got a call from your former governor this morning. That's right—it's the first call

I've gotten from him since his nomination. He called me in my room early this morning, said he just wanted to ask how the crusade was going—he told me, 'I just want you to know that Rosalynn and I are praying for your meetings out there.' I've known him since he was governor, you know. He's a friend of mine, has been for some time." Graham went on to note that he had heard that one of his own sermons had contributed to Carter's born-again experience.[131] Later, departing for a crusade in Detroit, Graham sent both candidates his good wishes. Carter replied with a handwritten letter, which greatly pleased Graham. "Thank you for your kind note," Carter wrote. "I pray that your crusade will be successful and that God will continue to use you grandly in his Kingdom's work. Your friend, Jimmy."[132]

Trying to maintain his neutrality, Graham kept telling reporters that in his view the two candidates had similar religious beliefs. When the press quoted Graham as saying, "We do not need any born-again candidates," frustrated Carter aides complained that all the famous preacher was doing was giving evangelicals an excuse to not vote for their candidate. In a moment of stress and anger even Carter snapped, apparently forgetting his efforts to woo Graham. "I think what people should look out for is people like Billy Graham, who go around telling people how to live their lives," Carter remarked in an unguarded moment. To this Carter's son Jeff added that Graham's doctorate was not legitimate, a false claim sure to inflame.[133] The sudden controversy helped neither Graham nor Carter, and both quickly sought to repair any damage. Graham dropped a note to Rosalynn, asking her to "give Jeff a hug. I have two sons and I understand." Later Graham explained that he had not intended his born-again comments as an attack on Carter, only against the establishment of a Christian party in America. The press had distorted his intent. To correct the matter, Graham left no confusion in his next remarks. While he would not reveal his personal vote, Graham explained that Carter was a "leader we can trust and follow."[134]

With the three presidential debates, scheduled for late September through late October, rapidly approaching, Carter obviously hoped that more people than just Graham harbored such sentiments. Carter had worked hard to win the votes of conservative Christians and the social liberals many of those Christians abhorred. It had not been easy with the issues of abortion, homosexuality, and feminism, among others, tearing at the fabric of American culture, but with the campaign entering its final, crucial stage, nothing yet had proved fatal. All Carter had to do was avoid mistakes and continue his delicate balancing act, and he would emerge a man for all seasons or, more appropriately, a candidate for all constituencies. The Oval Office appeared within his grasp.

Now in the political homestretch, Carter made perhaps his most obvious overture to religious conservatives, agreeing to appear on Pat Robertson's *700 Club* television program. Robertson and his film crew traveled to Plains, Georgia, and the twenty-minute interview took place on Carter's front porch. Robertson began by asking Carter why a good country boy would want to leave home for the turmoil in the nation's capital. He also asked Carter about the proper role of government. Aware of his audience, Carter struck a conservative tone, stressing his view of a smaller government. While Robertson asked almost as many questions about foreign policy as domestic, reflecting, perhaps, the evangelical concerns about Communism and Israel, Carter wanted to discuss the state of the American family, clearly assuming that appearing as a champion of family would resonate with Robertson's audience. The family was the building block of the nation, Carter concluded. If it faltered, little else mattered. When Robertson asked Carter about possible appointments, Carter implied that while he would not choose advisors on the basis of their religion, he wanted people who espoused good religious principles, for example, "unselfishness, truthfulness, honor, and a sense of compassion."[135]

For Carter, at least, the interview appeared a success. Robertson had avoided feminism and the controversies it engendered. In several instances Robertson had answered Carter's comments with an "amen" and afterward had asked Carter to do a promotion for a coming television revival. When Carter had remarked that he believed the 1948 founding of Israel was a fulfillment of biblical prophecy, Robertson obviously had assumed that it was an indication that the two shared a similar theology. Robertson had also assumed that Carter would accept suggestions for his "godly" appointments. In the following weeks Robertson spent considerable time developing a large pool of potential applicants, and according to Robert Maddox, there were "marathon conference calls with ministers to create the list."[136]

While not every evangelical supported Carter, almost all acknowledged the inroads Carter's professions of faith had made. "Evangelicals will give Carter solid support in November for both religious and cultural reasons," one pastor predicted, despite the fact that "a surprising number of clergymen have expressed reservations about his ambiguity on the issues."[137]

When Republican vice presidential candidate Robert Dole accused Carter of wanting to tax church property, *Christianity Today* noted that Carter had proposed no such thing. In fact, while governor of Georgia he had tried to amend the state constitution "so that sales taxes would not hit hospitals, nursing homes, and other church-affiliated organizations."[138] Just before the election, a senior editor, David Kucharsky, published a book that largely painted Carter and his background in a favorable light. Another book was even more favorable. Describing Carter's career as a "miracle" and stressing his "spiritual odyssey," the book benefited from ads placed prominently throughout the journal.[139]

Carter's inroads worried Congressman James Conlan, who contacted conservative activist Paul Weyrich. While Conlan complained about Carter's stance on homosexuality, abortion, and feminism, Weyrich listened but drew a different conclusion. If Carter really were a moral and religious man, Weyrich mused, Carter might ultimately prove more conservative than Ford. Carter had perhaps helped the conservative cause by stressing the family. Weyrich had long thought Ford insufficiently conservative, and, he tried to explain to Conlan, Carter might even appoint evangelicals to his administration, as he had implied to Robertson. Who knows, Weyrich concluded, Carter's election might not be such a bad thing. This was hardly what Conlan wanted to hear. Carter's overtures had apparently even begun to sway his own ideological allies.[140]

Carter denied that he was using his faith and insisted that he did not see himself as better than anyone else, a sentiment with a great deal of truth, given both Carter's firm beliefs and the fact that the press continued to see the issue as a boon to ratings. Nevertheless, Carter frequently mentioned that he prayed daily and welcomed the press to his small church in Plains, Georgia, where he still led a Bible study group. While Carter never claimed that people should vote for him because of his faith, his sister and his wife, Rosalynn, were not so reticent.[141] Carter did not want to overplay his religious hand. Not only did the politics of religion make him uncomfortable, but the downsides remained. He might demean his own faith, undermine the wall of separation between church and state that he still believed vital, or, of course, anger the liberal voters on which he also counted. He had to maintain his political balance. When a full-page ad appeared in *Christianity Today*, purchased by a group calling itself Citizens for Carter, the Carter campaign denied any connection. The ad asked directly, "Does a Dedicated Evangelical Belong in the White House?" The answer was clear:

Carter brought integrity to government and "morality to our national life." People in the "post-Watergate era" were "disillusioned with the moral corruption."[142]

It all worried the Ford campaign no less than it concerned Conlan. Ford had always been a religious man, and his son Michael was then a divinity student at Gordon-Conwell Theological Seminary, a multidenominational evangelical seminary in Massachusetts. Accordingly, Ford's aides encouraged him to speak more openly about his own views. Ford, however, was reluctant to "play the faith card" during the campaign. "I have always felt a closeness to God and have looked to a higher being for guidance and support," Ford explained, "but I don't think it was appropriate to advertise my religious beliefs." For its part, the Ford campaign had a weak grasp of the changes then sweeping religious communities across the land. A campaign briefing book included outdated information and even stereotypical portrayals of the various denominations.[143]

If Ford, like Carter, found religious politicking distasteful, his campaign staff, like his opponents, knew that he could not ignore it. "Jimmy Carter wears his religion on his sleeve but Jerry Ford wears it in his heart," the Ford campaign began to tell the press. Speaking of his faith more frequently, Ford granted interviews to Ben Armstrong, executive secretary of the National Religious Broadcasters, and Nathan Bailey, president of the National Association of Evangelicals. He told them that he and Betty read the Bible every night. His campaign released a private letter that Ford had written to Billy Zeoli, a well-known evangelical friend who headed Gospel Films, one month after Nixon's resignation. "Because I trusted Christ to be my savior, my life is His," the letter read. "When I walk into [the Oval Office] I realize that Man's wisdom and strength are not sufficient so I try to practice the truth of the proverbs."[144] In late September Ford entertained more than thirty evangelical leaders at the White House, which the *New York Times* concluded was evidence that Ford was "clearly challenging Carter, a born-again Southern Baptist, for the fundamentalist and often conservative Protestant vote."[145]

The first presidential debate did little to help Carter. Held at Philadelphia's Walnut Street Theater on September 23, the debate found Carter on the defensive. Not only did he have to rebut the old "fuzziness" charge, but he also appeared unduly nervous and stiff. Little of substance emerged from the debate. Perhaps the most memorable occurrence was the failure of the sound system and the fifty minutes of silence that followed.[146] While some polls suggested the incumbent had edged out the challenger in the contest, Carter had greater problems. Just as the debate took place, stories began to leak about an interview Carter had granted *Playboy* magazine, known for its celebration of sexual freedom and its soft-porn photos. Some have suggested that the disastrous interview was an attempt to allay the fears of many Catholics and Jews, wary that Carter's evangelical faith would lead to censorship. Others have suggested that it was an ill-advised attempt to demonstrate that he was not a religious fanatic or once again to explain how he separated his private morality from his public policy, another step in his balancing act.[147] More likely, Carter simply wanted to explain what he had learned from Christ's teachings against pride. In any event, Carter acknowledged that he had "committed adultery in my heart many times." All people were sinful and should not condemn others: "Don't consider yourself better than someone else because one guy screws a whole bunch of women while another guy is loyal to his wife." In many respects Carter's comments reflected long-held Baptist doctrine, but they also opened him up to direct questions on homosexuality. Faced with these questions, Carter repeated that he thought homosexuality was a sin and tried to carve a middle position by suggesting that the matter was best left to the states. Laws against homosexuality were understandable "because of their relationship to the Bible." For many years, "the Judeo-Christian moral standards were accepted as a basis for civil law." This kind of a standard was an "acceptable goal."[148]

The *Playboy* interviewer, Robert Scheer, pressed further. "The issue of homosexuality always makes me nervous," Carter replied, insisting that it was personal and moral more than political and obviously wishing to drop the matter. "I don't have any, you know, personal knowledge about homosexuality," Carter stumbled, "and I guess being a Baptist would contribute to my sense of being uneasy." Homosexuality was indeed a sin, but it was not for him to condemn. "Look," he finally snapped, "I can't change the teachings of Christ. I believe in them and a lot of people do in this country, as well."[149]

The *Playboy* interview did not win much support among homosexuals, while it shocked many in the evangelical community. Carter had hoped his comments about sin and pride would win him support, reflective of Jesus's Sermon on the Mount, but the very fact that he had chosen a magazine dedicated to sex to explain his views repulsed leading evangelicals. The choice made him appear to be the opposite of a true family man. Reverend Wallie Amos Criswell of Dallas, a leading Southern Baptist and pastor of its largest congregation, declared himself "highly offended."[150] Criswell invited Ford to one of his services and, with Ford in attendance, denounced Carter's interview. Ford and Criswell appeared friendly despite a rift that had developed the previous year. At the time First Lady Betty Ford had remarked that she would not be surprised if her daughter, Susan, had an affair, comments that Criswell had described as "shocking" and representative of "animal thinking." Now, however, all appeared forgiven. After his sermon Criswell told the press that Ford had declined a similar interview request from *Playboy*, an unconfirmed story but one that the Ford campaign relayed. Leaving the large red brick church building, Ford's campaign manager, James Baker, acknowledged that Criswell's support "will be important to us," and the following week the Ford campaign began to run television ads in the South depicting Betty Ford smiling in the congregation.[151] Columnist Jack Anderson added on *ABC News*, "President Ford's campaign aides have been researching Jimmy Carter's past for a sex scandal." Anderson claimed that Ford's staff had provided him with the names of women Carter had romanced but that he had investigated the claims and found them unsubstantiated. Carter, meanwhile, found the rumors infuriating.[152]

Trying to end the public relations debacle, Carter accepted the advice of advisor Charles Kilbo that the best way to handle the controversy was to face up to it directly, describe his intentions as laudatory (explaining his strong Christian faith), and then apologize. This would humanize him, Kilbo argued, making him appear like every mother's son who had ever misbehaved and deserved another chance. If he would take this approach, Kilbo insisted, Carter might not only diffuse the immediate controversy but also regain ground lost with women, particularly middle-class and suburban housewives.[153]

Falwell, who had for the most part quietly harbored reservations about Carter, was not so easily swayed, and the *Playboy* interview marked a severe downturn in their relationship. Falwell began to criticize Carter's remarks in a series of sermons entitled Sword of the Lord. With his television ministry, *The Old Time Gospel Hour*, now reaching over a million viewers, Falwell's comments won the attention of both campaigns. Richard Brannan from the Ford campaign wooed the evangelist, while an angry Jody Powell from the Carter campaign "delivered me an ultimatum," in the words of Falwell. A number of stations refused to air Falwell's criticism, fearing that it violated the Federal Communications Commission's "Fairness Doctrine," which required equal time for all political programming. Falwell told reporters that he had offered the Carter campaign a chance to rebut him but that he had received no reply. He assumed, therefore, that he was in full compliance with the law. When several stations told Falwell that they needed written proof of his offer for rebuttal, Falwell began to complain that the Carter camp was threatening retribution should Carter win the White House. It was, Falwell claimed, "pretty severe." The Carter campaign vehemently denied the charge, but Falwell called a press conference at the National Press Club in Washington to claim that the threats implied action by the Federal Communications Commission and violated his free speech rights. "I brought in some big guns," Falwell recalled, speaking of several prominent ministers present in support.[154]

The damage was done, Carter's carefully crafted balancing act apparently coming undone only weeks before the final vote. His once healthy ten-point lead in the polls evaporated overnight. Watching it all, *Newsweek* magazine ran a cover story declaring 1976 "The Year of the Evangelical."[155] It was no consolation to Carter. The world's most famous evangelical politician suddenly was in serious trouble.

The *Playboy* revelations appeared to be the proverbial "October Surprise," a sudden jolt late in the campaign season that many pundits characterized as a mortal blow to the challenger. The article was indeed a blow, but fatal it was not; enough time remained for Carter to stop the hemorrhaging. Both skill and luck played into Carter's rapid recovery, but even then the outcome was unclear. When voters went to the polls on November 2, an unusually warm and sunny day across much of the nation, the polls had the race as a virtual dead heat. Turnout was the key, and the election was anyone's call.

First, Criswell's prominent embrace of Ford offered Carter a chance to regain the initiative. With the *Playboy* interview still resonating, three former presidents of the Dallas Pastors Association issued a statement condemning Criswell's comments, describing them as a "blatant violation of the principle of separation of church and state." Supporting the statement were pastors from the Baptist, Methodist, and Presbyterian churches, along with one Jewish rabbi. Dr. James Landes, top executive of the 2.3-million-member Baptist General Convention of Texas, explained his objections to Criswell's actions: "Baptists are completely and fiercely independent in their thinking. Any Baptist member can take, under God, any position he feels like taking so long as he is speaking for himself. Once he steps outside the pulpit, he can endorse anyone of his choice." Landes and the other ministers believed that Criswell had not stepped outside the pulpit, although the question was open to debate. When Criswell had criticized Carter from the pulpit, he had not technically told his followers to vote for Ford. Likewise, while he had responded to media inquiries about his views on Ford by saying simply "I am for him," he had done so from the front steps of his church building, not from the pulpit itself.[156] In any event, the bright spotlight had obviously begun to shift away from Carter and onto his critics.

Falwell later acknowledged that the entire *Playboy* incident "cut both directions." While many people in the conservative Christian community thought Carter's remarks reprehensible, others did not feel as strongly as the critical ministers. Falwell finally admitted that he had picked the fight to "use as a platform" but that in hindsight "I was not that adept at using the media." Many of his followers still saw Carter's remarks as a sign of "openness and honesty in the wake of Watergate" and supported the Democrat in spite of Falwell's efforts.[157] For his part, Pat Robertson and his flock reflected more the optimism of Weyrich than Falwell's newfound skepticism. Robertson, like Graham, had put great faith in the religious pronouncements of Nixon and was still distraught over the Watergate disclosures. If nothing else, Robertson assumed, the *Playboy* incident proved Carter was open and genuine, the anti-Nixon. Still enamored with Carter's professions of his born-again faith, Robertson was willing to overlook *Playboy* and Carter's flirtation with the homosexual vote, the latter, he undoubtedly assumed, rhetoric necessary for elections but not really representative of the candidate's true views. To Robertson, Carter shared the same vocabulary and, therefore, the same theology.[158]

A Ford blunder helped. In the second nationally televised debate on October 6, journalist Max Frankel remarked that the recently signed Helsinki Accords officially recognized the Soviet sphere of influence in Eastern Europe. Ford replied: "We have an agreement where they notify us and we notify them of any military maneuvers that are to be undertaken. They have done it. In both cases where they've done so, there is no Soviet domination of Eastern Europe and there never will be under a Ford administration." When an incredulous Frankel pressed the matter, Ford did not recognize the political grave he was digging and argued that the Yugoslavians and Romanians did not consider themselves dominated. Not surprisingly, the Carter campaign wasted little time in labeling Ford as out of touch with reality and weak on national defense. Suddenly, the *Playboy* incident appeared to be old news. Ford had already faced questions about his own taxes and racist comments made by his secretary of agriculture, Earl Butz. Now, however, the press was abuzz with a new October Surprise, much to the delight of the Carter campaign.[159]

Carter did his part, returning yet again to the issue of family, the perfect antidote for *Playboy*. Just before the first presidential debate, Califano had submitted his report on the status of the American family to Carter, the report titled *American Families: Trends, Pressures, and Recommendations*. It concluded that the most severe threat arose from unemployment and lack of adequate income; not surprisingly, the report largely avoided the controversies surrounding feminism, homosexuality, and abortion. After reviewing Califano's work and in the wake of the *Playboy* revelations, Carter announced in a speech before the National Conference on Catholic Charities his plans for "a national conference on families." Carter had selected his words carefully, deciding on "families," not "family," to reflect the diversity of American family life.[160] It was a smart move, in a sense reflecting once again his political balancing act. By stressing the importance of family, he reiterated a major concern of conservative Christians. By using the word "families," he at least implied that he was open to a range of kinship groups. While many evangelicals believed that the only legitimate family was a married heterosexual couple with biological or adopted children, many liberals argued that the term encompassed single-parent homes, homosexual homes, extended family units, and simply people unrelated by blood but sharing a common abode and child-rearing duties. In the words of University of Wisconsin professor David Allen, "An overly rigid definition of the family and its responsibilities can contribute to limiting women's participation in the work force, constrict gender identities, and sustain a sense of entrapment." In the end, Allen concluded, "a plurality of definitions" was more appropriate. Carter's announcement was brief and short on specifics, and it had its intended effect. The devil may have been in the details, but the details could wait until after the election.[161]

In the waning weeks neither candidate distinguished himself. The final debate on October 22 brought no new bombshells and appeared to have little impact. The candidates battled over the nation's economic malaise and traded personal charges and countercharges, all apparently ineffectual. Carter's faith occasionally made its appearance, but Carter was always careful about his choice of words. When reporters pressed Carter about the expressed concerns of some Jewish leaders, he replied, "I hope that they have learned a little more about Southern Baptists." Members of the church believed in the separation of church and state in part because they believed in the "sainthood of the believer." The denomination stressed an individual relationship with God, and "no pastor has the right to interfere in that relationship." There was no "hierarchical arrangement whereby the church can send down a dictum." Simply put, Baptist leaders would not tell Carter what to do, a defense, hardly coincidental, that smacked of John F. Kennedy. Three days before the election, the press reported that Carter's Plains church would not allow a black family to join, with Carter's own cousin Hugh shouting that the church would not admit "negroes." Carter quickly issued a statement distancing himself, but a Gallup poll indicated that Ford had pulled ahead by one percentage point. The results were uncomfortable for Carter, but both political camps knew that the night of November 2 would be a long one.[162]

It was indeed long, but, for Carter at least, it ended well. When the election results came in, Carter had won the election with 297 electoral votes to Ford's 241. Out of almost 81.5 million votes cast, Carter came away with 1,680,974 more than his opponent, a bare majority at 50.1 percent and only slightly above Ford's 48 percent. Carter's narrow victory included only twenty-three states plus the District of Columbia; Ford won twenty-seven states. A key for Carter was the South, where it appeared that while he held on to the African American vote, traditionally Democratic, he also attracted low-income and rural whites. Carter carried eleven of the thirteen states in the old Confederacy, winning 53 percent of the total vote across the region and performing better than any Democrat since Harry Truman in 1948.

It all suggested that Carter's balancing act had succeeded. Carter apparently held his ground with Catholics, either matching the percentage won by previous Democratic candidates or only slightly losing ground. CBS claimed that Carter won 54 percent of the Catholic vote, four percentage points below the average for Democratic candidates, while other polls suggested that he won 57 percent, virtually the same as his predecessors. Carter improved among Protestants, however, CBS concluding that Carter took 46 percent compared to the average of past Democrats at 39 percent. Among self-described evangelicals, Ford captured 9.6 million votes to Carter's 6.4 million, a 3-million-vote shortfall that might suggest the impact of the *Playboy* article. In context, however, Carter fared significantly better among evangelicals than his predecessors, Hubert Humphrey and George McGovern, who lost the evangelicals by 7.2 million and 10 million votes, respectively. If Carter's campaign had worried that its candidate's evangelical rhetoric had scared Jewish voters, it appeared afterward to have had little cause for concern. Carter won a strong 68 percent of the Jewish vote.[163]

It did not take long for pundits and political scientists to attribute the election results to the politics of religion. Without his significant improvement among evangelicals, they noted, Carter would have lost such a close election. *Christianity Today* reported just after the election that while there had been no "nationally coordinated organization working to get evangelical Christians elected to public office," evangelicals remaining diverse both in their theology and politics, the campaign had spawned new regional organizations such as California Christians Active Politically that tended to favor the born-again Baptist.[164] Certainly, Carter's claim to be an honest "outsider" resonated in the post-Watergate era. In fact, one study of the election concluded: "Issues seem to have played a relatively minor role in determining the outcome." Concerns over honesty and integrity loomed over all specifics. "The only issue that more than half the voters said they considered influential on their own decisions was restoration of trust in government."[165]

Carter had worked diligently not to have the growing controversies surrounding feminism, abortion, and homosexuality disrupt his campaign, and, it appeared, he succeeded. Before the vote, many observers predicted that these issues would prove determinative, that their impact would be profound. At the time of the last presidential debate, for example, Marilyn Chandler, a former member of the President's Commission on Population Growth and the American Future, predicted that abortion would prove critical. The issue, she explained, "has reached ridiculous prominence in this Presidential campaign."[166] Gay rights advocates, confident that they had rallied the nation, assumed that their vote would prove equally pivotal, that the election would be, in the words of author William Turner, "the first in the nation's history in which lesbian and gay civil rights became a significant topic of debate."[167] Feminists predicted, with perhaps more weight, that the women's movement would finally confirm its importance. None of these predictions, thankfully to Carter, were wholly accurate. Still too new, still so relatively nonpartisan, the issues appeared to have had little overall impact. Whether a product of the similarities in the candidates' positions or a direct result of Carter's vagueness, the issues, almost all agreed, did not live up to their hype. Abortion, homosexuality, and feminism, among the other controversies surrounding the status of the American family, had indeed received much greater press before the election. They had not, however, swayed the majority in the voting booth.

Abortion was the most obvious example. Postelection surveys found attitudes on abortion poor predictors of voting behavior. Forty-seven percent of those polled who said that abortion should never be permitted voted for Carter, while 53 percent of those who said that it should always be permitted voted for him. When asked what were the most pressing issues facing the nation, less than one-tenth of 1 percent said abortion. Unemployment, inflation, and other economic issues, it appeared, determined the outcome, the media coverage of the vocal minority of abortion protesters hardly representative.[168] In fact, some polls placed Carter's support greater among Catholics who favored an antiabortion amendment than among those who opposed it. The official Catholic hierarchy, it appeared, did not represent the majority of American Catholics. Perhaps sensing this, the bishops had reaffirmed their "absolute neutrality" only weeks before the election. Moreover, the polls suggested that many voters did not understand each candidate's abortion position. In one poll 21 percent said Carter favored abortion rights, while 36 percent said he opposed them. The media had, at various times, called Carter's position "inconclusive" or "muddled," but Carter, it appeared, had successfully straddled the murky middle.[169]

Carter had achieved his delicate balance. In the end, Carter was able to hold on to enough evangelical followers while attracting a broader base to win the presidency. He had, for example, won the support of the Americans United for the Separation of Church and State, which declared him "vastly superior" to Ford, as well as the support of leading evangelist Pat Robertson. While Robertson drew up his list of conservative Christians for possible appointments, a group of feminists formed the Coalition for Women's Appointments to lobby for their own advocates. Carter had won the support of gay rights champions such as Bella Abzug as well as the majority of Falwell's flock, if not the pastor himself. Conservative Christians and liberal activists all looked to the new president-elect as one of their own.[170] This had put Carter into the Oval Office, but now the reality was simple: the campaign was over, and the job of governing had just begun. A new day had dawned, one that brought continuing economic woes, foreign policy challenges, and a clamor to save the American family, even if the definition of "family" was as inflammatory as the conflicting solutions offered. Everyone expected results, from the most militant feminist to the doctrinaire fundamentalist Christian. The future was not going to be easy for James Earl Carter Jr.

Pat Robertson, 1976
(Christian Broadcasting
Network)

Pat Robertson interviewing
Jimmy Carter, 1976
(Christian Broadcasting
Network)

Jimmy Carter and Gerald Ford
outside the White House, 1977
(Jimmy Carter Library, NARA)

Margaret Costanza being sworn in as director of the White House Office of Public Liaison, 1977 (Jimmy Carter Library, NARA)

Margaret Costanza, in white, meeting with the National Gay Task Force, March 1977 (Jimmy Carter Library, NARA)

Jimmy Carter, Rosalynn Carter, and
Amy Carter leaving church, 1977
(Jimmy Carter Library, NARA)

Carter addressing the National Prayer Breakfast, 1978 (Jimmy Carter Library, NARA)

ERA demonstrators outside the White House, 1978 (Jimmy Carter Library, NARA)

Sarah Weddington addressing the Interdepartmental Task Force for Women, December 1978 (Jimmy Carter Library, NARA)

Jimmy Carter and Rosalynn Carter departing church on Palm Sunday, 1978
(Jimmy Carter Library, NARA)

Jerry Falwell at the Liberty
University dedication, 1978
(Liberty University)

Billy Graham and Jimmy Carter, 1979 (Jimmy Carter Library, NARA)

Carter meeting with the National Advisory Committee on Women, 1979 (Bella Abzug is to Carter's immediate right) (Jimmy Carter Library, NARA)

Carter meeting with members of the National Advisory Committee of the White House Conference on Families in the East Room of the White House, 1979 (Jimmy Carter Library, NARA)

Antiabortion protesters, Washington, D.C., 1980 (Jimmy Carter Library, NARA)

White House breakfast for religious leaders, 1980 (Jimmy Carter Library, NARA)

Carter at prayer service in the National Cathedral, November 1979 (Vice President Walter Mondale is next to Carter) (Jimmy Carter Library, NARA)

Carter addressing the annual convention of the National Religious Broadcasters, January 1980 (Jimmy Carter Library, NARA)

Jerry Falwell, 1979
(Liberty University)

Ronald Reagan meets with Pope John Paul II, 1984 (Ronald Reagan Library, NARA)

CHAPTER THREE

Rootin' and Tootin'

THE INAUGURATION OF JIMMY CARTER on January 20, 1977, spoke volumes about how he envisioned himself and anticipated his presidency. He was not like those who came before, it suggested; he was truly a man of the people. Wearing a normal business suit that he had purchased in a small Georgia town, Carter abstained from much of the usual pomp. With Rosalynn and Amy at his side and with his security detail undoubtedly on pins and needles, Carter famously walked the mile and a half down Pennsylvania Avenue toward the White House after the ceremony. The populist message was obvious, as obvious as Carter's affirmation of his religion. A group of Baptist churches had held an early-morning People's Prayer Service on the steps of the Lincoln Memorial only days before the inaugural. Over five thousand people braved twenty-degree cold and the roar of jets taking off from nearby National Airport to sing and hear ministers pray for the president-elect.[1] Proclaiming a National Prayer for the President Day, a number of Baptists signed statements of prayer and forwarded them to Plains. In addition to asking Americans to pray for Carter, the statements declared that the "principles on which this nation was founded were from God."[2] With his inaugural address one of the briefest in history at only fourteen minutes, Carter took his oath of office on a Bible his mother had given him, opened, he told the press, "to a timeless admonition from the prophet Micah."[3] When well-wishers told him that they would pray for God to be with him, Carter acknowledged that he "experienced a sense of brotherhood with them."[4]

Only the third Baptist elected to the presidency in the nation's history, Carter surprised the press by attending the First Baptist Church of Washington on January 23, the first Sunday after his inauguration. Also surprised was Fred Gregg, who learned that his Bible class would include the new president. Arriving at the church to find hordes of reporters, Gregg introduced himself to Carter and asked him if he would like to teach. Carter declined, promising to do so in the future and adding that he was looking forward to the class. After the class reporters asked Gregg how the discussion had gone. Carter had been actively involved, Gregg answered approvingly. Like Carter, Gregg continued, he had just arrived in Washington. Also like Carter, "God clearly had some purpose in sending me up here."[5] The incident impressed many evangelicals. "By taking a Bible in hand and studying along with other members of his church, the President is showing that he is more than a spectator at an ecclesiastical event," *Christianity Today* editorialized. "He is demonstrating his need for instruction from God's Word." For this, all Christians should applaud him.[6] Within a month of the inauguration Carter was teaching a couple's class at the church. "God's law doesn't change, no matter if one is in Plains, Georgia, Washington, the Soviet Union, China, or Pakistan," Carter told his class. "Congress meets and goes home. God's law doesn't change."[7]

Four days after his first church visit Carter attended the National Prayer Breakfast and made some of his most forceful religious comments to date. Held annually by the Senate and House prayer groups, which convened every week at the Capitol, the breakfast drew four thousand attendees to the Washington Hilton hotel. Given the record turnout, over a thousand of the attendees had to listen from two large rooms adjoining the main ballroom. The crowd included a virtual Who's Who of the Washington elite, including the most powerful congressional members in both parties, members of the Supreme Court, and corporate leaders. Keynote speaker James Wright, the House majority leader, alluded to Carter in his remarks, describing events of the day as a new beginning in national life and a chance to recommit to God's forgiveness through Jesus Christ. When it was Carter's turn to speak, the crowd gave him a standing ovation. Carter hugged Wright and told him that he was "proud to be a brother with him" and a "child of God." Carter's remarks constituted a seventeen-minute sermon as he spoke, without notes, from chapters in 2 Chronicles. He appealed to government leaders to heed the exhortation of Jesus: "Whosoever shall be chief among you, let him be your servant." Carter added that he had already learned something from the White House receptions he had attended: military officers were usually the ones to say, "We are praying for you" or "God be with you." The crowd loved it, and a number of evangelical leaders spoke glowingly afterward.

Billy Graham noted approvingly that it was the first National Prayer Breakfast since 1953 where a president spoke of Jesus Christ in a personal way.[8]

Carter did not forget the importance of family. As if to remind him, Pope Paul VI called for a new commitment to the family just before the inauguration. Speaking to thousands at the Vatican, the pope did not mention Carter by name but urged his flock to defend the family "from the many evils that today can offend the unity, the stability, the fecundity, the educative function, and the spirit of union."[9] For his part, Carter stated in his inaugural address that he wanted his administration to be remembered as having "strengthened the American family, which is the basis of our society."[10] Carter told his new White House staff that despite the pressures they would surely face, they should not neglect their own families. "I want you to spend an adequate amount of time with your husbands, wives and children," he wrote in a memo. "We are all going to be here a long time and all of you will be more valuable to me and the country with rest and a stable home life."[11]

It was obvious that the new president's professions of faith and family, including the importance of forgiveness, were real. One of Carter's first actions was to invite Mary Fitzpatrick, a convicted murderer who had been assigned to work at the governor's mansion, to come to the White House and help care for nine-year-old Amy. Fitzpatrick had grown close to the Carters in Georgia, and after Carter personally requested her parole, she came to Washington and remained both out of trouble and, to Carter, a "close member of our White House family." Carter had no political reason to do this, and indeed, he received a significant degree of criticism. It was a true testament of his faith.[12]

Of course, Carter had not forgotten politics and still recognized that it was easy to drown in the waters where religion and politics both flowed. As Carter demonstrated that he would not leave religion at the door to the Oval Office, he continued to swim with care. Not wanting to appear to be using his religion, Carter declined an invitation to attend the Baptists' People's Prayer Service, sending sister Ruth in his place.[13] In his inaugural address he did not choose the passage from Micah lightly, at first rejecting a passage from Chronicles because he feared that some might interpret its condemnation of "sin" and "wicked ways" incorrectly. Micah's passage, which spoke of loving mercy and walking humbly with God, was less judgmental and thus avoided negative stereotypes.[14] While Carter spoke forcefully at the National Prayer Breakfast, he ensured religious balance at his inauguration. Catholic archbishop John Roach of Minnesota gave the benediction, while a Jewish cantor, Isaac Goodfriend, sang the national anthem. If Carter already knew that broadening his religious appeal was difficult, the reaction to his inaugural reminded him of the lesson. Rabbi Marc Tannenbaum of the American Jewish Committee complained that Goodfriend's anthem was not enough, only a "sop for the Jews." Father John Tavlarides of the Greek Orthodox Church added that not only was his religion absent but the entire inaugural too closely mixed religion and patriotism.[15]

In a sense, Carter's deft use of religion in the campaign ensured a bright light on his own religious activities as president if not criticism of any real or perceived administration misstep. If maintaining a balance in the campaign were difficult, the stakes appeared suddenly higher, a reality that Carter may have welcomed and encouraged at times but regretted at others. When his daughter, Amy, began fifth grade at the Thaddeus Stevens School, a public school in the District of Columbia, the media reported that her new teacher was the wife of a Methodist minister and had taught a Bible class.[16] When Amy had her baptism, complete with the Baptist tradition of immersion in water, the White House press corps dutifully reported the event, although, as *Christianity Today* wryly added, journalists "had some trouble handling details." Carter did not comment on the coverage, although one member of the congregation undoubtedly spoke for many by stating, "I think it's terrible how Amy's baptism has been played up by the press."[17]

All of the press added to the impression of conservative Christians that Carter was one of their own. Southern Baptists and evangelicals in particular harbored tremendous expectations for his presidency. In the words of Robert Maddox, not yet employed in Washington, people of faith "had great hopes that as president [Carter] could leverage the country spiritually and morally in ways that we had not seen in a long time." Carter's campaign message had resonated, just as he had hoped. Many conservative Christians, perhaps not fully cognizant of the nature of the new president's evangelism, knew only that he was someone different. He did love Jesus Christ; he did care about the family; the future, as a result, would indeed be different. As Carter undoubtedly knew, their expectations ran incredibly high.[18]

Carter's election was "exhilarating to [Pat] Robertson," biographer David Edwin Harrell noted. The following month Robertson began writing a newsletter to "track the progress of world events under the presidency of a Christian." The Reverend Bailey Smith reminded the Southern Baptist Convention that "[Carter's] initials are the same as our Lord's." Jerry Falwell, who now claimed that the idea that religion and politics did not mix was "invented by the Devil to keep Christians from running their own country," seemed at least temporarily to forget his problems with Carter during the campaign. Claiming that "the evangelical-fundamentalist vote went two to one to Democrat Jimmy Carter," Falwell spoke well of the new president and even implied that he had been instrumental in Carter's election. While acknowledging that he might oppose Carter "if he violates moral codes which in my opinion are in opposition to Scripture," Falwell said that Carter was, nevertheless, "my president-elect" and "has my respect and support."[19]

Both Billy Graham and Carter likewise seemed to forget any friction during the campaign. Graham acknowledged that he would be "rootin' and tootin' for [Carter]." Carter sent Graham a note: "I deeply appreciate your support and your prayers. They are very important to me. I will do my best to deserve your confidence. Please let me continue to benefit from your advice and counsel." Graham did not attend the inauguration—the first that he had missed since 1949—but did attend a special prayer breakfast a few days later that included a friendly exchange with the Carters. Carter invited Graham and his wife, Ruth, to the White House, with Rosalynn offering the Lincoln bedroom. Graham declined, joking that the bed had a hump in it. Obviously, he had been there before. Despite this public display of friendship, some observers continued to claim that Carter and Graham did not like one another. This was an untrue "rumor," a Graham admirer later insisted. Any distance between the two was simply because Carter wanted to "avoid giving the impression that he was packing the White House with Southern Baptists."[20] Graham continued to insist that he and Carter were "friends," and, indeed, Graham came to Carter's defense more than once. When some fundamentalists complained just after the election that Carter had the occasional alcoholic beverage, for example, Graham reminded them that "Jesus turned water into wine," adding cryptically, "That wasn't grape juice."[21] Claiming that "I'm very much for [Carter]," Graham donated $10,000 for a new Plains Baptist Church, then still struggling over racial integration.[22]

Just after the election Phil Strickland, a leader of the Baptist General Convention of Texas's Christian Life Commission, wrote Carter advocating that the new administration establish a "formal relationship with the religious community." Strickland noted that during the campaign Carter had been "appropriately concerned that your faith not be used for purely political ends." Strickland claimed that he had tried to honor that sentiment, but, now that the election was over, "it is important that the religious community not feel that they have been purposely ignored or excluded." Establishing formal "communication and support" with religious groups was not the same as "using the Church." Working together with the administration, churches could "advance social justice and meet human needs." To conclude, Strickland added somewhat vaguely that coordination might prove "a critical factor in the success or failure of administration proposals."[23]

If Strickland's note were rather presumptuous, he followed up with another lengthy memo to key Carter aides Hamilton Jordan and Landon Butler. The nine-page memo claimed that its "basic premise" was to emphasize that it was "critical for this administration to have a comprehensive understanding and effective working relationship" with religious groups and other significant public interests. Strickland then went into detail explaining the operations and organization of a number of religious groups and listing "priorities" for the new administration. Although Strickland still claimed to know that Carter did not like considering the political use of his faith, the memo listed "the political benefits to be derived by effective relations with these groups." Effective relations, Strickland continued, included initiatives from the White House before the groups formally pressed issues, direct lines of communication, and permanent structures to implement programs. Because religious groups were so diverse, "the task of relating to religious structures should not be the total job assignment of one office."[24] After sending the memo, Strickland and Butler had several telephone conversations, and Strickland offered to make overtures on behalf of the administration with his religious colleagues. "My offer to initiate some activities with the religious community still stands, if that is the way you choose to go," he wrote Butler in late February.[25]

Strickland also communicated with Carter's son Chip, undoubtedly aware that the younger Carter shared many of his religious concerns. Writing in late March, Strickland noted that relations with religious groups was "delicate," given that the "religious community is complex and fragmented." Attempts to bridge theological differences were foolish, and thus "cooperation among religious structures has evolved into being around issues." It was on this level that the administration should proceed. The White House should remember to deal only with the "top, recognized leadership." Otherwise, such leaders might feel "slighted" and work against the administration's objectives. In choosing issues to press, the White House should choose those that "cut across denominational and judicatory lines."[26] By the middle of 1977 Strickland had even taken it upon himself to volunteer to send the White House a list of key religious leaders in each state. "These are the people who it would be well to invite to the meetings," he wrote White House aide Laurie Lucey.[27]

Most correspondence was not nearly as presumptuous. James Sullivan, president of the Southern Baptist Convention, expressed his hopes for the new administration, to which Carter replied, "I deeply appreciate your comments and I assure you that I will do my best for God and for the citizens of our great nation."[28] Evangelist Robert Schuller wrote Carter, introducing himself and lavishing praise on the new president. "Someday I hope to shake your hand," Schuller wrote, adding, "Drop in and visit my church some Sunday when you are in California."[29] When letters did not simply express congratulations or good wishes, it was clear that the authors hoped that Carter's well-publicized faith might at least translate into improved access and influence. The Christian Embassy, for one, "offered its services" to the new president and requested a meeting for its leaders.[30] Pat Robertson, now familiar enough to address his letter "Dear Jimmy," once again congratulated Carter and requested a meeting for a friend, Dr. Charles Malik, a former president of the United Nations General Assembly and a "warmhearted evangelical Christian." If Carter would meet with Malik, Robertson promised to make his corporate jet available for Malik's use.[31] Jim Bakker also sent Carter a letter of congratulations and requested an appointment in the Department of Health, Education, and Welfare for a friend, Chuck Cannon, a "Christian."[32]

Bill Bright, head of Campus Crusade for Christ, proved particularly persistent in pressing for a meeting with Carter. "I commend you on your effective witness of your faith in Christ and can assure you that your example is making a profound impact on the lives of other leaders across America and throughout the world," Bright wrote. Listing his ministry's concerns and efforts, Bright was rather forward in his conclusion: "I shall look forward to discussing these matters with you personally at your earliest convenience."[33] Soon after Carter's inauguration, Oral Roberts requested a meeting with Carter, prompting his congressman, Oklahoma representative Jim Jones, to press for the meeting as well.[34] Carter's staff, clearly impressed by the volume of requests, recognized the need for formal procedures for all future replies. "We can't have folks just jumping in through the first White House window they come to," wrote aide Rick Merrill.[35]

Even Graham was not above making personal requests to Carter. "You have been much on my heart and in my prayers during recent days as you face mounting crucial decisions that affect people not only of this country but of the world," Graham diplomatically began one letter. Graham went on to note the case of a young woman, Marie-Christine Roberts, one of his in-laws through his oldest daughter's marriage, who faced deportation because of questions surrounding her dual citizenship. Her father, Graham noted, had fought with the American forces in World War II, and if Carter were to help, "it would probably make a good human relations story in the press, although she is not desirous of any publicity." Graham concluded that he would greatly appreciate any assistance Carter might provide.[36]

The letters were not just from outstanding and well-known evangelicals. Sent from charitable organizations and smaller congregations as well, they requested that Carter or members of his staff attend this church's ceremony or add their support to that church's cause. As his administration began, for example, the Centre for the Study of Religion and Communism, created at Britain's Keston College and dedicated to religious liberty in the Eastern bloc countries, pressed the new president for aid, playing off Carter's faith. "I hope that we will be able to maintain a close contact," wrote one of the group's leaders to the White House's Office of Public Liaison.[37] When a group of Mexican Mennonites faced deportation, a number of religious groups claimed religious persecution. The ensuing uproar reached *Newsweek* magazine, prompting Texas congressman George Mahon, in whose district the Mennonites resided, to complain to the White House. "The media continues to be very active in connection with this problem," one of Mahon's letters ominously warned.[38]

No matter where its origin, the deluge of letters was, perhaps, predictable. Every new administration faces congratulatory correspondence or efforts by various interest groups to gain an initial advantage on policy issues, to make the best first impressions. The widespread coverage of Carter's faith and the way the candidate had cast his campaign and his new administration, however, ensured the lobbying of religious advocates. Evangelicals and the broader conservative Christian community obviously held strong hopes for a man they anticipated would be an ally. Carter had raised their expectations, and, they obviously assumed, the time had finally arrived for action.

The administration might have welcomed the advice of Phil Strickland and others, presumptuous as it was, that Carter needed a developed, coordinated strategy to deal with religious issues and groups. The White House may not have done exactly as Strickland advised, cognizant that his advice was laden with self-interest, but his larger point had merit. In fact, Robert Maddox was suggesting the same thing. A Southern Baptist minister, Maddox had become good friends with Carter's son Jack while serving as a minister in Calhoun, Georgia. After the election the ambitious Maddox drew up a proposal for the position of White House religious liaison and began lobbying for it, noting the need for coordination and direction in policy and politics. "I knew exactly what I wanted to do," he later wrote. "Every president since Eisenhower had someone who worked with the religious community." Given Carter's "high profile as a religious man" and the volume of correspondence he would surely receive, Maddox reasoned, "it would be all the more important." Maddox developed a detailed prospectus and mailed it to Carter advisor Jody Powell.[39]

Nothing, however, happened. Weeks passed before Maddox received a short rejection letter. Strickland, who knew Carter better, received a more personal reply but hardly more satisfaction. "Your memos are good and will be of help," Carter wrote, even as he essentially dismissed the specifics.[40] Inside the White House advisor Butler thought the advice of Strickland and Maddox worth considering but convinced his superiors that the Office of Public Liaison (OPL) was sufficient. In the coming weeks Strickland continued to press his case but found his high access inhibited. All responses were brief and dismissive and came from OPL staffers. In reality, OPL's mandate was too broad to coordinate any comprehensive religious strategy, and the thought itself smacked of the politics of religion, something Carter did not like to entertain. The result was an almost ad hoc policy when it came to issues surrounding the family. Even as events brought more prominence to the battles of feminism, abortion, and homosexuality, among others, Carter relied on his own religious interpretations, which carried the potential of angering all sides. Without a coordinated strategy, the administration struggled, working to satisfy one group on one occasion and its opposite on another. Carter's delicate balancing act may have sufficed for the campaign, but moderation would not meet the high expectations of all after the election.[41]

The administration weighed every invitation and request individually, staffers, if not the president, always cognizant of political ramifications. In some instances, such as the invitation from the Christian Embassy, the White House gave its thanks but cited scheduling difficulties in regretting.[42] Not wanting to anger Robertson or Baker, the White House declined politely, promising that "your views will be given very serious and careful deliberation."[43] When Oral Roberts made his request, staffers debated it until Carter intervened and personally approved it.[44] The meeting took place in the Oval Office late in the afternoon of Wednesday, February 23, 1977, ending with Roberts leading a prayer. Roberts extended an invitation for Carter to attend commencement exercises at Oral Roberts University, but Carter regretted in a handwritten letter. "I thoroughly enjoyed your visit and appreciated the opportunity to pray together," Carter wrote. "Due to previous commitments, however, I will not be able to accept your kind invitation. I'm sorry."[45]

After the White House declined to meet with Robert Schuller, the evangelist continued to lobby, sending Carter a copy of his book *Reach Out for New Life*.[46] Carter sent a brief letter of thanks, and three months later Schuller sent copies of two of his other books, *The Peak to Peek Principle* and *Peace of Mind Through Possibility Thinking*, once again requesting a meeting with Carter. "Your interest in making your works available to the President is appreciated," the White House replied, adding that if it proved possible to arrange a meeting with Carter in the future, it would be in touch.[47] Bill Bright was equally persistent, but each time the White House demurred, citing scheduling difficulties. "It may be possible to arrange a meeting at some future date," Director of Scheduling Fran Voorde wrote, "and I will be in touch with you."[48] Several months later Bright invited the Carters to attend Campus Crusade for Christ's "executive seminar" scheduled for November in White Sulphur Springs, West Virginia. The White House once again sent its regrets but added, "They want you to know that they very much appreciate your thoughtfulness and send you their best regards."[49] In regard to Mahon's Mennonites, the White House arranged an extension for those in question, but, in the end, "the law was the law."[50]

Not surprisingly, given his prominence, Graham was a special case. The White House inquired with the Passport Office about Graham's in-law who was facing deportation and determined that "irregularities in the information given to this young woman means that she continues to be a citizen."[51] Carter called the woman personally to let her know of the decision, a gesture that Graham said "overwhelmed our entire family." Graham's letter, signed only "Billy," was profuse in its praise. "It has been my privilege to know several Presidents, but I have never had a more touching incident and I am eternally grateful." Graham then added "one more matter." The administration's stance on human rights "is something that you should hold on to without compromise."[52]

In many instances the politics was more overt. When, for example, the Church of God in Christ invited Martha Mitchell, special assistant to the president, to speak, she readily accepted, recognizing a chance to tie Carter's faith to his human rights agenda. Carter's religion, Mitchell explained, made the White House committed to African American civil rights.[53] Although unspoken, the fact that the congregation was predominantly black was no coincidence, and the talk apparently had its intended effect. "President Carter should be proud to have such an able ambassador as you," a letter of thanks read, adding that Carter himself was always welcome.[54] Moreover, early in the administration the staff quickly learned that correspondence from the National Association of Evangelicals deserved special attention. Referring one such invitation for Carter to speak to a colleague higher up the chain of command, White House staffer Sandra Adams wrote that the invitation was too important for "any standard procedure." It was "clearly an item on closer inspection that [top political appointees] should handle."[55] The annual convention of the National Religious Broadcasters was no different; the group represented over 650 Christian broadcasting stations and networks. With the president-elect invited to speak during the busy transition period, Carter's top aides cited the "hectic pace of these first days" in declining. Nevertheless, despite the loaded agenda, the importance the White House gave the invitation was evident. With the convention in Washington, the White House rushed by car a statement of welcome, which NRB leaders read to the delegates.[56]

Requests from the Southern Baptist Convention were always noteworthy as well, their expectations for obvious reasons among the highest. On the one hand, Carter felt an obligation to the denomination, but, on the other, he had to be careful lest he appear either to favor the Baptists in policy or practice or simply to do their bidding. Accordingly, when Porter Routh of the SBC's Executive Committee requested an interview with Carter for the SBC's Radio and Television Commission, the White House declined.[57] When the SBC leadership requested a presidential statement to commemorate the dedication of a new television studio, White House staffers noted that the request was for a "government licensed service of one religious denomination," and thus Carter should have nothing to do with the dedication. Once again the White House sent its regrets, citing scheduling difficulties.[58] As if to mollify any anger, Carter did agree a few weeks later to an Oval Office meeting with the SBC's board of directors. Staffers ensured that the meeting was not substantive, and it consisted only of introductions, a photograph, and a brief presidential Rose Garden statement.[59] If Carter hoped that this were sufficient to impress the participants, he apparently succeeded. "There is no group more concerned about you and your Presidency," wrote one director. "They still think of you as one of them and as a concerned layman."[60] To follow up, Carter also agreed to host a White House luncheon with the SBC's Missions Challenge Commission, established several years before to monitor the church's mission work.[61] Once again, staffers ensured that the luncheon was brief and that policy was not on the agenda.

Given the president's apparent concern for the SBC's mission work, Bright thought the time was ripe to press for more. He contacted the White House, informing it that he would soon arrive in Washington and asking to meet with the Carters. The reply noted that Carter's schedule was busy and thus a meeting on the designated date was impossible. It added, however, that in the future Carter "would enjoy having this opportunity," and should the occasion arrive, the Office of Scheduling "will be in touch with you."[62] At a church service in Washington weeks later, an acquaintance of Bright gave Carter and his wife, Rosalynn, an information booklet on the SBC's Mission Service Corps that Bright had given him. The booklet included the recent minutes of the Missions Volunteer Committee, which had adopted a resolution praying for Carter. Prominent Southern Baptist Jimmy Allen had also included in the minutes a hope that Carter might take an active role in the mission, perhaps filming videotapes.[63] A few days later Bright wrote Carter a laudatory letter noting Bright's "deep gratitude for your faithful virtue for our Lord." Bright promised to keep in touch. After receiving the letter, Rosalynn wrote a note thanking Bright for "your thoughtfulness and your prayers." Of all the SBC invitations, however, the one asking Carter to attend its annual convention promised the most publicity and, not surprisingly, the most consideration. Carter declined to attend, but, just as he had done with the NRB convention, he agreed to send a statement of welcome. If ever so subtly, Carter returned to the topic that he had long assumed was sure to please the faithful. The SBC, Carter wrote, has had a "positive influence on family life."[64]

Correspondence, of course, was not just in regard to requests for interview or invitations to events. The new administration had to deal with thousands of letters of application for employment or appointment. Carter might avoid offense in his personal schedule, but when it came to positions with impact on policy, balance was not so easily achieved. Religious conservatives may have hailed Carter's election and thus demanded personal attention, but they found many of his appointments both surprising and abhorrent. It was, perhaps, their first indication that when it came to specific matters of policy formation and implementation, the fears that they had harbored about Carter during the campaign were as real as their hopes, the fears that Carter, when it came to action, was not one of their own.

After his campaign interview with Carter, Pat Robertson had done his homework in submitting a list of evangelicals for possible appointment. Assuming that his meeting with Carter solidified an unwritten agreement (his support in exchange for appointments), Robertson had spent hours reading the Plum Book, the fat directory of positions in the federal government.[65] Now, however, Carter appeared to be ignoring the agreement; Carter had appointed virtually no prominent evangelicals. "I don't know if [Robertson's list] got to the president," Maddox later surmised, "but that was the last that was ever heard of it."[66] In fact, while surely dismissing any idea of quid pro quo, Carter had instructed advisor Stuart Eizenstat to draw up a list of all campaign promises. The result, totaling over a hundred pages, had three categories: promises to consider, promises to support, and promises to take some kind of action. The list included an amazing array of groups, from mine workers to senior citizens to Hispanics. Nowhere, however, were evangelicals listed, the new administration obviously concerned about the separation of church and state if not the balance of competing constituencies. Carter had "ignored the wishes of the Evangelicals," Robertson complained, and had come to rely too heavily on the "Eastern Establishment." Carter's choice for secretary of Health and Human Services, Patricia Harris, was an avowed enemy of Christianity because she had remarked that efforts to "Christianize America would be dangerous for democracy." Much of Robertson's criticism focused on foreign policy appointments, which he claimed were "under the control of the Council on Foreign Relations and the Trilateral Commission."[67] For Robertson, anyway, it all added up to only one conclusion: the Carter administration had gotten off on the wrong foot.

Feminists had also done their homework, with the result that was more to their liking. Not only had the Coalition for Women's Appointments submitted recommendations, but Carter's 51.3% Committee had established Talent Bank '77, a list of qualified women. Run on a volunteer basis by Joan Tobin, heiress to the Fleischmann food fortune, and given an office in the Democratic National Committee headquarters, Talent Bank '77 developed an impressive questionnaire that identified specific candidates for specific positions. Tobin ultimately turned the list over to transition officials, who ensured that the recommendations made Eizenstat's roster of promises.[68]

By the end of Carter's tenure, 22 percent of his appointments were women, the most by any president before Bill Clinton. These appointments included not only HUD secretary Harris but other high-level positions such as Eleanor Holmes Norton as head of the Equal Employment Opportunity Commission and Juanita Kreps as secretary of the Department of Commerce. Carter named Mary King to head volunteer programs such as VISTA and the Peace Corps and appointed forty women to federal judgeships, quadrupling the number of women who had served on the federal bench. Most notably (and controversially), he appointed the outspoken feminist Margaret "Midge" Costanza to lead the White House's Office of Public Liaison, the very office coordinating relations with religious groups. Costanza was known as a combative personality wholly dedicated to the cause of women's liberation. She had been active in New York Democratic politics for over two decades and had run for Rochester city council in 1973. Although she had won the most votes, the traditional determinant of who would serve as mayor, the all-male council had named her vice mayor. This brush with sexism had enraged Costanza and ensured her place as a leading feminist.[69] The appointment also thrilled gay rights activists, who wrote of their support. "Your distinguished career and deep humanity are so well known that is it very gratifying and reassuring to us," wrote Jean O'Leary and Bruce Voeller of the National Gay Task Force.[70]

After the election, all of the Ford appointees to the International Women's Year (IWY) Commission resigned as expected. With Costanza in charge of recommending replacements, the new commission included such ardent and controversial feminists as Eleanor Smeal, NOW president; Gloria Steinem, then editor of Ms. magazine; Elizabeth Carpenter, ERAmerica president; and Jean O'Leary of the NGTF. Costanza included a number of Republicans, such as Betty Ford, but the membership was obviously strongly in favor of the ERA. If this were not already obvious, Abzug was the designated chair. She would, the Washington Post reported, "manage Women's Year."[71] Abzug had lost her run for the Senate but remained determined to be a force for feminism. In the end the commission operated under the authority of the White House; the link between the two was obvious. At the same time, however, Costanza had stocked it with activists dedicated to the cause of women's rights and not necessarily what Carter thought was in the best political interests of his administration.[72]

Conservatives protested but largely in vain. "It has come to my attention," wrote one obviously annoyed conservative Christian, "that you have added more people to the National Commission on the Observance of International Women's Year." Of the forty-five members, "none represented the average Judeo-Christian woman." A good way to remedy the situation, the writer insisted, would be to appoint Phyllis Schlafly. Such an appointment was, of course, a nonstarter with Costanza, who tried to ignore those opposed to the ERA.[73] The conservative religious community found Costanza's appointment perplexing at best. Falwell thought her "obnoxious," although he was perhaps not as surprised as many other conservative Christians, while the appointment particularly dismayed Robertson.[74] Abzug's appointment to the IWY was another irritant to Robertson. "I wouldn't let Bella Abzug scrub the floors of any organization that I was head of," he stated, "but Carter put her in charge of all the women in America, and used our tax funds to support that [IWY] convention in Houston."[75]

Carter was always committed to women's rights, Sarah Weddington, one of the attorneys in *Roe v. Wade*, later recalled. After taking office he "sent out a memo to the various agency heads and cabinet officers, urging them to include women in their appointments when they were first making appointments." Carter, she claimed, would notice when a list of potential appointments arrived on his desk with the names of too few women.[76] Later invited to join the administration, Weddington had reason to applaud Carter's record in naming feminists. Indeed, many conservative Christians agreed with her conclusions even while lamenting, not applauding, the result. Nevertheless, other feminists still found fault, their expectations, just like those of their conservative opponents, raised so high that disappointment was inevitable. Out of the 103 ambassadors selected, they complained, only 6 were female. In retrospect, one such critic, feminist leader Jane McMichael, concluded reluctantly that the results were ambiguous. "The numbers aren't there, but for the first time an administration is appointing real feminists, rather than just any woman to fill out the quotas," she stated.[77]

The most troublesome appointment for many feminists was that of Joseph Califano for secretary of the Department of Health, Education, and Welfare (HEW), the department with perhaps the most obvious and direct impact on family policy. In his confirmation hearings Califano confidently declared that he opposed all abortions and would actively work to ban abortions under all federal health programs.[78] A week after Califano's controversial comments and confirmation, over 35,000 protesters walked from the Capitol to the White House in a March for Life. It was a political show of muscle, feminists complained, which caused Califano, if not the Carter administration at large, to curry favor with religious conservatives. The Religious Coalition for Abortion Rights wrote Carter a public letter concluding that Califano's appointment proved that under the new administration "women's rights will have a low priority." Carter, the letter stated, claimed that he supported the separation of church and state, but when push came to shove in the real world of politics, Carter caved.[79] "By denying access to abortions to one segment of society," the National Abortion Rights Action League (NARAL) added in an open letter to Carter, "you are apparently willing to openly discriminate against indigent women." The administration's "coercive policy" was not part of a "truly Democratic society."[80]

The NARAL letter spoke anew to the Hyde Amendment, which Califano supported in his confirmation hearings. Just after his confirmation the Supreme Court ruled 6–3 that the Constitution and current law did not require the states to spend Medicaid funds for elective or "nontherapeutic" abortions, thus clearing the path for renewed debate of the controversial amendment. The decision was "to the advantage of the family unit," declared the National Council of Catholic Bishops. It was a "national tragedy," countered the organization Planned Parenthood.[81] Less than two weeks later the Senate voted to forbid Medicaid funds for abortions except in cases when a threat existed to the life of the mother, or in cases of incest and rape, or when the procedure was "medically necessary." The House, meanwhile, passed a more restrictive prohibition, eliminating all exceptions, even those involving a threat to the mother's life.[82] This was no small distinction and illustrated the polarizing nature of the debate. For some, abortion was simply murder and could never be tolerated; all exceptions were a travesty. For others, any restrictions were a direct attack on basic individual freedoms and a clear assault on fairness. Simply put, as the House-Senate conference committee learned, this left little room for compromise. Those who attempted a middle ground faced criticism from all sides. The conference committee failed, and the issue returned to the respective chambers. The House quickly renewed its restrictive ban, only now allowing for exceptions when the mother's life was in danger. "We ought not to play God," declared a defiant Henry Hyde, his comments underscoring that he saw compromise as a challenge to his faith. The Senate, however, refused to budge, and the matter once again returned to a conference committee.[83]

Citing Califano's testimony, Hyde and a bipartisan group of congressmen sent to Carter a jointly signed letter to "heartily commend you for your forthright stand in opposition to the use of federal funds to pay for abortions." At the same time, however, a number of conservative Christians wrote letters complaining that Carter was not more forceful. "It would certainly be helpful," wrote one, "to see you take a stand against abortion and some of the other evils that seem to be tied to the thing you support so much, the Equal Rights Amendment."[84] The debate centered in Congress, but Carter was still in the middle.

Just as in the previous year, however, time was running short. The impasse over the Hyde Amendment once again threatened to derail passage of the entire appropriations for both the departments of HEW and Labor. Both were almost out of funds, and if nothing passed, their functions would cease, adversely affecting millions of people. Once again it appeared to be a high-stakes game of chicken. The debate, of course, garnered front-page coverage in the media, rallying supporters for each side and further entrenching legislators in their respective positions. Even as Congressman Mahon warned of "chaos" in government, his Pennsylvania colleague Daniel Flood acknowledged the problem to be one of "very strong personal convictions." Retreating on the issue invited the wrath of one side or the other and, in the words of one observer, "could destroy your career."[85]

With Califano now in office and Congress flustered over the Hyde Amendment, Carter tried to cool tensions in a nationally televised news conference. After Carter remarked that good people of faith could disagree on his appointments or on issues such as abortion, a reporter asked him if he thought it was "fair" that the government did not fund abortions for women who could not afford them. "Well," Carter answered, "as you know there are many things in life that are not fair." Recognizing that he had acknowledged a key argument of abortion rights advocates, that the Hyde Amendment hurt the poor, Carter then tried to recoup but only dug his hole deeper. The government could never make things exactly equal, he followed, "particularly when there is a moral factor involved."[86]

Watching the press conference, Costanza knew what to expect. The women's organizations would interpret Carter's comments to mean that those women who chose abortions were morally inferior. Indeed, Costanza's phone began ringing as groups such as Planned Parenthood, the Population Crisis Commission, and others called to complain. "I have received an overwhelming number of phone calls from interest groups, individuals, and White House staff members and Agency staff members expressing concern and anger," she wrote Carter the next day. "My opinion was well defined to the U.S. during the campaign," Carter cryptically replied, obviously annoyed. "My statement was more liberal than I feel personally." As if to remind her that he supported women's rights, he added, "If I had this much influence, ERA would have passed."[87]

The administration had only just begun, but the pressure was obvious. Carter had to produce, and for many on both sides, nothing but perfection appeared to suffice. He sought to remain close to evangelical leaders but not too close. He made many appointments of women but not enough to win universal praise. Compared to governing, campaigning had been a walk in the park.

The first order of business, of course, was the faltering economy. Carter's struggles to placate competing interests always played out within this context, not separate from it. Early in his term Carter submitted an economic stimulus bill that included small permanent tax reductions, a one-time tax rebate of $50, a public service jobs program, and increased spending on public works. He signed into law an increased minimum wage, but, in spite of it all, worried about growing deficits, he could not bring himself to embrace fully Keynesian economics. His proposals for increased spending were well below those advanced by his party's liberals, and Carter ended up abandoning his tax rebate program. This all angered many in his own party, who also demanded more forceful constraints on inflation. At the same time, Carter pardoned Vietnam era draft dodgers and proposed the creation of a new department to combat the ongoing energy crisis, which underlay so much of the inflationary economy. These actions, predictably, angered many conservatives who worried over the growth of new federal bureaucracies. Carter certainly inherited a difficult economy, but his many campaign promises ensured that at least some group met with disappointment. National health insurance promised to bust the budget; deregulation of energy threatened inflation and layoffs in the automotive industry; civil service reform mandated cuts in workers' pay; in short, the list of problematic trade-offs appeared endless. Faced with such difficult choices, within months Carter had already angered partisans on both sides of the aisle. In retrospect, Carter had already begun to erode his natural base of support. Without a firm constituency, the White House was left open to criticism on all fronts.[88]

On Father's Day Carter returned to an issue that he hoped would at least temporarily help stem the tide of complaint, the issue of family. In an interview given wide release Carter repeated his commitment to champion the American family, once again promising that every action his new administration took would "consider the integrity of the family." Formally proposing a revision of welfare programs and tax regulations along the lines that he and his opponent Shriver had advocated during the campaign, Carter struck themes sure to win substantial support. Carter explained that on average the standard tax deduction for unmarried couples was $1,200 greater than that of their married neighbors. "I would like to eliminate the disparity altogether," he remarked. In addition, the government provided greater welfare payments to single-parent families than to ones with both parents. This encouraged husbands to leave, he noted. Both policies hurt the family.[89]

In his proposals for appropriations, Carter once again tried to cool tensions. Carter's budget proposal for HEW included $35 million for "alternatives to abortion," programs such as family planning, adoption, and sex education. Califano, reflecting the White House's position, stated that the government "had an obligation to promote sex education in schools."[90] It was, the administration argued, a move all could agree upon because it would reduce the number of abortions. Unstated but obviously assumed was that it might defuse the political issue.[91] Moderation, however, was no longer politically viable. Sex education, religious conservatives cried, promoted unwed sexual activity. It further encouraged the breakdown of the family. Falwell, reflecting the views of many religious conservatives, argued that abstinence should be the only lesson and that matters of sex should be left to the parents and their church.[92]

In making his proposals, Carter might have foreseen what was coming, that the issue of family was no balm to the cracks in the nation's political culture but a debate sure to add to the deluge of complaints. Even as Carter spoke, a number of researchers held Family Impact Seminars to study the proper role of government in family life. The seminars, the *New York Times* reported, became "highly emotional and controversial."[93] When the national marketing and public opinion firm Yankelovich, Skelly and White released a report, "Raising Children in a Changing Society," it noted wide differences between what it termed the "new breed" of families and "traditionalists."[94] Adding to the debate, the Supreme Court held in *Moore v. City of East Cleveland* that a local ordinance restricting houses only to families based on marriage was "senseless and arbitrary" and rooted in "cultural myopia." This and a similar court ruling in California enraged such "traditionalists."[95] With tensions rising, a group of middle-aged women, alarmed by the contentious attitude they saw developing in academic and public debate, formed the Martha Movement. The movement, they claimed, was to "fill the gap between those [women] who devoted themselves slavishly and single-mindedly to the pursuit of their husband's happiness and the extreme feminists." There was a happy middle ground that encompassed most housewives, they argued.[96]

The family offered Carter no refuge from his troubles. In Carter's Father's Day interview, the reporter pressed him specifically on whether he thought it was appropriate for mothers with small children to work. "I think it's good," Carter replied, noting that his own wife had gone back to work when their oldest child was two years old. Pressed further on how he regarded homosexuality in relation to the family, Carter was blunt: "I don't see homosexuality as a threat to the family."[97] Such comments raised the ire of people like Connie Marshner, who had already gained some fame in the battle against federally supported child care and the publication of her *Family Protection Report*. Marshner knew more than most the controversies surrounding the issue of family and had already begun plans for a conservative presence at the family conference Carter had promised. In the words of Bill Billings, who had assisted his father, Robert Billings, in lobbying for Christian schools, the coming family conference represented "another battle to fight."[98]

Not surprisingly, given both the now obvious controversy and the economic stagflation, plans for the family conference languished, fueling speculation that Carter would not fulfill his promise. Indeed, planning for the conference had fallen to Laura Miller, an assistant to Califano at HEW, and Arabella Martinez, HEW's assistant secretary for human development services. Martinez had taken the lead in developing a mission statement, conference plan, and budget requests, but the two had only $3 million allocated for funding and faced a number of potential land mines.[99] Not only had Marshner and her allies begun organizing, but feminists associated with the International Women's Year also recognized the family conference as a way to advance their agenda. They had already prepared for the IWY conference, slated for Houston later in the year, but they also recognized the threat that Marshner and her allies, such as Phyllis Schlafly, posed for the family conference. As a result, behind the scenes several IWY staffers sought employment with the conference planners.[100]

With the family conference tentatively planned for December 1979, Califano selected the previous spring Wilbur Cohen as conference chairman and Patsy Fleming as executive secretary. Both, however, soon resigned. The former, dean of the School of Education at the University of Michigan and a man who had served as HEW secretary, did so for health reasons. The latter's resignation, however, grew from the divisions that threatened to paralyze the conference. Fleming, who had worked under Califano, was a black divorced mother of three teenage sons. Within days of her appointment the Reverend William Greeley, a Roman Catholic priest who wrote a syndicated column, complained that it was inappropriate for a divorced person to head a conference on families. Days after his column appeared Califano decided that Fleming would share her duties with a coexecutive secretary. This in turn enraged Fleming, who resigned, telling the press that Califano wanted a white, married individual to appease the Catholic lobby. A spokesman for Califano denied that Greeley's column played any role, while the Catholic Church insisted that it had brought no pressure to bear on the secretary. Others, however, suggested that the White House had intervened, which caused Stuart Eizenstat, Carter's top domestic advisor, to issue his own denial. "The idea didn't come from our shop or anybody I'm aware of over here," Eizenstat remarked.[101]

To promote the conference, a number of individual groups formed the independent Coalition for a White House Conference on Families. Watching the growing turmoil with frustration, some members began to speculate publicly that if differences over homosexuality, feminism, and abortion did not sink the conference, disagreements over whether the focus should be on intact middle-class families or poor minority families would do so. Robert Rice of the Family Service Association of America summarized the coalition's sentiments. "The great danger," he declared, "is that the conference . . . will be a demonstration of fragmentation and bitterness and that the subject of families will be politically poisoned for the next twenty years." As if to exacerbate the situation for the White House, California senator Alan Cranston called hearings to investigate whether Carter was doing all he could.[102]

It was difficult to separate the issue of family from the ratification battle over the ERA, which naturally began anew with the new administration and Congress. With Costanza out front, the new administration moved quickly to support the ERA. Just as Carter took the oath of office in January, Indiana became the thirty-fifth state to ratify the amendment—but not without the help of Rosalynn Carter. With the legislature virtually deadlocked, Rosalynn personally called wavering state Democratic senator Wayne Townsend. The honor had its intended effect; Townsend announced his support, and in the end, the ERA passed 26–24.[103] The press noted Rosalynn's role, and in her first interview as First Lady she promised to continue to press for ratification, both in the states and with her husband. "I will tell him what I think," she assured reporters.[104] This infuriated Schlafly, who accused the new First Lady of using taxpayer money for her lobbying, which Schlafly considered a violation of law. "Rosalynn Carter is part of the Executive Branch," Schlafly stated, explaining what she thought was an abuse of feminine wiles. "She wakes up every morning on an Executive Branch bed. She calls to a number of state legislators on an Executive Branch telephone. . . . The Executive Branch has nothing to do with [ERA ratification in the states]."[105]

As the remaining states resumed debate, both Carters lobbied state legislators but tried to do so in private. They did not want opponents to claim the influence of "Washington outsiders." After a series of defeats, however, proponents pressed the White House for a more public role. The Carters, aide Mark Siegel told the press, were "looking to see if a more prolonged effort might be helpful," an effort not only more public but more coordinated and strenuous.[106] Within weeks Carter had taken a new tack, telling reporters that failure to ratify the ERA hurt America in world opinion. "When I first met Soviet Ambassador [Anatoly] Dobrynin, I told him my position on human rights is strong," Carter stated. "He told me 'you are not without blame.' I asked what he meant by that, and he replied, 'You haven't passed the Equal Rights Amendment.'"[107]

Despite Carter's renewed push, however, Indiana remained the ERA's only bright spot. In the early months of the new presidency the amendment lost in Nevada, Mississippi, Virginia, North Carolina, Oklahoma, Missouri, Florida, and Illinois. In Georgia the ERA's proponents failed despite asking legislators to ratify it as a tribute to native daughter Rosalynn.[108] The defeats came, not surprisingly, at a cost to Carter. The election over, Schlafly now turned her guns more directly on the new administration. Eagle Forum declared Carter a hypocrite. "I think that for a President to try to influence directly members of [a state] legislature would be counterproductive," it quoted a Carter statement during the campaign. "There would be so much resentment against it, it would probably work against passage of the Amendment." "This," the forum sarcastically concluded, "from the man who promised never to tell a lie."[109] After the attacks of Schlafly and her allies, increas-

ing numbers of protest letters arrived at the White House. "[The Carters']
status as the Nation's First Family does not restrict their constitutional rights
under the First Amendment," came the administration's reply.[110] Soon Siegel
was left denying that the series of defeats "represented a political setback
for Carter." This was, obviously, a difficult task involving separating Carter's
reputation from the issue itself while promising that with Carter's support
in the future, the ERA would still become law.[111] "I think it's a great thing that
the President has gotten involved," Costanza added, worried, perhaps, that
such efforts might make Carter appear tepid to women's rights advocates.
"Critics who say otherwise don't understand leadership."[112]

The issue appeared to grow more complex and more partisan by the day.
Aware that their clock was ticking away, proponents of the ERA began to
push for legislation to extend the ratification period beyond March 1979. As
the Eagle Forum branded this unconstitutional, the White House requested
an opinion from the Department of Justice. While admitting that "the questions raised do not admit easy answers," Assistant Attorney General John
Harmon wrote, "We have found that there is no persuasive constitutional
foundation upon which to conclude that a reasonable extension of the present seven-year period would be impermissible."[113] In response, the administration announced its support of legislation in Congress, and Costanza
planned meetings with representatives from major pro-ERA organizations
to coordinate efforts.[114] At the same time Schlafly received an award for
her efforts in opposition from the Women's National Republican Club. As
she entered New York's Waldorf-Astoria Hotel, however, a woman threw a
pie in her face, yelling, "That's for ERA." It was "shocking," Schlafly angrily
remarked, but predictable given that "we're winning and they're losing."[115]
Equally angry, feminist Gloria Steinem declared that a "Radical Right coalition" held the ERA hostage. It was unfortunate, she insisted, that the issue
had become so partisan.[116] Later, several thousand supporters of the ERA
marched down Pennsylvania Avenue. Led by eighty-seven-year-old former
suffragette Hazel Hallinan, who had chained herself to the fence outside the
White House in 1917, the group received an official Rose Garden ceremony
from Carter. Proclaiming the day Women's Equality Day, Carter reiterated
his support for the ERA. "My commitment is the same as yours," he assured
the crowd.[117]

Most women's rights advocates welcomed Carter's efforts and recognized
the White House as an ally. Many increasingly felt, however, that the administration could do more. As debate intensified over extending the time

line for ratification, ERA opponents began to rally around efforts to rescind approval in the states that had already voted. Time had passed, opponents argued, and attitudes had shifted; opposition was greater. Even as the ERA faced defeat in many states, Idaho, Nebraska, and Tennessee voted to re-peal their earlier approval. Like the effort to extend ratification, however, these rescissions raised constitutional issues and posed another possible political time bomb. In a memo to the White House the Department of Justice noted that while the issue had come up in 1868 regarding ratification of the Fourteenth Amendment, constitutionality was unclear, and it was "virtually certain that the question will be put to Congress."[118] After a copy of the memo leaked to NOW, the organization cited it as proof that states could not rescind their approval and claimed that the administration had agreed the issue was one for Congress, where support for the ERA remained strong. This quickly prompted protests to the administration from states then considering rescission. In reaction to such protests the White House stated that, in fact, the issue remained under consideration and that the White House had drawn no final conclusion. To NOW, at least, this new White House statement appeared to be a retreat and raised questions about the administration's determination. Despite his strong support for the ERA, it appeared, Carter could not catch a break.[119]

Other issues, historian Susan Hartmann suggests, added to the doubt. According to Hartmann, Carter grew increasingly unresponsive to "the changing nature of the women's movement."[120] The movement's success had, in a sense, raised expectations and demands. While the ERA remained critical to the major women's rights organizations, the aspirations of many American women had broadened to all aspects of social and economic equality. Legal equality remained critical but in reality did little to address directly the daily deprivations faced by many working-class and minority women. Carter remained fixated on the ERA even as, just after the elec-tion, White House staffer Mary King submitted a formal recommendation that the administration review "all government budgets as they pertain to women." At the same time, early in the year representatives from over fifty women's organizations protested that Carter's proposed economic stimulus plan lacked sufficient emphasis on job training and welfare reform advanta-geous to poor women. It was a matter not only of equal legal rights but of resource distribution.[121]

Women, for example, increasingly demanded reimbursement and paid maternity leave for illnesses or pregnancy-related disabilities. This appeared too controversial for Carter, who did not want to anger conservatives unnecessarily. Even when representatives from his administration testified in April in favor of legislation in Congress, Carter remained quiet. "Leave me out of it for now," he wrote his subordinates. Carter did not want to "bring controversy in," recalled one aide. "It was best to keep it out [in the agencies]."[122] It was, in the end, almost two years before Carter came out in favor of a pregnancy disability act.[123] In another example, in June the Alliance for Displaced Homemakers (ADH) arranged a meeting with Costanza. During the campaign Carter had publicly identified the problems faced by housewives suddenly forced by divorce or widowhood to join the labor force. Now, however, Costanza and the ADH found top White House advisors largely indifferent. The White House was even unaware of legislation pending in Congress to address the matter. In the words of one advocate, the administration had "yet to fulfill its commitment." Once again, it took time for the administration to move. Even when Congress passed the Comprehensive Employment and Training Act, the administration budgeted only $5 million for displaced homemakers, a figure many activists recognized as wholly inadequate.[124]

Leading women's rights advocates loved the appointment of Costanza and welcomed Carter's promises of an open White House. They continued to harbor doubts, however, about some of Carter's other top advisors, most notably, Hamilton Jordan, now chief of staff, and Jody Powell, Carter's top press secretary. To Jordan, at least, Carter would never please many feminists no matter how much the administration did; they were, in short, unappreciative. One feminist, at least, urged First Lady Rosalynn to advise the president to consult with his female staff rather than Powell or Jordan. The two managed to "hurt the ERA and the women's movement with every move."[125] Domestic policy advisor Stuart Eizenstat, meanwhile, had lobbied for a weak party plank on abortion, an unforgivable sin for many women's rights advocates.[126] In fact, Carter's staff remained committed to gender equality, although commitments varied and tensions persisted.

As planning for the IWY conference in Houston continued, Carter worried that the conference, now on the immediate horizon, would devolve into a public spectacle of argument. He worried that Costanza, in the public's mind at least, had too closely tied the White House to the IWY commission while ensuring a controversial majority hardly open to compromise. The conference might explode in partisan bickering. As if making his point, congresswoman and delegate Barbara Jordan warned that women's rights were suffering "by a perceptible shift of America to the right." Anticipating a fight in Houston, she declared, "Our first task is to win over the other women."[127] This was, of course, no easy task with Marshner, Schlafly, and others lobbying from the opposite side. When the National Council of Jewish Women awarded Vice President Mondale its John F. Kennedy Award for Public Service, his wife, Joan, received the award for him. Joan selected her acceptance comments carefully, reiterating the importance of the family and the threats that it faced. "Family bonds are important as the recent television presentation of 'Roots' reminded us," she stated. The crowd applauded, but Marshner mocked the ceremony. Mondale, she argued, was no friend to the family. Not only had he proposed legislation to extend federally funded child care, but he supported radical feminists, the killing of unborn babies, and the acceptance of perversion. His administration's agenda destroyed the family.[128]

Marshner and Schlafly had a friend in Anita Bryant. Two days before Carter's inauguration, the Dade County Commission in Miami, Florida, approved an ordinance that prohibited discrimination against homosexuals in housing, public accommodations, and employment. While the 5–3 vote might have appeared of little import, it drew the ire of the thirty-seven-year-old singer and former Miss America, known nationally for her commercials on behalf of Florida orange juice. "We are not going to take this sitting down," Bryant warned, a promise she clearly intended to keep.[129] Hearings before the commission's vote had been, according to one pundit, "like watching the Scopes Monkey Trial." Protesters had argued that the word of God was above the law of man. When the vote had come, Bryant had fumed, while one supporter of the ordinance had proudly exclaimed, "The commission has come of age."[130] It was, of course, more the beginning than the end of a political battle that Bryant's efforts and celebrity cultivated. In many respects, it was a struggle that each side in the debate welcomed and hoped would set the tone for the future of their causes, posing yet another challenge to Carter's hopes for bipartisan peace and political moderation. For weeks homosexuality played prominently in the national media, rivaling the ERA and the Hyde Amendment for headlines. By May the *New York Times* summarized the debate with the byline, "Miami Debate Over the Rights of Homosexuals Directs Wide Attention to a National Issue."[131]

The National Gay Task Force wasted little time in pressing the advantage, asking its ally Constanza to use her new position on its behalf. "We seek your help both directly, and toward building a foundation to meeting with the President."[132] Constanza agreed and arranged a meeting for the NGTF with members of the White House staff on March 26. "I have been impressed," Constanza wrote the group, "and wish to explore more fully the role my office and I can play."[133] The NGTF began excitedly preparing for the meeting, which promised to win publicity as a precedent in the recognition and acceptance of homosexuals. O'Leary and Voeller selected fourteen homosexual rights activists from around the country and scheduled a meeting to organize an agenda several weeks before the White House visit. After getting permission to hold this planning session in California Democratic senator Alan Cranston's office in the Senate Russell Building, the two wrote participants that there would be time for fourteen five-minute presentations, each on a different aspect of discrimination. The participants were to define the key areas of concern, "include some facts and figures," and present each issue in a "separately bound package." The meeting promised "real changes for the gay community" if properly implemented, they concluded. "Everyone is excited, and we are getting mail from around the country offering suggestions, encouragement, and congratulations."[134] Inside the White House Costanza reviewed the anticipated agenda with her key assistant, Marilyn Haft. "You will be requested to respond with a commitment that we will attempt to set up appropriate meetings with the agencies for NGTF," Haft warned. "Of course time may be used by you to question or comment on the presentations as well."[135]

News of the White House meeting leaked out just as events in Florida began to gain steam. New York Democratic congressman Edward Koch wrote Carter personally to congratulate him, despite the fact that the president had not known of the meeting or of the efforts of his staff. "Your administrative support and action is well warranted," Koch concluded, given the growing reaction to the Florida ordinance.[136] Added Congressman John Burton in a separate letter, "I would hope that this dialogue will be fruitful and will continue throughout your term in office."[137] Both Koch and Burton sought to parlay Costanza's meeting and the Florida debate into support for the National Gay Civil Rights Bill that Koch had recently introduced in the House of Representatives. Similar to the one Bella Abzug had introduced in previous sessions of Congress, the bill would amend the Civil Rights Act of 1964 to add the words "affectional or sexual preference" to the list of protected groups. Koch had sent a "Dear Colleague" letter to every member of Congress just after the inauguration and clearly hoped that events would carry his bill farther than Abzug's.[138]

Although Koch's bill never earned a floor vote, nine congressmen added their names as sponsors, while Senator Cranston attempted to draft a similar version for his chamber. With the White House meeting approaching and the Miami controversy causing an increase in donations, the NGTF sought to raise its profile. The group created a new thirty-member board of directors with membership from around the country. In its first meetings the board added regional offices. It then launched a direct mail campaign and held a "national tea dance" to grow the budget. Lastly, it hired a media director.[139] The NGTF did not stop at Congress, citing as "the largest single factor in our ongoing oppression" the "restricted, stereotypical portrayal of lesbians and gay men perpetuated by the media."[140] Accordingly, the media director and the board wrote network executives and contacted talk shows. CBS responded that it was "happy to reaffirm to you" its standing policy to "recruit select, train, assign, promote, transfer, remunerate and administer . . . without regard to sexual preference."[141] ABC replied that an offending episode of the sitcom *Barney Miller* was not indicative of the company's views and that it too did not discriminate.[142] The NGTF had written to major corporations since 1975, and letters continued to arrive from companies such as AT&T, McDonald's, Bank of America, and Honeywell, all proclaiming that they did not discriminate against homosexuals.[143]

In addition to its support of Koch's bill in Congress, the NGTF pressured the White House to reverse a policy that denied gay literature at federal prisons. The Bureau of the Prisons (BOP) replied that it was policy to censor all publications "detrimental to the security, good order or discipline of the institution."[144] While the White House undoubtedly sought to downplay the issue, Costanza and Annie Gutierrez, associate director of Carter's Domestic Policy Staff, kept Carter's top advisors up-to-date on the matter. Writing to Gutierrez, an NGTF ally summed up the organization's sentiments: "I feel it is a gross waste of money for the government to be defending the indefensible."[145] The BOP tried to explain in a letter to Koch. "The reason for this decision focuses exclusively on the fact that homosexuality is major problem in correctional institutions," Director Norman Carlson wrote. "Publications which call attention or identify inmates who accept homosexuality can, in our opinion, be detrimental to their safety as well as to the safety of others."[146] This logic did not resonate at the NGTF, which filed suit to force the matter.[147] Prominent gay minister Troy Perry and his congregation added their support to the suit. "We are compiling much evidence against the Bureau at this time," Perry's church promised, "and if we can be of any assistance to you please contact this office."[148]

The White House remained silent in the face of the NGTF's momentum, but pressure was clearly building. For one, Koch was a Democrat who had assumed a very public role, while only one of the nine cosponsors of Koch's bill was a Republican.[149] Events during and since the campaign had added to a sense of partisanship, while local communities took up the fight. In early February, Tucson, Arizona, became the thirty-ninth community to pass a civil rights ordinance.[150] If it were difficult to avoid these events, no one could ignore the Florida debate, which by March had combined with developments in Washington to produce the perfect storm to match that over the ERA. The debate over homosexual rights had gone national in a way that not even the election months before had anticipated. Tempers flared and positions hardened, complicating Carter's moderate stance.

Lost in the voluminous correspondence was a letter from Harvey Milk. A gay man who had recently moved from New York City to the Castro District of San Francisco, Milk would later ignite a firestorm over gay rights and become one of the movement's foremost leaders. As the Miami controversy first brewed, however, Milk, still a political neophyte, wrote Carter and city leaders complaining that vandals had attacked his photography store and painted slurs on his walls as a direct by-product of the Florida controversy. "It is now open season on gay people," Milk pleaded to Carter. Milk's letter was personal and emotional. "Please," Milk begged. "I will come to Washington to meet you. The nation needs leadership, not violence." Milk was also, however, realistic. "I know that this letter will be passed on to someone else and that you will never see it."[151]

In some respects, perhaps, the Miami controversy was inevitable. For months prior to the county commissioner's January vote, a group of citizens had complained that homosexuals had "taken over" entire Fort Lauderdale hotels and that along Highway A1A gay nightclubs dominated. Fort Lauderdale mayor E. Clay Shaw had taken up such complaints, proclaiming that "straight businesses were losing regular customers by the droves."[152] This drew the ire of the gay community, which protested at city hall. Mocking the mayor, the city's gay press wrote that "Creeping Gayism Stirs Lauderdale," a not-so-subtle reference to the anti-Communist witch hunts of the McCarthy era.[153] Shaw refused to apologize and promised a crackdown on gay prostitution, prompting more protest at city hall and, ultimately, the county commissioner's vote.[154] In the following weeks, the battle raged in the media, prompting Bryant to declare in March that she would broaden her efforts into a national campaign. Homosexuality was a "disguised attack on God," and she would "lead such a crusade to stop it as this country has not seen before." She would call her campaign Save Our Children. Given Koch's gay civil rights bill and the NGTF's White House meeting, she had to act.[155]

Bryant had made herself a target, and the gay community responded by pressuring her orange juice sponsors. "The blacklisting of Anita Bryant has begun," Bryant declared, holding a telegram of complaint from a New York television producer. "It's quite obvious we have no right to control her private life," the Florida Citrus Commission replied, refusing to cancel Bryant's annual contract of $100,000.[156] While Bryant succeeded in saving her job, the gay community reveled in the exposure Bryant afforded them. "Bryant is really the perfect opponent," the NGTF notified its members. She was as useful to the gay civil rights struggle as "Bull Connor's cattle prods and police dogs" had been to the civil rights movement for blacks. Members should "watch your local media for coverage of the Dade County dispute."[157] Writing to the columnist Ann Landers, one gay rights supporter agreed, concluding that the Miami dispute "had taken the topic from the closet."[158] There was certainly much to watch. Save Our Children submitted a petition of over eleven thousand voters, forcing the county commission to schedule in June a popular referendum to overturn the ordinance. Other opponents filed suit, suggesting that a court ruling that the ordinance was unconstitutional would save the county $400,000, the cost of a special election.[159] As Florida governor Reubin Askew, known as "Reubin the Good" for his abstention from alcohol and tobacco, threw his support behind Save Our Children by declaring that the Constitution did not protect homosexuality, gay rights supporters formed their own group, known as the Miami Victory Campaign. Proclaiming "No Needa Anita," the campaign launched with a series of protests and meetings.[160]

Watching from the White House, Costanza wanted to join the fray. Her staff contacted gay rights leaders and others to seek their advice on whether she should attend the protests. The consensus was that she should not. It could, noted one, detract from efforts to pass the Equal Rights Amendment or help opponents cast Carter as antifamily. Perhaps another, less controversial White House official might attend, preferably a male. The Miami debate could assume too partisan an overtone, which could hamper the White House across a spectrum of issues. Bryant had never been too political before and even had registered as a Democrat. She had sung for President Johnson and at the Chicago Democratic National Convention in 1968. Now, however, she appeared to draw more of her support from Republicans, such as North Carolina conservative senator Jesse Helms, who declared that her fight and the battles against the ERA and abortion were for "decency and morality."[161] Many voters undoubtedly shared this view. If nothing else, at least one of the ordinance's biggest backers had contributed to the Carter campaign. In short, White House officials should tread lightly. Such advice raised doubts with Costanza, who ultimately chose to attend fund-raisers for the Miami Victory Campaign but not public protests.[162]

The Miami debate came to a head just when Costanza's long-anticipated White House meeting with the NGTF took place on March 26. The approach of the meeting brought a number of letters of support, many from congressional Democrats addressed directly to Carter. Representative Henry Waxman noted his "firm approval," while his fellow Californian Paul McCloskey called the meeting "one of your most courageous political initiatives." New Yorker Charles Rangel congratulated Carter for "directing" Costanza to hold the meeting, although, of course, Carter had done no such thing. "I found your decision in this matter to be representative of the laudable principles of equality which you voiced throughout the campaign." The congratulations, perhaps, represented the growing partisan nature of the debate, as no Republican letters arrived.[163] Nevertheless, congratulations came from the American Psychiatric Association and the National Organization for Women, undoubtedly demonstrating that while the meeting certainly carried a political cost, Costanza had tapped into a vein of support the White House could not ignore. The best avenue was to allow the meeting to continue but ensure that Carter did not associate with it personally, another attempt to maintain the administration's moderate stance.[164]

Costanza had selected a Saturday because she wanted the meeting to take place in the Roosevelt Room, a conference room with a long table directly across from the Oval Office and a room rich in history. When the delegation arrived, Costanza met it at the front gates and joked, trying to lighten the mood. With Costanza sitting at the head of the table, a commanding presence despite her small frame, thick glasses, and short black hair, the meeting lasted almost three hours. The group discussed discrimination in immigration, taxation, the military, housing, the penal system, and employment, among other issues. Troy Perry was most forceful—and the most unscripted. He noted that despite the growing public resistance to gay rights in many churches, there was a great deal of religious support for the homosexual movement.[165] As if to represent the growing partisan nature of the issue, a representative from the Democratic National Committee observed, later telling the press that the delegation had done "the most professional job I've seen."[166]

Costanza arranged for the members of the delegation to have follow-up meetings with the specific agencies related to each individual issue. Over the next two months Costanza often attended these meetings to ensure compliance from that agency's occasionally reticent staff. While in the end no major shifts in policy resulted and it would be easy to describe the entire episode as a failure, the press, already aware from the ongoing Miami controversy that the issue was good copy, highlighted the matter. Costanza and the delegation, not surprisingly, encouraged the coverage, with O'Leary describing the event as "the first time in the history of this country that a President has seen fit to acknowledge the rights and needs of some 28 million Americans."[167]

The coverage ensured a response from those critical of the meeting, of course, including Anita Bryant's Save Our Children campaign and Schlafly's Eagle Forum. "I protest the action of the White House in dignifying these activists for a special privilege with a serious discussion of their alleged 'human rights,'" Bryant said in a prepared statement for the media. "Behind the high-sounding appeal against discrimination in jobs and housing, which is not a problem to the 'closet' homosexual, they are really asking to be blessed in the abnormal life style by the President of the United States."[168] Bryant's comments associated Carter with the Miami gay rights movement despite the president's lack of involvement. When asked by the press if Carter knew of the meeting and undoubtedly aware of his political sentiments, Costanza replied that he did not—an untruth—and joked that they had planned the meeting in a bathroom. Carter had spent the weekend at Camp David, but the planning for the meeting and the press it had received had made the meeting obvious for weeks. Letters of complaint flooded the White House from conservative churches, prompting the White House, in the words of one aide, "to keep a negative/positive log for future reference to the Gay Rights issue."[169] As if to blunt this criticism, Jody Powell appeared the day after the meeting on CBS's popular news show *Meet the Press*. When host Bob Schieffer asked if Carter knew of the meeting in advance, Powell struggled for the correct answer: "I don't know if he knew in advance, but as I think—you know, Midge Costanza, who runs the public liaison office, and whose [sic] an assistant to the President, as I am, has as her primary function—I think she said this morning in one of the papers—dealing with organized America, making sure that there is a window to the White House for groups, that want to put before the President, and in a way, before the American public in the process, their concerns about our society. So, you know, I don't know how Midge feels or . . ." With Powell struggling, Schieffer mercifully interrupted, asking if Carter supported the gay rights movement. The question gave Powell a chance to recover. "Well, I don't want to speak to that," he quickly replied.[170]

Despite the White House's efforts, the emotional and controversial issue had clearly exacted a political cost. Even the tabloids picked up on the debate, with the *National Enquirer* conducting a "reader's poll." Almost 80 percent of respondents disapproved of the meeting, hardly a scientific poll but a representation of both the magnitude of the debate—now blanketed in the popular media—and the resistance the gay rights movement engendered.[171] Just over two weeks after the White House meeting, the Fifth Circuit ruled that the Miami ordinance was constitutional. Judge Sam Silver concluded, "It is in the public interest that the controversy be resolved swiftly." Although Carter would have certainly agreed, the Dade County Commission reaffirmed the ordinance in a 5–4 vote only four days later, thereby ensuring that the June referendum would take place.[172] There was now no doubt—the debate had become a political campaign, complete with fund-raisers, media consultants, polls, and stump speeches. It still promised a long, divisive struggle to come, and much to Carter's dismay, in this regard it resembled the ERA and abortion.

It was a hot summer in 1977 and, unfortunately for Carter, in more than one way. While the promised family conference languished, the passing weeks brought the November IWY conference closer, magnifying all the issues surrounding family and feminism. Under the auspices of the Department of State, the IWY commission was to sponsor fifty-six state meetings before July to prepare for the national conference. Delegates to the national conference, selected by the state conferences, were to make recommendations to eliminate the barriers that prevented women from full and equal participation in national life.[173] "The plans for these conferences are already underway, and lesbians must get involved immediately on their state level,"

Jean O'Leary declared early in the year. "We're contacting lesbian groups all across the country with information on how to participate." The gay community should encourage resolutions endorsing passage of laws "prohibiting discrimination on the basis of sexual or affectional preference in employment, housing, etc." It should also urge repeal of all laws "governing private sexual behavior between consenting adults." These resolutions were essential, O'Leary concluded, because "those passed at the national conference will be presented to the President and Congress."[174] O'Leary had more than simple optimism that such resolutions could pass. As one of the members of the national commission, she had won at the commission's first meeting in April approval to add "sexual or affectional preference" to the list of issues for consideration.[175]

O'Leary and her White House liaison, Costanza, were not alone in their preparation. In the preliminary state convention in Utah in July thousands of Mormon women registered "to ensure the support of correct principles," including the defeat of the ERA and any proabortion planks. The result was "a war," in the words of one of the minority of ERA advocates present: "I have never been treated so rudely in my life."[176] Flooded with complaints that IWY was only a stage for radical feminists, Senator Helms chaired ad hoc hearings to investigate a liberal bias. With cameras present, more than sixty women complained that in their own state conventions it was the feminists who tolerated no dissent. With the witnesses specifically selected, the hearings were as much a political show as Helms forecast for the national conference. In addition, the hearings added to the growing partisan nature of the debate. Recognizing that the Houston conference would be nothing like that held in Utah, the Mormons joined the John Birch Society in protesting the allocation of federal money to pay for the IWY expenses.[177] Phyllis Schlafly, of course, was not about to miss an opportunity to advance her cause and called for a profamily rally to be held simultaneously across town.

The White House watched these developments with apprehension. If Carter were associated with the conference too closely, Eizenstat warned, it could open a "can of worms." Much to Costanza's dismay, most advisors agreed and thus began to distance the White House from the conference. Facing new restrictions on the number of administration officials who could attend, Costanza protested futilely that "we do need that much representation." Rosalynn would attend, the White House added, but not Carter, despite an official invitation to speak.[178] Rosalynn would join former First Ladies Betty Ford and Lady Bird Johnson in making opening remarks. Rosalynn's daughter-in-law Judy Carter, who recently had spoken out in favor of the ERA, would also attend.

Still simmering over Carter's "life is not fair" defense of the Hyde Amendment, Costanza was angry. In July she arranged to meet with over forty Carter female appointees in the Old Executive Office Building. The informal group included women from the Environmental Protection Agency, the White House Domestic Policy Staff, and the departments of Labor, Agriculture, Defense, and HEW. Carter was, the group concluded, "legislating his personal views." To address the problem, they would draft a letter of complaint and try to schedule a meeting with Carter of poor women affected by the Hyde Amendment. They would also ensure that Califano met with representatives from the Religious Coalition for Abortion Rights, some complaining that he was deliberately avoiding the organization. When Califano promised to stress more alternatives to abortion, Connie Downey, a staffer in HEW's office of planning and evaluation, replied sarcastically, "The literal alternatives to it are suicide, motherhood, and some would add, madness." Carter, the feminists hoped, might change course once he realized that he had "underestimated the deep feelings of women across the country on the issue."[179]

Constanza began drafting the letter, which ended with a series of questions: "Is it moral to force a fifteen year girl on welfare to carry a pregnancy to term? Is it moral to ask a mother of five to have yet another child, to lose her job and forego any possibility of ever getting off welfare? Above all, is it moral for this country to advocate human rights and liberty abroad, while depriving the weakest in our society of their moral and human rights?"[180] The draft was, in many respects, a confrontational letter. Word had leaked out to the press about the meeting, and while Carter had not tried to prevent it, his opinion had been obvious in a cabinet meeting. The meeting of the women was unfortunate, Carter had stated, and holding it in the Old Executive Office Building was "inappropriate." Columnists Rowland Evans and Robert Novak had written that Carter's "blue eyes were chilly" when he described his "resentment." Now, Constanza worried, the press would highlight the disagreement further, so angering the White House that it might hurt the women's cause. It was wise, perhaps, to abandon the idea of a group letter and write private, individual letters.[181]

Within weeks the letters began to arrive, all respectful but some, argu-ably, controversial. The Equal Employment Opportunity Commission's Eleanor Holmes Norton wrote that "most who have abortions today are poor blacks." Access to safe abortions was "one of the few ways in which the wretched life of the ghetto has been relieved, with birth rates among such women showing sharp declines." Assistant Attorney General Barbara Ann Babcock wrote that the consequences of unwanted children included "child abuse, neglect, delinquency, crime and mental illness." Added White House advisor Esther Peterson, "I would hate to see even one more child come into the world under those conditions." The Hyde Amendment hurt the family; it did not help it.[182]

When the media asked about the matter, Constanza replied, "We shall abort the issue," her choice of words implying to some that she had no in-tention of surrendering the larger debate within the administration. Never-theless, many of the women involved worked to heal wounds. "It would be wrong to describe this as a rebellion," stated one, adding that overall "we're tremendously pleased with President Carter." While public statements of contriteness were wise politically, the publicity surrounding the meeting had, nevertheless, reverberated among both sides of the abortion divide. Just as the meeting began to fade from the newspapers, a group of twenty-seven women's groups released a statement praising Constanza and her al-lies. Likewise, members of the National Women's Political Caucus noted approvingly the internal administration disagreement in off-the-record comments to the media.[183]

For many abortion opponents, the entire public spat had a different ef-fect, highlighting the important role women such as Costanza played in the White House. If Carter truly supported the prolife cause, many argued, he would hardly tolerate such views or employ such advocates. Undoubtedly reflecting the views of many of his followers, Falwell sarcastically recalled that the publicity "didn't win [Carter] a great deal of support."[184] Trying not to offend either side, Carter declined numerous invitations to appear at antiabortion rallies or address their supporters. In one 1977 instance Nel-lie Gray, president of March for Life, requested to meet with Carter and sent him batches of red roses "representing the short life and martyrdom of pre-born human beings killed in our country." Replying for the White House, assistant Fran Voorde cited Carter's "extremely pressing schedule in the weeks ahead" to decline. "Once again," Voorde's letter concluded, "the

President thanks you for continuing to keep him apprised of your views in the area of human rights."[185]

The White House, it appeared, was pleasing no one, even as the publicity surrounding developments emboldened both sides. As the deadline for HEW appropriations approached, and with the Congress still divided over the Hyde Amendment, the House blinked first, allowing for exceptions for certain "medical procedures" such as dilation and curettage. Sensing that a resolution was near, both chambers approved an emergency month-long extension of appropriations. The conference committee then began to debate exceptions for both statutory and physical rape, only to have deliberations once again end in argument. No agreement existed as well over whether the victim had to report the rape to authorities prior to the abortion and over the larger issue of the threat to the mother's health. By the end of November another month-long extension passed as tempers continued to flare. Finally, in mid-December the conference committee hammered out an elaborate compromise that passed as a joint resolution. In the end Congress allowed exceptions when the abortion threatened the mother with "severe and long-lasting physical health damage"; when there was rape or incest properly reported to officials prior to the abortion; and when there was a necessity for certain medical procedures such as dilation and curettage. Relief at the bill's passage was palpable, although tempered with reality. Appropriation bills, after all, were an annual endeavor; the debate was not dead, only tabled.[186]

While the debate over the Hyde Amendment dragged from the hot summer into the cold winter, so did the debate over homosexual rights. As she promised, Anita Bryant traveled the country mobilizing support for the scheduled vote on the Miami gay rights ordinance, her speeches becoming more emphatic as the referendum neared. Homosexuals were "human garbage," and if the vote retained the ordinance, it would be legal to have "intercourse with beasts." She agreed when Jerry Falwell declared in support of her campaign that "so-called gay folks [would] just as soon kill you as look at you."[187] Around the country homosexual activists angrily disrupted many of Bryant's appearances. Gay rights groups organized boycotts of Florida orange juice, supporters wearing T-shirts proclaiming, "Squeeze a fruit for Anita." Carter said nothing about the dispute, although the White House was never far from the debate and a frequent object of scorn.[188] Less than ten days before the vote the Department of Housing and Urban Development opened public housing to homosexuals living in a "stable family relationship." The order, which included unmarried heterosexual couples as well, signified a broader interpretation of the term "family," a goal of the gay rights movement. Just as with Costanza's White House meeting, Carter had not been directly involved. Nevertheless, his administration's actions had once again cast him as a key player in the wars over homosexuality. If Judge Silver, whose ruling had cleared the way for the new referendum, had hoped that the controversy would dissolve quickly, he was, like Carter, surely disappointed.[189]

When the day for the June vote arrived, it was obvious the past was only prologue. Bryant had her victory, as county citizens voted by more than a 2–1 margin to repeal the gay rights ordinance. While Bryant did a jig in her Miami home as a way of celebrating and later agreed to join Falwell in a tour of Israel, she made it obvious that her campaign had only just begun: "All America and all the world will hear what the people have said, and with God's continued help, we will prevail in our fight to repeal similar laws throughout the nation." Robert Kunst, a leading figure in the defense of the ordinance, was clearly disappointed but, like Bryant, looked to the future. "This is just the beginning of the fight," he confidently proclaimed.[190] Indeed, the day after the vote over three hundred gay rights activists disrupted a Bryant appearance in Norfolk, Virginia, causing Bryant to flee the stage in tears. "Anita and the gays should cool it," pundit William Raspberry wrote, watching what he termed the "holy war" unfold. It might energize respective political bases, exacerbating partisanship, but it did the nation no good. Both sides should cease and desist.[191]

"Washington is next," declared Save Our Children spokesman Bob Brake.[192] In Washington, caught between a rock and a hard place, Carter continued to try to avoid the issue by taking a middle stance. Asked about the vote, he replied that he was "too busy" to deal with the issue.[193] No one, least of all the press, planned to let him off so easily. As Congress voted to override HUD's housing order, reporters asked him what he thought of the relationship between homosexuals and the family. "I don't see homosexuality as a threat to the family," Carter began but then added, "I don't feel that it is a normal interrelationship." American society should not have to approve homosexuality as normal, but neither "should it abuse or harass the homosexual." At the very least, Carter tried to conclude, the "highly publicized confrontations" were unfortunate. The reporters pressed further. Did Carter believe homosexuals should be able to adopt children or teach school? "That's something I'd rather not answer," Carter curtly replied, again in an effort to end the conversation. "Look, this is a subject I don't particularly want to involve myself in. I've got enough problems without taking on another."[194]

Of course, as Carter perhaps recognized, the issue was too emotional, too deep, and by the June vote, certainly too far advanced simply to evaporate. Even after the Miami vote thousands of gay rights supporters marched in cities from San Francisco to New York. "Two, four, six, eight, gay is better than being straight," many chanted. The controversy had gained so much steam and publicity that it had begun to spread abroad. In Barcelona, Spain, police used rubber bullets to break up a gay rights parade.[195] Given Carter's well-publicized efforts to encourage human rights abroad, gay rights activists had a handle with which to apply pressure. How could Carter champion human rights overseas while not more vigorously fighting abuses against homosexuals at home? After the Miami vote many in the gay community were in no mood for patience—or Carter's professed moderation.

Both sides in Raspberry's "holy war" thought Carter had let them down. After the Miami referendum both antiabortion and gay rights activists protested at New York's Waldorf-Astoria Hotel, where Carter was scheduled to appear for a Democratic Party fund-raiser. No one, it appeared, was satisfied with Carter's attempts at moderation. Four days earlier Vice President Mondale had appeared with San Francisco mayor George Moscone in Golden Gate Park only to face gay rights hecklers. Moscone managed to quiet the crowd, but when Mondale got up to begin his remarks, cries of "Gay rights are human rights" drowned out his speech. Frustrated, Mondale simply left the stage.[196]

By the fall of 1977 the nation appeared more conflicted than ever when it came to homosexuality, perhaps ensuring that the organized campaigns on both sides would only intensify. A Gallup poll noted that almost two-thirds of adults questioned thought that homosexuals should have equal rights when it came to job opportunities. When asked about specific jobs, however, the results were almost the opposite. Two-thirds of respondents said that gays and lesbians should not be schoolteachers. Almost as many rejected homosexuals as members of the clergy.[197] The media reported that homosexuals "have found new pride" in their orientation while noting that a thriving "gay market" in clothes and music had even made inroads into the broader popular culture. New to the radio was disco music, which, as *Time* magazine later noted, owed a great deal to the gay subculture.[198] Within a year one of the most popular pop groups was the Village People, whose chart-topping songs such as "Macho Man" and "YMCA" appeared to celebrate a hedonistic gay lifestyle. Increasingly, prominent individuals "came out," most notably the professional football player Dave Kopay. At the same time, however, the end of 1977 brought Save Our Children continued success. Cities such as St. Paul, Minnesota, and Wichita, Kansas, followed Dade County in overturning gay rights bills.

The issue of homosexual schoolteachers promised almost as many fireworks as the Miami controversy. Encouraged by Save Our Children, state senator John Briggs of Orange County, California, one of the most conservative counties in the state, announced plans to obtain the three hundred thousand required petition signatures to place on the ballot a requirement that school boards deny employment to "open and notorious" homosexuals. Determined not to lose again, opponents of the requirement organized as New Age, an umbrella group to rebut the "pseudo-religious" rants of "right-wing politicians."[199] In addition, in October the Supreme Court let stand a Washington state court ruling that school districts could dismiss teachers for being homosexuals. The case revolved around James Gaylord, who had been a teacher for thirteen years yet was fired despite—as all acknowledged—no improper conduct. Bryant praised the ruling, which infuriated the gay and lesbian community. It was, Bryant claimed, a ruling in support of the family.[200] Clearly, as the Dade vote faded, the overall controversy would not.

The IWY conference scheduled to begin on November 18, of course, loomed larger than ever. Assuming that homosexual rights polled less popular than rights for abortion or, in a general sense, feminism, Bryant and conservative activists such as Marshner and Schlafly continued to associate gay rights not only with pedophilia but with abortion, feminism, and in the broadest construct, a libertine attack on the family. In some respects it appeared an effective tactic; several leading advocates for women's rights suggested that gay rights helped explain ERA's stagnation. As the Houston conference approached, the White House reported that over 90 percent of calls about the conference complained that feminism meant abortion, homosexuality, and the demise of the nuclear family. Some gay rights activists even tried to argue that Bryant had fabricated the Miami controversy simply to stop ratification of the ERA. At least one state senator in Florida switched from supporting ratification to opposing it because Bryant and Schlafly convinced him that it would require legalization of same-sex marriages and destroy the family. As the conference approached, NOW banned gay pride banners from its rallies, confirming the wisdom of the conservatives' strategy.[201]

Carter worried as well that opposition to homosexuality might derail the conference. He had initially resisted appointing O'Leary to the national commission. "Does she have to use her title?" he had asked Costanza. "Sir," Costanza had replied, "that would be like asking if you had to use yours." Ultimately, Carter had given in, shamed a bit when Costanza noted that her own support for his campaign had carried risks for her career. Sometimes, she had implied, the correct move was tough politically. Now Carter realized that O'Leary's efforts had ensured homosexual rights a central debate at the conference. O'Leary was his appointment; her actions reflected on his administration. Perhaps, despite his best efforts, he had unwittingly tied the struggle for gay rights to his presidency. Perhaps in doing so he had helped ensure a raucous women's convention and the defeat of the ERA.[202] Perhaps he appeared to a majority of Americans not as a champion of the family but as one of its greatest threats.

To launch the IWY conference, scheduled for November 18–21, 1977, activists organized a symbolic run from Seneca Falls, New York, the site of the first conference for women's rights in 1848, to Houston. A series of female runners carried a torch the entire 2,612 miles. It was quickly apparent that even the run itself, although impressive, provoked protest, hardly a positive omen. The media reported that runners frequently "draw wolf whistles from truck drivers and sneers from many other women." Securing runners in the southern states proved problematic. "Now what would a woman want to get involved in something like that for?" asked one Alabaman.[203]

When the conference convened at the Albert Thomas Convention Center, approximately twenty thousand women attended, including two thousand delegates from fifty-six states and territories. Worried about possible violence between the approximately 350 self-designated "pro-family, prolife delegates" and the majority, who favored abortion rights and the ERA, the Houston police stationed additional off-duty officers around the convention hall. FBI agents also attended, "strictly on a stand-by basis," according to the Houston office.[204] In the end, there was no violence, but tensions ran high throughout each session. The conservative delegates wore yellow ribbons saying "majority," reiterating their claim that while organizers had forced them into the minority at the conference, they represented mainstream America. One reporter, pressed by conservatives, asked Abzug at a news conference if it were true that "the conference was dominated by lesbians and abortionists." A feminist colleague of Abzug interrupted with the sarcastic reply, "Well, they can't be both, can they?" When public debate over an abortion rights plank began, a woman rushed the stage with a large picture of an aborted fetus. As she was escorted off, her conservative supporters began to sing to the melody of a John Lennon song, "All we are saying is give life a chance." This enraged abortion rights advocates, who drowned them out with chants of "Choice!" When the prochoice plank passed, its supporters cheered and released balloons while opponents jeered. At the end of the conference the Pro-Family Coalition—as they now referred to themselves—sang loudly and unannounced "God Bless America," an obvious statement of protest.[205]

"The libs will learn that lesbian privileges and abortion are anti-family goals and not what the American people want," Schlafly confidently announced in an obvious attempt to tie feminism with homosexuality and couch both as threats to the nuclear family. Recognizing her tactics, a number of feminists spoke out against the homosexual rights plank, described as a "sticky wicket" by the lesbian delegate Kate Millett.[206] O'Leary had done her work, however, meeting with numerous delegates to ensure their support for the plank and had even arranged for a large celebration upon formal passage. Indeed, when the gay rights plank passed, thousands of gay activists in the gallery released yellow balloons inscribed with the slogan "We are everywhere." The balloons quickly filled the rafters, catching the eyes of the television cameras.[207]

"Why the full scale altercation between the two sides never took place is debatable," the *New York Times* mused. Undoubtedly, both sides recognized that the conference was primarily for publicity and that appearing to instigate violence might hurt their respective causes if not the status of women in general. In any event, of course, the fate of most resolutions was not in doubt, despite the activity. Abzug had assisted her majority with parliamentary procedures: a decision to use voice rather than roll-call votes and another to require only a simple majority, not two-thirds, for passage of a plank. Defending herself from criticism that she had "rigged the conference," Abzug insisted that all viewpoints had a chance at the microphone. When a group of feminists began to argue that a simple majority was sufficient to cut off debate, Abzug recognized that this gave credence to conservative complaints and objected.[208]

In addition, conservative critics had Schlafly's Pro-Family Rally to counter the conference, which proved no small consolation. Held five miles away at the Astro Arena, the rally drew an estimated fifteen thousand people, causing police to turn away several thousand more due to limited space. Schlafly, who was staying in a nearby Ramada Inn under armed guard, shuttled back and forth between the respective conferences, telling the conservative counterdemonstrators that the women's conference would prove to be the "death knell of the women's liberation movement." Schlafly made continued references to IWY. "If we had the $5 million Congress spent on the women's conference," she told the crowd, "we would have buried the ERA five years ago."[209] Speaking to the counterdemonstrators by video on a large screen, Anita Bryant also argued that lesbian rights defined feminism and destroyed the family. It seemed a coordinated campaign. Throughout, Schlafly ensured a patriotic, religious-oriented theme. The Stars and Stripes dominated a parade of state flags. In addition to patriotic music, the crowd prayed and sang spirituals. Speaker after speaker stressed the traditional role of women as wives and mothers, the sin of homosexuality, and the importance of overturning *Roe v. Wade*. Participants carried signs that not only called the ERA a "turkey" but also declared, "God Made Adam and Eve, not Adam and Steve." At the end of the rally one self-described housewife wore an orange tag with the words "God's Way." When asked what that meant, she replied, "That homosexuality is a sin, that God meant for a woman to take care of the family, and that every child that was conceived was a life that could not be taken."[210]

It all made for good political theater. While Imperial Wizard Robert Shelton declared that the Ku Klux Klan would protest the women's conference to "protect our women from all the militant lesbian women who will be there," Schlafly and her allies were largely successful in winning the public relations battle.[211] "Antifamily" now increasingly made its appearance in the media, continually, if not intentionally, lumping feminism and lesbianism together as a challenge to the traditional nuclear family. For many Americans, this gave conservatives the appearance of moral superiority, helping Schlafly to solidify an opposition. None of this boded well for Carter, who perhaps wisely avoided the conference. When First Lady Rosalynn Carter appeared on the first day, many conservatives bitterly complained. "I am sick and tired of the presidents' wives flim-flamming with these perverts," declared Texas state representative Clay Smothers. "Jimmy, we are here too," read one sign, an obvious reference to the gay rights balloons and an indication that many voters now joined Smothers in associating Carter with homosexuality and a threat to the family.[212]

While the counterdemonstrators adopted no resolutions, the IWY conference ended with a twenty-six-point National Plan of Action. As expected, every debated resolution passed with the exception of one calling for a cabinet-level Department of Women. In addition to the controversial planks supporting the ERA and lesbian and abortion rights, the resolutions included support for child care, battered women, women's health, and women in education. The president, one resolution directed, should direct all federal agencies regulating business to encourage the hiring of women. Another recommended social security benefits for housewives. When the convention was over, it was left to IWY commissioners to present the plan to the president and, hopefully, to assist in working out the language of specific legislative proposals.[213]

This worried Abzug, Costanza, and their allies. Legislation had set the commission's expiration for March 31, 1978, only four months away, and Carter might simply avoid controversy by taking no action. Indeed, pressed by the media, the White House was noncommittal when it came to the controversial planks adopted at the conference and only promised to continue to push for the ERA's ratification.[214] Not only had Carter obviously tried to distance himself from the conference, but, as the proceedings had ended, the IWY commissioners had angered the White House. They had issued a press release implying that some religious opposition to the conference's resolutions was akin to that of the KKK. In response, the Department of State, under whose Office of Public Information the commissioners had officially issued the release, canceled all funding for future commission mailings. It was unfortunate, Costanza knew, and did not speak well for the future. Aware of her concern, the press asked her what she expected Carter to do. She could offer no specifics, Costanza replied quietly, only that Carter would reiterate his support for the ERA in a coming "fireside chat."[215]

It was, perhaps, a bit ironic. Costanza, who had won the planks she sought at the conference, left Houston worried and a bit deflated. Schlafly, whose forces never had a chance, clearly departed optimistic. Feminists, Schlafly confidently declared, were "the most sexist women in the world." They could not solve their problems, so they wanted the government to do it for them: "God is on our side."[216] When the year had begun Schlafly had devoted much of her energies to foreign policy and the battle against Communism. Moreover, she had in some respects trod lightly on the new president's diplomacy. Rather than attack immediately Carter's positions, she had held out hope that he would grow firm against the Soviet Union. "[The Soviets] will surely test him in the coming months, probably in an ordeal of summitry," her *Phyllis Schlafly Report* had read in January, and only then would she know "if he is made of steel or cotton candy."[217] As the months had passed and the family issues had resonated, however, her emphasis had begun to shift slightly, with the battle against the ERA assuming an even greater prominence than before. Her rhetoric, already pointed and partisan, now became more acerbic. As the year passed, the *Phyllis Schlafly Report* ran an extended edition entirely on the need to defeat the ERA, its object of scorn obviously the Democratic Party. With the future of the family in doubt, the major threat was no longer simply external. With the situation so dire, an all-out assault was necessary.[218]

As the IWY conference concluded, Schlafly had obviously tacked wisely. She had become so famous that many supporters wanted her to challenge Republican senator Charles Percy, who was up for reelection in 1978. While she admitted the possibility as "exciting," her husband, Fred, said that he would not follow her to Washington. Schlafly, therefore, declined. "It's just plain different for a man leaving his wife home in the district to go to Washington than it is for a woman to leave her husband," she remarked.[219] If her regrets disappointed them, Schlafly's growing followers undoubtedly found her reasons more evidence of her exceptionalism.

The IWY conference did little to assist the White House, which appeared on the defensive as the year ended. Rosalynn Carter seemed to acknowledge as much in a televised interview with ABC's Barbara Walters. "[Carter] not campaigning harder for the ERA was an important mistake this year," the First Lady stated. "I know that he realizes that and has corrected it." The ERA was important to her as well, she reminded Walters. "I can look back and see maybe it would have made a difference if we had started a little earlier."[220] To regain the initiative, her husband obviously still hoped to cast himself as a champion of the family, the impact of IWY notwithstanding. As if to launch a new offensive, he reasserted White House control over planning for the family conference, removing much authority from HEW, and won several million additional dollars from Congress for the effort. While some advisors fretted over the possibility of another IWY and urged Carter to postpone a new conference until after his reelection, Carter still held out hopes for the originally scheduled date in late 1979.[221] At the same time, Carter moved again, proclaiming National Family Week. Conspicuously avoiding the controversies now so obvious to all, Carter simply declared, "The family teaches us responsibility and compassion, it encourages our best efforts and it forgives our failures."[222] On this, all would agree.

As the anniversary of his election elapsed and his first year drew to a close, it was more obvious than ever that Carter believed in what he said, that his concern for the family and his faith was no political charade. Throughout the year he had held "drop-in rap sessions with administration employees," in the words of reporter Helen Thomas. In these meetings he kept driving home the point that his staff should not let their jobs hurt their families. For Carter, concern about his staff was not simply a holiday greeting card. "It is important that the [White House] set the moral tone," he remarked. Staff should "not hold out false hopes" over controversial matters but treat all sides "respectfully." Both sides, after all, cared about their families. In one of these meetings Carter even went further, remarking, "Those of you who are living in sin, I hope you will get married." The comment evoked some nervous laughter but only emboldened the president. "I think it is important that we have stable family lives," he concluded. "I am serious about that."[223]

Carter still resisted using his faith as a political sword or, perhaps more appropriately given the momentum, a shield. When the Southern Baptist Convention requested permission to photograph Carter attending Christmas services and teaching his Sunday school class, an obvious attempt to paint once again the president as one of its own, the wise political move was to agree. In the light of IWY, it was just what the doctor ordered. Carter, however, would have none of it. Pictures were permissible only as the Carter family entered and exited the service, never inside the church. "Generally, the White House does not send a photographer to accompany the President to church," Powell wrote. "Because [church] is his one time with the family and away from business and the news media, I am very reluctant to suggest to him that any further photo coverage be made for whatever purpose."[224]

If the end of Carter's first year suggested that his motives were pure, it also demonstrated the truth in an observation by advisor Eizenstat: "The political process did not come naturally to Carter."[225] Indeed, as Carter worked to accommodate all sides on the controversial issues surrounding the family, now more prominent than ever before, the opposite was closer to the truth. Everyone, still with high expectations from the election, felt disappointed. Activists for gay rights complained that the White House had not done enough. Feminists shared similar sentiments. Conservative Christians, perhaps harboring the greatest expectations of all, had not found satisfaction in their opponents' disenchantment. They too demanded more, their frustrations growing with even the most trivial of slights. When Carter's Christmas cards arrived at the end of the year, the greetings simply depicted the White House. As Carter explained, he did not want to exclude "Jews, Muslims, Hindus, and even atheists." Christmas without Christ, critics complained, was not what they had anticipated from the nation's first born-again chief executive.[226] To make matters worse, the year ended with reports that an apparently inebriated Hamilton Jordan had insulted the wife of Egyptian Ambassador Ashraf Ghorbal at a Christmas party hosted by the journalist Barbara Walters. Staring at Mrs. Ghorbal's cleavage, visible in a low-cut dress, Jordan reportedly quipped, "I've always wanted to see the pyramids."[227] Accurate or not, it little mattered; the damage was done. Weeks later Jordan and his own wife divorced. Symbolic perhaps, but it appeared yet again to many social and religious conservatives that, rhetoric aside, the Carter administration was no friend to the institution of the family.

CHAPTER FOUR

His Faith and Virtue Were Not Enough

AT THE END OF 1977 CARTER expressed frustration that so many Americans doubted his leadership and that issues of competence bedeviled his administration. Twelve months earlier he had ridden a wave of optimism, but now polls indicated that a significant percentage of citizens questioned if he were up to the challenge. His legislative agenda appeared stalled in a reluctant Congress, Mondale explaining that an "overload of bills" undermined the administration's top priorities. A new year, however, offered new hope, a sentiment that Carter evidenced in his first State of the Union address on January 19, 1978. Carter spoke in the context of his domestic and foreign policy goals, but when he summarized them as "reconciliation, rebuilding and rebirth," he might have been speaking of his own political aspirations. The address, perhaps predictably, did not mention the controversial issues of abortion or homosexuality or even his support of the ERA. More surprisingly, the address did not even once mention the institution of family, suggesting that even in this general sense the events of his first year had made him increasingly gun-shy. Nevertheless, Carter's enumerated goals for the new year still included recommendations that continued the troublesome political dynamic established in the previous year.[1]

For one, Carter listed as a top priority the establishment of the Department of Education. While during his presidential campaign he had spoken fondly of private schools, music to the ears of conservative Protestants and Catholics, the new proposal was an obvious overture to the National Education Association (NEA), the nation's largest teachers' union, which had also supported Carter and had demanded the new bureaucracy. The NEA not only lobbied for more money for public schools but also advocated bilingual and multicultural education. Both assured the NEA the hostility of Christian school champions such as Robert Billings and self-described "family advocates" such as Connie Marshner.

Still publishing her *Family Protection Report* and committed to the defense of traditionalism in the planned family conference, Marshner published a book just after Carter's State of the Union address that summarized the arguments to keep government out of education, which, the book claimed, undermined the family as much as feminism, abortion, and homosexuality. In *Blackboard Tyranny* Marshner was not shy about laying blame on the Carter administration, noting in her first chapter that Vice President Mondale had always nurtured a "pet scheme." While still a senator, he had "paraded before the nation an HEW study [that] proposed elaborate policies to 'help' American children by meddling in their family lives." The book lambasted the "educational establishment" and savaged the NEA, both, it claimed, part of an "educational-political complex" that sought to usurp traditional values and parental autonomy. It denounced bussing of students for racial integration and demanded the return of "prayer to schools." Religion had no chance because of "secular humanism," presented as a "harmless, consensus-based universal morality" but actually a "poison." Marshner pressed for tax credits for private religious academies, noting sarcastically that "Democratic President Jimmy Carter and his HEW secretary, Joseph Califano, both sent their children to costly private schools," but both had "lobbied vigorously" against the credits. At the end of her book Marshner instructed her readers on how to effect change. If they became active, there was still hope for familial autonomy.[2]

The reaction to Carter's proposed department was, on occasion, withering. Evangelist Tim LaHaye tried to defeat the proposal with a unique use of the principle of separation of church and state, a sword that he had often faced from his own critics. "Our forefathers," LaHaye declared, "were simply preventing the establishment of a state religion." Carter's proposal for the Department of Education along with his funding proposals had, however, changed all that. "Since the educational system has been taken over by humanism, and since humanism is an officially declared religion, we find the government establishing a religion and giving the high priest a position on the president's cabinet."[3] Before Carter's address, *Christianity Today* had obviously anticipated the proposal but had been more muted if not diplomatic. "There should be equal time for evangelicals in the public schools," it had declared. After the address, as the fight for congressional approval began, letters began to pour in to members of Congress, a battle that promised to rage throughout the new year. Carter's State of the Union address, it appeared, had unintentionally ignited another controversial debate, one that had been relatively latent in his first year.[4]

As if to pour gas on the flames, the IRS announced what many conservative Christians had feared for almost a decade, a vigorous enforcement of its 1970 order revoking the tax-exempt status of racially discriminatory private schools. IRS commissioner Jerome Kurtz was obviously under pressure to make the announcement because a number of African American and civil rights organizations had pressed for action. Specifically, Kurtz ordered the IRS to label as "reviewable" any tax exemption for a school created in a district under a desegregation ruling. For these reviewable schools the IRS established a guideline to measure discrimination. A school could retain its tax status if it enrolled 5 percent of the proportion of minorities living in the area. If it could not meet this standard, it could still retain its exemption if it demonstrated a good-faith effort to recruit minority teachers and students. While some perceived this standard as fair or even lenient, a number of conservative religious groups began a letter-writing campaign. The IRS received over 120,000 letters of protest, an IRS record, according to officials, surpassing protests over the proposal for the Department of Education.[5]

People were so angry at the IRS, according to one conservative activist, that they wanted to "kill [Kurtz] and tell God it was an accident."[6] In the words of another protester, "The IRS uses its power to trod upon many things people consider moral issues. The IRS retribution [upon the traditional family structure], as best I can figure it, stems from a simple lust for money."[7] To harness this energy, Billings established a new lobbying organization, Christian School Action, and began producing a newsletter titled *Christian School Alert*. Billings's organization grew quickly, another indication that Carter's hopes for a political rebound still rested, at least in part, on controversial family issues.

Carter's State of the Union address listed another priority for the new year, a treaty with Panama over the country's historic canal. The United States had built the canal three-quarters of a century before during an age of imperialism, and it still operated it, to the chagrin of many Panamanians. With the cold war raging, the United States faced a problem with anti-Americanism throughout the region, suggesting that a resolution of the canal issue might better ensure not only the canal's long-term stability but also the United States' broader interests. By raising the canal in his speech, Carter seemed to suggest that foreign policy would also play a larger role in his new year's political renaissance. Indeed, after the holiday festivities Carter had begun his first major overseas trip, a six-nation, eighteen-thousand-mile diplomatic sojourn. Carter had not avoided foreign policy in his first year, and indeed, world events had been momentous. Nevertheless, Carter's administration had accomplished little. The Soviet Union had complained about Carter's emphasis on human rights, and negotiations over SALT II (Strategic Arms Limitation Talks), a new nuclear arms treaty, remained stalled. In Iran the American-backed leader, Shah Reza Pahlavi, still faced a growing insurrection as well as American criticism of his government's human rights record. Carter had met with leaders in the Middle East and welcomed a new Israeli prime minister, Menachem Begin, who appeared more open to negotiations with Egyptian leader Anwar al-Sadat, but peace still remained elusive. A civil war in Lebanon and the questions over Palestinian autonomy and Israeli-occupied lands still appeared intractable.[8]

Carter's address, of course, never referenced the role of religion in shaping his foreign policy agenda, but at closer inspection faith was never far below the surface. When his address spoke of achieving a more "just international system," his words smacked of Niebuhr. His emphasis on human rights alluded, if nothing else, to Jefferson's "inalienable rights," divinely ordained and protected. Abhorring violence, Carter spoke of "keeping lines of communication open in the Middle East" and "stopping the proliferation of nuclear weapons." The United States should "demonstrate good faith to the world" and "discourage the spread of hostile ideologies." SALT negotiations "have been long and difficult," Carter stated, but they were worth it because they brought the promise of peace. If Americans worked together and had faith, they could, "as the Bible says . . . move mountains."[9]

In the aggregate, playing the role of peacemaker won Carter religious applause. Specifically, however, many conservative Christians worried that Carter was not strong enough against "Godless Communism." Just after the State of the Union address, South Carolina senator Strom Thurmond sent Carter an edition of the *Presbyterian Journal* that included two articles, one written by prominent evangelist D. James Kennedy.[10] Kennedy's article stressed the need for a strong defense of America against the evils of Communism. "If the United States falls, the bastion of Christian missions goes with it," the article claimed.[11] Christians, the second article concluded, "too often are guided by their feelings rather than through their understanding of the Word of God." The Bible called for the faithful to be strong.[12] The White

House thanked Thurmond for the articles and added, "You may be sure that the viewpoint they reflect has been well noted."[13] Nevertheless, Thurmond worried. In his first year Carter had canceled the B-1 bomber and deferred deployment of the neutron bomb. His budget for the new year had called for an increase of only 3 percent in defense spending, which represented severe cutbacks from the Ford administration's projections. Carter had begun the new year by pressuring the Pentagon to curtail new shipbuilding by half. Carter clearly wanted to move beyond the cold war rhetoric, which all the faithful encouraged, but to the likes of Thurmond, Kennedy, and others, his emphasis on nonmilitary solutions still risked a threat to the nation, if not the church.[14]

Only weeks after the State of the Union address, Congress finally passed two treaties that settled the Panama Canal, assuring the canal's open access but promising to turn over entire control to Panamanian officials in just two decades, at the end of the millennium. To some, the treaties appeared to confirm that the wise peacemaker had become the foolish pacifist. The United States, Falwell argued for one, "had been politically bludgeoned into giving away the Panama Canal."[15] Moreover, Carter appeared determined to achieve a lasting peace between Israel and Egypt, hosting the respective leaders Begin and Sadat at his Camp David retreat, the presidential compound in the Maryland mountains outside the nation's capital. Reports indicated that Carter was demanding the Israelis cease settlement in the Palestinian-dominated lands they had recently occupied. Here, it appeared to many conservative Christians, Carter was unduly harsh on God's chosen people. Letters of complaint had arrived for some time, one early example protesting, "As one who openly voted and fought for you, as did many of my family and friends, I want to strongly and vehemently protest your immoral attempts to intimidate and coerce Israel." Israel was simply defending the Judeo-Christian tradition from heretics such as Sadat. "Can this be the same Jimmy Carter whose support of Israel in 1976 sounded so sincere?"[16]

Within weeks of the State of the Union address, delegates to the annual convention of the National Religious Broadcasters heard a message from the Soviet dissident Alexander Solzhenitsyn. "There is in our days a prevailing and entirely wrong belief that contemporary world disasters are the result of this or that political system's imperfections," Solzhenitsyn wrote. "It is not so, however. The truth is that they all stem from the relentless persecution of the religious spirit in the east, and the fading of that spirit in the West and Third World." Solzhenitsyn beseeched the group, dominated by evangelicals, to remain vigilant in the fight against Godless Communism if not the internal threat posed by the world's ascendant cultural liberalism.[17] Solzhenitsyn never mentioned Carter, but to many in the NRB his message added to the sense that the administration's actions, or inactions, had not lived up to its promise. Carter's first year had begun to cast doubt on his commitment to the traditional family, and now, with his new State of the Union address, it appeared the new year would bring new reasons for new complaints.

While the National Religious Broadcasters welcomed Solzhenitsyn's message, they still hoped that Carter would address convention delegates directly. While Carter had declined an invitation the previous year, most delegates had understood that he had been new to the White House, still learning the job and busy with his appointments. Now, however, their hopes were greater. Carter had settled into the Oval Office, and given his relatively rough first year, delegates assumed that the White House recognized the political benefits of accepting their invitation. In fact, after the official invitation, letters arrived from an array of NRB supporters. "Members of Congress and other government officials will be in attendance," wrote one state senator from Atlanta, "and I feel certain that President Carter would want to be a part."[18] If Carter were to accept, wrote one NRB member, he "will experience one of the warmest receptions ever received by any President."[19] It appeared from the letters that many members of the group were still willing to give Carter the benefit of the doubt, that after all the disappointments of his first year, indeed, after the State of the Union address and the IRS enforcement in the new year, many members still expected him to attend. Clearly, among some conservative Christians Carter already appeared a lost cause, but, to many others, hope sprang eternal.

Among the latter, the disappointment must have been familiar. Just as it had the previous year, the White House declined, again sending a formal statement of welcome. "I applaud your noble mission and hope you will gain from it as much satisfaction as the growing audiences you serve," the statement read.[20] Carter's regrets hit the NRB hard, its leaders telephoning the White House to press their case and ask if Rosalynn might attend in Carter's place. They "begged me to let [them] know if there was a last minute change of schedule or if [the First Lady] could go," recalled one of Rosalynn's aides.[21] Several months later the NRB pressed again. The group's Abe Van Der Puy requested a meeting with Carter for a small delegation. Van

Der Puy reminded Carter that before the 1976 election he had promised to meet with the group, which Van Der Puy now noted "reached over 115 million Americans by radio weekly and another 14 million unduplicated audience in television." He added that many members had supported Carter in 1976 and had been "impressed by the impetus you have given to evangelical Christianity."[22] The meeting made sense to some in the White House, with staffer Pat Bario suggesting forty-five minutes with both Carter and the First Lady before Christmas. The meeting could also include "some Jewish and Catholic publications, etc."[23] Recognizing that this was not what the NRB had in mind, the White House declined but, just as before, left the door open for future meetings. "While it has not been possible to work this out to date, we will keep your request in mind for the upcoming months," wrote Fran Voorde of the White House Scheduling Office.[24]

It had already been a year, but the administration still had no formal or comprehensive strategy to deal with the religious community. It continued its rather reactive, ad hoc policy, trying to locate a comfortable middle ground among groups resistant to compromise. Still seeking to please all sides on moral and family issues, the administration continued its political flirtations even as it sought to keep its distance. It wanted to be close enough to win votes but not so close that it lost others. In retrospect, even if the White House sought a new beginning with the new year, alienation was still sure to rule the day.

For one, the requests continued to arrive. In the early months of 1978 Carter declined to meet with evangelist Robert Schuller, who was in Washington to receive an award from the Daughters of the American Revolution, and to attend a Billy Graham crusade in Las Vegas, letters of invitation arriving from both Graham and city officials.[25] Rosalynn Carter declined an invitation to attend the annual seminar of the Christian Life Commission.[26] When Jerry Falwell wrote Carter requesting aid for a Baptist charity that his ministry sponsored, the White House sent its regrets: "It would not be fair to single out a favorite to support while excluding the others."[27] When Bill Bright requested a presidential message for the annual convention of Campus Crusade for Christ, the White House telephoned Bright that the convention did not "conform to the criteria for a Presidential message."[28]

Not all administration regrets were to invitations. When Jody Powell described Evan Dobelle, newly appointed as treasurer of the Democratic Party, as a "born-again Democrat," many evangelicals took offense. Pat Robertson's objections to what was obviously an unintended slight perhaps indicated just how far his reservoir of goodwill had evaporated. "Evangelical Christians across the country are shocked at the blasphemous utterance of press secretary Jody Powell," Robertson wrote. "The White House of the United States is hardly the forum to trample upon the sacred beliefs which are held by fifty million of your fellow Americans." Unless Powell were to issue an immediate apology, "there will be great damage to your administration."[29] The White House replied that Powell meant no offense: "He is a sincere young man who is the first to regret when his remarks are misinterpreted or considered as harmful." The letter was surprisingly deferential, suggesting that the White House still hoped for Robertson's vote. Indeed, it ended by thanking Robertson for "your continued concern and support."[30]

In fact, White House staffers had obviously crafted most letters of regret to avoid such offense. To Graham, it noted Carter's "appreciation for your thoughtfulness."[31] To the Christian Life Commission in a letter entitled "Friends," Rosalynn professed, "My family and my deep faith in God are the two most stabilizing influences in my life." While the White House regretted that Carter could not attend a meeting with the Christian Embassy, Landon Kite, the White House's director of correspondence, agreed to help coordinate a dinner in honor of the organization. Kite invited a number of high-ranking administration figures, including National Security Advisor Zbigniew Brzezinski and his wife.[32] When Schuller's thirteen-year-old daughter Carol lost her left leg in a motorcycle accident, Carter telegraphed the Schullers a letter of condolence, while advisor Anne Wexler arranged for a letter to Carol from Carter's daughter, Amy. Much later, when Schuller wrote Carter that he was taking the recovering Carol to "our nation's capitol, her dream," and requested a chance for her to "shake your hand," the White House declined in a gracious letter. When Senator Barry Goldwater then forwarded to Carter a copy of the diary the Schullers had written after the accident, since published as a book on hope, the White House sent its "best wishes for the Schuller family."[33]

The Southern Baptists remained a special concern. When early in January the SBC's new president, Jimmy Allen, requested a meeting of "leading Southern Baptist business people" to win support for the SBC's Mission Service Corporation, Carter handwrote a promise "to help raise funds." Allen, acquainted with Carter personally, knew that the president thought mission work critical and had supported the group the previous year. Allen correctly assumed that Carter wanted to do more. Suggesting a dinner, Carter remarked that he and Rosalynn were willing to host a reception but that the event could not be at the White House. "Perhaps a church or hotel," Carter wrote. "Be sure to set your sights high." The result was a small afternoon reception at the White House and a large evening dinner at the Mayflower Hotel.[34] In his remarks after the dinner, Carter stated that when he had arrived in Washington "I could see the need for a spiritual awakening in our nation." Such an awakening did not come from "laws, programs or political proposals" but from the "moral character of our people." The Baptist missions were an example of this moral character, and all present should support the Mission Service Corporation to the extent of their abilities. Jimmy Allen and the Baptists present thanked Carter profusely and sent him an ornamental pen afterward as a memento.[35]

The group of Baptists had been early and strong supporters of Carter's promised family conference, but, given the turmoil of the first year, many now worried that either the conference would fail to take place or, worse, that it would encourage the very threats to the family the conference should combat. Early in the new year Senator Alan Cranston chaired hearings on conference planning in his Subcommittee on Child and Human Development. Congressman John Brademas did the same in the House with his Subcommittee on Select Education. Both sought to assure the public that all organizational problems were in the past. When Carter, in one of his first comments of the year on the need to protect families, tried to do the same, his remarks gave many in the SBC pause. The conference, Carter promised, would "recognize the pluralism of family life in America."[36] This prompted the SBC to pass a resolution that while it still supported the conference, it had growing reservations. "Be it resolved," the resolution read, "that we urge the President to see that needed direction is given to this conference to insure that the Conference focuses on the strengths of the family rather than so-called alternatives to the family." The conference, the resolution continued, "should note carefully the impact on families of any proposed federal legislation."[37] In his remarks Carter announced plans to appoint a national advisory committee to guide the planning. With nominations open for the thirty to forty members Carter planned, the committee obviously stood as a venue for future confrontation.[38]

When Carter accepted an invitation to address the SBC convention in Atlanta, Powell wanted a special speech with appropriate religious overtones. Words clearly mattered. Still aware that Robert Maddox, a Southern Baptist minister, had applied to be a religious liaison the previous year and lived near Atlanta, Powell called Maddox and asked him to submit a draft.

Maddox agreed but took the opportunity to remind Powell that Carter's first year had cost him evangelical support. "I told [the White House] that I had picked up considerable concern from religious leaders over the approaches of the Carter Administration," Maddox recalled. After Carter approved Maddox's submission and the speech had gone over well, Rosalynn decided to attend one of Maddox's services while visiting family in Georgia. The First Lady mentioned that the White House planned to host a ceremony for the coming National Bible Week and asked informally if Maddox might suggest a list of religious leaders to invite. Maddox agreed, once again lobbying for the position of religious liaison and noting the need for a better-coordinated religious strategy. This time Maddox's pleas did not fall completely on deaf ears. While the White House did not immediately hire Maddox, it obviously recognized his talents if not some truth in his recommendations.[39]

Eight days into the new year a group of prominent writers and actors joined with political leaders from over half a dozen European countries to purchase a large advertisement in *Time* magazine. The bold headlines demonstrated that even as foreign policy and education promised to complicate any religious overture, the controversies that had so frustrated Carter in his first year had not evaporated. They had their own momentum, with Carter still caught in the whirlwind. "What's going on in America?" the ad read. "President Carter's human rights policy can gain credibility only if the rights of homosexuals in the United States of America are bound inseparably to human rights of all people." If Carter wanted to make human rights a centerpiece of his foreign policy, he should not forget the fight for homosexual rights at home. He should begin the new year by denouncing bigots such as Anita Bryant, "who preaches discrimination in the name of God."[40] Just as the ad appeared, Faye Wattleton, the new head of the Planned Parenthood Federation of America, announced that she was "putting the world on notice." From now on her organization, traditionally "low-key," was going to be more aggressive in the battle for abortion rights. "What has happened," Wattleton declared, "is that we have allowed [abortion opponents] to have center stage." After the *Roe v. Wade* decision too many abortion rights advocates assumed that the debate was largely settled. The growing controversies of Carter's first year and the White House's embrace of the Hyde Amendment, however, proved that advocates could no longer be complacent: "I'd like to say that those days are over."[41] Eleanor Smeal was no less emphatic. The new year, the NOW president announced, called for a "new campaign" to ratify the ERA. Smeal promised to hire additional staffers, begin a coordinated letter-writing campaign, stage more rallies, and increase an economic boycott announced the previous year of states that had yet to ratify the amendment. With her comments subtly suggesting how partisan the debate had become, Smeal claimed that the new campaign would "put additional pressure on Congress, the Democratic Party, and the President."[42]

Given the administration's unabashed support for the ERA, the struggle for ratification, now desperate, posed for Carter the potential for the greatest political embarrassment, if not the most damage to any religious liaison. As if to rebut Smeal, Missouri, one of the states NOW targeted in its boycott, filed suit, accusing the organization of antitrust violations. Led by a noted conservative state attorney general, John Ashcroft, the state argued that over ninety businesses had agreed to comply with the boycott, costing St. Louis, for example, over $10 million in lost convention fees.[43] In the White House the suit annoyed Costanza, who began to work even closer with Smeal and other NOW leaders. In meetings in late January and again in early February, Smeal reported on NOW's new efforts, while Costanza suggested that perhaps Carter might be willing to hold a White House reception for ERA supporters on Susan B. Anthony's birthday.[44]

With the birthday approaching, Costanza invited Carter to join the meeting. "I feel that your presence would give the [ERA] interest group representatives present the boost they need and would bring further press and public attention," her invitation read.[45] While Carter agreed with the meeting, he did not want to attend. Rosalynn, however, did stop by to lend encouragement. Without Carter's participation, the press was not what Costanza had hoped, but the meeting still illustrated the close relationship Costanza had developed with the many activists present. The group noted that a "new language" was needed, one that the opposition could not easily portray as "antifamily," and that additional fund-raising was essential. Costanza spoke of "the need for a flyer from the Department of Justice on why ERA extension is not unconstitutional" and promised to get a "fact sheet" to commentator Shana Alexander on the popular television show *60 Minutes*. As the meeting ended, Costanza added, "We should be meeting on a regular basis, perhaps monthly."[46]

With Carter set to accept formally the IWY's National Plan of Action in a March 22 ceremony, Costanza pressed for an executive order extending the IWY Commission beyond its date of expiration. She also pressed for the creation of an interdepartmental task force to work with the IWY and coordinate efforts in all government agencies. When Costanza completed a draft of the executive order she proposed, Eizenstat assistant Beth Abramowitz complained that the order placed Carter in a "box" by committing him to the full implementation of the National Plan of Action. Eizenstat agreed and also worried that both extending the IWY and creating another task force contradicted Carter's promises during the presidential campaign to reduce the size of government. Eizenstat, therefore, recommended to Carter that he let the IWY expire. If he felt the need to create a new task force, it should consist only of administration officials.[47]

When the March 22 ceremony arrived, Carter decided on a middle path to reconcile Costanza's and Eizenstat's recommendations. He let the IWY expire but still announced the creation of both the National Advisory Committee for Women (NACW) and the Interdepartmental Task Force for Women (IDTFW). By officially eliminating the IWY, he hoped to please conservative critics who continued to complain about the IWY's feminist bias. Eliminating the IWY removed the stigma and controversy attached since Houston, while naming the new body a "committee" and not a "commission" helped as well. At the same time, Carter promised Costanza and the IWY commissioners that the new NACW would include strong representation from their feminist constituency. Carter had given no indication of his plans, the media reported, which caught "even his aides by surprise." After Carter's brief comments, Abzug was polite but left no doubt that the White House's attempt at the middle had fallen short. "Mr. President, we welcome and appreciate what you've done," she remarked, "but it is not enough."[48]

The announcement did not end the debate. Carter initially intended to keep the NACW relatively small, but Costanza and her allies eventually prevailed in expanding its membership. The appointment of the committee's chair also provoked dissent. Carter agreed to name Abzug chair because it placated any feminists still simmering over IWY's demise and, in the words of Eizenstat, gave him "a strong card to play in 1980." If he did not appoint her, "there would be considerable vocal outrage." At the same time, Rosalynn worried, Abzug remained controversial with conservative critics. The appointment of a more conservative cochair might mute any criticism. Carter agreed and named former Puerto Rico IWY delegate Carmen Delgado Votaw to join Abzug in leading the new body.[49] Votaw, it turned out, was little consolation to the conservative Christians, who found Abzug even more "obnoxious" than Costanza. Falwell spoke out against the new committees on both radio and television, terming Abzug a "joke, exhibit A for the Left."[50]

Throughout the early months of 1978 the administration gave women's rights advocates much to applaud. Costanza apparently remained a powerful liaison within the halls of power, submitting to her colleagues suggested "ERA material to use in speeches." The recommended comments included acknowledging that "some may fear that the family may suffer if the Equal Rights Amendment is passed" but that in reality "families will benefit." If faced with religious objections, speakers could state vaguely that "in the teachings of Jesus Christ there is complete acceptance of women as whole and complete beings in the image of God."[51] Costanza was not alone, of course. When the National Governors Association conference convened at the Hyatt-Regency Hotel in Washington in late February, the administration successfully lobbied for a resolution "supporting full ratification and implementation of the Twenty-seventh Amendment to the U.S. Constitution."[52] When states such as Virginia held legislative debates on the ERA, administration staffers occasionally testified, careful as before not to appear too heavy-handed in a state matter.[53] When Abzug announced her intention to run for Congress to regain her old House seat, Carter endorsed her candidacy, while Mondale campaigned on her behalf. In what some thought inappropriate for a First Lady, Rosalynn auctioned herself off as a dance partner at an ERA fund-raiser. Daughter-in-law Judy had become so vocal in her support that Carter jokingly remarked that she was his "unofficial ambassador on ERA."[54]

Despite all this, however, a persistent skepticism among some women's rights advocates remained; the administration, they continued to believe, was simply not doing all it could. It was more than Carter refusing to show up personally at an ERA meeting or seeking compromise on the future of the IWY Commission. The White House had done little to support NOW even as a number of former IWY Commission members had begun to push for Carter to order federal departments and agencies to join the boycott. This was probably unconstitutional, Assistant Attorney General John Harmon reported, "because the Constitution carefully specifies that ratification is to be left to the States."[55] White House counsel Margaret McKenna agreed. "It would raise serious legal questions and would be viewed as improper," she wrote Costanza.[56] Supporting an action that would cause any American citizens economic hardship was obviously unwise, but many activists still insisted upon it.

The issue of affirmative action was similar. During the presidential campaign Carter had spoken in favor of including women in the government's affirmative action programs, and by 1978 there was evidence of some administration movement. The Department of Treasury, for example, had expanded its definition of "minority" to include women in its efforts to place federal deposits in minority-owned banks. According to the *New York Times*, "Increasingly, agencies that administer affirmative action plans involving minorities are basing their decisions on whether the people in question are 'socially or economically disadvantaged' rather than simply on race."[57] Rather than focusing on these developments, however, many women's rights advocates protested that Carter should do more. When Congress established the Small Business Administration 8(a) Business Development Program for minorities, Carter did not work to ensure that the program included women. Despite Carter's promises to follow up with new initiatives for female-owned businesses, many activists complained. "We are," the program director soon reported to the White House, "under some pressure to move quickly [to include women]."[58]

The frustration and skepticism that many feminists felt might have stemmed from the fact that the ERA remained stagnant as the spring ended.[59] Attacking Carter for his support, the opposition appeared to have all the momentum. In May a major committee of the National Conference of Catholic Bishops officially turned down a proposal to endorse ratification, citing the "consequences for family life" as one of its reasons, its wording— conscious or not—further tying the Catholic Church's resistance to that of the evangelists such as Falwell.[60] Even when a group of independent filmmakers produced a documentary depicting the ERA in a positive light, their choice of title unintentionally aided the opposition. *ERA: A Family Matter* tried to do as Costanza had urged and depict the ERA as a boon to family life, not a threat. The reality remained, however, that Falwell and his allies had so co-opted the term that even the use of it conjured up the arguments of the ERA's opposition.[61] Reflecting the growing partisanship, the NWPC adopted a "score card on women's rights" and awarded ten Democrats—but no Republicans—with a "perfect score." The Republican National Committee, meanwhile, announced that it would not honor NOW's boycott in its selection of potential convention sites. As many advocates anticipated, grow-ing partisanship at least complicated ratification prospects.[62]

When it came to homosexual rights, the dynamic was similar still. The administration's actions in the early months of 1978 might have given gay rights activists much to applaud. Nevertheless, those actions appeared in-adequate to such activists, and they demanded more. Early in the year the IRS granted homosexual organizations tax-exempt status, significantly in-creasing the ability of the National Gay Task Force (NGTF) and the Lambda Legal Defense and Education Fund, among others, to raise money and ex-pand their operations. The ruling was, to many conservative Christians, rather ironic, given the IRS enforcement against private education.[63] The Department of Defense also revised its policy of declaring gay bars near military bases off-limits for base personnel and, in a response to a suit by the Vietnam veteran Leonard Matlovich, ended its policy of dismissing homosexual soldiers with dishonorable discharges.[64] More notably, when Congress passed the Civil Service Reform Act of 1978, Carter signed it, hail-ing it as one of his most important legislative accomplishments.[65] While the law did not specifically mention homosexuality and the debate had centered on other matters, such as a cap on federal salaries to help fight inflation, the final bill did outlaw discrimination against private, non-job-related behavior. In short, it seemed to support the existing Civil Service Commission's policy of nondiscrimination against all homosexuals work-ing outside of sensitive positions. In many respects, all these developments represented a significant advance in the fight for gay and lesbian rights, but if anything they only increased the pressure the administration faced. To complicate matters further, the gay activist Harvey Milk, who had lobbied Carter the previous year, won election to the San Francisco Board of Super-visors. A former naval officer, Milk clearly was not shy about pressing his agenda. His first actions on the board in January were to criticize a state law banning homosexual marriage and to introduce a city ordinance banning discrimination against gays and lesbians.[66]

Milk's election came just before California prepared to vote on the ini-tiative proposed by Republican state senator John Briggs that required all school districts to fire "notorious homosexuals" from positions in which they could have contact with children. Along with the rest of the gay com-munity, Milk was not about to let the measure pass without a fight. He found a willing ally in Costanza, who praised his efforts as "one of the best defenses for human rights that I have read or heard in a good while." Advising Milk to use "actual statistics instead of distortions," Costanza asked to "borrow bits and pieces" of Milk's argument in her own efforts against the measure. Promising to enlist Carter, Costanza concluded, "Stay in touch and let me know when I can help."[67] Carter, however, refused to criticize the Briggs Initiative, which annoyed both Costanza and Milk. When San Francisco held a Gay Freedom Day parade in late spring, a celebration that included dozens of floats and attracted several hundred thousand people, Milk could not contain his criticism. "Most of all," Milk empathically declared, "I am tired of silence from the White House!" If Carter wanted to be a leader in human rights internationally, "well, then, damn it, lead." As thousands cheered, Milk closed his speech with what amounted to a threat. "If you don't [come to San Francisco and speak out against Briggs], then we will come to you." Milk was angry but smart enough to turn to his friend Costanza for assistance. "I believe it is vital that he do this," Milk wrote more diplomatically, "and I would be very grateful for any help you can give."[68]

Despite Milk's pleas and a similar Gay Freedom Day march in New York that attracted "tens of thousands," the aid never came; Carter remained quiet, angering the gay community more than ever.[69] Carter continued to seek the moderate, noncontroversial middle, to downplay an issue that appeared to please no one. As he remained quiet in regard to the Briggs Initiative, so too did he try to avoid the appearance of allying with Anita Bryant. When reports announced that Carter would appear with the outspoken singer, who continued her efforts in the new year, at the convention of the Southern Baptists, the White House quickly released a statement of denial. Carter would appear before the Brotherhood Commission, while Bryant would address the Pastors Conference. "The two groups in question not only have separate programs, spaced five days apart, but they also have separate memberships," the White House wrote.[70] Now into his second year in office, Carter's balancing act was no easier. Milk and the gay community were certainly forceful, but the *New York Times* also concluded that their efforts "are being caught in the snap of a backlash." By the time of the Gay Freedom Day parade, voters had overturned antidiscrimination measures in cities such as St. Paul, Minnesota, Wichita, Kansas, and even Eugene, Oregon, known for its liberal leanings.[71] There was ample evidence that the effort to combine gay rights with women's rights and abortion as "antifamily" continued to gain steam among theological conservatives. Bryant's address at the Southern Baptist Convention met with greater applause than did Carter's. In Kentucky efforts to defeat the ERA now included graphic pictures of lesbians, even distributed in the state's legislature.[72] A new book by author Tim LaHaye, *Unhappy Gays*, claimed that the religious community was only just beginning to recognize the threat that homosexuality posed. According to LaHaye, "The homosexual community, by militance and secret political maneuvering, is designing a program to increase the tidal wave of homosexuality that will drown our children in a polluted sea of sexual perversion—and will eventually destroy America as it did Rome, Greece, Pompeii, and Sodom."[73]

It was emotional rhetoric, but no less than that on abortion. Early in 1978 the National Broadcasting Corporation, undoubtedly fearing controversy, refused to air a scheduled broadcast of *The Lutheran Hour* because the sermon denounced abortion. Much to NBC's chagrin, however, its refusal engendered the very outrage it had hoped to avoid. NBC's censorship was, many critics claimed, an affront to "the Christian community and the American family." Also recognizing the emotional nature of the debate but taking a different tack, CBS anticipated a ratings bonanza. With correspondent Bill Moyers hosting, CBS ran an hour-long special entitled *Abortion: The Issue That Won't Go Away*.[74]

CBS's lament was hardly news to Carter, the abortion debate similar to that over feminism or homosexual rights not only in its often-professed relation to the American family but also in the way it continued to vex the administration. The new year brought Carter no relief, his actions continuing to satisfy no one. Compromise and the political middle remained elusive. "The more you talk, the more questions you raise," lamented one administration staffer in January.[75] Another acknowledged, "[Carter's] position on abortion has drawn confusion, disappointment, and vehement criticism from many circles, from those who feel that he has gone too far to those who feel that he has not gone far enough." Because abortion was part of "setting the proper moral tone for our social order, [the White House] is clearly struggling to make substantive progress in this area."[76] When the media reported in early February 1978 a surge of vandalism against abortion clinics, NARAL published a survey of violence that showed a marked increase since Carter's inauguration. Many clinics, the survey reported, experienced repeated vandalism, threatening telephone calls, and increasingly hostile picketers. Worse was an increase in bombings and arson, which, while denounced from all sides, still appeared to add to the momentum.[77] Carter may have spoken of respectful debate, but more abortion protesters began to equate the fight against abortion with the fight against slavery a century before. Americans now agreed that slavery was an unmitigated evil, and opponents, by speaking of abortion in the same context, reinforced their own sense of occupying the moral high ground. It made compromise less viable. Who would, after all, have compromised with an issue as evil as slavery?

When Califano announced in January new HEW rules to implement the previous year's agreement on the Hyde Amendment, it was easy to anticipate complaints. Victims of rape, Califano stated, would have sixty days to report the rape to gain federal funds to pay for an abortion. This was way too liberal, critics claimed. Reflecting these sentiments, Hyde said that only seven days were more appropriate. Anything more would increase the chance of fraud. In what appeared an attempt to appease Hyde, Carter told the press that any evidence of abuse would cause the administration to tighten the requirement.[78] HEW had to issue the regulations, columnist Philip Shabecoff wrote, but doing so was sure to pour gas on the fire. It was a "no-win situation" because abortion was such an "emotional and socially explosive issue." Drawing any conclusion about abortion was as "delicate as juggling eggs." When Califano arrived to review HEW's budget with the Senate Appropriations Committee, all senators wanted to discuss was the sixty-day requirement. In Shabecoff's words, Califano was "visibly nervous" and acted "like a man walking on egg shells."[79]

The budget discussions were scheduled as part of the annual appropriations process, which of course meant that senators would once again debate the Hyde Amendment. Indeed, as the new appropriations unfolded, the debate appeared to resemble the previous year's controversy. Once again, the House passed the more restrictive amendment, allowing for funding only to save the mother's life. The Senate bill provided funding for abortions when "medically necessary" or in cases of rape or incest. With the appropriations for the entire HEW department again in the balance, the House blinked, with a conference committee ultimately passing an amendment whose exceptions resembled the previous year's.[80] The debate was, however, different in one respect; the issue had spread to the appropriations for more departments, most notably the Department of Defense, whose funding stipulated restrictions similar to those of HEW. Even the Peace Corps was not exempt, with its appropriations mandating that none of the money allocated pay for abortions.[81] Outside of the appropriations process, legislators continued to introduce an array of abortion bills that spanned the spectrum from a constitutional ban to a constitutional endorsement. One abortion rights supporter introduced a bill to expand protections in the Civil Rights Act of 1964, while an abortion opponent introduced one prohibiting the U.S. Commission on Civil Rights from considering abortion as a fundamental right. None of these bills had a reasonable chance of passage, but each received press and added to the emotions that surrounded the issue.[82]

With the arrival of summer, the hard truth was difficult to ignore. The new year had brought no reprieve. Carter, biographer Peter Bourne concluded, "was in serious trouble."[83] His foreign policy and educational initiatives appeared only to add to the tensions that continued to surround the "family issues." There seemed no escape from the emotions that clouded the day.

On a hot, muggy July 9 in the nation's capital, a crowd of nearly one hundred thousand marched to the Mall in an attempt to revitalize the movement for the ERA and to encourage passage of a congressional resolution extending the ratification period. Organizers, including NOW, attempted to cast the rally as a "joyful family reunion," the description obviously chosen carefully and intended to help recapture the word "family." This was no easy task, as Schlafly lectured throughout the summer that the amendment was the best "symbol of the threat to traditional families." Her followers continued to work diligently to tie the ERA to abortion and homosexuality in the hope that the latter two would discredit the former.[84] In Kentucky, Carol Maddox, a member of Stop-ERA, wearing a badge that read "pro-family," tried to deliver to lawmakers graphic pictures of lesbian sex. If the ERA passed, she claimed, it "would encourage lesbians to advertise their sexual preferences which are immoral."[85] Frustrated, ERA supporters complained that when they contacted the White House for advice on how to repudiate the use of lesbian materials to attack the ERA, the White House referred them to the Gay Rights Alliance. "Well, I can't refer people in Oklahoma to them," one bemused caller stated. "How do you deal with something like that?"[86]

Speaker after speaker at the "family reunion" spoke on the importance of the ERA. Leading the marchers were Abzug, Smeal, Betty Friedan, and Gloria Steinem. Joining this impressive quartet of leading feminists were Costanza and HUD secretary Patricia Harris, both standing prominently in the front. Costanza was the most vocal, announcing that she carried a message from Carter that the ERA was the "bedrock for strengthening opportunities for women and minorities." Schlafly was not about to let the gathering pass without comment and noted that no Republicans had attended. The crowd was "a combination of government workers and lesbians."[87] After the rally and throughout the summer, Carter lobbied in a series of letters to wavering members of Congress and, specifically, members of the House Judiciary Committee, urging them to pass the extension resolution. "The Equal Rights Amendment is a long overdue addition to our Constitution," Carter wrote. "There is no constitutional requirement that ratification occur within a seven year period, nor within the period originally established for ratification."[88] Some in Congress complicated the extension debate by adding a rescission rider, congressional approval for states that had earlier ratified the ERA to withdraw their ratification. After some hesitancy over the constitutionality of rescission, the administration now voiced its opposition, to feminists belated but welcomed.[89]

Eleven days after the rally Carter sent a directive to the heads of all federal departments and agencies. Identifying the ERA as an "administration priority," Carter wrote, "I am convinced of the need to increase our effort to achieve equal treatment of women." He reiterated that Costanza would serve as his key assistant on the matter. She would, among other duties, "monitor and provide frequent and regular reports to me on our progress." In the interim, every agency or department was to designate a "policy representative" for women's issues, to "make the most of public appearances" in support of women's rights, and to "provide professional and clerical staff support" for the newly created Interdepartmental Task Force for Women.[90] A series of meetings followed throughout August and into September, most notably, with First Lady Rosalynn in the White House's East Room on September 18. Invited to this meeting were some of the key congressmen involved in the ongoing congressional debate.[91] In the Senate Assistant Attorney General Patricia Wald testified, "As I am sure you are aware by now, the Administration is in strong support of this [ERA extension] resolution."[92]

While women's rights advocates welcomed Carter's directive, they soon learned—much to their dismay—that at least in one regard it was disingenuous. The directive reiterated Carter's support for Costanza, but, in private, Carter had drawn the conclusion that Costanza was insufficiently loyal. She had always been the fiery, emotional, wisecracking New Yorker known for her outspokenness, but increasingly her public advocacy of women's rights, abortion, and homosexuality had leaked into criticism of the administration. Tension had existed for over a year since Costanza's open rebellion of female staff against the White House's support of the Hyde Amendment.

While she had, thankfully to Carter, followed this incident with a period of relative public silence, she had resumed her public advocacy in the summer.[93]

In many respects, Costanza's comments contributed to increasing the partisan nature of the debates. There was a "growing movement in the nation, sponsored by the 'right wing' and supported by large amounts of money," Costanza began to complain to the press. Citing the success of the ballot initiatives to overturn antidiscrimination laws against gays, she was as blunt as ever. The "right wing's aim was to strip minority groups of their human rights."[94] If Costanza was exasperated, so too was Carter. Costanza had become so outspoken that she had become a rallying cry for Falwell and others. She had energized the very groups she publicly demonized and thus made Carter's efforts to reach a compromise and avoid controversy almost impossible. In addition, she faced charges that she had held a political fund-raising event without reporting the proceeds. As part of a larger White House effort to gain better control over the administration's message, therefore, Carter demoted Costanza, relegating her to the basement—the very room where Nixon had stored his infamous tapes—and stripping her of her duties.[95] Costanza could still coordinate the fight for the ERA, but she would do so only as the chairman of the IDTFW, not as an official presidential assistant or as the head of the Office of Public Liaison.[96]

The loss of stature hit Costanza hard. In late July she scheduled, without Carter's knowledge, an appearance on ABC's *Good Morning America*. Upon learning of this, the White House sent Eizenstat in her place. The message was clear: she was on a tight leash and would have to muzzle her public advocacy. It was, Costanza quickly decided, too much. She resigned in August, citing differences in "method" as her reason.[97] Two weeks after her departure the National Advisory Committee for Women issued its first report. The committee, which Costanza had earlier advocated, titled the report "The Spirit of Houston." For many observers it appeared that the NACW and its chair, Abzug, would continue to press an activist, if controversial, agenda despite the loss of their White House champion.[98]

After Costanza's departure, Carter named in September Sarah Weddington as assistant to the president for women's affairs. Initially, at least, senior staff debated Weddington's role, asking her directly how she envisioned her job. After writing up a "brief synopsis for the President," Weddington met with Carter in the Oval Office. While stressing that she would not make the same mistakes Costanza had made, Weddington stressed her desire to advance "issues that have a particular significance to women, trying to see that women were included in all parts of the administration, assisting with the efforts to find women who were qualified and the best choices for various delegations, and just being sure that women were included in every aspect of the administration." Carter agreed, and Weddington settled into her new job, working closely with Eizenstat and Anne Wexler. "We were always working together to see that a large number of women were included for events," she recalled.[99]

From her very first meeting Weddington found the complexity of the ERA debate stressful.[100] "The President's Advisory Committee had actually been established and was functioning, but the Interdepartmental Task Force on Women was not actually functioning at the time I came," she recalled. Costanza had sent out memoranda to the various agencies and departments seeking representatives, "but we had to send out a new mailing to actually get those names in." The task force was "really into the formulative stages." Weddington's office quickly began to publish a monthly newsletter, *White House News on Women*, and its circulation soon surpassed fourteen thousand.[101]

In one sense, the women's rights lobby still had much to cheer. Weddington had, after all, argued the landmark *Roe v. Wade* case before the Supreme Court.[102] In another sense, however, it was not hard to conclude that Weddington would not pursue such an activist agenda. Selected in part because she wore "nylons and a bird's nest hair-do," in the words of one staffer, she appeared more conservative, less brash.[103] More important, she knew not to challenge her boss; she was a loyal employee and not an activist, a distinction that had apparently too often escaped Costanza. Some women's rights supporters feared that, at best, Weddington was a token in spite of her title or that, at worst, she would be too afraid of confrontation to advance her cause. Weddington appeared to lend credence to this concern when she told the press, "My primary loyalty is to the President." She acknowledged that "feminists have been critical of the administration" but insisted that "I don't think it was [Carter's] fault."[104] Most feminists, however, were willing to give Weddington the benefit of the doubt, hoping that if nothing else her prominence in the famous abortion case would give the ERA a push.

Costanza was philosophical. Writing to Carter, she explained that she thought they shared the same concerns but that "it is clear that our approaches to fulfilling them are different." It was "not my style," she understated, "not to voice my own opinions and ideas openly." She continued to claim that Carter supported human rights but explained to activists that he was just so "uncomfortable on [gay rights]."[105] In an ironic twist, Costanza appeared a team player in her resignation, informing gay rights advocates that the White House still received the leading gay newspaper, the *Advocate*, and that the gay rights movement should not lose all hope in the administration. Joining Costanza in resigning was her assistant, Marilyn Haft, another strong advocate for abortion and homosexual rights who left to become deputy counsel to Mondale. Assuming the responsibilities for serving as the liaison to the homosexual community was Bob Malson of Carter's Domestic Policy Staff. Staffer Wexler remained in contact with homosexual groups as well, although Weddington clearly hoped that the issue would fade. Malson and Wexler undoubtedly shared many of Costanza's sentiments but had no plans to stress abortion and homosexual rights in the manner she did. They were part of a team whose job it was to help Carter fulfill his objectives, not advance specific causes that they might personally champion.[106]

If many feminists interpreted Costanza's resignation as further evidence that the administration was, in the end, not a trustworthy ally, conservative Christians almost uniformly applauded the development. Regardless, events in the late summer swept the resignation out of the headlines. Costanza's ouster, the White House's realignment, and, in fact, almost all domestic matters appeared to pale in comparison to what followed. On September 17, 1978, after twelve days of secret meetings, Carter achieved his most notable diplomatic success, the famous Camp David Accords. With Israel agreeing to withdraw from the Sinai and Egypt agreeing to recognize the right of Israel to exist, the Camp David Accords ensured peace between the two longtime enemies, with a formal treaty signing scheduled for early the following year. With Israeli prime minister Begin and Egyptian president Sadat working with him, Carter understood that the accords were a major accomplishment for his administration. The agreement signaled a significant milestone not only in the relations between the two countries but also in the larger hope for peace between the Jewish and Islamic peoples of the region.[107]

As one might expect, the overall reaction from the American religious community was positive. Religion had never been far below the surface both in the dispute and in the new resolution. Carter's understanding of his own faith added to his respect for others, historian and sociologist Michael Lindsay concluded, a critical ingredient in the negotiations. As Carter recalled, "When I got to Camp David with Begin and Sadat, Doug Coe [leader of an international Christian fellowship] suggested that the three of us should issue a worldwide call for prayer that we would be successful. . . . [T]hat was the first thing we did at Camp David."[108] Accordingly, as *Christianity Today* reported, the Camp David Accords "had as religious an atmosphere as it did political."[109] After the agreement the Southern Baptist Convention forwarded a statement of congratulations to the White House. In a letter of thanks signed only "Jimmy," Carter replied, "I deeply appreciate the support of people of goodwill from across the Nation and around the world."[110]

As the occasional letter of protest had indicated during the negotiations, however, the reaction was not uniformly positive. The fear that Carter had hurt Israel and thus God's interests remained among some conservative Christians. The Camp David Accords had direct implications for believers in the dispensationalist, premillennial view that a complete restoration of ancient Israel was necessary for Jesus's Second Coming. What did the accords suggest about the prophecy of Armageddon? Looking to the end of the world, Pat Robertson melded the agreement into his theological worldview. The agreement did not counter the predictions of the book of Revelation, Robertson began to argue. Iraq and Syria would soon join Egypt in making peace with Israel, which would, in turn, prompt an attack by the Soviet Union. It was all part of God's plan. The final grand battle was near; Jesus would come again soon.[111]

The Camp David Accords complicated Falwell's message. "To stand against Israel is to stand against God," Jerry Falwell now regularly preached. American foreign policy should always encourage Israel's rise. At the same time, however, faith should always encourage peace, and the Camp David Accords were an undeniable step in that direction. Moreover, many of his followers clearly applauded the agreement. Unsure of how to react, Falwell was vague. The agreement, he stated, "was negotiated in good faith by men of goodwill." It was "the best agreement which could have been achieved given the conditions in the world in general and in the region in particular." If credit were due, however, it fell to Sadat and Begin more than Carter. Begin "was a good friend," but Carter was merely "support."[112] Even as much of the world—liberals and conservatives alike—praised Carter's efforts, Falwell could not find it in himself to join the chorus. Despite Costanza's departure and the relatively quiet summer, his relationship with Carter had already deteriorated beyond repair.

Carter declared October 7, 1978, the National Day of Prayer. It might as well have been the starting pistol for a new round of controversy. If the summer months had passed with relatively little turmoil over issues such as abortion, the ERA, and homosexual rights, in the fall they returned with a vengeance, Carter once again apparently caught in the dilemma of trying to reconcile the irreconcilable. Seeking to build on its momentum with conservative Christians, the White House sent to a number of ministers letters announcing the day of prayer.[113] Just over seven weeks later, on the eve of Thanksgiving, Carter hosted over three hundred religious leaders, including many members of the NRB, denied a meeting in January, for a dinner at the White House. The entertainment included the British actor Alec McCowen reciting the Gospel of Mark. The one-man show on a small stage constructed for the buffet was part of a celebration of the thirty-eighth annual National Bible Week. After the performance Carter thanked all for attending and remarked that he had spent the previous night rereading the Gospel of Mark in anticipation of McCowen's performance. He reminded the crowd of the importance of family and added that afterward he planned to leave for Camp David to share the holiday with thirty-three members of his own extended family.[114]

If Carter's overtures sought to build momentum with the conservative religious community, another of his goals ensured that he would make little headway. Only days after the National Day of Prayer Congress passed a joint resolution extending the deadline for ERA ratification almost three and a half years, until June 30, 1982.[115] It was another Carter victory in the wake of the Camp David Accords, but, unlike the accords, there was no ambiguity in the reaction of conservative Christians. Carter had lobbied hard for the extension, apparently shedding his administration's fear of influencing a matter constitutionally left to the states or, in his words, appearing a "nosy Washington outsider" to those still debating. He had sent a personal message to the legislatures of each of the fifteen states that had yet to ratify the amendment. When the extension resolution passed, Carter signed it with another plea for ratification. He was as forceful in his comments as he had ever been before while noting the achievements his administration claimed. Carter's actions were unusual; a joint resolution did not require a presidential signature. Carter simply took the chance to reiterate his support.[116]

After passage of the extension resolution, Carter publicized his efforts with women's rights advocates, undoubtedly aware of their growing skepti-

cism. The White House claimed that Carter's and Mondale's personal lobbying had "turned seven 'no' votes into pro-votes to pass the extension."[117]
It was true, and together with the way Carter now publicly touted his role,
it infuriated conservative Christians. For them, at least, it seemed to fly in
direct contrast to the National Day of Prayer, National Bible Week, and
Carter's own professions of love for family. Costanza's demotion, Falwell
recalled, was "surprising but certainly welcomed." White House announcements of days of prayer or Bible weeks were "expected and appropriate."
They suggested that maybe, after all, Carter was "still unwilling to go way
over the edge."[118] Nevertheless, at least for Falwell, the administration had
confirmed once again that when it came to matters of real policy such as the
ERA, Carter was no ally.

At the same time, however, it was soon clear that the extension victory
did little to assuage feminists, many of whom, like Falwell, saw no ally in
Carter. When Abzug insisted on additional funding for the NACW, the White
House resisted. To make matters worse, Weddington decided to assume
the chairmanship of the IDTFW in addition to her broader duties. As such,
she sought to develop a working relationship with the NACW. Still reeling
from her friend Costanza's dismissal, however, Abzug would have little of
it. When Weddington asked to attend a meeting of the NACW, Abzug said
no. Her committee should have direct access to Carter and not have to work
through Weddington. This rebuff, then, set the tone for future relations. In
November Abzug and her fellow NACW members requested a meeting with
Carter and his cabinet for the first anniversary of the IWY conference. They
sought a long meeting to discuss the administration's decision to cut the
budget to fight inflation, a decision that the NACW viewed as falling on poor
women. Weddington, however, said that the committee could have only fifteen minutes with the president the day after that requested, the last working day before the Thanksgiving holiday. The committee could, however,
have additional time with her or Wexler. This infuriated Abzug even more,
but she acquiesced, fearful that Carter would assume any additional strain
was her fault. Other members of the NACW, however, were not so reticent
and voted to refuse to meet at all with Carter on Weddington's schedule.
Their letter of regret, directed to Carter and released to the press, declared,
"We are particularly mindful that your Administration's priorities are being
shaped without any reference to how they will affect women." Even without
such strong words, an advisory committee canceling a meeting with a sitting president was unprecedented and an obvious slap.[119]

Weddington appeared conciliatory in public—an obvious attempt to minimize damage to the White House—and scheduled for the NACW a public meeting with Carter after January 1. The rift, however, had clearly grown quite wide. Only days after Thanksgiving, committee members again criticized Carter at a Democratic midterm convention in Memphis. In short, Abzug and her NACW allies seemed as determined as Falwell to denounce Carter. Costanza's departure and Carter's obviously growing friction with her ideological successor had, it appeared, done little to placate most conservative preachers. The ERA extension had, simultaneously, proved equally unimpressive to many of their political opponents.[120]

All sides looked to the ballot box, of course. The end of 1978 brought not only an off-year congressional election but also in California the long-anticipated referendum on the Briggs Initiative to ban homosexual school-teachers. On one side, a number of conservative ministers felt empowered. As the summer had passed, the IRS had responded to public pressure and reached an agreement with a key congressional subcommittee not to carry out immediately its desegregation enforcement on private schools, once again placing the matter on the proverbial shelf on which it had rested for the previous eight years. This was not enough for North Carolina senator Jesse Helms, however, who demanded further assurance. Using the congressional power of the purse, he pushed through in the fall an amendment denying the use of federal funds for investigating or enforcing the regulations. His efforts, predictably, thrilled many pastors who, according to Falwell, had "offered key individual and personal support."[121] Now, with the Briggs Initiative and the congressional election approaching, the same ministers readied to flex their muscles again.

On the other side, the homosexual and abortion rights lobbies mobilized as well. After Carter finally relented and declared his opposition to the Briggs Initiative, Harvey Milk and his colleagues pressed for more. The Civil Service Commission had followed an antidiscrimination policy since litigation had forced its hand just before Carter took office, and the newly signed Civil Service Reform Act had excluded discrimination in government hiring for nonsensitive positions based on private behavior. While the CSC had operated as though the law covered homosexuality, no statute had explicitly codified the group as a class. Milk and others, therefore, fearing a reversal of CSC policy, pressed Carter for redress. If the White House did not act, "the Hill," in the words of one aide, might move first and embarrass the president. Moreover, the homosexual lobby continued, Carter should end litigation, which had gone on for over a year, and order the Bureau of Prisons to revise its policy denying the distribution of gay literature. There was a need for a "more cooperative relationship," the NGTF wrote, implying that the alternative was ballot retribution. Carter, the message was clear, should not take the gay and lesbian vote for granted.[122]

Carter, of course, received a great deal of criticism from conservative Christians for opposing the Briggs Initiative. William Hann, president of the Southern Baptist General Convention of California, wrote Carter in early November that the president's stance "hurts us." Church members had worked hard for the proposition, just as all good Christians should. "Christians and even non-Christians alike are wondering why Southern Baptists are not together on moral issues." Hann included gay literature in his letter and noted to Carter, "I feel you would not want your daughter exposed to this any more than we do."[123] The White House's reply was polite but curt. "We have noted your comments and assure you that the president appreciates your interest in this legislation," read the form letter.[124] A month later, Hann's group mailed the White House a resolution it had passed and also forwarded it to former California governor Ronald Reagan, who the group obviously anticipated would make another run for the White House. The resolution "expresses our grave disappointment to President Jimmy Carter for his public opposition to an issue so strongly supported by his fellow Christians and Baptists."[125] The implication was, once again, ballot retribution.

For the congressional elections, pundits predicted that because of recent media attention and the fact that Watergate and the Vietnam War had faded, abortion would play the critical role so many people had predicted in 1976. A number of recent state elections had turned on abortion, and there appeared little to mute the issue in the national campaigns. Indeed, abortion appeared influential in a number of primaries as a new wave of politicians with firm positions challenged many incumbents still trying to straddle the middle. In Iowa, for example, Minette Doderer, a longtime leading political figure, lost the primary election for lieutenant governor. "It was the Right-to-Lifers," she acknowledged. "They won every race they were in."[126] According to the Associated Press, Massachusetts, "long regarded as one of the most liberal states politically," has experienced "the force of a conservative movement that embraces . . . restrictions on abortion." Abortion had even played a role in local elections that had little or nothing to do with the issue.[127]

With every congressman campaigning, the Vatican announced that the Catholic Church would excommunicate doctors who performed abortions. This obviously surpassed the National Conference of Catholic Bishop's earlier refusal to endorse the ERA, if not tying the two issues together in the minds of the Catholic flock. It was all too much for former First Lady Betty Ford, who again went public with her prochoice stance, noting as evidence of her interest the fact that she and the former president had a daughter.[128] Carter, however, remained relatively quiet as the elections approached. Other than pressing for the ERA, he largely avoided the issues of abortion and homosexual rights, undoubtedly frustrating those on both sides.

If anything, religion in all of its political manifestations continued to confound Carter. Just before the election a Southern Baptist named Hans Mullikin arrived at the White House gates. In an attempt to win souls for Jesus, Mullikin had spent two years crawling the sixteen hundred miles from his house to Washington, D.C. Assuming the effort was an inconsequential stunt, White House staffers did not realize the publicity Mullikin had garnered or the negative press their refusal to meet with him would receive. The prominent Baptist minister James Dunn, among others, protested. "[Mullikin] was told by one of your aides that you were too busy to see him," Dunn wrote Carter. "I realize that there are thousands of people who would like to see you, but of all people, you have been calling our country to humble themselves and pray, and here is a man who has done exactly what you have suggested over and over, and you could not take five minutes to meet with a fellow Baptist." Dunn went on to complain about Carter's policies on homosexual rights, suggesting that he assumed Carter would "throw equality at me." He was only stating God's word, Dunn concluded, and "I understand that you are only human."[129]

Once again Carter could not catch a break. Joining Mullikin in the news as the election approached was an odd dispute with the Church of Scientology. Although the church represented a cult to many conservative Christians, the controversy brought Carter more unfortunate headlines. After the South African government two years before had imprisoned two black "Scientologists," the FBI had begun its own scrutiny. The result was a raid into the church's American offices and, subsequently, a lawsuit by church leaders. The litigation came to a head just before the election and, although the FBI successfully defended itself, criticism poured into the White House. The noted jazz musician Chick Corea, for one, complained to Carter of "a vendetta by the Justice Department against my church."[130] Such criticism resonated across the spectrum of conservative denominations, already wary of the administration because of the IRS. While most conservative Christians had no love for the Church of Scientology, the entire incident suggested again a Carter administration willing to strong-arm religious groups. If the government were able to raid the Church of Scientology, then they too might be at risk. It was a matter of religious freedom.[131]

Carter still had no coordinated strategy to deal with religious-related issues, but two years in office had certainly taught him the difficulty attached to them. When his evangelist sister Ruth Stapleton scheduled an appearance at a Long Island convention of a Hebrew-Christian group, a group of Jews proclaiming Jesus's divinity, Carter contacted her about the political implications. It would surely anger the Jewish community, he noted. Stapleton agreed to cancel her appearance but denied that Carter had instructed her to do so: "He said he knew Jesus would guide me in what I must do."[132] At the same time, Carter agreed to meet with a group of Democrats, knowing full well that they sought to use religion to their political advantage. "The Congressional Black Caucus," District of Columbia congressman Walter Fauntroy wrote Carter, "has given me the responsibility of organizing black churchmen into a more cohesive [political] force." With the congressional elections approaching, African American ministers could coordinate an effective "get-out-the-vote effort."[133] Inside the White House aide Martha Mitchell encouraged the meeting despite Carter's well-known reservations. "One of the major objectives," she wrote, "is to organize Black churches in preparation for 1980."[134] As a result, several weeks before the November vote Carter met with the Black Clergy Planning Committee.[135] For her part, aide Wexler solicited the help of Jimmy Allen of the Southern Baptist Convention. In a laudatory letter Wexler wrote that Carter "can only be effective if we have the active assistance of influential people like yourself." Thanking Allen for his support, Wexler inquired when Allen would be in Washington and expressed her hopes for a meeting: "I am interested in hearing your ideas on how we might better mobilize the public on behalf of the President's priorities."[136] All of this suggested that while Carter still believed that an overt, coordinated campaign to use religion to win elections was a cynical betrayal of his faith, he had learned from his frustrations. According to advisor Eizenstat, by the 1978 elections Carter had grown more politically sophisticated. "Early on, he was very much, 'I only want to know what the best policy is and I'll worry about the politics of it later,'" Eizenstat recalled. "Later on those kind of bravado statements tended to disappear and he wanted to know what could pass, what we could get through, what did this committee chairman want, what did this interest group want. That was a function of worrying more about the reelection as we got closer to it."[137]

When Election Day, November 7, arrived, it must have been hard for Carter not to think of his own reelection. The results appeared an omen. While the incumbent party usually lost seats during off-year elections, a clear shift to the political right was evident. Republicans gained three senators, twelve congressmen, and six governors.[138] According to the National Right to Life Committee, five Senate seats switched from the abortion rights column to the antiabortion column. In the New Hampshire, Colorado, Minnesota, and Iowa contests, the effect of the abortion issue was most obvious. In the last of these, a group called the Pro-Life Action Council fought Senator Dick Clark because he refused to support a constitutional amendment on the issue. The council submitted three hundred thousand anti-Clark leaflets the Sunday before the election, and most observers argued that the leaflets turned the tide against him. In New York a newly reconstituted Right to Life Party attracted more than one hundred thousand votes for its candidate for governor, Mary Jane Tobin. This surprising result assured the party a place on all New York ballots for the next four years. After the election Tobin, whose campaign was managed by the veteran antiabortion protester Ellen McCormick, argued that her purpose was to force candidates to go on record regarding their abortion views. There could be no compromise; even elections for local tax assessors would face a litmus test on abortion. Surveying the 1978 election results, columnist Anthony Lewis recognized the connection the abortion issue had with other growing conservative causes. The election result, he wrote, "suggests that the anti-abortion sentiment goes along with a mood of resentment against Big Government." This was ironic because the advocates of smaller government were, in this instance at least, the very ones pushing for more federal restrictions. Nevertheless, the growing convergence of the various strains of conservative reform continued to foretell significant change to the American political system.[139]

On the surface at least, the Briggs Initiative appeared a salve to social liberals. The referendum to ban homosexual teachers failed 58 percent to 42 percent. Even in this regard, however, a growing social conservatism was evident. Reflecting on the vote, one homosexual lobbyist admitted that the opposition to Briggs had worked to make the election about discrimination, not homosexuality itself: "If it gets down to a plebiscite on homosexu-

ality, we lose."[140] In addition, Ronald Reagan, hardly a champion of homosexual rights, campaigned against Briggs. He did not want to encourage
homosexual activity, he explained, but saw the issue through a libertarian
perspective. Simply put, it was not the role of government, which resonated
among conservatives. When the results arrived, the gay and lesbian community celebrated through the night, the celebration itself winning national
publicity. "It was a valuable energizer for the movement," crowed one gay
rights lobbyist. It was also an engine for the social conservatives, who some
claimed had been complacent and overconfident after their victory in Miami. They were not about to make the same mistake again.[141]

The gay community's celebration did not last long. The Briggs Initiative
had conferred on Milk the particular aura of historical celebrity, and the
night of the victorious vote he led the raucous party, calling once again for
Carter to speak out. He called for a massive march on Washington the following year to force the president's hand. One of Milk's opponents, however,
had a different idea. Dan White, a former colleague of Milk's on the Board
of Supervisors, found the vote repulsive. Before his resignation he had
clashed with Milk at almost every meeting. On November 27 White took
a .38 caliber police revolver and crawled through an open window at city
hall to avoid the metal detectors. After shooting Mayor George Moscone,
White headed to Milk's office and murdered him as well. He then fled to
St. Mary's Cathedral before ultimately turning himself in to police. In the
trial that followed White admitted that he had committed the murders out
of alarm over the growing strength of the city's gay community. When his
sentence was only four to twelve years in state prison, protesters marched
with banners claiming that White had gotten away with murder.[142] In the
interim, predictably, Milk had assumed the status of martyr. "Civil rights
or civil war!" chanted more militant gays and lesbians. Eerily anticipating
the chance of both his murder and subsequent violence, Milk had recorded
a tape imploring his followers to channel their energy more positively in
Washington. Alas, it was not to be. The White Night Riots set for Carter a
tone as ominous as the election results.[143]

As this drama unfolded, the nation got another reminder that in matters of religion and morality, violence could lurk below the surface. On November 18 the tragic deaths of over nine hundred followers of the People's
Temple in Guyana shocked the world. Founded by Jim Jones, the church
had moved from California to Guyana the previous year both to establish a

religious society separate from the world's influence and to free itself from a possible tax investigation. After reports surfaced that the colony, known as Jonestown, had brainwashed and restrained its members, California congressman Leo Ryan flew down to South America to investigate. Jonestown security guards assassinated Ryan, which precipitated a Jones-orchestrated mass suicide. Across the nation newspapers carried front-page pictures of bodies by the hundreds lying bloated next to barrels of poisoned purple Kool-Aid. This quickly raised a public outcry for a crackdown on cults and, for the Carter administration, shades of the Scientology dispute and charges of government interference in religion. Carter did not want his administration, once burned, embroiled again in a similar dispute. The Justice Department, as a result, promised an investigation into the Jonestown tragedy but resisted a broader sweep of religious cults. It was a matter of religious freedom, Carter still insisted.[144]

For Carter, the election results, along with the Milk and Jonestown tragedies, set the tone for the end of the year. His second year in office ended no better than his first. When Carter announced that the United States would, on the first day of 1979, fully recognize the People's Republic of China, pundits seemed to forget that the recognition was the work of bipartisanship and two former presidents. For many conservatives, it was simply another example of Carter weakening the nation's defenses. When Carter agreed to travel to Salt Lake City over Thanksgiving to accept the Family Unity Award from the Mormon Church, criticism found him again. The trip appeared an obvious chance to remind the public that religion was not about angry confrontation or mass suicide but family, one of his true concerns and one of his signature issues. Nevertheless, if it proved a reminder of anything, it was that controversy always surrounded the issue of family. After a bitter internal debate the Mormon leadership had passed a resolution opposing the ERA as a threat to the family. With Carter's trip approaching, both sides lobbied the White House to comment on the debate.[145] "The passion for defeating the ERA as an anti-family evil is only in the minds of the leadership in Salt Lake City," the group Mormons for the ERA wrote Carter.[146] Aware of the correspondence, a staffer warned Weddington, "President Carter's appearance in Utah is already being perceived by the media and the members as acceptance of the Church's actions and position in regard to the ERA." The White House should "refute this notion clearly." In his remarks Carter might consider "making a case for his own concern for the family and the importance of the ERA in lending support to the family by strengthening individual family members."[147] Weddington agreed and sent Carter a memo concluding, "It would be good if you could even contribute to neutralizing their fear of the consequences of ERA."[148]

It was more of the same: more controversy, more criticism, and for Carter, more careful balancing of his rhetoric and actions. In the end, Carter decided against directly raising the issue of the ERA in his Utah remarks. As he had done before, he stressed in general terms the importance of the family and the threats that it faced, carefully avoiding any mention of abortion, homosexuality, and the ERA. He noted that "the church was my first family." Recounting Mormon history, however, Carter also noted that the college the religion had established was one of the first to educate women. "The State Constitution recognized in 1896 that women and men should have the same civil, political and religious rights and privileges," he added. "And we are trying now to spread that same commitment throughout our entire Nation."[149] Nowhere in his remarks did Carter directly advocate passage of any law or amendment. On its surface it was an homage to both the Mormons and the institution of the family. As everyone undoubtedly perceived, however, Carter's allusions walked a fine line in the hope of avoiding further controversy.

The results were more of the same. As 1978 ended, the brief joy among feminists that Congress had passed an extension for ERA ratification had begun to fade in the harsh light of the uphill struggle that still loomed, many activists still reeling from Costanza's departure. *Time* magazine reported that supporters of abortion rights were "in retreat" and blamed Carter.[150] Reflecting on the twelve months since their Houston conference, veterans of IWY acknowledged that recent developments had proved a "tragic defeat." It was obvious, one argued, that the women's movement had "missed the boat on abortion."[151] Their ideological cousins, the gay rights movement, remained in mourning over Milk's murder, his overt criticism of Carter just before his death still resonating. At the same time, however, it was more obvious than ever that Carter's first two years had disappointed growing numbers of conservative Christians. Illinois congressman John Anderson, who two years later would pose a third-party challenge to the incumbent, submitted an article to *Christianity Today*. Despite Carter's "good intentions," Anderson wrote, "his faith and virtue were not enough." Christians had placed great hope in Carter, but his "lack of experience had proved too difficult to overcome."[152]

By the end of 1978 it had been two long years since Carter's election, two bitter years of frustration and dashed hopes since the Year of the Evangelical.
Carter, with his faith his strength, remained resilient, still hopeful that he
could right the ship of state before his term expired. Behind the headlines,
however, a new reality slowly continued to form, a new political culture
that for Carter suggested that his continued optimism was unfounded. Few
spoke of a "Religious Right" by the end of 1978, but in retrospect the battles
over the previous twenty-four months—the frustrations born of abortion,
homosexuality, feminism, and the ERA, education and secular humanism,
and, as always, foreign policy—had laid a strong foundation for the movement. With Carter's political coalition fracturing, the roots for a new Republican alliance had begun to grow in its place.

Brown University historian William McLoughlin wrote in 1978 that a
"fourth Great Awakening" in American history was under way. With new
issues of gender and sexuality dominating religious discourse, the changing
dynamic promised to "restructure the general will."[153] By 1978 it was obvious
that the Year of the Evangelical was only the beginning. Polls indicated that
the number of Americans self-identifying as evangelical continued to swell.
According to one observer, Carter deserved much credit for "popularizing
the born-again movement," but the greatest growth remained among conservatives fearful of society's dynamism.[154] The evidence was everywhere.
Early in the year Southern Baptist Seminary in Louisville announced a new
doctoral program in evangelicalism, the first accredited seminary in the
nation to do so. During Mardi Gras in New Orleans over three hundred
young evangelicals fanned out across the French Quarter to win converts,
the largest Christian outreach ever during the famous celebration. A new
Bible translation designed for evangelicals sold more than 1.2 million copies
within only four weeks of its publication, breaking all records. Don Hillis,
associate director of conference ministries for the Evangelical Alliance Mission, noted approvingly that sixty thousand young people now studied at
Bible colleges and claimed that evangelical outreach in the United States
"far surpasses that of any other country."[155]

"I am far from predicting the demise of ecumenical Protestantism," author Donald Tinder wrote, but "the liberalizing winds" of recent years had
generated a need for something firm and absolute, an unchanging truth
strong enough to weather changing societal mores. The result solidified as a
defining doctrine in many churches issues of sexual liberation, among others. Concerns for the traditional family assumed a more prominent role in a

conservative theology that stretched across traditional religious lines. Issues surrounding modernity in a sense reshuffled the theological cards, splitting liberals from conservatives in a number of religions even as it brought conservatives together. The "inerrancy question," in the words of *Christianity Today*, ensured not only that the "older traditional denominations would barely hold their own" but also that a "new independent, conservative ecumenicalism" would continue to grow. Applauded one conservative evangelical, "Christianity now has a moral backbone."[156]

Again, the evidence by 1978 was manifold. When Paramount Pictures released in the summer a new movie starring Warren Beatty, *Heaven Can Wait*, it hoped to win a large evangelical audience and even distributed free tickets to pastors. The movie performed poorly at the box office, however, despite the endorsement by a number of liberal ministers in the National Council of Churches. Conservative pastors explained that the result was understandable; the film depicted an afterlife hardly represented in the Bible, an affront to true Christians.[157] In a more serious vein, Oxford scholar James Barr published a new book that put the ascendant theological conservatism into context. Modernity, he argued, had produced critical analysis of the Bible, which in turn had led to "nominal Christians" accepting a degree of religious relativism. This higher criticism undercut the need for faith and in reaction produced a new fundamentalism that insisted upon a rigid doctrine.[158]

In the middle of 1978 the Logos International Fellowship, a religious publisher, and the People of Hope, a New Jersey evangelical congregation, organized Jesus '78, a large religious revival in New Jersey's Meadowland Stadium. The purpose, the groups claimed, was to unite evangelicals and conservatives across denominational lines to share fellowship and win souls for the Lord. Catholics and Protestants of all stripes had to unite, they claimed, because the modern age posed threats that transcended traditional divides. "Nobody could have gotten us together . . . except the spirit of God," remarked Catholic bishop Peter Gerety of Newark, one of the speakers.[159] "Relations between Catholics and Protestants have greatly improved after decades of mutual suspicion and resentment," the *New York Times* concluded. Many in both camps now found common cause in the dynamics of the present day. The changes promised a "continued trend toward orthodoxy." Moreover, the newspaper noted, the Catholic Church was becoming more evangelistic, a characteristic that resembled many of the Protestant denominations. In the words of Archbishop Francis Hurley, the new evangelism focused more on "daily living experiences," in short, specific issues facing the present. Billy Graham agreed to a crusade at the University of Notre Dame and spoke in glowing terms of Catholics such as Mother Teresa. He had never asked anyone to renounce their past religious allegiance, Graham claimed, and assured his audience that he was not asking them to break from Rome.[160] Indeed, the famed evangelist thought the time was right to approach members of the Jewish faith, again seeking common cause in the challenges facing the world. Speaking to the American Jewish Committee's executive council in his first public address to a national Jewish group, Graham spoke of the "debt I owed to Israel, to Judaism, and to the Jewish people." Tensions between evangelical Protestantism and Judaism, he concluded, should be a thing of the past.[161] Later in the year a group of several hundred Protestant clergy across the denominational spectrum met in Illinois to draft a position paper on the importance of the Bible, later dubbed the "Chicago Statement on Biblical Inerrancy." The group shied away from potentially divisive specifics but declared that "scripture is without error or fault." On this they could all agree.[162]

Not all tensions, of course, had evaporated, as Carter well knew. When, for example, Carter announced an envoy to the Vatican, Baptist leader Jimmy Allen telegraphed his protest to the White House: "I regret your decision to continue the practice of appointing a personal envoy to the Vatican." It violated the First Amendment, Allen concluded, and amounted to special recognition of one individual faith. Four months later a group of Georgia Baptists signed a petition protesting Carter's appointment of Catholics to the Federal Communications Commission. It appeared the signers worried that a Catholic-dominated FCC would hinder the growing televised ministries of ministers such as Jerry Falwell. "Please appoint another faith or non [sic] at all," the petition read. "What's wrong with a Southern Baptist?"[163]

Nevertheless, the mutual concern for the family was hard to ignore. "We have begun to develop some unity," Dr. C. Brownlow Hastings, a Baptist pastor, remarked as the Hyde Amendment debate raged. "We are movingly encountering each other as brothers and sisters in Christ," Catholic bishop Bernard Shaw agreed. The Second Vatican Council had just emphasized interchurch relations, and a new organization, the Catholic-Baptist Ecumenical Institute in Winston-Salem, North Carolina, now worked to find common ground. Abortion was an obvious force to unite them. As 1978 began, the Reverend Charles LaFontaine acknowledged that positions on abortion had "hardened" since Carter's election but optimistically saw the fight against abortion as an issue that "transcended denominational and interfaith lines" and might encourage "ecumenism." Writing an article in the *New York Times*, LaFontaine pointed out that while much of the nation saw the fight against abortion as a "Catholic issue," conservatives in the American Catholic Church were now a minority, while in the evangelical Protestant faiths conservative strength was clearly growing. The article noted approvingly a "recent conference on abortion at the Graymore [New York] Ecumenical Institute." After condemning abortion, participants "went away friends, at least friendlier than before."[164]

The manner in which critics of abortion, homosexuality, and feminism equated all three as part of a larger threat to the traditional family contributed to conservative cohesion. There was, after all, power in numbers. Falwell, for example, learned quickly that working with activists across individual issues not only raised his own profile but assured a broader impact. "It was important to speak of ERA, the *Roe* decision, and protections for homosexuals as examples of laws contrary to the traditional American family," Falwell recalled. "It helped marshal the troops."[165] Like many Protestant pastors, Falwell had not traditionally focused on abortion. When the physician C. Everett Koop and the evangelist Francis Schaeffer, however, produced in 1978 a film and book denouncing abortion entitled *What Ever Happened to the Human Race?* Falwell thought their efforts superb. He congratulated them and soon became "close friends" with Schaeffer. The film and the press it received from pastors such as Falwell, historian Susan Field Harding concluded, "was widely credited with turning the tide of popular opinion against abortion."[166] "The traditional family is being threatened as never before in the history of the nation," Falwell now regularly claimed, listing abortion as one of the many evils society faced.[167]

Falwell loved to tie feminism, abortion, and homosexuality to the extremes of the counterculture of the 1960s. "Those who promote the Equal Rights Amendment were the same ones in the vanguard of the pro-abortion [movement] and . . . are still there. And they were in the anti–Vietnam War marches and they are the anti–nuclear power people and you know what they are saying," Falwell told his congregation.[168] Painting with broad strokes, Falwell never let Carter off easy. White House support for the Hyde Amendment "didn't win [Carter] a great deal of support," Falwell recalled, ignoring the fact that he had contacted his colleagues to ensure that very result. In 1978 Falwell was reluctant to join fellow ministers in protesting the new IRS regulations and enforcement, offering as an explanation, "We were totally integrated from the beginning." In reality, he later acknowledged, he worried that his earlier "Ministers and Marchers" sermon had placed him on the wrong side of history. If he joined the fight over the IRS, his critics could easily brand him a racist segregationist. The protest, however, caught fire, and it was apparent that he alone remained silent. In a "mood of common resistance," one columnist recalled, "representatives from Protestant, Roman Catholic, and Jewish bodies joined forces . . . to denounce the proposal."[169] Falwell quickly shifted course and sang with the chorus. The administration, he now echoed, was "seeking to control private and Christian schools."[170]

In any event, Falwell did not miss another opportunity to join forces with the like-minded, his many comments mimicking his colleagues. In the words of one biographer, Falwell covered his bases. He recognized the "dangerous influences" of "the use of humanistic textbooks, the expounding of evolution as fact, and the absence of prayer and patriotism in curriculum."[171] When Carter proposed the Department of Education, Falwell sounded like Connie Marshner or Robert Billings: "It was going to be a huge bureaucracy that takes control out of local school districts and moves it to Washington where the liberals can control it." It promised to "become a big monster."[172]

In her fight against homosexuality Anita Bryant moved quickly to embrace Falwell and other conservative pastors. At the recommendation of one of her admirers Bryant telephoned Falwell about her efforts in Miami. Falwell then invited Bryant and her husband and manager, Bob Green, to Lynchburg, where on a Saturday afternoon they barbecued in Falwell's backyard. While several of his friends advised him not to get involved, Falwell explained that he saw homosexuality as just one example of a larger threat to the family and had no choice but to react. The next day, a Sunday, Bryant spoke to an overflow crowd at Thomas Road Baptist Church and appeared on *The Old Time Gospel Hour*. God told him to go to Miami, Falwell told his audience. Ten days later over ten thousand people filled the Miami Beach Convention Center to hear Falwell, Bryant, and several other conservative pastors speak, the most for any religious gathering there since Billy Graham had visited in the 1950s. The crowd gave the speakers a standing ovation. Falwell spoke eloquently but was noticeably ill and had to be rushed by ambulance to the hospital just after the rally. Bryant was effusive in her praise and credited Falwell as an important factor in finally defeating the gay rights ordinance. "Dr. Jerry Falwell was one of the few preachers in this country whom [sic] openly rallied to our cause," she stated, although in reality he was far from alone.[173] The obvious crowds and the success of the Miami campaign guaranteed that at every subsequent rally or protest conservative clergy were at the fore. Impressed by the response as much as his colleagues were, Falwell ensured that homosexuality remained a center-piece of his agenda. It was, he wrote, "a symptom of a sin-sick society" that "at its root was a rebellion against God."[174] Treating homosexuals as equals would lead to the acceptance of rape and adultery and destroy the family. After Harvey Milk's murder Falwell was blunt, concluding, "Without question, San Francisco is undergoing a judgement from God today."[175] When several other conservative ministers repeated this charge, Milk's followers protested, and a rhetorical retreat followed. Many pastors insisted that their religions did not hate homosexuals, only that they were "people blinded by Satan, the God of this world." By 1978 many congregations had established counseling centers to help gays and lesbians recover and repent.[176]

In the long battle over the ERA, a number of conservative ministers rallied to the side of Phyllis Schlafly, their rhetoric remarkably similar. "It was a broad and well-coordinated campaign," Falwell recalled. Schlafly "engineered the state-by-state efforts but we offered all of our resources." Leading pastors were on the phone with Schlafly "constantly." She "was the quarterback but we carried the ball." The ultimate defeat of the ERA several years later "was another big victory for people of faith in this country," contributing mightily to "drawing the faithful into politics." In short, the ERA, like abortion and homosexuality, "brought the faithful together."[177]

With theological conservatism a force for unity, two additional trends were obvious by the midpoint of Carter's presidency. First, those ministers that chose to lead the charge grew enormously in stature and wealth. Second, the growing unity facilitated a parallel partisanship. The more conservative Christians coordinated to save the nuclear family, the more they turned to the Republican Party. The Carter administration now had a two-year record that for many conservative Christians strengthened a sense that the Democrats, in their zeal to lead the rights revolution, had championed immorality. Their sense of disillusionment in Carter, so profound given their initial expectations, had left a void that the Grand Old Party was more than willing to fill. As Carter hoped to prove a political phoenix in the second half of his term, the ascendant preachers' flirtations with Republican operatives and organizations signaled a growing theological unity with political teeth.

Falwell, for one, had certainly benefited from Carter's first two years. After graduating its largest class ever in 1978, 403 students, his Liberty Baptist College welcomed more than a thousand freshmen the following fall. Fund-raising exploded, $2.5 million arriving in February 1978, the most successful month to date. On "Miracle Day," September 24, 1978, $7 million arrived. It may have been a "miracle" in Falwell's words, but he had worked hard for it, campaigning during his travels and on his televised broadcasts. Liberty Baptist College underwent a construction boom, including new classrooms, an administration building, and a large gymnasium.[178] In April 1978 Falwell was among a handful of leading religious leaders invited to the Middle East by the Israeli and Egyptian governments. The group traveled first to Cairo and from there on an Egyptian jet south to meet Sadat. They then traveled to Amman, Jordan, and then to Israel. Falwell's reputation, it appeared, had preceded him overseas.[179] The secular press began to notice Falwell more, *Esquire* magazine describing him in 1978 as the "next Billy Graham."[180] Aware of his growing stature, Falwell thought himself important enough to submit a report on his trip to the Carter administration and then feel snubbed when the report did not receive the reception he thought that it deserved. "After returning from the Middle East, we put together all of our findings and mailed them to the White House," he remembered. "But they never responded or asked us to come and brief them."[181]

As more liberal congregations lost membership, Thomas Road Baptist Church expanded its seating. Falwell's official salary more than doubled, while he assumed a number of perks. No longer driving a Buick, he now flew around the country in a Jet Commander owned by his ministry. Late in 1978 Falwell took a group of selected Liberty students on a national tour. Extending the tour into the new year, Falwell combined music and preaching, tying all of his concerns together into a succinct warning to the nation. The tour's multimedia presentation, *America, You're Too Young to Die!* reflected a new sense of urgency. Before its conclusion the tour had visited almost 150 cities.[182]

In mid-1978 a headline in the *New York Times* read, "Religious Networks Blossom." *Christianity Today* added that the annual meeting of the NRB "now attracts top name personalities, from politicians, evangelists and prominent pastors to radio and TV stars, recording artists, and famous authors." The future was even brighter; religious broadcasting still had "room to grow."[183] None of this was news to Pat Robertson, of course, whose stature, like Falwell's, had exploded by the end of 1978. Robertson's Christian Broadcasting Network (CBN), the *New York Times* reported, was "well on its way to becoming a global presence."[184] Its 1978 telethon was four times larger than any previous event, for the first time raising more than $1 million per month in pledges. It now delivered twenty-four-hour programming to cable networks over the modern RCA SATCOM II. The success allowed Robertson to continue to expand his operations and fund-raising. Construction began on an impressive Georgian-style campus for CBN University, and within months the institution claimed a two-million-dollar endowment.[185] Paralleling his fund-raising, Robertson's rhetoric on his *700 Club* television show became increasingly conspiratorial and pointed, for example, specifically naming teachers as the engine of secular humanism.[186] It helped, apparently, to have enemies. Robertson's one-time employee, Jim Bakker, not only enjoyed his own growing television network, PTL, but established Heritage USA, a "Christian retreat." Six years earlier Bakker and his wife, Tammy, had lived in a travel trailer. They now owned two homes, including one with 4,500 square feet of living space. By the end of 1978 Bakker's rapid expansion and mismanagement quietly posed worrisome financial obligations. Outwardly, however, PTL still appeared prosperous and ready to expand further.[187]

The rhetoric on the importance of family throughout Carter's first two years certainly served the child psychologist James Dobson well. Dobson's radio program expanded rapidly, and when he began in 1978 to film and distribute a set of his lectures to churches, they proved popular, ultimately reaching millions of people. Dobson's frequent claims of having "rescued" homosexuals from their sin contributed to his growing audience. By 1978 Dobson assumed that his popularity and expertise on the family warranted an invitation to participate in the planning for Carter's family conference. When he did not receive an invitation, however, he began a well-coordinated lobbying campaign for inclusion. Dobson told his listeners that "liberal, secular humanists" were trying to recast the role of the American family and that if he received an invitation, he would insure the "correct perspective." His audience, he concluded, should write officials and urge them to issue the invitation.[188]

Throughout 1978 Bill Bright's Campus Crusade for Christ worked with a number of evangelical businessmen, including the chief officer of the Holiday Inn hotel chain, to implement a five-year fund-raising campaign launched at the end of the previous year. The group's astounding goal of $1 billion demonstrated their confidence. The money, they claimed, would help return the nation to traditional values and stem societal decay. In 1978 Bright announced the creation of the School of Theology of the International Christian Graduate University, the first component of what he hoped would become a major center for graduate-level Christian studies. Based in Arrowhead, Colorado, the university would also train future ministers to continue his evangelism.[189]

Billy Graham, of course, already had the stature the other ministers envied. Nevertheless, events during Carter's first two years expanded Graham's already famous ministry. Throughout 1978 Graham worked to raise over $30 million for his Billy Graham Center at Wheaton College in Illinois, which had agreed to house his papers. Charges of financial mismanagement annoyed the famed minister, but the episode faded, and Graham carried out well-publicized crusades in the Soviet Union and the Eastern European Communist bloc. He had enhanced, in the words of one writer, his impressive résumé as "a world Christian statesman."[190] In any event, he still enjoyed close access with Washington's power elite, Carter included. Upon his return from Europe, Graham sent Carter a report. Unlike Falwell, Graham received a reply. The White House thanked Graham and claimed that while Carter strongly supported the mission trip, he could not publicly comment. "The President would not want to endorse as explicitly Graham's activities," the letter read.[191] In a separate letter, Carter's foreign policy advisor, Zbigniew Brzezinski, characterized Graham's travels as "mutually beneficial."[192] The year's end brought more good news. "We thank God for your Christian witness," Graham wrote Carter, noting that Graham continued to pray for Carter's administration every day.[193]

It was a sentiment that few of Graham's colleagues shared, their movement to the political right increasingly overt by the end of 1978. John Conlan, the former Arizona Republican congressman who had long sought an alliance of conservative fiscal and religious leaders, took a position as special legal counsel to the National Religious Broadcasters, signaling to some observers that the NRB now officially acknowledged its support for the GOP.[194] Later in 1978 Gary Jarmin, a former disciple of Korean cult leader Sun Myung Moon, and Robert Grant, the leader of a group of California pastors who had backed the Briggs Initiative, united to form the organization Christian Voice, one of several new groups claiming to protect the traditional family. Drawing membership from the antipornography lobby Citizens for Decency Through Law, the two founders recruited sixteen members of Congress to serve as Christian Voice's first congressional advisory committee. The partisan nature of the committee was obvious from the start, its leadership including Republican senators Orrin Hatch of Utah,

Roger Jepsen of Iowa, James McClure of Idaho, and Gordon Humphrey of New Hampshire. Christian Voice began to use "moral report cards" to judge candidates on issues such as abortion and homosexuality, and its scores, if nothing else, indicated the organization's preference for Republicans. Contributions from its new political action committee, the Christian Voice Moral Government Fund, overwhelmingly went to Republicans. It was no small boon to the GOP; Christian Voice's budget soon reached $1.5 million from a donor base of 187,000 members.[195]

Now out of power, Republicans had the advantage of being on the political offense, with political discourse—and thus criticism—aimed primarily at Carter's initiatives and not their own. Terry Dolan's National Conservative Political Action Committee, Bright's Christian Embassy, and Howard Phillips's Conservative Caucus all flourished, the latter aided by the expanded fund-raising of Richard Viguerie and the connections of its new field director, Ed McAteer. Paul Weyrich remained as always the best cheerleader for a union of religious and fiscal conservatives, with his Survival of a Free Congress thriving just as its sister organizations were. The Heritage Society, perhaps Weyrich's most lasting contribution to the conservative cause, hired an outstanding new leader, Ed Feulner, who spent most of 1978 revamping the organization's staff and creating a "resource bank," a database of all conservative groups across the nation. The database, which eventually grew to over 2,200 experts and 475 organizations, facilitated coordination, Feulner explained. By 1978 all these organizations had close connections to both Republican congressional leaders and religious leaders such as Falwell. All spoke well of each other but hardly included Carter in their mutual admiration society. According to Falwell, for example, Jesse Helms, the arch-conservative Republican senator from North Carolina, had an "impeccable character and will do the right thing every time." When Dobson declared sarcastically that liberals sought a "society without families, a society without the moral hang-ups of the past," the Republican National Committee applauded.[196] When the IRS announced its enforcement of desegregation efforts in private schools, it was not just conservative school activists such as Connie Marshner and Robert Billings who were in an uproar. Traditional Republican organizations such as the Young Americans for Freedom (YAF) echoed their rhetoric, forming in 1978 a task force on affirmative action. Carter's efforts to help women, the YAF's report read, disrupted the nuclear family, with serious societal problems resulting. It was "just another example of the affirmative action mentality in action."[197]

The similarity in rhetoric did not stop there. Republicans had for years decried a liberal media bias. During the early cold war, the Republican-dominated House Un-American Activities Committee had focused on suspected Communists in the Hollywood elite, spawning the Hollywood Ten and contributing to McCarthyism. A decade later, the Republican Nixon, angry after a failed gubernatorial run in California, attacked the press, which, he complained, "would not have Dick Nixon to kick around any more." By 1978 Republican pundits regularly repeated charges of media bias among an array of issues. Now, however, critics of homosexuality, abortion, and feminism claimed the same.

Convinced that NBC and CBS gave their cause short shrift, abortion opponents complained that the broadcast and print media always portrayed them as "right-wing fanatics," radicals far outside the American mainstream. In 1978 a group calling itself the Ad Hoc Committee in Defense of Life began an effort to document specific cases of bias. Its periodical *LifeLetter* claimed that the fifth anniversary of the March for Life had not received the publicity it deserved; that broadcasting icon Walter Cronkite had done a "hatchet-job" on antiabortion leader Mark Gallagher; and that reviews of antiabortion books were always negative. By contrast, the periodical claimed, abortion rights advocates never received the negative press they deserved. In one case an advocate for abortion rights appeared on television to rave reviews when, in reality, he was "a basket case of frustration and bitter indignation."[198] When the IRS announced its enforcement decision, Falwell claimed that the liberal media encouraged the action. "Our critics wanted to tie evangelicals in with segregation," he argued. Conservative Christians "were made victims by the liberal press and by the liberal educational system." In any event, by mining a sense of media bias, many conservative Christians—intentionally or unintentionally—appeared to align themselves within a long Republican tradition.[199]

The IRS enforcement decision, of course, fit well with the Republican tradition of resistance to taxation, easily cast as an exemplar of big government run amok. Of all the developments encouraging a conservative alliance and partisanship, therefore, the IRS enforcement on private schools was one of the most notable. It was, Weyrich later claimed, one of the key impetuses for conservative Christians to form the modern Religious Right. "I had been trying to get these people interested in [abortion and the ERA] and I had utterly failed," Weyrich remembered. "What changed their mind was Jimmy Carter's intervention against the Christian schools, trying to deny them tax-exempt status on the basis of so-called defacto segrega-tion."[200] While Weyrich did not acknowledge the enforcement as just one part of a broader attack on the family and thus a concern with broader antecedents than he expressed, its impact was obvious. Weyrich immedi-ately began coordinating with Robert Billings and his new organization, Christian School Action. Billings enlisted Jerry Falwell, who complained in classic hyperbole, "In some states it's easier to open a massage parlor than a Christian school."[201] James Dobson, Pat Robertson, and Jim Bakker all contributed by inviting concerned guests to appear on their respective shows. Connie Marshner spoke against the IRS, as did evangelist Tim La-Haye. The connections they formed served all well, with the same elements uniting against Carter's proposal for the Department of Education. Chris-tian Voice, for example, added to its report cards legislators' stances against the new department. With Republicans leading the opposition, the results were predictable. In the Senate Republican Robert Packwood had for some time led efforts to relieve the tax burden of parents with children in private schools, and now Republicans throughout the party protested more vora-ciously than ever before. Many conservative Christians, it appeared, had found their new political home.[202]

Lawrence Lader, president of Abortion Rights Mobilization, an organi-zation that supported abortion rights through litigation, predicted in 1978 that this new partisan coalition would prove to be a political force in the fu-ture. Watching the IRS debate unfold, Lader forecast that his issue, abortion, would prove the "spearhead of political fanaticism" but that the coming "re-ligious right-wing alliance" would actively seek to extend its tentacles far beyond one issue. Abortion opponents would find common ground with the opponents of the equal rights amendment, homosexuality, and public education. This new Republican coalition, Lader warned, would draw its support from George Wallace's American Independent Party, which had polled approximately ten million supporters in 1968. Situated largely in the South, the Midwest, and strongholds of Catholic conservatism, the party would "revolve around all issues presumably posing a threat to the Ameri-can family." If abortion rights supporters did not unite similarly with their own allies, they would face certain defeat.[203]

If Lader did not realize the difficulty in coordinating a liberal counter-balance to the new Republican unity, Carter certainly understood. As 1978 drew to a close, the coalition that had elected him two years before appeared irrevocably fractured. While still occupying the Oval Office, the Democrats were in disarray and on the defensive. Every constituency demanded perfection from the administration and threatened to withdraw its support for Carter's reelection in 1980. Carter had pleased few. It was true that not all religious conservatives had joined the opposition, Graham being the most obvious example. Recognizing like Lader the shift in the political winds, Graham had refused to join Bryant's Miami crusade, its overt Republican overtones an obvious challenge to his nonpartisan, or at least bipartisan, traditions. Bryant's efforts, Graham proclaimed publicly, "single out one type of sin as being worse than another."[204] Nevertheless, the frustrations with Carter that many of Graham's conservative Christian colleagues now held had driven them into the arms of Weyrich, Conlan, and the Grand Old Party. The foundations for a new Religious Right were in place.

CHAPTER FIVE

The Formidable Conservative Barrage

"EVERY HERO BECOMES AT LAST A BORE," observed Ralph Waldo Emerson. By early 1979 little doubt remained among the odd coalition that had elected Jimmy Carter three years before. Carter was more than a bore; he was a nuisance, his presidency a failure undeserving of another term in office. From the political Left, the outspoken champions of the rights revolution, the feminists and gay community, among others, complained that Carter's brand of moderation had squandered a unique opportunity. Surely, many assumed, the Democratic Party could offer another hero in 1980 who would not disappoint. From the political Right, the seeds of the modern Religious Right were set to germinate. Many conservative Christians, ready for organization and anxious for a new hero of their own, now actively sought solace in the Republican Party. Caught in the middle remained the resolute Carter, still optimistically hoping that his own moral compass could craft a policy on family issues sufficient to hold his fragile constituency together.[1]

If the odds appeared bleak at the beginning of 1978, the early days of 1979 appeared to be the proverbial nail in the coffin. On the fourth day of the year Carter asserted that "new realities" must temper the nation's commitment to the poor. With inflation running at almost 10 percent and the administration's budget deficit estimated at $29 billion, Congressman Jack Kemp and Senator William Roth announced six days later a Republican plan to cut taxes by 30 percent over three years. The proposal won wide support from the conservative Christian community and added to the Republican Party's momentum. At the same time, the shah of Iran left his country, ostensibly for a short vacation but in reality never to return. Within weeks the fundamentalist Islamic clergyman Ayatollah Ruhollah Khomeini arrived in Iran from exile, and the country found itself in the midst of riots and political executions. At every turn, both domestic and foreign policy developments foretold a new political reality.[2]

At the White House Carter faced his own rebellion. The previous year Bella Abzug and the National Advisory Committee on Women had clashed with Sarah Weddington, and the ill will remained. When in the new year Abzug expressed additional criticism, suggesting that the White House was not a true champion of women's rights, Carter could take no more. He told his staff that the NACW only wanted meetings with him "for condemnation or for a public relations gimmick." Exiting the room, he shot back, "It saps our strength to be confrontational."[3]

The die was cast, and the result was what Gloria Steinem termed the "Friday Night Massacre," a not so subtle attempt to tie Carter to the Watergate-disgraced Nixon. The White House fired Abzug, who angrily retorted, "You're going to regret this."[4] Learning of her dismissal, twenty-four of the remaining forty NACW members also resigned. The number included every member of the original International Women's Year Commission. Moving quickly, the White House rallied the remaining women by naming as interim chair the respected president of the American Association of University Women, Marjorie Bell Chambers. Chambers had a strong reputation among feminists, but it was also obvious that a different body now existed.[5] Much smaller, it now carried the name President's Advisory Committee for Women (PACW) as if to emphasize its accountability to Carter. Moreover, the permanent chair fell to Lynda Johnson Robb, a woman without strong feminist credentials but the daughter of former president Lyndon Johnson and someone who knew the value of loyalty.[6]

Abzug made good on her threats, immediately beginning a nationwide speaking tour of women's groups, college campuses, and churches. Introduced as "one of the founding mothers of the women's movement," Abzug peppered her speeches with criticism of Carter, specifically that his proposed budget cuts would "hurt poor women the most." With the presidential election just over a year away, Abzug refused to endorse any candidate, which most observers interpreted as an additional slap at Carter. "[Abzug's speech] definitely has a negative effect on my opinion of Carter," commented one Swarthmore College coed, reflecting a sentiment many of her peers undoubtedly shared.[7] To make matters worse, only weeks later the White House cited executive privilege to block Weddington from appearing before the Senate Human Resources Committee. While it was long-standing policy that the balance of powers prevented presidential aides from testifying, Weddington had been unaware of this policy and had promised to attend. This offered Abzug a chance for additional criticism. "If Sarah hasn't seen the writing on the wall, she soon will," Abzug told the press, suggesting the White House sought to muzzle her: "I think the action speaks for itself." Questionable or not, Abzug's complaints apparently carried some weight. By early 1979 over 90 percent of the letters arriving at the White House did not support Weddington's appointment.[8]

It must have been frustrating for Weddington. While she continued to chair meetings of the Interdepartmental Task Force on Women, she was forced to acknowledge to members in early March, "We will not have a major ERA event this month, and possibly not for several months." The reason was simple: "It was not possible to get an appointment time on the President's calendar."[9] While the federal courts dismissed Missouri's lawsuit against NOW's boycott, little appeared positive for the women's rights lobby. Phyllis Schlafly continued to flagellate the administration as she tied the ERA to the "incompetent federal bureaucracy" and its desire to destroy traditional families by advancing abortion and lesbianism. Her language intentionally strengthened her conservative base, which kept ERA advocates on the defensive. "Although I am a Christian," one feminist stated on the popular *Phil Donahue Show*, "I still do support the Equal Rights Amendment." Implicit but unintentional, of course, was that Christianity opposed the ERA.[10] A new group, People of Faith for ERA, lobbied against such assumptions but found itself having to stress a negative—what the ERA would not do. First and foremost, it argued, the "ERA will not alter family structure." Schlafly, it appeared, continued to win the battle of perceptions.[11]

In late January Carter pressed for the ERA in his State of the Union address. The address "received great reviews from around the country and was a boost that was badly needed," Weddington reported to Carter.[12] It was, however, not enough. Defeats followed, with new votes held in Oklahoma, North Carolina, and Florida. Never one to miss an opportunity for press, Schlafly scheduled a victory celebration at Washington's Shoreham-Americana for March 22, the first anniversary of the IWY report to Carter. "We believe ERA died on March 22nd of this year," she said to cheers, noting that the original deadline for passage was only days away. With the crowd popping champagne corks, the entertainment included a show called *The ERA Follies of 1979*. Actors portraying Carter, Steinem, Abzug, and Weddington sang and danced. Schlafly wrote new lyrics for old songs, which the crowd enjoyed. "I've grown tired of Bella's face," the comedian playing Carter sang. "I could no longer take her chats, no longer stand her hats, I made her take a walk." Even as many women's rights advocates questioned her new role, Weddington faced the harshest criticism. She was "the number one supporter of killing babies." Like Carter, it appeared, Weddington proved an excellent foil. There was much hyperbole, but a conservative partisan bias was obvious throughout. Speakers lamented unnamed "federal bureaucrats," and the crowd remained almost exclusively Republican, including such notables as senators Orrin Hatch, Jake Garn, and Jesse Helms.[13]

Carter's obvious friction with feminists did not impress their conservative opponents. Robert Billings, his National Christian Action Coalition growing rapidly, did telegraph Carter to "applaud you on your recent firing of Ms. Bella Abzug." Abzug, Billings wrote, "did not represent the majority of American women."[14] She had not reared children or committed herself to her family, so firing her was wise. Weddington's reply reflected the White House's difficult position. Carter, Weddington responded, was "very conscious of the need to emphasize the role of wife and mother" but would always recognize a woman's individual right to choose her own path.[15]

More troublesome to many conservative Christians was Carter's refusal—once again—to attend the annual conference of the National Religious Broadcasters. Ben Armstrong, the group's executive director, lobbied particularly hard for Carter to attend the meeting, held at the beginning of each year. "As you know, in the past the evangelical community has largely been supportive of the President," Armstrong wrote White House aide Frank Moore, "but I believe that this year would be a very critical one to meet with us." Armstrong did not explain his reasoning, although his letter implied the looming election. "I recognize the demands on the President's time," Armstrong added, alluding to the White House's excuses from previous years, but the organization was willing to accommodate Carter's schedule.[16] In a separate plea NRB member Jimmy Waters reminded Moore, "Other presidents have appeared at our conventions in times past."[17] In regretting, the White House tried to be diplomatic. "This is a very busy month," Moore explained, citing a series of specific presidential commitments, details that had not appeared in previous regrets. "I can assure you, however, that the President gave your invitation every consideration." It was simply impossible for him to attend.[18] This excuse did not sit well with many NRB members, however, one bluntly writing of his frustrations: "It is the feeling of those of us who have been with NRB for a long time that Mr.

Carter has avoided us for some reason." There are some "bitter feelings." Most evangelicals had voted for Carter three years before, thrilled that "for the first time in American history we have a President who is committed to Christ."[19] Now, however, Carter needed to reaffirm this commitment.

Left unstated was the obvious alliance forming between many NRB members and the Republican Party. When Carter scheduled a trip to Dallas, members of the city's Cliff Temple Baptist Church invited him to speak at their service, obviously aware of the political dynamic. The congregation, the letter of invitation read, "was not insufferably Republican." The letter acknowledged that several Dallas Baptist leaders, including the prominent Reverend D. A. Criswell at Dallas's First Baptist Church, "had gone on some anti-Democratic tirades," which had met with "standing ovations." Nevertheless, if Carter agreed to come, Cliff Temple would greet him warmly. The White House clearly appreciated the sentiments but noted that Carter's schedule had been arranged far in advance.[20]

Following tradition, Carter agreed to attend the National Prayer Breakfast on January 18, traveling with Rosalynn by motorcade to the Washington Hilton Hotel. There Carter joined Billy Graham, who offered the opening prayer, and a number of prominent religious leaders and politicians.[21] In his comments Carter praised the role of faith in American history, but politics was never far below the surface. "It is not an easy course to follow when you believe deeply in something, not to try to impose the dictates of your conscience on the lives and choices of other people," Carter's speechwriters suggested, at least implying the frustration religious opposition had caused the White House politically. A lot of the hate in the world "is in the name of religion."[22] In his final draft Carter revised some of the phrases, but the message was similar. "We must guard against the abuse of our own religious faith," Carter declared. It was, in any event, obvious that Carter remained in the same dilemma that had so hampered his first two years. "Our Nation requires by law that the church and state must be separated," Carter declared. "The church cannot dominate our government." Nevertheless, he continued, "There is no way for a human being to separate in one's heart and mind those inevitable correlations—responsibilities of a secular life, even in government, on the one hand, and responsibilities to God on the other." The two were one and the same: "There is no way to sever [faith] from public events."[23]

Carter's State of the Union address did not contain such overt religious references but still left an impression of a president frustrated at every turn.

America needed a "new foundation" for greatness, Carter repeated several times, clearly hoping that the phrase would catch the popular imagination. This, however, was not the case, the speech arguably notable only in the tortured logic of Carter's appeal to all sides. On the one hand, Carter spoke of the need to "get control of the bureaucracy," proposing to reorganize and shrink the executive branch. He promised that his administration would "scrutinize the overall effect of regulation on our economy," adding that he favored a "sunset law" limiting federal programs that had "outlived their values." On the other hand, however, Carter quickly tacked from conservative to liberal. He noted that government "has helped to dismantle racial barriers, has provided assistance to the jobless and retired, has fed the hungry, has provided for the safety, health and bargaining rights of American workers, and has helped preserve our natural heritage." One was left to wonder, if government were so effective in promoting the common good, why diminish its functions?

Carter was not the only one giving speeches in early 1979, of course, and it was obvious that across the board the administration's critics had the upper hand. Early in the year Jerry Falwell spoke to followers on the steps of the Capitol, and his rhetoric was more politically pointed than ever before. Despite a downpour, approximately twelve thousand people attended, a number that included curious government workers on their lunch hour. He called for a massive voter registration drive and "urged the religious right to stand up and be counted." It was a message he repeated on the capitol steps of a number of key states during a campaign he dubbed Clean Up America![24] Falwell was clear about his intended targets. In a letter he sent simultaneously to his followers he criticized "obscene classroom textbooks" and "legalized abortion." Praising the traditional nuclear family, he denounced "practicing homosexuals" and "uncensored sex and violence." He concluded by asking his followers to mail "ballots" describing their views on these issues. When he received them, he promised, "the results will be tabulated and sent to each and every lawmaker, state legislator, governor, U.S. senator and representative, judge, school board, P.T.A. president, TV network, the fifty major advertisers in the country, and to President Carter himself."[25]

To mark the sixth anniversary of the *Roe v. Wade* decision, the now regular March for Life was particularly exuberant, many speakers clearly enamored with the GOP. Chanting "Life, life, life" and "No compromise," thousands of protesters braved bitter cold in walking from the White House to the Capitol. Carrying pictures of babies with captions reading "Thank God Jesus Wasn't Aborted," demonstrators pressed for more action. Underscoring the confidence of the march's leadership was its refusal to meet with groups favoring legal abortion. Eleanor Smeal, NOW's president, had called for the two sides to meet and seek areas of common interest, such as birth control. "They must stop killing babies forthwith," Nellie Gray, president of March for Life, retorted. "Pro-life people will not negotiate with baby killers."[26]

In February a local controversy in Dallas exploded into national headlines and proved another chance for conservative pastors to mobilize. The television station WFAA, Dallas's ABC affiliate, decided to drop evangelist James Robison's nationally syndicated program after the fiery preacher claimed on the air that homosexuals recruited children. Perhaps recognizing the unity that had begun to grow the previous year, Robison not only complained to the station but contacted fellow pastors, including Falwell, to organize a large protest rally at the Dallas Convention Center. Robison's staff handed out bumper stickers that read "Freedom of Speech, the Right to Preach." With a direct feed to WFAA, Robison threatened the station, which apparently worked. "The people at the station told me later that they just about got under the table," Robison remembered. "My goodness, they're going to come carry this station off, brick by brick."[27] The station argued at first that without equal time for homosexual groups to dispute the comments, the federal Fairness Doctrine governing public airways required the dismissal. With Falwell countering that stations "could not censor the content of sermons," the ministers indeed had a strong argument for religious freedom. It was this argument over censorship and freedom of religion that caused WFAA to reverse course and allow Robison's program back on the air, although Falwell jokingly acknowledged that "the packed house might have had something to do with it." As part of the protest, Reverend Criswell, already known for his partisan rhetoric, led members of his massive First Baptist Church in a march around the station. In covering the story, WFAA had become part of it, and thus ending the incident as quickly as possible was prudent.[28]

The controversy may have ended relatively quickly, but its ramifications were significant. Through the Dallas protest Falwell and Robison developed a much closer relationship with Paul Weyrich, Howard Phillips, and Ed McAteer, who had been working to unite conservative Christians into the

Republican fold. The latter had begun to organize seminars to encourage pastors to become politically active. Following the Dallas protest, Falwell joined approximately two dozen other conservative ministers in attending a seminar at the Crystal City Marriott just outside Washington. Here McAteer courted Falwell, impressing the ambitious preacher. McAteer, Falwell later remembered, was "a salesman for the new right." He "believed that the liberal church was involved [in politics] and now it was time for the conservative church to get involved too."[29] Weyrich, meanwhile, continued to impress upon the ministers that their followers would welcome more Republican-leaning political activism. He commissioned polls and publicized the results when they backed his claims.[30] With McAteer's seminars continuing, Falwell telephoned conservative school activist Billings, and the two agreed to meet in Richmond, Virginia. Falwell had met Billings the previous year, but their relationship had initially been cool, strained somewhat by the desires of both men to lead the growing conservative Christian unity. Now, however, Falwell, enthused by the Dallas protests and the McAteer seminars, argued that any competition was unwise. Working with the likes of McAteer, Weyrich, and Phillips, they would all benefit.[31]

Campus Crusade's Bill Bright had drawn the same conclusion, impressed as well by the success of the Dallas protest. Utilizing his many connections, Bright organized a meeting of leading evangelists in Dallas, a meeting that Robison later described in a flurry of hyperbole as "one of the most significant things that ever happened in the life of our country."[32] After speaking with Graham, Bright called Robison and explained that he and Graham were concerned about the direction America had taken and that they would like to meet to discuss the situation. When the group of a dozen pastors met at a hotel by the Dallas–Fort Worth Airport, the conversation centered on the spread of moral decay and the failure of Christians to stop it. The group included Billy Graham, Pat Robertson, the televangelist Rex Humbard, and prominent Southern Baptists such as Charles Stanley, among several others. Falwell, oddly, was not in attendance, suggesting, perhaps, that competition for the mantle of leader still simmered. After Graham stated that he thought America only had a "thousand days as a free nation" without change, the group readily agreed that new political activism was necessary. Bright added, "It's that serious." Graham explained, "I am uncomfortable politically" and "I cannot be publicly involved," an obvious reference to his long-stated desire to remain above partisanship. Humbard agreed with this sentiment, but most left with a new determination to press for political change, including new Republican associations.[33]

After the airport meeting, Stanley began to fulfill his pledge by holding Campaign Training Conferences to teach ministers how to engage their flocks politically without losing their church's tax-exempt status. If there were any doubt about the partisan nature of these sessions, Weyrich was a key instructor. The meetings increasingly crossed denominational lines and included Roman Catholics. The conservative columnist Robert Novak attended several of these sessions and recalled how minister after minister spoke against Carter. They had supported Carter in 1976 but felt let down by his actions since. "I decided at that point," Novak remembered, "that Jimmy Carter's goose was cooked because I saw the intensity of those people."[34]

As the leadership of a new Religious Right continued to coalesce, the greatest threat to Carter was that in denomination after denomination the theological issues that underlay much of the new political movement continued to resonate. With the election season almost begun, theological conservatives continued to gain strength as the evangelical movement grew more political still. Noting that a "problem threatens to divide contemporary evangelicalism," one conservative defended biblical inerrancy in an issue of *Christianity Today*. "Liberals confuse love with justice," the article concluded.[35] In Iowa a bill introduced at the same time in the state legislature sought to ensure equal time in the classroom for "scientific creationism." Reflecting an argument later known as "intelligent design," the bill's backers insisted that students should learn the debate surrounding evolution as well as the theory itself. The governor, the media reported, recognized the bill as "politically sensitive" and was moving "gingerly."[36] "Charles Darwin remains the bête noire of fundamentalist Christians," noted one amazed observer. Despite over a century of knowledge since the publication of *The Origin of Species*, the number of people challenging evolutionary science appeared to be growing. Even in the American Greek Orthodox community conservatives protested relativism in the church's theology, some attempting to form their own denomination, known as the Evangelical Orthodox Church. "We believe in the traditional creeds," a spokesman for the new church explained. People were no longer as "spontaneous as we said they were in the 1960s" and now longed for discipline and structure.[37]

Most notably, when the Southern Baptists held their convention in Houston in June, a "battle erupted with lines drawn according to one's interpretation of scriptural inerrancy," according to one report. The theological struggle, already intense in previous years, now was particularly caustic with "preconvention politicking." "[Conservatives] may be as orthodox as Peter," complained one Louisiana pastor, "but they are as mean as the devil." For months, Baptists Paige Patterson and Paul Pressler had led a grassroots movement against perceived liberalism in the church, advocating Adrian Rogers of Bellevue Baptist Church in Memphis, Tennessee, for the presidency. Rogers, who attended Bright's Dallas meeting, did not try to hide the direction he intended to take, praising "conservative, Bible-believing congregations . . . that believe in the inerrant, infallible word of God."[38] Complaining about liberal domination of the church's seminaries, conservatives ultimately prevailed, electing Rogers the new president of the thirteen-million-member denomination.[39]

Rogers immediately began to purge from church offices members who did not share his conservative doctrine. "The Baptist tradition of defending the autonomy of the church from the state and the state from the church was another casualty of the conservative takeover of the Southern Baptist Convention in 1979," author Randall Balmer writes. "The conservatives who took charge of the denomination quickly demonstrated that they had little interest in patrolling Roger Williams's 'wall of separation.'"[40] Within weeks, Wake Forest University broke its relationship with the North Carolina Baptist State Convention, the group having grown too conservative for the university.[41] As the Baptists met, impressive crowds of charismatics filled Shea and Giant stadiums in New York, proclaiming themselves a "charismatic revival movement" that drew from a large number of specific Christian faiths. This Jesus '79 festival surpassed even the large celebrations held the year before, many attendees insisting that their success lay in Americans' growing desire to return to the truth embodied in Jesus.[42]

With many of their members growing more political and with opponents claiming that their fund-raising was a scam, in March 1979 more than eleven hundred evangelical Christian groups formed the Evangelical Council for Financial Accountability (ECFA), an umbrella organization to ensure that its members were fiscally ethical and, without openly suggesting it, to preempt any government or external audits. Religious broadcasting, described by 1979 as "one of the fastest growing sectors in communications," had a vested interest in bills to deregulate the airwaves and thus, like every broadcaster, a self-interest in debates on Capitol Hill. If nothing else, the California attorney general had begun an investigation in early 1979 into the finances of several churches in his state, a reaction, no doubt, to the Jonestown massacre but a move that most churches continued to worry violated their First Amendment rights.[43] More in a partisan vein, Christian Voice expanded its mailing lists throughout 1979 with the intention of distributing to conservative churches a summary of its research and conclusions, a clear effort to influence the 1980 election. The Reverend Richard Zone, the organization's operations manager, acknowledged that opposition to abortion, feminism, and homosexuality ranked high on Christian Voice's agenda and that one could fairly describe the group as "right-wing." Announcing a new fundraising goal of $2 million to accompany the organization's research, Reverend Zone explained his motivation. "The [conservative] churches have been too passive," he suggested, "and a lot of Christians are fed up."[44]

Undoubtedly influencing the ECFA and the new push for self-regulation among evangelicals was a *Charlotte Observer* report that Jim Bakker's PTL had raised money for overseas missions but had used the money to pay Bakker's personal bills. The paper also reported charges that the network had helped one of its executives to skirt his creditors. The Federal Communications Commission promptly began an investigation, which ultimately lasted for years. At the time, however, Bakker obviously sought to gain conservative allies, casting the government's case as a "conspiracy." Although he failed to provide evidence, the clear implication was that the Carter administration had a vendetta. Bakker also employed the language that appealed to conservatives, describing the FCC as "back-room bureaucrats" who wanted to "put a black name on my ministry." When the IRS became involved, Bakker jumped at the opportunity to describe the tax agency as "vultures."[45] Attacking the IRS was sure to win allies among conservative Christians, still engaged in the struggle over the tax exemption for segregated private schools. Bakker, like James Dobson of Focus on the Family, began to book conservative activists and Christian attorneys on his show.[46]

The strategy made sense, as thousands of letters of protest against the IRS school regulations continued to flow into the White House and to members of Congress. The new year had hardly diminished conservative outrage. Predictably, Congress responded with hearings, which *Christianity Today* reported sent "shock waves throughout the religious community."[47] Bowing to the pressure, the IRS announced that it would loosen and suspend enforcement, including exempting ethnic schools. The emboldened opposition, recognizing that this promised to be arbitrary and unworkable, continued to demand final termination. The Southern Baptist Convention adopted a resolution denouncing the regulations, promptly forwarding a copy to Carter. "Your intervention in this matter would be greatly appreciated," James Wood Jr. of the Baptist Joint Commission on Public Affairs lobbied.[48] The administration's reply was noncommittal, if not dismissive. "This letter is to acknowledge receipt of the resolution," staffer Landon Kite wrote. "President Carter has asked that the appropriate staff be notified of your action."[49] At the same time, activists such as Billings, Grant, and Falwell pressed Congress to act. Moving quickly to settle the issue (and, perhaps unstated, to win the religious vote), two Republican congressmen, Robert Dornan of California and John Ashbrook of Ohio, introduced restrictive amendments to an appropriations bill that prohibited funds for enforcement. Largely embraced by the Senate, the legislation effectively ended the debate. It did not, however, eliminate a sense among the conservative religious community that Carter was not a friend and that an alliance with the GOP was wise.[50] In short, the political dynamic remained: Carter and his administration, seemingly frustrated at every turn, labored on, even as a new Religious Right gained momentum from his every move.

The only bright spot for Carter early in 1979 was the March signing of the Camp David Accords, negotiated the previous year. The ceremony, held on the North Lawn of the White House, offered Carter a brief respite from his critics, now regularly chastising the administration as weak and inept in foreign affairs. While the overwhelming reaction among the public was positive, it was clear that Falwell had grown more critical. The year before Falwell had appeared somewhat ambivalent, recognizing the agreement's popularity but also its implications for Israel and the dispensationalist, premillennial prophecies that many of his followers shared. Now, however, emboldened just like many of his theological colleagues, Falwell more easily dismissed the accords. He could no longer bring himself to give Carter even the least bit of credit. The Camp David Accords would not last, Falwell implied: "You and I know that there's not going to be any peace in the Middle East until one day the Lord Jesus sits down upon the throne of David in Jerusalem." The Soviet Union represented the forces of evil and would invade Israel in the fulfillment of prophecy. There the Soviet forces would face annihilation "on the mountains of Israel." This was the view Pat Robertson had embraced the previous year, but now Falwell more confidently reflected the same sentiments.[51]

The ongoing negotiations over the Strategic Arms Limitation Treaty re-

mained a different matter entirely, a much easier chance for critics to portray Carter as weak. Many legislators on both sides of the aisle continued to
complain that SALT II allowed the Soviets to remain strategically superior
in several categories of weapons and argued that it was symbolic of the decline of American power. Conservative Christians who had so long feared
the threat of Godless Communism remained among the most vocal in the
chorus of complaints. In an editorial *Christianity Today* chided those who
criticized the Camp David Accords on the basis of "predictive prophecy"
but seemed to agree that Carter's negotiating appeared naive and indecisive.[52] To counter this impression the White House began the new year by
wooing the Southern Baptists. The previous year the SBC had adopted a
resolution favoring the talks, and the White House clearly hoped for a new
resolution in 1979. Prominent Baptist Jimmy Allen warned the Department
of State prior to the denomination's June convention in Houston, however,
that conservatives had grown in strength. Allen promised to present SALT
in the brightest light possible at the coming convention and suggested the
best alternative was to gain the support of Billy Graham, who was scheduled
to speak. If the White House were to "brief Reverend Graham without any
reference to his speech, and if he is persuaded of the importance of SALT, he
will make the connection himself and include the issue in his message." The
State Department agreed, recommending that Carter consider a personal
meeting with Graham. The department then added "one last thought." A
division was growing among the Southern Baptists. "The energetic 'pro-
gressives' among the Southern Baptists are often out front and clearly more
visible on SALT. We must strive to keep the pro-SALT initiative within the
[Baptist] mainstream."[53]

After considering the issue, White House advisor Anne Wexler recommended that both Carter and Mondale meet with Graham.[54] Graham had
issued a statement that strongly supported arms limitations talks but had
not explicitly endorsed the SALT agreement. The statement had, however, at
least implied it. "This issue must concern every Christian," it read. "We have
a responsibility to be 'salt' and 'light' in our world, speaking out against the
madness which seems to have gripped whole nations."[55]

In early May the White House scheduled a private briefing for leading
opinion makers and included an invitation to Graham. "The SALT agreement is not a substitute for a strong defense," the invitation noted, adding that it was the "culmination of the work of three Administrations."[56]
Graham quickly replied by telegraph. "I deeply appreciate the White House

invitation to discuss the SALT treaty, but unfortunately I'm in the middle of our Sydney, Australia crusade and cannot possibly attend. Please be assured of my prayers."[57]

Without Graham's overt support the administration moved forward with the negotiations, and Carter and Soviet leader Leonid Brezhnev finally signed the agreement in Vienna in June. The month, however, ultimately proved pivotal in more than one way. Not only did Carter submit SALT II to the Senate for what proved to be a long ratification battle, but the conservative Rogers won the presidency of the SBC at the same time. The White House still hoped to win the support of Graham as the Senate debated, but clearly a new SBC resolution was now beyond hope.

By this point, the White House did have an important new connection to the Southern Baptists—Robert Maddox. Having earlier lobbied for the position of religious liaison to no avail, Maddox received a surprising phone call early in 1979, an offer to join Carter's speechwriting staff. It was not the religious position for which he had lobbied, but the ambitious Maddox was not about to miss an opportunity to come to Washington. Assuming his duties just as the Senate took up SALT, Maddox immediately began drafting a speech that summarized the difficult situation the nation faced. Later termed the "malaise speech," the address Carter delivered in mid-July came to symbolize all the frustrations that his administration encountered. The speech had a spiritual tone, not surprisingly, although it made only passing references to religion. Speaking of "our nation's hopes, our dreams, and our vision of the future," Carter declared that a "crisis of confidence" gripped the nation. Americans, he implied, overconsumed even as "consumption doesn't satisfy our longing for meaning." Calling for energy reform and conservation certainly made sense. Inflation, approaching an astonishing 13 percent, and oil shortages, resulting in long gas lines and frayed tempers at the pump, demanded a forceful response. Nevertheless, for many Americans the speech crystallized the impotence of the federal government generally and the administration specifically. It accentuated for others that Carter had more preachy moralism than competence, that America was no longer a great nation.[58]

This was not Maddox's intent, of course, and in any event a lot of truth lay in the remarks. The reality remained, however, that a majority of the public simply had little patience. Any goodwill for Carter had long since evaporated. It did not help when only days after the speech several dozen top administration officials abruptly resigned, including Secretary Califano at HEW. It was the largest such mass action in almost a century and a half, and it added to the sense that Carter had lost control. Critics now had additional ammunition, claiming that the White House had purged all independent thinkers. For Maddox, at least, the extensive administration reshuffling had a positive result, a transfer to the Office of Public Liaison, where he now reported to Wexler. It was a "happy development," Maddox recalled.[59] It gave him a chance to serve in a position similar to the one he had originally envisioned. Given a large office on the fourth floor of the Old Executive Office Building, Maddox claimed to have made a "strenuous effort to open the White House where it had been closed." His duties included a number of "fascinating" issues critical to the religious community, including "peace movements, struggles between the government and Christian schools, abortion and anti-abortion groups, gays versus straights, and attempts to correct bad legislation that hurt religious and charitable organizations."[60] Correspondence took up a lot of Maddox's time, the White House's new computer tracking system ensuring that every letter received a reply, and he traveled regularly to give speeches. He was, he remembered, "something of a fair-haired lad to the press," the preferred administration spokesman on matters of religious-related policy. Whatever the specific task, Maddox enjoyed a particularly close relationship with the Carters, especially Rosalynn and son Jack, who invited Maddox and his family to join them for films at the White House. Theological discussions frequently resulted, Carter once again impressing Maddox with his commitment to his faith and his efforts to embody in policy a Christian ideal. "I sensed that it was very important to him," Maddox recalled.[61]

It did not take Maddox long to recognize the sad state of affairs when it came to being religious liaison. Both the extent of conservative Christian organization and the caustic nature of the criticism caught him by surprise. "There was a split in the religious community," Maddox explained. "The mainline clergy . . . understood the ambiguity in the President's position. The really conservative clergy, however, were really upset by Jimmy Carter, and by then it was getting really nasty, an out-and-out hatchet job." His job, obviously, was not going to be easy. "I spent a great deal of my time trying to put out fires—unsuccessfully most of the time."[62] One of his first jobs was to write a speech for Carter to give to the new leaders of the Southern Baptist Convention, invited to the White House in the hopes of reconciliation. This struck Maddox as odd because "we Baptists do not write prayers." Maddox did what Wexler told him to do, however, although Carter avoided the prepared talking points and "prayed his own words—as he should have."[63] In any event, while preparing his proposed prayer, Maddox called a leading Baptist, only to have him "explode into the telephone about the difficulty he and others were having getting anything done with and in the Carter White House." Sadly, for Maddox it proved to be only one such contact. The meeting with the new SBC leaders in the Oval Office proved cordial but ended with the denomination's new president, Adrian Rogers, warning Carter not to abandon his religious roots. "I hope you will give up your secular humanism and return back to Christianity," Rogers stated.[64]

With the election just over a year away, the White House's critics were not about to let Carter off the defensive. Every development, it appeared, had political implications. When media outlets reported that a swamp rabbit had attacked Carter's boat while he was fishing—quickly dubbed the "killer rabbit story"—Jerry Falwell mocked him in speech after speech. The book of Revelation associated swamp rabbits with Satan, he joked, and Carter should have killed it. As he was in every other situation, Carter was simply too weak.[65] When reports arose that Carter's sister Ruth had used Democratic National Committee mailing lists in her evangelistic efforts, critics pounced. Ruth denied any knowledge of the connection and maintained that her business manager handled all such affairs. Still, she acknowledged hesitantly, her brother played a big role in her efforts. "A lot of people try to get through to Jimmy by using me," she stated, adding that it was "hard sometimes to see the political implications of things."[66] When the Greek Orthodox Church pressed for permission to hold a celebration of the twentieth anniversary of Archbishop Iakovos as part of a Greek American festival on the White House's South Lawn, administration staffers first thought of the political ramifications. Carter agreed to speak, but his staff wanted his involvement limited to "a smaller reception, held indoors, and in a dignified setting." In this way he could avoid an "ethnic type celebration with Greek music, food and dancing."[67] When the National Office for Black Catholics pressed for the Medal of Honor for the renowned sixty-nine-year-old jazz singer Mary Lou Williams, the White House declined. Williams had converted to Catholicism earlier in life, and despite the number of charitable causes in which she had participated, the award might prove too controversial.[68]

With the reelection campaign looming, politics magnified every move the White House made, every utterance that passed Carter's lips. New polls indicated that 70 percent of Americans assumed Carter faced certain defeat. His longtime friend and advisor Bert Lance faced conspiracy charges in violating banking law, and although a jury later acquitted him, the allegations alone added an uncomfortable tinge of corruption to the broader perception of White House incompetence. It appeared a gift to the likes of Weyrich and Falwell. Moreover, Carter's growing unpopularity with feminists and the gay community, among others on the political left, kept open the possibility of a nomination battle in his own party. Most notably, Massachusetts senator Edward "Ted" Kennedy had become increasingly critical, laying the obvious foundation for a troublesome challenge. The last thing Carter needed was more controversy, more criticism.[69]

The long-promised White House Conference on Families, of course, carried the seeds of both controversy and criticism. Planning for the conference had languished the previous year amidst energy and inflation concerns, not to mention the squabbling among the various constituencies that had for so long added to the sense of administration incompetence. The conference was, however, a campaign promise, and in theory at least it portended progress on an issue important to all, progress that if achieved would carry desperately needed political capital. Carter had to proceed and thus moved to get planning back on track.

In a detailed message sent to Congress accompanying his State of the Union address in January, Carter reminded the legislators of the importance of the family and promised that the administration would expedite planning for the conference.[70] Following up in April, Carter announced the appointment of James Guy Tucker as conference chairman. Tucker was a lawyer and former Arkansas congressman and, obviously, a man Carter hoped would be capable of reaching a compromise.[71] Within weeks Tucker selected five "deputy chairpersons." The group included several appointments pleasing to the women's rights movement, among them Mario Cuomo, lieutenant governor of New York; Coretta Scott King, the wife of Martin Luther King Jr.; and Maryann Mahaffey, a member of the Detroit City Council. "These outstanding individuals bring broad and diversified experience," Tucker stated. At the same time, however, Carter named John Carr the conference's executive secretary. Carr had been active in the fight against poverty and had worked with the Catholic hierarchy in Washington. He knew the concerns of conservative activists such as Connie Marshner and others, many of whom clearly hoped that he would help resist the efforts of homosexuals and abortion rights activists to manipulate the conference agenda. Forty individuals including an equal number of men and women with expertise in health care, education, law, labor, and religion agreed to round out the rest of the National Advisory Committee (NAC). By this point the White House had to confirm that the original date was impossible and publicly anticipated a date in the late summer of 1980.[72]

The appointments to the NAC, Tucker claimed, "mirror the nation's rich diversity and pluralism." Tucker sent the new members a memo announcing the NAC's first meeting in mid-July and outlining the goals of the conference. He stressed the importance of diversity of participation, citing the need for a "broad national discussion" and a "wide variety of activities."[73] Carter met with the NAC during its first meeting and reiterated the importance of family in a fifteen-minute speech. The problems facing American families were "very much a part of the crisis of confidence" afflicting the nation, Carter began. The speech included a little to please both conservatives and liberals. Families were "networks of relationships, rooted not only on kinship based in blood but a kinship based on shared experiences, shared joys and sorrows, and I think most of all, a shared love that crosses vast distances and also crosses very easily the barriers of generations." Americans, he continued, "often feel nostalgic about a past that seems to be simpler and sometimes seems to be better, and we can learn from the past, but we must not limit our vision of what a good family is just to what a family was in the past." Carter, it appeared, had adopted a broad definition of family. At the same time, however, Carter also remarked that the conference "will not be to set up some big, new, expensive Federal program. In fact, it may be just getting government out of the way." This certainly pleased Marshner and her allies.[74]

After Carter left, the NAC held its first full organizational meeting. As the White House intended, Tucker instructed the members that their purpose was not to dictate to Americans but to "listen to and involve families themselves." To accomplish this there would not be one big Washington conference but several conferences around the country. In preparation for these conferences the NAC would hold hearings in various locales beginning in the fall. This would provide individuals a chance to testify and help identify topics for further investigation. Each state was to have a coordinator, and there would be state conventions also beginning in the fall. The states would then select delegates to the national conferences. When these conferences concluded, an ad hoc task force of the NAC would report on the conferences to the president, and afterward the full committee would develop a six-month implementation strategy. Throughout this process the committee would keep the public up to date with a newsletter titled *Report from the White House Conference on Families*.[75]

The elaborate plans obviously established no rigid, central control, and undoubtedly, Carter hoped the inclusiveness would diminish any potential strife. As the state conventions began, however, the *New York Times* reported that the fight for delegates to the national conferences had devolved into a "test of strength between moderate and conservative factions." In the early conventions conservatives dominated in Virginia and Oklahoma, while moderates prevailed in South Dakota. While the *Times* acknowledged that it was difficult to "classify any delegates under one ideological heading," the issues of feminism, abortion, and homosexuality clearly divided participants into two camps. In fact, Marshner was hard at work organizing in the remaining states, and Tucker was already facing criticism that the White House had both rigged the national conferences with liberals and, secretly at least, planned to postpone the conference until after the elections. Such claims frustrated Tucker, who wrote a letter to the editor of the *Times* ensuring readers that such was not the case.[76]

Moreover, in the view of James Dobson, only "one Christian leader" had been invited to join the planning sessions. It was, he remarked, a "ratio we have come to expect." Dobson immediately began a lobbying campaign to join the committee, although he claimed to "simply mention on the air one day that I was very concerned . . . and would like to be a representative of the traditional family."[77] Thousands of letters advocating his participation arrived at the White House, which invited Dobson to come to Washington to participate in a research forum that preceded the conference. There he met Tucker, who later, Dobson claimed, told him over dinner at a nearby restaurant that Tucker had not originally wanted to issue the invitation because he feared that Dobson might cause problems. "I did not know that people like you existed," Dobson quoted Tucker. In any event, a few weeks later Dobson received his invitation to serve as a delegate at the conference and to participate in the task force that would summarize the conference's conclusions.[78]

As the elaborate planning unfolded, one reality was painfully obvious. The family conference begged the issues that had bedeviled the White House from the outset. The conference added fuel to the ongoing debates over feminism, abortion, and gay rights, each simmering as the election approached. At many of the press conferences surrounding the conference planning, for example, questions on abortion were omnipresent and difficult to ignore.[79] The questions were easy to understand, as both the Supreme Court and the renewed debate over the Hyde Amendment kept the issue prominent. To begin the year, the Court in a 6–3 decision declared unconstitutional a Pennsylvania law requiring doctors performing abortions to choose the method most likely to save the life of the fetus, provided that there was any chance the fetus might survive outside the womb.[80] In May the Court agreed to hear a new challenge to the Hyde Amendment that once again opened up the possibility that the courts might declare the amendment unconstitutional. The Court had earlier ruled that states were not required to pay for elective or "nontherapeutic" abortions. Now the justices would consider payment for "medically necessary" abortions. Finally, in July the Court in an 8–1 ruling declared unconstitutional a Massachusetts law that required unmarried minor girls to get the approval of their parents or a judge before undergoing an abortion.[81]

The decisions enraged abortion protesters and came just as demonstrators torched a Long Island abortion clinic. The *New York Times* reported that the antiabortion forces were particularly optimistic that in the new year's appropriations they might further expand the Hyde Amendment's restrictions. "We have to do battle every year," Hyde commented. "I think the situation will be much the same as last year, but increasingly this issue is being thought about and studied and I am optimistic."[82] Indeed, by the end of the year Congressman Henry Hyde and his allies had added abortion restrictions to an even wider array of appropriation bills. The list now included the appropriations for the Department of Justice, the District of Columbia, the Department of the Treasury, and the Postal Service. The latter two were particularly important because they prohibited abortion in the Federal Employees Health Benefits Program. Despite the efforts of the prochoice legislators, the coming years witnessed a further expansion and codification of these restrictions.[83]

Throughout 1979 the battle was, as Hyde predicted, as raucous as the previous years. The House and Senate once again deadlocked after unsuccessfully attempting to delete all riders to the appropriations process. Once again government offices appeared near a shutdown before legislators broached an emergency compromise just before the congressional Thanksgiving recess. As Hyde predicted, the compromise tilted further from abortion rights. While the Senate had held out the possibility of federal funds for women whose health would be severely restricted as confirmed by two doctors, the House had insisted only upon exceptions for the life of the mother and in cases of rape or incest, properly reported. In the end the Senate relented.[84] While this debated unfolded, all recognized that the Hyde Amendment had proved effective. Reports indicated that it had reduced federal funding for abortions by over 90 percent.[85]

The annual Hyde debate frustrated Carter, who undoubtedly still wished the issue would recede. Just as in previous years, he urged legislators to compromise and warned of the repercussions of a government shutdown. Unlike previous years, however, Carter made the point of meeting with groups of legislators to press his point.[86] The Carter administration had arguably maintained its centrist position. It supported the Hyde Amendment but was open to wider exceptions. Even as Congress debated, the administration hired Marjory Mecklenberg, president of an antiabortion group, as a consultant to its program to discourage teenage pregnancies. When Califano resigned as HEW secretary, Carter selected Patricia Roberts Harris as his replacement. When asked if she would depart from her predecessor's—and Carter's—position on the Hyde Amendment, Harris was clear that abortion rights would not be high on her agenda. "I have made it a habit of not differing with Administration decisions," she joked.[87]

Just as in the past, the administration's actions did little to stem the growing partisan divide on abortion. Although Harris's comments annoyed abortion rights advocates, much of the public increasingly saw Carter's party as the champion of abortion rights. At the annual National Right-to-Life Convention in Cincinnati in June, speakers lashed out at the Democratic Party. While Republican senator Robert Packwood remained an object of derision, Democratic senators Frank Church of Idaho, John Glenn of Ohio, John Culver of Iowa, Patrick Leahy of Vermont, Birch Bayh of Indiana, George McGovern of South Dakota, and, obviously given his expected presidential candidacy, Ted Kennedy of Massachusetts received far more criticism. Indeed, antiabortion protesters had recently begun following Kennedy, heckling him at many stops. In August two Democratic senators requested that the Postal Service investigate a mass mailing of fliers labeling them "baby-killers," a request that led to nothing but received a lot of press.[88] By the end of the summer, a former Carter supporter, Nevada businessman Sean Morton Downey Jr., announced that he would run for the Democratic nomination as a "right-to-life candidate." While Downey's campaign obviously held little chance of success, it nevertheless helped perpetuate the perception that Carter was no opponent of abortion. It helped lump Carter in the public's eye with the Democratic majority's support for abortion rights. Carter remained in the middle, it appeared, still satisfying few.[89]

Adding to the partisan dilemma of homosexual rights was the growing complexity of the issue. Lost in the milieu of events the previous year was the lingering matter of immigration reform, first raised by the National Gay Task Force (NGTF) in its 1977 White House meeting with Costanza but by mid-1979 grown into yet another well-publicized controversy that bedeviled Carter. Immigration law passed by Congress years before prohibited the immigration of "aliens afflicted with psychopathic personality" or those suffering from a mental disorder. Under the law, the U.S. Public Health Service (PHS) was to inspect new arrivals to check for these exclusions. The Supreme Court had ruled that the statute covered homosexuals, and in the 1950s Congress had added explicitly "sexual deviants." In 1973, however, the American Psychiatric Association had removed homosexuality from its list of mental disorders. In response, Carter's surgeon general, Julius Richmond, had announced in 1978 that since homosexuality was no longer considered a medical condition, the PHS would no longer investigate it. Faced with this dilemma, the Immigration and Naturalization Service (INS) had issued a rather vague "temporary directive" that it would no longer exclude homosexuals but rather "pardon" them into the country pending a final legal resolution of their cases. In short, by mid-1979 the issue had become a legal and administrative quagmire that rivaled the Hyde Amendment.[90] The homosexual community noted that many gays and lesbians previously denied entrance were still excluded, and it rallied behind the case of Zenaida Rebultan, a known Filipino lesbian unable to join the rest of her family in California. The gay press published stories of lesbians still asked by border guards—apparently in defiance of the temporary order—embarrassing questions about their sexual orientation. The questions ran the gamut from "Why are you traveling with only women?" to "What do you do in bed?" When London antique dealer Carl Hill arrived in San Francisco wearing a Gay Pride button, he faced exclusion and sued. Reports of men denied entrance because of earrings or even because they carried feminine-looking handbags further inflamed the homosexual community. While the INS reversed itself in the Hill case to avoid litigation, the issue arguably begged for strong executive action.[91]

With the exclusion still in the statute and confusion reigning, Senator Alan Cranston introduced legislation in Congress to remove "sexual deviants" from the law. The NGTF pressed the White House to clarify the situation, writing as well to the Department of Justice and the INS. In the words of one letter of complaint, "We believe it is time for you to take charge of this situation and instruct the INS to take a permanent and formal position that lesbians and gays are no longer excludable."[92] The NGTF continued to write and phone the White House but only gained one brief, private meeting with advisor Robert Malson. Publicly, the administration remained quiet as the year passed.[93] Finally, after consulting with its Office of Legal Counsel, the Department of Justice wrote the INS that "as long as the law remains unchanged, it is the duty of the Immigration and Naturalization Service to enforce it according to the intent of Congress at the time of enactment." The surgeon general was within his rights to conclude that a diagnosis of homosexuality was not a medical condition, but this did not relieve the INS of its statutory obligations.[94] When the decision was announced, the gay community was as exasperated as angry. The effect was to maintain the status quo; the decision said nothing about exactly how the INS was to conduct inquiries about sexuality without the PHS, and thus all would have to wait at least for further clarification by the INS if not for a final legislative remedy.[95]

The ongoing NGTF prison lawsuit, moreover, added to the complexity, although largely out of the headlines. Frustrated that the controversy surrounding the prohibition of homosexual literature appeared to be losing steam, members of Troy Perry's Metropolitan Community Church began to visit gay inmates in California prisons. Arguing that the visits identified gays and lesbians and thus encouraged violence much as the receipt of gay literature did, officials banned the church members. The church filed another suit, with the prison lawyers now basing a defense on the Eighth Amendment. The right to be "reasonably free from an atmosphere conducive of sexual assault falls within the right against cruel and unusual punishment," officials argued.[96] The result was to make the matter of prisons more complex and more divisive, as all sides awaited a decision from the courts or the administration.

When it came to women's rights and the ratification of the ERA, Phyllis Schlafly may have declared victory in her March celebration, but Weddington and Carter pressed on, continuing to deal with both the matter of state rescission and Schlafly's success at framing the ERA debate as a threat to the traditional family. Just as the other "family" issues, the matter had grown more complex by the end of the summer. After the legislatures of

Washington and Idaho voted to rescind their ratification vote, ERA supporters filed lawsuits. While the administration supported the litigation, the matter was complicated in Idaho. There the judge, Marion Callister of the federal district court in Boise, was Mormon, and publicity had grown surrounding his church's recent excommunication of an ERA advocate. The administration, Weddington suggested, might press for the judge to recuse himself.[97] While the White House rejected this recommendation as unwise political interference into the Justice Department, it accepted Weddington's suggestion that the White House begin a "magazine project," working with the editors of a number of women's periodicals to feature a pro-ERA article by Carter. Coordinating with Weddington, Sey Chassler, editor of *Redbook*, recruited over nineteen publications, including *Cosmopolitan*, *Vogue*, *Seventeen*, and most notably, *Family Circle*. Chassler suggested a meeting of the editors with Carter, which she told Weddington "would ensure wider media coverage."[98] As the magazine project unfolded, Carter followed up on his promise to do more for female-owned businesses by issuing an executive order establishing a women's business enterprise program designed to improve women's access to Small Business Administration loans and technical assistance.[99]

Carter's article for the women's magazines appeared in mid-August, just before he once again declared Women's Equality Day on August 26, the anniversary of the Nineteenth Amendment. Women's suffrage, Carter stated, "was only one step on the long journey toward full equality for women." The ERA was the next logical step. "I hope that in the future," Carter concluded, "we can celebrate the passage of the 19th Amendment and the passage of the Equal Rights Amendment."[100]

To fight it all—abortion and gay rights, feminism and the ERA—opponents had by mid-1979 advanced a nifty alternative that paralleled well the evolving family conference debate. Termed the Family Protection Act, the bill added to the growing partisanship that increasingly characterized the entire spectrum of family politics. First introduced by Nevada Republican senator Paul Laxalt, the legislation declared support for "traditional families" and the role of women as "traditionally understood." Among its many provisions, it prohibited abortion or any money that could be used to advance homosexuality or feminism. The legislation had little real chance of passage, but it played well in the media and won broad conservative support, most vocally that of Connie Marshner, still complaining about Guy Tucker's appointment as conference chairman and liberal meddling in the planning for the family conference. Recognizing another opportunity to assume the leadership of the emerging conservative Christian unity, Falwell began to stress the legislation throughout 1979, especially a provision for the Family Protection Administration. The purpose of family legislation, Falwell explained, was to "counteract disruptive federal intervention into family life in the United States and to encourage restoration of family unity, parental authority, and a climate of traditional morality."[101]

The planning for the family conference, the introduction of the Family Protection Act, and indeed the growing complexity and persistence of issues such as abortion, feminism, and the ERA were all vehicles for conservative Christians to unite politically into what some by mid-1979 had begun publicly to term the "new Religious Right." The battle over the IRS and schools, James Robison and the Dallas protests, and of course the efforts of Pat Robertson, Robert Billings, Bill Bright, Charles Stanley, and the others had all, to varying degrees and in their own ways, contributed to fulfilling the dreams of Paul Weyrich, Ed McAteer, and Howard Phillips. A new Republican majority now seemed a real possibility. It was, however, the ambitious Falwell who led the formation of an organization that signaled the true arrival of the Religious Right—the Moral Majority. In May 1979, after the Dallas protest and with the family conference, the Hyde Amendment, and the ERA all brewing, Falwell invited Weyrich, Phillips, and Billings to the Holiday Inn in Lynchburg, Virginia. As Weyrich remembered, Falwell had the desire but not the focus: "He didn't know what he wanted to do and he certainly didn't know how to do it."[102] When the group was eating lunch, Weyrich remarked, "Out there is what one might call a moral majority—people who agree on principles based on the Decalogue [the Ten Commandments], for example—but they have been separated by geographical and denominational differences and that has caused them to vote differently." If the ministers present could get this group together, they would prove a political force. Falwell quickly interrupted, saying, "Go back to what you said earlier." After Weyrich began to explain himself again, Falwell said, "No, you started out by saying there is something out there." Weyrich replied, "Oh, I said there was a moral majority." Turning to one of his subordinates, Falwell exclaimed excitedly, "That's it! That's the name of our organization." In this fashion the Moral Majority was born.[103]

Weyrich quickly led the discussion to the Republican Party, suggesting that the issue of abortion might help unify Catholics and evangelicals, which could impact the 1980 GOP platform. Some members of Falwell's Thomas Road Baptist Church still worried that by creating a political organization across religious boundaries, their pastor would neglect the Gospel. In response, Falwell cited the antiabortion evangelist and author Francis Schaeffer, popular among his congregation. Schaeffer, Falwell insisted, agreed with him. There was no biblical mandate against evangelical Christians joining hands for political and social causes as long as there was no compromise of theological integrity. The Bible contained numerous stories of persons from varying philosophical backgrounds uniting for a cause pleasing to God. After the meeting with Weyrich and the others, Falwell contacted Houston businessman Bob Perry, who agreed to loan Falwell $25,000 to start the organization. Falwell sent out fliers and letters to his associates and followers, characterizing the organization as "pro-life, pro–traditional family, pro-moral, and pro-American."[104] The fliers listed eight reasons for the "decline of America," noticeably adding the new evangelical concerns for the family to the older concerns about the spread of Communism. There was a "danger of capitulation to the Soviet Union, a very possible result." A "first cousin to communism," there was a "creeping socialism" spreading across America. There was also, however, a "vicious and determined attack on the family." If the nation continued down its present path, "the monogamous family—one man, for one woman, for one lifetime—may become extinct." As part of this assault on the family, there were "three to six million babies legally murdered through abortion on demand." Nothing in the flier was overtly partisan, although its criticism of "give away programs and welfare" smacked of the Democratic agenda and its claim that there was an "unprecedented lack of leadership" brought the obvious to mind—Jimmy Carter.[105]

The letters and fliers had the intended effect. Donations poured in, as did hundreds of people volunteering their time and efforts. Requests for interviews dotted Falwell's calendar. Within weeks Falwell paid Perry back his loan and hired a full-time staff. The national organization consisted of the Moral Majority Incorporated, a political lobbying organization, and the Moral Majority Foundation, an organization to publish newspapers and reports, conduct interviews, and in general, publicize the mission. The first board of directors included Charles Stanley, Tim LaHaye, James D. Kennedy, and Greg Dixon, pastor of Indianapolis Baptist Church. Falwell named Robert Billings the first executive director, but all recognized who represented the organization's heart and soul.[106] The group made great use of direct mail and its leaders' respective mailing lists. In the end, the Moral Majority included some Catholics and even a few Jews. The initial editor of the Moral Majority's periodical, *Moral Majority Report*, was Catholic, as one example. From the outset one could not join without "making the commitment to support the state of Israel," Falwell explained, a nation that he now stressed, in the words of author Grace Halsell, as "the landing base for the Second Coming." Whatever the specific requirements, evangelicals and fundamentalists dominated. Reflecting on the Moral Majority years later, Ralph Reed of the Christian Coalition argued that its creation "awakened the slumbering giant of the American evangelical church."[107] Given the Moral Majority's board, not surprisingly, a high percentage of new members hailed from independent Baptist churches.

Notably absent was Pat Robertson, which Weyrich thought "odd" and "unfortunate."[108] It was, however, understandable. The educated and connected Robertson was prospering in a way that even Falwell might envy. His CBN University was set to dedicate impressive new facilities, and Robertson operated almost two dozen counseling centers that were open twenty-four hours a day. The ratings for his telecasts continued to soar, and he had the use of over ten thousand volunteers to staff his telephone lines. While the fact that Robertson was a charismatic did not help, he clearly represented a challenge for leadership. Robertson's opinions, like Falwell's about the coming 1980 election were obvious, although, also like Falwell, he could still not directly or officially endorse any candidate for fear of losing his ministry's tax-exempt status. Carter was "personally devout," Robertson told his followers, but his administration had become "repugnant to many Christians." Carter had "offended" those "who were his ardent champions."[109] In any event, together Falwell and Robertson ensured a broad reach. According to a book by evangelist Ben Armstrong, *The Electric Church*, published at the time of the Moral Majority's formation, over 130 million Americans regularly watched religious-oriented television.[110]

With its headquarters in Washington, D.C., the Moral Majority knew what buttons to push. The organization sent out a direct mailing claiming that "we are losing the war against homosexuals." Gay and lesbian groups planned to lay a wreath on the Tomb of the Unknown Soldier, the flier exclaimed, turning it into the "tomb of the unknown sodomite." Stressing the fight against abortion to a degree that he never did before, Falwell became, in his own words, "close friends" with Schaeffer, whom he had never met before the Moral Majority's founding.[111] His friendship with Schlafly became even closer. "Without the gay rights and the women's movement," historians

John Gallagher and Chris Bull concluded, "Falwell's political ascendancy might well have crashed and burned far earlier than it did." Falwell kept insisting that the Moral Majority was nonpartisan, even as he explained that the Democratic Party "had capitulated to extremist liberal groups." Carter "sadly felt it unwise to fight the pressure and was unwilling to oppose the gay and lesbian agenda."[112] Falwell "had a good time with Jimmy Carter during that period," recalled one member of the Moral Majority. "I don't think he really disliked Jimmy Carter personally, but Carter practiced a version of Christianity that, if you were to use the term 'liberal,' you would probably be close to what he was, and that was not popular with evangelicals and fundamentalists."[113] Unfortunately for the White House, events continued to give the Moral Majority much ammunition. Just as the organization formed, Carter's elderly mother, Lillian, accepted an invitation to a fund-raising dinner at the swank Beverly Wilshire Hotel in Beverly Hills, California. She had no idea that the beneficiary was the Los Angeles Gay Community Services Center. When she arrived, a gaggle of reporters asked her if she were embarrassed. "No," she replied, "of what?" Learning of the cause and with cameras clicking, she had no choice but to enter. The story hit the papers, however, poking fun at Lillian but also, implicitly, at Carter. It all added up, and by the end of the year the Moral Majority reported contributions of $35 million from more than 2.5 million contributors.[114]

In forming the Moral Majority, Falwell passed over McAteer as executive director. While McAteer would have welcomed the appointment, he was not bitter or depressed. Instead, he set about forming his own organization, the Religious Roundtable. At first McAteer envisioned primarily a group of Southern Baptists and those conservative Christians who, for whatever reason, did not feel comfortable with the Moral Majority. In time, however, the Religious Roundtable thrived just as Falwell's group did, its membership in both numbers and breadth undoubtedly surpassing McAteer's initial expectations. By the end of the decade the Religious Roundtable, based in California and citing the sponsorship of 37,000 pastors from 45 denominations, boasted a total membership of 187,000. In no way did McAteer see his organization as a rival to the Moral Majority but rather as a sister entity dedicated to the same cause. In fact, McAteer signed Falwell, Robertson, and Robison, along with Stanley and Kennedy, as his "big five" directors. The incestuous relationship of the Religious Right was no coincidence, as many groups shared membership lists, communications, and resources of all kinds. Groups such as Phyllis Schlafly's Eagle Forum and the Heritage

Foundation all prospered together, all with similar connections to the same conservative politicians, such as Senator Jesse Helms.[115]

The new conservative organizations did not surprise Robert Maddox, but their obvious popularity did frighten him. As for the Carters, the new Religious Right pained as much as it angered them. In the early fall Maddox accompanied Rosalynn Carter on a trip to Thailand to highlight the humanitarian crisis of Cambodian refugees fleeing into the country. On the way the two lamented the recent developments. With tears in her eyes, Rosalynn stated, "It seems the harder we talk about love and caring for each other, the more some folks throw that back in our faces." Upon returning, Maddox began to work on a fund for the refugees and received a considerable amount of money from Jim Bakker. This gave Maddox hope that conservative Christians and the White House could still work together for a good cause or at least blunt the most overt partisanship.[116] Advisor Anne Wexler, like Maddox, had not completely abandoned hope of still winning over the Moral Majority, her optimism perhaps looking past all the friction that so pained Carter. "These people influence millions of people," she wrote. If the White House were to arrange a meeting with the organization's leadership, "the president can move some of these people to his point of view on energy, SALT, and hospital cost containment." Carter "often meets with groups more hostile than this, and meets with plenty of religious leaders. Why not? Let's do it!"[117]

Some lines of communication, at least, appeared still open. Perhaps intended as proof that the Moral Majority was indeed nonpartisan or perhaps in the faint hope of still altering the administration's positions, Falwell sent birthday wishes to Rosalynn. "May God guide you and keep you close to Himself during this next year," the letter read, surely an odd sentiment in light of Falwell's public chastising.[118] The Carters remained Southern Baptists, of course, and were still friends with such prominent figures as Jimmy Allen, who occasionally invited both to worship services, slyly adding in one invitation to a Baptist rally that television cameras ensured broadcast. Rosalynn remained active in the Christian Life Commission, the SBC's social action agency, and agreed to address its convention. Conservatives had the helm in the denomination, but Carter still recognized them as brothers in Christ, not robots in the service of the GOP. If Falwell still hoped to influence the administration, Carter still hoped to influence the Southern Baptists.[119]

For the White House, Billy Graham represented an excellent chance to win back ground from conservatives such as Falwell. While the evangelical community held Graham in high esteem, he had been notably absent from the Religious Right's nascent organizations. Win over the famous preacher, and one could win over his massive following. In late summer Rosalynn called Maddox and asked him to approach Graham to inquire again about the possibility of testifying in favor of the SALT agreement, still before Congress. Maddox flew to the evangelist's large and scenic mountain home in Montreat, North Carolina. Sitting on the front porch, Graham told Maddox that he remembered "with gratitude the President's willingness many years ago to host a Graham film event in Americus, Georgia," and his "role as Honorary Chairman of the Graham Crusade in Atlanta a few years ago."[120] Graham, Maddox reported to the White House after the meeting, "has complete confidence in, and admiration and love for the President." Graham remained distraught that the media had misquoted him during the campaign when it had reported that he had criticized Carter, and he now wished to be of service. "He would especially welcome private time with [Carter] for conversation," Maddox added, but he "does not care to be a highly visible figure at the White House." When Maddox pressed for the Senate testimony, however, Graham declined, although he promised to press for the treaty in other venues. "What I will promise the President," he explained, "is to talk about nuclear control every chance I get. I will do my part to help create a climate in which the Senate can debate the treaty with as little unnecessary clamor as possible." With their meeting cordial, Maddox then pressed Graham for a statement supporting the ERA. "He quickly, with nervous laughter, declined," Maddox reported, "although I got the impression that he himself has no problem with the amendment." With their meeting ending, Graham raised an issue that had permeated their discussions but that neither had yet raised directly. "The conservative right, fundamentalist evangelical political coalitions are a definite factor in American life," Graham noted. It would be wise for Carter "to take careful note of this group."[121] On this, Maddox needed no prompting.

After receiving Maddox's report, Carter's orders were clear. "Arrange a dinner" with Graham, he wrote in a memo to his staff.[122] Soon Maddox and Wexler wrote Carter that Graham had accepted an invitation but that his wife, Ruth, could not attend because of medical tests scheduled at the Mayo Clinic. The two recommended that in preparation for the dinner Carter read Jeremy Rifkin's book *The Emerging Order*: "This book speaks to the developing power and energy of the conservative evangelical movement in the country." In any event, the dinner would be a "great opportunity to get a new statement from Graham endorsing SALT." After rescheduling, the dinner took place in October, and Ruth was able to attend.[123] Graham was already in Washington, and both Carter and the First Lady agreed to wait for Ruth to arrive on another flight. Carter's daughter, Amy, joined the foursome in the Carter's private dining quarters, and Carter invited the Grahams to spend the night in the Lincoln Bedroom. The hospitality obviously impressed Graham, who wrote profusely of his gratitude. The entire reception "was far more than we ever expected or deserved," his letter of thanks read. "Ruth and I came away with a new insight into the dedication of both of you to the cause of peace and justice in the world and to your evangelistic urgency."[124] Carter did not request a new SALT statement, which undoubtedly contributed to the friendly atmosphere. Weeks later the Grahams sent the Carters a fruitcake, and Carter replied with a note "sending you our warm personal regards."[125]

As Carter and Graham clearly wooed each other, it was obvious that while Graham would not join the new Religious Right organizations, neither would he go public in any substantial way to help the White House. For his part, Maddox now more regularly met with conservative pastors in his own personal political offensive but later admitted, "I could not help them significantly other than to give them a hearing."[126] In the wake of his North Carolina trip, Maddox devoted considerable time to recruiting ministers to support the SALT agreement. He would contact ministers in states that had undeclared senators and mention SALT in a positive light, ultimately asking if the minister would like to receive information on the agreement. If the minister said yes, Maddox would then ask him if he knew of any other ministers who might want to receive the information. Maddox was always careful never to ask the minister directly to support the agreement or to request that the minister lobby the senator himself, which opponents might construe as using government funds for a political campaign. The system, Maddox acknowledged, was "novel."[127]

In early October the arrival of Pope John Paul II offered a chance to reach out to conservative American Catholics, one that Carter had no intention of downplaying. Moreover, the new pope had already begun to develop a reputation for theological conservatism that seemed to parallel the Religious Right. On his seven-day, six-city tour of the United States, for example, he strongly condemned homosexuality even as he attempted to distinguish sexual "activity" from "orientation." Such nuance made little difference to conservative pastors such as Falwell, who publicly interpreted the pope's remarks as support for their cause. At the same time, the nuance obviously did not impress homosexual activists either, who protested when the pope arrived in New York.[128] The pope's "doctrinal conservatism," the *New York Times* reported, gave hope for "a renewed enthusiasm for the church by loyalists." Anticipating the event, the *Times* speculated on the problems the new pope faced with so many divisions among his followers in America. It noted that, unlike in many other countries, "religious pluralism" and the pull of modernity posed "challenges."[129]

The political ramifications of the visit were obvious to White House staff, not only as a desperately needed outreach to conservative Christians but also as a way to shore up traditional Democratic constituencies. "A major portion of the labor leadership is Catholic," White House aide Landon Kite reminded his superiors. "I will need an adequate number of slots [in the White House reception] to make sure that Catholics in the labor movement are properly represented."[130] The planning involved logistics, including special instructions for the press and briefings of specific areas that might arise in discussions.[131] Foreign policy, all recognized, was sure to play a major role. The meeting would help the administration advance its human rights agenda, National Security Advisor Zbigniew Brzezinski noted. While the Vatican wanted to stress the visit as "nonpolitical, pastoral," Brzezinski wrote Carter, "the central fact remains that on October 6th millions of Americans, along with many more millions of people outside the United States, will observe a meeting between the world's two most prominent human rights activists." The White House should handle the visit carefully: "The occasion will carry enormous symbolic significance."[132] The National Security Council recommended a joint appeal to advance relief efforts in Cambodia, where refugees and famine combined for a potential disaster.[133] Secretary of State Cyrus Vance agreed that the visit presented an opportunity, listing in a memo to Carter "our objectives." Carter should "encourage the Pope to continue to support our foreign policy goals by convincing him we are firm in our pursuit of world peace." Carter might "enlist Vatican support on specific humanitarian policy questions" but remember that the pope would visit as a religious leader, not stressing his political role. Carter should avoid controversial political questions, especially those surrounding the pope's native Poland. Vance recognized that the visit had political implications, adding that Carter should "return the warmth that the Pope is so successful in projecting to the American people." Carter should "associate [himself]

with the Pope's sentiments" but prepare for questions over potential disagreements: "You may wish to stress that with your great responsibilities,
you constantly face moral dilemmas that require difficult and often unsat-
isfying compromises."[134]

When John Paul arrived on October 6, the president and First Lady were
on hand at Andrews Air Force Base to greet him. A reception followed at
the White House. Rosalynn's speech included phrases that resonated across
denominational lines. She spoke of the "values of family," already a code
word among many conservative Christians, and in a more obvious overture to the same group, praised the pope for speaking out "in a clear and
constant voice of the dangers of moral compromise." For his part, the pope
agreed to a meeting with clergy of different faiths the following day.[135]

At the White House an official "exchange of remarks" before the press
pool on the North Lawn launched the agenda. "May God be praised," Carter
remarked in Polish to applause, adding that he welcomed the pope "on behalf of every American of every faith." The pope's visit was an opportunity
to "renew our spiritual lives" and recommit to "the enhancement of human
rights, the compelling idea and goal of our time." The pope thanked Carter
and praised America's "mission as stewards of the common good."[136] The
two leaders retired inside the White House for a series of meetings, photographs, and a private discussion in Carter's personal residence. The White
House acknowledged that the discussions covered "particular situations of
concern to world peace and justice," including SALT II, Northern Ireland,
the Camp David Accords, and the problem of refugees in Cambodia, although in regard to the latter there was no joint statement along the lines
the NSC had recommended.[137] At the conclusion Carter issued a statement
on the South Lawn before the pope departed for Andrews Air Force Base.
Faith was relevant to the modern world, Carter stated, and the pope "has
reminded us of our responsibilities." Carter's comments covered a range of
areas but, intentional or not, alluded in one instance to the matter of abortion. "Let us vow that what our Creator has made—human life and human
spirit—we shall not destroy," Carter stated. Later, as the pope climbed into
his car, departing from the North Portico, Carter pointed to the throngs of
admirers nearby, reminding the pope that there were "all kinds of people in
America."[138]

By the fall of 1979, competing with the newly mobilized Religious Right for
the hearts and minds of the conservative Christian community may have

appeared a political Hail Mary, but to Robert Maddox it was only a start. Still meeting with conservative pastors, Maddox advised a larger, better-coordinated program. It was still not too late. The administration's recent efforts, while welcomed, still appeared ad hoc and lacking focus. Reporting that Baptist Jimmy Allen and Illinois evangelist James Wall had both warned him that a seismic political shift was about to occur, Maddox wrote Jody Powell, Hamilton Jordan, and other superiors that if Carter did not act faster and more authoritatively, waves of evangelicals would vote for the Republicans in the coming year. Mentioning specific denominations by name, Maddox wrote of the need for "symbolic acts to demonstrate [White House] solidarity." He advised against stressing "deeply divisive" issues, which "should be kept at a low profile." Given recent developments, Maddox surely knew that this was a tall order, not so easily achieved. Nevertheless, he tried to be positive. The conservative evangelical community loathed Ted Kennedy and, no matter what, would always prefer Carter.[139]

As Maddox obviously recognized, the fall signaled the official beginning of the 1980 campaign season. It brought, as expected, the announcements that Kennedy and Ronald Reagan had entered the race. The former joined California governor Edmund G. Brown Jr. in challenging the incumbent for the Democratic nomination. In a sign of the difficult task he faced, Carter initially trailed both Democrats in the polls, both clearly appealing to the more liberal elements of the party. In seeking the Republican nomination, Reagan, having made a name for himself four years before, appeared as the champion of the more conservative elements of his own party. In the middle was Carter, attacked from the both the political Left and Right and still desperately trying to hold together the coalition that had put him into the Oval Office.

With the Carter-Mondale campaign gearing up, Sarah Weddington received a promotion that expanded her responsibilities. She met with Hamilton Jordan to discuss whether it was wise to hire a new person to handle women's issues, but the two decided, Weddington recalled, that "it would be a break in the continuity of efforts and it would have meant three people in three years with those responsibilities." Weddington, therefore, continued to handle women's affairs as well as "coordinating with the Democratic National Committee and putting on a series of briefings for people from various states who were politically interested and politically active." She soon found, however, that much of her political work still revolved around feminism and the troublesome issues surrounding the family.[140]

This was not surprising, partly because the National Advisory Committee planning the family conference scheduled hearings for the last four months of the year. The NAC planned speakers on a "first-come, first-heard basis," each speaker limited to five minutes. In a summary of these hearings that was later published, the NAC noted that the "huge outpouring . . . both overwhelmed and challenged us."[141] At every hearing site from Hartford, Connecticut, to Seattle, Washington, additional days of testimony were necessary. In the end, over two thousand speakers had talked for a total of over six hundred hours. Transcripts surpassed ten thousand pages. The hearings were respectful but emotional, further illustrating how divisive the debate over the nature of the family had become. On one side, many speakers insisted that the government had a greater role to play in ensuring the availability of quality child care and equality of economic opportunity. They stressed both the prevalence and importance of single-parent families and the need for birth control and flexible employment. Others, however, recommended less money for family planning and the need to criminalize abortion and homosexuality. Many noted the importance of religious institutions, not the government, and recommended support for responsible parenting and the nuclear family.[142]

"Women's groups around the country, like other organized interests, are scrutinizing the candidates' records as the wary courtship dance between candidates and potential supporters begins in earnest," the *New York Times* reported in November. Carter, the paper concluded, appeared at a distinct disadvantage. "There are not many specific things we've asked that the President hasn't done, but I think there are a lot of things he could have done that have not been done," Suone Cother, executive director of ERAmerica, told the paper. Added Iris Mitgang, the new chair of the NWPC, "There is a general sense in the women's movement that if anyone could deliver the ERA, it was a President from the South, and I don't think Mr. Carter has used the full power of his Presidency for us."[143] All three Democratic candidates favored the ERA, but Carter was alone in not fighting the Hyde Amendment. Brown had even worked to have his own state assist in the abortions of poor women. Pressing his case, Kennedy described Carter as "passive and insensitive to women's needs." The Carter campaign replied that Kennedy had neglected the appointment of women among his own staff.[144]

After conspicuously adding several women to his campaign staff, Kennedy was more aggressive against Carter in a speech before an all-female audience in Washington. Two days later Weddington sent out a flier to women's groups citing the administration's accomplishments. Noting that the fliers were mailed from the White House, Kennedy questioned the timing. Carter, he claimed, was campaigning at taxpayers' expense. It was a "coincidence," Weddington shot back. "It was just an informational tool to show that women are making progress."[145]

Worse for the White House, NOW's executive board announced that it would oppose Carter's reelection, no matter whom he faced. The twenty-seven-member board cited Carter's "failure" to get the ERA ratified and his stance on the Hyde Amendment. Carter, board member Sue Errington declared, "must be held accountable" for his efforts to restrict abortion rights. Realizing that the board's decision might help the election of a Republican opponent of the ERA, Betty Friedan found it all too hard to believe. "I'm sure it didn't happen," she told reporters. "It would be ridiculous" to endorse somebody like Reagan. "My understanding was that it was just a very strong warning."[146] Recognizing how partisan the women's issue had become, the decision equally perplexed other feminists, some reacting with consternation. When the White House arranged a December meeting of women's rights advocates with Carter, the sad state of affairs was obvious. Meeting in the Cabinet Room for almost an hour, the group discussed the problems of ERA ratification and the complaints the administration faced. Among the "challenges" outlined was the necessity to "stress that no one person, even if it is 'the President' can pass ERA." When the discussion turned to the ongoing Idaho ratification litigation, which involved the constitutionality of the state's rescission, the participants understood that the matter promised great scrutiny and demanded careful handling. The judge assigned the case, Marion Callister, was a Mormon, and his church had come out strongly against the ERA. Church president Spencer Kimball, whose pronouncements represented God's word for the faithful, had declared that the ERA was "a threat to the family, which is a creation of God." The ERA was indeed a "moral issue," a dissident church group, Mormons for ERA, had replied. "What could be more moral than for those of us who make up approximately fifty-one percent of the population of our country to be included in the protections of the law?"[147] While some feminists continued to demand that the Justice Department remove Callister, who had refused to recuse himself, White House staffers still tried to explain that politics should have no role in judicial matters. To remove Callister would risk charges of politicizing the administration of justice, a throwback to Nixon.[148] The White House's lack of action, however, "does not lessen in any way the commitment of this Administration to the ERA." Within proper bounds, "we shall continue to pursue a positive decision in this case."[149]

In the end, the White House meeting received more publicity than anticipated. Given the decision of the board, Weddington had rescinded the invitation to NOW's Eleanor Smeal. Smeal, in turn, had promised the press that she would protest by chaining herself to the White House. When the meeting commenced, Smeal led a dozen activists in picketing the meeting as "fraudulent," only a "showcase." With this political theater outside, Carter told the advocates inside that he was open to meeting with them regularly. Afterward, Mitgang, who did attend, seemed to add at least a little credence to the protesters' claims. The meeting was as much political as substantive, she told the press. Observing it all was Bella Abzug, undoubtedly with a bit of glee. Carter, she wrote, deserved all the criticism he got.[150]

If Weddington thought her feminist colleagues ungrateful, she had even less patience for homosexual rights activists, many of whom shared Abzug's sentiments despite the administration's historic overtures. In fact, when gay rights protesters pressed her office, Weddington deflected the issue to Wexler and Robert Malson. "My office no longer deals with the gay issues in any substantive way," she insisted, forwarding all correspondence on the controversial issue to her subordinates.[151] One could hardly blame her. While the activist Milk was dead, the National Gay Task Force obviously still sought to raise its profile for the campaign and continued to organize the March on Washington that Milk had proposed before his assassination. With the march scheduled for mid-October, the NGTF began to circulate nationally a petition that it planned to submit to Carter. The petition called for an executive order banning all discrimination against homosexuals and asking that Carter more publicly support legislation to include sexual orientation in the Civil Rights Act of 1964, the legislation that Abzug and Edward Koch had unsuccessfully introduced several years before. The NGTF selected one of its board members, Kay Whitlock, to head the drive and to arrange a public meeting with White House staff to receive the petition.[152] At the same time, the NGTF sent a circular to its membership encouraging them to call a radio talk show that had scheduled Carter the day before the march. Callers, the NGTF instructed, should press Carter on such unresolved issues as prison literature, immigration, and civil service legislation.

When the day of the march, October 14, arrived, a crowd of 75,000 marched past the White House to the Washington Monument in support of homosexual rights. Recognizing that their movement had been branded antifamily, a number of activists tried to change the terms of the debate. "We are a family," noted one speaker. "When a heterosexual person shows a picture of their loved ones, it's called sharing," claimed another. "When we show a picture of our loved ones, it's called flaunting." A series of speakers urged Carter to stand up more forcibly against discrimination. In the words of one, "[Equality] will come much sooner if we stop assuming that the President . . . knows better than we."[153] At the same time, a coalition of conservative ministers met on Capitol Hill to organize the National Day of Prayer on Homosexuality. The group asked ministers from around the country to petition Carter and Congress to resist "efforts to give homosexuals special consideration under the law."[154]

The march proved all that Milk had hoped for, but the NGTF followed with a questionnaire to all presidential candidates. Explaining in a letter to Carter that the survey would "inform over 3,000 local lesbian and gay organizations nationwide" and that his answers would "be made available to more than fifty national lesbian and gay publications, reaching about two million readers," the NGTF posed five specific questions.[155] Wexler and Malson agreed to meet informally with members of the NGTF on separate occasions, but inside the White House debate over how to respond to the questionnaire grew. Wexler wrote Carter, noting that "the sensitivity of the press and general public to gay issues insure that the responses to this questionnaire will receive wider dissemination and analysis than in the typical case." In short, it demanded Carter's personal attention. The administration, Wexler and other advisors advised, should stress the accomplishments of the first term without adding a lot of specific promises for the future.[156] Some argued that Carter should become more personally involved because his main primary opponent, Kennedy, had not yet replied in a detailed or substantive way. Others suggested that Carter add forceful remarks in his upcoming 1980 State of the Union address.[157]

In the end, once again, the White House's response reflected its efforts to avoid controversy and carve for itself an acceptable middle position. The NGTF first asked if Carter would "continue the precedent you established of an 'open door' to White House and administration officials for lesbian and gay representatives." While the question itself acknowledged the gains made under Carter, the White House answered that "the President's policy is to expand the involvement of all the American people in their government." For too long, the "doors of the Federal government were closed to too many Americans," the statement read. "[Carter] has opened those doors and intends to see that they remain open." The reply to the second question was equally general. Asked if the administration intended to appoint qualified gays and lesbians to high office, the White House replied, "In all of his appointments to high office, the President has required that any nominee be sensitive to the civil rights and civil liberties of all Americans." All appointments "would be made without discrimination based on race, color, sex, religion, national origin, or sexual orientation." The final three questions were more specific. Would Carter support a strong statement of gay and lesbian rights in the Democratic platform? The White House, the answer came, "will make decisions on the platform as that process evolves." In following up the Civil Service Reform Act of 1978, would Carter issue an executive order explicitly naming gays and lesbians as a protected class? This was a difficult question, the White House replied, and "[Carter] will continue to explore whether other action is necessary, but no decision has been made at this time." Finally, would Carter support a strong gay rights bill? "The President supports many of the concepts contained in [HR 2074, the existing House bill], but has not yet committed his support to the details of any particular legislation dealing with this topic." The legislative process would have to continue.[158]

Wexler and Malson's meetings with the NGTF officials went without incident or publicity, the conversations centering on the still unresolved issues of immigration and civil service. Both staffers tried to explain the predicament the administration faced. In regard to the latter, even if Carter decided not to issue an executive order or support additional legislation to protect homosexuals in government service, the existing exceptions for sensitive positions only affected 5 percent of the workforce. In other words, protections already existed for almost all federal employees. Despite the debate's limited scope, the White House still received a number of letters from both sides. The Lesbian and Gay Democrats of Texas, for example, wrote that its six hundred thousand members would oppose the White House if it continued to stall. Alabama congressman Bill Nichols, on the other hand, wrote that he "had been contacted by many constituents over the past several months." All worried that allowing homosexuals in sensitive government positions would "endanger the country's national security."[159]

Letters regularly arrived at the White House, lobbying for this action or that. Perhaps one example of the potential power of groups such as the Moral Majority is the letter written by Texas pastor B. J. Willhite to Carter: "You should realize that [your position] is inconsistent with a Biblical understanding of homosexuality and inconsistent with a Christian perspective." It had more to do with "Sodom and Gomorrah" than America. "In the past I have supported you openly because of my belief that you were a committed Christian as have many of my congregation and friends," Willhite concluded. "I am sorry to say that I will no longer be able to do so."[160] The White House's response was, perhaps, telling. It did not reply directly to the complaint but simply referenced the Democratic Party's platform.[161] When the British comedy group Monty Python released a new movie, *Life of Brian*, satirizing the life of Jesus, conservatives across the Christian spectrum protested, some describing it as "blasphemy."[162] When Carter officially signed the Department of Education Organization Act, it spiked once again the conservative fear of big government, the fear of social engineering into family life. In what proved a fortuitous bit of timing, evangelist LaHaye rode the controversy by publishing another attack against secular humanism titled *Battle for the Mind*. LaHaye distributed the book free to preachers "so that the man on the street can both understand [secular humanism's] danger and be motivated to oppose it at the place it can be defeated—the ballot box."[163] To counter such efforts, groups such as Evangelicals for Social Action also mobilized. Committed to government activism on behalf of "justice and liberty," the group sought to unite theological liberals in much the same way that the conservatives had done among their own ranks. The group was, according to one description, "a modest counterattack on the formidable conservative barrage that is shaping up this election season."[164]

In the middle of it all, just as the campaign had begun, the year did not end quietly. First, in November thousands of militant Iranians stormed the American embassy in Teheran, seizing fifty-two Americans as hostages. Supposedly a group of students uncoordinated with the new government of revolutionary Iran, led by Ayatollah Khomeini, the militants demanded that Carter return the shah, recently admitted to the United States for cancer treatment. Events then unfolded quickly. Khomeini refused to meet with Ramsey Clark, a special American envoy sent to Iran, and Carter froze all Iranian assets. As the ripples from the Iranian provocation continued to sweep through the Middle East, including anti-American riots in several countries, Soviet troops attacked Afghanistan. The invasion, which continued for days and resulted in a Soviet puppet regime under Babrah Karmal, was another shock to the political system. Suddenly, events had turned the

nascent campaign on its head, no one sure of when or in what manner resolutions and peace might come.

At the outset, at least, Americans appeared to forget all about the family conference, homosexuality, abortion, the ERA, and even the economy.
When Carter proclaimed National Family Week in December, or when he
ordered all government departments to identify policies that affected families and recommend changes, few even noticed. With the media in a frenzy,
all other issues besides the international crisis paled, and Americans rallied
to the president in a tide of patriotism. Opinion polls suddenly indicated
the largest one-month reversal in history, Carter's approval rating soaring
from 32 to 61 percent. Although Carter had agreed to debate Kennedy, he
now reversed course, arguing that policy, not politics, demanded his attention. It seemed to most Americans an appropriate response.[165]

Most conservative Christians agreed. Rather than publicly criticize, some
offered praise, others advice. A number of religious leaders wrote the White
House of their prayers.[166] Baptist Jimmy Allen spoke with Carter directly
and emphasized that because the Iranian revolution was religious based,
economic sanctions would have little effect. After the Christian Life Commission adopted a similar stance that spoke of the "futility of political negotiations," its president, Phil Strickland, also wrote Carter: "We have a deep
concern that effective negotiations take into consideration the uniquely
religious nature of this crisis." The situation required "careful handling."[167]
With this, even the most liberal feminist agreed.

Quietly, however, behind the headlines the social and religious rifts were
way too deep by the end of the decade simply to vanish. However muffled,
the political campaign and all that it entailed had not evaporated. The Kennedy campaign let voters know that Carter's new "Rose Garden campaign
strategy" was indicative not of statesmanship but of political cowardice.
In fact, Kennedy staffers implied, Carter was taking political advantage of
the crisis. Among the Moral Majority, some began to complain that Iran
had simply exposed America's weakness. If the United States had not let
its guard down—as Carter had done—no rogue power would have been so
bold. Others suggested that Carter had weakened the shah of Iran by stressing human rights, precipitating the very crisis that he now faced. Either
way, the Republicans were willing to agree; the GOP wished to foster both
sentiments.[168]

The decade of the 1970s ended as tumultuously as it had begun. The
Vietnam War and a youthful counterculture may have given way to eco-

nomic stagflation and an emergent Religious Right, but the final months had witnessed a sudden burst of activity that appeared to promise a future as momentous and uncertain as the past. No one knew what the coming decade would bring, whether hellish wars or a Middle East at peace. Americans instinctively came together, although undoubtedly all knew that the new political dynamic would not last. Carter, amazingly it appeared, had one last opportunity to right his campaign's ship, to alter the public's dismal perception of his administration. If he could react firmly and resolve the crisis quickly and favorably, then the White House's fragile coalition might survive for another election after all. Despite the frustrations of the political Left and Right, perhaps Carter's political coffin had not yet been nailed shut. Delay and vacillation, however, and a long, agonizing hostage crisis would confirm Carter as inept and impotent, reminding voters of their latent disappointment. In this scenario, the new Religious Right would not be an extreme and lonely voice but rather a powerful constituency at the vanguard of a political tsunami.

CHAPTER SIX

The Profamily Movement

THE NEW DECADE OF THE 1980s begged for a strong leader. With inflation ravaging the economy and America disrespected abroad, voters sought a presidential candidate strong enough to order the chaos. Despite the obvious obstacles of his first term, a seemingly rejuvenated Carter was determined to take charge of the crisis and be that candidate. On January 20 he appeared on *Meet the Press* and in forceful language re-affirmed American resolve regarding Iran and Afghanistan. Countering charges of weakness, Carter appeared little fazed by the fact that most U.S. allies offered only tepid support. The next day, Carter crushed his main Democratic challenger, Ted Kennedy, in the Iowa caucus, signaling the official beginning of the campaign season and the reality that the incumbent still enjoyed a sense of national unity. Two days after his victory, Carter again attempted to project strength in his State of the Union address, confidently proclaiming a "Carter Doctrine," an American commitment to use armed force to counter any Soviet attempt to disrupt Persian Gulf oil supplies. He also asked for greater military spending and registration for a potential draft. When Congress approved a boycott of the upcoming Moscow Olympics to protest the Soviet invasion of Afghanistan, Carter applauded. Seeking to build on his momentum, Carter continued his Rose Garden campaign strategy, denouncing Kennedy's criticisms as "very damaging to our country."[1]

The White House's offensive involved more than simply its Rose Garden strategy. It included what the *New York Times* termed a "two-day blitz to sway evangelicals."[2] First, on the day of his Iowa victory, Carter attended the annual convention of the National Religious Broadcasters, held once again at the Washington Hilton. After three years of sending his regrets,

Carter reversed course for his reelection campaign, although by the new decade one certainly could understand if he had again declined. It was now quite obvious that the convention reflected the growing conservative tilt of the evangelical movement. In the lobby were representatives from the National Republican Committee, the American Conservative Union, and the Liberty Lobby. While many of the participants decried the "us versus them" mentality that had grown in the theological debate, conservatives clearly enjoyed both their majority and its potential impact on the coming election. "The liberals are apprehensive about the electric church because we seem to be succeeding," noted one enthusiastic convention participant.[3] Carter had "lost favor among evangelical leaders in the past three years," the *Times* noted, and his appearance at the convention was evidence of an attempt to shore up his support in the religious community.[4]

Ben Armstrong, the NRB's executive director, had worked hard to win Carter's attendance, playing on the election season. The invitation was gracious and made no mention of Carter's previous regrets.[5] Others lobbying were equally diplomatic although more direct in their allusions to politics. Elias Golonka of the Baptist Convention of New York noted that Carter's public faith "has had great implications for my ministry" but added that accepting Armstrong's offer might "enhance the cause of your Presidency in the coming difficult year."[6] When Carter accepted the invitation to speak, some broadcasters tinged their applause with a degree of sarcasm. "Eclipsing even the slightest election year motive," one general manager wrote, "is [the NRB's] prayer support." It was great, another wrote, to "finally" get to see the president.[7]

Leaving the White House by motorcade and arriving at the Hilton only five minutes later, Carter met Armstrong and the NRB's president, David Hofer, upon his arrival.[8] After quickly going onstage, Carter mentioned both the coming election and his support from conservative Christians in the past. "This is an election year and it is going to be quite different from the last one in 1976," Carter began. "This year I am going to let you spend your full time explaining what it means to be born again." As if to acknowledge the differences he had with many participants, he noted that God worked through "imperfect people" and argued that the broadcasters, with their "awesome power to shape public opinion," had an "obligation to show both sides of an issue." Carter mentioned Israel in several instances in what appeared to some observers to be an attempt to burnish his image as a friend to the beleaguered nation and asked for the group's prayers as his presidency moved forward in regard to Iran and Afghanistan.[9]

Carter did not stay long after his remarks, but to solidify any political gain, Rosalynn agreed to have tea with a group of NRB-related women the following morning. In addition, Robert Maddox, who had pressed hard for Carter's participation, agreed to attend the convention's closing banquet.[10] Nevertheless, tensions obviously remained, as no single speech could erase all the animosity that had developed. While Carter characterized his reception as "friendly," according to Maddox, many NRB members criticized his comments as "more political and less presidential."[11] A week after the convention, Armstrong requested that Carter meet with his executive committee. Such a meeting, he wrote, "would be extremely beneficial in the forthcoming election." Four years before, Armstrong added, Ford had agreed to meet with the committee just before that year's election. Noting both the efforts already undertaken and the group's continued conservative bias, Maddox recommended that Carter decline. "I do not think such a meeting is necessary at this time," he wrote.[12] Carter agreed, although the White House forwarded transcripts of his convention remarks as mementos. This overture apparently had at least some positive impact. Evangelist Rex Humbard later wrote Carter that he planned to replay a tape of Carter's convention remarks on his own televised broadcast, claiming with some hyperbole that over "one hundred million people" would see it.[13]

The president's attendance at the NRB convention was only the first half of its "two-day blitz." The following day, January 22, Carter welcomed a group of ministers to a White House breakfast. It was, Maddox recalled, a "tough assignment." The list of those invited was small "so conversation could take place." In deciding the list, the White House focused on "categories rather than personalities" and deliberately sought representatives of the burgeoning television ministries. Its intent was to invite "the left hand of the right," critics who could still work cooperatively.[14] Maddox developed topics for discussion and suggested that the ministers stick to the issues at hand in order to conserve time. The topics, Maddox noted, included all of the issues commonly debated in the religious community, including abortion and homosexuality. For each, Maddox prepared a possible response for Carter. On the day of the breakfast, the weather was gray and cold, and Maddox, nervous, arrived early from the subway. White House staff prepared an elaborate breakfast in a downstairs dining room that had long been the personal dining area for earlier presidents. Aware that many of the guests were southerners and attempting to cast a folksy atmosphere, the staff served grits. The attendees included Rex Humbard, Jerry Falwell, Jim Bakker, Oral Roberts, Demos Shakarian, James Kennedy, Tim LaHaye, and several other leading ministers. Pat Robertson declined his invitation. When Carter arrived, he made use of Maddox's preparatory briefs, "though he knew how to answer without much prompting." The schedule called for Carter to stay only twenty minutes, but the conversation was so "lively" that Carter stayed almost an hour. "We knew," Maddox recalled, "that three or four of them were essentially enemies. They said they had open minds but we knew that you can't just change your political enemies with a breakfast." At the closing, as planned, Roberts led the group in a prayer, and Carter pleased the attendees by asking them to pose for a photograph.[15]

In his own remarks, Carter once again stressed his born-again faith, obviously playing the same political card. He avoided any mention of abortion or the specifics of any controversial "family" issue but spoke in generalities about his faith in Jesus Christ. In many respects, the ministers appreciated his overtures. "I have been as critical of the President as anybody," remarked Bakker. "But it's easier to take potshots at the image on the screen than it is when you're in the same room with a warm, decent man confessing his faith in Jesus Christ." Robert Dugan of the National Association of Evangelicals added, "I've been to the White House for breakfast before but this is the first time that I've ever been served grits." Nevertheless, as Maddox predicted, the breakfast hardly wiped away all tensions. Several ministers pressed Carter on the specifics he had so carefully avoided. Dugan questioned Carter's support of school prayer and found him hesitant, worried about the pressure religious minorities would face. Reflecting his growing clout, Falwell was particularly aggressive, asking Carter if he supported a constitutional amendment outlawing abortion or realized that the ERA had no chance of ratification. Falwell also complained about the White House Conference on Families adopting a definition of family that included "any two people living together." Carter, Falwell told the press afterward, had reversed his position on the "right-to-life amendment." This piqued the media's interest and forced a denial from the White House. "The President's stance is unchanged," Anne Wexler replied. Carter would not advocate an amendment, "but if one passed, he would not oppose it. . . . [T]hat's all he said and nothing more." Predictably, it appeared the sort of middle-of-the-road stance that pleased no one.[16]

In what undoubtedly helped his renewed offensive, Carter attended the National Prayer Breakfast at the Washington Hilton, traveling by motorcade just as he had the year before but followed by a larger press contingent. "Spiritual growth depends partly on becoming more aware of others and praying for them," Carter told the more than three thousand attendees.[17] At the same time, he met with a group of twenty-six Hispanic Protestant ministers in the Oval Office, a group quite evangelical but, according to some White House staffers, more open to the Democratic Party. "The Hispanic Protestant population is larger than most people realize . . . and you have always felt that the direction which comes from ministers to a community is of the utmost importance," a memo briefing Carter read. At the meeting, the Reverend Ruben Cruz—"a strong supporter since the last election"—presented Carter with a new Spanish translation of the Bible. The White House ensured that the American Bible Society, so popular among all evangelicals, received a photograph of the meeting and that Maddox had the addresses of all attendees for future correspondence.[18]

Paralleling its overture to Hispanics, the White House also courted African American evangelicals, another group religiously conservative but more open to Democrats. In fact, with the primary season in full swing, Republicans complained that the Democrats were offering "walking around money" to black pastors in an effort to get them to endorse the party's agenda.[19] Democrats vehemently denied the accusations, and in any event, the administration was not involved. Still, at the White House Carter met with a large group of black pastors. Aware that the economy played a particularly important role to the pastors' parishioners, staffers arranged for a number of economic advisors to brief the group. Carter's comments highlighted both his faith and his efforts to combat inflation and unemployment. The meeting went well, and many of the pastors acknowledged that their support for Carter remained strong.[20]

Throughout it all, of course, the international crisis was never far below the surface. At the National Prayer Breakfast, conversations in the halls revolved around the hostage situation. Republican congressman Guy Vander Jagt, a Presbyterian minister and the keynote speaker, referred to the Iranian revolution by calling for a "spiritual awakening here at home." In his remarks Carter had to acknowledge the hostage crisis as well. "Every day I pray for the Ayatollah Khomeini, for the kidnappers that hold the Americans, and for those who are held hostage in innocence," Carter stated.[21] As Carter tried to repair his relations with evangelicals, Iran's Khomeini invited several American Christian clergymen to Teheran in what he claimed was an overture for peace. Noting that the pastors were on record against the deposed shah and more sympathetic to the ayatollah's position, critics cited the trip as a public relations stunt that helped the enemy. When an acquaintance of Carter's, the Southern Baptist pastor Jimmy Allen, followed with his own trip to Teheran at the invitation of the Iranian ambassador, the critics now complained that the White House was endorsing an appeasement policy. Although Allen had taken a firm stance against Iran and publicly distanced himself from the earlier trip, Carter was once again on the defensive against claims that he was too weak.[22] Ironically, the National Council of Churches complained at the same time that the Carter administration still employed ministers as CIA agents abroad, directly contradicting its own stated policy. The Senate Select Committee on Intelligence held hearings, and it was obvious that, regardless of the direction the White House chartered, it would face an avalanche of criticism: Carter was weak, he did not respect religion, or more often than not, he was simply inept. It was, obviously, an election season, and evidence of any national unity was fleeting.[23]

The White House's new election-year offensive to regain lost ground with evangelicals pleased Maddox but still did not represent the massive, coordinated agenda that he thought necessary. For one, campaign staff continued to decline numerous invitations for Carter to address religious audiences. Undoubtedly, Carter had to devote most of his time to crisis management as well as to his other campaign obligations, but the regrets still disappointed the churches in question and muted the White House's offensive. Moreover, Carter did not grant conservative pastors the well-publicized interviews that they continued to request. Most important, however, he coupled his election-year efforts to win conservative Christians with a similar offensive to retain the votes of the women's and gay rights movements. Carter had made promises to both groups and could not now repudiate his long-established positions, and he still believed that his advocacy of reform on these issues did not insult his evangelical faith. As Maddox recognized, however, this was not the theology of the new Religious Right. Attempts to maintain Carter's 1976 coalition would surely alienate all involved, dooming any campaign offensive and, in the end, the election itself.

Predictably, when it came to the matter of women's rights, the dawn of the new decade brought a wave of forecasts. "The 1980s may bring forth an increasingly conservative climate," wrote columnist Enid Nemy. "There will be a much more political bent to the [women's] movement," declared Eleanor Smeal, ignoring, it seemed, her already overt maneuvering. The new decade will doom the ERA, countered Phyllis Schlafly confidently.[24] For its part, the *Atlanta Constitution*, evidently ignoring all that had taken

place in the previous years, concluded, "The outcome of a close battle between President Carter and Senator Edward Kennedy for the Democratic
nomination may involve a crucial 'sleeper' issue: women's rights."[25] Given
it all, one could understand if Carter downplayed his earlier promises and
retreated in his advocacy of the ERA. Feminists such as Smeal had hardly
appreciated the administration's efforts to date, and new polls suggested
that the Republicans were increasingly united in regard to the amendment.
Republican voters would probably avoid the public spat that had characterized their primaries four years before. Nevertheless, Carter was true to
his word, continuing to meet regularly with women's rights advocates even
as Iran and Afghanistan consumed more and more of his time.[26] After appointing Juanita Kreps, who had resigned from the Department of Commerce to support the ERA at the League of Women Voters, Carter proposed
that the military require both sexes to register for the draft. Carter couched
his proposal not only as a women's rights issue but also as one of national
security, alluding to Iran and Afghanistan. "[The proposal] confirms what
is already obvious throughout our society—that women are providing all
types of skills in every profession, and the military should be no exception," Carter stated. It would also demonstrate "our resolve as a nation" to
resist "further Soviet aggression in the region around the Persian Gulf."[27]
Predictably, the proposal infuriated many conservatives. One group began
circulating a fictitious news report from "Manycities, U.S.A.," dated "198?."
It told a harrowing tale of a young woman returning from war maimed.
After she was awarded the "ERA Medal," her mother sobbed that she had
not thought that this is what women's equality would mean. The report
was "anonymous trash being circulated to congressmen," one of Weddington's staff complained. "I guess we can expect more of this from the un-
enlightened."[28]

Undeterred, Carter agreed to meet with the President's Advisory Committee for Women to hear its recommendations for ERA ratification. The
PACW had been working on its report since its inception twelve months
before, and the meeting in the Cabinet Room was substantive and lasted
for seventy minutes. "You may wish to reiterate that ERA cannot be passed
by one person," Weddington advised members beforehand, obviously not
forgetting the previous year.[29] Most of the report was general, but part of
it dealt with "target states." These states included Missouri, Georgia, Illinois, and Florida, all scheduled for new voting. States deemed unlikely to
ratify and thus not worthy of considerable effort included Alabama, Ar-

kansas, Louisiana, Mississippi, Nevada, Utah, and Virginia. It was possible that Oklahoma, along with North and South Carolina, might hold new votes, but most likely they would not. This was all confidential, denied to the press, as were recommendations to recruit more black leaders with the help of Coretta Scott King and prominent black lawyer Vernon Jordan, add individual briefings for opinion leaders, expand polling, and in total, involve the president more through letters of appreciation and encouragement.[30] Weddington added that she thought Virginia and Louisiana were still possible but noted that "many of the recommendations are already in operation." After the meeting, Carter issued a statement that resembled the promises made previously. He would "heighten and intensify" his efforts. This was enough for chairwoman Lynda Johnson Robb, who only added that Carter had approved the idea of distributing speech packets to cabinet members.[31]

In the weeks that followed, the White House held a number of symposia on the ERA recommended by PACW. Invited were business leaders, politicians, community activists, religious leaders, and journalists, among others. The agenda included a series of panels in the Old Executive Office Building.[32] In the first symposium, Carter addressed the issue of families, perhaps indicating once again the degree to which Schlafly had succeeded in framing the debate: "Some have claimed that the Equal Rights Amendment will destroy families. If I felt that the Equal Rights Amendment would destroy a single family, I would not support it. But that is not the case. It is not a threat to destroy a family if a wife feels that she is a first class citizen instead of a second class citizen. It certainly won't destroy a family for two working people at the head of a household to have a reasonable salary for the work they do." Carter also argued that the ERA would not "create an enormous Federal bureaucracy that would sprawl all over the United States," another obvious rebuttal to Schlafly. In the end, Carter's remarks suggested that he remained on the defensive, even as he renewed his push for the political initiative.[33]

Solidifying the gay and lesbian vote was no easier. Carter's stance was now well established and under constant criticism. His delicate balancing act made any political offensive problematic. Ever the champion of the gay community, Democratic California senator Alan Cranston reintroduced only days into the new year his legislation to repeal officially the ban on gay immigration, thereby ending the convoluted situation that most observers recognized as untenable. Kennedy quickly endorsed the legislation in anticipation of the coming California primary, beginning an obvious push to win the gay and lesbian vote. Wrestling with the issue, the White House bungled its response. First a spokesman stated that Carter would join Kennedy in supporting the bill, but then, only days later, the same spokesman claimed that it was a mistake. There was still no decision. "What bullshit," exclaimed Don Knutson, legal director of Gay Rights Activists, a new San Francisco organization. "They are just cowardly. It's typical Carter."[34] In the end, months passed until the administration announced its support for the bill, then couching it as necessary for compliance with the Helsinki Accords on human rights. Perhaps sensing the bill's fate, a Cranston spokesman declared, "An endorsement is nice, but who's going to work for it?"[35] Indeed, the administration did little to advance the legislation, which eventually failed. It was, in the words of the Washington Post, "immigration follies."[36] As if to recoup itself, the administration followed the bill's defeat with its own new directive. Immigration officials would now only exclude people who insisted upon making an "unambiguous, unsolicited declaration" of their homosexuality. Officials were not to consider appearance or other factors in their decision. While many activists welcomed the more forceful directive, it was, in the words of one gay activist, "a sidestep." It did nothing to resolve the central dilemma in enforcement of the law. In fact, the confusion continued to reign until Congress finally passed legislation to repeal the homosexual ban in 1990.[37]

With Kennedy now working hard to embrace homosexual rights, the White House moved quickly to end the long-running debate over homosexuals in the civil service. While Margaret Costanza, before her departure the previous year, had raised the possibility that Carter would support new civil service legislation explicitly banning discrimination based on sexual orientation, the White House continued to insist that the existing law's ban on discrimination based on private, nonrelated job behavior sufficed and that the exemptions for sensitive government jobs were necessary. If gay activists pushed the matter further, the White House warned, it might provoke a backlash. As if employing a play from its immigration playbook, however, the administration announced two new directives that it hoped would placate gay and lesbian voters. The first stated in the clearest terms to date that it was administration policy not to consider sexual orientation in government hiring. The second stated that civil service employees could consider volunteer work for homosexual groups acceptable work experience.[38]

To the homosexual community, the administration's policy appeared tepid at best, hypocritical at worst. If the White House really did believe that government workers should not discriminate against gays and lesbians, why rely on directives that might someday be reversed and instead ardently support legislation that explicitly named homosexuals as a protected class? Similarly, why not support legislation that explicitly allowed homosexual immigration rather than rely on a policy that later came to be known as "don't ask, don't tell" and that simply appeared to prolong a final resolution? As the election year unfolded, the administration did announce that it would relent and allow nonpornographic homosexual literature into prisons, a decision that finally ended that long-running debate and the litigation that surrounded it. This was, at least, one unmitigated gesture the gay community welcomed.[39] At the same time, the Federal Communications Commission announced that it would consider the views of the homosexual community in determining standards for broadcasting, another welcomed development.[40] Still, however, among many gays and lesbians a persistent sentiment remained: despite Carter's obvious election-year push for their votes, he was, at best, only a fickle friend.

In the midst of the primary season, the National Gay Task Force released a statement that acknowledged Carter's efforts. The administration's record was "solid." While its positions on civil service reform and immigration were "difficult to understand," Carter was more ally than enemy. At the same time, however, the organization Gay Vote 1980 reported that "support for President Carter within the gay community has eroded disastrously." The person most sympathetic to the cause had been Costanza, but she had been forced out.[41] Even as it released its public statement, the NGTF privately wrote Carter that it was "deeply disturbed and dismayed" that many issues remained unresolved.[42] The homosexual community had options, after all. Not only had Kennedy proved happily "outspoken on gay rights," in the words of the *Advocate*, but the battle for the Republican nomination included the Illinois congressman John Anderson, who had recently announced that he was leaving the First Evangelical Free Church of Rockford, Illinois, because of its opposition to abortion and gay rights.[43] "Unlike Carter," the NGTF concluded, "John Anderson is still promising changes for the better." It was "difficult finding gay voters who are not at least leaning toward Anderson." Even Reagan, the GOP front-runner, did not appear a huge threat, many activists not realizing that his opposition to the Briggs

Initiative had grown from a strong commitment to federalism, not equal rights for homosexuals. His campaign, the NGTF predicted, would try to "steer a middle course." Under a Reagan administration, the gay community "would fare about the same as under Carter."[44]

Given Kennedy's popularity and his strength in the primaries, a number of the White House staff wanted to move again to reassure the homosexual community that the administration's actions were not tepid and that uniting behind the president was wise politically. "Gays are looking for more public acknowledgment by the president," advisor Bob Malson wrote Stuart Eizenstat, who continued to coordinate all White House domestic initiatives. The president should consider an appearance at a gay forum or campaign event.[45] "Every incident," one of Malson's own staff warned, "has recently gotten extensive press coverage, especially in the [San Francisco] Bay area." California had a large gay constituency, and the administration could not afford to "appear to be operating in bad faith." It was "just what we don't need in an election year."[46] Tom Bastow of Gay Vote 1980 advised the Carter campaign that trying to straddle the middle was unwise, since the homosexual lobby was well organized in the states with the most convention delegates and electoral votes. The president "should begin to correct the situation before it is too late." As if reflecting Malson, Bastow suggested that Carter appear at a gay-oriented event and come out forcibly for a strong gay plank in the Democratic platform. After all, "Kennedy and [California governor Jerry] Brown are for it." If Carter did not support such a strong plank, "we are at least strong enough to make a long messy fight of it."[47]

Inside the White House, advisor Wexler acknowledged that Carter accepting a series of invitations to attend Gay Pride Week celebrations in San Francisco carried too much risk. "While obviously these requests will be turned down," she wrote, a strong statement of support "read by a local Carter person" would help.[48] In the end, the White House continued to profess its commitment to homosexual rights, a clear offensive to retain the gay vote. At the same time, the administration's political predicament remained never far below the surface. When the Carter campaign released a twelve-page summary of the administration's first-term accomplishments, it named everything from environmental policy to government reorganization to taxes. Nowhere, however, was homosexuality mentioned, not even in sections extolling Carter's record in defense of human rights or in protecting civil liberties.[49]

Carter had a lot on his political plate. He had to defend his handling of the economy amidst stagflation, the lingering combination of inflation and unemployment that offered critics on both the political Left and Right ammunition. He had to project strength in the international crisis in the hopes of recasting his administration's image, even as the early months of the new year predictably whittled away any sense of national unity. And, of course, he had to hold together his antagonistic 1976 coalition, a task that involved his troubled election-year offensive to pacify both the new Religious Right and the champions of the rights revolution. It would prove an active spring primary season.

As Carter won the January Iowa caucus, it was already obvious just how attractive Reagan was among many in the Religious Right. While some conservative Christians remained wary of the former actor and California governor because of his signing of a state bill that allowed for at least some abortions if not because of his Hollywood pedigree, most accepted his now frequent apologies and insistence that his signing had been a mistake. Moreover, his main opponent, former Texas congressman and Republican National Committee chairman George Bush, had recently denounced abortion but had been prochoice earlier in his career. Obviously failing to learn from Carter's abortion struggles, Bush claimed that he was personally opposed to abortion but would not support a constitutional amendment against it. Like Carter, he appeared still trying to carve out a middle, moderate stance. Accordingly, his candidacy worried the antiabortion lobby. Prior to the Iowa vote, the Pro-Life Action Council, the political arm of the state's antiabortion movement, wasted no time in endorsing Reagan. More organized than four years before, it employed an elaborate telephone network, voter identification, mailings, and a door-to-door campaign. More significantly, it stressed abortion as only part of a degenerating culture that threatened the family. From the official beginning of the campaign season, therefore, the growing unity among social conservatives was apparent. The day before the Iowa caucus, a new organization, the Life Amendment Action Committee, sponsored its first Respect Life Leadership Conference in Washington, scheduled to coincide with the seventh annual March for Life, coincidentally the day after the Iowa primary. At the conference leaders from over fifty antiabortion groups met and agreed that they should expand their agenda. They denounced abortion as well as the ERA, homosexuality, divorce, contraceptives, euthanasia, and most vehemently, "humanism." Simply put, America needed to return to its "Christian" roots. Just as their colleagues in Iowa, therefore, participants rallied around the antiabortion struggle but saw their agenda sweeping across the conservative spectrum. Also, just as in Iowa, the conference endorsed Reagan, with many Democrats promising to switch parties. "I am Democrat," declared Mary Beth Abraham, a delegate from Nebraska, "but I will be supporting Ronald Reagan if no one in my party comes forward."[50]

The results from Iowa thrilled the Pro-Life Action Council. Not only did Reagan win, but dozens of the council's members won seats as delegates to the coming Republican National Convention. When the March of Life followed on the next day in Washington, Reagan issued a statement in support, read to the thousands in attendance. "Jimmy Carter, stop the slaughter," proclaimed many banners. Once again, participants reflected a broader conservative critique. Anita Bryant, known for her fight against the homosexual rights movement, denounced abortion but added as she had before, "I am not just concerned about one issue." The nation's drift away from God had to stop.[51]

It remained a crowded field. As Ted Kennedy and Jerry Brown challenged Carter for the Democratic nomination, both attempting to pry disgruntled feminists and gay rights activists from the incumbent, Reagan led a large field of challengers. The group included not only Bush but also former Texas governor John Connally, Tennessee senator Howard Baker, Kansas senator Robert Dole, and two Illinois congressmen, Philip Crane and John Anderson. All sought to play off the momentous developments of the day, and they all, in varying degrees and from their own perspectives, found as much fault with Carter as with each other. The Iranian situation grew more troublesome with each passing day, but the crisis was in its early stage, and a United Nations mission to Iran still promised a "speedy release" of the hostages. In this context, Carter won a February caucus in Maine and a crucial primary in New Hampshire before Kennedy, as predicted, won his own state's primary on March 4. With Brown's campaign already faltering, a series of five primaries and seven state caucuses from March 11 to 22 clearly established Carter as the likely Democratic nominee. Although the United Nations mission had by now obviously failed, many of the votes were in southern states, which did not play well into Kennedy's more overt liberalism. In addition, Kennedy faltered in several interviews, in one instance clearly struggling when asked directly why he was running for president. Reagan, meanwhile, appeared in a commanding position in regard to the Republican nomination. While Bush won Michigan and remained the only possible threat, the nomination was essentially assured. Baker, who had seemed so promising at the outset, dropped out, as did Dole, Crane, and Connally, the latter having won only one delegate from Arkansas despite spending more than ten million dollars. Anderson, however, refused to yield and began what ultimately proved an effective third-party candidacy.[52]

Just as the primary season winnowed the competition and both parties began to focus more on the fall's general election campaign, one did not have to look far to see that the administration's offensive to placate the Religious Right had made little headway. In March a group of ministers submitted to Maddox a petition against homosexual rights signed by over seventy-five thousand people. "This so-called born-again Christian President is not acting very born-again," claimed Bob Jones III, president of Bob Jones University. "God's judgement is going to fall on America as on other societies that allowed homosexuality to become a protected way of life." Robert Billings added that the petition was a direct result of the NGTF's pressure on Carter.[53] More noticeably, after Carter's White House breakfast with leading ministers in January, Carter's staff began to receive complaints from conservative Christians who misquoted the president, many of the misquotes attributed to Falwell. One Baptist minister wrote Wexler, "I was talking with the leaders of the Southern Baptist Convention and they said that men like Jerry Falwell and others had tried in Christian love to share some concerns of the majority of people in this country with President Carter, but that he became very cold and would not discuss the matter further." Another writer complained about Maddox, who had arranged the January meeting and had been present. He had, the letter claimed, remarked that Carter "wanted nothing to do with James Robison and preachers like him." He had not shown "a loving Christian attitude" and should apologize. "Everybody I talk to is now voting for Reagan, and this time the black vote won't win it for [Carter] because the Christian vote is bigger."[54] Wexler replied that Maddox had never made the statement attributed to him, although "Dr. Maddox has said in private conversations with Reverend Robison, and on other occasions, that a meeting between President Carter and Reverend Robison would not be productive."[55]

Two months after the meeting, in March, Falwell spoke at a Moral Majority I Love America rally in Alaska and claimed to have asked Carter why he had "practicing homosexuals on [his] senior staff at the White House." Carter replied, according to Falwell, "Well, I am president of all the American people and I believe I should represent everyone." To this, Falwell told the Alaskan crowd, "I said why don't you have some murderers and bank robbers and so forth to represent?" The crowd applauded, and Falwell followed by printing the claim in the next edition of his *Moral Majority Report*. A Carter supporter was present at the Alaskan rally, however, and just before the Democratic National Convention sent a recording of the comments to Maddox. Comparing Falwell's comments to a tape he had recorded himself of the January meeting, Maddox quickly recognized Falwell's misrepresentation. Maddox's tape indicated that Falwell had asked Carter if it were correct to assume that two homosexuals living together would not fit Carter's definition of a family. Carter had not responded verbally, the transcript indicated, but had apparently nodded in agreement. Falwell had then stated, "Thank you—thank you very much."[56]

While Maddox knew that Falwell had been sharply critical of Carter, the brashness of his recent comments surprised Maddox. The tape recorder was "right under his face at the breakfast meeting," Maddox recalled, and, indeed, Falwell's staff had sought the recording in the first place. Had Falwell forgotten? Did he not think that his new claims would gain publicity? In any event, Maddox complained to several Falwell supporters, who initially denied that Falwell had made the claim. After Maddox played the recording, however, they reacted with surprise: "Oh my God, that is Jerry saying that."[57] Maddox contacted several newspapers, including the *Dallas Morning News* and the *New York Times*, whose subsequent stories suggested Falwell had lied. With the story gaining momentum, Maddox appeared on ABC's investigative news program, *20/20*. At first, it appeared, the sudden incident had caught Falwell off guard. "He is not going to take any calls today," his spokesman told newsmen. "He is with his family and promised them he wouldn't disrupt their day."[58] Soon, however, Falwell fought back. "I have stated as clearly and emphatically as I know how that my recent statement was not intended to be a verbatim report of our conversation with President Carter," Falwell told reporters. "Instead my statement was intended to be, and was, an honest portrayal of President Carter's position on gay rights. It was an anecdote, intended to dramatically get the attention of the audience. It was an absolutely accurate statement of the President's record and position on gay rights. It was meant to be nothing else." Far from backing down, Falwell then went on the attack, undoubtedly hoping to shift the focus of the debate. "The President has allowed homosexuals to place a wreath on the Tomb of the Unknown Soldier. He has issued orders to government agencies to refrain from inquiring about deviant sexual habits of people seeking government employment. The President is now supporting homosexual teachers in federally-supported classrooms such as on Army bases."[59]

Falwell's comments, in turn, brought a swift reaction from the administration. Maddox pointed out that the Department of Defense had abandoned its early resistance without White House interference. Recent court rulings ensured the protection of homosexual rights by holding that a person's activities outside of work could not be a factor in employment unless they affected performance. In general, Maddox argued, Carter did not sanction "the homosexual lifestyle," as Falwell claimed, but did believe that all Americans had civil rights. Many of Falwell's supporters agreed with his criticism of Carter's record but still had to acknowledge that the entire episode had hurt their message. While some insisted that the White House had ginned up the publicity "as a smokescreen to hide administration policy," Jimmy Allen, by then head of the Southern Baptist Radio and Television Commission, was more circumspect. "Anecdotes that do not tell the truth certainly ought to be avoided in any pulpit that I know of. I don't know that the person sitting in the crowd can tell the difference between that kind of an anecdote and the facts. [Falwell] should stick to the facts."[60] In any event, the entire episode stayed in the news for several days and allowed Falwell's many liberal critics to point out the irony of a man who believed in a literal interpretation of the Bible stressing the use of anecdotes. Years later, any anger on behalf of Falwell appeared to have waned. "I had a pretty good relationship with Robert Maddox," he recalled. "He was a nice man but from the moderate branch of the Southern Baptists. Like Carter, he was a good man but with a bad policy and philosophy."[61] In his own recollection of the incident, Maddox too had a broader perspective. "[Falwell] was becoming quite a celebrity," he surmised, and ego drove the controversy. "Well, by then Falwell was on a celebrity jazz and the Moral Majority had been formed as a conscious move by the political right to link up with the religious right."[62]

Throughout the spring primary season, the ongoing preparation for the White House Conference on Families, now definitively set as a series of three national conferences from June through July, exacerbated all such incidents. The succession of the preparatory state conventions offered family activist Connie Marshner additional opportunities to coordinate better her groundwork with both anti-ERA groups such as Schlafly's Eagle Forum and antiabortion groups such as the National Right to Life Committee. Marshner also cultivated strong connections with elements of the Catholic Church. Despite her efforts, feminists proved adept as well and increasingly took command in many states. In New York, for example, the leadership included representatives from the National Organization for Women, the Sisterhood of Black Single Mothers, and several homosexual activists. "Early in 1980, we saw that homosexuals were driving in," recalled Beverly LaHaye, wife of Tim LaHaye and head of the conservative group Concerned Women for America.[63] After the delegate selection, there was even a bit of violence as a representative of a group calling itself the Morality Action Committee attacked an abortion rights speaker. "He screamed at me that I couldn't be Catholic and ripped down our sign," the victim remembered. "Then he punched me in the arm and threw me and a man who tried to help me to the ground."[64]

In many states, the governors reserved the right to appoint a percentage of the delegates, and Marshner and her allies quickly complained that this benefited the liberals. The governors were rigging the conventions. In New York, Marshner ally and state senator John Marchi demanded that the governor appoint more "pro-family, pro-life individuals."[65] In Alabama, on the other hand, Governor Forrest James announced that his state would not participate in the conferences. Writing to conference chairman Guy Tucker, James's wife, Bobbie, explained that she was behind the boycott. Alabama, she wrote, "would not participate in this or other such conferences which do not establish traditional Judeo-Christian values concerning the family, the foundation of our nation under God."[66]

Tucker worked diligently to defuse the tensions. After sending all state coordinators a two-hundred-page manual of guidelines, Tucker wrote: "We are especially concerned . . . that you recognize and involve the broad diversity [of viewpoints]."[67] No one should be excluded, and the conventions should not favor one side or another. In a speech to the National Conference of Catholic Charities, Carter stressed that he had sent a directive to the heads of all federal agencies and departments instructing each to "establish a unique Office of Families to carry out the Conference's recommendations." It was critical, he reminded them, that they "do not limit themselves to what Washington officials think is important but learn from what American families believe is important to them."[68]

Given it all, Tucker could not help worrying that any plea for moderation was fruitless. An NBC television documentary titled *The American Family*

concluded that diversity was the new norm and that people would probably never agree on any standard. Collin Greer, editor of the periodical *Social Policy*, wrote that there was no longer an American family but rather a
"family question." "All groups have a right to be heard but it is difficult to
take a middle view on any issue," Tucker told a gathering of the American
Jewish Committee. Special interest groups dominated, and "you get battered
around by both sides."[69] In a memo to the National Advisory Committee,
he recommended "a delegate forum, more plenaries, and a possible varia-
tion of any 'yes/no' voting procedure." This would encourage compromise
and not confrontation. In short, the NAC should "reshape their proposals to
ensure more emphasis on broad participation."[70]

None of this impressed Marshner or her allies, who began to coordinate a lobbying campaign to oust Tucker as chairman. "He hates the pro-
family and pro-life groups and calls them every name in the book," wrote
one Catholic woman to Minnesota congressman Tom Hagedorn, who, con-
fused, contacted the White House to ensure that Tucker still had Carter's
support. "Recently Tucker criticized the traditional family," wrote another
woman from North Dakota, even more irate, adding that it was critical that
Carter overrule Tucker's guidelines.[71] The lobbying flustered many congressmen, who privately complained that the White House appeared un-
interested or preoccupied, an understandable truth given the international
and economic challenges. "Please provide me with adequate information to
respond to their concerns," wrote Florida representative Bill Nelson.[72]

As the summer approached, the larger crises facing Carter did not help.
The inflation rate hit an astounding 18 percent, and Kennedy, still stub-
bornly refusing to concede, won new momentum with primary victories
in New York and Connecticut. On April 1 Carter called a 7:00 a.m. press
conference and announced that he would delay imposing new sanctions on
Iran, and he implied that a breakthrough on the hostage crisis was imminent. That same day he won primaries in Wisconsin and Kansas. The good
news, however, did not last. As Carter narrowly won Pennsylvania, negotiations with Iran broke down, and Carter adopted a formal trade embargo.
When the U.S. Olympic Committee voted to boycott the Moscow games,
Carter encouraged other countries to follow, which engendered additional
criticism that the White House had abandoned the Olympic ideal. In the
middle of this, Cuba released a large number of prisoners—"scum" in leader
Fidel Castro's words—to come to America, beginning the infamous Cuban
"boatlift." While Carter won Texas, virtually guaranteeing his nomination,

Kennedy continued to attack, terming Carter's refusal to debate a "mockery of democracy" and the incumbent a "clone of Ronald Reagan." He would fight on to the convention, Kennedy announced, where he hoped delegates would be allowed to vote their "conscience."[73]

In the middle of this, former president Gerald Ford broke tradition and lambasted Carter as "the hero of the disasters he's created." Indeed, with the deteriorating international situation ensuring SALT II's defeat, Carter tried to avoid further embarrassment by pulling the treaty from Senate consideration. While Carter explained that he did so to protest the Soviet invasion of Afghanistan, it was obvious that all the effort and prestige the White House had invested in the agreement had, in the end, come to naught. The treaty's opponents celebrated, and its supporters sought to lay blame, but to both groups Carter emerged as weak and inept. Worse still, when Carter decided to launch a military rescue mission to free the Iranian hostages, equipment problems scrubbed the mission. While the mission withdrew from the desert, an accident killed eight of the rescuers, another "disaster" that had, proverbially at least, Carter's name on it. Iran quickly poured salt on the wounds by displaying the dead American soldiers, images that were promptly televised worldwide.[74]

Not all problems were so public or important, but with each mistake, each slight, the political task for Carter grew greater even as the primary season wound down. Following the failed rescue mission, Maddox invited a number of religious leaders for a briefing on the hostage situation but forgot to clear the invitations with the appropriate staff. The result was an angry bishop denied access to the White House as promised.[75] "This lack of communication," Maddox remembered, "smacked leaders of the more conservative religious community most painfully." Given their rapidly increasing audience and perceived power, they were "more easily rebuffed."[76] Carter could not easily complain because he committed his own faux pas. While discussing the apostle Paul's view of women in a Bible class at Washington's First Baptist Church, Carter explained that "there was a tremendous promotion in the status of women in God's sight as put forth by Paul." He then added with a smile, however, that "women have gone about as far as they ought to go now." The press quickly reported the comments out of context, causing one woman to complain, "I can't believe he would say that."[77] Several weeks later, Linda Tarr-Whelan, one of Sarah Weddington's key assistants, suddenly resigned. The press reported that the departure was due to "disagreements" with the White House. Known for her stringent feminism,

Tarr-Whelan had joined Weddington's staff "when Carter was seeking to strengthen his ties with women's groups." To many observers it appeared confirmation both that Weddington was too moderate and that the president had his own issues with women.[78]

Undoubtedly, Reagan and his Republican allies watched it all with a degree of satisfaction. Kennedy had increasingly played to his party's liberal base, Republicans assumed, and thus when Carter ultimately won the Democratic nomination he would be weak with some of his party's most important activists. Kennedy was making Carter appear more conservative than he was, deflating any zeal that was sure to be vital in the general election. Eventually, Republicans acknowledged, many of the feminists and abortion rights activists, faced with the possibility of a Reagan presidency, would probably fall in line behind Carter, but they would do so only reluctantly.[79] Others, however, might favor the independent candidacy of Anderson, weakening Carter further. While Anderson had been a Republican, he had a strong prochoice record and had won the scorn of many in his own party. This had also won him considerable press, promising more of a problem for Carter than Reagan.[80] In short, between the aftermath of Kennedy's campaign and the slice of the abortion rights lobby that Anderson would claim, Reagan would enter the general campaign in a stronger position than Carter.

In the Republican primaries, Reagan gained momentum, his resistance to abortion unwavering. "I believe," he declared in many of his stump speeches, "that abortion is the taking of human life." Obviously grasping the new unity of social conservatives around the banner of family, Reagan did not stop with abortion. He accused the Internal Revenue Service of harassing private schools connected to evangelical faiths, he advocated tax credits to help cover the costs of tuition to religious schools, and he denounced court rulings that "prohibited prayer in public schools." All of this, Reagan concluded, represented the "erosion of the American family," a line that the *New York Times* noted garnered "the most enthusiastic response." In what was surely music to the ears of the evangelical community, he added, "I don't believe that freedom of religion means freedom from religion."[81]

While such unequivocal rhetoric had already won over the majority of the social conservative vote, hesitancy about Reagan's candidacy still persisted among the most ardent antiabortion activists. Like his campaign four years before, Reagan still had to answer questions about his signature of the California bill allowing for some abortions. Moreover, rumors swirled that at the coming Republican convention he might try to unite the party by picking as his running mate George Bush, his opponent. Many abortion protesters insisted that Bush was unacceptable. Ellen McCormick, who had run as a single-issue, antiabortion activist in 1976, still refused to endorse Reagan and promised another run as a Right to Life Party candidate. This annoyed the Pro-Life Action Committee, which strongly endorsed Reagan, and led to public friction. Although McCormick had once served on the committee's board, the committee now argued that McCormick was a "purist" who was "holding up unreasonable and impractical standards." It annoyed the Republican Party as well, which perceived her as a potential impediment in commanding the new conservative religious vote.[82]

To solidify his support, Reagan hired Robert Billings to assist his campaign. Billings, who had worked with Christian Voice and the Moral Majority and, notably, was an associate of Paul Weyrich, seemed to suggest that Reagan promised more than just rhetoric. The Religious Right and the Reagan campaign had by this point become "unofficially close," Maddox recalled later. "Bob Billings was an executive director of the Moral Majority and when the Reagan campaign geared up, Billings left the Moral Majority and became a religious advisor kind of thing for the Reagan campaign." While Falwell always insisted that his organization did not endorse candidates, they "always portrayed Reagan as this paragon of Christian virtue and Carter as sort of an anti-Christ." The coordination of the conservative pastors and the Republican operatives was "terribly frustrating" for Maddox. "We had no effective way to combat it." The Religious Right had "cornered the market on religious radio and television."[83]

In this context, as Maddox warned, the Washington for Jesus rally on the National Mall in late April was hardly surprising. While the participants' disillusionment with Carter was as obvious as their support for Reagan, the rally in a larger sense demonstrated just how fractured much of American Christianity had become. Throughout the rally organizer John Gimenez stressed the Bible verse 2 Chronicles 7:14: "If my people who are called by my name humble themselves, and pray and seek my face, and turn from their wicked ways, then I shall hear from heaven, and will forgive their sin, and heal their land." To the rally's conservative participants, the verse was literal; God would heal the United States if it humbled itself before him. For theological liberals, however, the verse applied only to Israel in its historic context. God would heal any people who came to him. The distinction was not trivial, author Matthew Moen notes. The verse "transcends" the Washington for Jesus rally by representing a "statement of purpose" for the modern Religious Right. While the more liberal National Council of Churches could declare the rally nothing more than an attempt to "Christianize the Government," to Gimenez, Pat Robertson, and the rally's other conservative organizers the verse called to mind the nation's specific sins—its embrace of secular humanism, abortion, homosexuality, and the destruction of the family. As Gimenez intended, the verse was a call to arms, a call "to turn an immoral United States toward God so that He might forgive her and rebuild her glory."[84]

If April's Washington for Jesus rally represented an effective call to arms, the long-anticipated arrival of the White House Conference on Families in the early summer meant a perfect venue for the contest, a test of strength prior to the November elections, and a way to energize the political base. Now planned as three conferences in June and July, held consecutively in Baltimore, Minneapolis, and Los Angeles, the entire spectacle promised to ensure the debate over what constituted a family an important role in the presidential contest.

The series of state planning conventions had prepared Marshner well. Complaining about a broad definition of the family, she asked Tucker sarcastically if the infamous disciples of Charles Manson constituted a family. The tactic worked. After Marshner met with the conference's executive secretary, John Carr, Tucker agreed to name her an at-large delegate to the NAC, along with Jerry Regier, an acquaintance of Bill Bright's Christian Embassy and one of the organizers four years before of the evangelical Continental Conference on the Family. The two joined Dobson on the committee as a powerful voice for conservatives. While Marshner's flare for publicity annoyed Tucker, he thought snubbing her would be unwise. At the same time, however, Tucker refused to appoint Schlafly, who continued to complain about discrimination. Schlafly's group, the Eagle Forum, had failed to submit the required background information, Tucker claimed, although Schlafly's own public criticism undoubtedly made the decision easier. For its part, the Moral Majority did not apply. "We probably would have been rejected," Falwell concluded.[85] The "antifamily forces" had to be defeated, but the White House had already mapped "an agenda that proposes to sanction homosexuality for couples, expand day care, create new government programs to regulate families, and ensure federal funding for abortion."[86]

As part of her preparation, Marshner had formed the National Pro-

Family Coalition, a group that did include Falwell and Schlafly along with Dobson, Regier, and others. The coalition, Marshner explained, planned an organized presence at the national conferences. "What we're doing is to try to break the stranglehold that the professional human-services types and the bureaucrats have on family life," she concluded.[87] The group would stress the issues of abortion, homosexuality, and the ERA, the very divisive issues that Tucker feared as too disruptive. Marshner wrote to coalition members advising them on how to raise abortion, for example, even when conference debates appeared unrelated. If the issue were family violence, she explained, members should "propose that any society that professes to be concerned with the abuse of children should prohibit the ultimate form of abuse: abortion."[88]

Marshner was hardly done. She then announced that her coalition would work with Paul Weyrich's Free Congress Foundation to hold an American Family Forum, scheduled for Washington weeks after the initial national conference in Baltimore. Billed as the first convention of the profamily movement, it would counter the national family conferences—and, of course, raise publicity. Marshner began an active speaking campaign, visiting churches such as Falwell's Thomas Road Baptist Church.[89] Watching all of this with dismay was not only Tucker but a diverse array of organizations, each with its own specific, although perhaps less controversial, agenda. Many held great hope for the national conferences. One, the broad Coalition for the White House Conference on Families (CWHCF), represented fifty-two organizations, including not only groups such as Planned Parenthood of America but also institutions such as the American Red Cross. If the national conferences broke apart on wedge issues, the CWHCF worried, it would have accomplished nothing for American families. To avoid this failure and keep the conferences focused, the CWHCF stressed that single-issue debates were useless and that consensus was necessary to help families.[90]

Heading into the Baltimore conference, the NAC commissioned a Gallup poll on the status of the American family. As the NAC undoubtedly expected, the poll confirmed that citizens felt that a disaster loomed, thus underscoring the conference's importance.[91] Not surprisingly given the efforts of Marshner and others, Carter was reticent to attend the opening ceremonies in Baltimore. In late May, Tucker called Weddington and made a "strong plea" that Carter attend, explaining that if Carter did not, "we will be severely criticized for not supporting by his presence this initiative

on the family, especially after the rocky beginning the effort had." Moreover, Reagan would undoubtedly use Carter's absence to further his claim
as the champion of the American family. The Baltimore conference, Tucker
promised, "will be a good one with no disasters." Weddington agreed, noting that Tucker had "taken over what was obviously a very messy situation
and has done a good job with it."[92]

When top advisor Eizenstat heard that Carter might not attend, he protested directly to Carter. "I gather that a tentative decision not to go has
been made," Eizenstat began. Not attending would be "widely noticed and
would be taken as an indication of the administration's backing away from
its commitment to resolving a number of difficult issues facing families." In
the end, Eizenstat continued, "the White House Conference on Families is
the most visible demonstration of your commitment. Your presence would
go a long way to signal support for a strong family system; your absence
would bring forth considerable press and interest group criticism." Finally,
just as Tucker had warned of political ramifications in an election year, so
did Eizenstat. "Key constituencies who strongly support the Conference,
including Catholics and other religious and family-oriented organizations,"
were needed in November.[93]

Ultimately, Carter agreed to attend Baltimore's opening ceremonies,
while Eizenstat invited both Mondale and First Lady Rosalynn to attend
the subsequent conferences.[94] The advisors worked carefully on the address
Carter would give, revising several drafts. They eliminated sections praising the administration's record on behalf of families and deleted a comment
discussing the "controversy" on the issue.[95] In the end, Carter opened the
conference on June 5 at the Baltimore Convention Center with a speech that
appeared to continue Tucker's efforts to bridge differences. His only reference to the well-publicized disputes preceding the meeting was a joke to
diffuse tension. "I am very pleased to see that there's no violence in the audience or on the outside of the assembly area," he stated to laughter. Turning
serious, he straddled the middle when it came to the role of government.
"Where government involvement is helpful, let it be strengthened," he remarked. "Where it is harmful, let it be changed." He cited the nuclear family
of a mother, father, and children as the "standard that has been held up by
many traditions, including of course the Judeo-Christian tradition, and also
by thousands of years of human experience." At the same time, however,
he spoke of single-parent households and even noted that "family ties are
based on more than blood kinship," perhaps the most oblique of references

to the homosexual community. Throughout the speech he referenced his own family, at one point joking about his brother, Billy, whom the press had parodied as a bumpkin.[96]

A total of 671 delegates from fifteen states, Puerto Rico, and the Virgin Islands participated in the three-day Baltimore conference, attending twenty formal workshops on specific issues and debating resolutions. By the end, the conference had adopted a fifty-seven-point plan of action. On many issues there was general agreement, including resolutions to combat drug and alcohol abuse and to develop ways to assist families to care for elderly relatives at home rather than in institutions, the latter through changes in the tax code. Other resolutions that passed without much dissension were the elimination of the "marriage penalty" in the tax code, the revision of Social Security to recognize homemakers, additional aid for families with handicapped children, and more flexibility for employees in the workplace. Division and controversy were never far below the surface, however, as Marshner and—by her own estimates—the approximately 20 to 30 percent of "profamily" delegates that supported her positions remained determined to raise their voices. The NAC employed professional facilitators in each workshop, but leaders, obviously aware of Marshner's planning, had instructions to limit discussions to the specific issues at hand. NAC members wanted to encourage the broad diversity of viewpoints they had promised but only at the appropriate time and place; to do otherwise threatened anarchy. When Marshner's allies continued to raise abortion in every workshop and discussion, therefore, they were ruled out of order. Attempts to denounce gay and lesbian rights met with similar results. The NAC had already decided not to endorse any one view of what constituted a family, which continued to annoy Marshner. Finally, when the workshops arrived to discuss the controversial issues, Marshner and her allies were in the minority. Resolutions passed endorsing ratification of the ERA, the elimination of all discrimination, including sexual preference, and the right to abortion and family-planning services.[97]

By some accounts, an "us versus them" attitude spread among many delegates on both sides. On the second day of the conference, Marshner and ally Larry Pratt took their protest one step further. At the conference luncheon, Pratt wrestled the microphone from Tucker and told the crowd that the conference "was stacked and we should walk out."[98] Marshner then led approximately forty delegates out of the conference center, hoping, she said, to demonstrate that the conference lacked credibility. "We have become a pitiful minority and we are walking out on principle," she remarked. "I regret that even one delegate would leave," Tucker replied. "I've been beaten myself, but I believe in staying and going on."[99] In fact, Marshner had planned the walkout days before, according to several sources, and had even held an organizational meeting. To most observers the reason for the walkout was obvious—publicity. According to Carr, Marshner was "trying to make a point for the press rather than anything else."[100] Not all conservatives joined the walkout, Regier and Dobson among those who remained. Tucker claimed that had Marshner not led the walkout, the conference might have defeated the controversial resolutions that so outraged her. "Their decision to leave was directly responsible for their loss," he claimed. "They might have otherwise won by a comfortable margin."[101] This conclusion was questionable at best, certainly in regard to the ERA resolution, which passed 471 to 119, but it might have applied to the abortion and homosexual debates. Marshner denied that her boycott affected the outcome she still saw as inevitable, and Regier countered that the publicity earned "woke people up across the country."[102] It was, in Regier's view, a success, a seminal event. Gay activists, meanwhile, cited the support of the National Organization for Women, the Black Caucus, and other nongay groups in their "victory," a "victory in the face of right-wing pressure."[103] As if to support such claims, the Baltimore session ended with the playing of Sister Sledge's disco hit "We Are Family," the organizers apparently not recognizing the song as a well-known gay anthem.

When the second national conference convened in Minneapolis on June 19, approximately six hundred delegates from thirteen midwestern and southern states attended. Befitting the geographic area they represented, delegates included a larger contingent of conservatives. Just over half the Minnesota delegation was against abortion rights, for example, while two-thirds of the Illinois delegation publicly identified themselves as part of the profamily camp. Once again, a number of conservative delegates walked out, repeating the claim that the format limited their antiabortion stance. A majority, however, thought Marshner's tactics ill-advised and worried that another boycott would both discredit their cause and disrupt a conference that had a chance to make a difference in so many other areas. According to one profamily Tennessee delegate, "We're concerned about the economy, not as much gay rights." The result was less confrontation—and less press. Schlafly, still denied a position as a delegate, issued her own press release, decrying the conference as a "media event to promote an alternative lifestyle."[104] In the end, nevertheless, she undoubtedly found the conference's resolutions more to her liking. While the conference endorsed abortion rights and the ERA, just as in Baltimore, the vote was much narrower. Unlike the earlier conference, delegates voted to exclude homosexuals in the definition of the family and passed a resolution "opposing the imposition of a secular, humanist philosophy in public institutions." In most other respects, the Minneapolis resolutions reiterated those passed in Baltimore. Perhaps spinning the results, liberal members of the CWHCF denied that profamily forces had advanced, instead claiming for themselves the high ground of compromise. "It's not in our best interests," stated one man, "to get into polarizing tactics."[105]

Approximately three weeks passed before the third national conference convened in Los Angeles on July 10. In the interim, two Catholic groups withdrew from the CWHCF. The United States Catholic Conference and the National Conference of Catholic Churches, which together represented almost every Catholic in the nation, claimed that abortion and women's rights advocates "had taken unprecedented, unauthorized and inadvisable action in the name of the coalition." In short, the CWHCF now masked a more liberal agenda that the Catholic Church could no longer endorse.[106] Days before the Los Angeles convention, almost one thousand people came to Washington for the American Family Forum, the meeting promised by Marshner and Weyrich weeks earlier. The speakers surprised no one and included Schlafly and such well-known evangelists as Falwell, Dobson, Bright, and Beverly LaHaye. Attending as well was North Carolina Republican senator Jesse Helms, adding additional partisan flavor. In the words of conservative pundit James Kilpatrick, the forum was "as one-sidedly conservative as the Baltimore affair was one-sidedly liberal."[107] Falwell described the meeting as an "across the board rebuttal of the White House Conference on Families." It was, he proudly recalled, "one of the first times that we were able to mobilize pro-family conservatives."[108] At the same time as the American Family Forum, Dobson and several other evangelists met in a Washington hotel room and decided to form the Family Research Council (FRC), which, they envisioned, would continue the effort to lobby legislators. In the coming years, the FRC proved another formidable conservative entity, a reliable voice for the Religious Right.[109]

When the final national conference convened, most observers hoped that the composition of the delegates, representing nineteen western states and four territories, would prove more united than in either Baltimore or

Minneapolis. The second conference had witnessed less public strife than the first, but the midwestern delegates had still ventured into the definition of a family, which the NAC had hoped to avoid entirely. The 651 delegates in Los Angeles, by contrast, were 11 percent Hispanic, 9 percent black, and 4 percent Native American. With such a high percentage of minorities, most pundits anticipated that economic issues, not the more divisive social issues, would dominate.[110] In most respects, such predictions proved correct. Fifty-one delegates, mostly from Texas, tore up their ballots and staged a walkout to protest a lack of moral issues in the agenda. After the first two conferences, however, all expected the protest, which seemed almost obligatory and garnered little media coverage. In nearby Long Beach, several thousand people attended a profamily meeting to condemn abortion and homosexuality. They received even less coverage than their colleagues' walkout, while the group's call for a Senate investigation into delegate selection for the national conferences made them appear extreme.[111]

The final resolutions adopted in Los Angeles included an endorsement of the ERA and abortion rights, but the emphasis remained on ensuring equal opportunity in employment, transportation, health care, and housing as well as the need to improve education. In one departure from the earlier conferences, delegates voted to establish community advisory councils at local schools. The delegates adopted many of their predecessors' proposals, including revisions of the tax code and the need to combat drug and alcohol abuse. Tucker and the NAC were thankful that there was no great debate on the definition of family. With the close of the conference in mid-July, delegates submitted their resolutions to the NAC, just as their colleagues had done in Baltimore and Minneapolis. Just as the earlier participants did, they awaited the final summary report scheduled for presentation to the president and Congress.

In retrospect, the White House Conference on Families demonstrated the primacy of partisan politics. A problem that all Americans acknowledged—the deterioration of the family—might have originally appeared to be a force for consensus. Indeed, Carter had undoubtedly hoped for as much when he had first proposed the conference four years before. Looking back, however, the dissension and overt partisanship that emerged were probably inevitable, if compounded by delays and mismanagement. It was more than the conference's untimely concurrence with an election campaign. The rights revolution of the 1960s had assured issues such as homosexuality, abortion, and feminism a new prominence in political discourse, as Carter now recognized all too well. They were not easy to finesse, not open to compromise and moderation, and thus critical to the emerging Religious Right. The family conference, in the shadow of a presidential campaign, was simply the perfect platform to magnify all disagreements. After the conference concluded, evangelist Beverly LaHaye pointed the finger at Carter even as she embraced Republicans such as Reagan. "Jimmy Carter has falsely used his born-again image to hoodwink people into thinking he is one of us," she declared. "The White House Conference . . . does not represent the more traditionalist viewpoint of the family, but instead favors the feminist and the pro-homosexual viewpoints espoused by the liberal establishment."[112] On the other side, the activists LaHaye so loathed also looked to the realm of politics for redress, disappointed as so many were in Carter. For example, in the words of one gay activist who previously had been uninvolved in politics, "the White House Conference was my Stonewall," and "I am not going to put up with this."[113]

It was time for the national conventions, and this sense of exasperation permeated both parties. Americans were in debt, mired in stagflation, and still held hostage abroad, and they could not even agree on the nature of the family. Carter's inability to solve the international crisis had wasted any chance for political gain from what proved to be a fleeting sense of national unity. Divided and depressed, alienated and angry, Americans increasingly mobilized for what most anticipated would be an historic November vote. For many this meant turning to the new alliance between conservative Christians and the Republican Party. And for this the Religious Right was ready.

CHAPTER SEVEN

The Reagan Revolution

ONLY DAYS AFTER THE WHITE HOUSE Conference on Families concluded in Los Angeles, half a continent away the Republicans convened for their national convention. Held at Detroit's Joe Louis Arena from July 14 to 17, 1980, the convention demonstrated just how far the party and its charismatic candidate, Ronald Reagan, had united behind a conservative platform, an agenda that clearly welcomed the new Religious Right as a key constituency.

Before the convention Reagan had worked hard to win over conservative Christians. He had to do more than renounce his California bill, which sanctioned at least some abortions. Although he had been baptized a Disciple of Christ and attended Eureka College, an institution supported by the denomination, he remained in many respects an odd choice as the champion of theological conservatives. He had never been overtly religious and had divorced his first wife. For many evangelicals, divorce had always been unacceptable, citing a King James version of Matthew 5:22 that equated divorce with adultery. Several of his children had embraced the libertine 1960s culture, another sin to many evangelicals. Moreover, when the campaign released the candidate's 1979 tax returns, it was apparent that the millionaire had donated less than 1 percent of his adjusted gross income to charitable or religious causes, a percentage far below the 10 percent that many less wealthy religious conservatives thought scripturally mandated. Fortunately for Reagan, this was all damaging but not fatal. He was, simply put, somewhat fortuitous; the changing social mores of the 1960s had touched the conservative religious community even as it bemoaned the same. By the 1970s, for example, the divorce rate among evangelicals was virtually the same as that of the larger population, and the traditional prohibitions had begun to weaken. In the end, all factors considered, many in the Religious Right were now willing to tolerate personal imperfections if the candidate advanced their cause.[1]

Reagan had clearly come a long way since early in the primary season, when reporters had asked him if he considered himself "born again." "Well," Reagan had stumbled at the time, "I know what many of those who use that term mean by it. But in my own situation it was not in the religion of the church I was raised in, the Christian Church. But there you were baptized when you yourself decided that you were, as the Bible says, as the Bible puts it, that that is being born again. And so, it was, within the context of the Bible, yes, by being baptized."[2] Now, however, Reagan knew how to respond. He clearly and forcibly lauded born-again Christians, while his pollster, Richard Wirthlin, added publicly that the campaign expected to keep Carter from "cornering the market" on religious conservatives. Born-again voters, Wirthlin explained, constituted about a third of the population and were significant not only in the South but also in key states such as Ohio.[3]

As if to reiterate this point, approximately one thousand representatives from over thirty local Christian organizations met in Washington only weeks before the Republican convention to coordinate a profamily agenda. Naming their umbrella organization the Liberty Court Group, the representatives clearly sought to win Reagan's attention. The group included none of the major figures on the national scene, the Falwells or Robertsons of the Religious Right. This alone, however, perhaps added to their clout, an indication of the grassroots nature of the new conservative constituency.[4] When the group learned that Reagan planned to name Mary Louise Smith to his advisory Women's Policy Board, it flooded his campaign headquarters with letters of protest. A former IWY commissioner, Smith supported the ERA. Reacting quickly to the protest, Reagan announced the appointment of another advisory committee, the Family Policy Advisory Board. Included prominently were the noted abortion foe Henry Hyde and such antifeminists as Lottie Beth Hobbs and Beverly LaHaye. Also included was Marshner, by now the well-known champion of traditional families and celebrated Carter critic.[5] At the same time, Reagan began to note more publicly his opposition to the ERA and even began to hint that he wanted the party to drop its long-standing plank in support of the amendment, something he had never publicly acknowledged. The ERA, he stated, "has become a divisive symbol with people who are probably all together with regard to equal rights but who can be turned off or on by that as a symbol." In the very least, it was "disruptive" to the party. When asked directly if he supported repealing the plank, he replied, "I would support a plank that stresses our determination to oppose discrimination of any kind."[6]

As Reagan worked to ensure the support of the new Religious Right, he also feared that moderate Republicans might protest by disrupting the convention. Working to unite the party or at the very least paper over its divisions, Reagan's representatives suggested a "compromise" party plank on the ERA that acknowledged past support but stopped short of calling for ratification. When the platform committee passed a plank that suggested a stronger repudiation, promising to resist "any move that would give government more power over families," Reagan publicly approved but agreed to meet quietly with the moderates.[7] Assuring them that his obvious shift rightward did not negate his support for women's rights, he convinced Mary Louise Smith, still a Republican, to help placate her allies. Smith subsequently announced that while she still supported the ERA, she was "comfortable" with the plank and would support the platform. Reagan had, it appeared, moved deftly. "Obviously," platform committee John Tower summed up, "it's better to keep your political disputes to yourselves."[8]

As the Liberty Court Group formed and party activists haggled over their platform, Reagan agreed to meet with several leading conservatives, including Jerry Falwell, Paul Weyrich, Phyllis Schlafly, and Howard Phillips at Washington's Renaissance Hotel. Reports had indicated that Reagan was going to pick his running mate from a list of twenty-one politicians, including George Bush. The Texan was unacceptable, the assembled activists lobbied, because of his prochoice record. In his place Reagan should name Jesse Helms, the stalwart social conservative senator from North Carolina who had even threatened to put his own name forward at the convention to ensure ideological purity. As Falwell recalled the meeting, "I told Governor Reagan that conservatives just could not warm to Bush, and that with [Reagan's advanced age] and all that, this choice may endanger our vote." Reagan was polite but demurred.[9]

When the convention arrived, Reagan, clearly still trying to unite the party without alienating the Religious Right, selected Bush in spite of the warning. Maddox later recalled that the selection offered Carter a "flicker of hope."[10] It was soon obvious, nevertheless, that both men on the new Republican ticket had heard the larger conservative mandate. As Reagan stressed his prolife sentiments, once again describing his California abortion bill as a mistake, he stressed that his campaign chairman was Nevada senator Paul

Laxalt, a hero to many social conservatives. For his part, Bush denounced his earlier abortion stance in the most forceful and unambiguous language to date, an obvious tactical shift because of his nomination. When pressed by reporters to explain his reasoning, Bush tried to dodge the question. He would not be "nickel-and-dimed" on the social issues, he curtly replied, refusing to answer for his sudden change of heart.[11]

In any event, the Republican Party platform reflected in all respects a similar conservative shift. In 1976 the platform had been, in the words of one historian, "ambivalent" on the issue of abortion.[12] It had emphasized the disagreement among Republicans, terming the matter "one of the most difficult and controversial of our time," before briefly adding that the party "supports the efforts" of those seeking a constitutional ban. By 1980, with prolife forces packing the platform committee's subcommittee on human resources, including an organized presence by the Moral Majority, any ambivalence was long gone. The platform "affirm[ed] our support of a constitutional amendment to restore protection of the right to life for unborn children." The language was now forceful and direct, not only supporting the Hyde Amendment but even considering an antiabortion stance as a litmus test for federal judgeships, a position that at least one senator described as the "worst plank that has ever been in a platform."[13] The platform still supported "equal rights and opportunities for women" but promised to maintain the exemption of women from the military draft. In what amounted to the only display of division, a small number of moderate women quietly protested by donning the white dresses of the suffragettes. Much to Reagan's relief, however, the women were unable to garner enough support to require floor debates and roll-call votes. With only a voice vote on the issues, the party avoided any real public debate.[14]

Certainly, the moderates remained annoyed at both the party and its candidates for their drift rightward, some suggesting that Reagan's staff were, in the words of columnist Elizabeth Drew, "preoccupied elsewhere or asleep at the wheel."[15] Even former president Ford quietly complained during the convention about the shift away from the ERA. Nevertheless, the reality remained that the social and religious conservatives were simply better organized and prepared for the platform debate. As Drew observed, "There is a new element at the Republican Convention this year: the fundamentalist religious movement . . . a kind of counter-reformation against the growing acceptance of such things as abortion and homosexuality, the changing role of women." The Moral Majority, Drew added as one example, "controls the Alaska delegation."[16] "A number of single issue groups," the *New York Times* observed in a statement of the obvious, "are starting to form a loose coalition to fight abortion, the Equal Rights Amendment, pornography, and homosexuality."[17] Added Peter Gemma, director of the National Pro-Life Political Action Committee, "There is a sudden growing awareness on the part of all of us working in various single issues that if we pitched in together, we could get a lot more accomplished."[18]

The institution of family played prominently throughout the convention. "We affirm," the platform read, "our belief in the traditional role and values of the family in our society." The platform endorsed the Family Protection Act and protested "the Supreme Court's intrusion into the family structure." Several speakers commented on the "sanctity of family." The entire spectacle, the *New York Times* editorialized, lauded a Norman Rockwell image of family: "Nostalgia is a powerful political force in this country, but it provides no firmer theory of government than magazine covers."[19] To gay activists, the Republican view of family was decidedly antihomosexual. According to one such activist, "There is a real danger of the Republican party being taken over by people who don't think very much of our rights as gay people."[20]

In his keynote address, Reagan claimed that he "was ready to build a new consensus with all those across the land who share a community of values embodied in these words: family, work, neighborhood, peace and freedom." By naming family first, the *Times* concluded, "Mr. Reagan signaled the growing importance of a cluster of issues referred to as 'traditional moral values.'"[21] Clearly speaking to the grassroots elements as much as the prominent pastors, Reagan asked in an emotion-choked voice for a moment of silent prayer. "God bless America," he concluded to a twenty-minute standing ovation. When the festivities concluded, one fact was obvious: the Religious Right had little reason to complain.[22]

The Democrats, meanwhile, found much cause for complaint, not only in the Republican convention taking place in the Motor City but also in their own political backyard. Unity, of course, had never been Carter's forte, and the problems that he had faced for four years continued all the way through the Democratic convention in Madison Square Garden in New York City between August 11 and 14. As the convention approached, Carter worked to placate women's rights advocates, agreeing to meet with business leaders in the White House's East Room to press for both ERA ratification and the advancement of women in the corporate world, the proverbial two birds with one stone. After telling the attendees that it was "almost unbeliev-able, were we not witnessing it ourselves, the deliberate attempts to distort a simple proposition [the ERA]," Carter began to speak of "another area that we are pursuing ... discrimination that has existed with businesses." Elimi-nating discrimination on the job and in the marketplace was just as critical as ratification of the ERA.[23] As Carter spoke, administration efforts focused on the coming ratification vote in Illinois, scheduled just before the Repub-lican convention. Even with this, however, the divisions Carter still faced were evident. NOW had organized an impressive twenty-thousand-person march in the state, but Eleanor Smeal, NOW's president, still simmering at Carter, had invited no one from the White House. Recognizing that this was a public snub, the White House sent Eleanor Holmes Norton, a well-known African American connected to Carter. "Her appearance was," one White House staffer noted, "a slick maneuver on our part to have the Ad-ministration represented." Smeal "could not turn down such a prominent black woman because there has been a lot of friction lately between white and minority supporters."[24] Playing her part, Norton called for ratification and praised the administration's efforts.

When the Illinois vote came, all ERA supporters could at least agree that the result was unfortunate, ending any hope for momentum heading into the Democratic convention. The legislature rejected the ERA 102–71, and hope that the amendment would finally become part of the Constitution seemed as remote as ever. Addressing an ERA fund-raiser at Washington's Mazza Gallerie the day after the vote, Carter tried to be upbeat but had to acknowledge that the result was a "major disappointment." His administra-tion would press on, he promised. Indeed, behind the scenes staffers con-tinued to study the political dynamics in unratified states. Someone should call Arkansas governor Bill Clinton, one suggested, and "ask him if he's go-ing to get ERA passed for us." Clinton was, after all, "a real up and coming politician."[25]

Ted Kennedy, meanwhile, still threatened a floor fight at the convention. A coalition of women's groups, including the National Abortion Rights Ac-tion League, Women USA, the Women's Equity Action League, and even a group of matrons known as the Gray Panthers, declared that even with the primaries over, they considered the convention "open." Clearly hop-ing to use their noncommitted status as additional leverage even at this late date, the coalition proved that NOW was not the only group dissatisfied with Carter's performance. "Women are coming into this convention with a great deal of anger and a lot of demands," stated Abzug, perhaps exhibiting her own anger more than that of her colleagues.[26]

When the convention arrived, the Carter camp supported the ERA but resisted two proposals the women's rights delegates supported: one withholding financing and assistance to candidates who did not support ratification and the other supporting federal money for the abortions of poor women. The former, its advocates concluded, "would out-Republican Republicans," noting the opposition's well-known party discipline. To Carter, however, it helped Republicans by hurting Democratic unity. The latter proposal, of course, was the well-debated Hyde Amendment, on which Carter and the women's rights advocates had long disagreed.[27] Women delegates met with Weddington until 4:00 a.m. the night before the final vote, but she insisted that Carter would not abandon his opposition to either proposal. Less than an hour before the vote, however, the powerful National Education Association, which on other issues had been solidly behind Carter, dropped its resistance. The NEA commanded 302 delegates, the largest single block of any group, and the Carter camp knew further resistance was futile. After initially threatening to use its "whip system" of walkie-talkies on the convention floor to coordinate resistance, Carter's camp acquiesced. "We don't want further disagreement among Democratic women," advisor Anne Wexler told the press. "The ERA is the last issue in the world we want to fight about."[28] In the end, Carter issued a statement supporting the platform but still acknowledging that "my personal view [on abortion funding] remains unchanged."[29]

The question of a homosexual rights plank was even more difficult. When the National Gay Task Force had pressed the matter during the primaries, the Carter campaign had dodged the question. "To [endorse a strong plank] at this time," it had replied, "would be presumptuous on our part with the nominating process at an inconclusive stage."[30] Behind the scenes, however, the campaign had encouraged broad participation at regional hearings scheduled before the official platform meetings. This bought the campaign some time and provided a gauge of support for both sides. Reflecting later on these hearings, advisor Alison Thomas reported that a "split has developed between the gay activists and the Southerners." If the administration wanted to avoid "a fight on the floor of the convention or the issuance of a minority report," it would have to support a strong plank. These were real possibilities, "given the level of organization of the gay delegates."[31]

The gay lobby had, indeed, done its homework. Over thirty-five delegates to the Democratic convention were openly homosexual, while hundreds had pledged to support a strong gay plank. Even two delegates at the Republican convention were openly gay, a particular source of pride even if an acknowledgment of just how partisan the issue had grown.[32] It was, in short, enough to convince the Carter campaign. Testifying before the Democratic Platform Committee, Eizenstat declared that Carter supported a civil rights plank that protected "all groups from discrimination based on race, color, religion, national origin, sex, or sexual orientation." Four years earlier, Carter had successfully fought such a plank, but now, perhaps impressed both by the force of the gay lobby and by the political threat of Kennedy, he acquiesced. As if to tack toward the middle yet again, however, the administration resisted efforts to include specifically the words "gay" and "lesbian" in the plank. When it succeeded, many gay activists complained. It was, in a sense, classic Carter. He had not fully pleased the homosexual community, while to much of the American public his administration still remained the champion of gay and lesbian rights.[33]

A few days before the Democratic convention, another problem developed. Maddox suggested to Rosalynn that the White House invite Harold Bredeson, a friend with considerable influence in the conservative Christian community, to pray with Carter before the president's formal acceptance speech. When he received no official White House reply, Maddox told Bredeson to forget about the possibility; there would be no prayer. Bredeson, however, had other plans. A few days later, Maddox learned from Carter's staff that the pastor had arrived, telling security that the Lord wanted him to come anyway. As he sat fuming, Maddox suddenly received a phone call from Rosalynn's own staff. Carter, Maddox learned, wanted to pray with Bredeson after all, and Maddox should escort him. "If Harold Bredeson felt led of the Lord to go to the moon," Maddox laughingly recalled, "I would expect to see him waving from that place a few days later."[34]

While Carter was still defusing tensions as the convention approached, many in the media clearly expected a more public brawl than the placid production they had just witnessed in Detroit. While Carter certainly had the votes to defeat Kennedy, his persistent rival had engineered passage of a number of platform planks too liberal for the incumbent. This was "extraordinary," wrote pundits Jack Germond and Jules Witcover. "An incumbent president, his renomination secured, has been forced to accept a document that he did not fully support."[35] In the end, the Democrats avoided a disaster on the scale of their Chicago convention twelve years before. Nevertheless, the disgruntled feminists and gay rights supporters were more than willing to speak sarcastically to the press about their own candidate. Carter had "succeeded in stifling a potential eruption," the *New York Times* editorialized, but there was no doubt that pessimism and lethargy lingered just below the convention's cheers, festive music, and balloons. It was "Carter's fight at the Garden," the *Times* concluded, playing off the venue's fame for hosting boxing matches.[36]

When it came time for his acceptance speech, Carter obviously sought to rally his battered troops, describing the Republican vision of the future as a "make-believe world." If the GOP succeeded with their "dream," the nation would wake up to a "nightmare." Nevertheless, with hostages still in Iran, the Afghanistan war ongoing, and economic and energy woes intractable, Carter knew that he had his own nightmare. "I'm wiser tonight than I was four years ago," he stated in what appeared to be a prelude to an apology. "I've learned no easy answers are found." Carter spoke directly about Iran, suggesting that he prayed for the hostages as "though they were our own sons and daughters" and promising an aggressive economic agenda. Other than noting the importance of "compassion" and once referring to freedom of religion, his speech was devoid of all the controversial family issues that had so long bedeviled him. In fact, Carter did not once refer to the American family and ended his speech not with a resounding "God bless America" but with a simple "thank you."[37]

Carter did not leave New York City with much momentum. John Anderson's independent campaign had already shown a surprising resiliency and appeared to be gaining steam—at Carter's expense. With his prochoice position now well known, Anderson courted the feminist vote, selecting Mary Crisp as his national campaign manager. While Crisp had been a co-chair of the Republican Party, she had left the GOP over its new ERA opposition. The selection won Anderson additional historic publicity as the first female-led presidential campaign.[38] Anderson wasted no time in attacking both his opponents on the issue. Carter's support for women's rights was "half-hearted," Anderson claimed, while Reagan's was abhorrent. Anderson was aware as well of the political importance of family and strongly reflected the argument that feminists had been trying to make for some time. "The Republican platform has the effrontery to call itself pro-family," Anderson said. "I can't believe it's pro-family when the Government forces a 13-year-old to bear a child."[39] If Anderson were not enough, Carter's brother, Billy, was back in the news just as the conventions took place. With reports continuing to trickle in that Billy had lobbied for the Libyan government, the White House denied, at first quietly and then more forcibly, that the famous sibling had ever influenced American foreign policy. When just days before the convention Carter sheepishly acknowledged that "I cannot control him," the *New York Times* labeled the issue the "political sensation of the election year."[40] This was surely journalistic hyperbole but nevertheless somewhat symbolic. Carter, the would-be champion of the family, mired in the controversies surrounding the family, entered the general campaign with a personal family problem.

In the midst of convention season, evangelist James Robison invited all three presidential candidates to address a "major National Affairs Briefing" that his organization, the Religious Roundtable, scheduled for Dallas's Reunion Arena in late August, only days after the Democratic convention. The invitation was somewhat self-congratulatory and overtly political. "This will be the largest, most significant, political and spiritual gathering in the South this year," it read. "I can assure you we will be pressing people to action and how to organize the vote." In concluding, Robison added that besides the thousands in attendance, the meeting "will be telecast into another 100 cities on closed circuit television via satelite [*sic*]."[41] After receiving the invitation, Maddox was blunt: "It is a no-win situation. Mr. Reagan has been invited and most likely will be present. It would be a hostile crowd to the President. However, if the President does not attend, he will be soundly criticized."[42] After consideration, Maddox concluded, Carter should not attend. When advisors Wexler, Powell, and Jordan all concurred, aware of Robison's political inclinations, Carter declined. "President Carter shares your concern that Americans become more fully informed on the important issues confronting our Nation, especially issues of social justice and moral righteousness," the letter of regret stated. Carter would join the participants in "praying for the peace and well-being of the Nation."[43] Later, Anderson also declined, and according to Baptist Bailey Smith, the White House began pressing for moderate pastors to avoid the gathering as well.[44]

If the White House did indeed press for a boycott, its reasoning was as obvious as its failure. Over seven thousand ministers attended from forty-one states, the closing session on August 22 drawing thousands more. Speakers included not only the leading conservative pastors and social activists such as Schlafly but also outspoken lawmakers such as Jesse Helms. The organizers still clung to the description of the gathering as nonpartisan, but Republicans dominated. Texas governor John Connally, who by 1980 had shed his Democratic allegiance and openly embraced the GOP, also attended.[45] Across the arena, exhibits by such notable conservative organizations as Christian Voice, the Pro-Family Forum, the National Prayer Campaign, the Eagle Forum, the Right to Life Committee, the Fund to Restore an Educated Electorate, and the Institute for Christian Economics crowded the passageways. Every conservative religious leader was present, as were four hundred members of the press and over a dozen foreign correspondents. Participants took pride in the fact that the establishment press appeared to have noticed their movement and taken it seriously, or at least expected a good story. As seminars instructed participants on how to mobilize politically, a number of prominent speakers emboldened by the coverage complied and gave, to borrow a *Reader's Digest* phrase, "quotable quotes," inflammatory and colorful speeches sure to engender further controversy and coverage.[46]

Upon his arrival, Reagan immediately began courting the participants. In a press conference prior to his scheduled speech, he urged schools to teach the biblical story of creation alongside the theory of evolution. When pressed about his personal views, he claimed that he had "questions" about the evolutionary theory. As Reagan well knew, the question was a political landmine and required a delicate reply. Conservative activists in Arkansas and Louisiana were pressing successfully for legislation requiring schools to teach both evolution and "scientific creationism" as equally sanctioned options, an issue sure to spread to other states and throughout their judiciaries. Others saw the debate as "idiotic," the matter "settled in American politics fifty-five years ago at the Scopes Monkey trial." In any event, Reagan spoke directly in the press conference of the "increasing tendency of the state interfering with religion," and he described abortion as the "taking of human life."[47]

Falwell was among the first official speakers, stressing resistance to abortion and a defense of the family. Robison, ambitious like Falwell, arranged to speak directly before Reagan and fired up the crowd. While he did not mention abortion directly, he condemned Godless Communism and exhorted the crowd to get involved. God had to "take over the country." The government was "public enemy #1." With the crowd cheering, Robison concluded with a line he had used before: "I'm sick and tired of hearing about all of the radicals and the perverts and the liberals and the leftists and the Communists coming out of the closet. It's time for God's people to come out of the closet."[48] Reagan had planned to wait backstage during Robison's fiery and emotional address but decided to sit behind him onstage. Reagan advisors Michael Deaver and Edwin Meese cringed, but Reagan—and the over fourteen thousand then in attendance—loved it. When it came time for his keynote address, Reagan began with an introduction that Robison had suggested. "You can't endorse me," Reagan remarked in a bow to the event's supposedly nonpartisan nature, "but I endorse you." The crowd cheered, and according to Falwell, Deaver later admitted that "it turned out to be a good move for Reagan."[49]

Reagan had said everything the assembled conservatives wanted to hear, from denouncing abortion and Communism to stressing the role of the American family. He seemed to share a nostalgic vision of America with them, if not their mastery of image and the art of television. America, Reagan seemed to promise, was God's favorite country, and he would restore it to the stature a blessed nation deserved.[50] For some, it appeared to be the consummation of Reagan's marriage to the Religious Right. For others, it appeared to be confirmation that the newly united Religious Right was a potent voting block. It was a "significant moment," remarked one evangelist. "The candidate came to us; we didn't go to the candidate."[51]

If the National Affairs Briefing were controversial in itself, one comment stood out above the others and ensured a backlash. Oklahoma pastor Bailey Smith, newly elected as president of the Southern Baptist Convention, proclaimed that "God does not hear the prayers of a Jew." Smith's comment was a reflection of Baptist doctrine that those who had not accepted Jesus as their savior were doomed, but it nevertheless appeared too divisive and sensational for the press not to highlight. Falwell rushed in to defend his colleague. At first, he denied that Smith had made the comment, adding that the report "has to be of a political origin." If reporters would investigate, he claimed, "you'll probably find that the byline came from the White House." Later he tried to explain the theological foundations in more detail, stating, "I believe that God hears the prayer of any redeemed Jew or Gentile and I do not believe that God answers the prayer of any unredeemed Gentile or Jew."[52] With Falwell already a controversial figure, his claim fueled a new round of outrage as the press reported—incorrectly—that he had agreed with Smith. The *Washington Post*, the *Washington Star*, and *Newsweek* magazine, for example, all reported that he had, like Smith, said that God does not hear the prayers of Jews.[53] Theologically, of course, he had agreed with Smith, but, technically, he had not. God does hear the prayers of Jews, he had stated, but just does not answer them. After facing tough questions from reporter Marvin Kalb on the popular news program *Meet the Press*, Falwell eventually found his parsing of terms a reliable defense. He now insisted the press had deliberately misquoted him in an attempt to discredit him; he was a martyr, a victim of the liberal media. Working to repair any damage with the Jewish community, Falwell met in New York with Rabbi Marc Tannenbaum, director of interreligious affairs for the American Jewish Committee, and together they released a joint statement that "God hears the cry of any sincere person who calls on Him."[54]

While Smith undoubtedly suffered personally from the criticism he received, the entire National Affairs Briefing—and all the subsequent publicity it garnered, positive or negative—left one clear impression. In the words of author Dinesh D'Souza, "There was not much doubt about the power of the evangelical preachers."[55] Following the Dallas event, Harry Cook of the *Detroit Free Press* predicted that Falwell and his allies "will have a larger impact on the races than any religious leader has ever had in this country's 200-year history." The *New York Times* editorialized that the preachers had created "something very similar to a political party." Columnist Carl Rowan reassured worried liberals that it was not as bad as many predicted and that the country needed a "right-wing scare."[56]

In the weeks following the National Affairs Briefing, it was increasingly obvious to almost all observers that Reagan had apparently enhanced his reputation among the Christian conservative community while losing no real ground with moderates.[57] Once again it appeared obvious that the marriage of the Religious Right with fiscal conservatives was complete, with a new Republican Party as the immediate result. "It is the most important development on the right since 1964, the year conservatives took over the Republican Party," observed Wes McCune, head of Group Research Associates, a private polling firm. The Reverend Donald Shea, a Catholic and member of the National Republican Committee, was more circumspect but agreed that religious conservatives had found a home in his party. "They are new to the political scene and have come out in substantial numbers. It is quite a remarkable development." In the past conservative Protestants "would have been suspect of me because I am a Catholic," Shea continued. "But now they accept me and we get along quite well."[58] In some states such as Alaska, scholars noted, religious conservatives had completely taken over the state Republican Party. In others such as Iowa and Oklahoma, they proved influential in selecting candidates, Charles Grassley in the former and Don Nickles in the latter the best examples. In California, polls indicated that born-again Christians supported Reagan over Carter by a two-to-one margin. In Carter's own Georgia, conservative ministers formed the Georgia Pastors' Forum to fight for the "Christian issues," specifically the fight against abortion, homosexuality, and feminism. Larry Johnson, a spokesman for the group, explained: "In 1976 many pastors were sold on Jimmy Carter because of his 'born-again' Christian claims. Since then we've found out that this born-again man supports the ERA and is not against homosexuality as a life preference." The forum, Johnson concluded, supported Reagan.[59]

Still, not all religious conservatives supported Reagan. The most notable example was Ellen McCormack, the Right to Life Party candidate in New York who continued to argue with her followers that Reagan was not sufficiently prolife. After the National Affairs Briefing, McCormack begrudgingly acknowledged that this was a difficult argument to make, given both Reagan's overtures to her followers and his genial nature. Only days after the National Affairs Briefing, in fact, Reagan telephoned the Right to Life Party headquarters to ask for McCormack's support. "He was very pleasant and always polite," McCormack's campaign manager, Linda Zumpano, acknowledged to the press. As for the Reagan campaign, Roger Stone, northeast regional coordinator, displayed the candidate's confidence. "Voters who are interested in stopping abortion will vote for Ronald Reagan because he has a realistic chance of winning," Stone explained.[60] In the journal *Christianity Today* a series of articles debated the role of evangelicals in politics, some noting the danger of allying with one party, while others concluded that voting according to "biblical principles" was an excellent way to "declare the lordship of Christ." The articles generally agreed that the fight against homosexuality and abortion was among the principles that should guide voters.[61]

The conservative activist Paul Weyrich was certainly confident, granting an extended interview to the *New York Times*, which published a four-part exposé on the newfound prominence of "ultraconservative evangelical Christians as a political force within the Republican Party," the article intended to coincide with and explain the National Affairs Briefing. Weyrich traced the roots of the movement to the mid-1970s and the fight against "government red tape and the philosophy of humanism" that was gaining in the public schools. Weyrich mentioned the key players by name, including Robert Billings, Ed McAteer, and Howard Phillips, before turning to the prominent pastors such as Falwell and Robison. "Now the people who would become the centerpins of the Christian New Right were all in place," Weyrich reflected. More important, he confidently predicted that the 1980 election would produce the first fruits of the alliance.[62]

Reagan opened his "official" general campaign on Labor Day in Liberty Park on the New Jersey waterfront, the Statue of Liberty the backdrop for the television cameras. Reagan's campaign sought to portray the candidate as the embodiment of American values—leadership, competence, and strength—while painting Carter as indecisive and weak. In the electoral college Reagan sought to hold the western states plus traditional strongholds such as Indiana while gaining ground in the Democratic heartland, areas such as the industrial Midwest and the South. Key to these latter areas were southern white Protestants and Catholics, the largely blue-collar workers disillusioned by the economic and social tides since the 1960s. For these groups, Reagan would appear to be the champion of traditional values, including a strong Judeo-Christian faith. It was, in a sense, a version of Nixon's famous "Southern Strategy."[63] The economy worked to the challenger's advantage, as inflation still averaged 13 percent. Four years earlier Carter had created a "misery index," combining inflation and unemployment rates, and had chastised Ford for a score of 12 percent. Now Reagan saw an opening and pounced; after four years of Carter the misery index stood at 20 percent. Aware of the popularity of tax cuts for the constituencies he sought, Reagan proposed a 30 percent reduction in the individual tax rates along with large cuts in the business rates. He called for dramatic cuts in government, excluding the military, and for an end to oppressive regulations. New revenues from the unleashed and expanding economy, along with the reinvestment of new private capital, would more than offset the cost of the tax cuts, a policy later dubbed "Reaganomics." Carter fought back, claiming that Reagan's plans would swell the deficit, but Reagan cheerfully dismissed such claims, touting Carter as pessimistic on America.[64]

On the defensive economically, Carter sought to portray Reagan as unprepared and even dangerous in foreign affairs. Reagan made some notable gaffes, for example, in mid-August threatening to disrupt improving relations with the People's Republic of China by calling for the reestablishment of "official" relations with Taiwan. For the most part, however, Reagan successfully used the Soviet invasion of Afghanistan and the ongoing Iranian hostage crisis to couch the Carter administration as weak and to support calls for increased defense spending. Carter, Reagan continually drove home, simply did not fully grasp the threat that the Soviet Union posed. During Defense Week in mid-August, Reagan spoke to the Veterans of Foreign Wars and the American Legion, to the former describing America's mission as a "noble cause" while to the latter complaining that America's leadership had made the country "second to one."[65]

The debate over the nature of the family and all the controversial issues the subject begged were never far below the surface. As the Democratic convention concluded, the Department of Commerce reported that approximately one in five children was in a single-parent household, an increase of almost 80 percent over the previous decade. In late August Carter proclaimed the day before Labor Day as Working Mother's Day.[66] Weeks later, Spencer W. Kimball, president of the Church of Jesus Christ of Latter-day Saints, opened a conference celebrating the church's 150th anniversary by stressing the importance of family. "We know that when things go wrong in the family, things go wrong in every other institution in society," Kimball remarked. At the same time, the Supreme Court announced that it would hear oral arguments on a case involving involuntary termination of parental rights.[67]

The Supreme Court certainly added fuel to abortion's fire, the most notable case once again involving the Hyde Amendment. While the Court had earlier ruled that states were not required to pay for elective or "nontherapeutic" abortions, it now ruled 5–4 that the states were not even required to pay for "medically necessary" abortions. In *Harris v. McRae* the Court held, in essence, that the government does not have an obligation to equalize access to constitutional rights when poverty created conditions that prevented their exercise.[68] This was a difficult and ambiguous constitutional issue. In some other areas, such as the requirement that the government provide attorneys for indigent defendants, the Court seemed to suggest that the government had a duty to ensure proactively constitutional rights. Now the Court held that a basic difference existed between a law that interferes with a constitutional right and one that merely provides encouragement for an alternative behavior.[69]

Moreover, the Court held that the Hyde Amendment was not a violation of church and state separation. This, of course, added to the larger debate begged by the case. How much activism by religious organizations in the political process was legal? Frustrated by the momentum against abortion, critics pressed the Internal Revenue Service and the Department of the Treasury to strip the Catholic Church of its tax-exempt status. This effort held little realistic chance of success but reminded many conservative religious activists of the battle that activist Robert Billings had waged to keep private religious schools tax free. It arguably helped energize the evangelical community and unite it further with the Catholic Church.[70]

Perhaps not coincidentally, the Catholic archbishop of Boston, Cardinal Humberto Medeiros, released a letter read from the pulpit encouraging Catholics to vote for those who opposed abortion, a letter that "sent shock waves through [the election]," according to one observer. Cardinal Medeiros was hardly allied with the emerging leaders of the evangelical movement, but his letter clearly thrilled Howard Phillips, who declared in a flare of hyperbole that Medeiros "had joined the Moral Majority." Richard Viguerie, whose direct mail operation had tremendously assisted the conservative ministers, was more restrained. "This is an extremely exciting development," he remarked. "It certainly gives legitimacy to the whole process."[71] Falwell, who continued his travels around the country, noted the Medeiros letter and actively courted Catholics. He regularly cited the Republican platform as he continued to show audiences his ninety-minute video presentation, *America, You Are Too Young to Die!* The video showed repeated images of Charles Manson, sex-film theater marquees from New York's Times Square, atom bombs exploding, men kissing, and bloody fetuses lying in hospital pans. At the end, Falwell warned the crowds that the liberalism of the Democratic Party threatened the destruction of the nation. "God is very much a part of this campaign," stated one Republican activist in Oklahoma, encouraging the efforts of Falwell and his colleagues. "In a very real sense, the election in the Southern states is a religious battle," stated another. "Not since 1960 has politics hit the pulpit as it has here."[72]

The general campaign under way, a group calling itself Christians for Reagan ran television ads mentioning, among other issues, abortion. To be a true Christian, the ads implied, one had to be antiabortion. The National Conservative Political Action Committee ran ads condemning various Democratic senators for their support of abortion rights. Helping with the purchase of the ads was Viguerie, who had expanded his impressive list of direct mailings to conservative churches. The ads were, by at least one account, "unusually acid" and, unlike previously, appeared aimed as much at creating and expanding coalitions—such as the fight against abortion—as defeating the named Democrats. "This is an entirely new development in the political process," lamented one Democratic incumbent. Such appeals were effective and drew into the process citizens who had been relatively apolitical before. Working through their churches, they organized against abortion. "I used to be a Democrat," remarked one small-town Oklahoman, "but Carter reformed us."[73] The various antiabortion groups did not always support the Republicans in individual congressional races, but their support was, nevertheless, much more partisan than it had been in previous elections. The Right to Life Political Action Committee, for example, endorsed over three times as many Republicans as Democrats for the Senate. More activists began to note the role of the president and party in the selection of Supreme Court justices, a new tactic that perhaps reflected the realization that a constitutional amendment was unlikely. "We shudder at who [Carter] might appoint to the U.S. Supreme Court if given the chance," exclaimed Jack Willke of the National Right to Life Committee, "and we thank God every night that no opening appeared during his four year term of office."[74]

"They were all Republicans," historian Cynthia Gorney concluded, speaking of the numerous antiabortion groups. They were much more likely to "make sneering remarks about the Republican Party's timidity" than voting Democratic. Although perhaps somewhat hyperbolic, Gorney's conclusions were not far from reality. One member of the National Conference of Catholic Bishops worried that such overt partisanship might hurt the antiabortion movement. "If this situation is allowed to continue," remarked Monsignor George Higgins, "there is an increasingly grave danger that the right-to-life movement as a whole will be discredited as a right-wing sham."[75]

Carter, meanwhile, proclaimed Women's Equality Day in late August in an effort to unite his own partisans. Perhaps reflecting the bleak prognosis for the ERA, however, his statement was briefer than in previous years and concluded that "social and political change is never easy." Nevertheless, Carter continued, "I reaffirm my own commitment to make the Equal Rights Amendment part of our Constitution."[76] As Carter spoke, women staged a number of marches around the country. In New York City Bella Abzug led a march down 57th Street. She burned a copy of the Republican Party platform but hardly acknowledged the gains made during Carter's four years.[77] ERA opponents continued their pressure as well. God was against ERA ratification, Falwell told a crowd of fifteen hundred standing before the California capitol, American flags prominently displayed. "I'm not endorsing or supporting any candidate," he insisted, even as he indirectly attacked Carter. "People are saying to me, 'You're trying to get born-again Christians elected to office.' That's ridiculous. We're trying to get rid of some."[78] For her part, Schlafly pressed for a grand jury to investigate Carter's efforts to get the ERA passed in the recent Illinois vote. "Using White House telephones and White House staff for pro-ERA activities is an illegal expenditure of public money," Schlafly charged. As she spoke, supporters also claimed that various state legislators had been paid for their votes.[79] Falwell reiterated the claims, telling journalists that while he personally planned to vote for the Republicans, this did not represent an "official endorsement."[80]

An "official" endorsement was hardly necessary. Every observer knew where the Religious Right stood because it was hard to avoid its message. The Moral Majority now commanded local chapters in forty-seven states, almost all conducting voter registration drives and educational seminars. Surveys of the membership varied considerably, critics claiming only half a million members, while Falwell argued that it was six times as much.[81] Regardless, a Gallup poll revealed that almost half of Americans had heard of Jerry Falwell. His message aired on 373 local television stations and over 300 radio stations. A CBS/*New York Times* poll classified over sixty million Americans as potential supporters.[82] By early 1980 the Moral Majority reportedly had an income of over $1 million per week. Its periodical, *Moral Majority Report*, reached a circulation of 840,000, its articles increasingly instructing readers on the mechanics of organizing and influencing the coming election. Falwell now regularly flew around the country on his private jet, promising to defeat champions of "humanism" and saying that he was not "afraid" to criticize Carter directly.[83]

The Moral Majority's organization was impressive. Before he departed to work directly for the Reagan campaign, Robert Billings had suggested that the Moral Majority was open to any candidate of any party who was "pro-life, pro-American–free enterprise, et cetera, pro–Bible morality, and pro-family." Candidates who wanted the organization's endorsement had to have a state organization, be against a "bad incumbent," and attend a campaign school. This five-day training seminar cost $500 and taught participants how to raise money, organize precincts, and even select campaign staff. Despite the claims of nonpartisanship, Paul Weyrich taught the seminars, and almost all participants were Republicans. Now with the election imminent, the Moral Majority distributed a "hit list of liberal candidates" and a "support list" of candidates who promised traditional values. Again, one did not have to look far to see the partisanship.[84]

Falwell later claimed that he could not recall if the Moral Majority had helped the group Christians for Reagan, but the group mailed fliers to Moral Majority's members, obviously having acquired the membership and address lists. "My friend," the fliers read, "our world has been turned upside down and inside out because we Christians have been sitting back and allowing God to be expelled from our schools, allowed our Government to promote baby killings with our tax dollars, supported the so-called 'Equal Rights' for sexual perverts, and such." The Republican Reagan was the answer. "Mr. Carter is afraid of offending Gloria Steinem, the National Organization for Women, and the Equal Rights Amendment crowd but not afraid of turning his back on God." Whatever the official coordination, Richard Zone, president of Christians for Reagan and a minister from Pasadena, California, had met with Falwell at the recent NRB meeting. The same Reagan-Bush bumper stickers blanketed the parking lots in both Lynchburg and Pasadena.[85]

The principal driving force behind Christians for Reagan was Christian Voice and its political action committee, the Christian Voice Moral Government Fund (CVMGF). Maintaining an office in Washington, the CVMGF had for some months distributed a fifteen-page recruiting packet that contained accounts of the nation's moral failings along with selected comments from politicians, most presenting Carter and the Democrats in an unfavorable light.[86] Now, expanding its efforts, the CVMGF distributed two million pamphlets entitled *Make Your Christian Voice Count*. The pamphlets declared openly: "Ronald Reagan is the only candidate that has stood firmly behind his Christian principles at the risk of political loss. The American Christian community must support Ronald Reagan for President in 1980."[87] The bulk of the pamphlet reproduced an interview Reagan had given four years before during the nation's bicentennial. During that interview Reagan had remarked that the bicentennial was a chance to "reclaim those great principles embodied in [the] Judeo-Christian tradition and in ancient Scripture." At CVMGF's urging, a number of Christian radio stations across America ran the recorded interview regularly as the new vote approached. CVMGF recognized that Carter had won a majority of the southern evangelical vote in 1976 "from regional pride or Christian brotherhood." To ensure that this scenario did not repeat itself, it followed with several television ads that portrayed Carter not only as mean spirited but also as an ally to homosexuals and an opponent of American families.[88]

Roaming the halls of Congress was one of CVMGF's top lobbyists, Gary Jarmin. Befitting his job, Jarmin was blunt. Carter and the Democrats "have poor records on abortion, homosexual rights and other moral issues," he told all who would listen. "They deserve our prayers but not our votes." Jarmin, like Falwell, was adept at straddling the line separating free religious speech and political endorsement. When many Democrats complained about the partisanship of tax-exempt ministers speaking out on political matters, Jarmin explained that "any member of the clergy had the right to make a personal endorsement in church as long as it is a matter of personal opinion and not the endorsement of the entire church." It was a fine distinction, as all observers well knew. Moreover, attacking the ministers left the White House open to charges of stifling the free expression of religion, something the Carter campaign, still trying to stem the exodus of as many conservative Christians as possible, could not risk. To complaining Democrats, Maddox had little reply. "The President is aware of their feelings," he told the press.[89]

While not as direct or overt in its partisanship, the Religious Roundtable maintained its own voter registration and information campaign. The organization's newsletter, the *Roundtable Report*, kept readers informed on how to procure copies of House or Senate bills, how to check the status of legislation, how to be invited to testify before a congressional committee, and obviously, how to prepare for elections. The Roundtable's guide to the American political system, authored by Republican William Chasey, relied on a number of conservative think tanks for its statistics and arguments. Pat Robertson tried as well to tone down the more caustic partisanship, but there was no doubt where he stood. As only one example, programming on his Christian Broadcasting Network regularly praised Christian Voice and its advocacy.[90] James Dobson had not yet reached the level of Robertson, but with his radio program *Focus on the Family* growing rapidly and with his newfound prominence from the White House Conference on Families, his own fund-raising reached new heights, the coming election an obvious boon. As one former colleague recalled, "We repeatedly acknowledged to each other during those early days of political activism that it was a remarkably effective fund raising technique to talk to our constituents about the great danger secular humanists in Washington represented to their families and to offer our services as a shield against that danger." Accordingly, with the election only weeks away, Dobson met in a hotel room with Gary Bauer, a conservative Christian and, later, a member of the Reagan administration, along with several evangelists. There the group formed the Family Research Council (FRC), designed to continue the struggle for the traditional family beyond both the family conference and the election. The FRC was officially independent of Focus on the Family, but the two worked closely together and later merged.[91]

Billy Graham certainly recognized the conservative momentum among his colleagues, and while he continued his carefully crafted bipartisanship, he prepared for the election in his own way. Just after the conventions he enjoyed an extended—and well-publicized—stay at the Kennebunkport, Maine, retreat of vice presidential candidate George Bush. Only five weeks before the election, he announced that he would no longer use the term "born again." Graham made no reference to Carter, but as the president had widely popularized the term, Graham's announcement at least implied a rebuke.[92]

Watching it all, pleased that his long-sought goal of winning conservative Christians to the Republican fold appeared at last to be becoming a reality, Arizona congressman John Conlan invited Reagan to a gathering of evangelical ministers held at the Capitol Hilton in Washington. There Reagan, when asked by televangelist James Kennedy what he had done to enter heaven, replied that he could not "give God any reason for letting me in." He would simply have to ask for mercy in the name of Jesus. As Reagan undoubtedly anticipated, it was the perfect answer for his audience.[93] Coordinating with Conlan was not only Billings, now officially part of the Reagan campaign, but also Morton Blackwell. A Virginia delegate, Blackwell had served as the campaign's floor parliamentarian and now coordinated its efforts among young people, helping to establish "youth schools for Reagan, training over three hundred young people as political organizers." Blackwell was an associate of Viguerie, and his efforts had introduced him to a large number of conservative local pastors. Like Billings and Conlan, he remained a strong advocate for the union of religious and fiscal conservatives. Like the ministers and campaign staff he dealt with regularly, he assumed that his efforts were about to pay dividends.[94]

Reading the proverbial handwriting on the wall, Maddox was growing frantic. Earlier in the year, just before the Washington for Jesus rally, he had recommended an all-out offensive to retain the conservative Christian vote. The White House had indeed moved to regain lost ground, but, in Maddox's view, the offensive had still been uncoordinated and incomplete. Now, given the National Affairs Briefing, the situation appeared worse, and Maddox felt compelled to press the matter again. Writing a lengthy memo to Hamilton Jordan, Jody Powell, Anne Wexler, and the First Lady at the end of August, Maddox recommended an even broader offensive involving both White House events and non–White House events. In regard to the latter, Carter should consider meetings with interfaith councils. "All major cities have such councils," Maddox noted. "We could work it so that the Councils themselves extended the invitation . . . and took care of local logistics." If the administration handled the meetings properly, "the religious media will probably give better play than the secular media." In addition, Carter should consider attending the Labor-Management Prayer Breakfast in Pittsburgh in late October: "They have tried for three years to get the President." In regard to the former, Maddox recommended again lengthy interviews for religious television. As one example, Carter might consider an interview with Ben Armstrong, a "friend of the President." If he agreed, the interview "would go out live or on a 24-hour delay on all the nation's Christian radio (900 stations) and TV (35 stations)." Carter should also consider a "briefing and presidential drop by with major religious weekly and monthly magazines and journals." Staffers, Maddox added, "have done our homework with these people." Finally, Carter should consider a meeting with "lay and clergy opinion makers" and a "grass roots people's meeting." All of these meetings "are necessary for the Christian community to get a clearer idea of who the President is and why he has taken certain positions." In concluding, Maddox noted that he had arranged "an ad hoc group of laymen to prepare a brochure that will detail the President's positions." He promised to continue to "work closely with state coordinators in key states to insure the right kind of religious involvement in campaign stops for the First Family and Vice President."[95]

The reply Maddox received was, once again, not all that he thought necessary. Wexler and Powell recommended to Carter only an interview for religious television, with Bakker and Robertson sitting nearby. The two would not participate, but their "presence on camera would add great strength to the interview." Undoubtedly, Wexler and Powell noted, "both PTL and CBN would give full play to the interview" and hopefully make copies for other religious networks. The White House could produce an audio copy for distribution to religious radio stations. To conduct the interview, Wexler and Powell suggested Harold Bredeson, who had interviewed Egyptian president Sadat and Israeli prime minister Begin and who was, given his persistence at the convention, a "great admirer [of Carter]." In the end, conducting the interview was important to remind people that Carter was a man of faith: "Conservative Christians need to hear your views accurately and will not without such an interview."[96]

In the end Carter agreed, but Maddox, even more frustrated, learned of a problem. As Maddox wrote Powell, "When I began to work through the maze of religious television regulations, I discovered that the only way to avoid equal time and fairness problems and still get maximum coverage was to structure the interview as a news conference."[97] Maddox noted that Armstrong had offered to "moderate the discussion to control any possible troublemakers, although he minimizes the possibility of any kind of trouble." Such a format was unfortunate, Maddox noted, but Carter should still go ahead with the event. "The session would not be as informal and personal as I had wanted but this seems the only way to get the message beamed directly to conservative Christians. Dr. Armstrong believes the interview could be crucial. He says that when the people listen to the President and then to Mr. Reagan, especially on matters of faith, the President completely outdistances Mr. Reagan." Maddox acknowledged that a news conference format would require more of Carter's time and would require him to "prepare for questions on more than just the moral issues." It was not perfect, but the White House could "make sure no belligerents were recognized."[98]

The change in format was, however, more than Carter was willing to consider. It required too much time when time was at a premium, and it carried too much risk. It was, in the words of one aide, "no longer considered a priority for the President."[99] Carter still did not want to ignore pastors he thought he might still persuade, but Maddox knew that this would not prove the last-minute game-changer he feared was necessary. In the waning weeks of the campaign, Carter even welcomed Adrian Rogers and Bailey Smith to the Oval Office, the latter having just replaced the former as president of the Southern Baptist Convention. Both were archtheological conservatives, Maddox reported, but Smith claimed that he still prayed for Carter daily and "remembers the President's visit to his church a few years ago."[100] The ministers presented Carter with a videocassette produced by the SBC's Radio and Television Commission on the need for energy reform. Afterward, Carter sent a letter expressing his "great pleasure" in the meeting and thanking the participants for their advice on energy policy.[101] Rogers's wife, Joyce, who had met with Rosalynn, wrote her own letter of thanks but in doing so at least implied their theological differences. "I among many Southern Baptists and other Christians I know are very interested in understanding your viewpoints concerning women," she wrote. "It is difficult, however, working through the media to gain proper insights."[102]

In early September Robert Schuller's staff at his church, Garden Grove Community Church in California, wrote Maddox requesting a letter from Carter congratulating the church on the dedication of its massive new all-glass cathedral. The White House declined, but Maddox arranged for a letter from Carter to Schuller congratulating him on "the twenty-fifth anniversary of your dedication to the ministry." The same month, Carter wrote Billy Graham congratulating him on the dedication of the Billy Graham Center at Wheaton College, a "tribute to your unique ministry and enduring service to society."[103] More notably, Carter agreed to meet with Bakker, who had yet to make his personal endorsement despite his increasingly partisan rhetoric. An obviously proud Bakker had reprinted his communications with the White House in his PTL publications, and Maddox recognized an opportunity. Accordingly, with the election looming and the press following the campaign's every move, Carter met with Bakker on Air Force One in Memphis, Tennessee, and the two flew together to Jackson, Mississippi. During the flight the odd couple prayed together, which the press also reported. Afterward, Bakker wrote Carter that it was "indeed a pleasure for me to be with you, and it was a high-light of my life to have the honor of praying with you on Air Force One." Nevertheless, as Maddox could have perhaps predicted, Bakker still made no public endorsement of Carter and continued to comment favorably on Reagan.[104]

Reagan, meanwhile, was not about to lose ground with the Religious Right in the campaign's last weeks. Staff members from the Reagan-Bush campaign carried boxes of "Christians for Reagan" buttons and bumper stickers and coordinated their efforts with members of the Moral Majority. Billings obviously remained the key connection, Falwell describing his campaign job as "opening doors to the evangelical community."[105] Following up on his performance at the National Affairs Briefing, Reagan invited Falwell to one of his speeches in New Orleans. As Falwell recalled, "I met him at the airport and we rode together in the back of a limousine." During the ride the discussion turned to the Soviet Union, and Reagan remarked that at times he wondered if the world were headed toward Armageddon. He was not a fatalist, Reagan continued, but believed that God would respect those who made efforts toward world peace. The two then "prayed together." During Reagan's speech Falwell waited backstage. Afterward, they talked for an hour "about his faith in God."[106] As he spoke with Reagan,

Falwell wrote a laudatory introduction to Richard Viguerie's new book, *The New Right: We're Ready to Lead*. Released late in the campaign, it appeared to be just another indication of the Religious Right's marriage to the Republican Party.[107]

It was a marriage made in hell, according to the group Americans United for Separation of Church and State. According to one member, the "leaders of the evangelical right are uninformed, unrealistic about the issues, unfaithful to their own highest ideals, uncaring, unbrotherly, and untruthful."[108] At its annual convention in September, a series of panels explored how overt religious partisanship could corrupt the government and, in addition, how federal policy could restrict the faithful. Weeks later, a group of sixty-one prominent scholars and writers issued the "Secular Humanist Declaration," which warned that the "reappearance of dogmatic authoritarian religions threatens intellectual freedom, human rights, and scientific progress." The document assailed "fundamentalist, literalist, and doctrinaire Christianity" as well as religious extremism around the globe.[109] Liberal theologians spoke out more forcibly as well. Only weeks before the election various leaders in thirteen religious organizations, including the United Church of Christ, the Friends General Conference, and the United Presbyterian Church in the USA, denounced the actions of the Moral Majority and Christian Voice. "We find their selection of issues to be theologically inadequate," a statement read. "Their activities represent ideological preferences rather than the breadth of responsible Christian positions."[110] Even the Reverend Jimmy Allen, a moderate and former president of the Southern Baptist Convention, acknowledged that there had been "a total capitulation of a segment of the evangelical movement to right-wing politics and sword-rattling jingoism." Perhaps representing African Americans' traditional allegiance to the Democratic Party, a number of leading black evangelicals continued to question the Moral Majority and its ideological cousins. Sensing this division, the Congressional Black Caucus released a statement that painted the Moral Majority and others as a threat to black progress.[111]

Critics took every opportunity to lambaste the Religious Right. "What is troubling about the Robisons and Falwells is that they make checklists of politico-religious purity and urge that every candidate be judged by those tests," wrote one columnist. "It is as if all the complexities of the world could be reduced to a handful of black and white judgements, made by these ministers with the imprimatur of divine guidance." Some pundits were particularly harsh, others sarcastic. Writer Russell Baker was the latter. "If the reverend political clergy can be believed," he wrote, "God has spent a lot of time considering American domestic policy, concluded that it was a mess, and decided that it was all the Democrats' fault."[112]

With the election so near, the charges and countercharges flew, often to the point of hyperbole. Never one to guard her words, Phyllis Schlafly continued to suggest that Carter's reelection would sound the death knell for the American family. She even linked his support of the ERA to his problems with the Iranian hostage crisis. If he had paid less attention to ERA ratification, perhaps he would not have neglected problems in Iran and Afghanistan. "If this administration can't stand up to women's lib," she laughed sarcastically, "they can't stand up to the Russians." Falwell was no less sarcastic. When Secretary of the Army Clifford Alexander supported Carter's idea about drafting women, Falwell mocked him. Alexander, Falwell laughed, "has never been in combat and has only had six months of active military service in the Army National Guard as a private first class." If women were allowed in combat, their male colleagues would be distracted from the enemy because "they'd have to be watching out for the welfare of the little lady." The Moral Majority, countered Patricia Roberts Harris, secretary of the Department of Health and Human Services, was "at best exclusionary and at worst a dangerous, intolerant and polarizing influence in our political system."[113]

Looking back on it all, Maddox insisted that the tactics employed by the administration's critics, the "report cards and other campaign devices," far surpassed those of its own partisans. The Religious Right made Carter appear a "flaming liberal straight from the pits of hell," and the White House had to fight back as best it could. "I had preachers from east and west, north and south, sit in my office and make comments like, 'How can Jimmy Carter be a Christian and be for . . . ERA, not be for a constitutional amendment supporting prayer in public schools, not be for an anti-abortion amendment to the Constitution?'" He had, Maddox implied, no choice but to interrupt. "I had to say, 'Wait a minute. You can quarrel with his political stands all you want to. Vote against him if you don't like what he is doing. But be very careful about labeling him an unbeliever because you disagree with him on a certain issue or cluster of issues. As a matter of fact, there are people of strong, undeniable faith who come down on the other side of the very issues you are describing.'"[114]

Throughout September the candidates attacked each other. When in California Reagan blundered by suggesting that air pollution was under control and that the eruption of Mount St. Helens and the country's forests were responsible for much of the nation's pollution, the Carter campaign mocked the comments. At the same time, however, Reagan accused the Carter White House of deliberately leaking secret details of a radar-resistant warplane, the stealth bomber, in order to benefit Carter politically. Carter replied that the specifics were already well known and that no damage had taken place. In fact, there was damage, if only to Carter's campaign.[115]

One of the most contentious issues was over the first scheduled presidential debate, set for Baltimore on September 21. The sponsor, the League of Women Voters (LWV), had decided to invite the independent candidate, John Anderson, because several polls placed support for his National Unity campaign at more than 15 percent, the group's minimum threshold for participation. Carter still recognized that Anderson was more of a threat to his campaign than Reagan. While the maverick ex-Republican spoke of his "commitment to Jesus Christ," he had warned religious broadcasters that applying religious absolutism to the political system was "nothing less than an American version of religious intolerance" and might jeopardize their tax-exempt status.[116] In short, as Carter understood, the Religious Right was unlikely to vote for Anderson, while many feminists and gay rights supporters remained enamored with his campaign. When the LWV extended its invitation to debate, Reagan accepted and Carter did not, claiming that it was not fair for him to debate two Republicans. Reagan, meanwhile, refused to debate Carter without Anderson's inclusion. When the debate went ahead without Carter, both Reagan and Anderson trained their fire on the absent incumbent. Postelection polls debated whether Anderson or Reagan had won, but most agreed that the real loser was Carter.[117]

Just after the debate, Reagan attended a meeting of the National Religious Broadcasters held on October 3 in Lynchburg, the site of Falwell's church and the center of his ministry. As soon as Reagan exited the plane, reporters broached the issue once again of Bailey Smith's controversial comments at the National Affairs Briefing, asking Reagan if he agreed that God did not hear the prayers of Jews. In his reply Reagan walked a fine line. "No, because both the Christian and Judaic religions are based on the same God, the God of Moses, I am quite sure those prayers are heard," Reagan stated. Then, however, he continued, suggesting that Falwell's defense of Smith was valid as well: "I guess everyone can make his own interpretation

of the Bible, and many individuals had been making different interpretations for a long time."[118]

The broadcasters gave Reagan an enthusiastic reception. While Reagan
stressed the importance of family, he avoided any direct reference to abortion or the ERA. When he told the crowd that the Bible, not government,
was the answer to society's ills, the audience broke out in wild applause.
All expected partisan attacks, given the election, and Reagan delivered.
The crowd particularly responded to his charge that liberals were trying to
use the separation of church and state to keep conservative Christians out
of politics. "[Reagan] did a good job," Falwell later recalled.[119] Despite his
obvious success in Lynchburg, however, new polling gave Reagan pause.
Several surprising numbers suggested that while the Republican remained
the choice of most evangelicals, his overall popularity had slipped somewhat. While pundits debated the reasons, some suggesting that an apparent
decline in Anderson's numbers benefited Carter and others suggesting a
backlash to Reagan's courting of the Religious Right or the impact of his
advanced age, the Reagan campaign decided to switch its strategy. When
in early October the LWV announced that the new polling raised questions
about Anderson's eligibility for the second scheduled presidential debate,
set for Cleveland, Reagan agreed to debate the incumbent one-on-one.[120]

Neither candidate had time to rest. On October 16 both spoke at the
Alfred E. Smith dinner in New York City, a traditional milepost in campaigns where candidates usually demonstrated frivolity and goodwill in
their comments. Reagan recognized this and joked about his age. Despite
rumors, he deadpanned, he had not spoken at the first Smith dinner more
than half a century before. He looked young "because I keep riding older
and older horses." Carter, by contrast, unintentionally appeared defensive
and annoyed. He used the occasion to remind the audience of his success at
Camp David and of the Jewish prayer controversy. Carter launched into a
story about a young Palestinian boy who had inquired if he agreed with the
evangelist who had said that God didn't hear the prayers of Jews. "I said,"
Carter quoted his reply, "that I was sure that God heard all of our prayers,
Christian, Jewish and Moslem, because thirteen days before we had [the
Camp David] agreement." The audience hardly appeared impressed.[121]

Still hoping to keep the prayer controversy alive, the Democrats began to
run campaign commercials returning to Falwell's Jewish comments. Ignoring Falwell's many pro-Israel remarks, the ad began, "Dr. Jerry Falwell has
said that God does not hear the prayers of Jews." Running on 252 stations

in states with large Jewish populations, it continued, "If Reagan goes to the White House, Falwell will come with him, and they will purify the land as someone else did some years ago." The ads were undoubtedly harsh, and the Moral Majority immediately filed an eleven-million-dollar lawsuit against the Carter campaign and its coordinator, Gerald Rafshoon. The ad, the suit claimed, "implicitly portrays Dr. Jerry Falwell as a religious bigot." For its part, the campaign initially dismissed the suit but, after apparently learning that the ad was "not 100% accurate," decided to withdraw it. Falwell, in turn, decided to drop the suit.[122] He did not, however, drop his emotional appeals to his partisans. "What this country needs is Christians like you," read one letter mailed in the wake of the suit. "We've had enough of the anti-God, anti-American flag burning Americans who are disgracing our stars and stripes." Falwell continued to insist that he was a victim of a vendetta by Carter and the liberal media. "The Carter people knew I didn't say it, but they pushed it," he repeated as often as he could. The entire episode was "one of the most painful times of misunderstanding in the early Moral Majority years."[123]

The Carter campaign had backed down but was angry as well. In late October it appeared to press the issue, warning that a Republican victory would split the nation "black from white, Jew from Christian, North from South, rural from urban." The inclusion of the Jewish comment suggested to some the controversy surrounding Smith and Falwell, but Reagan did not take the bait. He was not "angry" at Carter's remarks, Reagan declared, only "saddened." It was the perfect reply in many respects, portraying him as the aggrieved party embodying the spirit of Christian forgiveness. In short, Reagan had further eroded Carter's reputation for compassion and, he hoped, augmented Reagan's support among conservative Christians. Even Eugene McCarthy, the antiwar Democratic candidate in 1968, complimented Reagan. Reagan ran a "more dignified campaign," he told the press. Carter, of course, vehemently disagreed. With the hard-hitting ads on both sides continuing, Carter, historian Andrew Busch notes, found questions about his character and morality a "particular source of bitterness."[124] Worried about potential damage from the "meanness" issue, Carter agreed to an interview on ABC News with reporter Barbara Walters. Walters pressed Carter for an apology, which clearly flustered him. Finally, Carter's comments seemed to acknowledge that he had taken the "low road."[125] Carter was becoming increasingly angry at the press, his staff complaining that the media never gave Reagan's controversial comments enough attention. In particular, according to columnist Elizabeth Drew, the staff assumed that Reagan had overplayed his Religious Right hand. The Carter campaign "was trying to think of ways to draw attention to Reagan's courtship of right-wing evangelicals without having Carter himself offend the 'born again' vote."[126]

Whether Reagan worried that he had overplayed his hand or not, he was not about to miss a chance to exploit every Carter weakness. Even as he courted Falwell, Reagan took a page from Carter's own playbook, reaching out to the women's rights activists still discontented with the administration. While Betty Friedan argued that "we don't have to love anybody personally, but we should fight to re-elect this administration," her feminist colleague Eleanor Smeal continued to attack Carter.[127] This offered Reagan an odd opening, which he adroitly took. He wrote Smeal and asked that NOW reconsider his candidacy. "I am as committed as you are to women's rights," Reagan wrote, releasing the letter to the press, undoubtedly aware that it would win wide coverage. "I'm convinced that what we disagree on is only the means . . . not the goal." In his letter Reagan complained about charges that he was sexist. "I regret even having to address this issue for fear that discussing it might lend a scintilla of credence to such a charge." He was against "tokenism," he wrote, but it was "time for a woman to sit among our highest jurists."[128] The promise to appoint a woman to the Supreme Court, Reagan understood, was a strong card to play, and Smeal's reaction showed that he had indeed succeeded in softening his image. "[Reagan] is finally waking up to the fact that this issue is a lot hotter than he realized," she replied, adding that he had supported fourteen separate bills on civil rights as governor of California and had promised to deal with discrimination against women on a case-by-case basis.[129]

Smeal was not alone. Final polls confirmed a split in the female electorate. Not only did Reagan still poll strong among women, but many opposed to him remained split between Carter and Anderson. The polls also noted that while those who shared Reagan's stance on both the ERA and abortion were a minority, social conservatives were more likely to "cast ballots solely on those issues."[130] Making a move that appeared almost desperate, the White House announced a reshuffling of advisors on the ERA. Whereas Weddington had coordinated the matter before, she would now share responsibilities with advisors Eugene Eidenberg, Frank Moore, and Wexler. Eidenberg had been involved in intergovernmental affairs and Moore in congressional relations. "If we're going to get ERA passed," a White House spokesman stated, "it can't be treated as a jurisdictional matter to be handled by one person on the President's staff."[131]

A week after the Alfred E. Smith dinner, on October 22, Carter received the National Advisory Committee's official report on the White House Conference on Families. While the issues of feminism and family in all its manifestations did not need any additional publicity, Chairman Tucker had argued for a public ceremony to unveil the results of the official report on the conference as an "opportunity to focus on the President's concerns for families and the actions he has taken to strengthen families," adding that it "could call attention to [Carter's] recent proposal to minimize the marriage penalty tax, a pledge Reagan has abandoned." Carter, Tucker added, need not worry about all the controversies the conference had fueled because the report diminished them.[132] Indeed, the report's final recommendations included homosexuals among the list of possible families—without, of course, endorsing one definition over another—but relegated an endorsement of abortion rights, family planning, and the ERA to "secondary" status. Ratification of the ERA, for example, ranked thirty-second among the report's recommendations. The primary recommendations included flexible working hours in the workplace; efforts to stem alcohol and drug abuse; changes in the tax code to eliminate the "marriage penalty" and to encourage home care of the elderly; financial assistance to families with handicapped members; and additional assistance in family violence prevention and day care arrangements.[133] In a statement released with the report, Carter praised the "consensus" that had produced the report, obviously choosing to diminish the dissension, just as the report itself had done. "We are already working to implement the recommendations," Carter remarked, adding that he had previously instructed all agencies to comply with the report's findings. Carter noted that he had urged Congress to revise the tax code and hoped that it would do so in the near future. For his part, Tucker conceded that implementation of the conference's recommendations hinged in large part on the results of the impending election. "If Reagan were to win," he told the press, "we would have to go back to him with it."[134]

Hope for real change came with a price tag, of course, which the report noted in numerous places. With the economy struggling, the NAC emphasized, states and local communities would have to bear a great deal of the responsibility and cost of implementation. Private industries would have to alter the way they do business. The struggling economy and ongoing turmoil in the Middle East promised to redirect much of the necessary energy, however, and some observers began to fear that the entire effort might have been for naught. Years later, Marshner concluded that the final report was "not going to be cited as a seminal document in the development of family policy in this country." It did little to change the direction of federal policy or stem the problems facing American families. It did, however, help ignite social conservatives as a powerful political force. "It got our people involved in a process that they hadn't been before," Marshner remembered. If nothing else, it geared them up for the election.[135]

The media gave the NAC report only scant coverage, a fact not surprising, given that the long-anticipated Carter-Reagan debate in Cleveland took place only six days later. Both candidates prepared well for the October 28 nationally televised contest. There had been a "radical departure of Governor Reagan from the principles or ideals of historical perspective of his party," Carter began, trying to put Reagan on the defensive. "I don't think that can be better illustrated than in the case of guaranteeing women equal rights." Reagan, however, would have none of it. He was for women's rights, he assured the audience, but was against "unelected judges" and big government. Smartly turning the question away from a focus on women's rights to an issue of repressive government regulation, Reagan put Carter back on the defensive. The debate predictably covered a broad range of topics, and throughout it all it was evident to many observers that Carter was struggling to keep the traditional Democratic coalition together. Even as he supported the ERA and courted the liberal elements of his party, he felt the need to answer Reagan's attacks. "I'm a Southerner," Carter replied, "and I too share the basic beliefs of my region against an excessive government intrusion into the private lives of American citizens." While most pundits termed the contest a draw, several large polls declared Reagan the clear winner. His well-publicized quip in admonishing Carter—"There you go again"—apparently resonated with the public.[136]

The final week of the long campaign was predictably frantic, the candidates looking for any last-minute advantage. Despite his hectic schedule, Reagan exuded an optimism, a certain charisma, that appealed to many voters. His followers worked to do the same. Falwell had always spoken in ominous terms about the condition of American morality. Now, however, even his rhetoric became more hopeful. "I am optimistic about America," Falwell stated without mentioning Reagan directly. "I am convinced that we can turn this nation back to God." At the same time, Carter appeared to many voters to stoke fear. Declaring that "peace is my passion," Carter nevertheless asserted that the Republicans would push the United States to the "nuclear precipice."[137]

Falwell was not the only one sensing the campaign's momentum. A week before the election, the Carter campaign finally mailed religious-oriented materials to about 250,000 ministers, the "only religious pieces mailed in favor of the president," in the words of a frustrated Maddox. While Maddox had long recommended a broad, coordinated offensive to win back the Religious Right, he personally did all that he could do, given his continued employment at the White House. "That's why I had to back off," he stated, even as he clearly applauded the last-minute mailings. Maddox spent that last week traveling, especially in the South, always ensuring that he was within the law by having the campaign, not the White House, pay his expenses. "I would get someone I knew in the area to set up a meeting," Maddox explained of his final efforts. That person would publish an advertisement in the paper, which would give the meetings publicity. This brought out everyone, and "I ran into some mighty rough people, ministers and lay people." By this point, he continued, "I knew all the answers." Sometimes Maddox felt a bit of success when critics acknowledged that Carter was indeed a Christian, even if he "wasn't much of a Christian." In reality, of course, such distinctions hardly mattered, as Maddox recognized. Most conservative Christians had already decided their vote. One of Maddox's last visits was with his son Ben to tour African American churches in Philadelphia. "We were enthusiastically received in the churches, but the Black community was Carter's already."[138]

The attack commercials continued to the bitter end. As an announcer stated that Carter embraced homosexuals in one ad, the screen showed men in bizarre drag costumes and other men kissing. Reagan, the announcer concluded, will defend the "traditional American family." Yet another ad depicted a woman in a cardigan sweater sitting in front of a middle-class wood-frame house. Staring into the camera, she explained that she was a "Christian mother." Unlike Carter, she did not want her children "taught that abortion and homosexuality were perfectly alright." When the Carter campaign complained, a spokesman for Reagan claimed that his candidate had nothing to do with the attacks. "We don't take a position on what [outside groups] do," he maintained. "We are completely separate and don't have input with these people."[139] Dobson's Focus on the Family, meanwhile, circulated an antiabortion video in conservative churches. Dobson claimed that over sixty million people saw it just before the election. Letters denouncing Carter continued to arrive at both the White House and the Democratic campaign headquarters. According to one evangelical, Carter owed the Christian community an apology because "Satan apparently has us right where he wants us, Christian against Christian."[140] Obviously annoyed, Maddox responded. "I agree with you about Christians fighting Christians," he stated, but the commercials did not have "accurate statements."[141] Fighting back on its own, Planned Parenthood, a major provider of abortions, announced a new patriotic publicity campaign to coincide with the election. With the Stars and Stripes waving in the background, words appeared on the television screen: "Planned Parenthood. Helping Build a Strong America by Helping Strong American Families."[142]

The big news of the final week was, of course, Iran. With the election literally only days away, reports that negotiations to release the hostages were nearing conclusion exploded into the headlines. If the hostages had found their freedom prior to Election Day, the situation might have worked to Carter's advantage. As it happened, however, the hostages remained captive as Americans went to the polls. Rather than the proverbial "October Surprise" feared by Republicans, the reports did little more than remind voters of Carter's ineptitude. Reagan adeptly used the campaign's last days to reiterate his claim that Carter was weak and that the entire hostage debacle was a direct result of that weakness. This resonated with conservative Christians more than most, many of whom had begun urging Carter to proclaim a national day of fasting and prayer for the captives. Even in the shadow of the election, however, Carter still declined, fearing that such a public prayer would cast the crisis as a religious dispute and that Reagan would criticize him for using his faith for political gain. This refusal, Maddox recalled, "only widened the gap between [Carter] and many conservative Christians," one final impetus for them to cast their ballots for the optimistic Republican. Heading to the polls, the Religious Right "could not understand how a born-again president could refuse to implore God in such a manner."[143]

For months the nightly newscasts had begun their programs by counting the days of American bondage, each passing day easily depicted as a testament to America's impotence. The economy remained mired in stagflation, interest rates rising as inflation continued at double-digit levels. According to most pundits, Anderson drained Carter's liberal base, and indeed, the day before the election Carter appealed to Anderson's voters to "return to the Democratic Party." As Maddox knew all too well, the Religious Right was a lost cause; conservative Christians would almost certainly not pull the same lever, cast the same ballot, as they had four years before. It all foretold a landslide—or did it? The final polls had some surprising news. The election was still close, some polls even declaring the race a dead heat. The numbers seemed to most pundits counterintuitive, perhaps an indication that Reagan did indeed seem to voters, after all, too extreme. Perhaps Americans were a bit hesitant to change metaphorical horses in the middle of a stream. Whatever their conclusions, the pundits had little time for analysis. It was, at long last, Election Day.[144]

November 4, 1980, dawned cold and rainy in Washington, perhaps for the Carter campaign the first indication that the surprising polls were far from the mark. At the end of the day, Maddox recalled, it was an "ineffably sad evening."[145] The challenger buried the incumbent by a plurality of nearly 9 million popular votes, 43,903,230 to 35,480,115. With Reagan carrying 50.7 percent of the total vote to Carter's 41 percent, it was indeed a landslide. Anderson's performance was impressive for a third-party candidate, 5,719,859 popular votes, or 6.6 percent of the total, while Ellen McCormack, running as the Right to Life Party's candidate, collected 32,320 votes. Reagan carried 44 states and won the Electoral College 489 to 49. While Carter carried his native state, the majority of the South went Republican for the first time since Reconstruction a century earlier, suggesting that the Reagan campaign's hope of attracting social and religious conservatives, the rural southern white Protestant vote, had succeeded. Worse still for the Democrats, the Republicans won the Senate for the first time since 1952. While the GOP did not reclaim the House, it reduced the Democratic majority by thirty-three seats. Democratic Speaker Tip O'Neill summed up the mood of his party: it was a "disaster for the Democrats."[146]

The Sunday following his defeat, Carter and his family attended services at the First Baptist Church of Washington, which quietly passed a resolution of condolence, "with love and prayerful support." Baptist Jimmy Allen sent his own letter of condolence, which Carter appreciated. "Your friendship is very important to me, and I thank you for your encouraging words," Carter replied, adding in a handwritten postscript, "I will pray for you. There is much to be done." Billy Graham's wife, Ruth, wrote Rosalynn a handwritten note on the loss. "May God bless you and the President as you enter a new phase of your ministry," she wrote.[147]

Members of the new Religious Right were not so restrained, clearly ecstatic about the result and quick to claim credit. Falwell staged a triumphant
display on the steps of the New Jersey statehouse, with dozens of flags and
performers in matching suits marching and singing patriotic songs before a
crowd of more than a thousand. Falwell explained that the Moral Majority
did not intend to rest after the presidential election. The New Jersey legislature was scheduled to meet in a special postelection session, and Falwell
wanted to make his presence known, a symbol to state legislatures across
the land. The Moral Majority was a "sleeping giant," an obviously exuberant
Falwell exclaimed. It had helped register more than four million new voters and had influenced another ten million. Whether in Congress or state-
houses, legislators "would do well to examine their records and get in step
with conservative values or be prepared to be unemployed." Watching the
spectacle, one critic worried that the Moral Majority would hold sway over
the new president-elect. The entire spectacle "reminds me of the begin-
nings of Fascism back in the 1930s."[148]

According to one of Falwell's colleagues, the attitude among the Moral
Majority was "Can you believe what we just did?" Falwell later termed the
election "my finest hour."[149] Of those highlighted on his organization's "hit
lists," senators John Culver of Iowa, Birch Bayh of Indiana, George McGovern of South Dakota, and Frank Church of Idaho all lost, along with lesser-
known senators in Georgia, North Carolina, and New York. Of the notables,
only California's Alan Cranston survived. Reflecting on the importance of
the election years later, the National Right to Life Political Action Committee claimed that eleven Senate seats changed from the prochoice to
the prolife column.[150] In the words of Falwell, "Of the forty-three races in
which a Moral Majority chapter was involved, the morally conservative
candidate won in forty. And of the twenty-eight political incumbents our
people opposed, twenty-three were defeated." He had reason to be ecstatic,
he claimed; his organization had earned it. Falwell later took a broader perspective but still claimed that the Moral Majority was crucial. "It was the
American people, not the Moral Majority, who elected Ronald Reagan," Falwell wrote. "But we helped."[151]

Evangelist Tim LaHaye was as excited as Falwell, declaring that God
"saw thousands of us working diligently to awaken his sleeping church to
its political responsibilities."[152] Richard Viguerie was more circumspect if
not equally pleased. The "ready-made network" of evangelical preachers,
Viguerie believed, enabled the Republicans to bypass the "liberal media."

Viguerie tipped his hat to the Moral Majority and the Religious Round-table, suggesting that such groups "numerically and perhaps historically" constituted "one of our most important assets." Combining both vanity and hyperbole, Richard Dolan of the National Conservative Political Action Committee declared that he was powerful enough to put Mickey Mouse in the presidency.[153]

In the first broadcast of his *700 Club* television show after the election, Pat Robertson began by applauding the gracious manner in which Carter had handled his defeat: "He has shown Christian virtue in a tremendous way, and I just want you to pray for him and his family." Robertson then moved on to Reagan and directly claimed that the votes of conservative Christians were critical to his victory: "This group provided Reagan with his clear margin of victory." As if to demonstrate the power of the new Religious Right, Robertson continued by listing "so-called liberal senators" who faced defeat. Using this as his cue, he pulled out a blackboard to explain the difference between liberalism and conservatism. While in the nineteenth century liberalism implied freedom, he explained, it now meant "usually Marxist, socialist, and big government." Liberalism "turns away from tradition, whatever tradition that happened to be." Now that conservatives were in charge, the people should expect and demand a limited government, a strong foreign policy, and a return to traditional assumptions, including those of the faith that had guided the nation since its founding.[154]

Robertson, it appeared, was trying to keep his show on a higher plane, dealing in the theoretical and acting like a gracious winner. As the show continued, however, this effort appeared to fade as Robertson obviously improvised more. He became more direct and harsh with personal attacks and innuendo against Carter's staff and allies. Staffer Tim Kraft had resigned because of "suspicion of cocaine." Midge Constanza had been "repugnant to Christians" by advocating gay rights. Peter Bourne had been "dispensing drugs in Washington," and all knew of top Carter aide Hamilton Jordan's "escapades." This type of behavior was the natural result of modern liberalism, and that was why Christians had turned to conservatism. Four years before, in 1976, Carter had appeared to be the anecdote to endemic corruption. Christians, Robertson concluded, had been "100% for Mr. Carter," who appeared one of their own. Now, in 1980, "we could only wish he had played it differently." Now it was the political conservatives who promised to implement "Judeo-Christian values," and this, in the end, explained the recent election.[155]

"A new and exciting spirit for evangelism is coming into the American religious community," pastor Peter Wagner, a professor at Fuller Theological Seminary, wrote just after the election. "I am optimistic." If it could happen in America, it could happen around the globe. Inspired by the American example, evangelicals in the Philippines pledged that by the year 2000 every political ward would have an evangelical church. America was only the start.[156] Watching the same developments but drawing an entirely different conclusion, columnist Flora Lewis agreed that conservative Christian evangelicalism was not just an American phenomenon, it was part of an "anti-intellectual, anti-science, anti-technology fundamentalism" that included Islamic radicalism and the likes of Ayatollah Khomeini. The involvement of religious conservatives in the political world was hardly cause for optimism. Lewis did not directly equate the American Religious Right with the extremes of radical Islam, but it was hardly the last time pundits drew the analogy.[157]

The obvious glee of the Religious Right was sure to provoke a reaction. As Christian Voice's Gary Jarmin remarked that the "victory of Christians" in the election "points to the beginning of a new era," the president of the Union of American Hebrew Congregations, Rabbi Alexander M. Schindler, could not restrain himself. "I do not accuse [conservative pastors] of deliberately inciting anti-Semitism but I do say that their preachments have an inevitable effect," Schindler explained. It was "no coincidence that the rise of right-wing fundamentalism has been accompanied by the most serious outbreak of anti-Semitism since the outbreak of World War II." Schindler's remarks brought a quick reaction from an angry Falwell: "I do not have to prove to Rabbi Schindler or anyone else my longstanding friendship for the Jewish people in America and around the world, and my strong and continuing advocacy of the cause of Israel."[158] In many respects, Schindler had employed a bit of hyperbole in his criticism, and Falwell, at least, had been outspoken in his defense of Israel, whatever his motives. Many Jewish voters were committed Democrats and had their own partisan reactions to the election. Rabbi Nathan Perlmutter, director of the Anti-Defamation League of B'nai B'rith, "respectfully reminded" Schindler that anti-Semitism was hardly confined to conservative Christians in America. It was also, for example, in the Soviet Union and in the Palestine Liberation Organization (PLO), which many leaders of the Religious Right staunchly opposed.[159]

Tensions were simply high after the historic election, and the issue was complex. The American Civil Liberties Union (ACLU), a frequent critic of Republicans, jumped into the fray, describing the "so-called Christian agenda of groups like the Moral Majority" an "anti–civil liberties agenda." The National Council of Churches, perhaps reflecting the growing liberal theology in its ranks, actively considered endorsing the recognition of the PLO, a move anathema to many conservatives. A Gallup poll indicated that almost two-thirds of Americans worried that religious groups might now wield too much power in government, a fact that perhaps underlaid the postelection snipping and political posturing on all sides. The reality remained that the election had tremendously altered the political landscape. From Falwell to Schindler, from Christian Voice to the ACLU, the future was unknown.[160]

While the antiabortion and anti-ERA lobbies celebrated, the election completely demoralized most women's rights advocates. "It's going to take a major effort not to go backward in the next four years," suggested Sarah Weddington, "let alone trying to move ahead." Perhaps feminists let Republicans too readily couch themselves as the champion of families, concluded Betty Friedan. "The future of families is not a right-wing concern but a feminist concern," she stated. "It was wrong to let the right wing get away with preempting it." Friedan's colleague Steinem was a bit more optimistic. "The women's movement didn't start in Washington," she remarked, "and it won't be stopped by it." In any event, having a "real threat in office" would galvanize supporters in a way that Carter's middle-of-the-road approach did not. While Steinem's view of Reagan had apparently soured, she did not blame her own criticism of Carter as part of the reason for Reagan's victory. In leaving the White House and anticipating the Reagan years, however, Carter advisor Wexler had a different view. Feminists, she suggested, would pay a "high price" for their lack of solidarity.[161]

Almost everyone, it appeared, proclaimed the power of the Religious Right. The award-winning ABC news program *Nightline* invited Falwell to appear on the show the night after the election, analyzing the results with an august cast that included the new president-elect and defeated senators McGovern, Bayh, and Church. The show won a wide audience and even an Emmy Award. Analyzing the new political reality, *Christianity Today* concluded that evangelicals now had the votes to lead the national agenda. An author employed by the *National Catholic Reporter* wrote that the key to Reagan's victory was that he attracted evangelicals without "scaring away" other, more moderate voters. *Time* magazine, reporting at the same time and quoting a Harris poll, concluded that as much as two-thirds of Reagan's constituency had evangelical roots. "The preachers gave it to Reagan," declared another headline.[162]

The Harris poll was notable because it clearly concluded that Reagan would have lost by one percentage point had it not been for the Religious Right.[163] Just after leaving the White House, Carter acknowledged to a reporter, "Yes, [the Religious Right] had a high level of influence in the 1980 election." Religious moderates, Carter explained, "were shot down, quite often by religious forces." The tactic was not new, "especially in the South," but it was effective. For her part, Rosalynn remembered the enthusiasm the Religious Right brought to her opponents. "Making my way through the crowd after a speech in a Texas shopping center," Rosalynn recalled, "I realized how organized the Moral Majority had become. All along the path the police had cleared for me were women holding their hands up with printed cards pasted in their palms that read, 'You don't love Jesus.'" It was annoying, she concluded. When Rosalynn tried to explain that, indeed, she did love Jesus, the reply was forceful and uniform: "If you loved Jesus, you wouldn't support the ERA."[164] While acknowledging the Religious Right's "very profound effect," both Carter and Rosalynn did not share the conclusion of the Harris poll. Too many other factors were at play, and the press, aware that the likes of Falwell and Robertson made good copy, exaggerated their influence.[165] "[Falwell] was not as powerful in 1976 as he was in 1980," Rosalynn explained, but he did not represent the vast majority of evangelicals or people of faith. "I've never equated my faith with that of the Jerry Falwells," Carter added.[166]

"Just because Reagan has won," an editorial in *Christianity Today* read just after the election, "the battle for righteousness and sane government is not over." The conservative evangelical vote was "significant" but "could not alone have elected Mr. Reagan." The best tactic for Christians was to "avoid pronouncing on every issue, particularly where they have no special expertise." They should be willing to work with moderates and guard against being "used as a tool of any particular party or candidate." It was "hard to say exactly how much credit the Religious Right can take for the electoral landslide," the journal studiously concluded. It may have been more influential in the surprising Republican takeover of the Senate, and in any event, most battles would play out in Congress, not the executive branch. Legislation to provide tax credits for private schools and to take prayer in the public schools out of the purview of the courts had excellent chances. A constitutional amendment to ban abortion "was somewhat less certain." In any event, conservative Christians should not get ahead of themselves and should continue the grassroots efforts that had accomplished so much.[167]

A wave of postelection polls added credence to such warnings, perhaps throwing doubt on the Harris poll and raining on Falwell's victory dance. If nothing else, with emotions cooling, the reality was increasingly obvious that a multitude of factors explained the "Reagan Revolution." It was not so easy to say that any one issue or group explained the results or that, had the Religious Right sat out the election, Carter would have been the one celebrating. Like so much else in political science and history, the influence of the Religious Right was a matter for debate. Some noted the overall low voter turnout—a little more than half of eligible voters went to the polls, 52 percent—and concluded that America had not embraced Reagan, it had simply endured Carter long enough. Voters had not accepted the Religious Right as much as rejected the status quo. Others noted the wide margin of victory and claimed that the Republicans hardly needed Falwell or Robertson. With the nation suffering economically and international crises dominating the news, the result was most likely inevitable, the close pre-election polls notwithstanding. "Reagan's winning margin was so large that even a split among evangelical sympathizers would still have elected him," political scientists Jeffrey Brudney and Gary Copeland concluded. "But if the contest had been closer, their overriding support would have been decisive—or if they had opposed Reagan as overwhelmingly as they supported him, he might not have won the election." In this view, the Religious Right had chosen the right horse but had not steered it to victory.[168]

Without a doubt, religious conservatives turned out strongly for Reagan. According to one poll, white evangelical Christians gave Reagan a two-to-one edge over Carter. While the total number was not sufficient to explain the overall results, Carter's share in this group had fallen by about one-fourth from 1976 to 1980. Evangelicals and conservative Christians proved more likely to participate in the election than others, and studies suggested that conservative Christians contributed mightily to Reagan's victories in North Carolina, Kentucky, Tennessee, Alabama, and Mississippi. According to another poll, 60 percent of white evangelicals who supported Carter in 1976 switched to Reagan in 1980. Yet a third poll even suggested that Reagan garnered 80 percent of the white evangelical vote. Reagan's victory in the South, 51 percent compared to Carter's 44 percent in one poll, was particularly noteworthy. Here, a traditionally Democratic region in which Carter had won 54 percent of the vote four years before, the force of conservative social issues undoubtedly played a role. In the words of one author, the New South's "Sunbelt Christianity," a white, middle-class evangelicalism that formed large "megachurches" and stressed a more doctrinaire approach to the Bible, played into Reagan's hands. In any event, the numbers varied depending upon the poll, any explanations always open to individual interpretation. Efforts to determine the effect of evangelicals depended on imprecise definitions. Both proponents and opponents tended to overstate the effect of religion, itself hard to separate from other issues. Moreover, evangelicalism remained diverse, many pundits—and pollsters—still equating it with the Moral Majority when, in reality, such had never been the case.[169]

What is obvious, nevertheless, is that Reagan's gains were virtually across the board in almost all demographic groups. Polls suggested that while Carter won among Catholics in 1976 by fifteen percentage points, he lost them to Reagan by an estimated two to seven points. Carter had won among blue-collar workers in 1976 by a three-to-two margin. In 1980 he only broke even, losing by one percentage point in one exit poll and winning by two in another. While African Americans still strongly supported Carter, three large ethnic blocs—Slavs, Italians, and Irish—all shifted Republican. Although Carter still won among Hispanics, Reagan gained more than a third of the vote. In 1976 Carter had won the Jewish vote by thirty percentage points; by 1980 his margin of victory was only six.[170] After the campaign, whatever the poll numbers, pundits spoke of "Reagan Democrats," a group of working-class Americans who had always remained loyal to the party of Franklin Roosevelt but now found themselves swayed by Reagan's optimism and his antigovernment, free-market promises. Conservative mistrust of government dovetailed nicely with the stagflation then facing the nation.[171]

To the degree that enthusiasm existed during the campaign, it was largely on Reagan's side. The campaign was the most expensive in American history, the total just over $275 million, $115 million more than four years before. These figures were in part the result of the new political action committees, the majority favoring the Republicans. The most influential PACs held strong connections to the most conservative voters, including religious and social conservatives. In addition, the election was the first since passage of the Nineteenth Amendment granting women suffrage rights that a "gender gap" existed in voting patterns, polls suggesting that women favored

Carter more than Reagan. While this might imply the importance of abortion and the ERA, women remained divided, splitting their anti-Republican majority between Carter and Anderson.[172]

The election dissection, to coin a phrase, was difficult to separate from postelection spin. Activist Viguerie, for example, who had contributed so much to the creation of the Republican PACs by uniting fiscal and theological conservatives, predictably explained the victory in the power of the new unity. "The white followers of TV evangelical preachers gave Ronald Reagan two-thirds of his ten-point margin," Viguerie announced, but they could not have won without allying with traditional small-government, big-business Republicans. If both groups wanted to sustain the Reagan Revolution, Viguerie implied, they had to continue to work together.[173] As Schlafly insisted that the election confirmed that the public rejected the ERA and that voters should be careful not to rest on their laurels, feminists countered that the election had more to do with other issues than the popularity of the amendment. Its supporters should rally anew. As the rhetorical battle went on, both the victors and losers had good reason to magnify the influence of groups such as the Moral Majority. After all, both sides in the political spectrum raised money by demonizing their opposition. If the enemy appeared a powerful juggernaut, donations grew. It was, in the words of writer Tina Rosenberg, a "peculiar kind of symbiotic ritual." In this sense, the election was simply one battle in a war that would never end.[174]

Demonized or praised, diminished or magnified, the Religious Right's "enthusiastic support" was, in the words of historian William Martin, "part of the wave that bore [Reagan] upward and moved other voters to take him seriously." It did not take long, after all, for pundits to recognize the historic nature of the vote. "For the first time in a generation," columnist David Broder mused, "it is sensible to ask whether we might be entering a new political era—an era of Republican dominance." Carter "found himself in an uncomfortable political environment," concluded one author. "The political coalition on which he depended for success was unraveling." The election suggested that "the New Deal coalition is no longer with us," added another observer. The "New Deal family is still alive," but its "relationships are strained and altered."[175]

Inside the White House, Carter and his close circle sensed that the election represented a seismic shift in American political history and wrestled with their role. As Reagan embarked on his transition, the Carters invited Maddox and his family for one last dinner at the executive mansion. The press had reported that Rosalynn was especially bitter at the defeat, but Maddox recalled her as calm and resigned. She believed in Romans 8:28, he explained: "All things work for the common good to them who love God, to them who are called according to his purposes." Rosalynn told Maddox that she could not explain why it was God's will, but if it were so, she accepted it. Carter's moderate Baptist allies were also at a loss to explain why so many of their denominational colleagues seemingly abandoned their faith. In the words of one Carter acquaintance, it was "one of the real puzzles." Reagan was "a Hollywood libertine ... had a child conceived out of wedlock before he and Nancy married, admitted to drug use during his Hollywood years, and according to [historian] Henry Steele Commager, was one of the least religious presidents in American history." It just made no sense. It was, however, real, influential, and not likely to change in the near future.[176]

America was a dynamic nation. Its religion was constantly changing, its politics never staid. It was, Maddox finally concluded, a reality that many Democrats were slow to grasp. "The Democratic Party, or at least some national leaders of the Party, being responsive to their own constituents, and listening to the rapidly fading drumbeats from the days of no limits on the American bounty, refused to see the conservative swing in the country," reflected Maddox. Carter was simply caught between "a riptide from the right and the final spasm of well-intentioned but dying liberalism on the left." It was the end of his coalition—the end of an era—but the beginning of a new one. Now it was Ronald Reagan's turn, Ronald Reagan's coalition under the microscope. Emboldened by the election, indeed often taking credit for it, the Religious Right assumed itself vital to the Reagan Revolution. It had, finally, arrived, and it demanded much in return.[177]

A Fault Line in American Society

IN *PARADISE LOST* JOHN MILTON WROTE, "The mind is its own place, and in itself can make a Heaven of Hell, and a Hell of Heaven."[1] Departing the White House on January 20, 1981, Reagan's inauguration day, it appeared the fifty-six-year-old Carter was a broken man, banished, as it were, to Hades. The Religious Right, meanwhile, like the ancient Israelites entering the Promised Land, had arrived in their political heaven. The reality, of course, was not so simple. The years following the Reagan Revolution spoke volumes about America's first born-again president as well as the Christian conservatives who had first embraced and then rejected him. Perhaps proving the truth in Milton, Carter refused to surrender what he had always seen as his religious duty and embarked on a remarkable post-presidency that was anything but hellish. Having arrived in its political Canaan, the Religious Right found no paradise but a struggle that in many ways demonstrated the movement's own limits.

For the Religious Right, the reality began to appear quickly. Senate majority leader Howard Baker suggested that cultural issues would have to wait until the economy recovered, a conclusion the White House apparently accepted. "Immediately after Ronald Reagan was elected," Paul Weyrich recalled years later, "the administration announced that its social agenda would have to be postponed for several years." Shocked given the campaign, Weyrich arranged for a conference call with his colleagues. "This cannot be tolerated," he told them. "If the idea that economic issues are more important than moral ones takes hold, then it says something about what we stand for."[2] In a sense, Weyrich's consternation was understandable. Despite the claims of many conservative pastors that they had made his success possible, Reagan made only a few appointments that pleased the Religious

Right. He appointed C. Everett Koop, the well-known prolife physician at Philadelphia's Children's Hospital, surgeon general. He also appointed James G. Watt, another evangelical, secretary of interior. A premillennialist who believed that Jesus's eminent return would set off an apocalyptic judgment day, Watt even testified before the House Interior Committee, "I do not know how many future generations we can count on before the Lord returns."[3] Moreover, Reagan appointed the evangelist Gary Bauer, a hearty champion of "family values," as a domestic policy advisor. Bauer developed a "very close relationship" with Morton Blackwell, who had worked with conservative pastors during the campaign. Given their similar views, Bauer and Blackwell remained close.[4] Among their administration allies was the evangelist Jerry Regier, selected to lead the new Office of Families, a result of the Carter struggles if nothing else. Finally, and perhaps most notably, Reagan appointed Robert Billings as an assistant secretary in the Department of Education in charge of nonpublic schools. "I had recommended him for this position," Falwell claimed.[5]

Riding their wave of high expectations, many pastors complained that these appointments were not enough. They appeared mere tokens, their small number confirmation that the new administration would stress tax cuts, deregulation, and defense in lieu of cultural issues. At the same time, some Catholics complained that the Baptist fundamentalist Billings would reign over parochial education, their complaints suggesting that old religious rifts were not quite dead after all.[6] Blackwell tried to explain to his allies that more was at play. Appointed special assistant to the president for public liaison, working under the office's first director, Elizabeth Dole, Blackwell had a difficult job. He had to ensure that appointees shared the administration's ideology, that they were "Reagan conservatives," and that they had adequate qualifications. The Religious Right had no problem with the former, Blackwell knew, but it did with the latter. "Many Reagan supporters had not worked in government and did not have the managerial or government experience," Blackwell recalled without mentioning the Religious Right specifically. "It was obvious from the outset that we were going to have a heterogeneous administration." This meant, of course, that he had to meet frequently with conservative pastors. "I knew that there were going to be a lot of people who would be disappointed when not everything they wanted was achieved all at once," Blackwell explained. "I had very good relations with the theological and politically conservative religious organizations," despite the many meetings the Religious Right demanded. "Certainly the religious groups wanted to be briefed."[7]

For his part, the new vice president, George Bush, a man roundly chastised by some conservative Christians during the campaign, treaded lightly. He obviously remembered the Religious Right's criticism and wanted to assure Americans that the new administration was not a tool for Falwell or anyone else who took credit for the victory. At the same time, like Reagan during the campaign, he did not want to alienate the conservative religious groups either, realizing that their support could help the administration's legislative agenda. In one of his first news conferences, Bush explained that Reagan was "no extremist" and that the new administration "would not be captive to any group." Turning directly to the issue of Falwell's organization, he went on to explain that "a lot of the so-called Moral Majority are not extreme views." The group reflected the timeless values of "strength of family and the belief that this is one nation under God . . . not extreme views." People of faith had a right to express their religious opinions, he explained, which the National Council of Churches certainly did from a liberal perspective. Conservative groups had their rights as well. Nevertheless, Bush said that he "took violent exception to certain individuals in some of these groups, some of their positions, and have stated it publicly, but I am not intimidated by those who suggest I better hew the line." The end of his comments was an obvious retort to the public warnings of Falwell and Weyrich, who also had directly pressed him after the election. To anyone who threatened him, Bush concluded, "Hell with them."[8]

Just after the election Reagan appeared to snub his conservative religious backers by declining to appear at the annual Washington convention of the National Religious Broadcasters, scheduled for only a week after the inauguration. The organizers had been so confident that he would attend that they had even printed his name on the official program.[9] Reports surfaced that one of Reagan's advisors had described abortion and school prayer as "no-win issues." Reagan, the advisor reportedly predicted, would reiterate his views on the social issues but do nothing about them. At the same time, another report quoted a top aide, Michael Deaver, as saying that the new president represented over two hundred million Americans, while the Religious Right constituted only 8 percent, a quote that if correct implied a strong shift to the middle. The Religious Right was welcome, Deaver reportedly concluded, but would have to come through the back door.[10] Months after the inauguration, the Religious Roundtable attempted a repeat of its Dallas convention held the previous year, obviously hoping that the meeting would attract a similar attendance and media attention. Organizers expected ten thousand, but only six thousand showed up, while neither Reagan nor any of his new advisors attended.[11]

In many respects, the administration's decision largely to table its social agenda made political sense. The economy remained mired in stagflation, and Reagan perceived economic recovery to be his foremost concern. Forcing controversial social issues such as abortion and homosexuality at the very outset would reward his loyal religious supporters but engender such righteous anger among his opponents that they might, out of spite alone, block congressional passage of his critical tax cuts. Some have suggested that Reagan passionately shared the social goals of the Religious Right, that he fully intended to press their issues when it was politically expedient to do so. Others, however, have argued that Reagan used the Religious Right and never actually believed—at least to the same extent—in its central tenets, a conclusion perhaps supported by his own background and relatively late conversion. In the words of historian Wilson McWilliams, "There is every reason to think that Reagan's social conservatism, though sincere, was also superficial."[12] To many observers, there was no sincerity at all. "Reagan very definitely played to the evangelical community, and did it rather skillfully," noted one reporter. He "played the themes" and "knew where he was going with that group."[13] According to another writer, Reagan did not share the beliefs of Falwell and others but saw them as a useful tool to drive a wedge between Southern Baptists and their historic allegiance to the Democratic Party. He hoped to accomplish just enough to woo them to the Republican fold but had no intention of highlighting their agenda.[14]

Having decided to emphasize its economic program but aware of the dismay of many of the religious conservatives, the administration worked to maintain its new conservative coalition. Although Deaver denied ever making the "back door" statement, Falwell called Blackwell for a chance to clear the air with Reagan. The resulting meeting obviously allayed many of the evangelist's concerns. Waiting to go into the Oval Office, Falwell met Deaver, who, Falwell claimed, was nervous and asked him not to bring up the back door comment. Once in, however, Reagan immediately joked, "Did you have to use the back door?" When Falwell replied that, no, he had come in through the front door, Reagan remarked, "Feel free. That door is always open." Whatever comments were made, Falwell was indeed one of the first to visit the White House after the inauguration.[15]

Only weeks after his inauguration, Reagan met at the White House with members of his Family Policy Advisory Board, a group that contained a number of religious conservatives. During the meeting Connie Marshner, now chairing the National Pro-Family Coalition, suggested that the White House make a "special overture to the evangelical and pro-family movement."[16] If Reagan were to meet with a large contingent of conservative religious leaders and press their agenda, they in turn would support more ardently his economic priorities. Economic and social goals were not mutually exclusive, Marshner seemed to suggest, and no choice between them was necessary. Marshner followed this conversation with a long memorandum. "The evangelical/pro-family movement would probably be willing to support the President's proposed budget cuts," Marshner wrote. "However they have not been asked." The administration needed to realize that "leaders of the religious revival, which overlaps but is not co-terminous with the evangelical right, are people . . . who do not ordinarily think in political or policy terms." Unfamiliar with the necessities of coalitions, "green to politics," they might simply abstain from the coming budget battles or even oppose the administration's economic proposals. If, however, the administration were to act more forcibly on Reagan's socially conservative rhetoric, conservative religious leaders would reciprocate. "With the predictable storm of protest that the budget cuts are going to provoke from the National Council of Churches and U.S. Catholic Conference types," Marshner continued, "some favorable editorializing and preaching from the religious community will be needed by the administration."[17] Obviously envisioning herself as a key player, Marshner offered to take the lead in any overture, suggesting almost forty religious leaders who might help. The list included relatively unknown individuals who had worked with her as well as the expected and famous: Falwell, Robertson, Robison, and Schlafly, along with James Kennedy and Tim and Beverly LaHaye.[18]

Marshner's proposal had merit, Blackwell argued, agreeing with his boss, Elizabeth Dole, and with Reagan confidant Lyn Nofziger that the White House should schedule a well-publicized meeting for the group with the president.[19] Blackwell and Dole hosted a luncheon with Weyrich in late March to coordinate the meeting, an indication, perhaps, that Marshner would not play the key role she envisioned. By late April, Weyrich and his

White House allies had selected a date for early May, and Dole had made a formal scheduling proposal to her superiors. "These groups are a key element of the President's winning coalition," Dole wrote. Building a "team spirit" would assist the administration's economic package.[20]

Much to Dole's dismay, however, the White House first delayed the meeting and then canceled it. "I hope and pray that this is a failure to communicate internally," Blackwell wrote Dole upon learning of the cancellation. "Per the information you gave me, I told Weyrich that this meeting had been approved by senior staff."[21] When word reached Congress that the White House had canceled a meeting with conservative religious leaders, their champions on Capitol Hill protested as well. Marshner was a "friend," Colorado Republican senator William Armstrong wrote Attorney General Edwin Meese. "I hope whoever made this decision can be encouraged to reconsider."[22] Armstrong's colleagues Orrin Hatch from Utah and Trent Lott from Mississippi agreed. The administration should reconsider, Hatch wrote Reagan directly: "I really believe that these people could help a great deal in providing grass roots support for your economic message."[23] Inside the administration, Blackwell lobbied key Reagan aide Michael Deaver. "The people to be invited have all decided that part of their role in life is to involve themselves in the public policy process," he wrote. "These people are not fully engaged in the fight for the President's economic package because, frankly, we have not paid adequate attention to briefing them."[24] The cancellation dumbfounded Blackwell. "The situation has become embarrassing for Mrs. Dole," he concluded. "I think it is essential for the credibility of Elizabeth's office that we break this log jam and schedule this meeting."[25]

The White House's reaction was, perhaps, telling. It claimed that it had followed developments "with interest" and was "optimistic ... that this meeting can take place in the future." In the meantime, however, "we may have to wait."[26] In the end, Reagan frequently welcomed conservative religious leaders to the White House, even if he never held the large formal meeting originally planned or, more important, placed a priority upon the social agenda that the meeting would have encouraged. James Dobson, for one, was a "regular consultant to President Reagan," according to one biographer, "sitting with him in the Cabinet Room or Oval Office." The White House even allowed Dobson to record one of his *Focus on the Family* radio broadcasts from the Oval Office. Others visited as well, Reagan always ensuring that his rhetoric and image, if not all of his actions, supported their cause. At his inauguration, Reagan stressed the nation's Judeo-Christian heritage by taking his oath with the Bible opened to 2 Chronicles 7:14: "If my people, which are called by my name, shall humble themselves, and pray, and seek my face, and turn from their wicked ways; then I will hear from heaven, and will forgive their sin, and will heal their land." The Bible selection was, in the words of one author, "a compliment to Falwell and the Christian Right."[27] In fact, Falwell gleefully wrote, Reagan "quoted the [biblical] text I had been quoting in my speeches across the country on his behalf."[28]

Even in stressing his primary goals, the economy and foreign policy, Reagan used language familiar to evangelicals. He spoke of the Soviet Union as the "evil empire" and the effort to contain it as a duel between "right and wrong and good and evil." In several instances, Reagan's comments suggested that he shared with many conservative Christians an apocalyptic view of the future. During the campaign he had remarked to evangelist Bakker, "We may be the generation that sees Armageddon." Now, in voicing his support of Israel, he declared the Jewish nation "the only stable democracy we can rely on as a spot where Armageddon could come."[29]

When it came to actions, however, the accomplishments remained few. When supporters reintroduced early in 1981 the Human Life Statute and the Family Protection Act, Reagan was surprisingly quiet.[30] With these bills the cornerstone of her agenda, Marshner relentlessly lobbied Blackwell, obviously enjoying her role as an experienced political insider. "In the current political environment," she wrote early in 1982, "feminist issue-makers are seeking to make daycare into the cause celebre once ERA is obsolete." The administration should include tax incentives in any bill because "opponents of the administration would like nothing better than to paint the administration as hard-hearted, depriving needy children of daycare and forcing mothers back onto welfare." Marshner was clearly growing impatient about the lack of progress and continually warned Blackwell that Reagan might lose the "pro-family vote."[31] Blackwell was frustrated as well. "Until now the President has avoided personally urging specific actions on the matter of abortion," he wrote Dole in 1982. "He has been outspokenly opposed to abortion, but he has not urged legislators to vote for or against any particular measure." Blackwell concluded that the stalling had been smart politically because abortion opponents had been divided between competing antiabortion bills by senators Helms and Hatch, but "now the situation has changed." The prolife groups had united in support of a Helms-backed initiative and turned to the White House: "If the President fails to take specific steps [to advance the Helms bill], that failure will be read as a betrayal." It was time to act, Blackwell warned, since they were at "a critical moment in the relationship between the President and the pro-life activists." If the White House were to forcibly enter the fray, the prolife community would "see that his actions speak as loudly as his words."[32]

At the same time, Blackwell worked closely with religious groups on proposals to extend tax credits to private schools and to assure school prayer. Given resistance in Congress and the array of competing interests, Blackwell found both issues frustrating. In regard to the tax credits, many conservative Protestant groups welcomed the idea but worried that accepting money "would make them vulnerable to all manner of regulations."[33] Because many Catholics did not share this concern, Blackwell struggled to unite the groups under one proposal. The subsequent bill failed just before the 1984 election, and the frustration boiled over, with a lot of finger pointing. In regard to school prayer, there was more unity among the religious groups for some form of voluntary prayer even as some expressed concern that a state-sanctioned prayer might result. Pressing the matter, the Moral Majority cosponsored with Weyrich's Free Congress Foundation the Family Forum II. At this event over five hundred delegates from thirty-seven states discussed ways to revive the "social agenda" as an administration priority and resolve the school prayer issue. In the summer of 1981, Senator Helms introduced legislation banning the Supreme Court from reviewing cases dealing with school prayer, a proposal that had no realistic chance of passing but that reignited evangelicals. By 1982 Falwell had highlighted the issue with a one-hour special on his *Old Time Gospel Hour* television program and even bussed his college students to Washington to form a human chain from the Supreme Court to the Capitol.[34]

Whether in response to this pressure or not, in 1982 Reagan proposed a school prayer amendment. Ultimately, the administration's proposal contained two clauses: "Nothing in this Constitution shall be construed to prohibit individual or group prayer in public schools" and "No person shall be required by the United States to pray." As Reagan unveiled his proposal in a Rose Garden ceremony, Falwell and other leading Christian conservatives stood next to him, Falwell hoping the proposal marked a new emphasis for the administration. Many of Falwell's followers were not so optimistic, assuming, correctly as it turned out, that the amendment had no real chance of winning the supermajority required.[35] In 1983 Falwell sought and won access to Reagan again, reiterating that he thought Christian conserva-

tives were crucial to continued Republican control and actually giving Reagan specific recommendations necessary for reelection. Reagan appeared
thankful and receptive and indeed repeated some of the points in speeches
in the following weeks.[36]

In the midst of this activity early in his administration, Reagan nomi-
nated Sandra Day O'Connor, an Arizona justice and protégée of Barry Goldwater, to the Supreme Court, a decision that fulfilled a campaign pledge to
appoint the first woman justice but one that rankled many religious conservatives. At the outset, at least, her record was unfamiliar. "I never knew
her," remarked Falwell. "I had never heard of her."[37] Quickly, however, reports raised questions about her commitment to the prolife cause. Writing
in the *Family Protection Report*, a publication of Weyrich's Free Congress
Foundation, Marshner noted that O'Connor's statement that she was personally against abortion was insufficient. "The Senate Judiciary Committee
did not successfully learn her judicial posture on the issue," Marshner bemoaned. "It may only learn it after she casts her first vote on the issue from
the bench."[38] When several prolife groups lodged more formal complaints,
it was obvious Reagan had damage to repair. Rather than pulling the nomination, Reagan decided on a direct appeal. He privately called Falwell and
other leaders. "You've got to trust me, Jerry," he asked Falwell. Reagan, it
appeared, knew that the political was often personal and that a direct plea
would help overcome both resistance to O'Connor's nomination and, in a
broader sense, reservations about the administration's emerging priorities.
Undoubtedly pleased that he had received a call from the president, Falwell agreed, although later claiming that he reserved the right to criticize
O'Connor if she wavered once she was on the bench.[39] In the end, the Senate confirmed O'Connor, and the administration continued with both its
original priorities and its rather symbolic and rhetorical efforts to placate
the Religious Right. This remained insufficient for Weyrich, who, more ac-
customed to the power elite, still hoped for more action to force more accomplishment. "What overshadowed all [conservative Christian leaders']
concerns was simply their pleasure in being able to get in even the back
door of the White House," he complained later. "They didn't want to do
anything to jeopardize that."[40]

The lack of real accomplishments particularly worried Pat Robertson,
who had begun to wrestle with the troubling thought that political involvement would never accomplish what needed to be done. It was, undoubtedly, a reaction to his disappointment in Carter. Reagan said the correct

things, but, then again, so had Carter.[41] Robertson resigned from the Religious Roundtable, claiming that he planned to focus more on spiritual matters. In fact, Robertson was not done with politics and founded in 1981 the Freedom Council, whose mandate was to "encourage, train, and equip Americans to exercise their civil [sic] responsibility to participate in government."[42] The key, Robertson and others now assumed, was to organize at the state and local level. The Freedom Council received much of its funding from the Christian Broadcasting Network (CBN) and utilized its mailing lists. Its membership was primarily evangelical and Republican, although Robertson worked to expand its influence outside these parameters. When Reagan took action that pleased the Religious Right, Robertson, like Falwell, was quick to take credit. Reagan agreed to appear three times on Robertson's *700 Club*, the first in 1983 and the second two in 1985. The tensions between Reagan and Robertson were never far below the surface. When the president declined an invitation to attend the dedication of CBN University's thirteen-million-dollar library, the centerpiece of its campus, Robertson assumed it represented another snub, another indication that Reagan was more talk than action.[43]

Nevertheless, despite it all, Reagan had for many in the Religious Right that something special. His continued references to his faith and to the Almighty were hard for conservative Christians to ignore, as were the grace and courage with which he handled an assassination attempt in March 1981. In addition, despite the dismay of some conservative Christians about the administration's domestic agenda, they continued to applaud Reagan's remilitarization and ardent stance against the atheistic Soviet Union, his "evil empire." Reagan may not have scored a touchdown in the game of abortion, but he seemed to have at least kicked a field goal against Communism. These "crusaders with nuclear swords," according to one author, did not support all of the new administration's efforts but nevertheless agreed that they represented a marked improvement over those of its predecessor.[44]

When his administration felt the need to shore up its support among religious conservatives, Reagan knew what to do. With his reelection on the horizon, he published an impressive lament in the *Human Life Review* on the upcoming tenth anniversary of the *Roe v. Wade* decision. In this article, titled "Abortion and the Conscience of a Nation," Reagan hit all the notes the Religious Right wanted to hear. "We cannot survive as a free nation when some men decide that others are not fit to live and should be abandoned to abortion or infanticide," Reagan wrote.[45] "Until now," one conservative columnist rejoiced, "[Reagan] has not gone much beyond code words fit for posters, nor has he used any forum except the occasional paragraph in a speech." Now that he had spoken out more forcibly than before, perhaps real actions would follow.[46]

Reagan did at least take several actions that pleased religious conservatives, even if some arguably proved more symbolic than restrictive. Most notable was an executive order requiring all new policy proposals to include a "family impact statement," a requirement reminiscent of the National Environmental Policy Act a decade before.[47] Marshner had been relentless in her lobbying for this order, writing cabinet secretaries as well as top White House officials: "I believe there is an opportunity now to begin the task of rethinking many of our current regulatory policies in terms of how they affect the American family." A "regulatory review" would "identify government policies which negatively impact strong families" and "determine possible policy alternatives."[48] The budget process had a more direct impact on advancing the priorities of social and religious conservatives, and for the most part, religious conservatives applauded the administration's direction. Cuts in government-funded social programs, Marshner and others believed, returned power to the family. Restrictive regulations by the Office of Management and Budget and various regulatory proposals by individual departments, the *Pro-Family Forum* declared, "should be commended."[49] The U.S. Senate Republican Policy Committee proudly declared that, working with Reagan, Congress had adopted "a number of changes in the tax laws which directly assist the family."[50] For his part, Blackwell maintained an "anti-pornography list" of religious leaders and civic groups that helped the administration launch an antipornography campaign headed by Attorney General Edwin Meese.[51] Blackwell continued to work well with leaders across the spectrum of religious conservatives, responding quickly to their inquiries and keeping his superiors knowledgeable about their complaints. "Morton," wrote David Williams of the American Family Association, "feel free to call upon me as an individual and as associated with the AFA for any assistance that I can render you." Williams added that his organization might help "when the White House needs allies on the outside."[52]

A number of religious and private organizations contacted Blackwell about the administration's efforts to battle homosexuality. In 1982 a Texas judge ruled that a state statute prohibiting "deviate [*sic*] sexual intercourse" between people of the same sex was unconstitutional, a decision that sparked outrage among the Religious Right.[53] "I am very concerned about the homosexual movement," wrote one religious leader. "Is there anyone in the FBI who is sympathetic?"[54] A group of activists formed the Institute for the Scientific Investigation of Sexuality and lobbied Blackwell frequently, although in terms that Blackwell undoubtedly thought inappropriate. "Gays are the fecal-eaters of our times" read the institute's first newsletter in 1983. "Almost all gays ingest significant amounts of fecal material every week of their sexually active lives."[55] Paul Cameron of the Fuller Theological Seminary and a frequent author kept Blackwell up to date on his unrelenting campaign against what he believed were the evils of homosexuality, on several occasions applauding the administration's efforts.[56] The Stop the Gay Bill of Rights Project contacted Blackwell about its efforts.[57] Blackwell obviously avoided the more controversial appeals, but the administration's position earned the praise of activists such as Phyllis Schlafly.[58]

Unlike his predecessor, Reagan clearly distanced himself from the homosexual community. Immediately after Reagan's inauguration, one representative of the National Gay Task Force, Jeff Levi, had a brief and unproductive meeting with a relatively low-level staffer in the Office of Public Liaison, Aram Bakshian. When the NGTF requested higher-level access, Dole's office recommended that she "just hold onto [the NGTF's request]." She could simply stall. "We can't really agree to meet—Aram already did. Any further contact is pointless. Can you think of a polite way to say the above?" In the end, the official reply simply noted "limitations upon Mrs. Dole's schedule."[59] Left unstated was the obvious: the gay and lesbian lobby would have no more access to the Reagan White House. All of this infuriated the NGTF's Charles Brydon, who claimed that a number of leading Republicans were closeted gays, a charge that journalist Taylor Branch expanded in *Harper's* magazine.[60]

The homosexual community, meanwhile, found Reagan's reaction to the emergent AIDS crisis outrageous. Acquired Immune Deficiency Syndrome first appeared as a rare cancer just as Reagan's term began. Although scientists soon determined that it could be transmitted through a variety of methods, it was most prominent among gay men and was referred to early as the "gay cancer." Conservative ministers soon began identifying the virus as God's wrath for homosexuality. Several Republicans, most notably the conservative pundit William F. Buckley, began to advocate drastic measures to combat the spread of the virus, including quarantines and tattoos for identification. When Koop began advocating compassion and condoms as a way to battle the disease, his strongest backers, the conservative religious community, began to criticize him. Apparently, the White House surmised, moving slowly was the best course politically. It simply did not want to alienate religious conservatives. While it discussed the crisis with a number of social conservatives, including members of the Moral Majority, it avoided the gay and lesbian community. The homosexual lobby and the Democrats would surely "attempt to politicize the issue," one White House staffer concluded.[61]

It was, in the end, five years before Reagan mentioned AIDS publicly. By this time, there were 36,000 cases in the United States alone. It was 1983 before the government allocated funds for the fight, and then only $33 million. A Department of Health and Human Services AIDS hotline employed only six people, with calls totaling more than ten thousand a day. Angered by the administration's weak response, gay activists formed ACT UP—the AIDS Coalition to Unleash Power. In sometimes outrageous fashion, ACT UP protested against Reagan. All of this exacerbated partisan tensions, solidifying not only the homosexual community in the Democratic camp but the Religious Right in the Republican.[62]

If nothing else, the Religious Right applauded the fate of the ERA. While ratification was already on life support, Reagan's victory represented the amendment's death knell. No longer did the Oval Office use its weight to encourage ratification. While Reagan named O'Connor to the bench and Jean Kirkpatrick the first female American ambassador to the United Nations, feminists responded that these appointments did little to advance true economic equality for most women. In particular, they protested, budget cuts in domestic programs hurt poor and minority women. After Reagan's inaugural, NOW formed the ERA YES Inaugural Watch, organizing forty thousand women to remind the new president of the majority's approval of the amendment. Litigation continued over rescission, with the Idaho case before the appellate courts as time ran out on amendment ratification. The court ruled the matter moot, and indeed, there was no need for the case to continue. By the June 1982 deadline, the ERA remained three states short of ratification. Polls suggested that Republicans deserted the ERA in large numbers, while Democratic support remained stagnant. NOW had scheduled "countdown rallies" in over 180 cities as the deadline approached, but its efforts proved as moot as the rescission litigation.[63]

Opponents of the ERA held a large party in Washington just after the June defeat. The editor of the *Conservative Digest*, John Lofton, presented Schla-

fly and Falwell with Special Service Awards for their efforts.[64] The two undoubtedly deserved it, the coalition of conservative Christians they helped
form now enjoying unparalleled access to the White House, the women
activists they loathed now banned. "Who Killed ERA?" asked one professor.
"Women, not men."[65] This was true as well, although the reality was larger
still. The era that had spawned the ERA in the first instance, the liberalism of
the 1960s, had run its course. In this sense, Reagan and the defeat of the ERA
were only symptomatic of a larger shift in the American populace. It was a
new age.[66] Indeed, advocates reintroduced the ERA as early as 1983 and have
done so virtually every session of Congress since. The result remains the
same, however. Conservative, largely Republican opposition is too great to
overcome. The past, it appears, is prologue.

By the 1984 election, it was apparent to all observers that the political
coalition that Reagan had created four years before, while strained, would
prevail yet again. Speaking at that year's Republican National Convention,
Reagan kept his rhetoric consistent. There was a "need" for religion in government, he told the cheering crowds. "The truth is, politics and morality
are inseparable." At the same time, his opponent, Minnesota senator Walter
Mondale, attempted to keep pace, all too aware of the trouble evangelical
leaders could pose from his years as Carter's vice president. "I don't know
if I've been born again, but I know that I was born into a Christian family,"
he remarked in the first presidential debate. "I have a deep religious faith."[67]
The public's interest in the Religious Right certainly had not waned. When
Memphis journalist Michael Clark wrote a series that explored the importance of the Moral Majority to the GOP, the exposé won a Pulitzer Prize.
In the end, the election was another Republican landslide. Once again, the
conservative religious vote fell Reagan's way, if, once again, it was not determinative in the final outcome. Following precedent, Falwell at least tried to
take credit, claiming to have "helped deliver eighty-five percent of the conservative religious vote to the Reagan-Bush team." He noted with obvious
pride that he and his wife, Macel, received personal invitations to the second inaugural. "I continue to travel 250,000 to 400,000 miles a year, speaking millions of words on thousands of platforms in every state," he wrote in
1987. "I appeared on hundreds of television and radio programs, and I was
interviewed by . . . journalists from what seemed to be every newspaper or
magazine in the world."[68]

Despite his overwhelming reelection, Reagan's second term suggested to
many observers that his "revolution" had waned. The economy grew, but

spiraling debt and the stock market crash in 1987 dimmed the luster. The Iran-Contra scandal eroded much of the public's confidence in Reagan, who earlier had carried the title of the "Teflon president" among some of his critics. While many conservative religious leaders still counted themselves part of his political team, the reality that their larger objectives remained unfulfilled continued to nag. In addition, revelations that First Lady Nancy Reagan dabbled in astrology hurt the president's popularity among the group. Finally, Blackwell was no longer in the White House. Just before the election he resigned, costing the Religious Right one of its most ardent allies. In leaving, Blackwell did not directly cite the frustration of the Religious Right but did acknowledge that "some people have been disappointed." The Reagan coalition remained, he knew, and still included the Religious Right as a key component. If the coalition were to continue to survive in the future, however, Republicans needed to return to the grassroots activism that had spawned their revolution in the first place. This, Blackwell insisted, was the reason for his resignation, a desire to return to his activist origins.[69]

By this point it was obvious that the Religious Right, while still a major political player, had more problems than just its apparent failure to achieve all of its political and cultural goals. Writing in 1989, author Michael D'Antonio was blunt. The Religious Right, he concluded, was a "failed crusade." It had been a movement "built on enchantment and unreason" but had come "face to face with reality."[70] The era of the Religious Right, author Steve Bruce concurred, had passed. Falwell allies Cal Thomas and Ed Dobson added to this sense by becoming particularly public in their disappointment, later writing a book concluding that their efforts had "brought us nothing."[71]

Such obituaries were, in a sense, easy. Perhaps victim to their own success, their own hubris, many evangelists suffered very public setbacks. While undoubtedly enjoying his access to the White House, Falwell's Moral Majority struggled as the 1980s progressed. Fund-raising dipped just as Falwell entertained loftier goals, overextending himself in an attempt to gain control of the Praise the Lord television empire of Jim and Tammy Bakker. The Federal Communications Commission had been investigating the Bakkers for some time, and the couple clearly hoped that the change in administrations would help their case. In fact, while both the FCC and PTL sought a way to "bow out gracefully," in the words of one observer, investigators could not ignore the continuing reports of financial impropriety. In 1987 the end finally came when reports surfaced that Bakker had had an affair with Jessica Hahn, one of his assistants, and had agreed to pay her hush money. The Bakkers checked themselves into the Betty Ford Center, Jim admitting to the regular use of Valium, and sold their televised empire to Falwell. Falwell, in turn, found the situation at PTL hopeless and turned the ministry's assets over to the courts. Ultimately sentenced to forty-five years for fraud, Bakker was released from prison in 1994. Falwell was left with only the financial headache and the bruise to his reputation.[72]

Struggling to maintain the outrage so critical for fund-raising, Falwell made statements that appeared outrageous to a majority of Americans. When AIDS broke among the homosexual community, for example, Falwell labeled the plague God's retribution. Not all of Falwell's problems, however, were self-inflicted. An interview he had given an independent journalist earlier in the decade appeared in the pornographic magazine *Penthouse*. In the interview, which Falwell claimed was illegally published, Falwell blasted Carter for his own 1976 interview in *Playboy*. It appeared to be obvious hypocrisy.[73] Insisting that he wanted to "go out on the top" but sensing that his political star had begun to wane, Falwell in 1986 merged the Moral Majority into a new group dubbed the Liberty Federation. This organization, however, subsequently received little press and, in essence, signaled the beginning of the end for what had become the most well known and controversial entity in the Religious Right.

Other major Religious Right organizations suffered as well. The Religious Roundtable lost income, while Robert Grant's Christian Voice fought to survive. With the departure of Billings to the Reagan White House, the National Christian Action Coalition declined, its functions often assumed by smaller, more grassroots activism. For example, conservatives began to push for vouchers allowing students to attend private schools with federal money and for charter schools freed of many regulations. Many conservative Christians began home schooling, a movement advocated by the Virginia activist Michael Farris, founder of the Home School Legal Defense Association.[74]

In a sense, many of the Religious Right's most notable leaders struggled to remain relevant. Almost comically, Falwell even denounced the animated character Tinky-Winky of the children's television show *Teletubbies* as a front for the gay rights movement.[75] Falwell was hardly alone in becoming fodder for jokes on late-night television. Well-known evangelist Oral Roberts, suffering like Falwell from financial obligations and declining revenue, declared in 1987 that if he did not raise sufficient funds, God would kill him. His colleague Jimmy Swaggart, long a champion of family values, cried before the cameras while admitting to an affair. One could argue that Bakker, Roberts, and Swaggart were not technically part of the Religious Right because they had not been as involved politically as Falwell, but the fact remains that they shared a religious constituency; the failures of even the less political impacted the fortunes of the overtly political.[76]

In addition, the emergence of the Religious Right had, by this time, led its opponents to organize better their own independent organizations, which had gained considerable steam. Most notable among these remained People for the American Way (PAW), operating under the leadership of television producer Norman Lear to encourage "pluralism, individuality, freedom of thought, expression and religion, a sense of community, and compassion for others." Noting that the Republicans had a firm grip on power, Lear predicted for the near future "troubled times." To expose the Religious Right, PAW worked to publicize the most controversial and inflammatory comments of the television preachers, a tactic that caused Robertson in 1986 to label PAW members "anti-Christian atheists."[77] With many religious conservatives now battling the American Civil Liberties Union in the courts, critics adopted an effective tactic, couching the Religious Right as a threat to the Constitution. According to Ira Glasser, ACLU president, "There is a strong anti–Bill of Rights movement building in America that is represented by a great deal of what the new evangelicals represent." When John Bennett, former president of Union Theological Seminary, appeared to support such comments, it was harder for conservatives to defend themselves as victims of partisan invective. The Religious Right, Bennett stated, has "an authoritarian tendency in religion which meshes with authoritarian secular structures."[78]

Despite the reality that much of its leadership appeared in disarray and its opponents had rallied, by the end of the Reagan years the Religious Right was far from dead. The obituaries were understandable, perhaps, but they hardly told the whole story. With their goals unfulfilled but still shared by millions, indeed divinely ordained, they believed, conservative Christians had no intention of surrendering in the realm of politics. Showing perhaps the same resilience their ancestors had shown, conservative Christians persisted, changing and adapting, far from stagnant. The Religious Right inherited the long American tradition of assuming that God's law, as understood in conservative readings of scripture, should be normative in determining the laws of the nation. "That the Religious Right had managed to

raise these concerns in the [secular-oriented social and political culture] of
the late twentieth-century was a remarkable achievement," concluded historian George Marsden.[79] The Religious Right was not dead, author Matthew
Moen added, only undergoing a "metamorphosis." It was in the process of
becoming "a more sophisticated political player." Its leaders were "gaining
some experience in politics."[80]

In many respects, perhaps as one result, Robertson had emerged as the
central figure in the Religious Right, even launching his own bid for the Republican nomination in 1988. While some interpreted his failure to gain the
nomination as further evidence of the movement's demise, in another sense
the fact that the public considered him a serious candidate at all challenged
the obituaries. In addition, because Robertson remained a charismatic, his
candidacy demonstrated the diversity and, thus, the continued vitality of
the movement. In its apparent troubles, the Religious Right had not nar-
rowed.[81] While some noted the demise of the American Coalition for Traditional Values, an umbrella group launched by Tim LaHaye with much fan-
fare earlier in the decade, other activists simply reorganized. For one, James
Dobson's Focus on the Family merged with the Family Research Council,
a conservative "think tank" headed by Gary Bauer, who had recently left
the White House. The union demonstrated that the activists themselves intended to maintain a strong presence in Washington for years to come.[82]

Certainly by the end of the decade any such presence had grown more
partisan than ever before, any pretensions for bipartisanship now obviously
a facade. The alliance between the Republican Party and the Religious
Right was as firm as ever, not easily broken by individual events. An array
of Republican congressional candidates now regularly marched under the
banner of "family values." Organizations in opposition, such as PAW and
even the ACLU, clearly had roots much deeper in the Democratic camp. The
chairman of the Democratic National Committee wrote to gay and lesbian
activists, describing their "common goal" and promising to work together.[83]
Indeed, even despite his administration's failure to champion strongly all of
the Religious Right's goals, the movement had grown more fond of Reagan
than ever before. In the words of historian Randall Balmer, Reagan had assumed "almost iconic status among many American evangelicals, despite
the fact that he had failed to deliver on his central promises to the Religious
Right."[84] His carefully cultivated image as "the Gipper," almost channel-
ing the lovable all-American persona of the Notre Dame gridiron legend,
demonstrated that Reagan had mastered the "art of the new politics of old

values," in the words of author John Kenneth White.[85] Religious conservatives across the board cherished such old values more than others, perhaps, ensuring that their new partisan political allegiance remained firm. The accomplishments appeared few, but the bonds were far from fleeting. Certainly, the Religious Right's continued support of Reagan paralleled a wider support among Republicans, who now credited Reagan with rejuvenating the country and winning the cold war. For religious conservatives, however, the sentiment also undoubtedly grew from another reality: with the end of the Reagan term came the possibility of something worse, a return to power of the Democrats. Given all of this, to use Balmer's words again, it had become almost impossible to "disentangle the agenda of the Republican Party from the goals of the Religious Right."[86] In the words of religious studies professor Fritz Detwiler, the Reagan era had helped brand the GOP with "the mythos and symbols of southern conservative white evangelical Protestantism."[87]

When George Bush won the 1988 election and succeeded Reagan in the Oval Office, religious conservatives were undoubtedly relieved. Most surely would have preferred Robertson, but Bush far surpassed his Democratic opponent, Massachusetts governor Michael Dukakis, in their esteem. While Bush benefited from the organization and votes of conservative Christians in that year's general election, in his four years of office he never enjoyed the same support as his predecessor. Many religious leaders still questioned his position on social issues. By 1990 rumors had circulated among many in the Religious Right that "evangelicals are being systematically excluded from and pushed out of staff positions at the White House." Bush's political consultant, Lee Atwater, arranged for a meeting early that year with key leaders, including Falwell, Robertson, Kennedy, Beverly LaHaye, and Adrian Rogers, but the meeting and subsequent creation of an advisory group on domestic policy did little to energize the Religious Right to Bush's defense.[88]

Hampered by a lack of enthusiasm, the long tenure of the Republicans, and a painful recession, Bush lost the 1992 election to the Democratic candidate, Arkansas governor Bill Clinton. Writing just after the election, political scientist Peter Kivisto once again wondered if the "Christian Right" had finally fallen. There were, he concluded, "conflicting reports from the frontlines."[89] In retrospect, the question once again appeared premature, the Religious Right far from dead. Indeed, not only did Clinton's election fail to be the death knell of the movement, it arguably helped rejuvenate it. After his defeat in 1988, Robertson met with Ralph Reed, a former head of the College Republicans who was then completing a doctorate in American history. "My goal," Reed later acknowledged, "was to become the next Lee Atwater—a bare-knuckled, brass tacks practitioner of hard ball politics."[90] He appeared just the person Robertson needed, a young activist to revitalize the movement. Using Robertson's mailing lists and connections, the two set about creating the Christian Coalition, arguably the primary successor to the Moral Majority as the champion of the Religious Right. With Reed as executive director running the daily operations and with Robertson as president, free to garner support and money, the new organization thrived.[91]

Secularists threatening the family still rallied the faithful, as homosexuality remained a key concern. In the early 1990s, Dobson joined with Colorado football coach Bill McCartney, founder of the group Promise Keepers, to champion a state referendum in Colorado to ban any legislation advocating homosexual rights. This referendum, dubbed Amendment 2, passed, only to have the Supreme Court strike it down. This court decision, together with a Texas case shortly before, created a new focus for Robertson and his allies: activist courts intent upon advancing the "gay agenda."[92] At the same time, a number of states, following the lead of Louisiana and Arkansas, continued to press for the teaching of the "debate" over evolution in science class. Well funded and now advocated by new organizations such as Seattle's Discovery Institute, the movement argued that the science of evolution was inconclusive, a new tactic in the old battle over "secular" education that its adherents claimed did not constitute teaching religion.

The new president, Clinton, perhaps ironically, ensured the Religious Right's momentum, his actions, both politically and personally, embodying for the movement all that it despised. In the words of one observer, Clinton served as "an enormous bull's eye for the arrows of the Christian Right."[93] From his early order to allow homosexuals in the military in his controversial and well-publicized "Don't Ask, Don't Tell" policy to his extramarital liaison with the intern Monica Lewinsky, Clinton inflamed conservative Christians. In addition, the battle over abortion evolved, shifting to the legal late-term abortions necessary for the health of the mother, termed "partial birth abortion" by critics. Clinton, perhaps more than anything or anyone else, ensured a return of the Religious Right to prominence. In the history of the Religious Right, he was, according to Balmer, an "interregnum."[94]

First with the Republican takeover of the House of Representatives in 1994 and then, more significantly, with the election in 2000 of Republican George W. Bush, the son of the former president, the Religious Right once again appeared ready to press its agenda. The younger Bush's election, Falwell later claimed, was the culmination of Falwell's political advocacy. Unlike his father, the younger Bush appeared a true believer, having undergone his own born-again experience in 1984 while recovering from his youthful alcoholism.[95] Bush prayed daily and reportedly began each morning with a devotional from *My Utmost for His Highest*, a collection of homilies by a nineteenth-century evangelist that, Bush maintained, helped him remain "in the Word." Evidence of Bush's sincerity was easy to find. According to journalist David Frum, some administration staffers felt pressure to attend Bible studies. Frum's colleague Bob Woodward claimed that Bush described himself as a "messenger" from God whose 2003 decision to invade Iraq was God's will.[96] In many respects, Bush's faith guided his policies much as Carter's faith had guided his own. They shared different brands of evangelicalism perhaps, but, in an odd sense, they were similar.[97]

If Carter disdained the use of his religion for political expediency, and subsequently, if living his faith proved problematic in the world of policy, the same was not true for Bush. Bush recognized the continued potency of the Religious Right and actively cultivated its support. Bush's chief political advisor, Karl Rove, coldly calculated the benefits of championing the long-standing agenda of conservative Christians, caring less about actual accomplishment than continued political alliance. In the end, the presidency of George W. Bush, which included the worst terrorist attack on American soil in New York on September 11, 2001, a lingering "War on Terror" that was reflected in the occupations of Iraq and Afghanistan, and a financial meltdown beginning in 2008, proved one of the most tumultuous in American history. After the Bush administration, America would never be the same, a reality that perhaps colored the Religious Right itself, much to its chagrin.

Certainly, during the Bush years conservative Christians enjoyed a level of accomplishment unsurpassed in even the vaunted Reagan administration. Bush appointed two conservative jurists to the Supreme Court, Samuel A. Alito Jr. and John G. Roberts Jr., both strongly backed by antiabortion activists. He denied funding for family planning that included abortion and restricted scientific research on embryonic stem cells to only those cell lines existing prior to his presidency. He advocated using federal money not only for private education but also for religious-based charities, this "faith-based initiative" resulting in a new office for implementation. He strongly opposed late-term abortions despite continued questions over the mother's health, and most notably during his 2004 reelection campaign, ardently opposed the recognition of gay marriages. In that year, Rove and others astutely encouraged states to place initiatives on the ballot that augmented conservative voter turnout. Throughout it all, Bush's rhetoric surpassed even that of Reagan, and like this Republican icon he cherished, Bush met regularly with conservative and evangelical ministers. Even as Bush's overall popularity dipped to historic lows, most conservative Christians defended their champion.

For the Religious Right, however, not all change was good. Despite it all, abortion remained legal, and gay rights continued to gain acceptance throughout American culture. More significantly, a new generation of younger evangelicals appeared, insisting that the Religious Right broaden its agenda. Led by pastors such as Rick Warren, the author of the best-selling book *The Purpose Driven Life*, these younger evangelicals shared much of the conservative social agenda of their theological ancestors but argued that their focus should also include a renewed commitment to fight poverty and combat global warming.[98] Warren was hardly alone, his success ensuring that others followed. Joel Hunter, for one, ran his own "megachurch" and also hit the best-seller lists with his *A New Kind of Conservative*. Man was destroying God's creation, this new generation argued, among other neglected concerns. They were, to one columnist, "the evangelicals you don't know."[99] More accepting of gay rights and viewing the issue of abortion as too divisive, these new conservative Christians did not share the firm partisanship of their elders. Many found the administration's Rovian political tactics unseemly. In fact, Rove's brass-knuckled politics resulted in several public relations debacles that exposed the dangers of overt partisanship. The media, for example, reported that not only had a recent graduate of Pat Robertson's law school, Monica Goodling, assumed a high-level Department of Justice position for which her qualifications were in doubt, she had been replacing federal prosecutors on a partisan basis. To make matters worse, two leaders of Bush's Office of Faith-Based and Community Initiatives, John J. Dilulio Jr. and David Koo, resigned, complaining that the poor had never benefited from the office's programs. The entire effort, they suggested, was simply political.[100] In total, much of the public had come to view such overtly partisan behavior as difficult to excuse, a perception many young evangelicals now shared. Some of the old-school evangelical leaders added to this momentum. In 2006 Ted Haggard, the leader of the National Association of Evangelicals and a longtime critic of homosexuality, became mired in his own public relations debacle, perhaps demonstrating that the earlier personal failures of Bakker, Swaggart, and others were not an aberration. A male prostitute claimed that he had shared a tryst and drugs with Haggard, forcing Haggard's resignation. Viewing this shifting theological tide, theologian and religion scholar David Gushee mused over a new "evangelical center" in his book *The Future of Faith in America*.[101] It seemed the birth of a new age with new leaders and a new agenda.

To the traditional leaders of the Religious Right, frustration was nothing new. In many respects, however, the changes in America's political culture appeared to them fundamentally different. The foundations of the movement, long rooted in the battles of the Carter years and afterward, appeared to be shifting. Even bumper stickers proclaimed the new sentiment: "Hate Is Not a Family Value" and "God Is Not a Republican" suggested support for the goal but not the means. Perhaps sensing this shift, the Democrats pressed anew for the religious vote, casting their own faith as a priority in a way many had been earlier reticent to do.[102] Bush's successor, Barack Obama, embodied this new sensibility, portraying himself as a committed Christian working in a postpartisan world. As if to make this point, Obama invited Warren to deliver his 2009 inaugural invocation. "The [evangelical] movement is undergoing one of its most important changes in a generation," wrote columnist William McKenzie. "The old leaders are fighting to keep their grip."[103]

Today the Religious Right, that unique coalition of theological conservatives and the Republican Party united over issues from the days of Carter, remains, even if the election of Barack Obama may have clipped its political wings and placed its future into question. Just as in the past, it would be foolish to write the movement's obituary once again. During the 2008 Republican primaries, the Baptist preacher and former Arkansas governor Michael Huckabee fought with committed Mormon and former Massachusetts governor Mitt Romney for the right to champion the causes long dear to conservative Christians. Neither won the nomination, which went to Arizona senator John McCain, but both still harbor presidential ambitions. From Huckabee to Romney to McCain's vice presidential running mate, Alaska governor Sarah Palin, the future will bring no shortage of politicians striving to revive the Reagan coalition. Even Robertson continues his televised advocacy, engaging in a very public "prayer offensive" to regain the momentum he senses that he has lost.[104] They may or may not succeed, but the theological underpinnings of the movement will survive, just as they have in the past, in power or not. The Religious Right has ebbed and flowed throughout American history; it has always adapted—and will undoubtedly continue to adapt—to the nation's changing demographic, social, economic, and perhaps most important, theological shifts. If altered, it will persist, representing a significant portion of voters and sure to manifest itself again in some form in the halls of power. In many respects, it has, in the words of author Sara Diamond, an "enduring political and cultural influence."[105]

The same, perhaps, could be said for the Religious Right's old nemesis. When Carter left the White House in 1981, much of the public viewed his one-term presidency as a failure. It would have been easy for Carter to retire to a life of solitude, bitter about his years in office. Carter, however, had no intention of fading gently into the good night. Like the religious conservatives he had both wooed and battled, he too has remained an enduring political and cultural force. He has remained as he has always been: an ambitious activist committed to the causes he championed in Washington. Now more than a quarter-century after leaving office, Carter has proved that his religious beliefs were no political facade, that his faith had always been his guide.[106] He has become a prolific author, for one, many of his best-selling books extolling the virtues of his faith. His memoirs recount how his faith guided him through the tumult of his presidency, while many of his works dispense moral advice for his readers.[107] His actions, perhaps, speak even louder. He has remained active in his church, still teaching occasionally a Bible study class. He became active in Habitat for Humanity, which solicits volunteers and donations to construct housing for the poor. Wielding a hammer alongside other volunteers, Carter brought the press, which, as all recognized, brought donations. "Almost everybody that works for Habitat is someone who out of a religious commitment just wants to do something for somebody less fortunate," explained Rosalynn.[108] According to Linda and Millard Fuller, the organization's founders, Jimmy Carter is a "devoted servant of God." His commitment to a project was genuine, and he never left after the cameras turned off. His "knowledge and understanding of the Bible are exceptional," and he is a "very serious student of the [scripture]."[109] Dan Ariail, the pastor of Carter's church in Plains, Georgia, the Maranatha Baptist Church, likewise sees in Carter a true believer, noting that Carter's work with Habitat for Humanity made him a carpenter, "like Jesus." Carter, Ariail remarked, "long ago determined to fashion his life along principles laid down by Christ." Carter's staffers, many of whom hardly shared the man's faith, joked among themselves that it was no coincidence that Carter's initials are "J.C.," given the importance of Christ in Carter's life.[110]

Carter has remained committed to human rights, traveling the globe, monitoring free elections, and serving almost as an American ambassador at large. From the Sudan to Haiti, from Pakistan to Bosnia, and, of course, always with advice for the troubled Middle East, Carter has appeared to many to be the conscience of America. The laurels came, from the J. William Fulbright Prize for International Understanding to, after five nominations, the famed Nobel Peace Prize in 2002. To advance his causes, Carter established the Carter Presidential Center as part of his presidential library complex at Emory University in Atlanta. While the library remains part of the U.S. National Archives and Records Administration, the Carter Center is a private nonprofit and nongovernmental entity free to pursue its own agenda. It focuses on the future as much as the past, a commitment to continue the struggle Carter began decades ago.

Not surprisingly, his struggles with the Religious Right have continued as well. Carter's evangelicalism still does not mesh with the theological views of his old foes, who, for much of his retirement, have relished the Republican resurgence. Carter now speaks more openly on the differences that divided his faith. "Christians and the general public must not condone, even by silence, the judgmental attitudes promoted by a few demagogic religions and political leaders," he wrote in 1996, the passage of more than a decade and a half obviously doing little to dull the sting of past battles. Self-righteously condemning others "was never Jesus' way."[111] When conservative Republicans in his home state of Georgia pushed to remove the word "evolution" from the state's public school curriculum in 2004, Carter called the effort an "embarrassment," an "attempt to censor and distort the education of Georgia's students."[112] Carter, now free from the constraints of politics and perhaps enjoying the freedoms brought by the winter of his life, continues his outspokenness, which, of course, enrages his old opponents. He criticized Israel for its treatment of Palestinians, even employing the term "apartheid" to describe the Jewish nation's policy. It was, to Robertson, Dobson, and others, an unforgivable sin, an outrage. To Carter it was simply a statement of reality and Christian compassion.[113] When Carter won the Nobel Peace Prize, the awards committee cited his "outstanding commitment to human rights" and his continuing interest in furthering democracy. Critics, however, including a number of Republicans, complained that Carter's version of human rights meant the slaughter of millions of unborn children and the endorsement of the sin of homosexuality. Noting Carter's continued outspokenness, they claimed that the award was as much a slight to the existing president, George W. Bush, as an actual endorsement of Carter's record.[114] At the dedication of the Gerald Ford Library several years after Reagan's election, Falwell recalled, "Carter wouldn't even speak to me." He and Rosalynn were "still bitter even as everyone else was quite nice." For Falwell's part, the feeling was mutual. "[Carter] allegedly represents America," he remarked sarcastically. "[Carter] wants to be the best former president ever, but he's been a disaster at that, putting his nose in where it doesn't belong and just complicating things for others."[115]

Throughout his "retirement"—if one can call it that—Carter continues to stress the importance of the family to the nation. As the millennium came to a close, he wrote that families were critical for the future as "a permanent foundation on which our lives can be fashioned."[116] Carter's rhetoric had little changed almost a quarter of a century after his presidency. Of course, both Republicans and Democrats continue to battle over the moniker "profamily." Having tied the nature of family to feminism, abortion, homosexuality, and freedom from government control, the Republicans' challenge was more than just the idyllic, stable family that Barack Obama presented or the problems surrounding many of the Religious Right's leaders. A number of Republican legislators were engaged in embarrassing affairs that captured headlines and belied their continued family rhetoric. From Idaho senator Larry Craig's 2007 arrest for lewd conduct in the solicitation of homosexual sex to the painful admission of an extramarital love affair by South Carolina governor Mark Sanford in 2009, Republicans proved that their actions did not always match their rhetoric.[117] Democrats shared the same human failings, of course, but many of them continued to be just as political as their Republican counterparts. In 1984, for example, New York governor Mario Cuomo declared in a speech to the Democratic National Convention, "Those who made our history taught us above all things the idea of family." Two years later his New York colleague Daniel Patrick Moynihan published *Family and Nation*, praising the family but noting that a range of "family modes" existed. Such rhetoric was necessary, writer Laura Gellott concluded, for "liberals to reappropriate 'family' as their issue, wrestling it away from . . . groups on the political right."[118] Genuinely concerned about the challenges facing the American family, Carter had helped launch the politics that surrounded them. In the new millennium he continued to express his angst even as the politics, like the Religious Right itself, proved fluid.

Surprising few, Carter proved a central figure in the growing rift that divided his own denomination, the Southern Baptists. The battles over the "family issues"—abortion, homosexuality, education, and feminism, among others—that had so challenged Carter during his presidency continued to tear at the fabric of the faith. The cracks that had emerged during the Carter years had become a chasm. Ten months into the new millennium, Carter renounced his membership in the Southern Baptist Convention, becoming, in the words of one media report, "an enlistee in the national public relations war between moderate and conservative Southern Baptists." In a letter to "my fellow Baptists," Carter explained, "I have been disappointed and feel excluded by the adoption of an increasingly rigid creed."[119] Since Carter's third year in office, conservatives had dominated the SBC. Moderates had complained and slowly had begun to form their own unaffiliated state conventions. In Texas, which contained the largest number of Baptists, moderates had formed the Baptist General Convention of Texas. The new state convention hardly represented all Texas Baptists but still held over $50 million in assets. A year later, in the summer of 2001, Carter called for a new national alliance for the growing number of moderate state conventions. To the conservative leaders at the SBC, Carter's call was a "publicity stunt." The former president was "out of step with the majority of Southern Baptists."[120] There appeared to be no love lost. When one of the leading conservative Baptist ministers, W. A. Criswell of the huge First Baptist Church of Dallas, died in 2002, theological scholars debated his legacy. To conservatives he was "quite extraordinary," but moderates disagreed with that assessment. "His theology was too narrow, his rhetorical appeal too regional, and his influence too limited to a particular subset within his denomination," they claimed.[121] Certainly, when it came to Carter's legacy, the debate was more animated still.

Of course, the Baptists remained hardly alone. The same issues that tore at Baptist unity still crossed denominational lines. In 2003 the Diocese of New Hampshire ordained the Episcopal Church's first gay bishop, Gene V. Robinson. Immediately, conservatives in the church threatened to align themselves with other, more conservative Anglican organizations in Africa and South America. The archbishop of Canterbury, Rowan Williams, already under fire for what critics described as theological liberalism, publicly worried about a major schism. "The struggle going on inside the Anglican communion . . . is not peculiar to Anglicanism," Sister Joan Chittister, a Roman Catholic nun, told the press in 2007, obviously reflecting on her own faith. John G. Green, a senior fellow at the Pew Forum on Religion and Public Life, agreed: "They know it's going to happen to them too."[122] Indeed, in the Evangelical Lutheran Church of America, the denomination's national assembly ended an emotional debate by urging its bishops not to defrock gay ministers in committed relationships. Realizing that this would anger conservatives, however, the assembly also created a task force to make future recommendations.[123] Unity was never easy. The American Presbyterian Church allowed gay clergy but required them to remain celibate, noting that such was the requirement for all unmarried church officers. The church, however, rejected gay marriage, instead favoring civil unions, which it maintained were not equivalent. The United Methodist Church took a similar stance but insisted that no same-sex ceremonies could take place in church facilities. Like Carter a quarter of a century earlier, these churches appeared in many respects to be searching for a middle ground, still no easy task. At the same time, the "family issues" not only split individual denominations, they pitted religions against each other. When in 2008 California voters debated Proposition 8, outlawing gay marriage, the Unitarian Universalist Church organized opposition. At the same time, the Church of Jesus Christ of Latter-day Saints countered by raising funds in support. After voters passed the prohibition, the Mormons complained that they faced harassment and religious bigotry by the proposition's defeated supporters.[124]

"Some Christians Reluctant to Share One Cup," blared a headline in the award-winning religion section of the *Dallas Morning News* in 2002.[125] Two years later, Furman University political scientist James Guth concluded, "Religion is more aligned with partisanship than in the past."[126] It was, as Carter undoubtedly knew, a potent and unfortunate combination. It was, in fact, a combination that had bedeviled American political culture since its founding. With the nation still struggling over the direction its culture should take, the "family issues" so long debated, President George W. Bush agreed to address the nation on the National Day of Prayer in 2005. In the East Room of the White House, Bush repeated an old story about Abraham Lincoln. A minister once remarked to the Great Emancipator that he hoped God was on the president's side. No, Bush quoted Lincoln's reply, it was the president's job to ensure that he was on the Lord's side.[127] The audience laughed, but Bush had hit upon a central dilemma that has always resided at that murky intersection of religion and politics. What is the role of religion in the realms of power? On this, of course, Americans have always disagreed, just as surely as they will continue to disagree in the future. With no consensus theologically, there will never be a consensus politically.

In the end, the Carter era stood at a fault line in the evolution of American culture, religion, and politics. Just as in the past, and undoubtedly in the future, a dynamic society had raised new issues for theological discourse, in turn assuring their manifestation in the realm of politics. A true man of faith, Carter had rallied the faithful only to learn that religious diversity ensured partisan discord. Carter did not create the modern Religious Right, but by following his faith in addressing the emerging issues of the day, by seeking common ground on the matter of family and all that it entailed, the moral issues such as feminism and sexuality that divided religions and resisted compromise, Carter ensured the movement's momentum. Reflecting on Carter's place in history, Robert Maddox concluded that the thirty-ninth president's public faith "may prove in the sweep of history to be among his most lasting contributions to the nation and to the Kingdom of God."[128] In fact, history will recall Carter's faith but also his battles over faith. Whatever the future holds, Jimmy Carter and the modern Religious Right share a common past.

Notes

ABBREVIATIONS

APSP   Office of Special Assistant to the President for Special Projects Files
APWA   Office of the Assistant to the President for Women's Affairs Files
DPS   Domestic Policy Staff Files
JCL   Jimmy Carter Library
MCPA   Miller Center for Public Affairs
OCS   Office of Chief of Staff Files
OPL   Office of Public Liaison Files
PSWF   Presidential Speechwriters Files
RRL   Ronald Reagan Presidential Library
WHCF   White House Central Office Files
WHNF   White House Names Files
WHPO   White House Press Office Files
WHSF   White House Staff Office Files

INTRODUCTION Washington for Jesus

1. *Washington Post*, April 30, 1980, 1; *New York Times*, April 30, 1980, 1; Cantor, *The Religious Right*, 61.

2. Gimenez quoted in Conn, "The New Christian Politics," 16; Marley, *Pat Robertson*, 63–64; Harrell, *Pat Robertson*, 177.

3. *Christianity Today*, April 4, 1980, 44, May 23, 1980, 40; Robertson quoted in Shriver, *The Bible Vote*, 24.

4. Flier, Washington for Jesus rally, folder ERA Strategy Group, box 33, Sarah Weddington Files, APWA, WHSF, JCL.

5. See MacArthur, *The Charismatics*, 13; Falwell, *The Fundamentalist Phenomenon*, 133–38; Woodbridge, *The New Evangelism*, 15; Ashbrook, *Evangelism*, 5; Ockenga, "From Fundamentalism."

6. Falwell, interview; Harding, *The Book of Jerry Falwell*, 21–22; Falwell, *Strength for the Journey*, 290, 337.

7. *Christianity Today*, May 23, 1980, 40; Martin, *With God on Our Side*, 212; Marley, *Pat Robertson*, 64.

8. Falwell, interview; quoted in Goodman and Price, *Jerry Falwell*, 109–10, 139–40.

9. Falwell, interview.

10. Robertson quoted in *Washington Post*, March 15, 1980, II, 1; Cantor, *The Religious Right*, 61–62.

11. Flier, Intercessors for Congress, folder ERA Strategy Group, box 33, Sarah Weddington Files, APWA, WHSF, JCL.

12. "Christian Declaration," March for Washington, folder ERA Strategy Group, box 33, Sarah Weddington Files, APWA, WHSF, JCL.

13. Maddox, interview; Robert Maddox, oral history audiotape, JCL.

14. Glad, *Jimmy Carter*, 108. See, for example, Nielson, *The Religion of Jimmy Carter*; Hefley and Hefley, *The Church That Produced a President*; Gaver, *The Faith of Jimmy Carter*; Ariail and Heckler-Feltz, *The Carpenter's Apprentice*. Carter has written widely on his faith, including *Sources of Strength* and *Living Faith*.

15. *Washington Post*, March 21, 1976, 7; Witcover, *Marathon*, 287–89; Glad, *Jimmy Carter*, 331.

16. *New York Times*, May 12, 1976, 41, June 17, 1976, 35; *Newsweek*, October 25, 1976, 31.

17. Falwell, interview.

18. Robertson and Carter quoted in Marley, *Pat Robertson*, 43.

19. Robertson quoted in ibid., 44; Balmer, *God in the White House*, 104–5.

20. Smith quoted in Martin, *With God on Our Side*, 157.

21. *Christianity Today*, June 18, 1976, 20; Marley, *Pat Robertson*, 45.

22. Maddox, interview; Lance quoted in Bourne, *Jimmy Carter*, 466.

23. Memo, Robert Maddox to Jody Powell, December 31, 1979, folder Religious Broadcasters 1980, 1980–1980, box 3, Ray Jenkins Files, WHPO, WHSF, JCL.

24. Memo, Ray Jenkins to Jody Powell, January 2, 1980, folder Religious Broadcasters 1980, 1980–1980, box 3, Ray Jenkins Files, WHPO, WHSF, JCL.

25. Memo, Robert Maddox to Jody Powell, January 6, 1980, folder Religious Broadcasters 1980, 1980–1980, box 3, Ray Jenkins Files, WHPO, WHSF, JCL.

26. Maddox, *Preacher at the White House*, 80–82.

27. Memo, Robert Maddox to Anne Wexler, March 8, 1980, WHNF Robert Schuller, WHCF, JCL; handwritten comments by Fran Voorde on memo, Robert Maddox to Anne Wexler, March 8, 1980, WHNF Robert Schuller, WHCF, JCL.

28. Maddox, interview; Maddox, oral history; Maddox, *Preacher at the White House*, 82.

29. Quoted in Moen, *The Christian Right and Congress*, 38.

30. Gimenez quoted in *New York Times*, April 27, 1980, 64, April 30, 1980, 1.

31. Bakker quoted in *New York Times*, April 30, 1980, 1.

32. Robertson quoted in *New York Times*, April 30, 1980, 1, and Cantor, *The Religious Right*, 16.

33. Robison quoted in D'Souza, *Falwell Before the Millennium*, 120–21.

34. Quoted in Dabney, "God's Own Network," 26.

35. Moen, *The Christian Right and Congress*, 38; Harrell, *Pat Robertson*, 178.

36. *Capitol Hill: The Newsletter of the Gay Rights National Lobby* 2, no. 2 (1980): 1–4.

37. Schlafly, interview; quoted in *New York Times*, January 23, 1980, 12.

38. *Washington Post*, April 30, 1980, 1; Marley, *Pat Robertson*, 63–64; Martin, *With God on Our Side*, 212.

39. Laxalt and Keene quoted in *New York Times*, April 21, 1980, II, 12.

40. *Christianity Today*, May 23, 1980, 40.

41. Maddox, interview; Shriver, *The Bible Vote*, 25; Bright and Robertson quoted in Cantor, *The Religious Right*, 62.

42. O'Connor, *No Neutral Ground*, 86; Robison quoted in Martin, *With God on Our Side*, 212; Falwell, interview.

43. Robertson quoted in Shriver, *The Bible Vote*, 26; Harrell, *Pat Robertson*, 178.

44. *Christianity Today*, May 23, 1980, 40.

45. Maguire, *The New Subversives*, 1–2; Drew, *Portrait of an Election*, 190; Fackre, *The Religious Right*, xi.

46. Schlafly, interview; Wilcox, *Onward Christian Soldiers?* 5; Reed, "What Do Religious Conservatives," 3.

47. Moen, *The Christian Right and Congress*, 4; Hill and Owen, *The New Religious Political Right*, 15.

48. Allen, interview; Fackre, *The Religious Right*, 6; Wilcox, *God's Warriors*, 43; Chandler, "The Wicked," 41.

49. Streiker and Strober, *Religion and the New Majority*, 141–44; Hill and Owen, *The New Religious Political Right*, 15–16; Fackre, *The Religious Right*, 6.

50. Hill and Owen, *The New Religious Right*, 15–16. See Wilcox, *God's Warriors*, 65–69; Lienesch, *Redeeming America*, 10; Guth, "The Politics of the Evangelical Right," 1.

51. Menendez, "Religious Lobbies," 5; Moen, *The Christian Right and Congress*, 4, 20. Niebuhr's books include *An Interpretation of Christian Ethics*, *Christian Realism*, and *Moral Man and Immoral Society*.

52. Allen, interview; Shriver, *The Bible Vote*, 34; Fackre, *The Religious Right*, 7.

53. The best overviews of the Religious Right are, perhaps, Martin, *With God on Our Side*, and Wilcox, *God's Warriors*; other strong academic overviews include Dionne and Diiulio, *What's God Got to Do*, and Capps, *The New Religious Right*.

54. Webber, *The Moral Majority*, 24; Moen, *The Christian Right and Congress*, 15–16.

55. Falwell, interview; Falwell, *Listen America!* 107.

56. Kater, *Christians on the Right*, 62; Finch, *God, Guts, and Guns*, 50–51; Moen, *The Christian Right and Congress*, 17; Falwell quoted in Webber, *The Moral Majority*, 27; Robertson, *Right on the Money*. Robertson's other books include *The New World Order*, *Miracles Can Be Yours Today*, and *Bring It On*.

57. 370 U.S. 421 (1962); Balmer, *Thy Kingdom Come*, 13–15.

58. Falwell, interview; Hastey and Ragsdale, "Right Religion, Right Politics?"; Billings quoted in Moen, *The Christian Right and Congress*, 27; *Time*, October 13, 1980, 35; Zwier, *Born-Again Politics*, 26.

59. Kincheloe, *Understanding the New Right*, 13, 19; Apple and Christian-Smith, *The Politics of the Textbook*, 3.

60. Zwier, *Born-Again Politics*, 23. See also Moen, *The Christian Right and Congress*, 31; Wilcox, "Evangelicals," 400–414; Hall and Combee, "The Moral Majority," 204–11; Moore and Whitt, "Multiple Dimensions," 423–39; D'Souza, "The Political Contributions," 20–25; Shriver, "The Religious Right," 26–30; Bell, "The Revolt," 42–63.

61. Zwier, *Born-Again Politics*, 29; Balmer, *God in the White House*, 80, 104–5; Wilcox, *God's Warriors*, 11; Moen, *The Christian Right and Congress*, 28. Numerous authors have noted this point; see, for example, Lienesch, *Redeeming America*, 1.

62. Martin, *With God on Our Side*, chaps. 6 and 7, 144–90.

63. Balmer, *God in the White House*, 94; Dobson quoted on 99; Baptist press quoted on 95.

64. Oldfield, *The Right and the Righteous*, 56; Watt, *A Transforming Faith*, 85.

65. Schlafly, interview; Stuart Eizenstat, interview, vol. 13, January 29–30, 1982, Jimmy Carter Presidential Materials Project, MCPA, 60.

66. Quoted in Jones, *The Trustee Presidency*, 2, 7; see also Jones, "Keeping Faith," 442, 444.

67. Maddox, interview; Maddox, *Preacher at the White House*, 157.

68. Maddox, *Preacher at the White House*, 136–37; Falwell, interview.

69. Bawer, *Stealing Jesus*, 6–8. See also Gannon, "The New Christian Right," 72; Wilcox, "Religious Attitudes," 70–71.

70. Wills, *Head and Heart*, 3.

71. Bourne, *Jimmy Carter*, 467. See also Fink, *Prelude to the Presidency*, 8.

72. Fink, *Prelude to the Presidency*, 191; Kucharsky, *The Man from Plains*, 23.

73. Allen, interview; Maddox, interview; Maddox, *Preacher at the White House*, 136–37.

74. See, for example, Leuchtenburg, "Jimmy Carter."

75. Eizenstat, interview, 102, 109.

76. Mueller, "In Search of a Constituency," 217.

77. Fink, *Prelude to the Presidency*, 8.

78. Eizenstat, interview, 117; Maddox, oral history.

79. Allen, interview; Cantor, *The Religious Right*, 59–60.

80. Phillips, interview; Cantor, *The Religious Right*, 60; Shriver, *The Bible Vote*, 13.

81. Bruce, *The Rise and Fall*, 57.

82. Morton Blackwell, oral history audiotape, RRL.

83. Marshner, interview; Lienesch, *Redeeming America*, 8.

ONE The Times They Are a-Changin'

1. Carter, *Why Not the Best?* 11; Carter quoted in Glad, *Jimmy Carter*, 345; Mazlish and Diamond, *Jimmy Carter*, 18–26.

2. National Park Service exit interview, Jimmy and Rosalynn Carter, II, JCL, 133.

3. Carter, exit interview, I, 12.

4. Carter, *Personal Beliefs*, 5–6, 44; Glad, *Jimmy Carter*, 66–67.

5. Glad, *Jimmy Carter*, 108. See McMorrow, *Jimmy*, chap. 4; and Carter, *Why Not the Best?*

6. Glad, *Jimmy Carter*, 111, 325, 333. For more on Niebuhr, see Niebuhr's books, *Moral Man and Immoral Society*, *An Interpretation of Christian Ethics*, and *Christian Realism*. Lovin provides a good overview of Niebuhr in *Reinhold Niebuhr*.

7. Eizenstat, interview, 116.

8. Carter and Anderson quoted in Anderson, *Electing Jimmy Carter*, 58.

9. Hargrove, *Jimmy Carter as President*, 5.

10. Daniel and Hart, *Addresses*, 74–76; Carter quoted in Glad, *Jimmy Carter*, 136.

11. Kirbo quoted in Hargrove, *Jimmy Carter as President*, 1.

12. Glad, *Jimmy Carter*, 333; Bourne, *Jimmy Carter*, 279.

13. Carter, exit interview, I, 40.

14. Ibid.; quoted in Fink, *Prelude to the Presidency*, 191; Kucharsky, *The Man from Plains*, 23.

15. Carter, exit interview, II, 156–57.

16. Wilcox, *God's Warriors*, 17.

17. Friedan, *Feminine Mystique*. See Hymowitz and Weissman, *A History of Women*; Davis, *Moving the Mountain*.

18. Bell, "The Revolt," 50.

19. See Morgan, *Sisterhood Is Powerful*.

20. Echols, *Daring to Be Bad*, 1–21.

21. Millet, *Sexual Politics*; Greer quoted in Christensen, *Utopia Against the Family*, 35. For more on Greer's views, see Greer, *The Female Eunuch* and *Sex and Destiny*.

22. Quoted in Whitney, *The Equal Rights Amendment*, 82.

23. Ryan, *Feminism and the Women's Movement*, 3; Cook, "Women White House Advisors," 11.

24. See Lunardini, *From Equal Suffrage*; Irwin, *The Story of Alice Paul*; and Becker, *The Origins*.

25. Schlafly, interview; Delsman, *Everything You Need to Know*, 30.

26. Delsman, *Everything You Need to Know*, 35; *Hearings on the Equal Rights Amendment*; *Hearings on Equal Rights 1970*; U.S. Congress, Senate, *Report No. 92-689*; U.S. Congress, House, *Report 92-359*.

27. Whitney, *The Equal Rights Amendment*, 28; Hatch, *The Equal Rights Amendment*, 1–2.

28. Rubin, *Abortion, Politics*, 11–16; Reed, "The Birth Control Movement," 22–52.

29. Blake, "Abortion and Public Opinion."

30. Gutierrez, interview; *Griswald v. Connecticut*, 381 U.S. 479 (1965).

31. Miller, *The Abandoned Middle*, 11–18. For a comparative discussion of abortion politics in other countries, see Lovenduski and Outshoorn, *The New Politics of Abortion*.

32. Kranz and Cusick, *Gay Rights*, 32. See also, for example, Murray and Roscoe, *Boy-Wives and Female Husbands*.

33. See Boswell, *Same-Sex Unions*.

34. Bronski, *Pleasure Principle*, 8.

35. Kranz and Cusick, *Gay Rights*, 122; Kinsey, *Sexual Behavior*.

36. Kranz and Cusick, *Gay Rights*, 33–34; PL 831, 81st Cong.

37. Galas, *Gay Rights*, 19.

38. Bilitis was supposedly the lesbian lover of the ancient Greek poet Sappho.

39. Kranz and Cusick, *Gay Rights*, 38, 71, 73; *Society for Individual Rights v. Hampton*, 63 F.R.D. 399 (1973).

40. Marotta, *The Politics of Homosexuality*, 134–35; Kranz and Cusick, *Gay Rights*, 123.

41. *Stonewall: Myth, Magic and Mobilization*, NPR, June 14, 1994.

42. Smith, "Full Moon," 109–12; Bronski, *Pleasure Principle*, 67.

43. See Gilbert, *A Cycle of Outrage*.

44. Moynihan, *The Negro Family*.

45. *New York Times*, June 20, 1975, 38.

46. Quoted in *New York Times*, August 22, 1975, 31.

47. Shoemaker quoted in *New York Times*, June 15, 1975, IV, 17.

48. Falwell, *Listen America!* 76; quoted in Whitney, *The Equal Rights Amendment*, 61. See Wills, *Under God*, for a summary of the biblical case against abortion.

49. Schlafly, interview; quoted in Whitney, *The Equal Rights Amendment*, 60–61.

50. Tedin, "Religious Preference"; Brady and Tedin, "Ladies in Pink."

51. Wilcox, "Religious Attitudes," 67. For one interpretation of the Bible's view of gender, see Robbins, *The Christian Church*, 11–32.

52. Deutchman and Prince-Embury, "Political Ideology."

53. Ephesians 5:23–33.

54. Quoted in *New York Times*, February 7, 1975, 37.

55. Silver, *The New Civil War*, 59–60.

56. Magnuson, *Are Gay Rights Right?* 115–16.

57. Silver, *The New Civil War*, 59–63, Hilton quoted on 61.

58. Johnson, *Gays under Grace*, 4. See also Johnson and Eaves, *Gays and the New Right*.

59. *New York Times*, June 16, 1976, 11; *Christianity Today*, January 25, 1980, 41, April 8, 1980, 22.

60. Quoted in *New York Times*, May 9, 1975, 30.

61. Galas, *Gay Rights*, 24–25; Kranz and Cusick, *Gay Rights*, 124.

62. *Rochester Democrat and Chronicle*, January 15, 1976, 9A.

63. McNeill quoted in *New York Times*, February 22, 1976, 26.

64. Glad, *Jimmy Carter*, 401; *New York Times*, September 10, 1976, 19, September 3, 1976, 9, Shannon quoted in September 5, 1976, IV, 13.

65. Herman, *Antigay Agenda*, 176–80; *U.S. News and World Report*, July 5, 1993, 42–48; Gallagher and Bull, *Perfect Enemies*, 6–7; Holbrook, *Fighting Back*, 24–26.

66. Falwell, interview; Allen, interview; *New York Times*, June 16, 1976, 11.

67. Falwell, interview; Allen, interview; *New York Times*, June 30, 1980, 30, November 28, 1980, II, 10.

68. Falwell, interview; quoted in *New York Times*, March 7, 1975, 10.

69. National Council of Churches, *Yearbook*, 53; *New York Times*, June 18, 1976, 11, June 8, 1980, 25.

70. *Theology Today* 32, no. 2 (1975): 189–93, quoted in *New York Times*, June 27, 1976, VI, 6. See also Darien, "Berger's Theology," 35–36.

71. Neuhaus later converted to Roman Catholicism and served as an informal advisor to George W. Bush; Neuhaus authored numerous books, for example, *American Babylon*, *The Naked Public Square*, and *Catholic Matters*.

72. White House Conference on Families, "A Brief History, National Advisory Committee, July, 1979," folder July 20, 1979—Remarks—Reception—White House Conference on the Family, box 51, Achsah Nesmith Files, PSWF, WHSF, JCL.

73. Moen, "School Prayer"; Hottois and Milner, *The Sex Education Controversy*, xvii; Kienel, *The Christian School*, 14–15; Moen, *The Christian Right and Congress*, 26; Martin, *With God on Our Side*, 169; *Bob Jones University v. U.S.*, 456 U.S. 922 (1983).

74. Spring, "Textbook Writing," 191–92.

75. Quoted in Martin, *With God on Our Side*, 106.

76. Quoted in ibid., 108. See also Steinbacher, *The Child Seducers*.

77. Marshner, interview; Moore quoted in Kincheloe, *Understanding the New Right*, 13, 19.

78. Kincheloe, *Understanding the New Right*, 9; Apple and Christian-Smith, *The Politics of the Textbook*, 3.

79. Kincheloe, *Understanding the New Right*, 7, 8, 22, 30; Kienel, *The Christian School*, 27, 35.

80. Quoted in Kincheloe, *Understanding the New Right*, 21. See also Larson, "Constitutional Challenges," 77.

81. Marshner, interview; *New York Times*, December 10, 1971; Ambrose, *Nixon*, 470; Martin, *With God on Our Side*, 174–75.

82. Mitchell, "The Politics of Child Care," 841.

83. Quoted in *New York Times*, September 14, 1975, IV, 17.

84. Bayh and Baker quoted in *New York Times*, October 6, 1975, 28, and March 28, 1976, VI, 9, respectively; see also *New York Times*, February 5, 1975, 41.

85. *New York Times*, May 2, 1976, IV, 16, March 16, 1975, 11.

86. *New York Times*, August 10, 1975, 1, December 13, 1975, 56, February 12, 1976, 1, April 27, 1976, 25, June 6, 1976, 11, February 18, 1976, 74.

87. *New York Times*, January 11, 1976, IV, 20.

88. Schaeffer quoted in Catherwood, *Five Evangelical Leaders*, 152. See also Schaeffer, *The Christian Manifesto*.

89. *New York Times*, January 11, 1976, IV, 20; Martin, *With God on Our Side*, 156.

90. Phillips, interview; Shriver, *The Bible Vote*, 13; Billings, *Guide to the Christian School*. See also History of the Christian Freedom Foundation, http://www.seekgod.ca/cff.htm, accessed March 11, 2009.

91. Richardson, interview; Richardson, *Amazing Faith*, 151.

92. Richardson, interview; Quebedeaux, *I Found It!* 35–44.

93. Shepard, *Forgiven*, 68.

94. Marley, *Pat Robertson*, 1–8, 10–13; Boston, *The Most Dangerous Man*, 23–27.

95. Shepard, *Forgiven*, 68, 133; *Christianity Today*, December 15, 1978, 41.

96. See, for example, Randi, *The Faith Healers*.

97. Gilbert, "Ballot Salvation," 2–3; Falwell, *Strength for the Journey*, 312–13.

98. See Pollock, *To All Nations*; Martin, *A Prophet with Honor*.

99. Graham quoted in Edgar Bundy Ministries, *Billy Graham*, 93–95.

100. Graham quoted in ibid., 98.

101. Martin, *With God on Our Side*, 32.

102. The release of new Nixon White House tapes in 2000 included a recording of Graham referring to a Jewish "stranglehold" on the media and denouncing the media as purveyors of pornography. See Vest, "Tangled Up in Tape," *Counterpunch*, http://www.counterpunch.org/vestgraham.html, accessed April 19, 2008; Dart, "Graham and Nixon," 7.

103. Graham quoted in Edgar Bundy Ministries, *Billy Graham*, 93.

104. Harrell, *Pat Robertson*, 60.

105. Falwell, interview; Martz with Carroll, *Ministry of Greed*, 107; Falwell, *Strength for the Journey*, 337.

106. Falwell, interview; quoted in Goodman and Price, *Jerry Falwell*, 109–10, 139–40.

107. Falwell, interview; Falwell, *Listen America!* 121, 128.

108. Lloyd, *Pioneers of Old Time Religion*, 19–20, 21–22, 25, 28; Falwell, *Strength for the Journey*, 327; Gilbert, "Ballot Salvation," 6.

109. Strober and Tomczak, *Jerry Falwell*, 72–74; Falwell, *Strength for the Journey*, 317.

110. Martin, *With God on Our Side*, 341; Bawer, *Stealing Jesus*, 248–49; Dobson, *What Wives Wished Their Husbands*; and Dobson, *Dare to Discipline*.

111. Schlafly, interview; Dobson quoted in Bawer, *Stealing Jesus*, 253.

112. Falwell, interview; Martin, *With God on Our Side*, 169–71.

113. Zwier, *Born-Again Politics*, 31–32.

114. Phillips, interview; Blackwell, oral history; Martin, *With God on Our Side*, 88–89, 204–5.

115. Phillips, interview; Lienesch, *Redeeming America*, 8; Shriver, *The Bible Vote*, 42; Cantor, *The Religious Right*, 60; Bruce, *The Rise and Fall*, 57; Martin, *With God on Our Side*, 153, 191–92.

TWO   The Year of the Evangelical

1. Anderson, *Electing Jimmy Carter*, 2, 10.

2. Glad, *Jimmy Carter*, 305, 321, 380.

3. Morris, *Jimmy Carter*, 229.

4. Schlafly, interview; Schlafly, *The Power of Positive Women* and *The Power of the Christian Woman*. See also Felsenthal, *The Sweetheart of the Moral Majority*.

5. Schlafly, interview. These senators were Barry Goldwater, Paul Fanin, Wallace Bennett, Norris Cotton, and Clifford Hansen; in addition, James Buckley of the Conservative Party is counted in the Republican fold.

6. Solinger, *Beggars and Choosers*, 11–12.

7. Buchanan quoted in O'Connor, *No Neutral Ground*, 71; Nixon quoted in Craig and O'Brien, *Abortion and American Politics*, 158.

8. See *A History of Conflict in High Court Appointments*, NPR, July 6, 2005; Aitken, *Nixon*, 391–93.

9. Rubin, *Abortion, Politics*, 155–57.

10. Ibid., 93–94; Schlafly, interview.

11. Cited in Vinovskis, "Abortion," 189–90.

12. Cook, Jelen, and Wilcox, *Between Two Absolutes*, 114–17.

13. The six states with an increase in opposition were Florida, Mississippi, North Carolina, South Carolina, Texas, and Virginia; Uslaner and Weber, "Public Support," 215–18.

14. McGovern quoted in *Congressional Quarterly Weekly Report*, May 6, 1972; Craig and O'Brien, *Abortion and American Politics*, 159.

15. Cook, Jelen, and Wilcox, *Between Two Absolutes*, 167.

16. Eagleton withdrew from the campaign after admitting he had received mental health care; Legislative Fact Sheet, Religious Coalition for Abortion Rights, March 1977, folder Women and Abortion, March, 1977–September, 1977, box 10, Margaret Costanza Files, OPL, WHSF, JCL; Gorney, *Articles of Faith*, 348.

17. Rubin, *Abortion, Politics*, 155–57. See also U.S. Commission on Civil Rights, *Report*.

18. *Congressional Record* 121, pt. 7 (March 25, 1975): 8581–82; Frank, "In Praise of Partisanship," 10–13. The Civil Service ban still applied to the Federal Bureau of Investigations and the intelligence agencies, where a fear of blackmail still existed.

19. *Gay Blade* 2, no. 5 (1971): 1; *Washington Blade* 7, no. 5 (1976): 2. See also Gay Rights National Lobby, *Does Support*.

20. Ide, *Idol Worshippers*, 9–10.

21. Gregory-Lewis, "The Republicans," 91–95, Way quoted on 93.

22. Robert Dole to Fellow Republicans, May 8, 1972, and Richard Nixon to Hugh Scott, March 18, 1972, both in folder ERA (notebook) (2), box 30, Sarah Weddington Files, APWA, WHSF, JCL.

23. Delsman, *Everything You Need to Know*, 36–44. Unlike the United Auto Workers, the AFL-CIO worried that gender equality would weaken union support.

24. Boles, "Systemic Factors," 5–22.

25. Schlafly, interview. The United Nations at first designated 1975 as IWY; see Tinker, *Women in Washington*, 18–23; Abzug and Kelber, *Gender Gap*, 63.

26. Schlafly, interview. Leading ERAmerica were Democrat Sharon Percy Rockefeller and Republican Helen Milliken; see Delsman, *Everything You Need to Know*, 36–44; *New York Times*, October 21, 1975, 46, December 3, 1975, 32, December 6, 1975, 28.

27. *It's Time: The Newsletter of the National Gay Task Force* (March 1976), folder Gay Rights Publications, 3/75–1/78 (O/A 5771), box 10, Margaret Costanza Files, OPL, WHSF, JCL.

28. Rubin, *Abortion, Politics*, 95; O'Connor, *No Neutral Ground?* 65.

29. *Christianity Today*, March 26, 1976, 230, 239–46.

30. Shriver quoted in *New York Times*, January 1, 1976, 24.

31. Young, *God's Bullies*, 26.

32. Quoted in *New York Times*, August 4, 1976, 12.

33. Carter quoted in Anderson, *Electing Jimmy Carter*, 10.

34. *New York Times*, April 4, 1976, 58, April 6, 1976, 35.

35. Schram, *Running for President*, 11.

36. Evans and Novak, Carter, and Paulson quoted in ibid., 11–12.

37. *New York Times*, January 25, 1976, IV, 3, January 30, 1976, 26.

38. *New York Times*, February 4, 1976, 4.

39. Rubin, *Abortion, Politics*, 98.

40. *New York Times*, February 28, 1976, 12, March 11, 1976, 34.

41. Reagan quoted in *New York Times*, February 8, 1976, 44.

42. *New York Times*, February 8, 1976, IV, 3; quoted in *New York Times*, April 4, 1976, II, 25.

43. Quoted in *New York Times*, February 9, 1976, 32.

44. Federal Election Campaign Act of 1974, PL 92-225; *Congressional Quarterly Weekly Report*, February 28, 1976, 463–65; *Washington Post*, February 26, 1976, 6; Rubin, *Abortion, Politics*, 99.

45. *School District of Abington Township v. Schempp* (consolidated with *Murray v. Curlett*), 374 U.S. 203 (1963); O'Hair quoted in Bates, *Battleground*, 49. See also O'Hair, *Nobody Has a Prayer* and *An Atheist Epic*.

46. McGraw, *Secular Humanism*, 4–5. See also *Christianity Today*, September 9, 1977, 60, September 22, 1978, 36.

47. Schaeffer, *How Should We Then Live?*; Detwiler, *Standing on the Premises*, 112–13; Catherwood, *Five Evangelical Leaders*, 153.

48. Schlafly, interview; Schlafly quoted in Carroll, *Famous in America*, 200–201.

49. Schlafly and Ward, *Ambush at Vladivostok*.

50. Phillips, interview; quoted in *Christianity Today*, March 26, 1976, 36.

51. Glad, *Jimmy Carter*, 330; See Carter, *Why Not the Best?*

52. *Washington Post*, March 21, 1976, 7; Witcover, *Marathon*, 287–89.

53. Glad, *Jimmy Carter*, 331.

54. *New York Times*, May 12, 1976, 41, June 17, 1976, 35.

55. *New York Times*, May 12, 1976, 41.

56. *New York Times*, April 20, 1976, 20, June 5, 1976, 25, June 6, 1976, 17.

57. Glad, *Jimmy Carter*, 331–32.

58. Ibid., 247, 332.

59. Strober and Marty quoted in *New York Times*, April 11, 1976, 41; Streiker and Strober, *Religion and the New Majority*.

60. Carter quoted in *New York Times*, August 1, 1976, IV, 9.

61. Colson, *Born Again*.

62. *Christianity Today*, March 12, 1976, 4.

63. *New York Times*, May 30, 1976, IV, 15.

64. Quoted in *New York Times*, June 20, 1976, 1.

65. Glad, *Jimmy Carter*, 286.

66. Quoted in ibid., 309.

67. Quoted in ibid., 336.

68. Carter and aide quoted in ibid., 188–89.

69. Quoted in Martin, *With God on Our Side*, 155.

70. Anderson, *Electing Jimmy Carter*, 77–78, 102.

71. *New York Times*, May 2, 1976, IV, 15.

72. Neuhaus quoted in Mitchell, *Billy Graham*, 31.

73. *New York Times*, September 12, 1976, 26, September 26, 1976, 32.

74. *Christianity Today*, April 9, 1976, 31, June 18, 1976, 32.

75. *Christianity Today*, August 6, 1976, 25.

76. Falwell, interview.

77. Ibid.; Falwell, *Strength for the Journey*, 345–46.

78. Falwell, interview.

79. Alexander-Moegerle, *James Dobson's War on America*, 188–89; Zettersten, *Dr. Dobson*, 98.

80. Richardson, interview; Robertson quoted in Harrell, *Pat Robertson*, 176; Bright, *A Movement of Miracles*, 46; Richardson, *Amazing Faith*, 151; Martin, *With God on Our Side*, 146.

81. *New York Times*, June 28, 1976, 31; quoted in Bronski, *Pleasure Principle*, 74; Kranz and Cusick, *Gay Rights*, 38. See also White, *States of Desire*.

82. Quoted in *New York Times*, June 28, 1976, 31.

83. *New York Times*, March 30, 1976, 1, July 4, 1976, 45.

84. Quoted in *New York Times*, March 30, 1976, 17.

85. Press release, National Gay Task Force, April 27, 1976, folder National Gay Task Force, Commission on Human Rights, 3/77 (O/A 4496), box 27, Seymour Wishman Files, OPL, WHSF, JCL.

86. Position paper, National Women's Political Caucus, June 1976, folder Gay Rights, box 7, DPS, WHSF, JCL.

87. Quoted in *New York Times*, August 22, 1975, 31, May 20, 1976, 31.

88. News release, Democratic Presidential Campaign Committee, California Gay People for Carter-Mondale, April 5, 1976, folder Gays, Jimmy Carter On, 3/76–3/77 (O/A 4499), 03/1976–03/1977, box 22, Seymour Wishman Files, OPL, WHSF, JCL; Carter quoted in Clendinen and Nagourney, *Out for Good*, 273.

89. Robert Hawley to Jean O'Leary, October 4, 1976, folder Gays, Jimmy Carter On, 3/76–3/77 (O/A 4499), 03/1976–03/1977, box 22, Seymour Wishman Files, OPL, WHSF, JCL.

90. Carter quoted in campaign press release, April 1976, folder Gay Rights: Publications, 3/75–1/78 (O/A 5771), 03/1975–01/1978, box 4, Margaret Costanza Files, OPL, WHSF, JCL.

91. Transcript, NBC, *The Tomorrow Show*, March 19, 1976, folder Gay Rights, box 7, DPS, WHSF, JCL.

92. Eizenstat quoted in Clendinen and Nagourney, *Out for Good*, 277.

93. "Special Report: The Gay Presence at the Democratic Convention," *Advocate*, August 12, 1976, 1.

94. Quoted in ibid., 4.

95. Hartmann, "Feminism," 225. See *Singleton v. Wulff*, 428 U.S. 106 (1976) and *Planned Parenthood v. Danforth*, 428 U.S. 52 (1976); quoted in *New York Times*, July 2, 1976, 1, July 4, 1976, 9, July 8, 1976, 9, July 12, 1976, III, 21.

96. Quoted in Bourne, *Jimmy Carter*, 315, 345.

97. Glad, *Jimmy Carter*, 273–74.

98. *New York Times*, August 12, 1976, 16.

99. *New York Times*, July 28, 1976, 9, August 13, 1976, 1.

100. Schlafly quoted in Carroll, *Famous in America*, 201.

101. *New York Times*, August 19, 1976, 26.

102. *New York Times*, August 17, 1976, 36.

103. Quoted in ibid.

104. Quoted in *New York Times*, July 2, 1976, 16, February 15, 1975, 31.

105. *New York Times*, February 14, 1976, 12.

106. Schlafly, interview; *New York Times*, February 25, 1976, 15, March 9, 1975, IV, 18, March 27, 1975, 33, October 30, 1975, 44.

107. Schlafly, interview; Glad, *Jimmy Carter*, 257–70. See also Witcover, *Marathon*, 16; Schram, *Running for President*, 111; Moore and Fraser, *Campaign for President*, 79; Drew, *American Journal*, 15; Shirley, *Reagan's Revolution*, 297–331.

108. Anderson, *Electing Jimmy Carter*, 78–79, Anderson quoted on 80; Jimmy Carter to Phil Strickland, December 17, 1976, folder (Christian Life Commission), 2/16/77–9/23/77, 02/16/1977–09/23/1977, Landon Butler Files, OCS, WHSF, JCL.

109. Quoted in *New York Times*, September 5, 1976, IV, 12.

110. Bernardin quoted in *New York Times*, September 11, 1976, 1; and Schram, *Running for President*, 225.

111. Quoted in Schram, *Running for President*, 226.

112. Haas, *Jimmy Carter*, 44; Carter quoted in *New York Times*, September 10, 1976, 20.

113. *New York Times*, September 1, 1976, 1; Powell quoted in Schram, *Running for President*, 277.

114. Gorney, *Articles of Faith*, 280–81.

115. Rubin, *Abortion, Politics*, 164; *New York Times*, September 29, 1976, 19, October 23, 1976, 1.

116. *New York Times*, September 11, 1976, 20.

117. *New York Times*, September 21, 1976, 27.

118. *New York Times*, September 8, 1976, 22, September 9, 1976, 32.

119. Quoted in *New York Times*, September 3, 1976, 9.

120. Quoted in Cook, "Women White House Advisors," 14; Klein, *Gender Politics*, 25; *New York Times*, August 28, 1976, 13.

121. Quoted in Hartmann, "Feminism," 224.

122. Quoted in *New York Times*, June 16, 1976, 26.

123. Carter Campaign press release, October 14, 1976, folder Gays, Jimmy Carter On, 3/76–3/77 (O/A 4499), 03/1976–03/1977, box 22, Seymour Wishman Files, OPL, WHSF, JCL.

124. Carter quoted in press release, Gays for Carter, August 1976, folder Gay Rights, box 7, DPS, WHSF, JCL; Carter Campaign press release, August 22, 1976, folder Gays, Jimmy Carter On, 3/76–3/77 (O/A 4499), 03/1976–03/1977, box 22, Seymour Wishman Files, OPL, WHSF, JCL.

125. Advertisement copy, Carter Campaign, September 1976, folder Gay Rights, box 7, DPS, WHSF, JCL.

126. *San Francisco Chronicle*, July 28, 1976, 26.

127. Charles Hill Graham to Bob Haverly, September 13, 1976, folder Gay Rights, box 7, DPS, WHSF, JCL.

128. Graham quoted in Frady, *Billy Graham*, 504.

129. Quoted in ibid.; and Martin, *A Prophet with Honor*, 461.

130. Quoted in Frady, *Billy Graham*, 504.

131. Quoted in ibid., 505.

132. Quoted in Pollock, *Billy Graham*, 278.

133. Carter quoted in Martin, *A Prophet with Honor*, 463.

134. Graham quoted in ibid.; Maddox, *Preacher at the White House*, 142.

135. Robertson and Carter quoted in Marley, *Pat Robertson*, 42–43.

136. Robert Maddox, oral history audiotape, JCL.

137. Quoted in *Christianity Today*, July 16, 1976, 48.

138. *Christianity Today*, October 22, 1976, 47.

139. Kucharsky, *The Man from Plains*; Norton and Slosser, *The Miracle of Jimmy Carter*.

140. Clendinen and Nagourney, *Out for Good*, 280.

141. See *Georgia Baptist Convention News Magazine*, May 27, 1976, 1; Charles Henderson, "The Politics of Love: Religion or Justice?" *Nation*, May 8, 1976, 56; Roger Rosenblatt, "The Carter Congregation," *New Republic*, August 7, 1976, 42.

142. Quoted in Martin, *With God on Our Side*, 148, 152; Clendinen and Nagourney, *Out for Good*, 279.

143. Ford quoted in Balmer, *God in the White House*, 88–89.

144. Quoted in *New York Times*, October 10, 1976, 42.

145. *New York Times*, October 11, 1976, 1.

146. Glad, *Jimmy Carter*, 383–87.

147. McWilliams, "The Meaning of the Election," 151.

148. "The Playboy Interview: Jimmy Carter," *Playboy* 23, no. 11 (1976): 63–86.

149. Ibid.

150. Schlafly, interview; Allen, interview; Criswell quoted in Martin, *With God on Our Side*, 158.

151. Criswell, Betty Ford, and Baker quoted in *New York Times*, October 11, 1976, 1.

152. Anderson quoted in Bourne, *Jimmy Carter*, 353–54.

153. Schram, *Running for President*, 336–37.

154. Falwell, interview; *Christianity Today*, November 19, 1976, 48.

155. Clendinen and Nagourney, *Out for Good*, 283; *Newsweek*, October 25, 1976, 68–70; Balmer, *God in the White House*, 109.

156. Landes and Criswell quoted in *New York Times*, October 13, 1976, 12.

157. Falwell, interview.

158. Marley, *Pat Robertson*, 41, 43–44.

159. *Washington Post*, October 7, 1976, 1; Glad, *Jimmy Carter*, 388–89.

160. Martin, *With God on Our Side*, 173; Jimmy Carter to Phil Strickland, December 17, 1976, folder (Christian Life Commission), 2/16/77–9/23/77, 02/16/1977–09/23/1977, box 91, Landon Butler Files, OCS, WHSF, JCL.

161. Allen quoted in Christensen, *Utopia Against the Family*, 36–37.

162. Glad, *Jimmy Carter*, 397–98; Carter quoted in *New York Times*, October 5, 1976, 8. See also Kraus, *The Great Debates*.

163. *Congressional Quarterly Guide*, 23. See also Stroud, *How Jimmy Won*; Clendinen and Nagourney, *Out for Good*, 283; Glad, *Jimmy Carter*, 400–405; Schram, *Running for President*, 361–63.

164. *Christianity Today*, December 13, 1976, 57; Marley, *Pat Robertson*, 45.

165. Bartley, *Jimmy Carter*, 12; Robinson, *Election Issues*, 11–21; McWilliams, "The Meaning of the Election," 155.

166. Quoted in *New York Times*, October 23, 1976, 29.

167. Turner, "Mirror Images," 5.

168. Schneider and Vinovskis, *The Law and Politics*, 199–201.

169. *New York Times*, February 13, 1976, 30, September 12, 1976, IV, 16, September 2, 1976, 30, September 3, 1976, 9, September 10, 1976, 19; Glad, *Jimmy Carter*, 310, 314, 319, 401.

170. Falwell, interview; Maddox, oral history; Lienesch, *Redeeming America*, 1; Glad, *Jimmy Carter*, 400–401; Martin, *With God on Our Side*, 157; Adams and Kavanagh-Baran, *Promise and Performance*, 78.

THREE Rootin' and Tootin'

1. *Christianity Today*, February 4, 1977, 51.

2. Prayer for the President, Pledging Prayerful Support to President-Elect Jimmy Carter, National Prayer for the President Day, January 16, 1977, folder National Prayer for the President Day, 01/16/1977–01/16/1977, box 91, Landon Butler Files, OCS, WHSF, JCL.

3. Carter quoted in Haas, *Jimmy Carter*, 3.

4. Quoted in *New York Times*, December 27, 1976, 28.

5. Gregg quoted in *Christianity Today*, April 1, 1977, 52.

6. *Christianity Today*, April 15, 1977, 38.

7. Carter quoted in Young, *God's Bullies*, 30.

8. James Allen to Martha Mitchell, November 16, 1977, and invitation, National Prayer Breakfast, February 2, 1978, both in folder National Prayer Breakfast, Washington Hilton 2/2/78 (O/A 5426), 02/1978–02/1978, box 91, Landon Butler Files, OCS, WHSF, JCL; Carter quoted in *Christianity Today*, February 18, 1977, 54.

9. Quoted in *New York Times*, December 27, 1976, 8.

10. Inaugural address, Jimmy Carter, January 20, 1977, Public Papers of the Presidents, American Presidency Project, University of California–Santa Barbara, http://www.presidency.ucsb.edu/ws/index.php?pid=6757&st=inaugural&st1, accessed January 19, 2008.

11. Quoted in *New York Times*, February 10, 1977, 39.

12. Carter, *Personal Beliefs*, 21–23, 106, 182, 217; Carter, *Keeping Faith*, 30.

13. *Christianity Today*, February 4, 1977, 51.

14. Carter, *Keeping Faith*, 19–20.

15. Tannenbaum quoted in *Christianity Today*, February 4, 1977, 51.

16. *Christianity Today*, January 7, 1977, 38.

17. Quoted in *Christianity Today*, March 4, 1977, 47.

18. Allen, interview; Maddox quoted in Martin, *With God on Our Side*, 401; *New York Times*, June 18, 1976, 11.

19. Harrell, *Pat Robertson*, 176–77; Smith quoted in Martin, *With God on Our Side*, 157; Falwell quoted in Adams and Kavanagh-Baran, *Promise and Performance*, 100, and Strober and Tomczak, *Jerry Falwell*, 179; Falwell, *Strength for the Journey*, 379.

20. John Pollock, *Billy Graham*, 278; Martin, *A Prophet with Honor*, 463; Mitchell, *Billy Graham*, 271.

21. Graham quoted in *Chicago Tribune*, December 28, 1976, 15.

22. *Chicago Daily News*, December 27, 1976, 8; *Chicago Sun-Times*, December 29, 1977, 11.

23. Memo, Phil Strickland to Jimmy Carter, December 3, 1976, folder (Christian Life Commission), 2/16/77–9/23/77, 02/16/1977–09/23/1977, box 91, Landon Butler Files, OCS, WHSF, JCL.

24. Memo, Phil Strickland to Jimmy Carter, Hamilton Jordan, and Landon Butler, February 16, 1977, folder (Christian Life Commission), 2/16/77–9/23/77, 02/16/1977–09/23/1977, box 91, Landon Butler Files, OCS, WHSF, JCL.

25. Memo, Phil Strickland to Landon Butler, February 27, 1977, folder (Christian Life Commission), 2/16/77–9/23/77, 02/16/1977–09/23/1977, box 91, Landon Butler Files, OCS, WHSF, JCL.

26. Memo, Phil Strickland to Midge Costanza and Chip Carter, March 21, 1977, folder (Christian Life Commission), 2/16/77–9/23/77, 02/16/1977–09/23/1977, box 91, Landon Butler Files, OCS, WHSF, JCL.

27. Memo, Phil Strickland to Laurie Lucey, July 15, 1977, folder (Christian Life Commission), 2/16/77–9/23/77, 02/16/1977–09/23/1977, box 91, Landon Butler Files, OCS, WHSF, JCL.

28. Jimmy Carter to James Sullivan, February 22, 1977, WHNF Southern Baptist Convention, WHCF, JCL.

29. Robert Schuller to Jimmy Carter, February 1, 1977, WHNF Robert Schuller, WHCF, JCL.

30. Jane Fenderson to R. H. Anderson, December 6, 1976, WHNF Christian Embassy, WHCF, JCL.

31. Pat Robertson to Jimmy Carter, December 19, 1976, WHNF Pat Robertson, WHCF, JCL.

32. Jim Bakker to President Jimmy Carter, March 3, 1977, and James King to Jim Bakker, September 26, 1977, both in WHNF Jim Bakker, WHCF, JCL.

33. Fran Voorde to Bill Bright, March 2, 1977, and Bill Bright to President Jimmy Carter, June 27, 1977, both in WHNF Campus Crusade, WHCF, JCL.

34. Memo, Fran Voorde to Tim Kraft, February 4, 1977, box 4, White House Subject Files, WHCF, JCL.

35. Memo, Rick Merrill to Kraft, February 22, 1977, box 4, White House Subject Files, WHCF, JCL.

36. Billy Graham to President Jimmy Carter, March 17, 1977, box 29, Zbigniew Brzezinski Files, White House Subject Files, WHCF, JCL.

37. Jane Ellis to Marilyn Haft, May 16, 1977, folder (Human Rights, Religion and Communism) 3/77–6/77 (O/A 4474), 03/1977–06/1977, box 75, Jane Wales Files, OPL, WHSF, JCL; *Right to Believe* 2 (March 1977): 1; *Washington Post*, February 20, 1977, 17.

38. George Mahon to Frank Moore, September 26, 1977, folder Mennonites (O/A 7290), box 28, Annie Gutierrez Files, DPS, WHSF, JCL.

39. Maddox, interview; Robert Maddox, oral history audiotape, JCL; Maddox, *Preacher at the White House*, 54–55.

40. Jimmy Carter to Phil Strickland, December 17, 1976, folder (Christian Life Commission), 2/16/77–9/23/77, 02/16/1977–09/23/1977, box 91, Landon Butler Files, OCS, WHSF, JCL.

41. Handwritten notes by Landon Butler on memo, Phil Strickland to Landon Butler, February 27, 1977, folder (Christian Life Commission), 2/16/77–9/23/77, 02/16/1977–09/23/1977, box 91, Landon Butler Files, OCS, WHSF, JCL; Maddox, oral history.

42. Jane Fenderson to R. H. Anderson, December 6, 1976, WHNF Christian Embassy, WHCF, JCL.

43. Jim Bakker to President Jimmy Carter, March 3, 1977, and James King to Jim Bakker, September 26, 1977, both in WHNF Jim Bakker, WHCF, JCL.

44. Memo, Fran Voorde to Rick Merrill, February 21, 1977, box 4, White House Subject Files, WHCF, JCL.

45. Jim Jones to Fran Voorde, February 28, 1977, Oral Roberts to President Jimmy Carter, February 24, 1977, and Jimmy Carter to Oral Roberts, February 27, 1977, all in box 4, White House Subject Files, WHCF, JCL.

46. Jimmy Carter to Robert Schuller, August 22, 1977, WHNF Robert Schuller, WHCF, JCL; Schuller, *Reach Out for New Life*.

47. Landon Kite to Robert Schuller, November 23, 1977, WHNF Robert Schuller, WHCF, JCL. See also Schuller, *The Peak to Peek Principle* and *Peace of Mind*.

48. Fran Voorde to Bill Bright, July 8, 1977, WHNF Campus Crusade, WHCF, JCL.

49. Eleanor Page to Rosalynn Carter, September 13, 1977, and James Fenderson to Eleanor Page, September 20, 1977, both in WHNF Campus Crusade, WHCF, JCL.

50. Hamilton Jordan to Melvin Todd, October 3, 1977, status report on Mennonites in Seminole, Texas, September 30, 1977, and memo, Leonel Castillo to Annie Gutierrez, October 28, 1977, all in folder Mennonites (O/A 7290), box 28, Annie Gutierrez Files, DPS, WHSF, JCL.

51. Memo, Zbigniew Brzezinski to Jimmy Carter, undated, box 29, Zbigniew Brzezinski Files, White House Subject Files, WHCF, JCL.

52. Marie-Christine Roberts to President Jimmy Carter, May 27, 1977, and Billy Graham to Jimmy Carter, April 9, 1977, both in box 29, Zbigniew Brzezinski Files, White House Subject Files, WHCF, JCL.

53. Remarks, Martha Mitchell to Business and Professional Association, Church of God in Christ, April 22, 1977, and Samuel Jackson to Martha Mitchell, March 23, 1977, both in folder Church of God in Christ 4/22/77 (O/A 5425), 04/1977–04/1977, box 4, Martha Mitchell Files, APSP, WHSF, JCL.

54. Samuel Jackson to Martha Mitchell, May 2, 1977, folder Church of God in Christ 4/22/77 (O/A 5425), 04/1977–04/1977, box 4, Martha Mitchell Files, APSP, WHSF, JCL.

55. Sandra Adams to Floyd Robertson, November 3, 1977, and memo, Sandra Adams to Seymour, December 6, 1977, both in folder National Association of Evangelicals 2/78 (O/A 4391) (1), 02/1978–02/1978, box 113, OPL, WHSF, JCL.

56. Statement of Welcome, Thirty-fourth Annual Convention of the National Religious Broadcasters, January 26, 1977, and memo, Hasek to S. Eizenstat, January 26, 1977, both in WHNF National Religious Broadcasters, WHCF, JCL.

57. Fran Voorde to Porter Routh, February 18, 1977, and Patricia Yaroch Bario to John C. Stevens, February 28, 1977, both in WHNF Southern Baptist Convention, WHCF, JCL.

58. Memo, Fran Voorde to Congressman Jim Wright, April 4, 1977, and Fran Voorde to Porter Routh, April 1, 1977, both in WHNF Southern Baptist Convention, WHCF, JCL.

59. Itinerary, meeting with directors, Southern Baptist Convention, May 13, 1977, WHNF Southern Baptist Convention, WHCF, JCL.

60. Glendon McCullough to President Jimmy Carter, May 19, 1977, WHNF Southern Baptist Convention, WHCF, JCL.

61. Itinerary, meeting with Missions Challenge Commission, Southern Baptist Convention, June 7, 1977, WHNF Southern Baptist Convention, WHCF, JCL.

62. Bill Bright to President Jimmy Carter, June 5, 1977, and Fran Voorde to Bill Bright, July 7, 1977, both in WHNF Bill Bright, WHCF, JCL.

63. Allen, interview; minutes, Mission Volunteer Committee, June 30, 1977, memo, C to Rita, August 10, 1977, Bill Bright to President and Mrs. Carter, August 14, 1977, and Rosalynn Carter to Bill Bright, August 22, 1977, all in WHNF Bill Bright, WHCF, JCL.

64. Presidential statement, Southern Baptist Convention, June 1977, WHNF Southern Baptist Convention, WHCF, JCL.

65. Clendinen and Nagourney, *Out for Good*, 283.

66. Maddox, oral history.

67. Quoted in Marley, *Pat Robertson*, 46, 50.

68. Adams and Kavanagh-Baran, *Promise and Performance*, 19–20.

69. Hartmann, "Feminism," 227, 230–31.

70. Bruce Voeller and Jean O'Leary to Margaret Costanza, February 1, 1977, folder (Gay Rights: Memos, Correspondence, Clippings) 5/76–8/78 (O/A 5771), 05/1976–08/1978, box 4, Margaret Costanza Files, OPL, WHSF, JCL.

71. *Washington Post*, March 20, 1977, 4; Cook, "Women White House Advisors," 92–94; Tinker, *Women in Washington*, 19–20.

72. *New York Times*, March 29, 1977, 27; Cook, "Women White House Advisors," 92.

73. Schlafly, interview; Dennis Atkinson to President Jimmy Carter, April 13, 1977, WHNF Phyllis Schlafly, WHCF, JCL.

74. Falwell, interview.

75. Robertson quoted in Martin, *With God on Our Side*, 166.

76. Exit interview, Sarah Weddington, January 2, 1981, JCL, 13.

77. McMichael quoted in Adams and Kavanagh-Baran, *Promise and Performance*, 79.

78. See Califano, *Governing America*.

79. *New York Times*, January 14, 1977, 14, January 24, 1977, 29, January 25, 1977, 10, January 31, 1977, 22.

80. NARAL to Jimmy Carter, March 17, 1977, folder 1/77–12/77 (O/A 5772), box 1, Margaret Costanza Files, OPL, WHSF, JCL.

81. *Maher v. Roe*, 432 U.S. 464 (1977); *Beal v. Doe*, 432 U.S. 438 (1977); quoted in *New York Times*, June 21, 1977, 20.

82. *New York Times*, June 18, 1977, 1, June 19, 1977, 24, June 22, 1977, 17. See also Lincoln et al., "The Court, the Congress," 207.

83. Hyde quoted in *New York Times*, August 3, 1977, 11, August 7, 1977, IV, 2, September 13, 1977, 14.

84. Henry Hyde et al. to Jimmy Carter, June 12, 1977, folder Abortion (O/A 6468), box 1, Annie Gutierrez Files, DPS, WHSF, JCL; Harold Brown to President Jimmy Carter, July 17, 1977, WHNF Harold Brown, WHCF, JCL.

85. Mahon quoted in *New York Times*, October 14, 1977, 14; Flood quoted in *New York Times*, October 6, 1977, 21.

86. Transcript, press conference, Jimmy Carter, July 12, 1977, folder 1/77–12/77 (O/A 5772), box 1, Margaret Costanza Files, OPL, WHSF, JCL.

87. Jan Peterson to Margaret Costanza, July 13, 1977, memo, Margaret Costanza to the president, July 13, 1977, and handwritten comments to Jimmy Carter on memo, Margaret Costanza to the president, July 13, 1977, all in folder 1/77–12/77 (O/A 5772), box 1, Margaret Costanza Files, OPL, WHSF, JCL.

88. Schulman, "Slouching toward the Supply Side," 51–61.

89. Quoted in *New York Times*, June 19, 1977, 16.

90. *New York Times*, February 23, 1977, II, 5; Califano quoted in *New York Times*, June 26, 1977, 22.

91. For an overview of the politics of family planning, see Finkle and McIntosh, *The New Politics of Population*, and Homans, *The Sexual Politics*.

92. Falwell, interview.

93. *New York Times*, June 24, 1977, 12.

94. Quoted in *New York Times*, August 21, 1977, III, 1.

95. Christensen, *Utopia Against the Family*, 39.

96. Quoted in *New York Times*, October 29, 1977, 17.

97. Quoted in *New York Times*, June 19, 1977, 16.

98. Marshner, interview; quoted in Martin, *With God on Our Side*, 174.

99. White House Conference on Families, "A Brief History, National Advisory Committee, July, 1979," folder July 20, 1979—Remarks—Reception—White House Conference on the Family, box 51, Achsah Nesmith Files, PSWF, WHSF, JCL; memo, Jane Wales to Margaret Costanza, February 13, 1978, folder White House Conference on Families 2/78 (O/A 4467), 02/1978–02/1978, box 67, Jane Wales Files, OPL, WHSF, JCL.

100. Memo, Jane Wales to Margaret Costanza, February 17, 1978, and memo, Diane Herrmann to Federal Women's Program Managers, January 30, 1978, both in folder White House Conference on Families 2/78 (O/A 4467), 02/1978–01/1978, box 67, Jane Wales Files, OPL, WHSF, JCL.

101. Eizenstat quoted in *New York Times*, June 19, 1977, 1, June 21, 1977, 18.

102. Rice quoted in *New York Times*, June 19, 1977, 1.

103. *New York Times*, January 20, 1977, 19.

104. *New York Times*, March 10, 1977, 18.

105. Felsenthal, *The Sweetheart of the Silent Majority*, 245–46; quoted in *St. Louis Post Dispatch*, February 5, 1977, 14.

106. *St. Louis Post Dispatch*, March 5, 1977, 16.

107. Quoted in *New York Times*, March 31, 1977, 22.

108. *New York Times*, April 1, 1977, 16; Hatch, *The Equal Rights Amendment*, 90–94.

109. *Eagle Forum*, March 1977, 2.

110. Margaret McKenna to J. K. Grier, March 21, 1977, folder Equal Rights Amendment, 1/77–10/77, 01/1977–10/1977, box 126, Margaret McKenna Files, White House Counsel Office Files, WHSF, JCL.

111. Siegel quoted in news summary, Office of Public Liaison, March 3, 1977, folder Women's Movement (Newsclippings), 2/77–11/77 (O/A 5771), 02/1977–11/1977, box 12, Margaret Costanza Files, OPL, WHSF, JCL.

112. Quoted in *New York Times*, April 13, 1977, II, 4.

113. Memo, John Harmon to Margaret McKenna, October 5, 1977, folder Equal Rights Amendment, 1/77–10/77, 01/1977–10/1977, box 126, Margaret McKenna Files, White House Counsel Office Files, WHSF, JCL.

114. Memo, Robert Lipshutz and Margaret McKenna to Jimmy Carter, October 11, 1977, folder Equal Rights Amendment, 1/77–10/77, 01/1977–10/1977, box 126, Margaret

McKenna Files, White House Counsel Office Files, WHSF, JCL; agenda, White House Meeting on ERA, October 12, 1977, folder (Equal Rights Amendment Strategy: National Organization for Women—NOW), 10/77–1/78 (O/A 4467), 10/1977–01/1978, box 66, Jane Wales Files, OPL, WHSF, JCL.

115. Schlafly, interview; *New York Times*, August 13, 1977, 9; Schlafly quoted in *New York Times*, April 17, 1977, 38.

116. Steinem quoted in *New York Times*, October 2, 1977, 24.

117. *New York Times*, August 23, 1977, 12; Carter quoted in *New York Times*, August 27, 1977, 8.

118. Memo, John Harmon to Robert Lipshutz, February 19, 1977, folder Equal Rights Amendment, 1/77–10/77, 01/1977–10/1977, box 126, Margaret McKenna Files, White House Counsel Office Files, WHSF, JCL.

119. *Miami Herald*, March 27, 1977, 4; William Zinkil to Jimmy Carter, March 28, 1977, and memo, Margaret McKenna to Annie Gutierrez, April 11, 1977, both in folder Equal Rights Amendment (O/A 8112), box 17, Annie Gutierrez Files, DPS, WHSF, JCL.

120. Hartmann, "Feminism," 228.

121. Ibid., 228–29; Costain, *Inviting Women's Rebellion*, 93–95.

122. Quoted in Hartmann, "Feminism," 232.

123. *Public Papers of the Presidents, Jimmy Carter*, 1978, 1643.

124. Hartmann, "Feminism," 233.

125. Quoted in ibid., 227; Bourne, *Jimmy Carter*, 314–15, 363. See also Jordan, *No Such Thing*.

126. Abzug and Kelber, *Gender Gap*, 46–47; *Washington Post*, January 23, 1977, 1.

127. Quoted in *New York Times*, June 28, 1977, 36.

128. Quoted in *New York Times*, March 11, 1977, 25.

129. Quoted in *New York Times*, January 19, 1977, 14.

130. Quoted in *Miami Herald*, January 19, 1977, 1; *Miami News*, January 18, 1977, 1.

131. *New York Times*, May 10, 1977, 18; *Christianity Today*, November 3, 1978, 46, July 8, 1977, 36.

132. Bruce Voeller and Jean O'Leary to Margaret Costanza, February 1, 1977, folder (Gay Rights: Memos, Correspondence, Clippings) 5/76–8/78 (O/A 5771), 05/1976–08/1978, box 4, Margaret Costanza Files, OPL, WHSF, JCL.

133. Costanza quoted in *New York Times*, February 16, 1977, 14.

134. Jean O'Leary and Bruce Voeller to Franklin Kelly et al., March 15, 1977, folder (Gay) Civil Rights 10/76–2/78 (O/A 4609), 10/1976–02/1978, box 22, Seymour Wishman Files, OPL, WHSF, JCL.

135. Memo, Marilyn Haft to Margaret Costanza, March 25, 1977, folder (National Gay Task Force: Agency Meetings) 3/77–10/77 (O/A 4499), 03/1977–10/1977, box 27, Seymour Wishman Files, OPL, WHSF, JCL.

136. Edward Koch to Jimmy Carter, March 21, 1977, folder (Gay Rights: Support Letters) 2/77–3/77 (O/A 5771), 02/1977–03/1977, box 4, Margaret Costanza Files, OPL, WHSF, JCL.

137. John Burton to Jimmy Carter, March 11, 1977, folder (Gay Rights: Support Letters) 2/77–3/77 (O/A 5771), 02/1977–03/1977, box 4, Margaret Costanza Files, OPL, WHSF, JCL.

138. HR 2998, *Capitol Hill: The Newsletter of the Gay Rights National Lobby* 1, no. 1 (1977): 1; "Gay Rights Bill Gathers Steam," *Washington Blade* 8, no. 4 (1977): 8.

139. Memo, Bruce Voeller and Jean O'Leary to NGTF Board of Directors, February 3, 1977, position description, February 1977, and memo, Bruce Voeller and Jean O'Leary to NGTF Board of Directors, February 7, 1977, all in folder National Gay Task Force Flyers and Publications, 12/76–3/77 (O/A 4499), 12/1976–03/1977, box 27, OPL, WHSF, JCL.

140. *It's Time: The Newsletter of the National Gay Task Force* (special bonus issue, 1977), folder (Gay Rights Publications) 3/75–1/78 (O/A 5771), 03/1975–01/1978, box 4, OPL, WHSF, JCL.

141. Drew Brinckerhoff to Loretta Lotman, June 24, 1977, folder (Gay Rights Publications) 3/75–1/78 (O/A 5771), 03/1975–01/1978, box 4, OPL, WHSF, JCL.

142. Peter Cusack to Robert Livingston and Loretta Lotman, April 10, 1977, folder (Gay Rights Publications) 3/75–1/78 (O/A 5771), 03/1975–01/1978, box 4, OPL, WHSF, JCL.

143. Support Statements Packet, National Gay Task Force, folder (Gay Rights Publications) 3/75–1/78 (O/A 5771), 03/1975–01/1978, box 4, OPL, WHSF, JCL.

144. Policy statement, Bureau of the Prisons, folder Prisons—Homosexuals (O/A 7291), box 31, Annie Gutierrez Files, DPS, WHSF, JCL.

145. Gutierrez, interview; Paul Albert to Annie Gutierrez, February 25, 1977, folder Prisons—Homosexuals (O/A 7291), box 31, Annie Gutierrez Files, DPS, WHSF, JCL.

146. Norman Carlson to Edward Koch, December 10, 1976, folder Prisons—Homosexuals (O/A 7291), box 31, Annie Gutierrez Files, DPS, WHSF, JCL.

147. *The National Gay Task Force v. Carlson*, No. C.A. 27-0809 (D.D.C. 1980); *Arizona Gay News*, April 14, 1978, 1.

148. Moss Teller to NGTF, February 9, 1977, folder Prisons—Homosexuals (O/A 7291), box 31, Annie Gutierrez Files, DPS, WHSF, JCL.

149. The cosponsors were Stewart McKinney, (R-Conn.), William Clay (D-Mo.), Louis Stokes (D-Ohio), John Conyers (D-Mich.), Yvonne Burke (D-Calif.), Augustus Hawkins (D-Calif.), Norman Mineta (D-Calif.), Abner Mikva (D-Ill.), and Charles Diggs (D-Mich.).

150. Press release, NGTF, February 8, 1977, folder National Gay Task Force—Need for Federal Legislation, 3/77 (O/A 4496), 03/1977–03/1977, box 28, Seymour Wishman Files, OPL, WHSF, JCL.

151. Harvey Milk to Jimmy Carter, July 4, 1977, WHNF Harvey Milk, WHCF, JCL.

152. Shaw quoted in *Variety*, December 8, 1976, 23.

153. *Gay Community News*, December 25, 1976, 1.

154. *Miami Herald*, December 3, 1976, 1.

155. Quoted in *Washington Post*, March 28, 1977, 3.

156. *New York Times*, February 25, 1977, II, 7, March 3, 1977, 27.

157. Action report, NGTF, April 1977, folder National Gay Task Force, 4/77–5/77 (O/A 4461), 04/1977–05/1977, box 91, Jane Wales Files, OPL, WHSF, JCL.

158. Quoted in *Santa Barbara, California, News-Press*, February 24, 1977, B-6.

159. *New York Times*, March 30, 1977, 10.

160. *New York Times*, May 10, 1977, 18; action report, NGTF, May 1977, folder National Gay Task Force, 4/77–5/77 (O/A 4461), 04/1977–05/1977, box 91, Jane Wales Files, OPL, WHSF, JCL; *Christianity Today*, May 20, 1977, 46.

161. *Christianity Today*, March 18, 1977, 30; Helms quoted in Clendinen and Nagourney, *Out for Good*, 300.

162. Memo, Marilyn Haft to Margaret Costanza, March 31, 1977, folder (National Gay

Task Force: Agency Meetings) 3/77–10/77 (O/A 4499), 03/1977–10/1977, box 27, Seymour Wishman Files, OPL, WHSF, JCL.

163. Henry Waxman to Jimmy Carter, March 3, 1977, Paul McCloskey to Jimmy Carter, March 8, 1977, and Charles Rangel to Jimmy Carter, March 2, 1977, all in folder (Gay Rights: Support Letters) 2/77–3/77 (O/A 5771), 02/1977–03/1977, box 4, Margaret Costanza Files, OPL, WHSF.

164. Robert Gibson to Jimmy Carter, March 14, 1977, and Karen DeCrow to Jimmy Carter, February 26, 1977, both in folder (Gay Rights: Support Letters) 2/77–3/77 (O/A 5771), 02/1977–03/1977, box 4, Margaret Costanza Files, OPL, WHSF, JCL; memo, Marilyn Haft to Margaret Costanza, March 25, 1977, folder Gay Rights—Civil Rights, box 7, Robert Malson Files, DPS, WHSF, JCL.

165. Agenda, NGTF Meeting, March 26, 1977, folder National Gay Task Force Correspondence, 9/76–2/78 (O/A 4499), 09/1976–02/1978, box 27, Seymour Wishman Files, OPL, WHSF, JCL; notes of White House NGTF meeting, Bob Malson, March 26, 1977, folder Gay Rights—Civil Rights, box 7, Robert Malson Files, DPS, WHSF, JCL; Clendinen and Nagourney, *Out for Good*, 288–89; Lou Romano, "Gays Meet with Carter Aides," *Washington Blade* 8, no. 4 (1977): 1, 6.

166. David Dahlquist, "The White House Delegation," *Washington Blade* 8, no. 5 (1977): 10–11; quoted in *It's Time: The Newsletter of the National Gay Task Force* 3, no. 7 (1977): 3.

167. Ibid.; Clendinen and Nagourney, *Out for Good*, 289–90; *New York Times*, March 27, 1977, 13; O'Leary quoted in *Richmond Times-Dispatch*, March 27, 1977, A7.

168. Schlafly, interview; quoted in *New York Times*, March 28, 1977, 56.

169. Memo, Richie Reiman to Margaret Costanza, March 28, 1977, folder (Gays, Jimmy Carter on) 3/76–3/77 (O/A 4499), 03/1976–03/1977, box 22, Seymour Wishman Files, OPL, WHSF, JCL.

170. Transcript, Jody Powell on *Meet the Press*, March 27, 1977, folder (Gays, Jimmy Carter on) 3/76–3/77 (O/A 4499), 03/1976–03/1977, box 22, Seymour Wishman Files, OPL, WHSF, JCL.

171. Photocopy, *National Enquirer*, undated, folder Gay Rights: Memos, Correspondence, Clippings, 5/76–8/78 (O/A 5771), 05/1976–08/1978, box 4, Margaret Costanza Files, OPL, WHSF, JCL.

172. Quoted in *New York Times*, April 16, 1977, 12, April 20, 1977, 16.

173. PL 94-167.

174. Quoted in *It's Time: The Newsletter of the National Gay Task Force* 1, no. 5 (1977): 1.

175. Press release, NGTF, "Sexual Preference Added to List of IWY Issues," April 15, 1977, folder National Gay Task Force, 4/77–5/77 (O/A 4461), 04/1977–05/1977, box 91, Jane Wales Files, OPL, WHSF, JCL.

176. Quoted in *New York Times*, July 25, 1977, 26.

177. *New York Times*, August 16, 1977, II, 10, October 27, 1977, II, 17.

178. Eizenstat and Costanza both quoted in Cook, "Women White House Advisors," 94.

179. Memo, Jan Peterson to Margaret Midge Costanza, July 20, 1977, folder 1/77–12/77 (O/A 5772), box 1, Margaret Costanza Files, OPL, WHSF, JCL; memo, Jan Peterson to Margaret Costanza, July 26, 1977, folder Women and Abortion, 4/77–9/77 (O/A 5772), box 10, Margaret Costanza Files, OPL, WHSF, JCL; Downey quoted in Hartmann, "Feminism," 231.

180. Draft of letter, Margaret Costanza to Jimmy Carter, undated, folder Abortion, 1/77–12/77 (O/A 5772), box 1, Margaret Costanza Files, OPL, WHSF, JCL.

181. Carter quoted in *New York Times*, August 27, 1977, 22; Rowland Evans and Robert Novak, "Quashing an In-House Revolt on Abortion," undated copy, folder Abortion, 1/77–12/77 (O/A 5772), box 1, Margaret Costanza Files, OPL, WHSF, JCL.

182. Eleanor Holmes Norton to Jimmy Carter, August 16, 1977, Barbara Ann Babcock to Jimmy Carter, August 12, 1977, and Esther Peterson to Jimmy Carter, August 7, 1977, all in folder Women and Abortion, 4/77–9/77 (O/A 5772), box 10, Margaret Costanza Files, OPL, WHSF, JCL.

183. For an overview of Carter's relationship with the feminist movement, see Cook, "Women White House Advisors"; Costanza quoted in *New York Times*, August 27, 1977; quoted in *New York Times*, July 29, 1977, 16.

184. Falwell, interview.

185. Nellie Gray to Jimmy Carter, June 18, 1977, and Fran Voorde to Nellie Gray, June 23, 1977, both in folder Abortion (O/A 6468), box 1, Annie Gutierrez Files, DPS, WHSF, JCL.

186. *New York Times*, October 13, 1977, 15, October 14, 1977, 14, November 1, 1977, 29, November 2, 1977, 19, November 4, 1977, 1, November 28, 1977, 19, November 30, 1977, 20, November 12, 1977, IV, 1.

187. Bryant and Falwell quoted in Clendinen and Nagourney, *Out for Good*, 306.

188. *Christianity Today*, November 4, 1977, 52.

189. *New York Times*, May 29, 1977, 22.

190. *Christianity Today*, June 17, 1977, 6; Bryant and Kunst quoted in *Christianity Today*, June 8, 1977, 1; Falwell, interview.

191. *Washington Post*, June 17, 1977, 25.

192. Quoted in *Washington Post*, June 9, 1977, 28.

193. Carter quoted in memo, Marilyn Haft to Dick Pettigrew, November 28, 1977, folder (Gay Rights: Jimmy Carter's Views On) 10/76 (O/A 5772), 10/1976–10/1976, box 4, Margaret Costanza Files, OPL, WHSF, JCL.

194. Carter quoted in *New York Times*, June 19, 1977, 16.

195. *New York Times*, June 27, 1977, 1, 20.

196. *Christianity Today*, July 8, 1977, 25; Turner, "Mirror Images," 14.

197. *New York Times*, July 17, 1977, 34.

198. *New York Times*, October 25, 1977, 41, July 17, 1977, VII, 31; *Time*, December 4, 1978, 68; Altman, "What Changed," 52, 57.

199. *New York Times*, August 8, 1977, 47.

200. *New York Times*, October 10, 1977, 24.

201. Schlafly, interview; Turner, "Mirror Images," 17–18; Gallagher and Bull, *Perfect Enemies*, 12.

202. Carter and Costanza quoted in Marcus, *Making History*, 271.

203. Quoted in *New York Times*, November 4, 1977, 14.

204. Whitney, *The Equal Rights Amendment*, 28–29; *New York Times*, November 18, 1977, II, 4.

205. Schlafly, interview; *New York Times*, November 19, 1977, 22, November 20, 1977, 1, quoted in November 21, 1977, 44.

206. Schlafly and Millett quoted in *New York Times*, November 15, 1977, 46.

207. *New York Times*, November 21, 1977, 44.

208. *New York Times*, November 23, 1977, 14; Whitney, *The Equal Rights Amendment*, 29.

209. Schlafly, interview; *New York Times*, November 20, 1977, 32.

210. Schlafly, interview; quoted in *New York Times*, November 20, 1977, 32.

211. Marcus, *Making History*, 272–73; Shelton quoted in *New York Times*, November 15, 1977, 46.

212. Schlafly and Smothers quoted in *New York Times*, November 20, 1977, 32.

213. *New York Times*, November 21, 1977, 44; *To Form a More Perfect Union*; *Christianity Today*, December 30, 1977, 38.

214. Schlafly and Smothers quoted in *New York Times*, November 20, 1977, 32.

215. *New York Times*, November 21, 1977, 44, November 24, 1977, II, 4.

216. Schlafly, interview; *Newsweek*, July 27, 1977, 35; quoted in Carroll, *Famous in America*, 245.

217. *Phyllis Schlafly Report* 10, no. 6 (1977): sec. 1, 4.

218. *Phyllis Schlafly Report* 10, no. 9 (1977): sec. 2, 1–4. Schlafly did praise Democratic senator Sam Ervin.

219. Quoted in Carroll, *Famous in America*, 245.

220. Quoted in *New York Times*, December 19, 1977, 20.

221. *National Association of Social Workers News*, March 1978, 1; *Report from the White House Conference on Families* 1, no. 1 (1979): 1–2.

222. Proclamation 4536, November 9, 1977; *New York Times*, November 13, 1977, 16.

223. Thomas and Carter quoted in *Idaho Statesman*, February 19, 1977, B5; Carter quoted in Midge Costanza, handwritten notes, undated, folder Anti-Abortion Groups, January, 1978, (O/A 5773), 1/1978–1/1978, box 1, Margaret Costanza Files, OPL, WHSF, JCL.

224. Joseph L. Powell Jr. to Walker L. Knight, December 9, 1977, WHNF Southern Baptist Convention, WHCF, JCL.

225. Audiotape, Exit Interview, Maddox, JCL.

226. Carter, *Christmas in Plains*, 109.

227. Bourne, *Jimmy Carter*, 428.

FOUR   His Faith and Virtue Were Not Enough

1. Lankevich, *James E. Carter*, 99–102; *Washington Post*, January 20, 1978, 1.

2. Marshner, interview; Marshner, *Blackboard Tyranny*, 35, 40, 61, 128–29, 147, 290.

3. LaHaye quoted in Edel, *Defenders of the Faith*, 136–37.

4. *Christianity Today*, December 30, 1977, 8.

5. Zwier, *Born-Again Politics*, 25–26.

6. Quoted in Moen, *The Christian Right and Congress*, 27; *Los Angeles Times*, May 19, 1980, 21.

7. Quoted in Moen, *The Christian Right and Congress*, 11; see also Diamond, *Not by Politics Alone*, 65–66.

8. See Stueck, "Placing Jimmy Carter's Foreign Policy," 244–66; and Lankevich, *James E. Carter*, 8–25; Carter, *The Blood of Abraham*, xviii.

9. Lankevich, *James E. Carter*, 99–102.

10. Strom Thurmond to Dan C. Tate, February 23, 1978, WHNF James Kennedy, WHCF, JCL.

11. D. James Kennedy, "Revival or Removal," *Presbyterian Journal*, June 4, 1978, 7–9.

12. R. J. Sproul, "The Sensuous Christian," *Presbyterian Journal*, January 4, 1978, 10–13.

13. Landon Kite to John G. Farmer, February 28, 1978, and Landon Kite to Strom Thurmond, February 28, 1978, both in WHNF James Kennedy, WHCF, JCL.

14. Lankevich, *James E. Carter*, 28; Stueck, "Placing Jimmy Carter's Foreign Policy," 251–52.

15. Falwell, *Strength for the Journey*, 380.

16. Howard Phillips to Jimmy Carter, February 12, 1989, WHNF Howard Phillips, WHCF, JCL.

17. Solzhenitsyn quoted in D'Souza, *Falwell Before the Millennium*, 107.

18. Ed Barker to Fran Voorde, December 22, 1978, WHNF National Religious Broadcasters, WHCF, JCL.

19. Carl Richardson to President Jimmy Carter, December 20, 1977, WHNF National Religious Broadcasters, WHCF, JCL.

20. Presidential Statement of Welcome, Thirty-fifth Annual Convention of the National Religious Broadcasters, January 23, 1978, WHNF National Religious Broadcasters, WHCF, JCL.

21. Memo, Hallie to Rosalynn Carter, undated, WHNF National Religious Broadcasters, WHCF, JCL.

22. Abe Van Der Puy to President Jimmy Carter, July 14, 1978, WHNF National Religious Broadcasters, WHCF, JCL.

23. Memo, Pat Bario to Fran Voorde, September 5, 1978, WHNF National Religious Broadcasters, WHCF, JCL.

24. Fran Voorde to Abe Van Der Puy, September 18, 1978, WHNF National Religious Broadcasters, WHCF, JCL.

25. Linda Beversluis to Fran Voorde, February 15, 1978, and Fran Voorde to Linda Beversluis, March 6, 1978, both in WHNF Robert Schuller, WHCF, JCL; William Briare to President Jimmy Carter, January 12, 1978, and Fran Voorde to Kenneth Forshee, January 24, 1978, both in WHNF Billy Graham, WHCF, JCL.

26. Rosalynn Carter to Friends, Christian Life Commission, March 23, 1978, WHNF Christian Life Commission, WHCF, JCL.

27. Jerry Falwell to President Jimmy Carter, February 1, 1978, and Landon Kite to Jerry Falwell, March 2, 1978, both in WHNF Jerry Falwell, WHCF, JCL.

28. Memo, Landon Kite to Eliska Coolidge, June 15, 1978, WHNF Campus Crusade, WHCF, JCL.

29. Telegraph, Pat Robertson to President Jimmy Carter, April 26, 1978, WHNF Pat Robertson, WHCF, JCL.

30. Jim Purks to Pat Robertson, May 9, 1978, WHNF Pat Robertson, WHCF, JCL.

31. William Briare to President Jimmy Carter, January 12, 1978, and Fran Voorde to Kenneth Forshee, January 24, 1978, both in WHNF Billy Graham, WHCF, JCL.

32. Rosalynn Carter to Friends, Christian Life Commission, March 23, 1978, WHNF Christian Life Commission, WHCF, JCL; Landon Kite to Dr. and Mrs. Zbigniew Brzezinski, January 1978, WHNF Campus Crusade, WHCF, JCL.

33. Jimmy Carter to Robert Schuller, July 23, 1978, memo, Charles Vanwagenen to Anne Wexler, August 21, 1978, Robert Schuller to Jimmy Carter, January 9, 1979, and Landon Kite to Robert Schuller, February 5, 1979, all in WHNF Robert Schuller, WHCF, JCL.

34. Jimmy Carter to Jimmy Allen, January 1978, Jimmy Allen to Fran Voorde, March 3, 1978, and itinerary, Mission Services Corporation Dinner, May 2, 1978, all in WHNF Southern Baptist Convention, WHCF, JCL.

35. Allen, interview; transcript, remarks of the president, Mission Services Corporation Dinner, May 2, 1978, and Jimmy Carter to William Cockrill, May 8, 1978, both in WHNF Southern Baptist Convention, WHCF, JCL.

36. White House Conference on Families, "A Brief History, National Advisory Committee, July, 1979," folder July 20, 1979—Remarks—Reception—White House Conference on the Family, box 51, Achsah Nesmith Files, PSWF, WHSF, JCL.

37. "Resolution on the White House Conference on Family Life, Adopted by the Southern Baptist Convention June 15, 1978," WHNF Southern Baptist Convention, WHCF, JCL.

38. *National Association of Social Workers News*, March 1978, 1; *Report from the White House Conference on Families* 1, no. 1 (1979): 1–2.

39. Jack Harwell to Fran Voorde, April 14, 1978, WHNF Southern Baptist Convention, WHCF, JCL; Robert Maddox, oral history audiotape, JCL; Maddox, interview.

40. *Time*, January 9, 1978; Turner, "Mirror Images," 13.

41. Wattleton quoted in *New York Times*, February 3, 1978, 14, March 2, 1978, 16.

42. Quoted in *New York Times*, February 11, 1978, 18.

43. *New York Times*, March 1, 1978, 14.

44. Memo, Jane Wales to Margaret Costanza, January 31, 1978, and memo, Jane Wales and Shelly Weinstein to Margaret Costanza, February 11, 1978, both in folder (Equal Rights Amendment Strategy: National Organization for Women—NOW), 10/77–1/78 (O/A 4467) 10/1977–01/1978, box 66, Jane Wales Files, OPL, WHSF, JCL.

45. Memo, Margaret Costanza to Jimmy Carter, February 14, 1978, folder (Equal Rights Amendment Strategy: National Organization for Women—NOW), 10/77–1/78 (O/A 4467) 10/1977–01/1978, box 66, Jane Wales Files, OPL, WHSF, JCL.

46. Minutes and agenda of February 15, 1978, ERA strategy meeting, folder (Equal Rights Amendment Strategy: National Organization for Women—NOW), 10/77–1/78 (O/A 4467) 10/1977–01/1978, box 66, Jane Wales Files, OPL, WHSF, JCL.

47. Cook, "Women White House Advisors," 95–96.

48. Ibid., 97; *Washington Post*, March 23, 1978, 1; quoted in *New York Times*, March 23, 1978, II, 13.

49. Eizenstat and Wexler quoted in Cook, "Women White House Advisors," 99; *Washington Post*, May 13, 1978, 8.

50. Falwell, interview.

51. Memo, Margaret Costanza, undated, 1978, folder ERA (notebook) (1), box 29, APWA, WHSF, JCL.

52. Statement of policy resolutions, National Governors Association Conference, Washington, D.C., February 26–28, 1978, and memo, Heather Pars to Margaret Costanza, February 17, 1978, both in folder (Equal Rights Amendment Strategy) 2/78 (O/A 4467), 02/1978–02/1978, box 66, Jane Wales Files, OPL, WHSF, JCL.

53. Raymond Vickory to Jimmy Carter, February 16, 1978, folder Equal Rights Amendment, 11/77–1/79, 11/1977–01/1979, box 126, Margaret McKenna Files, White House Counsel Office Files, WHSF, JCL.

54. *New York Times*, February 1, 1978, 19, February 19, 1978, 18, April 4, 1978, III, 18.

55. Memo, John Harmon to Margaret McKenna, March 21, 1978, folder Equal Rights Amendment, 11/77–1/79, 11/1977–01/1979, box 126, Margaret McKenna Files, White House Counsel Office Files, WHSF, JCL.

56. Memo, Margaret McKenna to Midge Costanza, March 22, 1978, folder Equal Rights Amendment, 11/77–1/79, 11/1977–01/1979, box 126, Margaret McKenna Files, White House Counsel Office Files, WHSF, JCL.

57. *New York Times*, July 30, 1978, 1.

58. Quoted in Hartmann, "Feminism," 233–34.

59. *Christianity Today*, July 21, 1978, 54.

60. *New York Times*, May 2, 1978, 18, July 7, 1978, 21.

61. Schlafly, interview; press release, Transcultural Communications, Inc., July 28, 1978, folder ERA (2–7), box 29, APWA, WHSF, JCL; *New York Times*, August 8, 1978, IV, 3.

62. *New York Times*, May 12, 1978, II, 4, April 9, 1978, 26.

63. Holbrook, *Fighting Back*, 67.

64. National Defense Research Institute, *Sexual Orientation*, 3–9. See also Hippler, *Matlovich*.

65. PL 95-454.

66. *New York Times*, January 12, 1978, 14, March 22, 1978, 21.

67. Margaret Costanza to Harvey Milk, July 10, 1978, folder Gay Rights—Harvey Milk Speech and Letter, 6/78–7/78 (O/A 5771), 06/1978–07/1978, box 4, Margaret Costanza Files, OPL, WHSF, JCL; Margaret Costanza to Robert Hutchinson, July 21, 1978, folder Gay Rights Correspondence, 5/76–7/78 (O/A 5771), 05/1976–07/1978, box 4, Margaret Costanza Files, OPL, WHSF, JCL; Margaret Costanza to Harvey Milk, July 30, 1978, WHNF Harvey Milk, WHCF, JCL.

68. Transcript, Gay Freedom Day remarks, Harvey Milk, San Francisco, June 25, 1978, and Harvey Milk to Margaret Costanza, June 28, 1978, both in folder Gay Rights—Harvey Milk Speech and Letter, 6/78–7/78 (O/A 5771), 06/1978–07/1978, box 4, Margaret Costanza Files, OPL, WHSF, JCL.

69. *New York Times*, June 26, 1978, 15.

70. Landon Kite to Clayton Wells, June 2, 1978, folder Gay Rights Correspondence, 5/76–7/78 (O/A 5771), 05/1976–07/1978, box 4, Margaret Costanza Files, OPL, WHSF, JCL.

71. *New York Times*, April 30, 1978, IV, 8, April 28, 1978, 1, May 10, 1978, 18, May 25, 1978, 13.

72. *New York Times*, February 12, 1978, 16, June 12, 1978, 16.

73. LaHaye, *Unhappy Gays*, 179.

74. Quoted in *New York Times*, March 25, 1978, 31, April 21, 1978, 27; *Christianity Today*, November 4, 1977, 63.

75. Patrick Swygert to Margaret McKenna, January 18, 1978, folder Abortion, 5/77–1/78, 05/1977–01/1978, box 118, White House Counsel Office Files, WHSF, JCL.

76. Quoted in Edward C. Smith, "The President's Position on Abortion," *Human Life Review* 4, no. 1 (1978): 55–59.

77. Wattleton quoted in *New York Times*, February 3, 1978, 14, March 2, 1978, 16.

78. *New York Times*, January 27, 1978, 1, February 18, 1978, 10.

79. Shabecoff quoted in *New York Times*, February 5, 1978, IV, 5.

80. *New York Times*, June 2, 1978, II, 6, August 8, 1978, supplement, 128, October 4, 1978, supplement, 75, October 16, 1978, 5.

81. *New York Times*, August 5, 1978, 5, October 13, 1978, 7.

82. *New York Times*, July 3, 1978, 20, July 18, 1978, 16.

83. Bourne, *Jimmy Carter*, 426.

84. *Phyllis Schlafly Report* 12, no. 2 (1978): 4.

85. Schlafly, interview; quoted in *Washington Star*, February 12, 1978, 12.

86. Quoted in *New York Times*, May 28, 1978, 44.

87. Carter and Schlafly quotes in *New York Times*, July 10, 1978, 1.

88. *New York Times*, July 13, 1978, 11; Jimmy Carter to Don Edwards, July 12, 1978, folder Meetings—ERA 9/18/78, 09/18/1978–09/18/1978, box 34, APWA, WHSF, JCL.

89. Margaret McKenna to Claiborne Pell, September 29, 1978, folder Equal Rights Amendment, 11/77–1/79, 11/1977–01/1979, box 126, White House Counsel Office Files, WHSF, JCL; John Harmon to Birch Bayh, September 14, 1978, folder ERA (notebook) (2), box 30, APWA, WHSF, JCL.

90. Directive to Heads of Departments and Agencies, Jimmy Carter, July 20, 1978, folder Equal Rights Amendment, 11/77–1/79, 11/1977–01/1979, box 126, White House Counsel Office Files, WHSF, JCL.

91. Memo, Stuart Eizenstat to Frank Moore, September 8, 1978, folder ERA (2–7), box 29, APWA, WHSF, JCL; memo, Margaret Costanza to Senior Staff, July 24, 1978, folder Equal Rights Amendment, 11/77–1/79, 11/1977–01/1979, box 126, White House Counsel Office Files, WHSF, JCL; agenda, White House meeting with Mrs. Carter, September 18, 1978, and memo, Fredi Wechsler to Mrs. Carter, September 18, 1978, folder Meetings—ERA 9/18/78, 09/18/1978–09/18/1978, box 34, APWA, WHSF, JCL.

92. Testimony of Patricia M. Wald, assistant attorney general, Office of Legislative Affairs, before the Subcommittee on Constitution, Committee of the Judiciary, United States Senate, concerning SJ Res. 134, August 2, 1978, and memo, Phoebe Felk to Robert Lipshutz, July 31, 1978, both in folder Equal Rights Amendment, 11/77–1/79, 11/1977–01/1979, box 126, Margaret Costanza Files, OPL, WHSF, JCL.

93. *Washington Star*, April 4, 1978; Cook, "Women White House Advisors," 72–73.

94. Costanza quoted in *New York Times*, May 10, 1978, 18.

95. Glad, *Jimmy Carter*, 441; Hartmann, "Feminism," 227; Cook, "Women White House Advisors," 20–25, 58–76; Falwell, interview.

96. Kaufman, *The Presidency of James Earl Carter*, 107; Cook, "Women White House Advisors," 73.

97. *New York Times*, July 4, 1978, 22, July 26, 1978, 1, August 2, 1978, 1, Cook, "Women White House Advisors," 74.

98. *New York Times*, August 18, 1978, 68.

99. Sarah Weddington, exit interview, January 2, 1981, JCL, 2, 6.

100. Ibid., 3.

101. Ibid., 8, 17–18.

102. *Christianity Today*, October 20, 1978, 64.

103. Quoted in Cook, "Women White House Advisors," 86.

104. Quoted in *New York Times*, September 2, 1978, 49, November 6, 1978, 58.

105. Costanza quoted in Clendinen and Nagourney, *Out for Good*, 406.

106. Gutierrez, interview; Bob Malson to Sarah Weddington, December 27, 1979, folder Gay Views, 1980, 12/79–12/31/79, 12/1979–12/31/1979, box 8, Robert Malson Files, DPS, WHSF, JCL.

107. See Telham, *Power and Leadership*; and Miller, *Shadow and Substance*.

108. Quoted in Lindsay, *Faith in the Halls of Power*, 30–31.

109. *Christianity Today*, October 6, 1978, 20, 48.

110. Jimmy Carter to members of the Executive Committee, Southern Baptist Convention, September 27, 1978, WHNF Southern Baptist Convention, WHCF, JCL.

111. Marley, *Pat Robertson*, 62.

112. Falwell, interview; Falwell, *Fundamentalist Phenomenon*, 215; Simon, *Jerry Falwell and the Jews*, 3–51, 81.

113. Anne Wexler to Foy Valentine, October 6, 1978, and Anne Wexler to Jimmy Allen, October 6, 1978, both in WHNF Southern Baptist Convention, WHCF, JCL.

114. Press release, news service of the Southern Baptist Convention, November 28, 1978, WHNF Southern Baptist Convention, WHCF, JCL.

115. SJ Res. 134; Whitney, *The Equal Rights Amendment*, 84; Hatch, *The Equal Rights Amendment*, 2.

116. Press release, Office of the White House Press Secretary, Statement of the President of the United States on the Extension of the Time Period for Ratification of the Equal Rights Amendment, October 20, 1978, folder ERA (notebook) (1), box 29, APWA, WHSF, JCL; *New York Times*, October 21, 1978, 13. The fifteen states that had yet to ratify were Alabama, Arizona, Arkansas, Florida, Georgia, Illinois, Louisiana, Mississippi, Missouri, Nevada, North Carolina, Oklahoma, South Carolina, Utah, and Virginia.

117. Summary of Jimmy Carter's Efforts to Pass ERA, July 1978, folder ERA (2–7), box 29, APWA, WHSF, JCL.

118. Falwell, interview.

119. *New York Times*, November 23, 1978, 18; Cook, "Women White House Advisors," 105–6.

120. *New York Times*, January 7, 1979, 36; quoted in Cook, "Women White House Advisors," 109–10.

121. Falwell, interview; Martin, *With God on Our Side*, 172–73.

122. Jean O'Leary to Robert Maulson, September 22, 1978, folder Gay Task Force, National, box 7, Robert Malson Files, White House Counsel Office Files, WHSF, JCL; memo, Seymore Wishman to Midge Costanza, February 14, 1978, folder (Gay) Civil Rights, 10/76–2/78 (O/A 4609), 10/1976–02/1978, box 22, OPL, WHSF, JCL.

123. William Hann to President Jimmy Carter, November 7, 1978, WHNF Southern Baptist Convention, WHCF, JCL.

124. Landon Kite to William Hann, November 29, 1978, WHNF Southern Baptist Convention, WHCF, JCL.

125. Robert Hughes to Jimmy Carter, December 7, 1978, and Resolution on California Proposition #6, both in Southern Baptist General Convention of California, WHNF Southern Baptist Convention, WHCF, JCL.

126. Quoted in *New York Times*, June 20, 1978, 1.

127. *New York Times*, September 21, 1978, supplement, 7.

128. *New York Times*, May 2, 1978, 18, June 16, 1978, 9, October 18, 1978, supplement, 37.

129. James Dunn to President Jimmy Carter, December 4, 1978, WHNF James Dunn, WHCF, JCL.

130. *Federal Times*, November 14, 1977, 1; *Quash: Newsletter of the Grand Jury Report* 2, no. 7 (1977); *New York Times*, September 3, 1977, 13; Hugh Wilhere to Annie Gutierrez, March 23, 1978, and Chick Corea to Jimmy Carter, October 8, 1978, both in folder Church of Scientology (O/A 7293), box 7, Annie Gutierrez Files, DPS, WHSF, JCL.

131. Memo, Assistant Attorney General, Criminal Division, to Annie Gutierrez, and press release, Church of Scientology, undated, both in folder Church of Scientology (O/A 7293), box 7, Annie Gutierrez Files, DPS, WHSF, JCL; Falwell, interview.

132. Stapleton quoted in *New York Times*, June 3, 1978, 23.

133. Walter Fauntroy to Jimmy Carter, February 15, 1978, folder Black Religious Leaders 2/78–9/78 (O/A 5419), 02/1978–09/1978, box 29, Martha Mitchell Files, APSP, WHSF, JCL.

134. Memo, Bunny Mitchell to Fran Voorde, April 25, 1978, folder Black Religious Leaders 2/78–9/78 (O/A 5419), 02/1978–09/1978, box 29, Martha Mitchell Files, APSP, WHSF, JCL.

135. Walter Fauntroy to Martha Mitchell, May 25, 1978, folder Black Clergy Meeting

with the President 5/78–6/78 (O/A 5404), 05/1978–06/1978, box 2, Martha Mitchell Files, APSP, WHSF, JCL.

136. Allen, interview; Anne Wexler to Jimmy Allen, December 29, 1978, WHNF Southern Baptist Convention, WHCF, JCL.

137. Eizenstat quoted in Hargrove, *Jimmy Carter as President*, 21.

138. *Washington Post*, November 8, 1978, 1; Lankevich, *Jimmy Carter*, 37.

139. Press release, Carol Long, National Right-to-Life Political Action Committee Director, January 1998, http://www.nrle.org/news/1998/NRL1.98/long.html, accessed May 6, 2007; Gorney, *Articles of Faith*, 330–31; Craig and O'Brien, *Abortion and American Politics*, 48; Anthony Lewis, "A Singular Issue," *New York Times*, November 16, 1978, 27.

140. *Washington Post*, November 8, 1978, 1; quoted in Clendinen and Nagourney, *Out for Good*, 389; Gallagher and Bull, *Perfect Enemies*, 19.

141. Quoted in Gomez, "Out of the Past," 52.

142. After serving five years, White was released and committed suicide; replacing Moscone as mayor was Dianne Feinstein. See Holbrook, *Fighting Back*, 80; Galas, *Gay Rights*, 30–33; Clendinen and Nagourney, *Out for Good*, 403–5.

143. Quoted in Clendinen and Nagourney, *Out for Good*, 403; *New York Times*, November 28, 1978, II, 12.

144. *New York Times*, November 24, 1978, 1, November 25, 1978, 9, November 28, 1978, 14.

145. Resolution on the Equal Rights Amendment, Church of Jesus Christ of Latter-day Saints, October 12, 1978, folder Mormons for the ERA, box 35, APWA, WHSF, JCL.

146. Teddie Wood, November 15, 1978, folder Mormons for the ERA, box 35, APWA, WHSF, JCL.

147. Memo, Barbara to Sarah Weddington, November 13, 1978, folder Mormons for the ERA, box 35, APWA, WHSF, JCL.

148. Memo, Sarah Weddington to President Carter, November 22, 1978, folder Mormons for the ERA, box 35, APWA, WHSF, JCL.

149. Press release, remarks of the president at Family Unity Awards Ceremony, Mormon Tabernacle, Salt Lake City, Utah, November 27, 1978, folder Mormons for the ERA, box 35, APWA, WHSF, JCL.

150. *Time Magazine*, December 19, 1977, 12.

151. *New York Times*, November 18, 1978, 48.

152. *Christianity Today*, November 3, 1978, 14.

153. Allen, interview; Schlafly, interview; *New York Times*, August 5, 1978, 19.

154. *New York Times*, June 13, 1978, II, 1; *Christianity Today*, February 10, 1978, 52.

155. *Christianity Today*, February 10, 1978, 61, March 10, 1978, 64; *The Holy Bible: New International Version*.

156. Tinder quoted in *Christianity Today*, October 21, 1977, 10, April 21, 1978, 16, October 6, 1978, 54.

157. *Christianity Today*, September 8, 1978, 75.

158. Barr, *Fundamentalism*.

159. *New York Times*, May 7, 1978, XI, 18, May 14, 1978, 29; Gerety quoted in *Christianity Today*, June 2, 1978, 46.

160. *New York Times*, May 4, 1978, 17, July 3, 1977, 10, November 11, 1977, 16; Martin, *A Prophet with Honor*, 460.

161. Graham quoted in *Christianity Today*, November 18, 1977, 49.

162. *Christianity Today*, November 17, 1978, 36.

163. Telegraph, Jimmy Allen to President Jimmy Carter, July 7, 1977, Ted Wayne et al. to President Jimmy Carter, October 2, 1977, and James Gammill Jr. to Gentlemen, October 12, 1977, all in WHNF Southern Baptist Convention, WHCF, JCL; *Christianity Today*, July 29, 1977, 37.

164. Hastings and Shaw quoted in *New York Times*, March 3, 1978, 8; Charles LaFontaine, "Ecumenism and the Abortion Issue," *New York Times*, January 22, 1978, 14.

165. Falwell, interview; Falwell, *Listen America!* 130.

166. Falwell, *Listen America!* 130; Harding, *Book of Jerry Falwell*, 191. See also Schaeffer and Koop, *What Ever Happened*.

167. Marshner, interview; Falwell, interview; Falwell, *Strength for the Journey*, 359.

168. Falwell quoted in Goodman and Price, *Jerry Falwell*, 134.

169. Falwell, interview; *New York Times*, December 10, 1978, IV, 7; *Christianity Today*, November 17, 1978, 52.

170. Falwell, *Listen America!* 131.

171. Pingry, *Jerry Falwell*, 9.

172. Falwell, interview.

173. Falwell, interview; Bryant quoted in Strober and Tomczak, *Jerry Falwell*, 180–82.

174. Falwell, *Listen America!* 183.

175. Falwell quoted in Strober and Tomczak, *Jerry Falwell*, 183.

176. Falwell, interview; Simon, *Jerry Falwell and the Jews*, 152–53; Falwell quoted in Goodman and Price, *Jerry Falwell*, 46.

177. Schlafly, interview; Falwell, interview; Gilbert, "Ballot Salvation," 4; Falwell, *Listen America!* 124, 150; Pingry, *Jerry Falwell*, 7; *Life's Answer: The Newsletter of the James Robison Association*, December 1980, 2.

178. Strober and Tomczak, *Jerry Falwell*, 77–79, 82.

179. Ibid., 167; Falwell, interview.

180. Mary Murphy, "The Next Billy Graham," *Esquire*, October 10, 1978, 25–32.

181. Falwell, interview.

182. D'Souza, *Falwell Before the Millennium*, 89, 91; Falwell, *Strength for the Journey*, 256.

183. *New York Times*, July 23, 1978, II, 1; *Christianity Today*, February 24, 1978, 41, March 10, 1978, 54.

184. *New York Times*, July 23, 1978, II, 4.

185. Harrell, *Pat Robertson*, 63, 72–73; Marley, *Pat Robertson*, 102; *Christianity Today*, May 20, 1977, 43.

186. Detwiler, *Standing on the Premises*, 64.

187. *Christianity Today*, December 15, 1978, 41, September 21, 1979, 28; Shepard, *Forgiven*, 68–69, 133.

188. Bawer, *Stealing Jesus*, 254; Martin, *With God on Our Side*, 342; Alexander-Moegerle, *James Dobson's War on America*, 40–41.

189. Richardson, interview; Quebedeaux, *I Found It!* 46–47, 175; *New York Times*, November 11, 1977, 19, December 1, 1977, II, 1.

190. Richardson, *Amazing Faith*, 100–102, 105–6; Pollock, *To All Nations*, 144; *Christianity Today*, October 21, 1977, 27. See also Griffin and Dienert, *The Faithful Christian*; quoted in Catherwood, *Five Evangelical Leaders*, 220.

191. Memo, Rick Inderfurth to Christine Dodson, November 1, 1978, memo, Stephen Larrabee to Zbigniew Brzezinski, November 3, 1978, and memo, Stephen Larrabee to

Zbigniew Brzezinski, November 8, 1978, all in White House Subject Files, Zbigniew Brzezinski, WHCF, JCL.

192. Zbigniew Brzezinski to Billy Graham, November 9, 1978, White House Subject Files, Zbigniew Brzezinski, WHCF, JCL.

193. Billy Graham to Rosalynn Carter, December 28, 1978, WHNF Billy Graham, WHCF, JCL.

194. *New York Times*, January 29, 1978, IV, 18.

195. Diamond, *Not by Politics Alone*, 68–69; Zwier, *Born-Again Politics*, 20–21.

196. Falwell, interview; Pingry, *Jerry Falwell*, 66; history of the Heritage Society, http://www.heritage.org/support/about.cfm, accessed July 27, 2009.

197. Phillips, interview; Young Americans for Freedom, *Task Force Report*, 10.

198. *LifeLetter* 2 (1978): 1–4; *Christianity Today*, April 7, 1978, 56; see also Sheppard, *The Partisan Press*.

199. Falwell, interview; Falwell, *Strength for the Journey*, 369.

200. Weyrich quoted in Balmer, *Thy Kingdom Come*, 15; Balmer, *God in the White House*, 96–97; Martin, *With God on Our Side*, 173.

201. Falwell quoted in Martin, *With God on Our Side*, 172.

202. Phillips, interview; Martin, *With God on Our Side*, 169; *Christianity Today*, April 21, 1978, 43; Graham, "Civil Rights in the Carter Presidency," 205–6, 213; Harrell, *Pat Robertson*, 184; Zwier, *Born-Again Politics*, 51.

203. Lader quoted in *New York Times*, January 11, 1978, 7.

204. Graham quoted in *Toronto Star*, June 5, 1978, 8.

FIVE The Formidable Conservative Barrage

1. See Delbanco, *Representative Men*, 236.

2. *New York Times*, January 5, 1979, 5, January 11, 1979, 1; Lankevich, *James E. Carter*, 39–40.

3. *New York Times*, January 7, 1979, 36; quoted in Cook, "Women White House Advisors," 109–10.

4. Quoted in *New York Times*, January 13, 1979, 1.

5. *New York Times*, January 14, 1979, January 15, 1979, IV, 9, January 16, 1979, 9, January 7, 1979, 21, January 31, 1979, 8.

6. *New York Times*, May 9, 1979, 14.

7. Quoted in *New York Times*, April 11, 1979, 14.

8. *New York Times*, February 1, 1979, 19; memo, Hugh Carter to Jimmy Carter, September 29, 1978, folder ERA (2–7), box 29, APWA, WHSF, JCL.

9. Memo, Sarah Weddington to ERA Task Force, February 26, 1979, and memo, Sarah Weddington to ERA Task Force, March 14, 1979, both in folder Equal Rights Amendment, 2/26/79–8/23/79 (O/A 608), 02/26/1979–08/23/1979, box 174, Stephen Selig Files, OCS, WHSF, JCL.

10. *New York Times*, February 22, 1979, 18; quoted in January 7, 1979, 36.

11. Flyer, People of Faith for ERA, December 1978, folder ERA (notebook) (2), box 30, APWA, WHSF, JCL; Anne Fullis, "Coming Through: Christians and the Equal Rights Amendment," *Interpreter*, July–August 1978, 2–5.

12. Memo, Sarah Weddington to Jimmy Carter, January 25, 1979, folder ERA Strategy Group, box 33, APWA, WHSF, JCL; *Christianity Today*, May 4, 1979, 48; State of the

Union address, Jimmy Carter, January 23, 1979, Public Papers of the Presidents, American Presidency Project, University of California–Santa Barbara, http://www.presidency.ucsb.edu/ws/indexphp?pid=32675, accessed May 18, 2008.

13. Schlafly, interview; *New York Times*, March 21, 1979, 1; quoted in March 23, 1979, 18, October 14, 1979, 26.

14. Telegraph, Robert Billings to President Jimmy Carter, January 14, 1979, WHNF Robert Billings, WHCF, JCL.

15. Sarah Weddington to Robert Billings, March 9, 1979, WHNF Robert Billings, WHCF, JCL.

16. Ben Armstrong to Frank Moore, December 27, 1978, WHNF National Religious Broadcasters, WHCF, JCL.

17. Jimmy Waters to Frank Moore, December 5, 1978, WHNF National Religious Broadcasters, WHCF, JCL.

18. Frank Moore to Ben Armstrong, January 5, 1979, WHNF National Religious Broadcasters, WHCF, JCL.

19. Jay D. Cole to President Carter, January 30, 1979, WHNF National Religious Broadcasters, WHCF, JCL.

20. James Dunn to Phil Wise, March 5, 1979, memo, Sarah Weddington to Fran Voorde, March 13, 1979, and handwritten comments on letter, James Dunn to Tim Craft, March 5, 1979, all in WHNF James Dunn, WHCF, JCL.

21. Memo, Achsah Nesmith and Bernie Aronson to President Jimmy Carter, January 16, 1979, and itinerary, President and Mrs. Carter's Attendance at National Prayer Breakfast, Washington Hilton, January 18, 1979, folder 1/18/79—National Prayer Breakfast, 01/18/1979–01/18/1979, box 2, Advance Office Files, WHPO, WHSF, JCL.

22. Draft, remarks for National Prayer Breakfast, January 16, 1979, folder 1/18/79—National Prayer Breakfast, 01/18/1979–01/18/1979, box 2, Advance Office Files, WHPO, WHSF, JCL.

23. Allen, interview; remarks, President Jimmy Carter, National Prayer Breakfast, January 18, 1979, Public Papers of the Presidents, American Presidency Project, University of California–Santa Barbara, http://www.presidency.ucsb.edu/ws/index.php?pid=32335&st=&st1, accessed May 18, 2008.

24. Falwell, *Strength for the Journey*, 358; Strober and Tomczak, *Jerry Falwell*, 176.

25. Falwell quoted in Strober and Tomczak, *Jerry Falwell*, 175; Falwell, interview.

26. Flier, National March for Life, Inc., 1978, folder Anti-Abortion Groups, 1/78 (O/A 5773), 01/1978–01/1978, box 1, OPL, WHSF, JCL; *New York Times*, January 23, 1979, III, 10.

27. Robison quoted in Martin, *With God on Our Side*, 199.

28. Falwell, interview; *New York Times*, April 1, 1979, 43; *Dallas Morning News*, April 3, 1979, 3.

29. Falwell, interview.

30. Oldfield, *The Right and the Righteous*, 101.

31. Phillips, interview; Falwell, interview; Willoughby, *Does America Need*, 38–39.

32. Robison quoted in Martin, *With God on Our Side*, 205.

33. Graham quoted in ibid., 206.

34. Novak quoted in ibid., 207.

35. *Christianity Today*, March 23, 1979, 24.

36. *New York Times*, April 25, 1979, 14.

37. Quoted in *New York Times*, September 18, 1979, 25, March 11, 1979, 25.

38. Rogers quoted in *New York Times*, June 13, 1979, 9; Balmer, *God in the White House*, 101–2.

39. Allen, interview; *Christianity Today*, July 20, 1979, 32.

40. Balmer, *God in the White House*, 103.

41. *Christianity Today*, September 7, 1979, 58.

42. *New York Times*, June 2, 1979, 26, June 3, 1979, 37.

43. *New York Times*, March 3, 1979, 21, February 2, 1979, 19, December 2, 1979, 1, November 11, 1979, 53.

44. Quoted in *New York Times*, September 20, 1979, 13.

45. Bakker quoted in Shepard, *Forgiven*, 125, 137, 206; *Christianity Today*, June 6, 1980, 47, May 4, 1979, 44.

46. Martin, *With God on Our Side*, 172.

47. *Christianity Today*, January 5, 1979, 42, March 23, 1979, 60.

48. James Wood Jr. to President Jimmy Carter, June 21, 1979, WHNF Southern Baptist Convention, WHCF, JCL.

49. Landon Kite to James Wood, July 10, 1979, WHNF Southern Baptist Convention, WHCF, JCL.

50. *Christianity Today*, October 5, 1979, 58.

51. Falwell, interview; Falwell quoted in Halsell, *Prophecy and Politics*, 33–35.

52. *Christianity Today*, April 20, 1979, 8.

53. Allen, interview; memo, Bill Ayers to Anne Wexler, March 29, 1979, WHNF Billy Graham, WHCF, JCL.

54. Memo, Anne Wexler to Phil Wise, March 30, 1979, WHNF Billy Graham, WHCF, JCL.

55. Statement by Billy Graham on the Convocation on Southern Baptist Resolution Number Five, Peacemaking and Nuclear Arms Control, 1978, WHNF Billy Graham, WHCF, JCL.

56. Jimmy Carter to Billy Graham, May 9, 1979, WHNF Billy Graham, WHCF, JCL.

57. Telegraph, Billy Graham to President Jimmy Carter, May 12, 1979, WHNF Billy Graham, WHCF, JCL.

58. Maddox, interview; Maddox, *Preacher at the White House*, 63; Address to the Nation on Energy and National Goals, Jimmy Carter, July 15, 1979, Public Papers of the Presidents, American Presidency Project, University of California–Santa Barbara, http://www.presidency.ucsb.edu/ws/index.php?=2596&st=st1, accessed May 18, 2008.

59. Maddox, *Preacher at the White House*, 73, 1; Moss, *Moving On*, 296–97; Lankevich, *James E. Carter*, 47.

60. Maddox, interview; Maddox, *Preacher at the White House*, 73, 78.

61. Maddox, *Preacher at the White House*, 77, 83.

62. Robert Maddox, oral history audiotape, JCL.

63. Maddox, *Preacher at the White House*, 85.

64. Ibid., 135; Rogers quoted in Bourne, *Jimmy Carter*, 467.

65. Falwell, interview; Morris, *Jimmy Carter*, 275.

66. Ruth Carter Stapleton quoted in *New York Times*, January 21, 1979, 27.

67. Memo, Gretchen Poston to Landon Butler, July 19, 1979, and memo, Victoria Mongiardo to Anne Wexler, August 6, 1979, both in folder Archbishop Iakovos, 6/26/79–10/2/79, 06/26/1979–10/02/1979, box 90, Landon Butler Files, OCS, WHSF, JCL.

68. Raymond S. Blanks to Julia Dobbs, September 6, 1979, and Raymond Blanks to Gretchen Poston, May 24, 1979, both in folder National Black Catholics, box 69, Louis

Martin Files, Office of the Special Assistant to the President Files, WHSF, JCL; *New York Times*, February 18, 1979, D10; National Office for Black Catholics, *Black Perspectives*.

69. Lankevich, *James E. Carter*, 45–46. See also Morris, *Jimmy Carter*, 258, 278–79.

70. White House Conference on Families, "A Brief History, National Advisory Committee, July, 1979," folder July 20, 1979—Remarks—Reception—White House Conference on the Family, box 51, Achsah Nesmith Files, PSWF, WHSF, JCL.

71. Press release, April 12, 1979, Office of the White House Press Secretary, Appointment of Jim Guy Tucker to Lead White House Conference on Families, folder July 20, 1979—Remarks—Reception—White House Conference on the Family, box 51, Achsah Nesmith Files, PSWF, WHSF, JCL.

72. *Report from the White House Conference on Families* 1, no. 1 (1979): 1–4; *New York Times*, July 12, 1979, III, 7.

73. Memo, Jim Guy Tucker to National Advisory Committee Members, July 6, 1979, folder July 20, 1979—Remarks—Reception—White House Conference on the Family, box 51, Achsah Nesmith Files, PSWF, WHSF, JCL.

74. Press release, July 20, 1979, Office of the White House Press Secretary, Remarks of the President at Reception for the White House Conference on the Family, folder July 20, 1979—Remarks—Reception—White House Conference on the Family, box 51, Achsah Nesmith Files, PSWF, WHSF, JCL; quoted in *New York Times*, July 21, 1979, 20.

75. *New York Times*, July 21, 1979, 20; *Report from the White House Conference on Families* 1, no. 1 (1979): 1–11, Tucker quoted on 1.

76. Marshner, interview; *New York Times*, January 7, 1980, IV, 8, December 16, 1979, VI, 15.

77. Dobson quoted in Zettersten, *Dr. Dobson*, 150.

78. Marshner, interview; quoted in Zettersten, *Dr. Dobson*, 150–51.

79. Transcript, news conference, November 10, 1977, transcript, remarks at question-and-answer session, public meeting, July 21, 1977, transcript, interview with National Black Network, July 18, 1977, memo, Charles Goodwin to Seymour, March 8, 1978, and memo, Jane Wales to Midge Costanza, March 8, 1978, all in folder Women and Reproductive Freedom, June 1970–March 1978 (O/A 5772), 6/1970–3/1978, box 11, Margaret Costanza Files, OPL, WHSF, JCL.

80. *Colautti v. Franklin*, 439 U.S. 379 (1979).

81. *Belloti v. Baird*, 443 U.S. 622 (1979).

82. *New York Times*, February 16, 1979, II, 1; Hyde quoted in March 1, 1979, II, 20.

83. Wilcox et al., "Federal Abortion Policy," 6.

84. *New York Times*, June 28, 1979, II, 14, July 12, 1979, 1, July 18, 1979, 18, September 29, 1979, 1, October 11, 1979, 20, October 13, 1979, 1, November 14, 1979, 22, November 16, 1979, 9, November 17, 1979, 10.

85. Alan Guttmacher Institute, *Fact Sheet*.

86. *New York Times*, October 2, 1979, II, 13.

87. *New York Times*, February 8, 1979, 16; Harris quoted in July 21, 1979, 7.

88. *New York Times*, June 24, 1979, 16, November 13, 1979, II, 14, August 23, 1979, 20.

89. *New York Times*, June 8, 1979, 21, June 24, 1979, 16.

90. Gutierrez, interview; *Immigration and Nationality Act of 1952*, PL 82-414, 66 Stat. 163 (1952); Turner, "Mirror Images," 11.

91. *It's Time: The Newsletter of the National Gay Task Force* 6, no. 7 (1979): 1–2; *New York Times*, December 27, 1979, 16.

92. Lucia Valeska to Benjamin Civiletti, August 31, 1979, folder Gay Rights, box 7, Robert Malson Files, DPS, WHSF, JCL.

93. Lucia Valeska to Michael Egan, July 11, 1979, and White House phone log, June 1979, both in folder Gay Rights, box 7, Robert Malson Files, DPS, WHSF, JCL.

94. Memo, John Harmon to David Crosland, December 10, 1979, and memo, David Crosland to Robert Malson, December 11, 1979, folder Gay Task Force, National (10/79–3/24/80), 10/1979–03/24/1980, box 7, Robert Malson Files, DPS, WHSF, JCL.

95. *New York Times*, December 27, 1979, 16.

96. Memo, Norman Carlson to Frank White, December 26, 1979, folder Gays, box 8, DPS, WHSF, JCL.

97. *New York Times*, November 18, 1979, 26, December 6, 1979, 26; memo, Sarah Weddington to Ben Civiletti, November 20, 1979, folder ERA—Callister in Idaho v. Freeman, 11/1979–11/1979, box 78, OCS, WHSF, JCL; *Christianity Today*, January 4, 1980, 64.

98. Sarah Weddington to Phyllis Starr Wilson, July 26, 1979, folder Presidential Statement on ERA, box 36, APWA, WHSF, JCL; memo, Carol Coleman to Gail West, May 9, 1979, folder Equal Rights Amendment, 4/1/79–8/31/80, 04/01/1979–08/31/1980, box 8, PSWF, WHCF, JCL; Sey Chassler to Sarah Weddington, April 17, 1979, folder Presidential Statement on ERA, box 36, APWA, WHSF, JCL.

99. Hartmann, "Feminism," 234; Tinker, *Women in Washington*, 293–94.

100. Press release, Women's Equality Day, 1979, Office of the White House Press Secretary, August 20, 1979, folder Equal Rights Amendment, 4/1/79–8/31/80, 04/01/1979–08/31/1980, box 8, PSWF, WHCF, JCL.

101. Schlafly, interview; Falwell, interview; Falwell, *Listen America!* 136.

102. Quoted in Martin, *With God on Our Side*, 200.

103. Quoted in ibid.; Phillips, interview; Falwell, interview; Fallwell, *Strength for the Journey*, 359.

104. Falwell, interview; Falwell, *Strength for the Journey*, 361–63.

105. Goodman and Price, *Jerry Falwell*, 25.

106. Falwell, interview; Falwell, *Strength for the Journey*, 363.

107. Falwell, *Listen America!* 107; Zwier, *Born-Again Politics*, 48; Halsell, *Prophecy and Politics*, 9–10; Reed quoted in Bawer, *Stealing Jesus*, 163.

108. Tamney and Johnson, "The Moral Majority," 155–56; Wilcox, "Evangelicals," 355–61; Hall and Combee, "The Moral Majority," 205; Oldfield, *The Right and the Righteous*, 91, Weyrich quoted on 139.

109. Marley, *Pat Robertson*, 50; Robertson quoted in *Washington Post*, October 4, 1980, 7.

110. Harrell, *Pat Robertson*, 61–62, 76–77; Armstrong, *The Electric Church*; Kater, *Christians on the Right*, 18.

111. Falwell, interview; Steve Martz, "Wreath Laying at the Unknown Soldier Tomb," *Washington Blade*, May 29, 1980, 3.

112. Falwell, interview; Gallagher and Bull, *Perfect Enemies*, 24, 31; Herman, *Antigay Agenda*, 50.

113. Quoted in Martin, *With God on Our Side*, 207.

114. Quoted in *New York Times*, October 27, 1979, 43; O'Connor, *No Neutral Ground*, 85; Utter and Storey, *The Religious Right*, 10.

115. Phillips, interview; Falwell, interview; Maddox, oral history; Harrell, *Pat Robertson*, 185, 187; Brown, *For a Christian Nation*, 205; Utter and Storey, *The Religious Right*, 9–10, 51–52, 56–57, 62–63, 68–70, 73–74.

116. Maddox, interview; Maddox, *Preacher at the White House*, 148–49, 153.

117. Memo, Anne Wexler to Phil Wise, September 10, 1979, WHNF Moral Majority, WHCF, JCL.

118. Jerry Falwell to Rosalynn Carter, August 15, 1979, WHNF Jerry Falwell, WHCF, JCL.

119. Jimmy Allen to Jimmy Carter, June 6, 1979, WHNF Southern Baptist Convention, WHCF, JCL; fact sheet, First Lady Rosalynn Carter's Scheduling Office, March 26, 1979, and Kathryn Cade to David Edens, April 2, 1979, both in WHNF Christian Life Commission, WHCF, JCL.

120. Maddox, interview; memo, Robert Maddox to President Jimmy Carter, September 5, 1979, WHNF Billy Graham, WHCF, JCL.

121. Maddox, interview; Graham in quoted in Maddox, *Preacher at the White House*, 141.

122. Carter handwritten comments on memo, Robert Maddox to President Jimmy Carter, September 5, 1979, WHNF Billy Graham, WHCF, JCL.

123. Memo, Anne Wexler and Robert Maddox to the president, October 26, 1979, and memo, Phil Wise to Bob Maddox, October 18, 1979, both in WHNF Billy Graham, WHCF, JCL.

124. Billy Graham to President and Mrs. Jimmy Carter, November 6, 1979, WHNF Billy Graham, WHCF, JCL.

125. Jimmy Carter to Ruth and Billy Graham, December 14, 1979, WHNF Billy Graham, WHCF, JCL.

126. Maddox, interview; Maddox, *Preacher at the White House*, 154.

127. Maddox, *Preacher at the White House*, 144.

128. Gallagher and Bull, *Perfect Enemies*, 19–20; *New York Times*, October 1, 1979, 1, October 6, 1979, 6.

129. *New York Times*, September 30, 1979, 1, December 30, 1979, XII, 8.

130. Memo, Landon Kite to Hamilton Jordan, September 5, 1979, folder Pope John Paul II Visit to U.S., 9/79, 09/1979–09/1979, box 69, Jody Powell Files, WHPO, WHSF, JCL.

131. Notice to the press, October 6, 1979, memo, Phil Larson and Gretchen Poston to White House Staff, October 4, 1979, and memo, unsigned, October 5, 1979, Aftermath of the Pope's Visit, all in folder Pope John Paul II Visit to U.S., 9/79, 09/1979–09/1979, box 69, Jody Powell Files, WHPO, WHSF, JCL.

132. Memo, Zbigniew Brzezinski to Jimmy Carter, undated (September 1979), folder Pope John Paul II Visit to U.S., 9/79, 09/1979–09/1979, box 69, Jody Powell Files, WHPO, WHSF, JCL.

133. Memo, James Rentschler to Jerry Schecter, October 5, 1979, folder Pope John Paul II Visit to U.S., 9/79, 09/1979–09/1979, box 69, Jody Powell Files, WHPO, WHSF, JCL.

134. Memo, Cyrus Vance to Jimmy Carter, September 20, 1979, folder Pope John Paul II Visit to U.S., 9/79, 09/1979–09/1979, box 69, Jody Powell Files, WHPO, WHSF, JCL.

135. Memo, Gretchen Poston to White House Staff, October 1, 1979, transcript, remarks of the First Lady, Arrival of His Holiness Pope John Paul II, undated, Frank Dominguez to Esteban Torres, October 31, 1979, and itinerary, Visit of Pope John Paul, all in folder Pope John Paul's Visit, 9/7/79–10/31/79, 09/07/1979–10/31/1979, box 30, Esteban Torres Files, Office of Hispanic Affairs Files, WHSF, JCL.

136. Transcript, Exchange of Remarks Between the President and His Holiness John Paul II, North Lawn, October 6, 1979, folder Pope John Paul II Visit to U.S., 9/79, 09/1979–09/1979, box 69, Jody Powell Files, WHPO, WHSF, JCL.

137. Transcript, White House Press Statement Following Meeting Between President Carter and His Holiness John Paul II, October 6, 1979, folder Pope John Paul II Visit to U.S., 9/79, 09/1979–09/1979, box 69, Jody Powell Files, WHPO, WHSF, JCL.

138. Transcript, Remarks of the President After White House Reception for His Holiness John Paul II, October 6, 1979, and White House Press Pool Report, Pope's Departure at North Portico, both in folder Pope John Paul II Visit to U.S., 9/79, 09/1979–09/1979, box 69, Jody Powell Files, WHPO, WHSF, JCL.

139. Maddox, interview; memo, Robert Maddox to Jody Powell, December 31, 1979, folder Religious Broadcasters 1980, 1980–1980, box 3, Ray Jenkins Files, WHPO, WHSF, JCL.

140. Exit interview, Sarah Weddington, January 2, 1981, JCL, 4.

141. National Institute for Advanced Studies, *Summary*, 1.

142. Ibid., sec. 3.

143. Cother and Mitgang quoted in *New York Times*, November 11, 1979, 25.

144. Quoted in *New York Times*, November 30, 1979, 22.

145. *New York Times*, December 5, 1979, 28; Weddington quoted in December 9, 1979, 38.

146. Errington quoted in *New York Times*, December 11, 1979, 1; Friedan quoted in December 11, 1979, 22.

147. Kimball quoted in *Charlotte Observer*, January 15, 1979, 4; quoted in *Newsletter: Mormons for ERA*, November 1979, 3.

148. Quoted in *Los Angeles Times*, December 5, 1979, 4.

149. Agenda, Meeting with Presidents of Women's Organizations, December 13, 1979, talking points, Meeting with Presidents of Women's Organizations, December 13, 1979, and memo, Sarah Weddington to Jimmy Carter, December 13, 1979, all in folder Equal Rights Amendment, 4/1/79–8/31/80, 04/01/1979–08/31/1980, box 8, PSWF, WHSF, JCL.

150. *New York Times*, December 12, 1979, II, 8, quoted in December 14, 1979, II, 10, December 27, 1979, 22.

151. Handwritten comments by Sarah Weddington on White House Correspondence Tracking Worksheet, December 1979, folder Gay Views, 1980 (12/79–12/31/79), 12/1979–12/31/1979, box 8, Robert Malson Files, DPS, WHCF, JCL.

152. Memo, Jane Wells to Anne Wexler, October 4, 1979, folder Gay Rights, box 7, Robert Malson Files, DPS, WHCF, JCL; memo, Allison Thomas to Anne Wexler, December 18, 1979, folder Gay Views, 1980 (12/79–12/31/79), 12/1979–12/31/1979, box 8, Robert Malson Files, DPS, WHCF, JCL.

153. Quoted in *New York Times*, October 15, 1978, 14; Marcus, *Making History*, 258.

154. Marcus, *Making History*, 258; *Washington Post*, October 12, 1979, C4; Clendinen and Nagourney, *Out for Good*, 408.

155. Lucia Valeska and C. F. Brydon to Jimmy Carter, November 9, 1979, folder Gay Views, 1980 (12/79–12/31/79), 12/1979–12/31/1979, box 8, Robert Malson Files, DPS, WHCF, JCL.

156. Memo, Anne Wexler and Stu Eisenstat to Jimmy Carter, December 19, 1979, folder Gay Views, 1980 (12/79–12/31/79), 12/1979–12/31/1979, box 8, Robert Malson Files, DPS, WHCF, JCL.

157. Transcript, meeting of Allison Thomas, Bob Malson, Dianna Rock, and Mike Chanin, December 10, 1979, and memo, Allison Thomas to Bob Malson, December 10,

1979, both in folder Homosexuals (7/20/79–5/31/80), 07/20/1979–05/31/1980, box 7, Robert Malson Files, DPS, WHSF, JCL.

158. White House Position Statement on Issues of Concern to the Gay Community, December 1979, and Tim Kraft to Lucia Valeska and Charles Brydon, December 14, 1979, both in folder Gays, box 211, Stuart Eizenstat Files, DPS, WHSF, JCL.

159. Lucia Valeska and C. F. Brydon to Robert Malson, December 20, 1979, and Bill Nichols to Jimmy Carter, February 19, 1980, both in folder Gay Views, 1980 (1/2/80–n.d.), 01/02/1980–01/02/1980, box 8, Robert Malson Files, DPS, WHSF, JCL.

160. B. J. Willhite to Jimmy Carter, December 11, 1979, folder Gay Rights, box 58, Bill Albers Files, APWA, WHSF, JCL.

161. Memo, Mike Chanin to Jane Leclerc, December 31, 1979, folder Gay Rights, box 58, Bill Albers Files, APWA, WHSF, JCL.

162. *Christianity Today*, October 5, 1979, 68, November 16, 1979, 32.

163. PL 96-88, signed October 17, 1979; LaHaye quoted in Bates, *Battleground*, 54–55; LaHaye, *Battle for the Mind*.

164. *Christianity Today*, November 2, 1979, 76.

165. Anne Wexler to Jerry Falwell, December 27, 1979, WHNF Jerry Falwell, WHCF, JCL; Anne Wexler to Pat Robertson, December 27, 1979, WHNF Pat Robertson, WHCF, JCL; memorandum for the Heads of Executive Departments and Agencies, Jimmy Carter, October 15, 1979, WHNF John Carr, WHCF, JCL; Lankevich, *James E. Carter*, 52–53.

166. Falwell, interview; Robert Hughes to President Jimmy Carter, December 21, 1979, and Daniel Chew to Members of the Southern Baptist Convention of California, December 31, 1979, both in WHNF Southern Baptist Convention, WHCF, JCL.

167. Allen, interview; Phil Strickland to President Jimmy Carter, January 17, 1980, and Frank Moore to Phil Strickland, January 23, 1980, both in WHNF Christian Life Commission, WHCF, JCL.

168. Falwell, interview; *New York Times*, December 30, 1979, IV, 15, December 24, 1979, 15; Lankevich, *James E. Carter*, 55.

SIX The Profamily Movement

1. Lankevich, *James E. Carter*, 56–57; State of the Union address, Jimmy Carter, January 23, 1980, American Presidency Project, University of California–Santa Barbara, http://www.presidency.ucsb.edu/ws/index.php?pid=33079&st=&st1, accessed May 18, 2008.

2. *New York Times*, January 28, 1980, II, 5.

3. *Christianity Today*, February 22, 1980, 48; quoted in March 7, 1980, 66.

4. *New York Times*, January 28, 1980, II, 5.

5. Ben Armstrong to President Jimmy Carter, July 18, 1979, and Fran Voorde to Ben Armstrong, August 2, 1980, both in WHNF National Religious Broadcasters, WHCF, JCL.

6. Elias Golonka to President Jimmy Carter, July 17, 1979, WHNF National Religious Broadcasters, WHCF, JCL.

7. Bill Freeman to President Jimmy Carter, January 4, 1980, and Sur Bahner to President Jimmy Carter, January 3, 1980, both in WHNF National Religious Broadcasters, WHCF, JCL.

8. Itinerary, President's Appearance at the National Religious Broadcasters' 37th Annual Convention, January 21, 1980, WHNF National Religious Broadcasters, WHCF, JCL.

9. Allen, interview; press release, transcript, President's Address to the National Religious Broadcasters, January 21, 1980, WHNF National Religious Broadcasters, WHCF, JCL; memo, Achsah Nesmith to Anne Wexler, January 16, 1980, and final draft, President's Remarks to National Religious Broadcasters, January 21, 1980, both in folder Religion, box 6, Achsah Nesmith Files, PSWF, WHSF, JCL.

10. Memo, Robert Maddox to Carol Emig, January 18, 1980, WHNF National Religious Broadcasters, WHCF, JCL.

11. Maddox, *Preacher at the White House*, 154.

12. Ben Armstrong to Robert Maddox, January 29, 1980, and memo, Bob Maddox to Fran Voorde, February 5, 1980, both in WHNF National Religious Broadcasters, WHCF, JCL.

13. Robert Maddox to Ben Armstrong, February 5, 1980, Jim Purks to Cecil Todd, February 27, 1980, and Rex Humbard to President Jimmy Carter, May 20, 1980, all in WHNF National Religious Broadcasters, WHCF, JCL.

14. Maddox, interview; Maddox, *Preacher at the White House*, 162–63.

15. Maddox, *Preacher at the White House*, 164–65; Robert Maddox, oral history audiotape, JCL.

16. Dugan, Bakker, and Wexler quoted in *New York Times*, January 28, 1980, II, 5, January 28, 1980, II, 5; Falwell, interview.

17. Allen, interview; itinerary, President and Mrs. Carter's Attendance at National Prayer Breakfast, Washington Hilton, February 7, 1980, folder 2/7/80—National Prayer Breakfast—Washington Hilton, box 3, Advance Office Files, WHPO, WHSF, JCL; Carter quoted in *Christianity Today*, March 7, 1980, 61.

18. Itinerary, brief meeting with Hispanic Protestant Ministers, February 13, 1980, memo, Miriam Cruz to Bill Albers, February 19, 1980, and Michael Lynch to Esteban Torres, January 7, 1980, all in folder Christian Embassy, 1/7/80, 01/07/1980–01/07/1980, box 15, Esteban Torres Files, Office of Hispanic Affairs Files, WHSF, JCL.

19. *New York Times*, March 8, 1980, 8.

20. Talking points, Black Ministers Meeting, memo to the President, March 19, 1980, and William Coffin to Jimmy Carter, March 20, 1980, all in folder Black Ministers Meeting, 03/21/1980–03/21/1980, box 66, PSWF, WHSF, JCL.

21. Vander Jagt and Carter quoted in *Christianity Today*, March 7, 1980, 61.

22. *Christianity Today*, January 25, 1980, 50.

23. *New York Times*, February 24, 1980, 22, February 27, 1980, 16, March 1, 1980, 22, May 2, 1980, 1, May 6, 1980, 24.

24. *New York Times*, January 18, 1980, II, 6, quoted in July 7, 1980, II, 12, January 24, 1980, III, 2; Schlafly, interview.

25. *Atlanta Constitution*, January 8, 1980, 24.

26. Summary, Harris Poll on Women and ERA, January 1980, folder ERA (2–7), box 29, APWA, WHSF, JCL.

27. Carter quoted in *New York Times*, February 9, 1980, 1; Whitney, *The Equal Rights Amendment*, 87.

28. *New York Times*, February 9, 1980, 9; memo, Barbara to Sarah Weddington, February 8, 1980, folder ERA (2–7), box 29, APWA, WHSF, JCL.

29. Memo, Sarah Weddington to Jimmy Carter, January 8, 1980, folder ERA (1), box 28, APWA, WHSF, JCL.

30. Executive Summary of the President's Advisory Committee Report on ERA, January 8, 1980, folder ERA (1), box 28, APWA, WHSF, JCL.

31. Memo, Sarah Weddington to Jimmy Carter, January 7, 1980, folder ERA (1), box 28, APWA, WHSF, JCL; *New York Times*, January 9, 1980, 18.

32. Agenda, ERA Briefing, February 12, 1980, and Jack Gordon to Linda Tarr-Whelan, February 19, 1980, both in folder ERA Briefing 2/12/80, 02/12/1980–02/12/1980, box 16, Kathy Cade Files, Office of the First Lady Files, WHSF, JCL.

33. Transcript, Remarks of the President, ERA Briefing, February 12, 1980, folder ERA Briefing 2/12/80, 02/12/1980–02/12/1980, box 16, Kathy Cade Files, Office of the First Lady Files, WHSF, JCL.

34. Quoted in *Blade*, June 26, 1980, 1; memo, Bob Malson to Mike Chanin, June 18, 1980, folder Gays, box 211, Stuart Eizenstat Files, WHSF, JCL.

35. Robert Strauss to John Shenefield, April 8, 1980, and Alan Parker to Alan Cranston, June 18, 1980, both in folder Gays, box 211, Stuart Eizenstat Files, WHSF, JCL; quoted in *Blade*, June 26, 1980, 1.

36. *Washington Post*, July 8, 1980, 16.

37. Quoted in *Washington Post*, September 10, 1980, 15; Turner, "Mirror Images," 12; Turner, "Lesbian/Gay Rights," 208–25.

38. Robert Malson to Jerod Krieger, July 30, 1980, folder Gay/Lesbians (7/1/80–n.d.), 07/01/1980–07/01/1980, box 7, Robert Malson Files, DPS, WHSF, JCL; *Washington Post*, May 14, 1980, C2; Turner, "Mirror Images," 15.

39. Norman Carlson to Robert Kastenmeier, February 1, 1980, and Robert Kastenmeier to Norman Carlson, January 7, 1980, both in folder Gay Task Force, National (10/79–3/24/80), 10/1979–03/24/1980, box 7, Robert Malson Files, DPS, WHSF, JCL; Turner, "Mirror Images," 14.

40. *Washington Star*, March 13, 1980, 10; Turner, "Mirror Images," 14.

41. News release, NGTF, March 6, 1980, folder Gay Task Force, National (10/79–3/24/80), 10/1979–03/24/1980, box 7, Robert Malson Files, DPS, WHSF, JCL; *Charlotte Observer*, March 13, 1980, 13; news release, Gay Vote 1980, March 12, 1980, folder Gay/Lesbians (2/8/79–6/30/80), 02/08/1979–06/30/1980, box 7, Robert Malson Files, DPS, WHSF, JCL.

42. C. F. Brydon and Lucia Valeska to Jimmy Carter, April 1, 1980, folder Gay Task Force, National (4/1/80–n.d.), 04/01/1980–04/01/1980, box 7, Robert Malson Files, DPS, WHSF, JCL.

43. *New York Times*, April 5, 1980, 7.

44. C. F. Brydon and Lucia Valeska to Jimmy Carter, April 1, 1980, folder Gay Task Force, National (4/1/80–n.d.), 04/01/1980–04/01/1980, box 7, Robert Malson Files, DPS, WHSF, JCL; *Advocate*, June 12, 1980, 7.

45. Memo, Bob Malson to Stu Eizenstat, May 8, 1980, folder Gay Task Force, National (4/1/80–n.d.), 04/01/1980–04/01/1980, box 7, Robert Malson Files, DPS, WHSF, JCL.

46. Memo, Robert Montague to Bob Malson, March 25, 1980, folder Homosexuals (7/20/79–5/31/80), 07/20/1979–05/31/1980, box 7, Robert Malson Files, DPS, WHSF, JCL.

47. Tom Bastow to Diane Rock, January 24, 1980, folder Gay Views, 1980 (1/2/80–n.d.), 01/02/1980–01/02/1980, box 8, Robert Malson Files, DPS, WHSF, JCL.

48. Memo, Allison Thomas to Anne Wexler, May 28, 1980, and Bob Malson to Bert Carp, June 7, 1980, both in folder Homosexuals (6/1/80–10/10/80), 06/01/1980–10/10/1980, box 7, Robert Malson Files, DPS, WHSF, JCL.

49. Record of the Carter Administration, January 1980, folder Gay Rights, box 58, Bill Albers Files, APWA, WHSF, JCL.

50. Quoted in *New York Times*, January 13, 1980, 22, January 21, 1980, 18.

51. Quoted in *New York Times*, January 23, 1980, 12.

52. Lankevich, *James E. Carter*, 58–59. See also Pomper, *The Election of 1980*.

53. Quoted in *New York Times*, March 23, 1980, 47.

54. Tom Lester to Anne Wexler, July 2, 1980, White House Subject Files, Public Relations Files, WHCF, JCL.

55. Anne Wexler to Tom Lester, July 11, 1980, White House Subject Files, Public Relations Files, WHCF, JCL.

56. Maddox, interview; Falwell and Carter quoted in *Washington Star*, August 23, 1980, B6.

57. Maddox, interview; quoted in Martin, *With God on Our Side*, 211.

58. Maddox, interview; quoted in *New York Times*, August 8, 1980, 16.

59. Falwell quoted in *Washington Star*, August 23, 1980, B6.

60. Allen quoted in ibid.; Allen, interview.

61. Falwell, interview.

62. Maddox, oral history.

63. Marshner, interview; quoted in Martin, *With God on Our Side*, 177, 178.

64. Quoted in *New York Times*, January 28, 1980, IV, 10.

65. *New York Times*, February 3, 1980, XXI, 16, February 10, 1980, XXII, 22, quoted on February 6, 1980, III, 15; Marshner, interview.

66. Quoted in *New York Times*, February 12, 1980, II, 6.

67. Tucker quoted in *Report from the White House Conference on Families* 1, no. 2 (1979): 4.

68. Carter quoted in ibid., 8; press release, White House Conference on Families, February 12, 1980, folder Families, White House Conference On, 2/78 (O/A 4467), 02/1978–02/1978, box 67, Jane Wales Files, OPL, WHSF, JCL.

69. *New York Times*, January 2, 1979, III, 10, October 14, 1979, IV, 19; Tucker quoted in March 26, 1980, III, 18.

70. Memo, Jim Guy Tucker and John L. Carr to National Advisory Committee, April 3, 1980, folder Families, WH Conference On, box 58, Bill Albers Files, APWA, WHSF, JCL.

71. Marshner, interview; Mrs. Henry Thrisher to Tom Hagedorn, February 28, 1980, Tom Hagedorn to Frank Moore, March 14, 1980, and Betty Permes to Senator Young, March 10, 1980, all in WHNF Jim Tucker, WHCF, JCL.

72. Bill Nelson to Frank Moore, March 21, 1980, WHNF Jim Tucker, WHCF, JCL.

73. Lankevich, *James E. Carter*, 61–62. See also Stanley, *Kennedy vs. Carter*; Glad, *Jimmy Carter*, 469.

74. Lankevich, *James E. Carter*, 58–59. See also Ryan, *The Iranian Rescue Mission*.

75. Maddox, interview; Maddox, *Preacher at the White House*, 98–99.

76. Maddox, *Preacher at the White House*, 136.

77. Quoted in *New York Times*, April 14, 1980, II, 6.

78. *New York Times*, July 6, 1980, 14.

79. Hartmann, "Feminism," 225.

80. *New York Times*, March 23, 1980, IV, 21, April 5, 1980, 7. See also Bisnow, *Diary of a Dark Horse*.

81. Reagan quoted in *New York Times*, April 21, 1980, II, 12.

82. Quoted in *New York Times*, June 22, 1980, 28.

83. Maddox, oral history.

84. Moen, *The Christian Right and Congress*, 38; quoted in *New York Times*, April 27, 1980, 64.

85. Falwell, interview; Martin, *With God on Our Side*, 179–81; Schlafly, interview.

86. Falwell, *Listen America!* 133.

87. Marshner, interview; Marshner quoted in *Los Angeles Times*, February 1, 1980, IV, 8.

88. Marshner quoted in *New York Times*, June 6, 1980, II, 4.

89. Falwell, interview; Marshner, interview; Martin, *With God on Our Side*, 181.

90. *New York Times*, June 6, 1980, II, 4.

91. *New York Times*, June 3, 1980, II, 12.

92. Memo, Sarah Weddington to Fran Voorde and Phil Wise, May 29, 1980, WHNF Jim Tucker, WHCF, JCL.

93. Memo, Stu Eizenstat to the President, May 31, 1980, WHNF Jim Tucker, WHCF, JCL.

94. Stuart Eizenstat to Rosalynn Carter, May 8, 1980, and Stuart Eizenstat to Walter Mondale, May 8, 1978, both in folder (White House Conference on Families), 5/6/80 & 6/2/80, 05/06/1980–06/02/1980, box 113, DPS, WHSF, JCL.

95. Draft, Suggested Remarks for President Jimmy Carter at White House Conference on Families, June 3, 1980, memo, Achsah Nesmith to Sarah Weddington, June 3, 1980, memo, John Carr to Rick Hertzberg, undated, and draft, President's WHCF [White House Conference on Families] Address, undated, all in folder White House Conference on Families, Baltimore, MD RH/AN, 06/05/1980–06/05/1980, box 70, Achsah Nesmith Files, PSWF, WHSF, JCL.

96. Press release, Remarks of the President to the White House Conference on Families, June 5, 1980, folder White House Conference on Families, Baltimore, MD RH/AN, 06/05/1980–06/05/1980, box 70, Achsah Nesmith Files, PSWF, WHSF, JCL.

97. Marshner, interview; Martin, *With God on Our Side*, 182–83; *New York Times*, June 8, 1980, 24, June 9, 1980, III, 16.

98. Quoted in Martin, *With God on Our Side*, 183.

99. Marshner, interview; Marshner and Tucker quoted in *New York Times*, June 7, 1980, 46.

100. Marshner, interview; Carr quoted in Martin, *With God on Our Side*, 184.

101. Tucker quoted in *New York Times*, June 9, 1980, III, 16.

102. Regier quoted in Martin, *With God on Our Side*, 185.

103. *New York Times*, June 22, 1980, 24; quoted in *It's Time: The Newsletter of the National Gay Task Force* 7, no. 5 (1980): 1.

104. Quoted in *New York Times*, June 20, 1980, 18; Schlafly quoted in June 23, 1980, II, 8.

105. Quoted in *New York Times*, June 22, 1980, 24.

106. *New York Times*, June 27, 1980, 20.

107. Kilpatrick quoted in Martin, *With God on Our Side*, 186.

108. Falwell, interview.

109. *Christianity Today*, September 19, 1980, 40; Martin, *With God on Our Side*, 342.

110. *New York Times*, July 11, 1980, 14.

111. Ibid.; Marshner, interview.

112. Schlafly, interview; Marshner, interview; quoted in Clendinen and Nagourney, *Out for Good*, 423.

113. Quoted in Martin, *With God on Our Side*, 185.

SEVEN The Reagan Revolution

1. *Christianity Today*, September 19, 1980, 50; Balmer, *God in the White House*, 112–14; Busch, *Reagan's Victory*, 50; Cannon, *Reagan*, 131.

2. Reagan quoted in Drew, *Portrait of an Election*, 173.

3. Wirthlin quoted in ibid., 172.

4. *New York Times*, July 30, 1980, 1.

5. Martin, *With God on Our Side*, 214.

6. Quoted in *New York Times*, June 21, 1980, 8.

7. *New York Times*, July 8, 1980, 1, July 9, 1980, 1, July 10, 1980, 1.

8. *New York Times*, July 7, 1980, II, 8, July 14, 1980, 14, July 16, 1980, 14.

9. Phillips, interview; Busch, *Reagan's Victory*, 82; Falwell quoted in D'Souza, *Falwell Before the Millennium*, 126.

10. Maddox, *Preacher at the White House*, 166.

11. Bush quoted on Balmer, *God in the White House*, 116.

12. Busch, *Reagan's Victory*, 81.

13. Ibid.; Falwell, interview; Craig and O'Brien, *Abortion and American Politics*, 166; quoted in Martin, *With God on Our Side*, 212.

14. Busch, *Reagan's Victory*, 81–82.

15. Drew, *Portrait of an Election*, 189–90.

16. Ibid., 190–91, 193.

17. *New York Times*, July 30, 1980, 1.

18. Quoted in ibid., B6.

19. *New York Times*, July 9, 1980, 1, July 10, 1980, 18.

20. Rosalind Petchesky, "Antiabortion, Antifeminism, and the Rise of the New Right," 206–46, quoted in Clendinen and Nagourney, *Out for Good*, 423–24.

21. *New York Times*, July 30, 1980, 1.

22. Gorney, *Articles of Faith*, 336, 346; quoted in Martin, *With God on Our Side*, 214. See also Hunter, *Culture Wars*, 275.

23. Agenda, Briefing with Business Executives, May 15, 1980, folder Briefing for Business Executives on ERA, 5/15/80, 05/15/1980–05/15/1980, box 3, Briefing Files, APWA, WHSF, JCL; transcript, Remarks of the President to Business Executives, May 15, 1980, folder ERA (2–7), box 29, APWA, WHSF, JCL.

24. Memo, Barbara Haugen to Bill Albers, May 12, 1980, folder ERA (2–7), box 29, APWA, WHSF, JCL.

25. Memo, Marie to Sarah Weddington, June 21, 1980, folder ERA Strategy Group, box 33, APWA, WHSF, JCL.

26. Quoted in *New York Times*, June 5, 1980, II, 9.

27. Quoted in *New York Times*, August 13, 1980, II, 3.

28. Wexler quoted in ibid.

29. Statement of President Jimmy Carter on the 1980 Democratic Party Platform, August 13, 1980, folder ERA (2–7), box 29, APWA, WHSF, JCL.

30. Martin Franks to C. R. Brydon and Lucia Valeska, March 17, 1980, folder Gay Task Force, National (10/79–3/24/80), 10/1979–03/24/1980, box 7, Robert Malson Files, DPS, WHSF, JCL.

31. Memo, Alison Thomas to Anne Wexler, May 23, 1980, folder Gay Task Force, National (4/1/80–n.d.), 04/01/1980–04/01/1980, box 7, Robert Malson Files, DPS, WHSF, JCL.

32. *Gay Community News*, June 21, 1980, 1.

33. *Sentinel*, June 13, 1980, 1; Clendinen and Nagourney, *Out for Good*, 417–18.

34. Maddox, interview; Maddox, *Preacher at the White House*, 168–69.

35. Busch, *Reagan's Victory*, 89; Germond and Witcover, *Blue Smoke and Mirrors*, 203.

36. *New York Times*, August 13, 1980, II, 13, August 15, 1980, 22.

37. Remarks, Acceptance of Democratic Party Nomination, Jimmy Carter, Democratic Party National Convention, August 14, 1980, American Presidency Project, University of California–Santa Barbara, http://www.presidency.ucsb.edu/ws/index.php?pid=44909, accessed May 19, 2008.

38. *New York Times*, August 15, 1980, II, 3.

39. Quoted in *New York Times*, September 16, 1980, II, 4.

40. *New York Times*, August 3, 1980, 1.

41. James Robison to President Jimmy Carter, June 3, 1980, WHNF James Robison, WHCF, JCL.

42. Maddox, interview; memo, Bob Maddox to Fran Voorde et al., June 12, 1980, WHNF James Robison, WHCF, JCL.

43. Fran Voorde to James Robison, July 17, 1980, WHNF James Robison, WHCF, JCL.

44. *Christianity Today*, September 19, 1980, 50; *New York Times*, August 17, 1980, 1.

45. *New York Times*, August 21, 1980, II, 9.

46. Shriver, *The Bible Vote*, 28–29; Moen, *The Christian Right and Congress*, 40.

47. Kater, *Christians on the Right*, 65.

48. Robison quoted in Balmer, *God in the White House*, 118.

49. Falwell, interview; O'Connor, *No Neutral Ground*, 87; Robison and Reagan quoted in Martin, *With God on Our Side*, 216, 217.

50. D'Antonio, *Fall from Grace*, 9.

51. Quoted in Martin, *With God on Our Side*, 217.

52. Falwell, interview; quoted in Goodman and Price, *Jerry Falwell*, 3; D'Souza, *Falwell Before the Millennium*, 122–23.

53. *Newsweek*, November 10, 1980, 76; *Washington Star*, October 13, 1980, 4; *Washington Post*, October 4, 1980, 6.

54. Price and Goodman, *Jerry Falwell*, 5–8, quoted on 5.

55. D'Souza, *Falwell Before the Millennium*, 121.

56. Cook, *New York Times*, and Rowan quoted in ibid.

57. Allen, interview; quoted in Haas, *Jimmy Carter*, 158.

58. McCune and Shea quoted in *New York Times*, August 17, 1980, 1.

59. *New York Times*, August 8, 1980, II, 7; Johnson quoted in July 12, 1980, 6.

60. Zumpano and Stone quoted in *New York Times*, August 27, 1980, 17.

61. *Christianity Today*, September 19, 1980, 10, 14, October 24, 1980, 20.

62. Phillips, interview; Weyrich quoted in *New York Times*, August 18, 1980, II, 7.

63. Balmer, *God in the White House*, 117; Haas, *Jimmy Carter*, 154–55.

64. Haas, *Jimmy Carter*, 154–55.

65. Ibid., 156.

66. *New York Times*, August 17, 1980, 29, August 30, 1980, 44.

67. Kimball quoted in *New York Times*, October 5, 1980, 28, October 6, 1980, II, 8; *Doe v. Delaware*, 450 U.S. 382 (1981).

68. *Harris v. McRae*, 449 U.S. 297 (1980). See also Ambrose, "The *McRae* Case," 26–28.

69. Tompkins, *Roe v. Wade*, 112–13; Solinger, *Beggars and Choosers*, 19; Rubin, *Abortion, Politics*, 173; Tribe, *American Constitutional Law*, 1135.

70. *New York Times*, October 3, 1980, 22.

71. Phillips and Viguerie quoted in *New York Times*, September 18, 1980, 31.

72. *New York Times*, August 20, 1980, II, 22; quoted in September 29, 1980, IV, 13, September 25, 1980, II, 14.

73. Falwell, interview; *New York Times*, March 24, 1980, II, 6; quoted in Brown, *For a Christian Nation*, 90.

74. O'Connor, *No Neutral Ground*, 87; Willke quoted in Gorney, *Articles of Faith*, 336.

75. Gorney, *Articles of Faith*, 347, Higgins quoted on 348.

76. Transcript, Proclamation by the President on Women's Equality Day, 1980, folder ERA (2–7), box 29, APWA, WHSF, JCL.

77. *New York Times*, August 27, 1980, 12.

78. Falwell quoted in *Dallas Times Herald*, October 31, 1980, 17.

79. Schlafly quoted in *Chicago Tribune*, August 12, 1980, 13.

80. Falwell, interview.

81. Hadden and Swann, *Prime Time Preachers*, 164–65; Sigelman and Presser, "Measuring Public Support," 325–37.

82. Yankelovich, "Stepchildren," 5–10.

83. Snowball, *Continuity and Change*, 66; O'Connor, *No Neutral Ground*, 85; Utter and Storey, *The Religious Right*, 10; Falwell quoted in *New York Times*, January 21, 1980, 21; Falwell, interview.

84. *Christianity Today*, March 21, 1980, 48.

85. Falwell, interview; quoted in *New York Times*, August 18, 1980, II, 7; Goodman and Price, *Jerry Falwell*, 32–33.

86. Diamond, *Not by Politics Alone*, 68–69; Zwier, *Born-Again Politics*, 20–22; Shriver, *The Bible Vote*, 13–14; Hill and Owen, *The New Religious Political Right*, 61.

87. Quoted in Hill and Owen, *The New Religious Political Right*, 59–60.

88. Quoted in ibid., 60–61.

89. Jarmin quoted in *New York Times*, March 31, 1980, IV, 10; Maddox quoted in January 21, 1980, 21.

90. Chasey, *The Legislative Scenario*; Snowball, *Continuity and Change*, 43.

91. Alexander-Moegerle, *James Dobson's War on America*, 42.

92. Edgar Bundy Ministries, *Billy Graham*, 140, 142.

93. Reagan quoted in Martin, *With God on Our Side*, 209.

94. Morton Blackwell, oral history audiotape, RRL.

95. Maddox, interview; memo, Robert Maddox to Rosalynn Carter, Anne Wexler, Jody Powell, and Hamilton Jordan, August 22, 1980, Public Relations Files, White House Subject Files, WHCF, JCL.

96. Memo, Jody Powell and Anne Wexler to President Carter, September 8, 1980, Public Relations Files, White House Subject Files, WHCF, JCL.

97. Carter, handwritten notes on ibid.; memo, Rick Hutchinson to Jody Powell, September 11, 1980, Public Relations Files, White House Subject Files, WHCF, JCL; memo, Bob Maddox to Anne Wexler and Jody Powell, September 18, 1980, folder Religious Broadcasters 1980, 1980–1980, box 3, Ray Jenkins Files, WHPO, WHSF, JCL.

98. Memo, Maddox to Wexler and Powell, September 18, 1980.

99. Memo, Mary Hoyt to RSC, October 15, 1980, WHNF Jim Bakker, WHCF, JCL.

100. Memo, Robert Maddox, Talking Points, Meeting with Newly Elected Officers of SBC, August 7, 1980, memo, Bob Maddox to Mrs. Carter, June 11, 1980, and memo,

Phil Wise to Bob Maddox, July 23, 1980, all in WHNF Southern Baptist Convention, WHCF, JCL.

101. Jimmy Carter to Adrian Rogers, August 14, 1980, WHNF Southern Baptist Convention, WHCF, JCL.

102. Joyce Rogers to Rosalynn Carter, August 24, 1980, WHNF Southern Baptist Convention, WHCF, JCL.

103. Marjorie Kelley to Robert Maddox, September 5, 1980, and Robert Maddox to Marjorie Kelley, September 12, 1980, both in WHNF Robert Schuller, WHCF, JCL; Jimmy Carter to Billy Graham, September 9, 1980, WHNF Billy Graham, WHCF, JCL.

104. Shepard, *Forgiven*, 159–60; Jim Bakker to the President, November 3, 1980, WHNF Jim Bakker, WHCF, JCL.

105. Falwell, interview; Goodman and Price, *Jerry Falwell*, 29, 33; Falwell, *Strength for the Journey*, 365.

106. Falwell, interview; *Los Angeles Times*, March 4, 1981, 15.

107. Viguerie, *The New Right*.

108. Quoted in *Christianity Today*, October 24, 1980, 62.

109. Quoted in *New York Times*, October 15, 1980, 18.

110. Quoted in *New York Times*, October 21, 1980, 6.

111. Allen quoted in *New York Times*, October 25, 1980, 9, October 7, 1980, IV, 21, September 29, 1980, IV, 13.

112. Quoted in *New York Times*, September 25, 1980, 27, October 19, 1980, VI, 24.

113. Carroll, *Famous in America*, 246–47; Falwell, *Listen America!* 162; Simon, *Jerry Falwell and the Jews*, 149; Falwell quoted in *Atlanta Journal-Constitution*, August 23, 1980, B1; Harris quoted in *Atlanta Journal-Constitution*, September 25, 1980, II, 10; *Chicago Tribune*, January 29, 1980, 7; Falwell, interview; Schlafly, interview.

114. Maddox, *Preacher at the White House*, 166.

115. Haas, *Jimmy Carter*, 159.

116. *New York Times*, September 30, 1980, 22, August 24, 1980, 28.

117. Haas, *Jimmy Carter*, 160; Germond and Witcover, *Blue Smoke and Mirrors*, 264–65.

118. Reagan quoted in Germond and Witcover, *Blue Smoke and Mirrors*, 255.

119. Falwell, interview.

120. Germond and Witcover, *Blue Smoke and Mirrors*, 268.

121. Reagan and Carter quoted in ibid., 269.

122. Falwell, interview; *Lynchburg News and Daily Advance*, October 31, 1980, 1; *Washington Star*, October 31, 1980, 1; D'Souza, *Falwell Before the Millennium*, 124.

123. Falwell, interview; Shiver, *The Bible Vote*, 20–21; Falwell, *Strength for the Journey*, 375–76; Price and Goodman, *Jerry Falwell*, 9.

124. Quoted in Haas, *Jimmy Carter*, 161, McCarthy quoted on 166; Busch, *Reagan's Victory*, 107.

125. Germond and Witcover, *Blue Smoke and Mirrors*, 256–63.

126. Drew, *Portrait of an Election*, 289.

127. Quoted in *New York Times*, October 6, 1980, 2.

128. *New York Times*, October 16, 1980, 1; quoted in October 15, 1980, 1.

129. Quoted in *New York Times*, October 21, 1980, II, 7.

130. *New York Times*, October 4, 1980, 8, October 30, 1980, II, 14.

131. Quoted in *New York Times*, October 18, 1980, 8.

132. Memo, Jim Guy Tucker to Phil Wise, October 9, 1980, WHNF Jim Tucker, WHCF, JCL.

133. White House Conference on Families, *Listening to America*.

134. Carter and Tucker quoted in *New York Times*, October 23, 1980, III, 1.

135. Marshner quoted in Martin, *With God on Our Side*, 187.

136. Haas, *Jimmy Carter*, 167; transcript, Commission on Presidential Debates, Carter-Reagan Debate, October 28, 1980, http://www.debates.org/pages/trans8ob.html.

137. Falwell, interview; Falwell quoted in D'Souza, *Falwell Before the Millennium*, 100; Reagan quoted in Lankevich, *James E. Carter*, 69.

138. Maddox, interview; Robert Maddox, oral history audiotape, JCL; Maddox, *Preacher at the White House*, 170.

139. Quoted in *Washington Post*, October 31, 1980, 5.

140. Brown, *For a Christian Nation*, 175; W. B. Sanders to President Jimmy Carter, September 28, 1980, Public Relations Files, White House Subject Files, WHCF, JCL.

141. Robert Maddox to W. B. Sanders, October 17, 1980, Public Relations Files, White House Subject Files, WHCF, JCL.

142. Maddox, oral history; *New York Times*, October 5, 1980, 25.

143. Maddox, interview; Maddox, oral history; Maddox, *Preacher at the White House*, 160.

144. *Washington Post*, November 3, 1980, 1; Maddox, oral history; Lankevich, *James E. Carter*, 69; Drew, *Portrait of an Election*, 343.

145. *Washington Post*, November 5, 1980, 1; Maddox, *Preacher at the White House*, 170–71.

146. *New York Times*, November 5, 1980, 1.

147. *New York Times*, November 17, 1980, IV, 12; Jimmy Carter to Jimmy Allen, November 13, 1980, WHNF Southern Baptist Convention, WHCF, JCL; Ruth Graham to Rosalynn Carter, December 11, 1980, WHNF Billy Graham, WHCF, JCL.

148. Quoted in *New York Times*, November 11, 1980, II, 2; see Bonafede, "New Right Preaches," 779–81.

149. Quoted in Martin, *With God on Our Side*, 220.

150. Brown, *For a Christian Nation*, 159; press release, Carol Long, National Right-to-Life Political Action Committee Director, January 1998, http://www.nrle.org/news/1998/NRL1.98/long.html, accessed May 6, 2007.

151. Falwell, *Strength for the Journey*, 365–66.

152. LaHaye quoted in Balmer, *God in the White House*, 119.

153. Viguerie quoted in Kater, *Christians on the Right*, 36; D'Souza, *Falwell Before the Millennium*, 127.

154. Transcript, *700 Club*, November 6, 1980, WHNF 700 Club, WHCF, JCL.

155. Ibid.

156. *Christianity Today*, November 21, 1980, 24, January 23, 1981, 46.

157. *New York Times*, November 28, 1980, 27.

158. Jarmin quoted in *New York Times*, November 9, 1980, 31; Schindler quoted in November 23, 1980, 29; Falwell quoted in November 26, 1980, 17.

159. Perimutter quoted in *New York Times*, December 14, 1980, 32.

160. *New York Times*, November 7, 1980, 7, November 9, 1980, 31.

161. Weddington quoted in *New York Times*, November 7, 1980, 16; Friedan and Steinem quoted in November 11, 1980, 16; Wexler quoted in Cook, "Women White House Advisors," 226.

162. Rosenberg, "How the Media Made," 28; Tom Minnery, "The Religious Right: How Much Credit Can It Take for the Electoral Landslide," *Christianity Today*, December 12, 1980, 1510–11; Castelli, "The Religious Vote," 650; Brown, *For a Christian Nation*, 159; *Time*, December 8, 1980, 24–27; Rubin, *Abortion, Politics*, 113.

163. D'Souza, *Falwell Before the Millennium*, 127.

164. Quoted in Carter, *First Lady from Plains*, 335.

165. Quoted in Harrell, *Pat Robertson*, 181.

166. Jimmy and Rosalynn Carter quoted in Young, *God's Bullies*, 20.

167. *Christianity Today*, December 12, 1980, 14, 52.

168. Brudney and Copeland, "Evangelicals," 1072–107. See also Abramson, Aldrich, and Rohde, *Change and Continuity*; Sandoz and Crab, *A Tide of Discontent*; Lerner, *The Left Hand of God*, 194; Buell and Sigelman, "An Army"; Shriver, *The Bible Vote*, 91; Tamney and Johnson, "The Moral Majority," 145–46.

169. Busch, *Reagan's Victory*, 128; Pinsky, *A Jew among Evangelicals*, 15. See also Himmelstein and McRae, "Social Conservatism"; Lipset and Raab, "Evangelicals," 25–31; Miller and Wattenberg, "Politics from the Pulpit"; Edel, *Defenders of the Faith*, 139.

170. Busch, *Reagan's Victory*, 127–28.

171. Germond and Witcover, *Blue Smoke and Mirrors*, xvii. For a good overview of the results of the 1980 election, see Zwier, "The New Christian Right"; Diamond, *Roads to Dominion*, 209–10; and Cantor, *The Religious Right*, 62–63.

172. Haas, *Jimmy Carter*, 169–71; Busch, *Reagan's Victory*, 128; O'Connor, *No Neutral Ground*, 88. Eight percent fewer women than men voted for the GOP, 46 to 54 percent.

173. Viguerie quoted in Utter and Storey, *The Religious Right*, 10.

174. Rosenberg, "How the Media Made," 27–28; Cook, "Women White House Advisors," 225.

175. Martin, *With God on Our Side*, 220; Broder quoted in Haas, *Jimmy Carter*, 171; Busch, *Reagan's Victory*, 32; McWilliams, *The Politics of Disappointment*, 49.

176. Maddox, *Preacher at the White House*, 179; quoted in Bourne, *Jimmy Carter*, 468.

177. Maddox, *Preacher at the White House*, 120; Busch, *Reagan's Victory*, 23. See also Shirley, *Reagan's Revolution*.

EPILOGUE A Fault Line in American Society

1. Milton, *Paradise Lost*, 253.

2. Weyrich quoted in Balmer, *God in the White House*, 121–22; Martin, *With God on Our Side*, 222.

3. Watt quoted in *New York Times*, August 22, 1981, 6.

4. Morton Blackwell, oral history audiotape, RRL.

5. Falwell, interview.

6. Marshner, interview; Balmer, *God in the White House*, 119–20; Woods, "Christian Faith," 69; Evans and Novak, *The Reagan Revolution*, 204–21.

7. Blackwell, oral history.

8. Bush quoted in *New York Times*, November 11, 1980, II, 8.

9. Pierard, "An Innocent in Babylon," 191.

10. *Conservative Digest* 8 (February 1982): 11; Martin, *With God on Our Side*, 223; Falwell, interview.

11. *Chicago Tribune*, September 5, 1981, 2.

12. McWilliams, *The Politics of Disappointment*, 59.

13. Quoted in Martin, *With God on Our Side*, 208–9.

14. See Blumenthal, "The Righteous Empire," 18–24.

15. Martin, *With God on Our Side*, 223; Falwell, interview; Goodman and Price, *Jerry Falwell*, 61.

16. Memo, Connie Marshner to Rich Williamson, February 17, 1981, folder Pro-Family Activists (1), OA12450, Morton Blackwell Files, RRL.

17. Ibid.

18. Marshner, interview; memo, Richard Williamson to Lyn Nofziger, March 5, 1981, folder Pro-Family Activists (1), OA12450, Morton Blackwell Files, RRL.

19. Memo, Morton Blackwell to Red Cavaney, April 28, 1981, folder Pro-Family Activists (1), OA12450, Morton Blackwell Files, RRL.

20. Memo, Morton Blackwell to Red Cavaney, April 30, 1981, and schedule proposal, Elizabeth Dole, May 5, 1981, both in folder Pro-Family Activists (1), OA12450, Morton Blackwell Files, RRL.

21. Memo, Gregory J. Newell to Morton Blackwell, June 8, 1981, and memo, Morton Blackwell to Elizabeth Dole, June 11, 1981, both in folder Pro-Family Activists (1), OA12450, Morton Blackwell Files, RRL.

22. William Armstrong to Edwin Meese, May 29, 1981, folder Pro-Family Activists (1), OA12450, Morton Blackwell Files, RRL.

23. Orrin Hatch to Ronald Reagan, May 28, 1981, and Trent Lott to Ronald Reagan, May 21, 1981, both in folder Pro-Family Activists (1), OA12450, Morton Blackwell Files, RRL.

24. Memo, Morton Blackwell to Michael Deaver, June 24, 1981, folder Pro-Family Activists (1), OA12450, Morton Blackwell Files, RRL.

25. Memo, Morton Blackwell to Red Cavaney, June 30, 1981, folder Pro-Family Activists (1), OA12450, Morton Blackwell Files, RRL.

26. Max Friedersdorf to Trent Lott, June 4, 1981, folder Pro-Family Activists (1), OA12450, Morton Blackwell Files, RRL.

27. Zettersten, *Dr. Dobson*, 152; Busch, *Reagan's Victory*, 174; D'Souza, *Falwell Before the Millennium*, 132.

28. Falwell, *Strength for the Journey*, 365–66.

29. Reagan quoted in Balmer, *God in the White House*, 121, and in Halsell, *Prophecy and Politics*, 47.

30. Marshner, interview; Smith, *Faith and the Presidency*, 349; Willoughby, *Does America Need*, 76–78.

31. Marshner, interview; memo, Connie Marshner to Morton Blackwell, February 4, 1982, folder Pro-Family Activists (3), OA12450, Morton Blackwell Files, RRL.

32. Memo, Morton Blackwell to Elizabeth Dole, August 20, 1982, folder Pro-Family Activists (3), OA12450, Morton Blackwell Files, RRL; Blackwell, oral history.

33. Blackwell, oral history.

34. Ibid.; Martin, *With God on Our Side*, 232–33.

35. Martin, *With God on Our Side*, 233; Falwell, interview.

36. *Lynchburg News and Daily Advance*, April 2, 1983, 1; Falwell, interview; Martin, *With God on Our Side*, 234.

37. Falwell quoted on D'Souza, *Falwell Before the Millennium*, 133.

38. *Family Protection Report* 3, no. 9 (1981): 4.

39. Reagan quoted in D'Souza, *Falwell Before the Millennium*, 133.

40. Weyrich quoted in Balmer, *God in the White House*, 122.

41. Marley, *Pat Robertson*, 50–51.

42. Boston, *Most Dangerous Man*, 29.

43. Martin, *With God on Our Side*, 235. Reagan did invite Robertson to serve on the task force studying victims of crimes; see Marley, *Pat Robertson*, 45–75, 79, 82.

44. Edel, *Defenders of the Faith*, 193.

45. Reagan, "Abortion," 7–16, quote on 16. The article was reprinted in the Knights of Columbus journal, *Columbia* 63, no. 8 (1983): 4–9.

46. *Washington Post*, May 21, 1983, 14.

47. Busch, *Reagan's Victory*, 174.

48. Marshner, interview; Connie Marshner to William French Smith, April 21, 1983, folder Pro-Family Activists (1), OA12450, Morton Blackwell Files, RRL.

49. *Pro-Family Forum* 10, no. 3 (1983): 1.

50. The changes included spousal IRAS, deductions for adoptions, and a number of new exemptions; see press release, U.S. Senate Republican Policy Committee, "Major Family-Related Tax Changes of the 97th Congress," March 1983, folder Pro-Family Activists (3), OA12450, Morton Blackwell Files, RRL.

51. Draft, Anti-Pornography List, Morton Blackwell, June 24, 1983, folder Pro-Family Activists (4), OA12450, Morton Blackwell Files, RRL.

52. David Williams to Morton Blackwell, February 25, 1983, folder Pro-Family Activists (4), OA12450, Morton Blackwell Files, RRL.

53. *Dallas Morning News*, August 18, 1982, 17; *Dallas Times Herald*, August 18, 1982, 1; memo, Consequences of Court Decision Striking Texas Sodomy Statute, August 1982, folder Homosexuals (2), OA9088, Morton Blackwell Files, RRL.

54. Kenneth Lisenbee to Morton Blackwell, November 15, 1982, folder Homosexuals (2), OA9088, Morton Blackwell Files, RRL.

55. *Newsletter of the Institute for the Scientific Investigation of Sexuality* 1, no. 1 (1983): 1.

56. Cameron, "A Case Against Homosexuality," 17–47; Cameron, *The Life Cycle*; Paul Cameron to Morton Blackwell, July 12, 1982, and press release, Paul Cameron, March 18, 1983, both in folder Homosexuals (3), OA9088, Morton Blackwell Files, RRL.

57. Executive Director, SGBRP, to Morton Blackwell, undated, folder Homosexuals (2), OA9088, Morton Blackwell Files, RRL.

58. *Texas Tribune*, June 9, 1983, 3.

59. Quoted in ibid., 20.

60. Taylor Branch, "Closets of Power," *Harper's*, October 1982, 34–50.

61. Gallagher and Bull, *Perfect Enemies*, 21–22; Kranz and Cusick, *Gay Rights*, 41; quoted in Turner, "Mirror Images," 21.

62. Kranz and Cusick, *Gay Rights*, 41.

63. Cook, "Women White House Advisors," 229–30.

64. Whitney, *The Equal Rights Amendment*, 55.

65. Quoted in *Washington Post*, September 14, 1980, III, 1.

66. Schlafly, interview. For overviews of the cyclical nature of American politics, see Schlesinger's seminal *The Cycles of American History* and Alexander, *Cycles in American Politics*.

67. Smith, *Faith and the Presidency*, 346; Mondale quoted in Balmer, *God in the White House*, 122; Reagan quoted in Martin, *With God on Our Side*, 235.

68. Clark reported for the Memphis newspaper *Commercial Appeal*; Falwell, *Strength for the Journey*, 379.

69. Blackwell, oral history.

70. D'Antonio, *Fall from Grace*, 13. See also Kivisto, "The Rise or Fall," 1–5.

71. See Bruce, *The Rise and Fall*; Thomas and Dobson, *Blinded by the Might*, 24. See also Lienesch, *Redeeming America*, 2–3.

72. Shepard, *Forgiven*, 202; Martin, *With God on Our Side*, 276.

73. D'Souza, *Falwell Before the Millennium*, 136–37.

74. Detwiler, *Standing on the Premises*, 54.

75. Falwell, interview; Harrell, *Pat Robertson*, 39.

76. Cantor, *The Religious Right*, 64–65.

77. Lear and Robertson quoted in Harrell, *Pat Robertson*, 213.

78. Glasser and Bennett quoted in D'Souza, *Falwell Before the Millennium*, 143.

79. Marsden, "The Religious Right," 12.

80. Moen, *The Transformation*, 3.

81. Wilcox, *God's Warriors*, 14–15.

82. Diamond, *Not by Politics Alone*, 32; Cantor, *The Religious Right*, 64.

83. Charles Manatt to Tom Chorlton, August 30, 1982, folder Homosexuals (1), OA9088, Morton Blackwell Files, RRL.

84. Balmer, *God in the White House*, 124.

85. White, *The New Politics*, 11.

86. Balmer, *Thy Kingdom Come*, 170.

87. Detwiler, *Standing on the Premises*, 13.

88. Balmer, *God in the White House*, 127–28.

89. Kivisto, "The Rise or Fall," 1–5.

90. Reed quoted in Balmer, *God in the White House*, 125.

91. Boston, *Most Dangerous Man*, 35; Martin, *With God on Our Side*, 329. See also Vaughn, *The Rise and Fall*; Watson, *The Christian Coalition*; and Reed, *After the Revolution*.

92. Balmer, *Thy Kingdom Come*, 25.

93. Diamond, *Not by Politics Alone*, ix.

94. Balmer, *God in the White House*, 133.

95. Mansfield, *The Faith of George W. Bush*, 53–56.

96. Falwell, interview; quoted in *New York Times*, October 28, 2004, 14; Frum, *The Right Man*; Woodward, *Plan of Attack*.

97. Mansfield, *The Faith of George W. Bush*, 67–73; Balmer, *God in the White House*, 143–47.

98. Warren, *The Purpose Driven Life*; *Time*, August 18, 2008, 36–42.

99. *Dallas Morning News*, June 2, 2008, 11.

100. See Koo, *Tempting Faith*.

101. Gushee, *The Future of Faith*.

102. Balmer, "Jesus Is Not a Republican," 6–9.

103. *Dallas Morning News*, March 18, 2008, 12.

104. *Virginian Pilot*, July 20, 2003, J2.

105. Diamond, *Not by Politics Alone*, vii. See also Shibley, *Resurgent Evangelicalism*; Miller, "Striving to Understand," A17–A18.

106. For the best summary of Carter's postpresidency, see Brinkley, *The Unfinished Presidency*.

107. Carter entitled his memoirs *Keeping Faith*; his other books include *Sources of Strength, Turning Point: A Candidate, A State and a Nation Come of Age, Talking Peace: A Vision for the Next Generation, An Outdoor Journal, Everything to Gain: Making the Most of the Rest of Your Life, The Blood of Abraham: Insights into the Middle East, A Government as Good as Its People, Why Not the Best?* and *Palestine: Peace Not Apartheid.* Carter has also produced a children's book, *The Little Baby Snoogle-Fleejer*, and a book of poetry, *Always a Reckoning.*

108. Rosalynn Carter, National Park Service exit interview, 3:12, JCL.

109. Quoted in Ariail and Heckler-Feltz, *The Carpenter's Apprentice*, 9–10.

110. Ibid., 11–12, 35.

111. Carter, *Living Faith*, 187.

112. Carter quoted in *Dallas Morning News*, January 31, 2004.

113. Carter, *Palestine.*

114. *Dallas Morning News*, October 12, 2002, 1, 22.

115. Falwell, interview.

116. Carter, *Living Faith*, 13.

117. See, for example, *Newsweek*, August 3, 2009, 5; *Dallas Morning News*, September 6, 2009, 4.

118. Cuomo quoted in Christensen, *Utopia Against the Family*, 40; Moynihan, *Family and Nation*; Gellott quoted in Christensen, *Utopia Against the Family*, 41.

119. Carter quoted in *Dallas Morning News*, October 20, 2000, 1.

120. Quoted in *Dallas Morning News*, July 7, 2001, G1.

121. Quoted in *Dallas Morning News*, January 19, 2002, G1.

122. Chittister and Green quoted in *Los Angeles Times*, October 14, 2007, 12.

123. *Los Angeles Times*, October 14, 2007, 12; *National Post*, May 15, 2008, 1.

124. *USA Today*, October 23, 2008, 1.

125. *Dallas Morning News*, January 12, 2002, G1.

126. *Washington Post*, August 28, 2004, B7.

127. *Newsweek*, November 13, 2006, 37.

128. Maddox, *Preacher at the White House*, 123.

Bibliography

PRIMARY SOURCES

Archival Materials

Jimmy Carter Library, Emory University, Atlanta, Georgia (JCL)

National Park Service Exit Interview
    Jimmy Carter
    Rosalynn Carter

Oral History Audiotapes
    Robert Maddox
    Sarah Weddington

White House Central Office Files (WHCF)

    White House Names Files (WHNF)
        Jim Bakker
        Robert Billings
        Bill Bright
        Harold Brown
        Campus Crusade
        John Carr
        Christian Embassy
        Christian Life Commission
        James Dunn
        Jerry Falwell
        Billy Graham
        James Kennedy
        Harvey Milk
        Moral Majority
        National Religious Broadcasters
        Pat Robertson
        James Robison
        Phyllis Schlafly
        Robert Schuller
        700 Club
        Southern Baptist Convention
        Jim Tucker

    White House Subject Files
        Public Relations Files
        Zbigniew Brzezinski Files

White House Staff Office Files (WHSF)

Domestic Policy Staff Files (DPS)
Stuart Eizenstat Files
Annie Gutierrez Files
Robert Malson Files

Office of the Assistant to the President for Women's Affairs Files (APWA)
Bill Albers Files
Briefing Files
Sarah Weddington Files

Office of Chief of Staff Files (OCS)
Landon Butler Files
Stephen Selig Files

Office of the First Lady Files
Kathy Cade Files

Office of Hispanic Affairs Files
Esteban Torres Files

Office of Public Liaison Files (OPL)
Margaret Costanza Files
Jane Wales Files
Seymour Wishman Files

Office of the Special Assistant to the President Files
Louis Martin Files

Office of Special Assistant to the President for Special Projects Files (APSP)
Martha Mitchell Files

Presidential Speechwriters Files (PSWF)
Achsah Nesmith Files

White House Counsel Office Files
Margaret McKenna Files

White House Press Office Files (WHPO)
Advance Office Files
Ray Jenkins Files
Jody Powell Files

Miller Center for Public Affairs, University of Virginia, Charlottesville, Virginia (MCPA)

Jimmy Carter Presidential Materials Project
Stuart Eizenstat, interview, vol. 13, January 29–30, 1982

Ronald Reagan Presidential Library, Simi Valley, California (RRL)

Morton Blackwell Files
OA9088
OA12450

Oral History Audiotape
Morton Blackwell

Interviews

Jimmy Allen, December 4, 2009
Jerry Falwell, July 24, 2003
Annie Gutierrez, December 3, 2009
Robert Maddox, December 2, 2009
Connie Marshner, December 4, 2009
Howard Phillips, December 6, 2009
Michael Richardson, July 15, 2003
Phyllis Schlafly, December 4, 2009

Newspapers

Atlanta Constitution
Atlanta Journal-Constitution
Charlotte Observer
Chicago Daily News
Chicago Sun-Times
Chicago Tribune
Dallas Morning News
Dallas Times Herald
Idaho Statesman
Los Angeles Times
Lynchburg News and Daily Advance
Memphis Commercial Appeal
Miami Herald
Miami News

National Post
New York Times
Richmond Times-Dispatch
Rochester Democrat and Chronicle
San Francisco Chronicle
Santa Barbara, California, News-Press
St. Louis Post Dispatch
Texas Tribune
Toronto Star
USA Today
Virginian Pilot
Washington Post
Washington Star

Periodicals

Arizona Gay News
Capitol Hill: The Newsletter of the Gay Rights National Lobby
Christianity Today
Commentary
Commonweal
Congressional Quarterly Weekly Report
Congressional Record
Conservative Digest
Eagle Forum
Esquire
Family Protection Report
Federal Times
Gay Blade

Gay Community News
Georgia Baptist Convention News Magazine
Human Life Review
Interpreter
It's Time: The Newsletter of the National Gay Task Force
LifeLetter
Life's Answer: The Newsletter of the James Robison Association
Nation
National Association of Social Workers News
National Enquirer
National Journal

New Republic
Newsletter: Mormons for ERA
Newsletter of the Institute for the
   Scientific Investigation of Sexuality
Newsweek
Phyllis Schlafly Report
Playboy
Presbyterian Journal
Pro-Family Forum
Quash: Newsletter of the Grand Jury
   Report

Report from the White House
   Conference on Families
Right to Believe: Newsletter of the
   Centre for the Study of Religion
   and Communism Sentinel
Sentinel
Theology Today
Time
U.S. News and World Report
Washington Blade
Washington Monthly

Government Publications

Hearings on Equal Rights 1970, Before the Committee on the Judiciary, United States Senate, September 9, 10, 11, 15, 1970. Washington, D.C.: U.S. Government Printing Office, 1970.

Hearings on the Equal Rights Amendment, Before Subcommittee #4 of the Committee on the Judiciary, United States House of Representatives, March 24, 25, 31; April 1, 2, 5, 1971. Washington, D.C.: U.S. Government Printing Office, 1971.

National Institute for Advanced Studies. Summary of National Hearings of the White House Conference on Families. Washington, D.C.: White House Conference on Families and the Department of Health, Education, and Welfare, 1980.

Public Papers of the Presidents, Jimmy Carter, 1977–1980. Washington, D.C.: U.S. Government Printing Office, 1977–80.

To Form a More Perfect Union: Report of the National Commission of International Women's Year 1976. Washington, D.C.: U.S. Government Printing Office, 1977.

U.S. Commission on Civil Rights. Report on the Constitutional Aspects of the Right to Limit Childbearing. Washington, D.C.: U.S. Government Printing Office, 1975.

U.S. Congress. House. Report 92-359, 92nd Congress, 1st Session, 1971. Washington, D.C.: U.S. Government Printing Office, 1971.

U.S. Congress. Senate. Report No. 92-689, 92nd Congress, 2nd Session, 1972. Washington, D.C.: U.S. Government Printing Office, 1972.

White House Conference on Families. Listening to America: Action for the 80s: The Report to the President, Congress and Families of the Nation. Washington, D.C.: White House Conference on Families, 1980.

Memoirs

Abzug, Bella, and Mim Kelber. Gender Gap: Bella Abzug's Guide to Political Power for American Women. Boston: Houghton Mifflin, 1984.

Armstrong, Ben. The Electric Church. Nashville: T. Nelson, 1979.

Bright, Bill. A Movement of Miracles. San Bernardino, Calif.: Campus Crusade for Christ, 1977.

Califano, Joseph, Jr. Governing America: An Insider's Report from the White House and the Cabinet. New York: Simon and Schuster, 1981.

Carter, Jimmy. *The Blood of Abraham*. Boston: Houghton Mifflin, 1985.

———. *Christmas in Plains*. New York: Simon and Schuster, 2001.

———. *Keeping Faith: Memoirs of a President*. New York: Bantam Books, 1982.

———. *Living Faith*. New York: Random House, 1996.

———. *Palestine: Peace Not Apartheid*. New York: Simon and Schuster, 2006.

———. *The Personal Beliefs of Jimmy Carter*. New York: Three Rivers Press, 2002.

———. *Sources of Strength*. New York: Random House, 1977.

———. *Why Not the Best?* New York: Bantam Books, 1976.

Carter, Rosalynn. *First Lady from Plains*. Boston: Houghton Mifflin, 1984.

Daniel, Frank, and Carroll Hart, eds. *Addresses of Jimmy Carter (James Earl Carter), Governor of Georgia, 1971–1975*. Atlanta: Georgia Department of Archives and History, 1975.

Dobson, James. *Dare to Discipline*. New York: Bantam, 1980.

———. *The Strong-Willed Child*. Las Vegas: Living Books, 1992.

———. *What Wives Wished Their Husbands Knew About Women*. Las Vegas: Living Books, 1981.

Falwell, Jerry, ed. *The Fundamentalist Phenomenon: The Resurgence of Conservative Christianity*. Garden City, N.Y.: Doubleday, 1981.

———. *Listen America!* Garden City, N.Y.: Doubleday, 1980.

———. *Strength for the Journey: An Autobiography*. New York: Simon and Schuster, 1987.

Jordan, Hamilton. *No Such Thing as a Bad Day*. Atlanta: Longstreet Press, 2000.

LaHaye, Tim. *Battle for the Mind*. Ada, Mich.: Fleming H. Revell, 1980.

———. *Unhappy Gays: What Everyone Should Know About Homosexuality*. Carol Stream, Ill.: Tyndale House, 1978.

Maddox, Robert. *Preacher at the White House*. Nashville: Broadman, 1984.

Marshner, Connaught. *Blackboard Tyranny*. New Rochelle, N.Y.: Arlington House Publishers, 1978.

Robertson, Pat. *Bring It On*. Nashville: Thomas Nelson, 2008.

———. *Miracles Can Be Yours Today*. Nashville: Thomas Nelson, 2006.

———. *The New World Order*. Nashville: Thomas Nelson, 1992.

———. *Right on the Money: Financial Advice for Tough Times*. New York: FaithWords Publishing, 2009.

Schaeffer, Francis. *The Christian Manifesto*. Wheaton, Ill.: Crossway Books, 1982.

———. *How Should We Then Live?* Wheaton, Ill.: Crossway Books, 1983.

Schaeffer, Francis, and C. Everett Koop. *What Ever Happened to the Human Race?* Wheaton, Ill.: Crossway Books, 1983.

Schlafly, Phyllis. *The Power of Positive Women*. New York: Jove Publications, 1978.

———. *The Power of the Christian Woman*. Cincinnati: Standard Publishing, 1981.

Schlafly, Phyllis, and Chester Ward. *Ambush at Vladivostok*. Milwaukee: Pere Marquette Press, 1976.

Schuller, Robert. *Peace of Mind Through Possibility Thinking*. Old Tappan, N.J.: F. H. Revell, 1977.

———. *The Peak to Peek Principle*. Old Tappan, N.J.: F. H. Revell, 1975.

———. *Reach Out for New Life*. New York: Bantam, 1977.

Viguerie, Richard. *The New Right: We're Ready to Lead*. Falls Church, Va.: Viguerie Company, 1980.

SECONDARY SOURCES

Abramson, Paul, John Aldrich, and David Rohde. *Change and Continuity in the 1980 Election*. Washington, D.C.: Congressional Quarterly Press, 1982.

Adams, Bruce, and Kathryn Kavanagh-Baran. *Promise and Performance: Carter Builds a New Administration*. Lexington, Mass.: D. C. Heath, 1979.

Aitken, Jonathan. *Nixon: A Life*. Washington, D.C.: Regnery Publishing, 1993.

Alan Guttmacher Institute. *Fact Sheet: Abortion in the United States*. New York: AGI, 1995.

Alexander, Michael. *Cycles in American Politics: How Political, Economic, and Cultural Trends Have Shaped the Nation*. Bloomington, Ind.: iUniverse, 2004.

Alexander-Moegerle, Gil. *James Dobson's War on America*. Amherst, N.Y.: Prometheus Books, 1997.

Altman, Dennis. "What Changed in the Seventies?" In *Homosexuality: Power and Politics*, ed. Gay Left Collective. New York: Allison and Busby, 1980.

Ambrose, Linda. "The *McRae* Case: A Record of the Hyde Amendment's Impact on Religious Freedom and Health Care." *Family Planning–Population Reporter* 7 (April 1978): 26–28.

Ambrose, Stephen. *Nixon: The Triumph of a Politician, 1962–1972*. New York: Simon and Schuster, 1989.

Anderson, Patrick. *Electing Jimmy Carter: The Campaign of 1976*. Baton Rouge: Louisiana State University Press, 1994.

Apple, Michael W., and Linda K. Christian-Smith. *The Politics of the Textbook*. New York: Routledge, 1991.

Ariail, Dan, and Cheryl Heckler-Feltz. *The Carpenter's Apprentice: The Spiritual Biography of Jimmy Carter*. Grand Rapids, Mich.: Zondervan Publishing, 1996.

Ashbrook, William. *Evangelism: The New Neutralism*. Columbus, Ohio: Calvary Baptist Church, 1963.

Balmer, Randall. *God in the White House: How Faith Shaped the Presidency from John F. Kennedy to George W. Bush*. New York: HarperCollins, 2008.

———. "Jesus Is Not a Republican." *Chronicle Review*, sec. B of *Chronicle of Higher Education*, June 23, 2006.

———. *Thy Kingdom Come: An Evangelical's Lament*. New York: Basic Books, 2006.

Barr, James. *Fundamentalism*. Santa Ana, Calif.: Westminster, 1978.

Bartley, Numan V. *Jimmy Carter and the Politics of the New South*. St. Louis, Mo.: Forum Press, 1979.

Bates, Stephen. *Battleground: One Mother's Crusade, the Religious Right, and the Struggle for Control of Our Classrooms*. New York: Poseidon Press, 1993.

Bawer, Bruce. *Stealing Jesus: How Fundamentalism Betrays Christianity*. New York: Three Rivers Press, 1997.

Becker, Susan. *The Origins of the Equal Rights Amendment: American Feminism Between the Wars*. Westport, Conn.: Greenwood Press, 1981.

Beckman, Linda, and S. Marie Harvey, eds. *The New Civil War: The Psychology, Culture, and Politics of Abortion*. Washington, D.C.: American Psychological Association, 1998.

Bell, Daniel. "The Revolt Against Modernity." *Public Interest* 81 (1985): 42–63.

Billings, Robert. *A Guide to the Christian School*. Metairie, La.: ACTion Press, 1978.

Bisnow, Mark. *Diary of a Dark Horse: The 1980 Anderson Presidential Campaign*. Carbondale: Southern Illinois University Press, 1983.

Blake, Judith. "Abortion and Public Opinion: 1960–1970." *Science*, February 12, 1971, 540–49.

Blumenthal, Sidney. "The Righteous Empire: A Short History of the End of History and Maybe Even of the GOP." *New Republic*, October 22, 1984, 18–24.

Boles, Janet K. "Systemic Factors Underlying Legislative Responses to Woman Suffrage and the Equal Rights Amendment." In *The Equal Rights Amendment: The Politics and Process of Ratification of the 27th Amendment to the U.S. Constitution*, ed. Sarah Slavin. New York: Haworth Press, 1982.

Bonafede, Dom. "New Right Preaches a New Religion and Ronald Reagan Is Its Prophet." *National Journal*, May 2, 1981, 779–81.

Boston, Robert. *The Most Dangerous Man in America? Pat Robertson and the Rise of the Christian Coalition*. Amherst, N.Y.: Prometheus Books, 1996.

Boswell, John. *Same-Sex Unions in Premodern Europe*. New York: Vintage, 1995.

Bourne, Peter G. *Jimmy Carter: A Comprehensive Biography from Plains to Post-presidency*. New York: Scribner, 1997.

Brady, D., and K. Tedin. "Ladies in Pink: Religion and Political Ideology in the Anti-ERA Movement." *Social Science Quarterly* 56 (1976): 564–75.

Brinkley, Douglas. *The Unfinished Presidency: Jimmy Carter's Journey Beyond the White House*. New York: Penguin Books, 1998.

Bronski, Michael. *The Pleasure Principle: Sex, Backlash and the Struggle for Gay Freedom*. New York: St. Martin's Press, 1998.

Brown, Ruth Murray. *For a Christian Nation: A History of the Religious Right*. Amherst, N.Y.: Prometheus Books, 2002.

Bruce, Steve. *The Rise and Fall of the New Christian Right*. New York: Oxford University Press, 1990.

Brudney, Jeffrey, and Gary Copeland. "Evangelicals as a Political Force: Reagan and the 1980 Religious Vote." *Social Science Quarterly* 65 (1984): 1072–79.

Buell, Emmet, and Lee Sigelman. "An Army that Meets Every Sunday? Popular Support for the Moral Majority in 1980." *Social Science Quarterly* 66 (1985): 426–34.

Busch, Andrew E. *Reagan's Victory: The Presidential Election of 1980 and the Rise of the Right*. Lawrence: University Press of Kansas, 2005.

Cameron, Paul. "A Case Against Homosexuality." *Human Life Review* 4, no. 1 (1978): 17–47.

———. *The Life Cycle*. Oceanside, N.Y.: Dabor Science Publishers, 1977.

Cannon, Lou. *Reagan*. New York: G. P. Putnam's Sons, 1982.

Cantor, David. *The Religious Right: The Assault on Tolerance and Pluralism in America*. Washington, D.C.: Anti-Defamation League, 1994.

Capps, Walter H. *The New Religious Right: Piety, Patriotism, and Politics*. Columbia: University of South Carolina Press, 1990.

Carroll, Peter N. *Famous in America: The Passion to Succeed*. New York: E. P. Dutton, 1985.

Castelli, Jim. "The Religious Vote." *Commonweal*, November 21, 1980, 650–51.

Catherwood, Christopher. *Five Evangelical Leaders*. Wheaton, Ill.: Harold Shaw Publishers, 1985.

Chandler, Ralph Clark. "The Wicked Shall Not Bear Rule: The Fundamentalist Heritage of the New Christian Right." In *New Christian Politics*, ed. David G. Bromley and Anson Shupe. Macon, Ga.: Mercer University Press, 1984.

Chasey, William. *The Legislative Scenario*. Washington, D.C.: Religious Roundtable, 1980.

Christensen, Bryce J. *Utopia Against the Family*. San Francisco: Ignatius Press, 1990.

Clendinen, Didley, and Adam Nagourney. *Out for Good: The Struggle for a Gay Rights Movement in America*. New York: Simon and Schuster, 1999.

Colson, Charles. *Born Again*. Ada, Mich.: Chosen Books, 1976.

Congressional Quarterly Guide to the 1976 Election. Washington, D.C.: Congressional Quarterly, 1977.

Conn, Joseph L. "The New Christian Politics." *Church and State* 33 (July–August 1980): 15–19.

Cook, Elizabeth Adell, Ted G. Jelen, and Clyde Wilcox. *Between Two Absolutes: Public Opinion and the Politics of Abortion*. Boulder, Colo.: Westview Press, 1992.

Cook, Emily Walker. "Women White House Advisors in the Carter Administration: Presidential Stalwarts or Feminist Activists." PhD diss., Vanderbilt University, 1995.

Costain, Anne A. *Inviting Women's Rebellion: A Political Process Interpretation of the Women's Movement*. Baltimore, Md.: Johns Hopkins University Press, 1992.

Craig, Barbara Hinkson, and David M. O'Brien. *Abortion and American Politics*. Chatham, N.J.: Chatham House Publishers, 1993.

Dabney, Dick. "God's Own Network." *Harper's*, August 1980, 33–52.

D'Antonio, Michael. *Fall from Grace: The Failed Crusade of the Christian Right*. New York: Farrar, Straus and Giroux, 1989.

Darien, Gary. "Berger's Theology and Sociology." In *Peter Berger and the Study of Religion*, ed. Linda Woodhead et al. New York: Routledge, 2003.

Dart, John. "Graham and Nixon: Anti-Jewish Words on Tape." *Christian Century*, March 13, 2002, 7–9.

Davis, Flora. *Moving the Mountain: The Women's Movement in America since 1960*. New York: Simon and Schuster, 1991.

Delbanco, Andrew, ed. *Representative Men: The Collected Works of Ralph Waldo Emerson*, vol. 4. Cambridge, Mass.: Harvard University Press, 1996.

Delsman, Mary A. *Everything You Need to Know about ERA*. Riverside, Calif.: Meranza Press, 1975.

Detwiler, Fritz. *Standing on the Premises of God: The Christian Right's Fight to Redefine America's Public Schools*. New York: New York University Press, 1999.

Deutchman, Iva E., and Sandra Prince-Embury. "Political Ideology of Pro- and Anti-ERA Women." In *The Equal Rights Amendment: The Politics and Process of Ratification of the 27th Amendment to the U.S. Constitution*, ed. Sarah Slavin, 39–55. New York: Haworth Press, 1982.

Diamond, Sara. *Not by Politics Alone: The Enduring Influence of the Christian Right*. New York: Guilford Press, 1998.

———. *Roads to Dominion: Right-Wing Movements and Political Power in the United States*. New York: Guilford Press, 1995.

Dionne, E. J., Jr., and John J. Diiulio Jr., eds. *What's God Got to Do with the American Experiment?* Washington, D.C.: Brookings Institution Press, 2000.

Drew, Elizabeth. *American Journal: The Events of 1976*. New York: Vintage, 1978.

———. *Portrait of an Election: The 1980 Presidential Campaign*. New York: Simon and Schuster, 1981.

D'Souza, Dinesh. *Falwell Before the Millennium: A Critical Biography*. Chicago: Regnery Gateway, 1984.

——. "The Political Contributions of the Religious Right." In *The Religious Right*, ed. Gary McCuen. Hudson, Wis.: Gary McCuen, 1989.

Echols, Alice. *Daring to Be Bad: Radical Feminism in America, 1967–1975.* Minneapolis: University of Minnesota Press, 1989.

Edel, Wilbue. *Defenders of the Faith: Religion and Politics from the Pilgrim Fathers to Ronald Reagan.* New York: Praeger, 1987.

Edgar Bundy Ministries. *Billy Graham: Performer? Politician? Preacher? Prophet?* Miami: Edgar Bundy Ministries, 1982.

Evans, Rowland, and Robert Novak. *The Reagan Revolution.* New York: Dutton, 1981.

Fackre, Gabriel. *The Religious Right and the Christian Faith.* Grand Rapids, Mich.: William Eerdmans Publishing, 1982.

Felsenthal, Carol. *The Sweetheart of the Moral Majority.* Garden City, N.Y.: Doubleday, 1981.

Finch, Phillip. *God, Guts, and Guns.* New York: Seaview, 1983.

Fink, Gary M. *Prelude to the Presidency: The Political Character and Legislative Leadership Style of Governor Jimmy Carter.* Westport, Conn.: Greenwood Press, 1980.

Fink, Gary, and Hugh Davis Graham, eds. *The Carter Presidency: Policy Choices in the Post–New Deal Era.* Lawrence: University Press of Kansas, 1998.

Finkle, Jason L., and C. Alison McIntosh, eds. *The New Politics of Population: Conflict and Consensus in Family Planning.* Washington, D.C.: Population Council, 1994.

Frady, Marshall. *Billy Graham: A Parable of American Righteousness.* Boston: Little, Brown, 1979.

Frank, Barney. "In Praise of Partisanship." *Gay and Lesbian Review* 11, no. 5 (2004).

Friedan, Betty. *The Feminine Mystique.* New York: W. W. Norton, 1963.

Frum, David. *The Right Man: The Surprise Presidency of George W. Bush.* New York: Random House, 2003.

Galas, Judith C. *Gay Rights.* San Diego: Lucent Books, 1996.

Gallagher, John, and Chris Bull. *Perfect Enemies: The Religious Right, the Gay Movement, and the Politics of the 1990s.* New York: Crown Publishers, 1996.

Gannon, Thomas. "The New Christian Right in America." *Archives de Sciences Sociales des Religions* 52, no. 1 (1981).

Gaver, Jessyca. *The Faith of Jimmy Carter.* New York: Manor Books, 1977.

Gay Rights National Lobby. *Does Support for Gay Rights Spell Political Suicide? A Close Look at Some Long-Held Myths.* Washington, D.C.: Gay Rights National Lobby, 1981.

Germond, Jack W., and Jules Witcover. *Blue Smoke and Mirrors: How Reagan Won and Why Carter Lost the Election of 1980.* New York: Viking Press, 1981.

Gilbert, J. E. "Ballot Salvation." *Journal of Popular Culture* 18, no. 1 (1984).

Gilbert, James. *A Cycle of Outrage: America's Reaction to the Juvenile Delinquent in the 1950s.* New York: Oxford University Press, 1986.

Glad, Betty. *Jimmy Carter: In Search of the Great White House.* New York: W. W. Norton, 1980.

Gomez, Jewelle. "Out of the Past." In *The Question of Equality*, ed. David Deitcher. New York: Scribner, 1995.

Goodman, William R., Jr., and James J. H. Price. *Jerry Falwell: An Unauthorized Profile.* Lynchburg, Va.: Paris and Associates, 1981.

Gorney, Cynthia. *Articles of Faith: A Frontline History of the Abortion Wars.* New York: Simon and Schuster, 1998.

Graham, Hugh Davis. "Civil Rights in the Carter Presidency." In Fink and Graham, *The Carter Presidency,* 202–23.

Greer, Germaine. *The Female Eunuch*. London: MacGibbon and Kee, 1970.

———. *Sex and Destiny: The Politics of Human Fertility*. New York: Harper Collins, 1984.

Gregory-Lewis, Sasha. "The Republicans: Embracing Homophobes and Gay Rights Backers: A Fresh Look at the Grand Old Party." In *Witness to Revolution: The Advocate Reports on Gay and Lesbian Politics*, ed. Chris Bull. Los Angeles: Alyson Books, 1999.

Griffin, William, and Ruth Graham Dienert, eds. *The Faithful Christian: An Anthology of Billy Graham*. New York: McCracken Press, 1994.

Gushee, David. *The Future of Faith in America: The Public Witness of the Evangelical Center*. Waco, Tex.: Baylor University Press, 2008.

Guth, James L. "The Politics of the Evangelical Right: An Interpretive Essay." Paper presented at the annual meeting of the American Political Science Association, New York, September 1981.

Haas, Garland A. *Jimmy Carter and the Politics of Frustration*. Jefferson, N.C.: McFarland, 1992.

Hadden, Jeffrey, and Charles Swann. *Prime Time Preachers: The Rising Power of Televangelism*. Reading, Mass.: Addison-Wesley, 1981.

Hall, Cline, and Jerry Combee. "The Moral Majority: Is It a New Ecumenicalism?" *Foundations* 25, no. 2 (1982).

Halsell, Grace. *Prophecy and Politics: The Secret Alliance Between Israel and the U.S. Christian Right*. Chicago: Lawrence Hill Books, 1986.

Harding, Susan Field. *The Book of Jerry Falwell: Fundamentalist Language and Politics*. Princeton, N.J.: Princeton University Press, 2000.

Hargrove, Erwin C. *Jimmy Carter as President: Leadership and the Politics of the Public Good*. Baton Rouge: Louisiana State University Press, 1988.

Harrell, David Edwin, Jr. *Pat Robertson: A Personal, Religious, and Political Portrait*. San Francisco: Harper and Row, 1987.

Hartmann, Susan. "Feminism, Public Policy, and the Carter Administration." In Fink and Graham, *The Carter Presidency*.

Hastey, Stan, and Warren Ragsdale. "Right Religion, Right Politics?" *Homer Missions* 51 (October 1980).

Hatch, Orrin G. *The Equal Rights Amendment: Myths and Realities*. New York: Savant Press, 1983.

Hefley, James, and Marti Hefley. *The Church that Produced a President: The Remarkable Spiritual Roots of Jimmy Carter*. New York: Weyden Books, 1977.

Herman, Didi. *The Antigay Agenda: Orthodox Vision and the Christian Right*. Chicago: University of Chicago Press, 1997.

Hill, Simon S., and Dennis E. Owen. *The New Religious Political Right in America*. Nashville: Abington Press, 1982.

Himmelstein, Jerome, and J. A. McRae Jr. "Social Conservatism, New Republicans, and the 1980 Election." *Public Opinion Quarterly* 48 (1984): 596–605.

Hippler, Mike. *Matlovich: The Good Soldier*. Boston: Alyson Publications, 1989.

Holbrook, Sabra. *Fighting Back: The Struggle for Gay Rights*. New York: E. P. Dutton, 1987.

The Holy Bible: New International Version. Grand Rapids, Mich.: Zondervan, 1977.

Homans, Hilary, ed. *The Sexual Politics of Reproduction*. Brookfield, Vt.: Gower Publishing, 1985.

Hottois, James, and Neal Milner. *The Sex Education Controversy: A Study of Politics, Education and Morality.* Lexington, Mass.: D. C. Heath, 1975.

Hunter, James D. *Culture Wars: The Struggle to Define America.* New York: Basic Books, 1991.

Hunter, Joel. *A New Kind of Conservative.* Ventura, Calif.: Regal Books, 2008.

Hymowitz, Carol, and Michaele Weissman. *A History of Women in America.* New York: Bantam Books, 1988.

Ide, Arthur Frederick. *Idol Worshippers in 20th Century America.* Dallas: Monument Press, 1985.

Irwin, Inez. *The Story of Alice Paul and the National Women's Party.* New York: Harcourt, 1920.

Johnson, Maury. *Gays under Grace: A Gay Christian's Response to the Moral Majority.* Nashville: Winston-Derek Publishers, 1983.

Johnson, Paul, and Thomas Eaves. *Gays and the New Right: A Debate on Homosexuality.* Los Angeles: T & P Bookshelf, 1981.

Jones, Charles O. "Keeping Faith and Losing Congress: The Carter Experience in Washington." *Presidential Studies Quarterly* 14, no. 3 (1984).

——. *The Trustee Presidency: Jimmy Carter and the United States Congress.* Baton Rouge: Louisiana State University Press, 1988.

Kater, John L., Jr. *Christians on the Right: The Moral Majority in Perspective.* New York: Seabury Press, 1982.

Kaufman, Burton. *The Presidency of James Earl Carter, Jr.* Lawrence: University Press of Kansas, 1993.

Kienel, Paul A. *The Christian School: Why It Is Right for Your Child.* Wheaton, Ill.: Victor Books, 1974.

Kincheloe, Joe L. *Understanding the New Right and Its Impact on Education.* Bloomington, Ind.: Phi Delta Kappa Educational Foundation, 1983.

Kinsey, Alfred. *Sexual Behavior in the Human Male.* Philadelphia: W. B. Saunders, 1948.

Kivisto, Peter. "The Rise or Fall of the Christian Right? Conflicting Reports from the Frontline." In *The Rapture of Politics: The Christian Right as the United States Approaches the Year 2000*, ed. Steve Bruce, Peter Kivisto, and William Swatos Jr. New Brunswick, N.J.: Transaction Publishers, 1995.

Klein, Ethel. *Gender Politics: From Consciousness to Mass Politics.* Cambridge, Mass.: Harvard University Press, 1984.

Koo, David. *Tempting Faith: The Inside Story of Political Seduction.* New York: Free Press, 2007.

Kranz, Rachel, and Tim Cusick. *Gay Rights.* New York: Facts on File, 2000.

Kraus, Sidney. *The Great Debates, Carter vs. Ford, 1976.* Bloomington: Indiana University Press, 1979.

Kucharsky, David. *The Man from Plains: The Mind and Spirit of Jimmy Carter.* New York: Harper and Row, 1976.

Lankevich, George J., ed. *James E. Carter: Chronology, Documents, Bibliographic Aids.* Dobbs Ferry, N.Y.: Oceana Publications, 1981.

Larson, Edward J. "Constitutional Challenges to Textbooks." In *Textbooks in American Society: Politics, Policy, and Pedagogy*, ed. Philip Altback, Gail Kelly, Hugh Petrie, and Lois Weis. Albany: State University of New York Press, 1991.

Lerner, Michael. *The Left Hand of God.* New York: HarperCollins, 2006.

Leuchtenburg, William E. "Jimmy Carter and the Post–New Deal Presidency." In Fink and Graham, *The Carter Presidency*.

Lienesch, Michael. *Redeeming America: Piety and Politics in the New Christian Right*. Chapel Hill: University of North Carolina Press, 1993.

Lincoln, Richard, et al. "The Court, the Congress, and the President: Turning Back the Clock on the Pregnant Poor." *Family Planning Perspectives* 9, no. 5 (1977).

Lindsay, Michael. *Faith in the Halls of Power: How Evangelicals Joined the American Elite*. New York: Oxford University Press, 2007.

Lipset, S. M., and E. Raab. "Evangelicals and the Elections." *Commentary* 71 (1981): 25–31.

Lloyd, Mark. *Pioneers of Old Time Religion: Jerry Falwell, Rex Humbard, Oral Roberts*. Dubuque, Iowa: Kendall-Hunt, 1988.

Lovenduski, Joni, and Joyce Outshoorn, eds. *The New Politics of Abortion*. London: Sage Publications, 1986.

Lovin, Robin W. *Reinhold Niebuhr and Christian Realism*. Cambridge: Cambridge University Press, 1995.

Lunardini, Christine. *From Equal Suffrage to Equal Rights: Alice Paul and the National Women's Party, 1910–1928*. New York: New York University Press, 1986.

MacArthur, John, Jr. *The Charismatics: A Doctrinal Perspective*. Grand Rapids, Mich.: Zondervan, 1978.

Magnuson, Roger. *Are Gay Rights Right?* Portland, Ore.: Multnomah, 1990.

Maguire, Daniel C. *The New Subversives: Anti-Americanism of the Religious Right*. New York: Continuum Publishing, 1982.

Mansfield, Stephen. *The Faith of George W. Bush*. New York: Penguin, 2003.

Marcus, Eric. *Making History: The Struggle for Gay and Lesbian Equal Rights*. New York: HarperCollins, 1992.

Marley, David John. *Pat Robertson: An American Life*. New York: Rowman and Littlefield, 2007.

Marotta, Toby. *The Politics of Homosexuality*. Boston: Houghton Mifflin, 1981.

Marsden, George. "The Religious Right: An Historical Overview." In *No Longer Exiles: The New Religious Right in American Politics*, ed. Michael Cromartie. Washington, D.C.: Ethics and Policy Center, 1993.

Martin, William. *A Prophet with Honor: The Billy Graham Story*. New York: William Morrow, 1992.

———. *With God on Our Side: The Rise of the Religious Right in America*. New York: Broadway Books, 1996.

Martz, Larry, with Ginny Carroll. *Ministry of Greed: The Inside Story of the Televangelists and Their Holy Wars*. New York: Weidenfeld and Nicholson, 1988.

Mazlish, Bruce, and Edwin Diamond. *Jimmy Carter: An Interpretive Biography*. New York: Simon and Schuster, 1979.

McGraw, Onalee. *Secular Humanism and the Schools: The Issue Whose Time Has Come*. Washington, D.C.: Heritage Foundation, 1976.

McMorrow, Fred. *Jimmy: The Candidacy of Carter*. New York: Whirlwind Books, 1976.

McWilliams, Wilson Carey. "The Meaning of the Election." In *The Election of 1976: Reports and Interpretations*, ed. Marlene M. Pomper. New York: David McKay, 1977.

———. *The Politics of Disappointment: American Elections, 1976–1994*. Chatham, N.J.: Chatham House Publishers, 1995.

Menendez, Albert J. "Religious Lobbies." *Liberty* 77 (March–April 1982).

Miller, Arthur, and Martin Wattenberg. "Politics from the Pulpit: Religiosity and the 1980 Elections." *Public Opinion Quarterly* 48 (1984): 300–312.

Miller, D. A. "Striving to Understand the Christian Right." *Chronicle of Higher Education*, June 30, 2000.

Miller, Hal. *The Abandoned Middle: The Ethics and Politics of Abortion in America*. Salem, Mass.: Penumbra Press, 1988.

Miller, Linda B. *Shadow and Substance: Jimmy Carter and the Camp David Accords*. Washington, D.C.: Georgetown University Press, 1992.

Millet, Kate. *Sexual Politics*. London: Rupert Hart Davis, 1970.

Milton, John. *Paradise Lost*. New York: Oxford University Press, 2005.

Mitchell, Curtis. *Billy Graham: Saint or Sinner?* Old Tappan, N.J.: F. H. Revell, 1979.

Mitchell, Sonya. "The Politics of Child Care in America's Public/Private Welfare State." In *Families in the U.S.: Kinship and Domestic Politics*, ed. Karen Hansen and Anita Garey. Philadelphia: Temple University Press, 1998.

Moen, Matthew C. *The Christian Right and Congress*. Tuscaloosa: University of Alabama Press, 1989.

———. "School Prayer and the Politics of Lifestyle Concern." *Social Science Quarterly* 65, no. 4 (1984): 1065–71.

———. *The Transformation of the Christian Right*. Tuscaloosa: University of Alabama Press, 1992.

Moore, Helen, and Hugh Whitt. "Multiple Dimensions of the Moral Majority Platform: Shifting Interest Group Coalitions." *Sociological Quarterly* 27, no. 3 (1986).

Moore, Jonathan, and Janet Fraser. *Campaign for President: The Managers Look at 1976*. Cambridge, Mass.: Ballinger, 1977.

Morgan, Robin, ed. *Sisterhood Is Powerful*. New York: Vintage Books, 1970.

Morris, Kenneth. *Jimmy Carter: American Moralist*. Athens: University of Georgia Press, 1996.

Moss, George Donelson. *Moving On: The American People since 1945*. 2nd ed. Upper Saddle River, N.J.: Prentice Hall, 2001.

Moynihan, Daniel Patrick. *Family and Nation*. San Diego: Harcourt Brace Jovanovich, 1986.

———. *The Negro Family: The Case for National Action*. Washington, D.C.: Office of Policy and Research, Department of Labor, 1965.

Mueller, Carol. "In Search of a Constituency for the New Religious Right." *Public Opinion Quarterly* 47 (1983).

Murray, Stephen O., and Will Roscoe, eds. *Boy-Wives and Female Husbands: Studies of African Homosexualities*. New York: Palgrave Macmillan, 2001.

National Council of Churches. *Yearbook of American and Canadian Churches, 1976*. New York: NCC, 1976.

National Defense Research Institute. *Sexual Orientation and U.S. Military Personnel Policy: Options and Assessment*. Santa Monica, Calif.: Rand, 1993.

National Office for Black Catholics. *Black Perspectives on the Evangelization of the Modern World*. Washington, D.C.: NOBC, 1974.

National Public Radio. *A History of Conflict in High Court Appointments*. July 2005.

———. *Stonewall: Myth, Magic and Mobilization*. June 1994.

Neuhaus, Richard John. *American Babylon*. New York: Basic Books, 2009.

———. *Catholic Matters: Confusion, Controversy, and the Splendor of Truth*. New York: Basic Books, 2007.

——. *The Naked Public Square: Religion and Democracy in America*. Grand Rapids, Mich.: Eerdmans Publications, 1986.

Niebuhr, Reinhold. *Christian Realism and Political Problems*. New York: Charles Scribner's Sons, 1953.

——. *An Interpretation of Christian Ethics*. New York: Charles Scribner's Sons, 1935.

——. *Moral Man and Immoral Society*. New York: Charles Scribner's Sons, 1932.

Nielson, Niels, Jr. *The Religion of Jimmy Carter*. Nashville: T. Nelson, 1977.

Norton, Howard, and Bob Slosser. *The Miracle of Jimmy Carter*. Plainfield, N.J.: Logos International, 1976.

Ockenga, Harold. "From Fundamentalism, through New Evangelism, to Evangelism." In *Evangelical Roots*, ed. Kenneth Kantzer. Nashville: Thomas Nelson, 1978.

O'Connor, Karen. *No Neutral Ground: Abortion Politics in an Age of Absolutes*. Boulder, Colo.: Westview Press, 1996.

O'Hair, Madalyn Murray. *An Atheist Epic: The Complete Unexpurgated Story of How Bibles and Prayers Were Removed from Public Schools of the United States*. Austin, Tex.: American Atheist Press, 1989.

——. *Nobody Has a Prayer*. Austin, Tex.: American Atheist Press, 1982.

Oldfield, Duane Murray. *The Right and the Righteous: The Christian Right Confronts the Republican Party*. New York: Rowman and Littlefield, 1996.

Petchesky, Rosalind. "Antiabortion, Antifeminism, and the Rise of the New Right." *Feminist Studies* 7 (1981).

Pierard, Richard V. "An Innocent in Babylon." *Christian Century*, February 25, 1981.

Pingry, Patricia. *Jerry Falwell: Man of Vision*. Milwaukee, Wis.: Ideals Publishing, 1980.

Pinsky, Mark. *A Jew among Evangelicals*. Louisville, Ky.: Westminster John Knox Press, 2006.

Pollock, John. *Billy Graham: Evangelist to the World*. New York: Harper and Row, 1979.

——. *To All Nations: The Billy Graham Story*. San Francisco: Harper and Row, 1985.

Pomper, Gerald M. *The Election of 1980: Reports and Interpretations*. New York: Chatham House, 1981.

Quebedeaux, Richard. *I Found It! The Story of Bill Bright and Campus Crusade*. New York: Harper and Row, 1979.

Randi, James. *The Faith Healers*. Buffalo, N.Y.: Prometheus Books, 1987.

Reagan, Ronald. "Abortion and the Conscience of a Nation." *Human Life Review* 9, no. 2 (1983): 7–16.

Reed, James W. "The Birth Control Movement Before *Roe v. Wade*." In *The Politics of Abortion and Birth Control in Historical Perspective*, ed. Donald T. Critchlow. University Park: Pennsylvania State University Press, 1996.

Reed, Ralph. *After the Revolution*. Nashville: Thomas Nelson, 1996.

——. "What Do Religious Conservatives Really Want?" In *Disciples and Democracy: Religious Conservatives and the Future of American Politics*, ed. Michael Cromartie. Grand Rapids, Mich.: Eerdmans Publishing, 1994.

Richardson, Michael. *Amazing Faith: The Authorized Biography of Bill Bright*. Colorado Springs, Colo.: Waterbrook Press, 2000.

Rifkin, Jeremy. *The Emerging Order: God in the Age of Scarcity*. New York: Putnam, 1979.

Robbins, Edward Morris. *The Christian Church and the Equal Rights Amendment*. Nashville: Winston-Derek Publishers, 1986.

Robinson, Herbert W. *Election Issues, 1976*. Washington, D.C.: International Management Systems Corporation, 1976.

Rosenberg, Tina. "How the Media Made the Moral Majority." *Washington Monthly*, May 1982, 26–32.

Rubin, Eva R. *Abortion, Politics, and the Courts: "Roe v. Wade" and Its Aftermath*. Westport, Conn.: Greenwood Press, 1987.

Ryan, Barbara. *Feminism and the Women's Movement: Dynamics of Change in Social Movement, Ideology, and Activism*. New York: Routledge, 1992.

Ryan, Paul B. *The Iranian Rescue Mission: Why It Failed*. Annapolis, Md.: Naval Institute Press, 1985.

Sandoz, Ellis, and Cecil Crab, eds. *A Tide of Discontent: The 1980 Elections and Their Meaning*. Washington, D.C.: Congressional Quarterly Press, 1981.

Schlesinger, Arthur, Jr. *The Cycles of American History*. Boston: Houghton Mifflin, 1986.

Schneider, Carl E., and Maris A. Vinovskis, eds. *The Law and Politics of Abortion*. Lexington, Mass.: D. C. Heath, 1980.

Schram, Martin. *Running for President, 1976: The Carter Campaign*. New York: Stein and Day, 1977.

Schulman, Bruce J. "Slouching toward the Supply Side: Jimmy Carter and the New American Political Economy." In Fink and Graham, *The Carter Presidency*.

Shepard, Charles E. *Forgiven: The Rise and Fall of Jim Bakker and the PTL Ministry*. New York: Atlantic Monthly, 1989.

Sheppard, Si. *The Partisan Press: A History of Media Bias in the United States*. Jefferson, N.C.: McFarland, 2007.

Shibley, Mark A. *Resurgent Evangelicalism in the United States*. Columbia: University of South Carolina Press, 1996.

Shirley, Craig. *Reagan's Revolution: The Untold Story of the Campaign that Started It All*. Nashville: Nelson Current, 2005.

Shriver, Peggy L. *The Bible Vote: Religion and the New Right*. New York: Pilgrim Press, 1981.

———. "The Religious Right: A Program of Intolerance and Coercion." In *The Religious Right*, ed. Gary McCuen. Hudson, Wis.: Gary McCuen, 1989.

Sigelman, Lee, and Stanley Presser. "Measuring Public Support for the New Christian Right: The Perils of Point Estimation." *Public Opinion Quarterly* 53, no. 3 (1988).

Silver, Diane. *The New Civil War: The Lesbian and Gay Struggle for Civil Rights*. New York: Franklin Watts, 1997.

Simon, Merrill. *Jerry Falwell and the Jews*. Middle Village, N.Y.: Jonathan David, 1984.

Smith, Gary Scott. *Faith and the Presidency: From George Washington to George W. Bush*. New York: Oxford University Press, 2006.

Smith, Howard. "Full Moon over the Stonewall." In *The Village Voice Anthology: Twenty-five Years of Writing from the Village Voice*, ed. Geoffrey Stokes. New York: William Morrow, 1982.

Snowball, David. *Continuity and Change in the Rhetoric of the Moral Majority*. New York: Praeger, 1991.

Solinger, Rickie. *Beggars and Choosers: How the Politics of Choice Shapes Adoption, Abortion, and Welfare in the United States*. New York: Hill and Wang, 2001.

Spring, Joel. "Textbook Writing and Ideological Management." In *Textbooks in Ameri-*

can Society: Politics, Policy, and Pedagogy, ed. Philip Altback, Gail Kelly, Hugh Petrie, and Lois Weis. Albany: State University of New York Press, 1991.

Stanley, Timothy. *Kennedy vs. Carter: The 1980 Battle for the Democratic Party's Soul.* Lawrence: University Press of Kansas, 2010.

Steinbacher, John. *The Child Seducers.* Fullerton, Calif.: Educator Publications, 1971.

Streiker, Lowell D., and Gerald S. Strober. *Religion and the New Majority: Billy Graham, Middle America, and the Politics of the 1970s.* New York: Association Press, 1972.

Strober, Jerry, and Ruth Tomczak. *Jerry Falwell: Aflame for God.* Nashville: Thomas Nelson, 1979.

Stroud, Kandy. *How Jimmy Won.* New York: William Morrow, 1977.

Stueck, William. "Placing Jimmy Carter's Foreign Policy." In Fink and Graham, *The Carter Presidency.*

Tamney, Joseph, and Stephen Johnson. "The Moral Majority in Middletown." *Journal for the Scientific Study of Religion* 22, no. 2 (1983).

Tedin, K. "Religious Preference and Pro/Anti Activism on the Equal Rights Amendment Issue." *Pacific Sociological Review* 21, no. 1 (1978): 55–65.

Telham, Shibley. *Power and Leadership in International Bargaining: The Park to the Camp David Accords.* New York: Columbia University Press, 1990.

Thomas, Cal, and Ed Dobson. *Blinded by the Might: Can the Religious Right Save America?* Grand Rapids, Mich.: Zondervan, 1999.

Tinker, Irene. *Women in Washington: Advocates for Public Policy.* London: Sage, 1982.

Tompkins, Nancy. *Roe v. Wade and the Fight over Life and Liberty.* New York: Franklin Watts, 1996.

Tribe, Laurence. *American Constitutional Law.* Minneola, N.Y.: Foundation Press, 1978.

Turner, William. "Lesbian/Gay Rights and Immigration Policy: Lobbying to End the Medical Model." *Journal of Policy History* 7, no. 2 (1995).

———. "Mirror Images: Lesbian/Gay Civil Rights in the Carter and Reagan Administrations." In *Creating Change: Sexuality, Public Policy, and Civil Rights*, ed. John D'Emilio, William Turner, Urvashi Viad. New York: St. Martin's Press, 2000.

Uslaner, Eric M., and Ronald Weber. "Public Support for Pro-Choice Abortion Policies in the Nation and States: Changes and Stability after the *Roe* and *Doe* Decisions." In *The Law and Politics of Abortion*, ed. Carl E. Schneider and Maris A. Vinovskis. Lexington, Mass.: D. C. Heath, 1980.

Utter, Glenn, and John Storey. *The Religious Right: A Reference Handbook.* Denver, Colo.: ABC-CLIO, 1995.

Vaughn, Joel. *The Rise and Fall of the Christian Coalition.* San Jose, Calif.: Resource Publications, 2009.

Vest, David. "Tangled Up in Tape." *Counterpunch*, March 5, 2002, http://www.counterpunch.org/vestgraham.html, accessed April 19, 2008.

Vinovskis, Maris. "Abortion and the Presidential Election of 1976: A Multivariate Analysis of Voting Behavior." In *The Law and Politics of Abortion*, ed. Carl E. Schneider and Maris A. Vinovskis. Lexington, Mass.: D. C. Heath, 1980.

Warren, Rick. *The Purpose Driven Life: What on Earth Am I Here For?* Philadelphia: Running Press, 2003.

Watson, Justin. *The Christian Coalition: Dreams of Restoration, Dreams of Recognition.* New York: Palgrave Macmillan, 1999.

Watt, David Harrington. *A Transforming Faith: Explorations of Twentieth Century American Evangelicalism.* New Brunswick, N.J.: Rutgers University Press, 1991.

Webber, Robert E. *The Moral Majority: Right or Wrong?* Westchester, Ill.: Cornerstone Books, 1981.

White, Edmund. *States of Desire: Travels in Gay America*. New York: E. P. Dutton, 1980.

White, John Kenneth. *The New Politics of Old Values*. Hanover, N.H.: University Press of New England, 1988.

Whitney, Sharon. *The Equal Rights Amendment: The History and the Movement*. New York: Franklin Watts, 1984.

Wilcox, Brian, et al. "Federal Abortion Policy and Politics: 1973 to 1996." In Beckman and Harvey, *The New Civil War*.

Wilcox, Clyde. "Evangelicals and the Moral Majority." *Journal for the Scientific Study of Religion* 28, no. 4 (1989).

———. *God's Warriors: The Christian Right in 20th-Century America*. Baltimore, Md.: Johns Hopkins University Press, 1992.

———. *Onward Christian Soldiers? The Religious Right in American Politics*. 2nd ed. Boulder, Colo.: Westview Press, 2000.

———. "Religious Attitudes and Anti-feminism: An Analysis of the Ohio Moral Majority." *Women and Politics* 7, no. 2 (1987): 70–71.

Willoughby, William. *Does America Need the Moral Majority?* Plainfield, N.J.: Haven Books, 1981.

Wills, Garry. *Head and Heart: American Christianities*. New York: Penguin Press, 2007.

———. *Under God: Religion and American Politics*. New York: Simon and Schuster, 1990.

Witcover, Jules. *Marathon: The Pursuit of the Presidency, 1972–1976*. New York: Viking, 1977.

Woodbridge, Charles. *The New Evangelism*. Greenville, S.C.: Bob Jones University Press, 1969.

Woods, James E., Jr. "Christian Faith and Political Society." In *Religion and Politics*, ed. James E. Woods. Waco, Tex.: Baylor University Press, 1983.

Woodward, Bob. *Plan of Attack*. New York: Simon and Schuster, 2004.

Yankelovich, Daniel. "Stepchildren of the Moral Majority." *Psychology Today* 15, no. 11 (1981).

Young Americans for Freedom. *Task Force Report on Affirmative Action*. Sterling, Va.: YAF, 1978.

Young, Perry Deane. *God's Bullies: Native Reflections on Preachers and Politics*. New York: Holt, Rinehart and Winston, 1982.

Zettersten, Rolf. *Dr. Dobson: Turning Hearts Toward Home*. Dallas, Tex.: Word Publishing, 1989.

Zwier, Robert. *Born-Again Politics: The New Christian Right in America*. Downers Grove, Ill.: InterVarsity Press, 1982.

———. "The New Christian Right and the 1980 Elections." In *New Christian Politics*, ed. David G. Bromley and Anson Shupe, 73–194. Macon, Ga.: Mercer University Press, 1984.

Index

ABC News, 100, 304

abortion rights: ACLU and, 64; African
Americans and, 65; blanket
restrictions on, 86; British Parliament
and, 32; Democratic National
Convention and, 85–86, 89–90; ERA
and, 32, 38, 62, 69, 87, 137, 139, 150,
173, 176, 179, 205; Hartford Manifesto
and, 44; Hyde Amendment and, 91,
141–43, 278, 290; Medicaid and, 91,
122; Moral Majority and, 278–79; NAC
and, 272; nontherapeutic abortions
and, 122; publications regarding, 188,
192, 222, 279; *Roe v. Wade* and, 28, 52,
164; Supreme Court rulings regarding,
33, 86, 93, 122, 222, 290; White House
Conference on Families and, 271
—views on: Anderson's, 264, 283, 318;
Blackwell's, 327–28; Bryant's, 257;
Bush's, 265, 341–42; Califano's, 122,
141; Carter's, 72–73, 183; Catholic
Church's, 90–91, 183; Costanza's,
142; Democratic Party's, 65–67, 86;
Eizenstat's, 131; Falwell's, 56, 142,
192–95, 266; Ford's, 73; Graham's,
42; Helms's, 64, 137, 327; House of
Representatives', 66; LaHaye's, 276;
Maddox's, 308–10; Marshner's, 221,
329; McCormick's, 86, 185, 288;
McGovern's, 65–66, 223; Milk's,
181, 194; Neuhaus's, 44; Powell's, 91;
Reagan's, 73–74; Republican Party's,

66–67, 92, 278; Senate's, 122; Southern
Baptists', 42, 347; Tucker's, 262, 272;
Weddington's, 314

Abortion Rights Mobilization, 200

Abortion: The Issue That Won't Go Away
(television broadcast), 171

Abraham, Mary Beth, 257

Abramowitz, Beth, 166

Abzug, Bella: ERA and, 173; on gay
rights, 64, 71, 84, 106, 148, 239;
Hyde Amendment and, 91; IWY
Commission and, 121, 166–67; NACW
and, 180–81, 204–5; women's caucus
and, 86; on women's rights, 69, 150,
292

ACLU. *See* American Civil Liberties Union

Acquired Immune Deficiency Syndrome,
332–33

activist judges criticism, 63–64

ACT UP, 333

Adams, Sandra, 117

ADH (Alliance for Displaced
Homemakers), 131

Ad Hoc Committee in Defense of Life,
199

Advocate (newspaper), 36, 85, 254

Afghanistan, 246, 251, 301; Soviet invasion
of, 242, 245, 263, 289; War on Terror
and, 341

AFL-CIO, 68

African Americans: abortion and, 65;
Carter's support of, 104; civil rights

CPSIA information can be obtained at www.ICGtesting.com
Printed in the USA
LVOW06s0029181115

463097LV00001B/57/P